Memorial Book of Sochaczew (Poland)

Translation of
Pinkas Sochaczew

Original Book edited by: A. Sh. Sztejn, G. Wejszman

Published in Jerusalem, 1962

Published by JewishGen

An Affiliate of the Museum of Jewish Heritage—A Living Memorial to the Holocaust
New York

Memorial Book of Sochaczew

Translation of *Pinkas Sochaczew*

Copyright © 2021 by JewishGen, Inc.
All rights reserved.
First Printing: April 2021, Iyyar 5781

Editors of Original Yizkor Book: A. Sh. Sztejn, G. Wejszman
Project Coordinator: Jan Meisels Allen
Layout and Name Indexing: Jonathan Wind
Cover Design: Rachel Kolokoff-Hopper

This book may not be reproduced, in whole or in part, including illustrations in any form (beyond that copying permitted by Sections 107 and 108 of the U.S. Copyright Law and except by reviewers for public press), without written permission from the publisher.

Published by JewishGen, Inc.
An Affiliate of the Museum of Jewish Heritage
A Living Memorial to the Holocaust
36 Battery Place, New York, NY 10280

JewishGen, Inc. is not responsible for inaccuracies or omissions in the original work and makes no representations regarding the accuracy of this translation. Digital images of the original book's contents can be seen online at the New York Public Library website.

The mission of the JewishGen organization is to produce a translation of the original work, and we cannot verify the accuracy of statements or alter facts cited.

Printed in the United States of America by Lightning Source, Inc.

Library of Congress Control Number (LCCN): 2021933438

ISBN: 978-1-954176-05-8 (hard cover: 670 pages, alk. paper)

Cover Credits

All photos and illustrations are from the original Yizkor book.

Front Cover: Illustration from page 8, background map from page 582

Front and Back Cover Background: Color, texture and design by Rachel Kolokoff Hopper

Top of Spine: *The Synagogue* from page 10

Back Cover Top Left Clockwise:

The sister of Yossel Chazen with her child, page 325

Reb Hirsch (Shalom Zvi) Friedman, page 188

The Synagogue, page 10

Shabtai Weinberg's wife page 418

The Zibola twins – Yitzchak of blessed memory and Eliahu may he live long, page 103

Reb Mendl Frydman: one of the prominent community leaders, page 135

Reb Leib Zawadski, the founder of the Bible study society, and his wife Frimet, page 260

Reb Hershel Brzezinski, page 167

Back Cover Poem: *My Grandfather's Home* by Esther Shoham, page 381

JewishGen and the Yizkor Books in Print Project

This book has been published by the **Yizkor Books in Print Project**, as part of the **Yizkor Book Project** of JewishGen, Inc.

JewishGen, Inc. is a non-profit organization founded in 1987 as a resource for Jewish genealogy. Its website [www.jewishgen.org] serves as an international clearinghouse and resource center to assist individuals who are researching the history of their Jewish families and the places where they lived. JewishGen provides databases, facilitates discussion groups, and coordinates projects relating to Jewish genealogy and the history of the Jewish people. In 2003, JewishGen became an affiliate of the **Museum of Jewish Heritage—A Living Memorial to the Holocaust** in New York.

The **JewishGen Yizkor Book Project** was organized to make more widely known the existence of Yizkor (Memorial) Books written by survivors and former residents of various Jewish communities throughout the world. Later, volunteers connected to the different destroyed communities began cooperating to have these books translated from the original language—usually Hebrew or Yiddish—into English, thus enabling a wider audience to have access to the valuable information contained within them. As each chapter of these books was translated, it was posted on the JewishGen website and made available to the general public.

The **Yizkor Books in Print Project** began in 2011 as an initiative to print and publish Yizkor Books that had been fully translated, so that hard copies would be available for purchase by the descendants of these communities and also by scholars, universities, synagogues, libraries, and museums.

These Yizkor books have been produced almost entirely through the volunteer effort of researchers from around the world, assisted by donations from private individuals. The books are printed and sold at near cost, so as to make them as affordable as possible. Our goal is to make this important genre of Jewish literature and history available in English in book form, so that people can have the personal histories of their ancestral towns on their bookshelves for themselves and for their children and grandchildren.

A list of all published translated Yizkor Books in the project with prices and ordering information can be found at:
http://www.jewishgen.org/Yizkor/ybip.html

Lance Ackerfeld, Yizkor Book Project Manager
Joel Alpert, Yizkor-Book-in-Print Project Coordinator
Susan Rosin, Yizkor-Book-in-Print Project Associate Coordinator

This book is presented by the
Yizkor-Books-In-Print Project
Project Coordinator: Joel Alpert

Part of the Yizkor Books Project of JewishGen. Inc.
Project Manager: Lance Ackerfeld

These books have been produced solely through efforts of volunteers from around the world. The books are printed using the Print-on-Demand technology and sold at near cost, to make them as affordable as possible.

Our goal is to make this intimate history of the destroyed Jewish shtetls of Eastern Europe available in book form in English, so that people can experience the near-personal histories of their ancestral town on their bookshelves and those of their children and grandchildren.

All donations to the Yizkor Books Project, which translated the books, are sincerely appreciated.

Please send donations to:

Yizkor Book Project
JewishGen, Inc.
36 Battery Place
New York, NY, 10280

JewishGen, Inc. is an affiliate of the
Museum of Jewish Heritage
A Living Memorial to the Holocaust

Notes to the Reader:

We apologize ahead of time for the poor quality of images in the book. Often these images had been scanned from the original Yizkor books which were of poor quality to begin with, being copies of old photographs. Each transfer results in loss of quality. We have done the best we could, given the original material and the resources and technology at hand. Even though images often appear of higher quality on computer screens, that does not transfer to high quality images in print. A reader can view the original scans on the web sites listed below.

Within the text the reader will note "{34}" standing ahead of a paragraph. This indicates that the material translated below was on page 34 of the original book. However, when a paragraph was split between two pages in the original book, the marker is placed in this book after the end of the paragraph for ease of reading.

Also please note that all references within the text of the book to page numbers, refer to the page numbers of the original Yizkor Book.

The original book can be seen online at the New York Public Library site:

https://digitalcollections.nypl.org/items/0598c600-3a18-0133-f68f-00505686a51c

or at the Yiddish Book Center web site:

https://www.yiddishbookcenter.org/collections/yizkor-books/yzk-nybc314003/shtain-a-sh-vaysman-pinkes-sokhatshev

In order to obtain a list of all Shoah victims from Sochaczew, the reader should access the Yad Vashem web site listed below; one can also search for specific family names using family name option. These lists are continually updated by Yad Vashem, so it is worthwhile to periodically search these lists.

There is much valuable information available on this web site, including the Pages of Testimony, etc.
http://yvng.yadvashem.org

A list of this book and all books available in the Yizkor-Book-In-Print Project along with prices is available at:
http://www.jewishgen.org/Yizkor/ybip.html

Acknowledgements

Our sincere appreciation to Yosef Grundwag, Secretary, The Committee of Sochaczewites in Israel, for permission to put this material on the JewishGen web site.

Our thanks to Jerrold Landau, translator extraordinaire! Jerrold translated both the Hebrew and Yiddish portions of the book. His attention to detail and knowledge about Judaism and how our ancestors lived added to the depth and wealth of our knowledge.

Jan Meisels Allen
Translation Project Coordinator, Sochaczew, Poland Yizkor Book

Geopolitical Information:

Sochaczew, Poland 52°14' N 20°15' E 32 miles W of Warszawa

	Town	District	Province	Country
Before WWI (c. 1900):	Sochaczew	Sochaczew	Warszawa	Russian Empire
Between the wars (c. 1930):	Sochaczew	Sochaczew	Warszawa	Poland
After WWII (c. 1950):	Sochaczew			Poland
Today (c. 2000):	Sochaczew			Poland

Alternate names for the town:
Sochaczew [Pol], Sochatshev [Yid], Sokhachev [Rus], Sochatchev, Sochoczew

Nearby Jewish Communities:

Wyszogród 11 miles NNW
Bolimów 11 miles SSW
Czerwińsk nad Wisłą 12 miles N
Wiskitki 12 miles SSE
Żyrardów 14 miles SE
Leszno 15 miles E
Łowicz 16 miles WSW
Błonie 16 miles E
Kiernozia 16 miles W
Sanniki 18 miles WNW
Grodzisk Mazowiecki 18 miles ESE
Skierniewice 19 miles SSW
Mszczonów 21 miles SE

Bodzanów 21 miles NNW
Zakroczym 21 miles NE
Łyszkowice 22 miles SW
Nowy Dwór Mazowiecki 24 miles NE
Gąbin 25 miles WNW
Nadarzyn 25 miles ESE
Pruszków 25 miles E
Sobota 25 miles WSW
Żychlin 27 miles W
Bielawy 28 miles WSW
Płońsk 28 miles N
Głowno 29 miles SW
Jabłonna 30 miles ENE

Jewish Population: 3,776 (in 1897), 3,011 (in 1931)

Map of Poland with Sochaczew

Title Page of Original Yizkor Book

מוקדש לזכר קדושי עירנו
געהייליקט דעם אנדענק פון אונדזערע קדושים

Translation of Previous Page

Pinkas Sochaczew

Dedicated to the Martyrs of Our Town

TABLE OF CONTENTS

From The Past

Introduction, by Gavriel Wejszman	4
From the Editorial Committee	6
The Jewish Community of Sochaczew from the Olden Days until the 19th Century by Yeshaya Trunk	9
Sochaczew takes on a Yiddish character, by Julian Niemcewicz	13
The History of the City and Area of Sochaczew and its Jews, by Mrs. Janina Swierzynska	14
A Score of Years as the Rabbi of Sochaczew, by Nachman Blumental	20

The Rabbi's Court

The Inscription of the Tombstone of Sara Tzina	31
A Spiritual Center, by A. Chetzroni	32
The Voice and Echo, by Eliezer Sztejnman	38
The Admor Rabbi Shmuel of Blessed Memory by A. Ch.	46
The Admor Rabbi Dovid of Holy Blessed Memory by Rabbi Yehoshua Moshe Aharonson	50
Rabbi Dovid Borenstein, the Admor of Sochaczew by B. Tzemach	57
Reb Avrahamele Sochaczewer by Aharon Cejtlin	62
The Rebbi's Court by M. B. Sztejn	66
The Rebbe's Funeral by David Wolrat	70
The Shem Mishmuel by A. Chetzroni	73

Social and Spiritual Life

Sochaczew between the Two World Wars, by Menachem Frydman	77
The Local Thearer by Yosef Grundwag	94
Sochaczew as I Remember It by Yerucham Ines	100
The Destroyed Home, by Moshe Szwarc	106
Organized Institutions, by Sh. Swiatlowski	114
The Birthpangs of Zionism in Sochaczew, by S. Grundwag	117
The Pioneers of the Hebrew School, by Yaakov Frydman	120
Hashomer Hatzair, by Yaakov Frydman	122
The Worker's Movement, by A. Shtshafa	125
The First Amateur Theater by David Wolrat	127

The Wind Orchestra, by Yitzchak Weinstock	130
"The Sochaczever Newspaper", by Yaakov Frydman	131
"Chevra Tehillim", by Elchanan Kac	135
"Chevra Kadisha" (Burial Society), by Yitzchak Frydman	139
Life of the Spirit, by Meir Goldfarb	140
The Cooperative People's Bank, by Shlomo Swiatlowski	145
The Teacher of Children, by Leib Fursztenberg	148

Rabbis of Sochaczew

Rabbis of Sochaczew, by Moshe Levanon	156
Rabbi Elazar Hakohen, by M. B. Sztejn	163
My Father of Blessed Memory, by Zeev Wolf Yechiel Landau	166

Sochaczevers – Their Role in Cultural and Spiritual Life

Alexander Zisha Frydman, by M. B. Sztejn	170
Ozer Warszawski, by Lea Kenig	175
Biographical Notes, by Melech Rawicz	182
Shmuel Lehman of blessed memory, by Yeshaya Trunk	184
Pinchas Graubard, by Y. Frydman	186
Pinchas Graubard, by A. Alemi	186
Wolf (Vove) Rozenberg, by Moshe Szwarc	190

Personalities

Reb Alexander Zisha Frydman by Dr. Hillel Zeidman	193
A Shining Personality - Reb Zishe, by Pesia Shorashewski	204
Simcha Grundwag, by Yaakov Frydman	210
Frejman Hirsch (Shalom Tzvi Frejdman), by Yaakov Frejdman	212
Reb Menashe Czemerynski, by Elchanan Kac	216
Communal Activists of Sochaczew, by Shlomo Swiatlowski	218
Reb Hershel Kluska of blessed memory, by Shlomo Swiatlowski	220
Men of the People, by Y. F.	221
My Parents' Home, by Shlomo Frydman	225
My Father of Blessed Memory (Avraham Rechtman), by Yaakov Tzidkoni	231
The Courtyard of Moshe Rechtman, by Yaakov Tzidkoni	233
Bernard Kampelmacher - the Teacher of our City, by Yisrael Rozen	235
The Woman Chaikel the Wagon Driver, by Leib Fursztenberg	238
Happenings Herein, by Yaakov Frydman	241
Moshe Aharon Shulklaper, by Yaakov Frydman	241
Reb Meir Binyamin, by Yaakov Frydman	243

Avraham Meir Lejzers, by Yaakov Frydman	244
Chaikel Baal Agala (Chaikel the Wagon Driver), by Yaakov Frydman	245

Common Happenings and Memories

Anski Questionaire, by Yaakov Frydman	247
In Those Days, by Pinchas Graubard	253
The Lamed-Vavnik, by M. B. Sztejn	259
Did He Not Promise You, by Moshe Levanon	260
From the Book "Poland", by Y. Y. Trunk	264
Smugglers, by Ozer Warszawski	268
Unkosher Merchandise, by Pinchas Graubard	271
At the Bzura, by Tzvi Cohen	273
From my Experiences, by Machla Lewin-Boteler	276
Moshe Festman, by Yaakov Frydman	278
The Zionist Minyan[7], by Yaakov Frydman	281
Yosef Wolkovitch, by Yaakov Frydman	284
Yechiel Meir Telman, by Yaakov Frydman	284
The Murder of the Regional Official Baragow, by Yaakov Frydman	285
Delights, by Yakov Tsidkoni	286
Episodes, by Yakov Tsidkoni	288
Father Was Sentensed to Death	288
The Blind Man	289
The Death of the Rabbi	289
A Desire Which Was Fulfilled	290
Lusovniks	291
Early Morning Excursions	291

The Holocaust

The Martyrdom of the Elders and the Youth, by M. Rajc	293
The Destruction of Sochaczew, by Reizel Rozenberg (Rosenkopf)	301
Thus was I Saved, by Tova Moszenberg	305
In the Skarzysko Camp, by Zeev Sheynwald	307
In the Villages and Forests, by Hirsch Gothilf	308
Pinchas of Blessed Memory (Pinia)	311
Who Would Make it that my Head Would be Water..., by Chana Frydman	312
The German Murderers, by Lewkowicz	315
My Frightful Days, by Tauba Moszenberg	320
My Experiences Under the Nazi Regime, by M. Sh. Frejdenberg	326
Memories, by Moshe Geier	327
Dates to Remember, by Chaim Weisz	328

Expiring from Hunger and Cold, by A. Sochaczever	330
On the Aryan Side, by Rosa (Wejnberg) Goldsztejn[8]	331
From Aryan Documents, by Leib Lurie	335
Thus Was the Sochaczew Community Tortured, by B. Jarlicht	340
A Few Words, by Hersch Gothilf	339
Recall me – Remember, by Esther Shoham	346
Memories from my Time in Hiding, by Tzvi Taubenfeld	347
A Letter to the Grundwag's Children, by Yozka Grosman	351
In the Ghetto, by Mordechai Gebirtig	353
Numbers – Thousands, Millions, by H. Lejwik	354
What I Saw and Heard in Sochaczew in 1939, by Yitzchak Telman	355
From the Last Days of the Warsaw Ghetto, by Miriam Flajszman	357
The Partisans of Sochaczew, related by Yechiel Silber	360
The Last Ones of a Family, by Machla Lewin-Boteler	376
From Among the First Victims, by Rozka Szmulewicz	378
A Memorial to our Fellow Native Yechezkel Adamczyk, by M. L.	380
My Grandfather's Home, by Esther Shoham	381
The "Transfer", by Y. P.	382
The Publication of the Book Du Prel, by Magistrate Blumental	384
On the Ruins, by L. Fursztenberg	384

Sochaczewers In the Land of Israel / In America

Sochaczevers in Israel, by Yerucham Ines	392
A Monument for a Dear Soul Sh. Swiatlowski	398
Eliezer Meir Libert, by Yaakov Frydman	401
The Sochaczew Mutual Benefit Organization of Chicago, by Louis Libert	402
Sochaczevers in New York, by Ch. L. Ludzki	405
The Activities of our Women's Help Organization in New York	415

Those That Passed Away

In Memory of Mother of Blessed Memory, by Chana Frydman	421
Aharon Ish-Shalom (Frydman), by Y. P.	423
Tzipora Baum (Albert) , by Y. P.	426
Tzipora Baum, by Yisrael Rozen	429
Yaakov Frydman of Blessed Memory, by Yisrael Rozen	431
Moshe Eliezer Bornsztejn of Blessed Memory, by M. B. Stein	434
Chana Kaplan (nee Greenberg), by Yerucham Ines	436
Those Who Fell in the Battle for the Homeland	437

Epilogue, by Yaakov Tzidkoni	444

Names of the Martyrs	448
Index of the Yiddish Section	495
Index of the Hebrew Section	556

Appendices

Sochaczew Map, by Yosef Grundwag	581
The Committee of Sochaczewites in Israel, by Joseph Grundwag	585
The Sochaczew Memorial, by Yosef Grundwag	586
Poland Trip 2001 (July), Photographs by Jan Meisels Allen	590
Photographs from Treblika by Jan Meisels Allen	606
Aerial photographs of Sochaczew	615
World War II German Captured photographs	617
Sochotzover Society of Greater New York, Membership 1977	622

Index of Names for this Publication — 633

Memorial Book of Sochaczew (Poland)

52°14' / 20°15'

Translation of *Pinkas Sochaczew*

Edited by: **A. Sh. Sztejn, G. Wejszman**
Published in Jerusalem, 1962

Acknowledgments

Project Coordinator:

Jan Meisels Allen

Our sincere appreciation to Yosef Grundwag, Secretary, The Committee of Sochaczewites in Israel, for permission to put this material on the JewishGen web site.

This is a translation of: Pinkas Sochaczew (Memorial Book of Sochaczew)
Editors: A. Sh. Sztejn and G. Wejszman, Jerusalem
Former residents of Sochaczew in Israel, 1962,
843 p. (Hebrew and Yiddish)

PINKAS SOCHACZEW

JOURNAL OF SOCHACZEW

Edited by A. Sh. Sztejn
Gavriel Wejszman

Editorial committee:
Yaakov Frydman of blessed memory
Mendel Frydman
Moshe Levanon (Brzezinski)
Yerucham Ines

{second title page, with illustration}
PINKAS SOCHACZEW
Dedicated in memory of the martyrs of our city

{opposite to title page}
Published by the Organization of Sochaczew Émigrés of Israel
With the participation of the United Committee of Sochaczew Landsmanschaft Organizations of America
Printed in Israel, 1962
All rights reserved
Printed in Jerusalem, 5722
Produced on paper of Hamashbir Ltd.

TRANSLATOR'S FOOTNOTES:

1. The word used for 'echo' is 'bas kol'. This phrase is difficult to translate into English. It means literally 'daughter of a voice'. It refers to a 'divine voice', i.e. an echo of divine inspiration that is not of the level of prophecy.
2. This literally means "The name from Samuel", and is a pseudonym for Rabbi Shmuel Bornsztejn, 1856-1926, the head of the Aleksandrow Hassidic group.
3. Hashomer Hatzair, literally "Young Guard" is the youth group of the extreme left wing Zionist movement.
4. Literally "Organization of Psalms", referring to an organization of men who would gather together on a regular basis to recite Psalms.
5. I am not sure of the translation of this. The Yiddish is "Anski-Ankete". Ankete is a poll.
6. Lamed Vav is the numerical equivalent of 36. This is a reference to a Jewish legend that in every generation, there are 36 saintly people who are not known to society in general. A 'Lamed Vavnik' would be a reference to someone as one of these 36 saintly people, and would refer to an extremely righteous, modest and unassuming person.
7. Minyan (in Hebrew/Yiddish literally 'quorum'), is a quorum of ten adult Jewish males necessary for Jewish public prayer services.
8. In the 'arisher' times. Meaning of 'arisher' is unclear.
9. Admor is a title used for a Chassidic Rabbinical leader.
10. This work translates from Yiddish as "the knocker of the synagogue", who may have been the person who knocked on people's doors early in the morning to wake them up for synagogue services, or alternatively may have been the person who knocked on the synagogue's lectern to quiet the people.
11. A quote from the book of Lamentations "Who would make it that my head would be water, and my eyes a fountain of tears, and I would weep day and night over the destruction of my people".
12. From the context of the table of contents, it is not clear if this refers to thirty days or thirty years. 'Shloshim', the Hebrew word used here, is often used as a reference to the thirty day mourning period that follows the death of a close relative.

(3 Yiddish 601 Hebrew)

FROM THE PAST

Introduction
Translated by Jerrold Landau

As we approached the task of preparing the book of Sochaczew, we set the following goal: to describe the Jewish character of Sochaczew as it was in the past, the development of the Jews there, as well as the perpetuation of the final drama of Sochaczew – the era of Hitler. Today, this is not easy at all, for to our sorrow, everything is now in the past, much of the historical material was lost along with the destruction of the Jews, and whatever survives in the archives is not accessible today to the Jewish historian. Nevertheless we have succeeded in including in this book historical chapters that are authoritative and worthwhile, and which present somewhat of a picture from the beginning of Sochaczew Jewry.

The older history of Sochaczew occupies a relatively small part of the book relative to the history from the period of the 20th century. This is understandable, since to our great sorrow, the events during the time of Hitler are equal to all the past difficult periods of our history.

The material of the second part is drawn for the most part from memory. Its chapters describe the ups and downs, the negative aspects of Jewish life in Sochaczew along with the high points, the embodiment of Jewish life – and along with this, the final fire before the complete annihilation of this city.

In the chapters of memories, there are descriptions that portray and perpetuate the various aspects of Jewish Sochaczew: the institutions, organizations and groups, as well as the personalities who worked in these institutions.

Wondrous is the strength and dedication of the activists and leaders who involved themselves in Jewish activity in all spheres of communal life, and who help to raise the level of Jewish culture. It is especially wondrous given that the relationship with the outside world was difficult – and especially during the 1930s – unfriendly and hostile, and it required much spiritual strength to oppose the world which was becoming more distant and treacherous. The Jews of Sochaczew possessed this strength.

Jewish Sochaczew had a special character, which gave rise to its great and well-known people, its great Admorim (Hassidic Masters), scribes and wagon drivers, as well as working intelligentsia. Great personalities shine out from the pages of the "Pinkas", such as: Alexander Zusha Friedman, Ozer Warshawski, Pinchas Graubard, Shmuel Lehman, Vove Rosenberg, and others who raised themselves above the local scene, and left their mark on Jewish life in Poland in general. The Admorim of Sochaczew, of blessed memory, who were among the establishers of Polish Hassidism, spread their light beyond the borders of Poland. The Hassidic world absorbed the spiritual radiance of "The House of Sochaczew", which was a gathering place for the wise. Jewish Sochaczew was comparable to any large city in Poland in quality. This well connected city, which lies on the banks of the peaceful Bzura, was turned into a vale of tears during the evil days of Hitler, a place where the lives of its dear Jews were stamped out.

In the Pinkas Sochaczew, there is an expression of deep agony as well as a fierce pining for the world that was destroyed – the wonderful Jewish world that was destroyed. However, alongside, these pages awaken feelings of great pride, as they point out the heartening fact that complete and pure Jews such as these had their dwelling place in Sochaczew. These are not just the Jews of the Sabbath and festivals – but also the personalities of Jews during the six work days, filled with purity and warmth, such as: Chaikel the wagon driver, Yakir the shoemaker, and many others like them, simple Jews, common-folk, sublime souls.

Regarding the era of the destruction, this book will describe those who suffered the frightening tortures with their own bodies, that is the few brands who survived the destruction of the city of Sochaczew. These survivors, who were saved in a miraculous manner from the ghettos, the crematoria, the forests and the bunkers, as well as the modern-day Conversos[1] – they describe here what they experienced with their bodies: tribulations, oppression, degradation, the full load of evil which afflicted them during the days of Hitler, may his name be blotted out. From this material, the heartening fact emerges that even during the terrible conditions that prevailed during the oppression of Hitler, the Jews of Sochaczew did not lose the Divine shadow from their faces. This was the way of Sochaczew.

Someone looking in from outside may get the impression that the wounds of these survivors have been healed over time. However when their heart opens, the wounds appear unbandaged to any onlooker. The wounds have been dressed externally, however they will never heal.

As has been mentioned, the memories described in this section are based on the personal experiences of the eyewitnesses. However their content is so true and convincing – described in almost a stoic manner – that we can see through this personal lens the tragedy of the entire people of Israel – the frightening demise of eastern European Jewry.

Without doubt, a linguist who examines this work carefully will find here a word that is not appropriate, and there a sentence that is not organized. However, is it possible to tune a cry of grief with a tuning fork? Since all of their words are one collective cry, a voice from the depths of despair, we did not want to edit the material that we received, and we left it in its original fashion. In our opinion, the manner of presentation is not important here, but rather the frightening content.

Therefore, the words are brought down here without paint or comb, without any change, in the simple manner in which they were written. However, due to their simplicity, they are so stirring, and they connect us with the most frightful drama that overtook our nation that knows grief, from the time that it became a nation.

On occasion there will be some repetition, and even contradictions, however we did not permit ourselves to "fix" the content and to resolve the contradictions. On the contrary, it is possible that a historian will find in this text new facts, which will enable him to complete and fully understand material that is already known from other sources.

We made every attempt to retain the style of the writers in order to stress the collective character of this book. For this reason, we retained the different writing style of material that we have copied from other sources.

May the Pinkas Sochaczew be a spiritual monument to the Jewish life of Sochaczew that was annihilated, and may it be an addition to the Holocaust literature of Jewry in general.

Gavriel Weissman

{7 - Yiddish} {603 - Hebrew}

From the Editorial Committee
Translated by Jerrold Landau

With feelings of trepidation and holy trembling, we – a group of Sochaczew natives in Israel – succeeded after ten years of effort in publishing a Yizkor book to perpetuate the destroyed community of Sochaczew. This activity demanded great dedication and communal responsibility. We were unsure if we were worthy of describing the tribulations, and of eulogizing our most dear ones and relatives.

We knew from the outset about the great difficulties that overtook them, and about the great responsibility that was placed upon us, and therefore we decided, with seriousness and deep faith, to gather documents and testimonies about the lives and deaths of our relatives and friends. We gathered photographs of organizations, institutions, schools, rabbis, and simple folk – all of which had ethnographic value.

We were faced with the challenges of recalling things from the forgotten recesses of the memory, and of perpetuating the era of destruction. The time was pressing, as it was still possible to rescue the information from oblivion, as it was possible that tomorrow or the next day would, G-d forbid, be too late.

We set out the goal, to the extent that it was possible, to present an authentic and non-divisive picture of Jewish life in Sochaczew; not to diminish the value of one faction and to glorify another. We attempted to portray the cooperation between members of different groups. If it happens that a group or faction was not described to the appropriate extent, it was because there was nobody available to fill the gap.

We can only lament this fact. As far as possible, we avoided tendentious descriptions, and even more so unintentional negative descriptions. We attempted to portray an accurate picture even of the time of the Holocaust, and if distressing events took place due to the pressures of the era – we also recorded them. Nevertheless, the negative events are few in comparison to the sublime moral tales – even in the face of the Nazi enemy. It is wondrous how our martyrs maintained their faith – despite everything – and guarded their divine spark. Not only the martyrs, but also the warriors among the people of Sochaczew, maintained their faith. All of them light up in front of us as an eternal flame. We will remember their memory in our hearts forever.

Very few Sochaczew natives survived – however the survivors also preserved their faith in the eternal existence of our people – and they stubbornly persisted in continuing their creativity and constructive activity despite everything.

It was obvious to us even before we began collecting material for this book, that it would only be possible to collect and publish a small portion of the great sea of tears and troubles – however we have not succeeded in collecting more than this at this time.

It is also quite conceivable that we neglected to mention the names of some of the martyrs whom should have been mentioned, and to describe their lives and deaths. However, we cannot be blamed, as we were not able through any means to obtain any more information than we present here.

Pinkas Sochaczew is a communal Kaddish[2] prayer for the Jews of Sochaczew as they were, a memorial to the 5,000 pure victims, and a gravestone on their unmarked graves.

Jewish Sochaczew was viciously destroyed and its voice is silenced. Pinkas Sochaczew will transfer the melodious echo to the descendents of Sochaczew from generation to generation.

We must give our best wishes to all of those who participated in the production of this book. To our great distress, not all of the participants merited to witness the publication of this Yizkor book. Those that passed on include our dear Sochaczew natives Yaakov Friedman, Moshe Eliezer Bornstein, Pinchas Graubard, Vove Rosenberg – of blessed memories.

We remember with deep gratitude the editor A. Sh. Stein, who gave a great deal to consolidate the format of this book. He was snatched away by a cruel death in the midst of his work. It is an honor to memorialize him.

With feelings of holiness, and full of somber respect to the martyrs of our city, we present this book to our readers, with the hope that our goal to establish a monument to the former life in our city has been realized.

Tel Aviv, Shvat 5722 (1962)

ספר סאכאטשעוו

מוקדש לזכר קדושי עירנו
געהייליקט דעם אנדענק פון אונדזערע קדושים

{11 - Yiddish} {607 - Hebrew}

The Jewish Community of Sochaczew from the Olden Days Until the 19th Century

(a translation and digest)

by Y. Trunk

Translated by Jerrold Landau

The Jewish community of Sochaczew is not among the oldest of Poland. It is numbered among the Jewish settlements from the middle era of Poland-Mazowsze[3]. The first official document that we have of Jews in the locality is from 1426, and its content is a debate between the "szlachta", that is the nobleman, and the Jew of the "land" of Sochaczew.

However, there is no proof from here that Jews settled in the city only in 1426. On the contrary, the above mentioned dispute seems to indicate that there was a Jewish settlement there already predating this time. We have knowledge of Jewish settlements in the vicinity from earlier times – and all of these are links in the general trend of population settlement. (The community of Plock is an exception, as we have the first records of a community there from 1237.)

According to a survey conducted by the Starostowa (mayor) of Sochaczew in 1599, the Jews of the city owned twenty houses. If we estimate that four families lived in each house, the Jewish Population at that time would be 320 people (with an estimate of four people per family).

Twenty years later, in 1620, there were already 22 houses, which would translate to a population of 352, approximately. Mention is already made of a synagogue in the survey of 1599.

We have in our possession records of the Jewish population of 1,349 in Sochaczew and environs from 1765.

In 1800, the Jewish population numbered 972 souls, and eight years later – 1,085. In 1827 – the population was 2,322 souls, in 1857 – 2,936, and at the end of 1897 – 3,776. To sum up, the population increased fourfold in ninety years. According to the census of 1921, the Jewish population of the city was 2,419 souls. The reduction in population was due to the First World War. At the outbreak of the Second World War, the population was 4,000.

Year	Jewish Population	Total Population[4]	% Jews
1599	320 (approx.)	–	–
1620	352 (approx.)	–	–
1765	1,349 (including environs)	–	–
1808	1,085	1,342	80.8
1827	2,322	3,142	73.9
1857	2,936	3,848	76.3

1897	3,776	5,763	65.5
1908	4,520	6,397	70.6
1921	2,419	5,070	47.7
1931	–	10,800	–
1939	4,000	–	–

The facts in this table prove that –

1) From the 17th century, the Jewish population grew continuously, in particular during the last quarter of the 19th century. Between 1857 and 1897, the population grew by 28.6%. The city was almost completely destroyed in the First World War, due to the battles that were fought along the Bzura.

2) Nevertheless, in relation to the non-Jewish population, there is a continuous relative decrease of the Jewish population. At the beginning of the 19th century, the Jews were 80.8% of the population, in the middle (1857) – 76.3%, in 1897 – 65.5 %, and in 1921 – 47.7%. This was a general trend in Poland at that time.

There are few sources about the economic activity of the Jews. During the 16th century, the Jews were mainly occupied in credit activities – granting loans with interest to Christians, noblemen, and other Jews. There were regulations that set out the conditions of the loans, and were meant to protect the lender.

The Synagogue

It appears that the role of Jews in business was very small. We do not find mention of them in the list of taxpayers and in the international fairs. However, at the beginning of the 18th century, a large tannery began to operate.

The Jews of Sochaczew paid a special tax to the Starostowa (mayor), over and above their general taxes. Each Easter, the Jewish homeowners supplied a liter of pepper, and the renters supplied one half a liter. From this, we can deduce that they lived in the area that belonged to the fortress, and were under the jurisdiction of civic law.

In 1599, we know of two Jewish royal stewards from Sochaczew – Michael and Mordechai (Marek) the sons of Shlomo. At the beginning of the 17th century, there was a Jewish physician named Felix.

Sochaczew belonged to region of Greater Poland, according to the Jewish organizational structure.

Sochaczew was represented at the first congress of the communities of Greater Poland that is known to us, that is the congress of 1519 that dealt with the division of national taxes for the years 1519-1521 at the rate of 200 guilder annually.

The physician (or rabbi) Yaakov was one of the five regional parnassim (administrators) appointed for tax collection.

In 1569, Sochaczew was counted among 33 communities of Greater Poland, the income of which, to the tune of fifty guilder per year, was granted by King Zygmunt August to one of the members of his court.

As it was a small community, it did not fill a recognizable role in the activities of the regional council, however the regional council convened there more than once.

Reb Moshe Sochaczewer, a Sochaczew native, was known as "A parnas and leader in the region of Poznan" in the latter half of the 17th century. His son-in-law Rabbi Meir Eisenstat, known as the "Panim Meorot"[5], praised him in the introduction to his book for his role in saving 24 people who were convicted on false charges.

Fort ruins..

Justice in Sochaczew (1556-1557)

Natural disasters, such as fires and epidemics, affected Sochaczew, as did man-made disasters, such as blood libels, destruction, and wars.

One such blood libel cost three Jews of Sochaczew their lives, and started a wave or persecutions against Jews of the entire region.

Four Jews – Beinish the sexton, his son Yaakov, and the two brothers Yosef and Yaakov Socha (during the court case, their father Tritel was also indicted), were convicted in April 1556 (on the eve of Passover) on the count that one of them – the sexton – enticed a Christian woman, Dorota Lawancka (or Lazancka) to steal the host from the nearby village church, which they then purchased for the price of three Taller and a piece of cloth[6]. Afterward, they were accused of piercing the host and collecting the blood in a vessel... They were imprisoned together with their wives in the Plock fortress (with the exception of Beinish, who was imprisoned in the Sochaczew jail) and subject to severe interrogation by the interrogators of the diocese. They were not able to stand up to their oppressors and were sentenced to death. The sentence was carried out, and the only one saved was Yaakov, the son of Beinish who escaped. Prior to this, they executed the Christian woman Dorota. The bodies of the three who were executed in Plock were hung until January 1557. After the intervention of the king, the bodies were turned over to the community of Plock. The king, who was a fine but weak person, did not intervene, even though the Christian woman confessed before her death that the accusation was false, which was made only because of her desire for revenge.

After the conviction became known, persecutions against the Jews took place in all areas of Mazowsze [3]. Many were imprisoned and killed. Only later, on June 3rd, 1556, did the king issue an edict in the form of "an iron letter"[7], to protect the lives and property of the Jews.

Nevertheless, the persecutions did not stop, and king was forced to issue other such "iron letters", and made it clear that the confessions of the accused were extracted by torture.

Representatives of the Jews, who were leaders of the community of Plock then appeared before the king in person to complain against the regional rule Rawe and the mayor of Sochaczew, who broke the law, trampled on the rights of the Jews, mocked the edicts of the king, extracted confessions from their victims via torture, and sentenced them to death. On January 15th, 1557, the royal court of law decreed that the accused were free from any wrongdoing, and that from now on, any case against the Jews with regard to desecration of Christian holy objects or blood accusations must only be tried by the royal court.

In 1619, the community of Sochaczew had another martyr, who was sentenced to death for the "murder" of a Christian child.

During the war between Poland and Sweden (1656-1657), the city was besieged by the enemy, and the fortress was destroyed by fire. We assume that the community was destroyed.

With all this, there was no shortage of disputes between the Jews and Christians in the area of economic competition.

Jews of Sochaczew tended to move to the capital city of Warsaw. In 1765, there were 8 families from Sochaczew (39 people) in Warsaw, and in 1781, there were 27 families (61 people). In 1784 (after the temporary expulsion from Warsaw), there were 5 families (16 people), and in 1792, there were 10 families (35 people).

Since the community of Warsaw did not have its own cemetery until 1806, they would bring the dead for burial in Sochaczew or Grodzisk.

The Jewish court of law in Warsaw issued a decision that if a Jew was brought for burial to Sochaczew, the heirs would have to pay 1/3 of the burial cost – 18 red coins.

The administrator of the cemetery of Prague[8] was a Jew from Sochaczew, Shimon the son of Natan. His salary was 6 guilder per week. He was the trusted advisor and aid to the leader Shmuel Zwitkower.

The community of Sochaczew financially assisted the revolt of Kosciuszko[9], as did other communities. The community collected 300 guilder for this purpose. The Jews showed patriotism to their land.

The Prussian occupation (from the partition of Poland in 1795 until 1807) was filled with decrees against the Jews. Included with these decrees was the requirement to obtain a permit for marriage, which was only granted with proof of age and property ownership.

Yochanan, a Jew from Sochaczew, was well known as a surgeon and the local obstetrician. His son Levi Noelson completed his studies in medicine in Frankfurt auf Oder. Two young men of Sochaczew completed their studies at the rabbinical seminary of Warsaw in January 1830 – that institution was regarded at that time as a bastion of heresy. [10]

{29}

Sochaczew takes on a Yiddish Character
Julian Niemcewicz
Translated by Jerrold Landau

In 1817, a well-known Polish writer and political activist [1] , Julian Ursyna Niemcewicz, made a journey through Poland and Imperial Prussia, and wrote about the impressions of his trip, as well about his earlier and later journeys. Sochaczew was among the towns that he visited, and he devoted a few lines to that town. Of course, he took an interest in the Jews of the town, and he did not forget about them.

He writes regarding Sochaczew:

"Once it was a Polish city, but today (1817), it has become completely Judaised. Only Jews live on the Rynek (the town center), and in the best streets of the city. The remaining Christians live in the suburbs."

One must admit that Niemcewicz was a liberal Polish politician and writer, and he even wrote "sympathetic" words about the Jews in a few of his works. One of his novels, "Lyuba and Siara" even had a Jewish theme, in which he speaks out against the backward and "dark" Jews, and praised the few that are "progressive", that is to say, assimilated.

{30}

The History of the City and Area of Sochaczew and its Jews
Mrs. Janina Swierzynska
Translated by Jerrold Landau

The soil around the middle of the course of the Bzura River is particularly fertile, and therefore, it was settled very early. The earliest vestiges of human life on that soil are from approximately 12,000 years ago. Remnants of structures and implements from prehistoric epochs have been found by chance in over forty places: archeological remains of ancient settlements, cemeteries, and fortresses.

According to Professor Arnold, Sochaczew already existed as a fortified settlement in the ninth century, that is at a time before there was a united Polish nation and kingdom, which was founded, as is known, in the tenth century. The fortress served as a political, administrative and military center for the tribe that lived around the area of the Bzura. According to other sources, the fortress was built in the midst of the tenth century, but before that time there was already a settlement there in the form of a city and a business center. The settlement was established in a favorable location, at the crossroads of several land routes as well as in the middle of the water route of the Bzura River. Various economic enterprises were also centered in that area in agriculture and forestry. On account of this, a business center for the barter of goods was established very early on. Thanks to the business center ("Targowisko") [2] and fortress, Sochaczew celebrated its millenium in the year 1962.

At the time of the first Polish rules of the Piast dynasty, the fortress of Sochaczew became the seat and residence of the representative of the ruler, who was known as the Kasztelan. In truth, that title was first used in the thirteenth century, but the position existed previously. Sochaczew became not only a center of a Kasztelan district, but also for a larger territory, which consisted of several Kasztelan districts, known in Polish as "Ziemia" (a land).

As can be understood, the Sochaczew fortress had a positive influence on the development of business. Various excavations reveal that by the end of the eleventh and beginning of the twelfth century, Sochaczew became a very vibrant and flourishing business center.

According to a tradition that is apparently correct, the ruler of all of Poland, King Boleslaw III Krzywausti ("with the curved mouth") died in the Benedictine monastery of Sochaczew in the year 1138.

The first written records about Sochaczew come from the time of Konrad I, the Duke of Mazowia who brought a Knight of the Cross into Poland, who, according to a document from 1221, represented Konrad in Wiskiti, and who appears in the documents with the signature: "Palanta, Kasztelan of Sochaczew".

Konrad granted the second document, with the same signature, in 1222 in Trojanow (the duke had two residences: In Wiskiti and Trojanow). There were two churches in Sochaczew in 1257. One is called "Saint Wawrzyniec [3], Holy Maria Magdalena and Eleven Thousand Virgins", and is located on the grounds of the old Benedictine Church (today one can find the grottos there, across from the house of the Szepietowskis). The second is the Dominican Church, which was the seat of the Sochaczew parish during the nineteenth and twentieth centuries, until the time of the Second World War.

In the thirteenth century, several dukes of Mazowia along with their entourages resided in Sochaczew. It was also the residence of bishops. One bishop of Posen (Poznan) even held his induction ceremony in Sochaczew. According to church records, Sochaczew was the seat of the diocese of Posen, the oldest in Poland.

The fact that Sochaczew was situated on a place where paths crossed did indeed have a positive influence on the development of business; however it had a fatal influence on the security situation. Not only businessmen traveled along the routes, but also foreign armies...

Lithuanian and Byelorussian dukes, who waged wars against the dukes of Mazowia or became intermingled in their own controversies, would plunder and destroy the town, the fortress and the surrounding area. The wooden fortress was not sufficient to protect this type of open settlement. Therefore, in the first half of the fourteenth century, Ziemowit II the Duke of Rawa, Wiskiti and Sochaczew (1313-1349) built a stronger fortress in Sochaczew. Its ruins can be seen until today.

The fortress – in Gothic style – is similar to the fortresses that were built at that time by the builders of Kazimierz the Great, as well as the fortresses of the Knights of the Cross.

The territory that was ruled by the ruler of Sochaczew was at that time not called a "land", but rather a "duchy" [4].

After the death of Ziemowit II, who left behind no children, his brother's son, Duke Kazimierz of Mazowia, inherited the Duchy of Sochaczew. He was the last lifelong pawn of the Duchy of Sochaczew under the auspices by the Polish king Kazimierz the Great. After his death, Sochaczew returned to the control of the duke of the entire Mazowia region, Ziemowit III, called "the Elder". He was the brother of the interim late Duke Kazimierz. Ziemowit III called a meeting of the Mazowian nobility in order to carry out a reform of the existing statute. This convention took place in the fortress of Sochaczew. There, the new statutes were proclaimed in the year 1377. These statutes applied to the entire Mazowia, and were called "The Mazowian Statutes" or "The Sochaczew Statutes", which were more just than the previous ones were. Among other things, the new statutes repealed what was known as "God's Law", which used to apply to the prohibition against witchcraft. (The accused used to have to go through a "fire test" or a "water test", which would generally end with his death. This was considered to be a punishment from god.)

After Ziemowit's death, his son Ziemowit IV, called "The Younger" ruled in Sochaczew and in Plock. After the death of the Hungarian and Polish King Ludwig (1382) Ziemowit IV ascended to the Polish throne. However, he was overthrown. Wladyslaw Jagiello (1386-1434), who married the daughter of the previous King Ludwig, became the king of Poland. As a result of the rivalry, Hungarian soldiers, backed by the ruler of Krakow, fell upon and destroyed Sochaczew. Later, Jagiello, wanting to have his formal rival Ziemowit on his side, married his sister Alexandra. Ziemowit remained the ruler over his territory, officially recognized by his overlord, the King of Poland.

In the battle of Grunwald (1410), he directed the battle from Mazowsze. One of his sons was the commander of the king's bodyguards and another son, known as an "able person to conduct battles", was a member of the royal war council. Jagiello's army marched through the entire Duchy of Sochaczew, from south to north, on its way to Grunwald.

After Grunwald, he had to fight again for the area of Sochaczew, for this was one of his duties. To conduct his duties in ensuring the security of the city, he was given a war chariot, hitched to four horses and laden with battle paraphernalia, as well as riders for the horses and a guard for the wagon.

From the time of the Hungarian attack (1384) after the death of King Ludwig, until the Swedish "flood" (1956-1957) [5], the Duchy of Sochaczew lived in peace. Obviously, this helped the economic development.

The end of the 14th century, the 15th century and the beginning of the 16th century – this was the time of the greatest development of the Sochaczew artisans. Business was not able to flourish as greatly for there were two large competitors in the neighborhood – Lowicz and Warsaw. Lowicz (24 kilometers from Sochaczew) administratively subordinate to Sochaczew – later became the property and residence of the archbishops of Gniezn, the first dignitaries of the Polish kingdom whose court was not subordinate to the kings. Furthermore, the clergy was freed from various taxes, as were the merchants of Lowicz, who were subordinate to the archbishop. Therefore, the merchants of Sochaczew, who exported their grain by water to Danzig along the same rivers as did the Lowiczer merchants, the Bzura and Wisla, were not able to compete with the merchants of Lowicz, for the former were required to pay a water duty and the latter were not. Warsaw, which was not far away (56 kilometers), became a competitor not by defeat, since the city belonged to Crown Poland during the time of the royal decrees (at the first half of the 14th century).

The sources surmise that before that time, the grain business in Sochaczew played a very major role. It is known that the city had its own unit of measure, known as the "Sochaczew horseshoe" (a unit of measure that was used by the loaders who loaded the ferries that went to Danzig), and the "Sochaczew Kortz" [6]. The Sochaczew units of measure were larger than the Danzig units of measure. The meat trade also flourished greatly.

The development of artisanship was very rapid. In the 16th century, artisans from forty different trades worked in Sochaczew. The rug makers were the most prominent. The rugs from Sochaczew were very fine and expensive.

Kings and bishops purchased them. They were written in wills. Sochaczew textiles, on the other hand, were quite cheap. Those textiles were used by the common folk. In the Sochaczew castle, only the guards wore clothes made from that cloth. However, this cloth was produced in great quantities and sent throughout Poland. It went to Krakow and Poznan and into Prussia via Lublin and Zamosc.

The first privilege that we know of in Sochaczew stems from 1407. Ziemowit IV granted it. There certainly must have been older privileges, since sources from prior to the year 1368 call the city "civitas", a name (Latin) that was given only to a large city. Specialists in medieval history believe that the first privilege was granted in Sochaczew at the beginning of that century, or even earlier. We do not know very much about the privilege of 1407, which was not preserved, and of which we only know from second hand sources. We know more about the privilege of 1434, granted by Ziemowit V, of whom we have heard regarding the war council of Wadyslaw Jagiello. This was the prototype of all later rights granted in the city. All Polish kings later confirmed this privilege. This privilege was similar to those of the other "king's cities": Radom and Kazimierz [7].

In the 15th century, there was a hospital, and old age home and a hospital church in Sochaczew.

The dynasty of the dukes of Mazowia, who reigned in Plock, Rawa and Sochaczew, died out in 1426. Duchess Anna, mother of the recently deceased former duke and the widow of Duke Wladyslaw (who fought with the king's bodyguards under Grunwald) was bequeathed the Sochaczewer Duchy along with the castle in the city for life by her husband. In 1476, Anna, out of her own goodwill – without reckoning with the opposition of the Duke of Warsaw – gave everything to King Kazimierz Jagiellonczyk, who thereby received four cities: Bolimow, Brdow, Mszcsonow (Amszczenow) and Kolo. Earlier, the Duchy of Rawa –- relying on an agreement – united with Crown Poland and became a woyewoyda (province). In 1476, the Duchy of Sochaczew again became "The

Sochaczew Land", the motto of the fortress (which was the seat of the central administration of the entire land). The economic life of the city again began to develop normally. The kings, as has been stated, again renewed all of the privileges.

The development of the city became inhibited during the second half of the 16th century and first half of the 17th century. This was a result of the privileged positions held by the szlachta [8] in Poland, which had a similar negative influence on the economic life of all Polish cities, with the exception of the largest cities of Krakow and Warsaw. In Sochaczew, this caused only a recession in the economy, but not a catastrophe.

The catastrophe first came in the middle of the 17th century. This was caused by the Swedish war ("the flood"). The city and the castle were burnt. A portion of the population was killed, a portion was expelled, and the largest portion died from the epidemics that erupted in the wake of the war. From that time until the end of the Polish Republic (1795), Sochaczew vegetated as a small town, populated almost exclusively by Jewish poor people. It also used to serve as the confluence of the various szlachta. The churches of the Dominican and Friar-Dominican parishes were rebuilt. Since the castle had been burnt, they used to have to meet in the Dominican church.

At the time of the large scale Sejm [9] (1768-1772), when it was decided to strengthen Poland militarily, expand the army to 100,000 men, etc., a series of fortresses were rebuilt, including in Sochaczew. Unfortunately, this was only for a short duration. In 1793, at the time of the second partition of Poland in the year 1794, when the generals Duke Jozef Poniatowski and Henryk Dombrowski participated in the Kosciuszko uprising that came to a head near the Bzura behind Kamion and Sochaczew, the castle was again destroyed, and remains a ruin until this day.

In 1793, at the time of the warwith Prussia, the church parish was again burnt, and was never rebuilt.

II

The first information about Jews in Sochaczew comes from the 16th century. At first they were required to settle only in a few houses, and they were forbidden to circulate among Christians and to assemble publicly [10]. Only at the fairs, that is to say on the market days, were they permitted todisplay their merchandise for sale. That implies that the Jews of Sochaczew– similar to the Jews in all of the middle-sized cities of Europe – had to live in their own Jewish quarter (ghetto) at that time. In Sochaczew, this was on the Podzamcze (behind the castle).

At the time of the reign of Zygmunt August (1548-1572), there were eight houses there, and the number of individuals was approximately thirty. The Jews had their elders who governed them. The Jews, like all the other citizens of the city, paid the royal tolls and the silver tax, with the exception of the war tax, which they paid double; for Jews did not serve in the military.

The Jews paid a portion of their taxes in a natural fashion. Yearly at Wielkanoc (Easter), the owners of the houses paid the Starosta (mayor) a pound of pepper, and the tenants paid a half a pound.

The relations between the Christians and Jews at that time were not very good. The Christian citizens of the city complained that the Jews were "for us not very necessary" – for they purchase and export from the city merchandise that we need for our work such as fat, wool, leather and other items, and therefore the price of these items rises. The Polish artisans lacked raw materials; this situation caused a great opportunity for the Jews. It is very possible that the economic terrain was the cause of the legal case alleging that Jews desecrated Catholic holy places. As a result of this litigation that was caused by a Christian woman who served as a maid among Jews, Dorota

Lawancka, several Jews were beheaded and burnt (a few sources, report these things differently) in the Market Place of Sochaczew. [11]

The Papal emissary Alojzy Lipoan had an influence on this evil verdict, and thanks to him, the sentence was immediately executed. On the other hand, King Stanislaw August felt very bad about this situation when he found out about it.

The delegation of szlachta of the Polish Sejm, headed by the Hetman [12] Jan Tarnowski, exploited the next sitting of the Sejm in their struggle against the Polish bishops, in order to exclude them from the Polish senate.

As is known, the delegates lost this battle.

At that time (1564), the following Jews lived in Sochaczew: Izak (Yitzchak) Roczimek who was the owner of orchards; Moshe – a carpenter; and Michael – an owner of a house.

At the time of the reign of Zygmunt III (1587-1632), there were already 22 Jewish houses in Sochaczew. However, when those houses were burnt down during a fire in the entire city (Sochaczew was often burnt down), the Jews did not hasten to rebuild them. In accordance with the royal decree, it was forbidden for "strangers" to live in Polish cities, and this was punishable by the confiscation of property and exile from the land.

Nevertheless, it was possible for them to rebuild, for the son and heir of Zygmunt III, King Wadyslaw IV (1632-1648) granted a privilege to the Jews of Sochaczew permitting them to have their own well and bathhouse as well as a synagogue upon the original property. This privilege also freed the rabbi, the teacher and the cantor of the synagogue from all taxes and statutory duties. The Jewish community possessed a synagogue and a cemetery. Apparently the community was sufficiently well to do so as to be able to build and maintain all of these institutions, even though the population was so small. It is significant that, first and foremost, they were able to have their own well.

There were always few wells in Sochaczew. Until our time, water carriers would carry water from the Bzura through the town and sell it by the bucket.

During the war with Sweden (in the middle of the 17th century), the city was completely destroyed and the population was exiled. Jews took over the abandoned houses and nobody interfered with them. Just the opposite, King Jan Kazimierz (1648-1668) issued an edict in 1658 permitting Jews to build houses in the cities of Mazowia. According to Surowiec, only Jews, on account of their low lifestyle and level of solidarity, were able to tolerate the poor conditions that prevailed in Polish cities since the middle of the 17th century.

In the second half of the 17th century as well as in the 18th century, the Jews in Sochaczew became a significant majority of the population.

Their livelihood for the most part came from business with the military. For example, we know that Siemanowska, the Kasztelan of Wielun, gave a loan of 3,000 zloty to Jews. Jews also worked as artisans. At the time of the four-year Sejm (1768-1772) a Jew was employed as a tailor even in the church. He sewed all of the vestments and items that were needed for the Christian prayer services.

In the year 1749, a resident of Sochaczew, the Jew Lewka (Leib) Moszkowicz (the son of Moshe) received a certificate from King August III (1733-1763) confirming the privilege that was given to the Jews of Sochaczew by King Wladyslaw IV (the privilege that granted the right to own houses, fields, and gardens, as well as the right to deal with various businesses, including the distillation of liquor, slaughtering of animals, and selling meat in the old market).

At the time of the Kosciuszko uprising (1794), Jews, along with the other citizens of the city, donated money to assist the uprising.

The fire station.

When the parish church burnt down in 1793, the Jewish community took the remaining materials and built a synagogue for themselves (this was certainly the synagogue that the Germans destroyed in the last war). Thereby, the Jews were obligated that, if the church were to be rebuilt, they would have to provide either bricks, or pay 5,000 zloty. The church was not rebuilt, and the Jews never had to pay this obligation. As far as I know, the parish itself never demanded payment of this obligation.

When the city fell under Russian rule, the relations between the Polish and Jewish citizens were matter-of-fact and good. In 1905, at the time of the Polish nationalist demonstrations, the painter Rozenfeld gave a public speech which began: "I am a Jew and a Pole", and burst out in tears.

{There is a half page footnote at the conclusion of this section, as follows:}

Janina Swierzynska, a Magister [13] of History, is an elderly woman who is currently concluding a major work "The History of Sochaczew from Olden Days until 1795" (the third partition of Poland). She sent us a précis of her work (in Polish).

Sochaczew natives know Mrs. Swierzynska due to her friendly relations with Jews prior to the war in Poland. She also provided a series of reminiscences regarding her former contacts with Jews:

In 1931 Jozek Monia was a member of the planning committee for the 50th anniversary Jubilee of the fire station. Chil Widelec excelled in his ten years of services with the fire station.

Moszek Tykocziner was a member of the first department. Yoel Gelbsztejn, Yitzchak Weinstock and Hersch Graubert played in the orchestra.

Before the First World War, the widow Rozen was employed by her father in his brewery. After her death, at the time of the First World War, her son opened up a shop on Staszic Street.

A group of pioneers studied agricultural work on a farm that belonged to the Swierzynska family, and later immigrated to the Land of Israel. This was after the First World War.

At the time of the last war, the younger citizens would sneak out the Jewish quarter. This was prior to the Jews being shipped off to Warsaw and from there to their deaths. When she came back, Szwiezsinska inquired about the fate of her brother, who was at that time in German captivity.

Mrs. Swierzynska also relates that a few years ago, archeological excavations were conducted at the market place. At that time, the magistrate's office was discovered. If she is not mistaken, prior to the war, there were three Jewish sewing stores on that area of land, which were run by the three Frumer brothers. Among other things, they found many torn Jewish books. All of these were shipped to Warsaw, and are now in the possession of the Woyewoda (regional) Conservatory.

{40}

A Score of Years as the Rabbi of Sochaczew
by Nachman Blumental
(Rabbi Shmuel Yitzchak Landau of blessed memory)
Translated by Jerrold Landau

The Organization of Sochaczew Émigrés owns a very interesting ledger, maintained most certainly by the pre First World War Sochaczew Rabbi with his own handwriting from the years 1902-1912. A score of years of Jewish life is portrayed with through his vivid view.

Truth be told, the name "ledger" does not appropriately describe this manuscript. For in it we see a chronicle of all of the occurrences that took place during a certain slice of time in a certain place, which the chronicler recorded and collected. He described everything that took place in a natural fashion. From the second side, I understand that this work is not merely a protocol book of either communal council or a specific institution (synagogue, Beis Midrash, a Mishna learning society, etc.) from the old times.

In our case, we have something more and something less than such a "simple" ledger. Something less: because its author, Rabbi Shmuel Yitzchak Landau of blessed memory, did not generally chronicle the events of his community, although this might be the most important. He made note of that which transpired as he served as the officiating rabbi in his city. He described that which he, as can be said, took care of in an official capacity. One can therefore regard this manuscript, from an observer's viewpoint, as a notation book of the communal activity of the rabbi in his time, when he lived and worked in Sochaczew. (After that, he apparently left Sochaczew.)

On the other hand, the manuscript is perhaps more than a "simple" ledger. It is tantamount to a document book, as we shall see. In that manuscript, we find documents of claim certified by others, by the interested parties, who came to the rabbi of the town, to "their" local rabbi, to ask his advice.

If the rabbi drew up some sort of agreement between the two sides, we see his signature under the agreement. If somebody had to pay a portion or the entire sum of money that was owed to someone and used the rabbi as an intermediary, the rabbi would write a confirmation in the ledger. He would do so in the language that he knew: Hebrew, Yiddish, Polish or Russian.

Thereby, that ledger contains a great amount of words of faith. It is not dry and drab. One gets a feel of variegated colors in his full language.

Externally: The manuscript consists of two parts. One is written as a bookkeeping ledger in large format with red and blue lines – horizontal and vertical – and is written solely in Russian. It consists of 22 pages, written on both sides. Apparently, the beginning is missing from the book. Since the pages are not numbered, and we only have one hard tablet of the binding (the second), we cannot estimate how much is missing.

The note book was apparently written for the authorities. That explains the language – Sochaczew belonged at the time to the Warsaw Gubernia and was a part of Congress Poland, which belonged to Russia. It contains lists, certificates from people, mainly from people who were getting married. These certificates were read out three times in the synagogue, as was required by the law [14].

That portion of the manuscript begins from 1902 and ends in 1905. We have 54 such certificates from 1902, 76 from 1903, and 54 from 1904. (The final note is from December 27th. Following it is number 55, but without any contents.)

We have 25 such certificates from 1905 (the final certificate is from May 31, which is from slightly less than half of the year).

The numbers 26-31 are written in the first column from the year 1905, but further contents are missing. Evidently, the end of the book is also missing.

On the empty area of the last side, there are notices of paid money with names, written with a feather and lead in Polish. This is evidently from a later era.

These lists – the total number is 209 – tell us the number of weddings that took place between Sochaczewer Jews – at the minimum with one side being from Sochaczew – in the aforementioned years. The first note, bearing the number 1, is from January 8, 1902 (perhaps until that time there were no weddings) until May 31, 1905.

Here is the contents of the first notice, in Yiddish translation: "On January 8, 1902, a certificate of banns was issued for the wedding in the Sochaczew Jewish synagogue between the young man Moshe Bendkower, 23 years old, the son of the late Yankel and Chana, and the young woman Hinda Ester Szpigiel, 29 years old, the daughter of the late Shlomo and Pesel Chaya. The first reading took place on the 22nd, the second on the 29th of December 1901, and the third on January 5th of the current year." On the side, the word "signed" is written with a different pen and different handwriting. (Perhaps someone from the authorities, who audited the books, signed.) For someone who seeks knowledge about family life in Sochaczew of that time, this book is obviously an important source.

Aside from that certificate, we have here twelve notes about documents that were given over by the authorities through the rabbinate, as follows:

1. On January 24, 1902, a declaration was sent to the court of peace that Moshe Kohan and Perl Lea Diamant are in agreement regarding the 4 Rubles and 20 Kopeks that Kohan demanded from Diamant. Since the judge desired an oath from Kohan, it fell away, since Kohan declared that he had no more demands from the woman. Evidently, the claimant decided to forego his demand in order to avoid swearing.

The fear of an oath (possibly even of a true oath) held many Orthodox Jews from having a judgement and having his rights taken care of in an public, non-Jewish court [15].

There was a similar document regarding another judgment between Efraim Kac and Wolf Litowski, and others.

Again on the 3rd of May of the same year, the rabbinate issued a certificate to Itzik Izak Najman that he was well versed in the laws of the Jewish faith and in the Hebrew language. Evidently this relates to the issue of whether he ought to be able to teach Jewish children "Zakon Bozi" [16] in an open school, or perhaps open his own cheder. Such a certificate was also issued to Shaya Yona Nut, Yisrael Zelwer, Michael Rozen and others in the same year.

Among the certificates, we find also one that confirmed that such and such a Jew was a resident of the city, and therefore should be protected from expulsion from the city.

On the tablet of the manuscript we also find a certificate with the date 1912 in an orthographical, error-ridden Polish with a signature of Jakob Morgensztern from Czekanow confirming that he owes the rabbi 30,000 (?) rubles.

Aside from this manuscript, we have a second, notated in a wide-ruled notebook, unnumbered, in which a great amount was certainly missing. As with the first, this book, which is smaller, has only one hard tablet. That book is missing the beginning, and evidently the end.

That book includes various cards, notes, letters, and... promissory notes.

That manuscript is a sort of a catchall; a hodge-podge of various types of issues (including private matters), that a rabbi in a city such as Sochaczew (which is a regional city) had to take care of. We can find matters there that would normally pertain to various offices of the secular society. First of all, we have there a row of annotated Gets [17], which is the work of a rabbi. Second, there are records of all sorts of controversies among the Jewish residents that were brought to the rabbi for adjudication, rather than before the "Kazionem" court [18]. However what is novel is that disputes between Jews and Poles also came before the rabbi. The rabbi issued decisions even on such matters. The Poles evidently had more trust in the Jewish rabbi than the Russian judge... who in general did not have an overly positive reputation. Czarist Russia, as is known, was known throughout the world for bribery. That local official would have certainly taken from whoever would have given something to him in that regard.

That second section of manuscripts numbers 73 cards (aside from the empty ones), mostly written on both sides; aside from 50 various cards and notes (in a different format from the book).

The portion that was recorded with care and is of interest to us begins with the year 5663 (1903). It begins with a list – from the month of Adar – of people to whom the rabbi issued a hechsher [19] for a variety of items and products. Following that, there is information about Gets, exemptions, etc.

The first notice: "Today, Wednesday, 13th of Tammuz 5663, the woman Rachel the daughter of Yitzchak Meir was divorced from her husband, Mordechai Yisrael Yehoshua, and received a notice confirming such."

Then there is a long list of names of people who received exemptions from various "bonds" so that they would be able to marry of a son or a daughter. For a researcher of Jewish family life in general, and of Jewish life in Sochaczew itself and the surrounding area, this material is first class.

Suddenly, there is this type of announcement: "To make note of the fact that on Wednesday, 5663 (1903) the woman Chana Rachel the wife of Reb Yechezkel Zimler from the village of Witkowicz in this region came and announced that a few weeks prior from this time, her daughter, the young girl Dvora Reizel, approximately 4 years old, lost her virginity by jumping." [20]

After that there is another list of Gets, in accordance with the appropriate style.

After that, there is a long chain of certificates stating that certain Jews left the rabbi money in order to repay debts that they owed to others; afterwards there are certificates from those whose debts were in official hands – delivered from the rabbi's hand. An entire accounting! How much trust did the people have in their rabbi! For the most part, it deals with decision which the two sides fulfilled. The rabbi was the judge and also the executor of the decision. The rabbi conducted correspondence with both parties, warned them, made sure that both sides would be in peace, and finally come to an agreement that both sides would agree to.

A little bit later, there is a promissory note written by the rabbi, indicating that the signer of the note could not pay the amount on one occasion. The rabbi dragged out the money slowly from the signer until the entire promissory note was paid off. The plaintiff signed underneath – all in the same ledger – that he has no more complaints against the defendant.

And now there was a difficult problem that tormented the rabbi, regarding how to write the Jewish name in a Get so that it will be in accordance with the law. It should not, G-d forbid, be missing a letter, and that there should not be any superfluous mark in the text of the Get, so that it should not be invalid [21]. The Rabbi writes: On Thursday of the Torah portion of Shoftim, 4th Elul 5670 (1910), the woman Branah (it was written with an 'h' at the end because thus did she sign, and with an aleph after the resh, and a he after the nun) the daughter of Berish (in the book Mayim Chaim, Berish is written without the yod) was divorced. It was unclear if his Hebrew name was Yisachar or Dov; therefore it is written that everybody calls him Berish). She was divorced from her husband who was known as Hershel. (There were two Gets there. In one, Hershel was written in accordance with the Hatam Sofer. Everyone reads the name with a segol [22] should write the name Hershel with an ayin after the he, without a yod. It was written with a nickname as Hershil [23], the reason being because his signature was always such. The opinion of the decision is already known, and therefore to remove all doubt, I have written two Gets.). The son of Moshe Aharon – – –

In order not to, Heaven forbid, make an error, the rabbi had to write two Gets: one with the name Hershel and the other with the name Hershil.

The same thing happened with the name Gedalia, where he wrote it once with the name Gedaliahu (with a vov at the end). On another occasion, the rabbi had difficulty with the name Leibish or Libish – this took place with regard to some sort of dispute between Hirsch Leib Jakubowicz (who could barely sign) and the gentile Stanislaw Bondanowicz. The rabbi obligated the Jew to pay "to Herr [24] Stanislaw" the sum of 8.75 rubles each Rosh Chodesh – until he has paid off the entire loan of 35 rubles.

The gentile, unfortunately, had to know when Rosh Chodesh [25] occurred in order to know when to expect a payment.

The "uncircumcised" [26] Stanislaw was not the only one who came to the rabbi for litigation and one the case!

There is even a contract of sale in which a Jew rents to a gentile a mill and sells to him horses and saddles of all types, for a non-insignificant sum in those days – 15,000 rubles. The contract is written in Hebrew (which was certainly explained and translated for the Pole). It explicitly states, "I have rented to the uncircumcised Szikorski". The uncircumcised man seemed to have not found an explanation for the words and sooner went to the rabbi than a non-Jewish notary. It is also quite possible that, aside from his trust in the rabbi, the gentile was certain that Jew would sooner obey a contract signed by the rabbi – as the Poles would call it "Pod Cherm" – than a contract signed by a Russian official.

It is also possible that the situation was helped by the fact that the rabbi would certainly have been cheaper than a gentile notary!

Here is another type of issue: a young man came and complained that his wife had not become pregnant. A difficult matter. What should the rabbinical court (consisting of three judges) do? It did not issue a decision on the spot. However, it did obligate the woman to travel to Warsaw to visit "an expert doctor", so that he could investigate and assert "if she is according to the way of all the woman, or if, through some sort of therapy, she could be the way of all the woman". With one word, the court understood the matter as would a modern court. I wish to add, not strictly in accordance with halacha [27]. They turned to an expert, a person, a scientist, to express his opinion, so that they would know how to deal with the situation.

There is recorded something that would arouse the suspense of the reader – a sort of criminal story.

A woman came to the rabbi and complained that her husband had disappeared a little while previously. They did not know where he had perished. She gave some details about what happened, a description of her husband, and the like. A little time later, the rabbi accepted a testimony from a Jew who saw a corpse out in the field. He gave a description of the corpse as he had seen it. He declared, "He had slightly white, yellowish {!} eyebrows, and the hairs of his beard were yellowish". On the basis of this testimony, the rabbi determined that this was the husband of the woman who had earlier come with her complaint that her husband had disappeared.

It is a shame that we do not have any further details regarding this case. Perhaps this is because we did not have the entire ledger, but only a section of it. On the other side, the case, being a capital case, was not in the jurisdiction of the rabbi but rather of the local governing authorities, who had certainly investigated such a matter. The rabbi would have had no connection with this case. He only had interest in the question of the woman: is she an aguna or a widow? [28] From so far away, we see the matter being played out in the ledger of the rabbi. If the ledger had been written somewhat differently there would have been a great deal of writing there – about the murder itself, where it took place, why, etc. The rabbi, on the other hand, in his official capacity, did not include any description of private matters or experiences. It was strictly a journal of his activities as a rabbi – had he taken interest in the case, he would have gone beyond the bounds of his legal capacity.

Here we have a second case of the same type.

About six years earlier, a man left his wife in the town of Leczyza and never returned. Then it mentions that a Jew from Sochaczew, approximately six years previously (on the day after the Festival of Shavuot, 5662 – 1902) found a drowned man on the banks of the Wisla River near Sochaczew. He had a scald mark on his hand. This was the exact sign that the widow had given...

And a third case...

A Jewish woman came to the rabbi and explained that her husband had left and not returned. He had been sick, and she went with him to several doctors. Some of the doctors told her that he had a very weak heart, and some of them told her that he was nervous. He indeed appeared nervous, for he always told her that he was going to die..." Indeed, when the Wisla calmed down in the summertime, they found a dead body on the banks of the river, with the same signs and same clothing that the woman had described (he was wearing suspenders with flowers, and a collar with a black tie. She also said that he was wore a silver watch with dviske [29] chain, with embedded pebbles of various colors.)

Only the clock with the "dviske" chain did the woman not describe, for they are "under the hand of the sledevatil" [30], investigator (why explicitly this?!). The woman also recognized the blue pen that was on him, since she had seen that blue pen being given by her husband to their son to play with... A fascinating and sad story! Even here the rabbi does not give any excess details.

Of the great many deeds, relating to various matters, that the rabbi deal with in an official capacity, a reasonable number [31] – as is understandable in our situation – were devoted to disputes between partners (monetary matters). People came to the rabbi for litigation. He issued a decision, and the sides accepted his decision and signed accordingly. The promissory notes and receipts were deposited with the rabbi on contingency; people also pay through him into the various councils, and he returns the written notes of obligation. Everything is recorded in the same ledger.

The rabbi in this case was not only the judge (in important cases, he served as the head of the rabbinical court, and took two other rabbis to assist him, or he acts as an arbitrator and the two sides choose adjudicators), but he also served as executor. If one of the sides does not uphold the agreement, he sends a warning to him, threatens him, and pesters him until he gives in.

The rabbi is also the confidant of both sides, and plays the role of a bank. He lends out money, pays out, etc. All of this belongs to the rabbi of a small town.

And among the debts that he pays, he also has his own, private ones.

Contracts sealed between two Jews for a partnership for a specific period of time form another section of work that is conducted by the rabbi. This is a very interesting chapter, and one can learn a great deal from it regarding the economic life of the Jews in those places in those times. A large number of Jews were occupied with leasing summer orchards from the farmers. These contracts specify precisely what the partners put into the business, what they must do, and how they will divide up the profits. One side of the business is the "arel" (uncircumcised person) from whom one rents the orchard. His participation is also precisely defined. That work in the orchard is sometimes referred to as "haganot" [32] in the ledger. Jews were also occupied in the grain business. They did not only enter into business ties with "arels", but also with the "poretz" [33], the owner of the village, the possessor. The rabbi does not refer to him as the "arel", but rather as the "adon" ("master" (Master Gorecki, Master Sendziekowski, who leased the "shveig" to Jews, etc.[34]). Such a master sells a large quantity of wheat to Jews, or released a large orchard to Jews, etc.

An other type of trade that the Jews in the city occupied themselves with was the "shmatte trade" [35]. Here as well, a partnership was created for the work. Three types of "shmattes" (cloths) were specified in the contracts: 1) smooth cloths; 2) scraps; 3) singed cloth. Incidentally, specialists defined the difference between these types.

We did not record all of the trades that are listed in the ledger, and with which Jews from Sochaczew and its environs occupied themselves. I wish to emphasize that it was not only with trades that Jews were occupied, sitting an entire day in a store waiting for a purchaser to come in, who would often return to Jews and non-Jews [36].

Issues of weddings, divorces, breaking of matches, and birth of children occupy more place in the ledger than business dealings do. More than once, these are all recorded on one and the same side: it is specified that on a certain day, the wedding took place between the groom – who is so and so years old – with the bride – who is so and so years old.

(Incidentally, I noticed that in many cases, the bride was significantly older than the groom. Was this perhaps a problem that is worthwhile for us to take interest in?)

Then, the parents of the engaged couple come to the rabbi and wish to break off the engagement. The rabbi was called upon to return the gifts that the groom had received from the bride's side. The bride also had to return the gifts that she had received from the groom's side, etc. Only after the end of the long negotiations does the rabbi make a point: if the sides regret what is presently taking place… that if there is a way out for the angry groom and bride to reconcile, perhaps they can become appeased…

In apposition to the brief notices of weddings, we have even briefer notices regarding the death of so and so. The rabbi recorded who brought the news to him, and where the even took place.

A little further on, we have a notice that such and such a woman gave information that she had given birth to a child on such and such a day. Sometimes he dealt with a birth that had taken place several years earlier! One would come to inform the rabbi when there was a need to do so. To simply go to an office to present information that a child had been born was not "wishing words" [37] in those days. Jews did not hurry to do so.

From the large scale and broad work of the rabbi, which encompassed dozens of small settlements that did not have their own judge – one can see the level of trust that people placed in him – both Jews and gentiles.

Among the numerous cards that are lying in manuscript, one finds a letter written in Polish from a Pole to a Jew, informing him that he should come on a specific day to the "Sendzia" (that is the government judge) and sign an deed – "in accordance with what the rabbi has decreed".

He noted everything with such modesty and restraint. There were no overly "harsh" words. The sides understood the hints, so the sides did not have to annotate a long "deed of sale". An agreement, a compromise, or a legal decision. He shunned branding the debtor, he sought a way of compromise, a way out for the two sides. With few words, he gives over the essence of the matter, without deliberating over the details.

We can imagine how much time the rabbi spent hearing out the sides, how many cuss-words each of the disputants honored the other side with (and perhaps even more than cuss-words), how many complaints and reasons they placed before the rabbi – all of this is not registered in the protocol. The rabbi issued his decisions briefly and sharply. His words resulted in "Peace upon Israel"!

From the following notice, we can see how far the authority and influence of the rabbi extended:

"We accept upon ourselves to make peace between us from this day forward, not to cause any controversy, Heaven forbid, not to pursue each other in matters of livelihood, and not to cause damage, Heaven forbid, in matters regarding the body or money. We forgive each other completely with regard to any matters that took place up to this time, and with regard to all types of disputes and arguments that took place between us. We affix our signatures to this on Thursday, the fourth Intermediate Day of Sukkot, and we accept all of the above upon ourselves."

Four signatures appear under this.

We do not know at this time what the basis of dispute was between the four Jews, and we also do not know who they four Jews were. We do know that these were four toiling Jews, and from their signatures we can deduce that holding a pen in their hand was not a simple matter for them! These Jews had significant worries abut livelihood, and therefore the disputes (usually with regard to competition). However, finally, the goodwill between the sides, and certainly also the influence of the rabbi, prevailed upon them to come together and forgive each other completely. This did not take place on the eve of Yom Kipper (when such events usually take place), but rather on the Intermediate Days of Sukkot! [38]

Aside from such items, we find in the manuscript – on various pages – lists of Jews who sold their Chometz to the rabbi on the eve of Passover, so that the rabbi can sell it afterwards to an "arel". [39]

One list, from the year 5668 (1908) contains 206 entries. Only number 20 is missing.

In order to characterize the typical material that is found in this list, you will permit me to bring down one such entry.

"97. Reb Aharon Bester from the village of Tranow of the community of Chodokruw [40] rented the storehouse that he owns in the aforementioned village, and also the attic above his place of residence; and he sold all types of Chometz, questionable Chometz, vessels and sacks of Chometz. He retained the rights of walking through those areas. He also sold all of the standing fowl (!) in that aforementioned attic, aside from one turkey... [41]"

The second list from the year 5660 (1900) contains 213 entries (it is missing everything until number 20). A third list, from the year 5671 (1911), numbers 211. So many Jews signed over their Chometz to the rabbi!

What can we learn from the dry and sparse facts that we find in these lists?

First of all, we discover [42] that we find here the names of many Jews who lived in villages in the near and far vicinity of the city of Sochaczew. This includes a few small villages where Jews later did not live on account of the anti-Semitic situation. However, 50-60 years ago, the Jews lived and work peacefully there. From these lists we also see that, on more than one occasion, a Jew lived together with a gentile in a house. On more than one occasion, a Jew rented a room or a stable from an arel (as they were called by the author), and peacefully earned their peace of bread (they were certainly not excessively wealthy individuals!)

From the "things" that the Jews signed over in their sale of Chometz, we can derive their occupations. It should be emphasized that a large number of Jews – both in the regional city of Sochaczew and in the province – had stalls with horses or cows. That means that they were coachmen, horse dealers, or dairymen – selling milk or producing "products that are derived from milk", as they are called in our manuscript.

From other things that are recorded in those lists, grain stands out, which Jews held in their granaries (as they are indeed called in the Hebrew of the rabbi [43].

The language of the ledger is interesting. As is known, our rabbis were not expert in grammar. The gender of the word, especially in a verb, does not interest them. A present tense instead of a past tense, or vice versa, is also not an error to them.

The large number of Yiddish words that we find in the text is also characteristic. I believe that in such cases, the rabbi did not know the appropriate Hebrew word. It is clear that this is a reason, but not the only one. There is also another, more important, reason. This is the precision which typifies our author. A Hebrew word might not describe the thing with exact precision. The meaning that the old Hebrew word (that the rabbi knew from the Bible) connoted might have become obsolete with the passage of time. The former Hebrew noun may not portray today's reality. Therefore, the writer must use a Yiddish word that designates the matter in a unique manner, is understood by everybody, and is not prone to misinterpretation. He was dealing here with important judicial documents; things must be the clearest of the clear.

A rabbi would certainly not be familiar with new Hebrew words, and a half a century ago, he would certainly not have used such [44]. Only Yiddish words remained.

Another category of foreign words in our manuscript are those of international application, or those that would be impressive to the Russian authorities. For example, the word "sond" stands out – the Russian court. By the use of this word, the author makes it clear to everybody that he is not referring to a Beis Din (rabbinical court). A Hebrew word here could only cripple the situation.

Here is a partial list of Yiddish and other foreign words that we encounter very often in our ledger, which was written in Hebrew.

The Apotek, near a hreient, the balkon, a broiz, viorst, hotelmacher, hatovoziszstvoya [45].

Oysgeshikevet for a gevelb, virok, sond, smattes (shmattes), on nochname, handshlag. [46].

Veksl, em Novirok (Gentile for New Year) [47].

In the matter of trepin, the oficina, the fatziat, regarding the plimp (from a well), a tzentin (a tenth person), regarding the plan, a store of bakalia, restaratzia, to give him reyentovey, akt, fierkosa, kastenes, flashin, the striz, the stall that is zayzod, frachtstantzia, servetet [48], the shenkl, the bofet, the shank, the first shtok, the second shtok, etc., the platz [49].

An address is written as none other than in the following example: "In the city of Lodz, old city, number [50]...", or "under number". Protestn [to protest], kvitel [a note], receptn [probably receipts], podlage, shines, kvitantzia [a receipt of check], kavtzia, the tzene [cost] on the new dwelling, according to the tzene, the stall, the stall of birds (lul!) [lul being a known Hebrew word for chicken coop], the beidl [booth]. Shetzkarnia (shetshkarnia, where one cuts straw on sietshke), three morges [three acres], a room called magazin, a measure of wheat of 4 zere [evidently a measure of volume], 3 zere... rozovka.

There are also words that later fell into disuse. Thus, we encounter a few times the words "Shveig" or "Shvag". This means that Jews leased from the poretz the entire quantity of milk that came from his cow, and made dairy products from it (cheese, sour cream, etc.). Similar words, such as sodzinkes and yarkelech belong to this category.

From this standpoint as well, the ledger is an interesting and educational document.

This manuscript has an entirely different value for Jews of Sochaczew. It reminds them of their own past. Among the lists of names, among the written incidents, they might perhaps find themselves. If not, they will certainly find their acquaintances, relatives. Who knows if perhaps they might find their own parents, and certainly their grandparents!

This dry, matter-of-fact document will be near and homelike to us. It is a bit of our cut off past, a piece of our own essence!

We bring down here one of the characteristic agreements that we find in the ledger. We bring it down word for word, without changing anything. Our own remarks appear in parentheses.

This is a memorial that on Tuesday of the year 5669 (1909) Reb Mordechai Pinczewski and Reb Binem Frumer from this holy city came before me. Reb Mordechai Pinczewski gave a contract to Reb Binem Frumer that he could live in the dwelling that he had lived in from today for another two (!) years, from Rosh Chodesh Cheshvan of the year 5670 until Rosh Chodesh Cheshvan of the year 5672 for the sum of 450 Rubles a year. A condition exists between them that if during the course of the two years [51] Reb Mordechai increases the payment that he set for this house, and if he furnishes another shop [52], then the aforementioned Reb Binem Frumer can live there for a third year, that is until Rosh Chodesh Cheshvan of the year 5673 for the aforementioned sum of 450 rubles. However the choice shall be in the hands of Reb Mordechai Pinczewski to decide regarding Reb Binem Frumer, that is, he has the authority to give the aforementioned Reb Binem another store (!) with living quarters in the aforementioned house. However, the tzene (!) [53] of the new dwelling with the store will be as is recorded (!) by three men who are expert in the value of the new store with the dwellings. All of this was agreed upon by means of a kinyan sudar [54] to establish the situation as stated above. They also affixed their signatures to affirm the aforementioned.

On such and such a day, such and such a year

Mordechai Pinczewski

Simcha Binem the son of Yitzchak Menachem of blessed memory Frumer

TRANSLATOR'S FOOTNOTES:

1. There is a Polish footnote here at the bottom of the page, as follows: "Juliana Ursyna Niemcewicz. Podroze historyezne po ziemiach polskich miedzy rokiem 1811 a 1828 odbyte – Paryz 1858".
2. Polish for marketplace.
3. Polish for Lawrence.
4. The word used here is "fuerstentum", which is German for duchy.
5. The dates given here are obviously incorrect. They should be in the 1600s.
6. A unit of measure, possibly a quart.
7. The Yiddish spelling here is closer to Czwizmir or Tzuizmir, and does not resemble the spelling of the occurrences of the proper name 'Kazimierz' in this section – however I could not identify a town with that spelling.
8. Szlachta are the Polish noblemen (literally 'landed gentry').
9. Polish parliamentary gathering.
10. There is a footnote on this page: This is according to the work of Y. Trunk, which in this connection is accurate.
11. See the history section by Y. Trunk on page 607 for more detail on this incident.
12. 'Hetman' is an official Polish government position.
13. The Polish equivalent of a Master's Degree.
14. This is obviously referring to the secular law at the time. These certificates would be marriage banns.
15. An oath is considered a serious matter in Jewish law at the best of times. This would be particularly true if administered in a gentile court.
16. Zakon means "monastery" or "convent", Bozi refers to god. I suspect that this is a Polish term for religious studies.
17. A Get is a Jewish bill of divorce. The Get is given by the husband (or emissary) to the wife. Then it is returned to the rabbinical court for safekeeping, and a document is given to the wife certifying that a Get was given, and that she is divorced.
18. Seemingly a secular court.
19. A certificate of kashruth.
20. Evidently, such a note was meant to protect the girl's status of a virgin upon marriage, should a question arise. Interestingly, the specific date is missing in this note.

21. The consequences of an invalid Get are quite severe in Jewish law. If the wife remarried without a proper Get, the children of the second marriage would be considered 'mamzerim' ('bastards' for want of a better word).
22. The soft 'e' vowel.
23. With a yod after the shin. The correct spelling of a name on a Get is a prerequisite for validity. This is the reason for the entire complex spelling discussion here.
24. Literally "Herl", seemingly a Yiddish diminutive of the German 'Herr' – Mr.
25. The New Moon, which marks the beginning of the Jewish month.
26. 'Arel' – a term stressing his gentile status. r
27. Traditional Halacha did not deal with the possibility of therapy for infertility.
28. An aguna is a woman who is bound to her husband, whose death cannot be determined definitively. Such a woman is not allowed to remarry. The term is used in modern parlance for a woman who is bound to a husband who refused to issue a Get.
29. I am not sure of the meaning of this term. It is evidently a type of watch, perhaps a brand name.
30. This word means 'investigator'.
31. The word really means "economical" or "thrifty". I am not sure if this means "a small amount", or "a reasonable amount". I chose the latter from the context.
32. Hebrew for "the gardens".
33. A "poretz" is the landowner.
34. I am not sure what "shveig" means here. It usually means "under one's hat", or "quiet".
35. A shmatte is a rag, but in this connotation refers to cloth. Interestingly enough, the term used here is 'smatte' (with the s rather than the sh sound). However, the term is defined in parentheses as 'shmatte'. The sh sound is pronounced as s by Lithuanian Jews, so I am not sure what the implication is here.
36. This sentence is garbled in the original. I am not sure of its intended meaning.
37. Seemingly a term for "appropriate custom".
38. The fourth Intermediate Day of Sukkot occurs ten days after Yom Kippur.
39. It is forbidden for a Jew to own leavened products on Passover (let alone eat them). As it is often impractical to dispose of one's entire stock of leavened products, it is possible to arrange a sale of such to a gentile. These leavened products then do not have to be moved out of the house, but they do have to be cordoned off. The individual Jews designate the rabbi as the agent to transact the sale with a gentile. After Passover, the sale in terminated (the legal intricacies are beyond the scope of this footnote), and the ownership reverts to the individual Jews.
40. I could not identify these locations.
41. The text itself inserted the exclamation mark here – as the selling of livestock as Chometz is not the usual custom.
42. The literal term used here is "it is thrown in our eyes".
43. The Yiddish term here is "shpeichler", meaning granary. The implication here is that the rabbi recorded his notes in Hebrew, but used the Yiddish word in a Hebrew sentence.
44. The early 1900s was the very beginning of the renaissance of the modern Hebrew language. This renaissance brought with it many new words for concepts that did not exist in ancient Hebrew.
45. I am not able to identify many of these words in this and the following paragraph. Apotek is a pharmacy. Balkon is a balcony. Broiz is Yiddish for brewery. Viorst (verst) is a Russian unit of distance. Hatelmacher might be a hat-maker, although the spelling here is unconventional.
46. Oysgeshikevet a gevelb is Yiddish for "to furnish a store". Virok has something to do with the Slavic word for year (see next paragraph). Sond seems to be Russian for a court, as previously mentioned.

Shmattes / Smattes are dealt with in a previous footnote. Nochname might mean surname – but it is unconventional. Handshlag might mean a beating administered with the hands.

47. Veksl is a promissory note or I.O.U.
48. The text inserts a note here indicating that the end part 'tet' has variation with an aleph and an ayin.
49. Plimp is a pump. Fierkosa is a safe (i.e. a place to store valuables). Kastenes might mean 'chests' (i.e. places to store valuables). Flashin are bottles. Frachtstanzia might have something to do with freight. Shenkl is a locker or cabinet. Shank is a cabinet. Shtok is a story of a building, so the first shtok is the first story. Platz is a space or lot.
50. The word 'number' is here in Yiddish. For the rest of the paragraph I will put my comments in square brackets.
51. The original switches from Hebrew to Yiddish here, in mid-sentence. The Yiddish in the next line is spelled very unconventionally.
52. The text switches back to Hebrew here.
53. A term for cost or payment.
54. A 'kinyan sudar' (contract sealed by the cloth), is a form of transferring ownership within Jewish law, whereas the owner picks up a piece of cloth or other simple object in lieu of the object that is transferring ownership. The picking up of the cloth effects the formal transfer of ownership. The kinyan sudar is frequently used today in Jewish ritual contracts – including at the sale of Chometz prior to Passover.

{64 - Yiddish} {612 - Hebrew}

{56}

The Rabbi's Court

The Inscription of the Tombstone of Sara Tzina
Translated by Jerrold Landau

The wife of the Admor Reb Avraham Borensztejn of Sochaczew (the author of Avnei Nezer).
She was the daughter of the holy Admor Reb Menachem Mendel of Kock.
She died in Sochaczew on 24 Kislev, 5670 (1910) and there is her resting place. [1]

I dwelt in the countries, the daughter of a flying angel
The chariot of G-d was in the holy Sinai
The glory of her righteousness flies through the world
Her excellence and merchandise are a new offering
The eyelids should weep and drop water
The Rabbi will supplicate to the heavens
The holy one of the honorable G-d, who reveals secrets
Menachem [2] of the house of Judah awoke those slumbering
The holy composition the Gaon of our strength and glory
A nest for wisdom, the key to our locked hearts
A woman of valor and wisdom, who excelled greatly
The sprout of her righteousness blossoms as a splendid vine
Holy ones assist her among the pure ones

She shines in the Heavenly treasuries
Her righteousness shall shine like the light of the seven days [3]
She will arise to life [4] after resting in peace
May her soul be bound in the bonds of eternal life

{57}

A Spiritual Center
A. Chetzroni
Translated by Jerrold Landau

Sochaczew – what Polish Jew does not recognize that name? Its name was also known far beyond its borders. It was apparently a town like several hundred other Jewish towns in Poland. What made it so well known among Jews? Sochaczew has to thank the Rebbe's court, the residence of the Rebbes who were known throughout the world by the name of Sochaczew. It was almost as if these were bound into a concept: Sochaczew Torah and Sochaczew Hassidism!

Sochaczew had a special success with its rabbis. It was a small town, but from way back, famous Gaonim occupied its rabbinical chair. Among others were the Gaon Reb Moshe (the brother of the Shach [5]); Reb Meir Ashkenazi, the author of "Panim Meirot"; later the Gaon Reb Leybish Charyf Helpern. Such greats in Hassidism as the holy Jew and Reb Yeshaya of Przeworsk would come to his Yeshiva. It is assumed that the Rebbe, Reb Bunim of Przysucha also studied with him in Sochaczew. Continuing on with the list: The Gaon and Kabbalist Reb Leybish of Korew; the Gaon Reb Elazar the Cohen of Pultusk the brother-in-law of Reb Yaakov of Lissa the "Chavat Daat". What was actually the attractive force of Sochaczew? It is possibly that the town permitted its rabbis to conduct a Yeshiva there, that the householders displayed love and respect for Torah scholars, and understood the need to create a home for students who left their homes and came to study in Sochaczew. What more did those Gaonim desire than that they be given the possibility to spread Torah?

It seems that this was also what attracted the renowned genius and Gaon Reb Avrahamel Borensztejn. He was a son-in-law of the Kocker Rebbe, Reb Mendel. He left his rabbinate in Nasielsk and took up the rabbinate in Sochaczew after the death of Reb Elazar the Cohen in 5643 – 1883. That rabbi, Reb Avrahamel, was the founder of the dynasty of Sochaczew Hassidism, through which the town obtained a place on the east [6] in Jewish history in Poland.

A new epoch in life in the town began with the arrival of Reb Avrahamel. It became a force of attraction, and turned into a center of Torah and Hassidism. Youths with sharp minds and a deep striving for perfection, who had a feeling for the new path of the intermingling of Torah with Hassidism which was promoted so basically and consistently by Reb Avrahamel, were attracted here. Kocker Hassidism, which strived for the pinnacle of truth, and the scholarship and sharpness of Reb Yitzchak Meir the Gerrer Rebbe (Chidushei Harim) were united in a novel and captivating manner. This Hassidism implied completeness – the harmony of the soul with the body, both towards the service of the Creator; as well as Torah – the Torah of truth through the clarity of halacha, which were intermingled into a unified concept in the hot-glowing and crystal clear sprit of the Gaon. Well-known rabbis came to the great Torah center, which had already taken an important place in the world of scholarship. They came to the sparkling Torah spring and bound themselves with eternity. Such greats as the Konicker rabbi, Gaon and decisor of Jewish law Reb Yoav Yehoshua (the author of "Cheklat Yoav"); the Gaon of Krakow Reb Yosef Engel, famous for his dozens of books; the head of the Warsaw court of Jewish law Reb Yitzchak Feigenbaum, and others. As well, Gaonim from

Lithuania, sharp minds and even sharper Misnagdim (opponents of Hassidism), would come to discuss and study, or to verify points of Halacha, without concerning themselves that the Gaon is simultaneously a Hassidic Rebbe. Kest-youths [7] and scholarly young men who searched for their way in learning with depth, wholeness and Hassidism, remained there for months or even years.

Aside from this, he maintained a constant exchange of correspondence with all of the Torah giants from around the world. They would turn to him from all Jewish communities with questions and difficult halachic dilemmas. The thousands of responsa that he wrote were later published in the seven volumes of "Responsa of Avnei Nezer", gave him the name in the Jewish world as the final arbiter. He became the decisor for Poland, in the same way as did Reb Yitzchak Elchanan of Kovno become such a generation later.

מצבת מרת שרה צינא

אשת האדמו"ר ר' אברהם בורנשטין מסוכצ'וב [בעל אבני נזר]
היא בתו של האדמו"ר הק' ר' מנחם מענדל מקוצק.

נפטרה בסוכצ'וב כ"ד כסלו תר"ע ושם מנו"כ.

שרתי במדינות בת שרף מעופף
רכב אלקים שם סיני בקודש
הדר צדקתה עלי ארץ ינופף
צינה וסוחרה זאת עולת החדש
בת עין תדמע ותזל מים
הרב תאני' אל בת השמים
קדוש ה' מכובד מפענח נעלמים
מנחם לבית יהודה מקיץ נרדמים
מחברת הקודש גאון עזינו ותפארתנו
קן לחכמה מפתח סגור לבבנו
אשת חיל וחכמה מאד גוברת
צמח צדקתה פורח כגפן אדרת
קדושים יתנו לה יד בין תמימים
זורחת היא בגנזי מרומים
צדקתה תזהיר כאור שבעת הימים
לקום לתחי' אחרי שנת שלומים

תנצב"ה

However, it was not solely rabbis and scholars who arrived in Sochaczew. Hassidim, and ordinary Jews who knew only a simple page of Talmud also came. They realized that they would not be permitted to go to the lesson that Reb Avraham taught in the Beis Midrash daily for an entire morning – and even if they were to be allowed in, they would understand very little. Very few students had the head to follow the deep class – however they came in as Hassidim. Reb Avrahamel was not only a Gaon in the revealed Torah [8], but he was also a Hassidic Rebbe. He would deliver

Torah talks during his "tish" [9], but during private encounters, he would elevate souls, and ignite the holy flame of sublimity and fear of Heaven.

He even warded off the Hassidim who came only for Hassidism. However he treated with love and devotion those stubborn ones who remained, and he learned with them in accordance with their understanding.

A Hassid tells as follows: When he came to Sochaczew as a young men, in the first place, when he came to the Rebbe to greet him, he asked: "Can you learn anything?" The young man answered: "I study the laws of Israel". "So why did you come to me?" The Rebbe asked with veiled hurt. The young man was shamed. The Rebbe noted the young man's hurt feelings and quickly said: "Don't be hurt, if you conduct yourself honorably, it is as if you are learned." Jews came and indeed learned how to conduct themselves honorably, how to be honest with one's fellow and furthermore – with oneself; not to deceive oneself and go around irking others, but only to concern oneself with being a Jew, an honorable Jew!

There was no contradiction between the Gaon and the Rebbe, both melded into one unit. Revealed and hidden were both studied simultaneously, like two expressions of the same essence. Both were the essence of striving for truth. When he studied the revealed, he was striving for the clarification of the foundations of halacha, and when he studied Hassidism he was striving for the completion of the person, the unanimity of thinking, feeling, speaking and doing (thought, speech, and deed), or as it is referred to by Hassidim: completeness of the soul, spirit, and inner essence.

Thus was Sochaczew known in the world as a center of Torah and Hassidism. Sochaczewer shtibels were established in dozens of towns, where people worshipped, learned and indeed also conducted Hassidic meals, all with the Sochaczew style. If a young man or a son-in-law on kest[7], or a mischievous boy needed a friend to study with, or simply needed a rabbi, he knew and address: the Sochaczewer shtibel. Groups were founded in dozens of towns, who perhaps did not even know where Sochaczew was located, but who wanted to have a part of the learning in the Sochaczew style. For a new methodology in learning was created there, a methodology that stresses the essence, not explanations leading to didactics – only the clarification of halacha in accordance with deep reasoning.

Thus was Sochaczew a spiritual center for Jews in Poland, beginning from the 1880s. It remained an important place until this day. For even after the death of Reb Avrahamel (11 Adar, 5670 – 1910), and his place was filled by his only son Reb Shmuel, who was known in the Hassidic world as the "Shem Mishmuel" after the name of his magnum opus – the stream of Hassidim and students who came to Sochaczew did not abate. This new methodology of Torah consolidated itself and broadened itself under the successor of Reb Avrahamel, and in the hundreds of students who were literally spread around the entire world.

The Yeshiva as well, which almost did not exist in the final years of Reb Avrahamel due to the Rebbe's poor health, was renovated with great scope under Rev Shmuel. Its peak was established by the young Gaon Reb Aryeh Tzvi Fromer, an expert student of Reb Avrahamel, who later became known as the Kozieglower rabbi and the head of the Yeshiva of the famous Yeshiva Chachmei Lublin. A new stream of students filled up the Beis Midrash and court.

Even when Sochaczew was destroyed during the First World War, and the Rebbe Reb Shmuel moved his court first to Lodz and later to Zgierz – the name of Sochaczew remained as the trademark of that branch of Hassidism, as a symbol. This was the same with the third Sochaczewer Rebbe, Reb David, the eldest son of Reb Shmuel, who became Rebbe after the death of his father (24 Tevet, 5686 – 1926). He lived in various cities, first as the rabbi in Wyszogrod, and later as the rabbi in Otwock,

Pabianice, and in Lodz at the outbreak of the Second World War. He died in the Warsaw Ghetto (8 Kislev 5603 – 1942) – but he always was known in the world as the Sochaczewer Rebbe. Similarly, the name remains with the current Sochaczewer Rebbe, Reb Chanoch may he live long, the second son of Reb Shmuel, who lives today in the Bayit Vagan neighborhood of Jerusalem. Sochaczewer Hassidism survived beyond the city of Sochaczew.

It is understandable that life in Sochaczew itself willingly or unwillingly followed the rhythms of the life in the "court". They ate the Sabbath meal hastily in dozens of homes, so that the father could go to the "tish". Many others went away to worship in the Rebbe's Beis Midrash, and completely conducted their private lives in accordance with the daily schedule of the Rebbe. The young and the curious peered in on the arriving students, and they were proud of their renown. If a boy was fortunate enough to ask a question of the illustrious rabbi, he would be in seventh heaven. It was a dream to be part of the Rebbe's class. He indeed spread Torah among the Sochaczew boys and young men. Older Jews has the aroma of Hassidism.

During a time of tribulation, Heaven forbid, one ran to the Rebbe. If one needed advice, one went to the Rebbe in his home. If one had news, one hastened to share it with the Rebbe. Thus did the court become a center for the residents of Sochaczew, a participant in joy and sorrow. It is obvious that no communal affair in the town took place without taking into account the opinion of the court. And although Reb Avrahamel no longer served as a rabbi (he resigned from the rabbinate in the 1890s due to various reasons, and from then on he occupied himself with being a Rebbe, with writing response, and with his own students), Jewish life in Sochaczew continued to be under the direct influence of the "court".

The "court" itself was not in the center of town, in the Jewish neighborhood, but rather almost in the outskirts of the town, in the gentile neighborhood. Shortly after Reb Avrahamel was accepted as rabbi, Hassidim did not agree that their Rebbe should live in a communal house, and, having no option, the city agreed with this, based on the claim that Reb Avrahamele was not merely the rabbi of the city of Sochaczew itself. They proposed to purchase an old manor house near the edge of the city, along the way to the slaughterhouse. The Hassidim purchased it for the Rebbe. Various legends arose regarding the origins of the house and the reasons for its purchase. As was told, one of its merits is that it has the aroma of Sanctification of the Divine Name. In the opposite place (in the priest's garden), once, three Jews were burnt in Sanctification of the Divine Name [10].

Indeed , the "court" was like a world unto itself. It was a massive brick house, with large green windows and a high red roof. It was in a little from the street, and had a flower garden in front with a picketed fence, and chestnut trees and lilac trees, which gave off an intoxicating aroma in the spring. It was a large, angular courtyard, paved with stones. On one side, there was a large Beis Midrash with windows on all sides, with the eastern window looking out over the garden. On the other side, there was a small Mikva and a Sukka. A fence closed off the access from the court to the garden, with its stubble walkways and its laden fruit trees. Upon entering the court through the small door (the large gate was always locked), one felt as if one was in another world. Despite the incessant movement of the Yeshiva students and the arriving Hassidim, a calm rested upon everyone. Politeness ruled the mood. Quiet, this is the house of Torah!

On a festival or an ordinary day of celebration, when a large number of Hassidim arrived, and the paths in the garden were full of groups that were walking, moving back and forth and talking about learning or Hassidism – the mood was solemn, like a family who were arriving together for a joyous occasion. However, the politeness pervaded over everybody and tamed the bubbly joy.

The "court" also served as a type of window to the outside world. Hassidim from large cities bought with them the breadth of the large cities, with their tall, high streimels and elegant silk kapotes. The constant traffic of Hassidim, arriving from near and far, brought in a closeness from far away places. People met each other, became friends, and on occasion matches were made. Often this was between a Sochaczewer householder with a visiting Hassid, and frequently with a Yeshiva student.

The "court" was not only a spiritual well and source of pride for Sochaczew, but it was also an important source of business. The "court" itself was a good employer of all types of people, including shopkeepers and craftsmen. Visiting Hassidim required lodging. Not infrequently, householders took advantage of a festival to earn some extra rubles by taking in Hassidim. It was like a Jewish fair in the town.

The relations between the town and the "court" were not always harmonious. There was also friction. Young people rebelled against the domineering attitude of the "court". Zionism and Socialism were natural opponents of the "court". When it came time to deal with appointing a rabbi (and Reb Avrahamel was no longer serving as a rabbi by the end of the 1890s – and rabbis were changed a few times), or to appoint a shochet – the mood flared up, and sides were formed. Sometimes a controversy broke out, with all of its accompanying negative manifestations. This picture was quite well known in the Polish towns. However, when the mood calmed down, normal relations with the "court" resumed.

The "court" was conducted in Sochaczew for three decades – until the outbreak of the First World War. It was secluded but also bound up with countless aspects of Jewish life in Sochaczew.

The outbreak of the First World War brought an end to an era of Polish Judaism. Life was changed beyond recognition. This also caused great changes in the "court". On account of the war and later the destruction of the town, Reb Shmuel settled first in Lodz and later (in the year 5678 – 1918) in Zgierz. The Yeshiva was dissolved and the Beis Midrash was destroyed during the time of the battles. The house was also badly damaged. Even when the town was rebuilt, the "court" remained in Zgierz after the war. Still later, during the time of the third Sochaczewer Rebbe, Reb David, it was not returned to Sochaczew. However, the name Sochaczew remained with this Hassidic stream forever. Neither Krosniewice, where Reb Avrahamel began his tenure as a Hassidic Rebbe, nor Nasielsk where Reb Shmuel settled, nor Pabianice where Reb David lived,, became bound with the name of Hassidim. Sochaczew alone merited being perpetuated, and the famous unique Hassidic-scholarly methodology of Kocker Hassidism was perpetuated through its name.

Sochaczew was destroyed as a city during the First World War – but it was rebuilt. Jewish Sochaczew was finally destroyed by the Nazi beasts. It is no more. A portion of its spirit remains in Sochaczewer Hassidism, the only bearer of its name in its living memory.

TRANSLATOR'S FOOTNOTES:

1. This tombstone inscription is written in very cryptic fashion.
2. The name 'Menachem' literally means 'the comforter', and often has Messianic connotations.
3. A reference to the seven days of creation.
4. A reference to the resurrection of the dead.
5. Siftei Cohen, a well known commentator on the Shulchan Aruch (Code of Jewish Law).
6. A reference to the eastern wall of the synagogue, where the most important people sit.

7. Young men who are supported by their father's-in-law for some period after their marriage, in order to enable them to continue with their Torah studies.

8. The revealed Torah refers to the study of Bible, Talmud, and Jewish law. The hidden Torah refers to the study of Kabbalah and mysticism. Hassidism is considered to be a manifestation of the hidden Torah.

9. Literally 'table', but here referring to a 'table gathering', where Hassidim gather around a table to hear the words the Rebbe, and to partake jointly of food.

10. When a Jew dies a martyr's death, it is considered to be in sanctification of the divine name (Al Kiddush Hashem).

The Voice and the Echo
by Eliezer Sztejnman
Translated by Jerrold Landau

Between Kotzk and Sochaczew

Translator's note: This long section extends from page 612 – 627. Only the first half of this section was translated, up to page 619. This section is not written from a historical perspective, but rather presents in a lengthy fashion the spiritual foundations of the leader of Sochaczew Hassidism. It is somewhat repetitive, very esoteric, and replete with mystical innuendoes, Kabalistic thoughts, and spiritual messages. This translation hardly does it justice, however it is included here as it does present to the reader a glimpse of the mindset of the sublime form of Hassidism that was represented by Rabbi Avraham of Sochaczew. Note that the other sections of the Hassidic dynasty of Sochaczew, which immediately follow this section, are not written in the same style, are much easier to read, and present a more historical viewpoint of the Hassidic dynasty of Sochaczew.

i. The Sochaczew Version of Hassidism

The Besht[11] was born in 5460 (1700), and Rabbi Avraham of Sochaczew died in 5670 (1910). For approximately two hundred years, the banner of the kingdom of Hassidism fluttered in the heights of the people of Israel, and the wellspring of Hassidism flowed and spread out in the deepest recesses of Jewish existence. In Kotzk they used to say: "until the Holy Jew[12]all of Hassidism was explained by the teachings of the Besht, and from the time of the Holy Jew and onwards all of Hassidism was explained by Pshischa". It is possible to state that Rabbi Avraham of Sochaczew was the last expositor of the house of Pshischa, that is to say of Hassidism in general. The Holy Jew died in 5574 (1804). We have before us two timeframes, from 5460 until 5574, and from 5574 until 5670. There were approximately one hundred years in each timeframe. Just as the Holy Jew was the first prince of Pshischa, Rabbi Avraham was the final prince.

The kingdom of Hassidism spread over our heads a firmament of lofty souls and spread before us a mosaic of lofty Jews; the rabbis were referred to only as wonderful Jews in conversations among Jews in the entire Jewish Diaspora. The Hassidim did not praise their rabbis because they were erudite and great scholars, and also not because they were workers of portents and miracles. In the study hall of Pshischa there was no talk of miracles or signs. They used to say "signs and miracles on the land of Ham[13], only Ham goes after miracles – but rather each Jew praised his rabbi that he was a fine Jew, a proper and G-d fearing Jew. There is no higher praise than being considered G-d fearing. What is wisdom worth without the precursor to wisdom[14]? What is the praiseworthiness of wisdom? Even the Satan (lehavdil)[15] and the evil inclination, Heaven forbid, can engage in great learning of they so desire, and can have great power in Torah debates. Therefore the purpose of everything is good deeds. Of course, someone with fine character traits will also excel in Torah and wisdom. For a master of fine character traits, his Torah knowledge will also be a fine character trait, and all of intentions will be for its sake, for the honor of Torah. A proper and upright Jew will also have a straightforward intellect, and will not convolute his reasoning, but will rather always be diligent in pursuing the truth.

It is not, Heaven forbid, that the Hassidim did not consider the Torah to be at the pinnacle of the world of Israel, but rather they attempted to learn with love and modesty, and not for the purposes of pride, and certainly not for the purposes of instigating disputes, or to be able to claim that they possessed the title of Rabbi. Since the Hassidim did not extol a sharp wit in its own right, and did not consider the accumulation of knowledge to be a fitting cause for honor, they attained a reputation among the opponents to Hassidim as well as among those who were neutral that their rabbis were not diligent in Torah learning, and were not masters of Torah (with my apologies to their honor for stating this). It is difficult to disprove wisdom that is passed down from person to person via tradition and constant repetition. The world may ask questions, provide excuses, and suspect – however the suspicions of the world are of no value. A faulty idea such as this is destined to become popular and be passed down from generation to generation. Thus did think members of the community who were not expert in even the minute part of the Torah of the Hassidic teachers. They believed that this was the truth, and that there was no point in disproving the matter. However in truth, even in a place where nobody protests the lie, a person himself will not budge from his opinion. The truth is that the great Hassidic teachers were almost without exception prominent sages. Were not all the rabbis experts in Torah? This was not only two for the rabbis, but also for almost all of the Admorim[16] who was an expert in Hassidism was also an expert in the revealed[17] Torah, with the exception of a very small number of the famous Tzadikim who were not great Torah scholars. Many people already had denigrated the Besht himself, and minimized his knowledge of the revealed Torah, only for the reason that he did not want to publicize his great knowledge of the revealed Torah. In truth, he was sharp and expert in all areas of Torah. One cannot find a statement from him that is not full of innuendoes to a verse of the Torah or a statement of the sages of blessed memory. His eyes scanned all of Jewish law and lore, and he was very familiar with the Zohar, the Shela, Maimonides' commentary on the Mishna, books of exposition and books of character refinement[18]. In short, he was a great sage, while at the same time a cautious sage, terrified and frightened that people should find out about the extent of his erudition. He was not only pious, acting beyond the letter of the law, but he also studies his books with greater care than was customary. He was public in his Hassidism but private in his Torah. The two very great students of the Besht, pillars of the teachings of Hassidism, the author of "Toldot" and the Maggid of Mezerich were prior to their embracing of Hassidism, lions in the council of the scholars. Rabbi Pinchas of Koretz, a student and associate of the Besht, was also a great sage. Rabbi Levi Yitzchak of Berdichev, the Maggid of Koznitz, rabbi Shmelke of Nikolsburg, the author of "Haflaah", Rabbi Elimelech, and it goes without stating Rabbi Shneur Zalman, the Holy Jew, Rabbi Menachem Mendel of Kotzk, Rabbi Chaim of Tzanz, Rabbi Avraham of Czechnow, as well as many other Admorim of the early and late period were all outstanding scholars.

Now go forth and learn: how great was the level of Rabbi Avraham of Sochaczew in Torah, in that he had the title of Gaon even among the Misnagdim [19], who desired to decisively remove the crown of Torah from the Hassidim. Those that argued did not argue with Rabbi Avraham. All of them stated in unison that he was the elite of the geniuses. His sun already shone brightly as a wonder child. He was a wonderful navigator through the sea of Talmud, Jewish Law, and responsa throughout all his days until his old age. We do not at all have to prove his greatness in Torah, however it can be said about him that in the same way as you can find his greatness in Torah, you can also find his greatness in the teachings of Hassidism.

Some people have their greatness revealed through their revelations of new methodologies in Torah, wisdom, actions, or character traits. There are other great people, who are even superior to the aforementioned, who do not present us with any new ideas, and who in all routine matters appear to be average, however their great praiseworthiness is in that they do not invite praise upon themselves by strange mannerisms and exceptional deeds. On the contrary, they restrain themselves, behave discreetly, and conduct themselves with simplicity. They are diligent in their judgements, and diligent as well in the trait of grace that surrounds them. They are modest, discreet, and go about without fanfare. Apparently, they repeat over old matters, but with a novel charm. They do not formulate their own doctrine – therefore they do not follow their own systematic method, but rather they march to their own tune. They are very careful not to separate themselves from the community. They hide themselves, and even hide their own state of concealment. It is wondrous that they do not go after wonders, lest they enchant the masses and cause actions that are not sanctioned by law. Such completely modest people are found in the midst of the community of Hassidim, and among the teachers of Hassidism. They always found for themselves a shadow in which to hide and stand off to the side, to hide for days and years under the canopy of the tallis of the rabbi, even when they themselves had already reached the top of the ladder and were fitting to lead a congregation. They would say: it is not for us to influence, it would be sufficient that we would be worthy of receiving influence. A proper Jew flees from the position of leadership as long as he is not forced into it.

Rabbi Avraham of Sochaczew, who was as great in Torah as he was in Hassidism, spent many years under the cloak of the Kotzker, and he also relied on the rest of his rabbis. He spent seven years in the house of his father-in-law Menachem Mendel, and he learned Torah and fine character from him. After the death of the Kotzker, he subordinated himself to the "Chidushei Harim". Afterwards, he cleaved to Rabbi Henech of Alexander. He used to say: "all my days I suckled from Kotzk". At the Bar Mitzvah feast of his grandson, he stated: "until this day I have not forgotten even one word from what I had learned in Kotzk". He was of fine character, he made himself small and always had a superior rabbi from whom he could gain influence. He was not only a master of fine character traits and modesty, but he also had a sharp mind, was mighty and was a master over his inclinations. It took a large measure of might to fulfil for himself the verse "do not awaken or stir up the love until the desirable time"[20]. That is, to restrain the brimming wellspring for himself until the appropriate time, to gain knowledge, to know how to investigate and deliberate, and even so to restrain his mouth. Rabbi Avraham of Sochaczew was blessed with a large measure of the power of silence and the trait of humbleness.

Once the Rabbi of Kotzk, who was already well on in years, said about him: "I never saw someone as mighty as him even amongst ten thousand brave warriors. The physicians cannot imagine what type of proper vessel laden with might he is unto me." This statement was made about the fourteen-year-old prodigy just after his marriage, and at that time he was dangerously ill with jaundice. Indeed, he was dangerously ill all of his life, however the illness did not in any way drain his power for Torah. This was so much the case that the Hassidim used to say of him that he lives and breathes through the power of the Kotzker lung, that is to say, in the merit of the blessing given to him by the Kotzker he was able to live even though his own lungs were weak by nature. The admiration of Rabbi Menachem Mendel with regard to the might of his illustrious son-in-law also applied, in an even greater measure, to his spiritual power. Rabbi Avraham was a mighty man in all of his ways. He was mighty in thought and deed, in his conceptual prowess and the modesty of his spirit, in his diligence in Torah and his immersion in Hassidism, in his new ideas on Torah and in his novel mannerisms. His most admirable characteristic was his powerful ability to master his various powers, some of them contradictory to each other, and to bind them together in a pleasant manner, so that they would not oppose or struggle with each other. He made great peace in the depths of his soul. His multi-facetedness brought him to unity. The contradictions, which would have been apparent in others, presented a vision of wholesomeness in him. He possessed nobility without stuffiness. He had an enthusiastic spirit without being bitter. Even though he was humble, he was not downcast. His spirit was not oppressive. Rather than being weak minded, he was always of clear mind and settled. His ideas wee clear, and he was pure in his deeds. Even when he was broken hearted, he did not lose his reason or his hope. In this area he was opposite of his father-in-law, his revered rabbi and teacher. The Rabbi of Kotzk was almost not in the realm of flesh and blood, he was like a mass of black gall, a living embodiment of existential despair. The Rabbi of Kotzk was like a type of adversary, whom no detractor could touch at all anything that belonged to him, no foreign army could smite his disciples by sword, he was a man of G-d who could not set fire to his sheep and cattle – and nevertheless, the wrath of G-d was poured upon him, for the creator of the world sent fire to his bones, overtook his spirit with a great wandering, and brought trembling to all the recesses of his soul. Rabbi Menachem Mendel stood in solitude for many years, trembling and fearful in the midst of the congregation and community. The holy flock of Hassidim surrounded him, pining and waiting for their holy rabbi to speak to them some words of comfort, or even some words of wrath and indignation which would be as bitter as gall and as tough as sinews, just not to leave them on their own. He stood in front of them startled and pensive, for the most part mute without word, with only grumbling coming from his mouth, or a shout or cold curse from his lips. Even Rabbi Avraham, the youth he fostered and the child of his delights, stood in fear and trepidation in his presence, relying on him and hoping that he would utter something. However, Rabbi Avraham did not tremble. The quaking did not affect his soul. He was calm externally, and perhaps even internally, for apparently the trait of peacefulness was his lot from Above. Is not such a sublime grace, which was guarded in him throughout all difficult times, a wondrous thing?

Rabbi Avraham appears to us as a type of wonder within a wonder. He always remained as the embodiment of purity and might, yet nevertheless Kotzk was the root of his soul and the traditions of Kotzk his birthright. He suckled from Kotzk. Nevertheless Kotzk flowed with blood, but with him the blood was uprooted and turned into good milk. His soul flowed with milk and honey.

This was a tale of two people, who were both walking on the same path designated for very special people, and one of them went out on a path on his own. This was a path that was already trodden by many before him. However, the path of the many, which is walked on without any specific intention, following established custom, is not similar to the path of the many which is reached after exploration and searching. Rabbi Avraham went out from the remorse to the level-headedness, and from the isolation to the community, to public prayer to communal life, and to the spreading of Torah as the head of the Yeshiva before the community of his students. Even greater than this, during the years that Rabbi Avraham lived with his father-in-law, that is until the death of Rabbi Menachem Mendel, the Kotzker would teach his students the ways of isolation and separation from the community. It would come to pass that the Hassidism would flock to their Rabbi and stand before him waiting and imploring him for his words. At that time, Rabbi Menachem Mendel would say to his son-in-law: "Go and see, my son Avraham, what has happened to me. In my youth, when I had my full strength, I did not permit the mixed multitude to come close to me. And now look at what has happened in the end. You should be careful to always stand your ground, so that you will not G-d forbid come to this state."

Rabbi Avraham was indeed careful not to go out from the confines of isolation. He trod in the path of Kotzk. He fled from positions of authority. He attached himself to the dust of the feet of other rabbis, so that people would not attach themselves to the dust of his feet. He stood strong in Torah, and minimized himself in Hassidism, as his Rabbi of Kotzk advised him, in order that he should not come to neglect the Torah.

The Rabbi of Kotzk examined and found that in the world there is no vessel as fitting as Rabbi Avraham to fill up with Torah. Even Rabbi Chaim of Tzanz, himself a genius in Torah, acted from the authority of the wisdom of Rabbi Avraham. For years after the death of the Kotzker, Rabbi Avraham still resided in the home of his father-in-law and gave himself over completely to Torah. He no longer had anyone to support him, and he saw poverty himself. Finally, due to the great hunger, he was forced to leave the sanctuary of Torah and accept a rabbinical position in Parczow. However, even as he sat on the rabbinic seat, the Kotzker spark overtook him, which prevented him from becoming involved with people. In order to counteract this, Rabbi Avraham attempted to become involved in communal matters, and to conduct learning sessions in the city, without showing favoritism to the trustees and parnassim. He took hold of the trait of truth, and he was not silent for the sake of the honor of the Torah. He quickly stirred up the ire of the leaders of the community, and became an antagonist to them. As a general principal, a rabbi who is not yielding is persecuted. Rabbi Avraham, who was humble in all his ways, was forced to enter into constant controversy not only in Parczow, the first city in which he held the rabbinate, but also in all other cities in which he held the rabbinate for temporary periods. From this there is not proof at all that Rabbi Avraham imposed his authority upon the community through the strength of his opinion. A rabbi does not have to be forceful in order not to be at peace with his congregation. Even the modest and good Rabbi Levi Yitzchak suffered from persecution in several cities in which he served as the rabbi, and he had to move from one place to another due to the difficulties which came upon him, until he was accepted as rabbi in Berdichev. There, they respected him, and the name of Hassidism was made beloved by him. The same experiences came to Rabbi Avraham, who at the end of his movement from city to city finally arrived in Sochaczew, where he fortified himself with honor and greatness. It is said that he was elevated, and elevated others in his city. This proves the adage in "Pirke Avot"[21], "There is no person who does not have his place". Every person comes to his source when he comes to the city that is prepared for him due to divine providence. Just as there is a 'root soul', there is also a 'root city'. Rabbi Levi Yitzchak and Berdichev, Rabbi Avraham and Sochaczew, were pairs paired up from heaven. Rabbi Avraham derived joy from Sochaczew. Beauty to you, oh Sochaczew.

After Rabbi Avraham had been sorely tried through the tribulations of the rabbinate, he was chosen by the quorum of Hassidim to be their rabbi and spiritual guide. He avoided the rabbinate for many years, but in the end it caught up with him. For one whose mission is to be a shepherd to a holy flock, there is no alternative other than accepting the mission. Whether with consent or per force, there is no choice but to ascend the seat. One does not refuse the public. If one attempts to refuse, they force him. He may claim: "I do not want, I cannot, I am not fitting". One answers him: "so want, and you will be able to, and you will be fitting. But what then? Is it your desire to be only modest, hiding among the vessels, but is that not invalid modesty? There are those who flee so that they might be pursued. It is better not to flee, and that one should not be pursued. Is it your desire to be diligent in Torah? You will be. The masses have not yet come. Will you also distance yourself from the individuals?" One may try to desist... there are many excuses. However it comes down to this: there is a time when a man is forbidden from separating himself from the community.

Such a time came to Rabbi Avraham. In the year 5630 (1870), this time came upon his window and said to him: "go out from your current path, become a rabbi." Rabbi Chanoch Henech of Alexander died that year. Rabbi Chanoch Henech was at peace with Kotzk, very emotional. Even more accurately: he was a chord from the Kotzk violin, a thin and fine chord. He knew how to bear the burden of the Kotzker groan, even though he did not bear the heavy headedness of Kotzk. Nevertheless, he was the continuation of Kotzk, a memory of the Kotzk movement, and a living testimony to that greatness. When Rabbi Chanoch Henech went to his eternal rest, the pillars of Kotzk shook to their foundations. In 5619 (1859) the sun of Kotzk set, and in 5630 the moon of Kotzk set. Rabbi Avraham was called to the seat. There was no other Kotzker like him in the world. Therefore, Rabbi Avraham, the dandled child of the elder Rabbi, the true ornament, should stand up to preserve the greatness of Kotzk.

The situation was slightly strange. In the study of hall of Kotzk they taught that a person is required to be fearful of the rabbinical seat, just as one is fearful of a snake or scorpion. And now the command, through the authority of Kotzk, came to Rabbi Avraham to take honor for himself and occupy the seat. Is this not contradictory to the main point? The beautiful soul should be in dread of such a situation. Nevertheless, Rabbi Avraham was in the deepest sense of good disposition, a soul that desired propriety; he was level headed, and his spirit was even and deliberate. Rather than complicate matters, he would loosen the bonds, burn out the difficulties, and bring problems close to the mind. The Kotzker himself taught him on several occasions how to extricate himself from difficulties. He said to him: "Avraham, if it is decreed unto you that you should become a rabbi, when the day comes, lead only a small congregation. Do not turn to the masses. Get close only to the special people. Prayers ascend much better from a small quorum, and there will also be time to learn. The larger the congregation, the more neglect of Torah there will be. The glory of a Tzadik is in a small community, and in a place of the masses there is no joy and no peace for the soul."

After lengthy deliberation, Rabbi Avraham agreed to accept the yoke of the rabbinate upon himself. He explicitly made a condition that he should be the rabbi of a small group of Hassidim, and that anyone who is not diligent in Torah should not become close to him, and that they should let him lead a large Yeshiva, and not take him away from the study of the Torah by spending time around the table, and requests for advice. At that time, a new leader came into the world of Hassidism, and he set out on his path, which was not yet trodden, but was later trodden by other people. To be more accurate, a new style of Hassidism arose, that of Sochaczew. The style of a leader and Rabbi, head of a Yeshiva and Admor, all in one body, the style of Hassidim who sit before their Tzadik in the tent of Torah. This was an innovation, whose foundation was in the unique way of Kotzk, with the enthusiasm of Kotzk for isolation, with the desire of the Kotzkers for a sublime and exalted Hassidism, ennobled by exalted people, special people of noble character, all beloved and clear, masters of sublime and exalted intellects. The way of Kotzk was thus: with thunder and lightning, indignation and strong emphasis, being brazen toward heaven, knocking on the locked gate, presenting complaints before the Master of the World, by debating and litigating with Him and with man who was created in His image: with a great shout, calling out incessantly: arise, awaken, become alert, shine. However, the style of Sochaczew was quiet and deliberate, without fanfare or force, without a stormy wind, but rather with the power of Torah and with peace. Perforce, if anger and bitterness ascend like a ladder to heaven in a holy manner toward the sky, even more so would the Torah, whose ways are ways of pleasantness, would serve as a ladder to the heavens. This was the style of Sochaczew, which did not come at all to contradict Kotzk, but rather came out of Kotzk as an infant from its mother's womb. Rabbi Avraham did not at all come to argue, to define a new path, for this was the path from old. A simple person cannot be righteous. It is assumed that a righteous person would have been taught well. Whomever is not immersed in Torah, how could he be immersed in Hassidism? Who is a Hassid? Someone of refined character – and there is nothing as refined as Torah. The Torah teaches us to be wise and good. It plants in us the love of righteousness and uprightness, graciousness and truth. And behold, these are the traits which glorify the Hassidim. Rabbi Avraham would say that there are many paths in the worship of the Creator. The best of them all is the study of Torah. Only the Torah can open the gates of light, and instill in us the heavenly influence. Rabbi Avraham held the opinion that above all levels is the level of receiving divine influence. The learning of Torah is what helps one receive this influence. He who learns Torah will become a vessel that collects, for he will expend much energy in understanding the hidden and revealed aspects of it. You might ask as to why we say in the blessings of the Torah "He who gives the Torah" rather than "gave" in the past tense. That is because the Torah is given on a constant basis. As it says "From the desert it was given as a gift". We dwell in the desert, and if it were not for the Torah that stands before us we would die of thirst. The sages said: "Anyone who sits and learns Torah, the Holy One Blessed Be He sits and learns with him." Due to the exercise of learning, a divine influence comes upon him at all times. The Torah is constant. As long as a Jew sits and learns, he is in the category of those who receive Torah, of course he cannot come to haughtiness at such a time. The Torah teaches us modesty. From the source of modesty all other good traits flow. A haughty person cannot be upright. A haughty person does not even have a straight intellect, since his mind is always scheming. A true learned person is truly modest. The Torah is the pillar of light in our paths.

Rabbi Avraham never ceased to speak of the praise of Torah study. He who learns Torah sees the world through the eyes of a freeman, and is saved from fear due to strange thoughts and evil contemplation. He who learns Torah inherits joy. The primary aspect of the commandment to learn Torah is to be happy and derive pleasure from one's learning. Therefore it can be said about him, that he came to renew Hassidism in the light of Torah. There were many learned Hassidim and rabbis who were expert in Torah. However only Rabbi Avraham made the Torah into the coat of many colors for Hassidism, and was diligent to pour into the Kiddush cup of Hassidism wine that was steeped in Torah and to fill the cup to the brim. He did not say that it is sufficient to have a little Torah, but rather he aspired to an abundance of Torah. The aim of his soul was to dig a deep well for Torah from which water would come out for the many, that the knowledge of Torah would fill the souls of his Hassidim as water to a large sea. Great lovers love the object of their love with great love, and therefore they aspire to attain a great amount, not only Torah itself, but also the sea of Torah. The Torah is compared to fire and this fire quenches other fires. This was the main point of the Hassidism of Sochaczew. The Torah is a tree of life and the potion of life, a medicine for all ills. In Kotzk there was a frightful wound that was not healed. He left after him broken hearts, tormented spirits, downtrodden souls, who were more pained due to their knowledge. The style of Sochaczew prepared for the trembling of Kotzk a healing remedy of old, whose power is always new: the light of Torah. However, this light was blended with the light of Hassidism. Just as there is fire on top of fire, there is also light on top of light. Kotzk is fire on top of fire, and Sochaczew was light on top of light. He who says "light" also says "it is good"[22]. A voice came out of Kotzk: "it is bad", and Rabbi Avraham answered peacefully: "it is good"!

TRANSLATOR'S FOOTNOTES:

1. Conversos were Jews who disguised their Judaism and presented themselves externally as Christian during the time of the Spanish Inquisition, while secretly maintaining their Judaism. The term Marranos is often used for these people, however it has been deemed inappropriate as it originated as a derogatory term meaning "pig".

The reference here is to Jews who disguised themselves as Christians in order to survive the Holocaust.

2. Kaddish (literally "sanctification") is among other functions in the daily Jewish prayer services, is recited by mourners in memory of dead relatives. It affirms the meaningfulness of life and Jewish belief despite loss.

3. Mazowsze, known in English as Mazovia or Masovia, is the Polish province surrounding and including Warsaw.

4. The column heading, which I have translated as 'Total Population', is actually 'Non-Jewish Population' in the original. However, the percentages given are actually the percentage of column 2 (Jewish Population), in relation to column 3. Since the percentage column is entitled "% of Jews', I interpreted the third column as being the general population (Jews + non-Jews), in order to make the statistic meaningful. The percentage of Jews relative to the non-Jews is a meaningless statistic, whereas the percentage of Jews relative to the general population is a meaningful statistic, and is probably what was intended. If the third column was indeed the non-Jewish population, then the % in column 4 should have been calculated by (column 2 / (column 2 + column 3), rather than column 2 / column 3. This footnote also applies to point 2 below the table.

5. Literally "Face of Splendor". Often Rabbinical leaders who published significant works were known by the title of their major publication.

6. This is describing a classic medieval style of blood libel, known as the 'desecration of the host'. Jews were accused of obtaining a 'host' (a wafer used in Church services, which according to Christian tradition, acts as a 'host' to the body of Jesus), piercing it so that it would exude blood (obviously a fictitious charge, but based on the Christian belief that the wafer actually contains an embodiment of Jesus), and using the blood for the baking of matza (unleavened bread) for Passover. This is a variant on the more common blood libel, where Jews were accused of murdering a Christian child so that they could use the blood for the baking of matza for Passover. These types of libels were the cause of untold suffering for the Jews of Europe during the middle ages.

7. An iron letter is a document protecting one's right to travel or reside in a given area.

8. Most probably, this refers to Prague, the capital of Bohemia (currently the capital of the Czech republic), but it may possibly be referring to the Polish town Praga.

9. Tadeusz Kosciuszko was a Polish general who led "Powstanie Kosciuszkowskie" – the Kosciuszko uprising against the Russian oppressor. Kosciuszko is well known in the United States for his contribution, together with General Pulaski, during the War of Independence.

10. The Hebrew word used here is Apikorsut, which roughly translates as heresy or religious skepticism, although the full flavor of the word cannot be described in English. The word derives from the Greek philosopher Epicurus, who was well known for his philosophic outlook on life that stressed unbridled enjoyment of this world, since there is no future world. The Jewish concept of heresy took its name from Epicurus. This seminary must have been known at the time for a liberal outlook on religion.

11. The acronym of Rabbi Yisrael Baal Shem Tov, the founder of Hassidism.

12. From the context, this is referring to Rabbi Simcha Bunem of Pshischa, the founder of the Pshischa dynasty of Hassidism.

13. "He Who performed signs and miracles in the land of Ham" is a quote from the daily evening (maariv) service, referring to G-d's sending of plagues and performance of miracles in Egypt at the time of the exodus. The ancient Egyptians were descended from Ham, the son of Noach. Here this phrase is lifted from the maariv service and its meaning is altered to indicate that the performance of miracles and signs are not appropriate for

the Jewish leaders. Other Hassidic groups were very involved in the performance of miracles, and this was obviously a point of debate.

14. A reference from the daily morning (shacharit) service: "The precursor to wisdom is fear of G-d".

15. The interjection 'lehavdil' appears here. This is used when talking about a bad subject just after talking about a sublime idea. Here the Satan is referred to just after a reference to the fear of G-d.

16. An Admor is a Hassidic master. Admorim is the plural.

17. The revealed Torah generally refers to the study of the Bible, Talmud, and Jewish law. Hassidism stresses study of the 'hidden Torah', which refers to Kaballah and mysticism.

18. Various traditional books of Jewish wisdom. The Zohar is the main book of Jewish mysticism (Kabbalah), and the Shela was a medieval commentator.

19. Misnaged, plural Misnagdim, are the opponents of Hassidism.

20. A verse from the Song of Songs.

21. Pirke Avot is the Mishnaic tractate "Chapters of the Fathers" or "Ethics of the Fathers", which is an anthology of saying of the sages, primarily about the topic of character refinement.

22. A reference from Genesis, where G-d created light, and then said that the light was good.

{628}

The Admor Rabbi Shmuel of Holy Blessed Memory
by A. Ch.
Translated by Jerrold Landau

The Second of the house of Sochaczew (known by the name of his book "Shem Mishmuel") 4 Chesvhan 5617 (1856) – 24 Tevet 5686 (1926)

Notes about his personality

Rabbi Shmuel of holy blessed memory was born in the year 5617 in the house of his holy grandfather Rabbi Menachem Mendel of Kotzk (his righteous mother was Sara Tzina the daughter of the fiery Admor of Kotzk) during the time that his father the Gaon Rabbi Avrahamele was supported at the table of his father-in-law. His youth was spent in Parczow and Krosniewice, places that Rabbi Avrahamele served as rabbi and spread Torah publicly. During those days the young Reb Shmuel soaked up most of his Torah from his father – for the rabbinate did not take much of his time, as he was coronated as a Rebbe only in 5630, -- and even at that time the lines of Hassidim that knocked on his door were not too long, and did not disturb him from his learning. Therefore, he was able to give of his time freely to the education and teaching of his only son who was fitting, and to give him to taste of his treasures.

In 5634 (1874) he married Yuta Lea the daughter of the well-known Kotzker Hassid Rabbi Eliezer Lipman, the son-in-law of the holy Rabbi Shlomo of Radomsk, the author of "Tiferet Shlomo" (this did not prevent Rabbi Eliezer Lipman from being an enthusiastic Hassid of Kotzk). Even after his marriage he did not leave his father's house, as was customary in those days, to be supported at the house of his father-in-law. He rather remained to live near his father in Krosniewice, for it was difficult for the two of them to part. The couple moved together with Rabbi Avrhamale of holy blessed memory to Nasielsk and later to Sochaczerw. There they lived in a separate dwelling on Warsaw Street, and they made their livelihood from a wine store. In truth, he did not ever spend much time with his business, for a trusted associate ran it.

After his first wife died after a reasonably long life, he married (in 5663 – 1903) Mirel the daughter of the Gaon Rabbi Moshe Natan Shapira, the head of the rabbinical court of Kaszionz (the author of "Shemen Lemaor").

After the passing of his father the Gaon Rabbi Avraham of holy blessed memory in 5670 (1910), the Hassidim coronated him to take his father's place as the Admor of Sochaczew, and he then moved to live in the home of his father in the Hassidic courtyard.

At the outbreak of the First World War, (Av 5674), he was with a healer in Germany. He was arrested there as a Russian citizen, and only after great efforts did he succeed – along with other Admorim who were in the same position – to return to Poland. However due to the persecutions of the Jews by the Czarist government and the scheming of the officials, it was dangerous for him to return to Sochaczew, a small town, and therefore he decided to remain for a period of time in Lodz. He lived there during the days of the war, and was not in Sochaczew at the time of its destruction in 5675 (1915).

In Lodz, in the midst of a large community of his Hassidim and friends, he spent the difficult days of the war, he suffered with all of their sufferings, and was available to encourage and assist them, and to guide them with advice and counsel during the days of confusion. It is interesting that during those days he excelled in his energetic activity to raise up the stature of Torah and Hassidism, as is testified to by his humorous essays – printed in the book Shem Mishmuel – which he produced for his community of faithful, and which occupy most of that book. Not only did Hassidim of Sochaczew come early in the morning to his door, but most of those that turned to him were Hassidim of other dynasties, as well as many non-Hassidim.

However, the life in the big city with its large population was difficult for him, and the many who turned to him distracted him from his holy work, and his state of health also suffered due to this. The many tribulations weighted down to him as a heavy burden, and therefore he left in 5679 (1919) to live in Zagorze, a small town near Lodz, in order to distance himself somewhat from the tumult and crowds of this active city. He settled there and established his Yeshiva there only temporarily, and he never ceased to make plans to return to the destroyed Sochaczew.

In 5686 (1926) his illness became more severe. On the advice of his physicians, he moved to Otwock, a resort near Warsaw, however not long thereafter he passed away at the age of 70, on the 24 of Tevet 5686. He was brought to eternal rest near the grave of his father in Sochaczew, and the entire house of Israel mourned the loss bitterly.

He was the only son of his parents (aside from him they had a daughter by the name of Esther, who was married to Rabbi Meir Borenstein, the brother of her father. They lived in Sochaczew and she died there during her father's lifetime). from his youth he never moved from the side of his father. He was always with him, and he saw himself as his student in every way, and he revered him without bound. Even as time went on, and he himself was the father of a large family, not one day passed when they did not see each other. Even afterward, when he filled the place of his father, when he himself was already an Admor, he did not see himself as standing upon his own authority, setting out his own path. It was always to him as if he was resting upon the shoulders of his father the Gaon, as if he was only an interpreter of his father's words.

This was not because he was weak minded and always required support to stand up. On the contrary, Reb Shmuel of holy blessed memory was strong in his opinions and did not give in to anybody. He stood his own very firmly with a clear and sharp wit. However it was different with respect to his father, since he would always give into him, and he was always an attentive son and student.

On the other hand, the relationship of his father to him was also extraordinary. The famous Gaon of his generation, the halachic decisor whom nobody could dispute, related to his son with respect and reverence. He valued greatly his opinions in Torah, both in the revealed and hidden Torah, and he looked upon him as a person of worth. He would refer to him (not in his presence), my Reb Shmuel ("Mein Reb Shmuel"). Most of those who would turn to him with respect to matters of spirituality or matters of the world he would send to Reb Shmuel, by saying: "Have you already been to my Reb Shmuel?". He was always interested to hear his opinion on important matters. This powerful man did not do a small or large matter without soliciting the advice of his son.

Here is an interesting tidbit. The author of "Avnei Nezer"[1] did not have the custom (in particular during the latter years) to have a communal third Sabbath meal. Therefore the Hassidim would gather in the house of Reb Shmuel of holy blessed memory, who would arrange the third Sabbath meal, replete with words of Torah as was the custom among Admorim (and this was in the life of his father, and in the same city!). The father would advise the Hassidim who gathered before him at this time to go to the table of Reb Shmuel of holy blessed memory, and he would even show some anger to those who did not do so.

Thus did they live together for 35 years, acting jointly in all areas. It was as if they possessed the same soul – and the legacy of their soul was one, together the breathed the air of the heights of Kotzk On occasions it seemed as if the father, the famous Gaon before whose utterances many trembled, found support from the solid Kotzk shoulders of the son. (It should be pointed out that Reb Shmuel was also impressive and strong in body build, he was tall and had a glorious countenance, he walked upright and his face was glowing and splendorous despite the seriousness of his expression.) For here, perhaps, we can begin to understand the unusual relation between these two, the father and the son. Who, aside from Reb Shmuel, had such intimate contact with the internal world of the 'Avnei Nezer", and merited to recognize his internal greatness in Torah and fear of Heaven, – and from that comes the boundless reverence of the son to the father. He was more a prized student than a son – due to his knowledge of him. The respect of the father to the Kotzker son, very strong and powerful, comes from the reverence which is beyond description, and the cloak of his fiery father-in-law from Kotzk, who from a young age merited to enter into the inner sanctum of his courtyard, and subordinated himself to him completely, to the exclusion of any personal desire and youthful whims, and did not free himself from this subordination all the way through his old age.

This strong line – the way of Kotzk – accompanied him through all of his days of activity, and influenced all of his deeds and words. He expressed himself through his books – the eight volumes of "Shem Mishmuel" which appeared posthumously – in which he published words of Torah and Hassidism organized according to the weekly Torah portion, words which he spoke before his congregation of Hassidim during the years 5670-5686 (1910-1926). These words are written clearly with rich expression, with a warm breath – as if these words are only now coming out of his holy mouth.

The main point of his words, the recurring theme, serve as a means to peek into the inner depths of his personality and to recognize the great yearning which he yearned, and for which he worked without tiring. He constantly stove for completeness of the soul and for a complete unity in worship of G-d. This unification of personality was the main point of his words. The desire of the heart for the Creator of all, with constant enthusiasm, and without ever letting it out of his mind, and his task to direct the waves of yearning for the object of his yearning – the unification of the soul with G-d and his Torah, – this was the purpose of this elite man, it was about this that he preached, and it was this that he demanded of others as well as himself, first and foremost of himself. With regard to the life of activity – in his words: " the six days of effort – one will only see the scattering of the soul, the scattering of the desire, at a time when most of a person's effort is centered around one goal; and if a person is able to direct his thoughts and desires to one point, thus he will succeed in understanding the depths of it, – obviously, I am referring to coming close to G-d, – this is signified by the Sabbath, when all work is forbidden, and the soul is free to direct itself specifically to this holy purpose. The Sabbath is a taste of the World to Come, the barriers fall down on it, and particularly those whose root is in the physical nature of man, and he is able to come close to his Creator." These words and others give us a key to understanding his mighty personality, and the also mark his outward behavior. This is the Hassidism of Pshischa and Kotzk in the style of Sochaczew.

He was also involved in the communal life of Polish Jewry. He took a clear stand, without fear, with respect to all of the problems that afflicted that era, including also mockery[2]. He expressed his opinions in a clear fashion, without wavering. His words were not always acceptable to his opponents, however they were forced to respect the earnestness, uprightness, and lack of personal interest in his words.

All his days, he desired to settle in the Land of Israel. In 5651 (1891), he visited the Land of Israel with the encouragement of his father, the author of "Avnei Nezer", in order to acquire land and found a Hassidic settlement. However, the prohibition of selling land in the Land of Israel to citizens of Russia interfered with their plans. On this occasion, he traversed the length and breadth of the Land of Israel, and he always spoke about this wonderful experience of his. During the time of the awakening surrounding the Balfour Declaration, he took the view that it was required to settle in the Land of Israel – and to establish agricultural settlements of Hassidim, and he spoke about that topic in his capacity of participant in all of the leadership councils of Agudas Yisrael. He urged Agudas Yisrael to include effort for the Land of Israel on its agenda. Even in his latter years when it was impossible for him to acquire land in the Land of Israel for many reasons, he never ceased to desire and to speak about his desire to settle in the Land of Israel.

With the passing of his father the Gaon Rabbi Avraham of blessed memory (5670 – 1910), the Hassidim of Sochaczew coronated him as their Admor. All the elder Hassidim including famous Gaonim, such as the Gaon Rabbi Yoav Yehoshua the head of the rabbinical court of Kinczek (the author of the book "Chelkat Yoav"), the Gaon Rabbi Yitzchak Feigenbaum the head of the rabbinical court of Warsaw, and many other elite spiritual men, Hassidim and men of worthy deeds, gathered around him and accepted his authority. He continued in the path of his father of holy blessed memory – a blend of Torah and Hassidism, resting in the depths of halacha with enthusiasm and spirit, however he added his own breath, and wove a fundamental thread in the tapestry of Kotzk-Sochaczew Hassidism. His rich and powerfully expressive manner of speech established Sochaczew Hassidism and added an important layer upon the glorious edifice that was Polish Hassidism. His books were accepted in wide circles, and became fundamental texts of Polish Hassidism.

He also had an important role in the spreading of Torah. He renewed the Yeshiva of Sochaczew and appointed the young sage Rabbi Aryeh Tzvi Frumer, may G-d avenge his soul (who later became the head of the Yeshiva Chachmei Lublin) to head it. This Yeshiva existed until the outbreak of the First World War. Many of the rabbis and sages of Poland came from that Yeshiva. He also founded a Yeshiva "Beis Avraham" in Lodz, which existed until the Holocaust.

He expended great effort in organizing and publishing the manuscripts of his father the Gaon of holy blessed memory, and he published the seven-volume responsa set "Avnei Nezer". He include his own glosses on the content on almost every page, noted discreetly in the name of the publisher, and sometimes only noted by parentheses.

He occupied the seat of the Admor of Sochaczew for sixteen years. Only part of those years were spent in Sochaczew itself, and most of them outside of the city. However, he always saw himself – and others saw him – as tied to Sochaczew and whatever transpired in it. He was laid to rest honorably in Sochacze

---

{632}

The Admor Rabbi Dovid of Holy Blessed Memory
Translated by Jerrold Landau
Iyar 5638 – 8 Kislev 5703 (1878 – 1942)
By Rabbi Yehoshua Moshe Aharonson

The last rabbi of Sanok, which was near Sochaczew.
Currently a member of the chief rabbinate of Petach Tikva.

Our master the honorable Admor of Sochaczew the holy Rabbi Dovid Borenstein, may his blood be avenged, was born in 5638 in the city of Nasielsk, to his father the holy Gaon the middle Admor Rabbi Shmuel of blessed memory, the author of the book "Shem Mishmuel". He in turn was the son of Rabbi Avraham of blessed memory, the author of the books "Avnei Nezer" and "Eglei Tal", who was the son-in-law of the holy glorious elder Rabbi of Kotzk of blessed memory.

From his earliest youth, exceptional traits were noticed in him, a wonderful sublimity Torah and Hassidism. He was a quick learner and had a phenomenal memory, clearness of thought, uprightness of the heart, and a beautiful sublime soul.

The kindness of his grandfather and the might of his father were blended in him to form the glory of truth and peace.

His private tutor was the Hassid Rabbi Yitzchak Shlomo Lieberman of blessed memory of Ozorkow, however he was mainly educated from his childhood by his grandfather, the Gaon and sign of the generation. He learned both the revealed and hidden Torah from him, along with his unique methodology in understanding the depths of the early sages. He was dear to him as his own son, and his hand never left his grandfather's hand. As he got older he became closer to his exalted grandfather, until his soul was bound up with his soul.

As he became Bar Mitzva, his grandfather the "Avnei Nezer" said about him: "He is already a complete man".

At the time when he was being propositioned for marriage prospects, the "Avnei Nezer" said to one of the examiners: "Behold my grandson has a broad intellect, which extends from one end to the other end. However, I do not permit him to express new ideas about Torah at such an early age. For the righteous Gaon Rabbi Chaim Halberstam of blessed memory, the Admor of Tzanz may his virtue stand us in good stead, told my father the Rabbi of Biala that it would be best not to permit me to innovate at such an early age."

At the age of 17 he married Esther, the daughter of the Hassid Rabbi Mottel Weingut (a relative of the author of the Tur) of Zadnoska Wola. However the "Avnei Nezer" did not permit his grandson to leave the house of study of Sochaczew. Even later, the spiritual connection between him and his grandfather did not cease (see the Avnei Nezer on Choshen Mishpat, paragraphs 60-63).

He acquired for himself the Torah and character of his grandfather: excellence in Torah and Hassidism, a deep sharpness along with common sense and a clear mind, diligence and self sacrifice in his efforts to search out the absolute truth, and to distance himself from premises that are distant and contradictory to the truth.

The elder Admor of blessed memory rejoiced greatly in his beloved grandson, his Torah and Hassidism, his diligence and character. He saw in him his spiritual heir, who would carry on his path into the future.

In approximately 5668 (1908) he accepted upon himself the rabbinate of Wyszogrod. His grandfather traveled with him in order to be present during his coronation as the rabbi of that city. He conducted the rabbinate sublimely as did his father, and he also set up a Yeshiva in the city, where the learned true Torah day and night according to the method of Sochaczew. After the outbreak of the First World War, the rabbi lived in a temporary dwelling in Lodz, in the home of Rabbi Dovid Proshinowsky of blessed memory. However after the termination of the war he did not wish to return to Wyszogrod, due to the persecutions that he suffered there at the hands of the strong-handed people, due to his not knowing how to flatter the parnassim who walk at the head of the people, but he rather would tell them off without worrying about their rank.

Just like his grandfather, he knew no rest during the time of his service. Since he was already famous as one of the Torah giants of his generation, many important communities turned to him, such as Bendin, Pabianice, and others, with requests to serve on the rabbinical seat. Ultimately, he was appointed rabbi of Tomaszew.

He lived in Tomaszew for several years, and he did not find rest there either. However, before he had even found his bearings there, and begun to spread the light of his Torah and wisdom upon the communal structure, his father the author of "Shem Mishmuel" was summoned to the Heavenly court, and immediately during the funeral, on the 24 of Tevet 5686 (1926), all of the Hassidim of Sochaczew appointed him to fill his father's place.

He first lived in Otwock, later in Pabianice, Kolumna, and again in Lodz. In that active city, he spread the Torah of Hassidism according to his own unique style, and influenced people with his Torah and wisdom. His countenance was sublime, since the glory of kingship was anointed upon him, he radiated honor and glory.

He very quickly became famous as one of the great and important Admorim in Poland. The Hassidic masses, learned people, and people of good deeds from all sectors related to him with honor and reverence, and saw in him the continuation of the way of the Gaon of Sochaczew.

He walked in the footsteps of his holy father the "Shem Mishmuel" who founded a large and magnificent Yeshiva called "Beis Avraham" on the first yahrzeit of the "Avnei Nezer". The head of the

Yeshiva was the Gaon Rabbi Aryeh Leib Frumer the head of the rabbinical court of Kozieglowy, may G-d avenge his blood. The pious Rabbi Mendel Borenstein of Siedlec taught the second level. The Yeshiva was run by his son-in-law Rabbi Aharon Rotenberg of blessed memory. The Yeshiva existed until the outbreak of the First World War, and hundreds of boys were educated in it. Many of them were outstanding in Torah and fear of heaven, and they received their path in life from that Yeshiva.

After the war, the Yeshiva "Beis Avraham" was established in Lodz. Its chief activist was Rabbi Meir Bunim Hakohen Neihaus of blessed memory, with the support and proper assistance of the Admor Rabbi Shmuel of holy blessed memory.

There was also an attempt to establish a Yeshiva in Zagorze in 5684 (1924), under the direction of the son of our rabbi, Rabbi Avraham Yisrael, may he live a long life. The head of the Yeshiva was Rabbi Mendel Wachsler of blessed memory. However, after the death of the "Shem Mishmuel", this yeshiva ceased to exists.

His son the Admor Rabbi Dovid of holy blessed memory also established a network of "Beis Avraham" Yeshivas in cities of Poland – Warsaw, Lodz, and others, in which was educated a generation of learned Hassidim, lofty thinkers and people of worthy deeds.

An honorable monthly publication was published in Warsaw called "Beis Avraham". Its purpose was to promote the Sochaczew style of learning. It was published by Rabbi Leibel Elbinger may his blood be avenged – as well as, may he be granted life, the author of this essay. Torah giants of that generation as well as the elders of the Sochaczew Hassidim may their blood be avenged participated in this publication.

As did his holy father, he also played an active role in communal life, in that he was the leader of the rabbinical organization of Poland. As a member of the leadership of the Council of Torah Sages and one of the heads of Agudas Yisrael, he was always very interested in communal affairs, and his opinions were decisive.

Many of his followers who were closest to him were renowned people of Poland. They were famous Torah giants, such as: the Gaon Rabbi Avraham Weinberg may G-d avenge his blood the author of "Reishit Bikkurim"; the Gaon Rabbi Aryeh Leib Frumer may G-d avenge his blood, the author of "Siach Sadeh", the book of responsa "Eretz Hatzvi", and the head of the Yeshiva "Chachmei Lublin"; Rabbi Eliahu Laskowski may G-d avenge his blood, the head of the rabbinical court of Dobrut (who was hung in the marketplace of his city by the German Nazis may their names be eradicated, after he had sanctified the name of heaven and the Jewish people in public by giving a lecture – while upon the gallows – as is recorded in the chronicles of the days of the Holocaust and the uprising); Rabbi Velvish Borenstein of holy blessed memory from Czestochowa; Rabbi Baruch Laznowski may G-d avenge his blood, the head of the rabbinical court of Ujazd; Rabbi Chaim the head of the rabbinical court of Konstantyno; Rabbi Goldschlag the head of the rabbinical court of Pieszyce; The Rabbi of Piniatki; Rabbi Eliezer Shalom the righteous teacher of Wola; Rabbi Yisrael the righteous teacher of Radomsk; Rabbi Eliezer Lipman Leventhal may G-d avenge his blood, the head of the rabbinical court of Cieladz; and others.

Along with his great zealousness for G-d and His Torah – which he inherited from his father of strong character – he was also very deliberate in his words and actions, he walked deliberately and spoke deliberately, he weighted and measured his actions, he was pleasant to his fellowman, always took the opinions of others into account, received every person pleasantly, and excelled in the trait of true love of his fellow Jew.

His prayers were also calm and deliberate, with a soulful voice, word for word, properly enunciated, measured and precise, coming from the depths of a sensitive and pure heart with a special tune, which penetrated into the hearts of the congregation with pleasantness and splendor.

He felt a definite obligation with regard to the upbuilding of the Land of Israel, just as did his holy fathers the "Avnei Nezer" and the "Shem Mishmuel". (see Avnei Nezer on Yoreh Deah part 2 section 454 and 455 which where he addressed the holy Rabbi of Pilow of blessed memory in a lengthy fashion; and in the collection of responsa Avnei Nezer for the end of Choshen Mishpat, section 95; and in the book "Abir Haroim" pages 106 and 107.) His pining for the Land came to the fore during the Sabbath meals, when he would deliver a discourse on Torah at the table with his congregation of Hassidim, for there was pretty much not one Sabbath in which he did not mention in his discourse the holiness of Torah, the Sabbath and the Land, all three of which were intertwined together by him with the weekly Torah portion. His Torah discourses were said with great devotion, with the wisdom and understanding of the mind influencing the emotions of the heart.

In similar fashion to his father Rabbi Shmuel of holy blessed memory, who visited the Land of Israel in 5651 (1891) along with his brother-in-law and uncle Rabbi Meir of holy blessed memory on a mission of the "Avnei Nezer", who did not suffice himself with acquiring a portion of our holy land in his inner room in Sochaczew, by means of explaining the deep laws and commandments which are dependent on the land; he also sent his son and aforementioned son-in-law with a large sum of money in order to purchase a plot of land in the Land of Israel. They remained in the Land for three months, and traversed its length and breadth in order to actively acquire it. To their distress, their plan was aborted, since the government of Turkey at that time forbade the sale of land to Jews of Russia.

His son as well, Rabbi Dovid of holy blessed memory, visited the Land of Israel twice. At first he came there in the summer of 5684 (1924) with a complete plan to start a Hassidic settlement in wide areas, and he also purchased land for this purpose.

His words upon his return to Poland still ring in my ears. They were delivered in a large public gathering in a hall on 31 Zamenhof, where he lectured with great enthusiasm on the commandment of settling the Land of Israel. He called upon the well to do of his Hassidim to purchase properties, to go there and settle.

The depression that broke out in Poland immediately after his visit prevented the materialization of his plans.

On the 20th of Tevet 5684 (1924), at the festive opening of the fourth national convention of Agudas Yisrael in Poland, he called out to the convention in a fiery speech for practical activity for the sake of settling the Land. Thus were his words:

"Blessed are you who come in the name of G-d – blessed are those who are brought here through the will of G-d, Whose spirit gathered you here, for His spirit brought you to the service of G-d, in order to strengthen the religion and the Torah.

We bless you from the house of G-d, that is the Land of Israel. For it was from there that G-d commanded the blessing of life to the world. From there will come the everlasting life of Israel, for ever – until the days of the Messiah, and He acts gracefully toward his Messiah, to David and his children forever. Our rabbi, my revered father of holy blessed memory used to call out all the days of his life for the work for the Land of Israel, and in the last convention in which he participated, he declared it to be his pure will that everyone should act with all his might for the sake of settlement of the Land of Israel. Our rabbi, my grandfather the Admor of blessed memory taught in the Avnei

Nezer that it is in accordance with halacha (Jewish Law) that the commandment to settle the Land of Israel applies in this day and age.

The holy Jew used to say: "Is it not true that every Jew is required to fulfil all of the commandments of the Torah, the 248 positive commandments and 365 negative commandments, however everyone has special commandments, one positive commandment and one negative commandment which are set aside for him, for whose sake he came into the world, as it says in the Gemara, 'your father, what was he most careful about', however how do we know which is the special commandment for any person? That is the commandment for which the person has a desire, he pines for it, that is his commandment, it belongs to him. And even if there is a negative commandment for which he has a desire to transgress, G-d forbid, he has to watch himself extra carefully from it, so that he will G-d forbid not stumble in it. And that is his task in this world.

Therefore when we see that the desire for our holy Land is revealed and growing, that a mighty desire is awakened from observant people who seek G-d and concern themselves with His commandments, and all Jews now desire to go up to the holy Land, it is a sign that now is the special time to busy oneself with the commandment of settling in the Land of Israel.

However the foundation and cornerstone of settling in the Land of Israel is the keeping of Torah and the commandments. Even after the four expressions of redemption, "I will take you out", "I will save you", "I will redeem you", and "I will take you"[3], the condition follows "For I am the L-rd your G-d", and only after that does it say "I will bring you to the land". It is explained in the Or Hachayim, for there is no damage G-d forbid to the command of G-d that is worse[4], and now that everyone is gathered together for this great commandment, to strengthen the religion and the Torah by settling the Land of Israel, at the time that the community does this commandment, the blessing "His community is founded upon the Land" will belong to them. When the "community" is banded together to build the Land, in a strong and proper foundation, they will be successful, for only then will our service for the Land of Israel come to the point of a peaceful and mighty fulfillment." Thus far were his words.

His holy words made a mighty impression upon those gathered, and the seal of the Land of Israel was stamped upon the convention.

In the winter of 5684 (1925), our rabbi visited the Land of Israel for the second time, accompanied by the Gaon of Kozieglowy, may G-d avenge his blood. They spent Purim in Tel Aviv, Passover in Jerusalem, and the left the Land on Lag Baomer[5].

On Rosh Hashana 5699 (1938), he preached to his Hassidim, especially to the youth, that they should learn Mishna off by heart, for there will be a time when books will not be available...

When the German legions broke into Lodz at the beginning of the Second World War, they broke into his house, tortured him, and dragged him through the streets of Lodz. When he was saved from them he fled to Warsaw with his entire family, broken and crushed from the many disasters which befell the world, from persecution and torture, expulsion and humiliation of the Jewish people, who were now found in distress, trouble and straits, who were now caught in the lowest recesses of hell in this world.

The rabbi of holy blessed memory took the terrible situation deeply to heart, and his sublime face was etched with the bitterness and sorrow that was in his heart that was pained for the troubles of the Jewish people. He was completely frightened from the terrible news that his ears heard, that was worsening from day to day, and from the troubles of his people that his eyes witnessed. Nevertheless, he attempted to show a pleasant face, and to give spiritual protection for those who came to the shadow of his protection in order to hear words of comfort and support from his mouth.

On the festival of Shavuot 5700 (1940), I still merited to be among those who sat at his table that he set up in his hidden dwelling in Warsaw, opposite the Zaks garden, together with a community of prominent Hassidim. With emotion and outpouring of the soul he expounded the verse "You shall be straight with the L-rd your G-d" (Deuteronomy 18:13) with Rashi's commentary on that verse, that you should go with Him in a straight path and you should wait for Him, and do not try to divine the future, etc. In those days our rabbi of holy blessed memory still hoped that he would merit to ascend to the Holy Land. At the time that my brother the prominent Rabbi Avigdor Leibish may G-d avenge his blood fled from Warsaw to Lodz, our rabbi requested that he should inquire if the missing documents that were needed to arrange his emigration had arrived to his address in Lodz. When I received a negative reply in a letter from my brother, in which he described the tribulations of the Lodz Ghetto, I went to the Admor of holy blessed memory and informed him of these matters. He sat steeped in his thoughts about the tidings of Job that I had brought him, and in front of him on the table was a book of the Bible. He turned to me and said: "You know that the purpose of the creation of man and his coming into this world is to rectify and complete his soul, and a Jewish person is required to strive and act to attain this completeness that is required of him until the goal is reached, in order to fulfil the intent of creation, however not every person merits to complete his soul by virtue of his spiritual work during the days of his life in this world. On the contrary, most people destroy rather than rectify, go down rather than ascend, and from where can come their completeness? Therefore there are times when G-d looks and gazes unto the end of all generations, and arranges things so they can be completed in a different fashion, according to the statement "there are some people who can acquire their world in one hour"...

I was brazen enough to stop him and ask him: "Did not our sages say in Pirke Avot that one hour of repentance and good deeds in this world is better than the entire life of the world to come?"

He answered me: "Certainly we desire and pray that we shall merit to fulfil our souls through life, repentance and good deeds, however if we do not merit that, Heaven bestows upon us the opportunity to attain eternal life in other means... We learn this from the first section of our holy Torah, where Abel was righteous and Cain evil, and nevertheless the blood of Abel was spilled, and Cain the murderer lived ..." And the holy rabbi continued on with similar words, and this is not the place to publish them.

With regard to the above, see what is written in the book Maggid Meisharim on the portion of Vaerah, that the angel informed the house of Joseph: "And you will merit to be a burnt offering before Me, and to be burnt for the sake of My holy name, your flesh and bones will be completely burnt before Me, and left cut up and will be removed like queen wool". And see the book Bikurei Aviv page 3, by the holy Rabbi of Radzymin of holy blessed memory.

It is related that in those gloomy days he would say: "I reflect, I was in the Land of Israel, and I had intention to settle there, even though at that time it was possible to live in the exile, but nevertheless I did not merit at that time to set up my residence in our Holy Land. Now when it is not possible at all to live here, am I not worthy to ascend to the Land of Israel?"

Before Rosh Hashana 5741 (1940), our rabbi of blessed memory published a proclamation (published in stencil) with words of encouragement and awakening for repentance. I remember that the words of Torah were based on a statement of the holy Zohar, section 3:168: "A tree to which light does not rise will be knocked down and lit, a body in which the light of the soul does not rise will be knocked down and lit".

The Admor of holy blessed memory encouraged the Gaon Rabbi Frumer and the Gaon Rabbi Stuciner to establish a Yeshiva and teach Torah even in the darkness of the shadow of death of the

Warsaw Ghetto. The groups of Rabbi Avrahamele Weinberg and of the Gaon of Kozieglowy were among those who were well known during the time of the Holocaust for their strength of spirit, and for keeping the tradition of Hassidism – and also for their preparations for the revolt. The youth studied Torah with diligence in an underground bunker below the house on 14 Mila. Every night after midnight they would go out to search for food in the abandoned and empty houses in order to sustain themselves.

The Rabbi of Sochaczew advised me to leave Warsaw and to return to my family and community in Sanok, where I had served as a rabbi, and from where I had fled since the Gestapo interrogated me. When I came back to my house in the Sanok Ghetto, it became clearly evident to me – after about a year – at the beginning of the winter of 5702 (1941) about the establishment of a death camp in Chelmno (Kolmnhauf) by Kaul, and about the many acts of murder in the forests of Kozmir. From the information that I gathered and the terrifying news that was transmitted to me by the sons of Rabbi Yissachar Cohen of Gostynin, may G-d avenge his blood, and after I investigated the truth of the matter, I wanted to debunk the lie, for the Jews of the Ghettos were not sent out for work alone. I wrote a letter to the Rabbi of Sochaczew of holy blessed memory, in cryptic language, that the aunt Esther from Megilla street, house 7, dwelling 4 is coming... the innuendo was clear, for it says in verse 4 of chapter 7 of the Scroll of Esther "for me and my nation are given over to be annihilated, killed, and destroyed, and if we were only to be sold as slaves and maidservants I would have maintained my silence". The hint was clear, for after a very brief period of time I received a response that advised me to draw strength from verse 4 in chapter 23 of the book of Psalms[6].

It became known to me only know, from the essay "in the vale of murder" by the eyewitness Mr. Feingold that "a short time before the deportations, the Rabbi of Sochaczew was the first to sound an alarm to the Jewish community that an evil decree was about to come upon the Jewish people. He, of blessed memory, said that this decree would be enacted by the men of the S.S. from Lublin, whom have bands tied to their sleeves with the inscription Fernichtungs Komand ("Extermination Unit").

Adam Chernikov inquired about this matter to the governors Leist and Fischer, to the Commissar of the Ghetto Aaurswald, and the Gestapo chief Brand may his name be blotted out. They did not know about this new decree, but the Rabbi of Sochaczew did not rest, he called together people, and requested that they enter into council. In his house, meetings were held with regard to the uprising..."

On July 19, 1942, when the word of the impending expulsion began to spread, a top-secret meeting of activists and important people was called in the upper wall of the Warsaw Ghetto on 27 Nowalipki Street. The Admor of Sochaczew was there along with the Admor of Alexander of holy blessed memory, as well as the Rabbis of Pawianice and Kalice, and other honorable people of various affiliations. The topic of discussion was the difficult question: Are the rumors of extermination true?...

He lived in various different dwellings until the closing of the Warsaw Ghetto, for he feared to live in a set place. Later he traveled to Otwock, and then he returned to the Warsaw Ghetto and took up residence on 24 Murnowski at the home of Reb Yosef and later Reb Yitzchak Meir Elbinger, may G-d avenge their blood. They were former parnassim of Warsaw and among his closest Hassidim.

His home in the Ghetto was a central place for counsel, gatherings and meetings. He preached words of comfort, encouragement, strength, and hope in general and in detail. It is told that during the times of the deportations, he found refuge in a hidden room in a shop on 67 Genesha Street. He died there of heart failure on the 8th of Kislev 5703 (1942), caused by the great tribulations of the Jewish people which weighed on his pure heart.

On this day, a cold and snowy winter day, for a brief moment the honor of the dead returned to the Ghetto, which had been desecrated by that time just as had been desecrated the honor of the living. For there was arranged a funeral according to the former custom, in which a recognizable community participated. He was laid to rest with honor in the cemetery on Genesha Street, near the grave of the first head of the rabbinical court of Warsaw (the grandfather of my father of holy blessed memory) the Gaon Rabbi Shlomo Lipschitz of blessed memory, the author of the book of responsa "Chemdat Shlomo".

The righteous one will be remembered forever. May G-d avenge his blood, and may his merit protect over us.

{639}

Rabbi Dovid Borenstein, the Admor of Sochaczew

by B. Tzemach

Translated by Jerrold Landau

(Biographical notes)

He was a rabbi and Admor, a decisor of Torah law and an expositor of secret innuendoes of the Midrashic treasury, a deep thinker in novel ideas on the Torah and full of heartfelt emotion in prayer. His mind was for halachic decisions and his devoutness for Hassidism.

He was like his grandfather, the Admor Reb Dovidel of holy blessed memory was a rabbi and Admor, a decisor in halachot of milk and meat[7], and ways to raise up the soul. He occupied himself with expositing on the permitted and forbidden, laws of divorce documents and marriage, on the one hand, and a yearning for spiritual uplifting on the other hand.

Torah and Hassidism were combined one with the other – as was the way of the Admorim of Sochaczew.

This was a covenant between the youthful grandchild and the exalted grandfather, the author of the "Avnei Nezer". The hand of this Torah giant and halachic leader did not turn from the tender child, and later from the youth Dovidel. The hand of the youth was tied to the belt of the grandfather, who transmitted to his grandson the secrets of Torah from the pure wellspring of Kotzk.

The Admor Reb Dovidel of holy blessed memory. He died in the Warsaw Ghetto.

Aside from the education that he received in his own father's house, the youth absorbed the spirit that was bestowed upon him by his exalted grandfather.

After the lessons in the Beis Midrash (study hall) along with the other yeshiva students, the grandfather gave over to the grandson that which can only be exposited in a one-on-one fashion, that which he in turn had received from his great teacher, his father-in-law of Kotzk.

The youth was a youth, serving before his grandfather. He listened, heard, and paid attention, and felt the love that his grandfather-teacher felt toward him, as he was transmitting his legacy to his grandson-student.

The tender and noble child was already almost a man. He studied the true Torah in a true fashion. Just as the Torah is true, the path toward it is also true.

The sharpness in learning was only a means in the Sochaczew style, in order to clear the thoughts, in order to discover similarities and connections, to understand what is taught. The main thing is the true path, the straightforward intellect, and the thoughts that come forth from the pure spring, the freedom of choice that is before the sin.

The grandson received the true path from the grandfather, the clearness of thought, and the righteousness in judgement. All of this was gleaned from the Beis Midrash when the "Avnei Nezer" conducted classes. However above this, he was educated by his grandfather in the inner sanctum, privately. Thus did the grandfather give over to the grandson that which he himself had received from the holy wellspring of Kotzk.

He married the daughter of a scholar. His in-laws were not from the family of Admorim, and they were also not of rabbinical or judicial stock. His wife was the daughter of good people from an old Hassidic household (not of Sochaczew Hassidim), and she brought with her the nobility and good-heartedness of a rich and noble Jewish home. Along with communal spirit and secular education, she brought the spirit of moderation into the Hassidic court.

The young married man Reb Dovidel continued his education at the house of his grandfather, and he also gave lessons to other youths. He received and gave. He sat in the tents of Torah and his personality spread its influence beyond. He influenced and glowed out to the environs.

His sharpness, clearness of thought, vast erudition, and his way in Torah amazed his reverential followers. The pleasantness of his ways and facial expression endeared him to everyone. The noble young man who was great in Torah was beloved by everyone and acceptable to his fellowman. However, the time came for Dovidel to go out on his own path, on an independent path. Thus decided his grandfather.

Rev Dovidel who was already famous as a Torah giant wished to serve as a rabbi. Several respectable communities offered the rabbinical seat to the young student. The "Avnei Nezer" realized that his grandson must find his own path, however the grandfather who was very attached to the grandson decided that, at least, he should go to a city that is near to Sochaczew. Thus Reb Dovidel became the rabbi of the town of Wyszogrod.

Wyszogrod, on the banks of the Wisla, was a city of workers. The Jews worked all week in the gardens and fruit orchards, or they worked in river transportation. These simple and healthy Jews were not Torah scholars. The young scholar, who only recently had left the tent that was completely Torah and Hassidism, met the masses, average people, who did not necessarily understand even the words of their prayers. He served as a rabbi, teacher and guide in day to day life. Very few people were scholars in this town of gardeners, and there were also some who participated in the Haskala (enlightenment). These people would gather in the house of the rabbi on winter nights, and conduct discussions on matters of Torah and books of Torah research, which were also familiar to the young rabbi.

Nevertheless, the rabbi lived in Wyszogrod as if on a lonely island, and he found rest for his yearning soul in the books of halacha and Hassidism. There, far from the centers of Torah, he filled the wide margin of his Gemara with notes – short notes that explained matters in a simple and sharp fashion, replete with comparisons, connections, and sources. His friends were the shelves of books that filled the room of the court of law. Behold, there was not one book from among the thousands of books of halacha and responsa, both regarding the revealed and hidden Torah, that was not decorated with notes and glosses in his own handwriting.

Very soon, the fury of the war that broke out in 5674 (1914) caught up with him. The lot of the community of Wyszogrod was similar the lot of other Jewish communities, which were destroyed by the German invaders. The governments changed in quick succession, and the Jews of the small towns, weak and vulnerable, sought refuge in the larger cities. The rabbi of Wyszogrod sough refuge, empty handed, in Lodz. After a time, he was invited to serve as rabbi in the city of Tomaszew Mazowick. In contrast to the divergent opinions between the different Hassidic factions which existed in most of the cities, a spirit of unity existed in Tomaszew, and the entire large community of Hassidim and followers of Torah accepted his authority as rabbi of the city. However, a controversy broke out between the Hassidim on the one side, and the simple folk on the other side, who were suspicious that the rabbi was "too orthodox". His tenure in Tomaszew disturbed his peacefulness, and he finally decided to give up the rabbinical seat of that city.

Prior to that, he attempted to actualize his desire and to settle in the Land of Israel. Still during the lifetime of the "Avnei Nezer", he absorbed a love of the Holy Land, and the idea of ascending to the Land of Israel was comforting to his soul. During the time of the fourth Aliya, it appeared as if the opportunity presented itself, and the Rabbi of Tomaszew organized a delegation to be sent to the Land of Israel, headed by himself, with the intention of founding a religious settlement in the Holy

Land. He visited the land, and acquired land for the organization for the purpose of setting up the settlement. When he returned to Poland, he was enthusiastic, and he engaged in activity to realize the objective; to his distress, the new conditions in Poland frustrated his plans. However the desire to ascent to the Land never ceased. All the days of his life he placed Jerusalem at the pinnacle of his joy and the pinnacle of his concerns.

His father, the Admor "Shem Mishmuel", died in the year 5686 (1926), and he was coronated as the Admor of Sochaczew. Nothing changed in his lifestyle, since even before that time he was revered as a Rebbe by his followers, and even before that time, he occupied himself in Hassidism and Kabbalah, just as he occupied himself in the revealed Torah. However, now the sealed wellspring of Torah and Hassidism was opened, it overflowed and waxed very great. A great many people came to drink with thirst of his words. His prayers were full of feeling, and poured out to his Hassidim with a broken heart. His Torah discourses during the Sabbath and festival meals were replete with words of his predecessors and hints of Kabbalah, and they encouraged his community of Hassidim also during the six days of work. Through his words, the thoughts that were hidden and locked in his own world were expressed, and all of his discourses were tied with a string of grace expressing his yearning for the Holy Land.

His sharpness in halacha and halachic decisions, his expertise in words in books of Kabbalah and Hassidism, his piercing power in jurisprudence, his deep understanding also of the ways of the world – all of these traits caused to be gathered around him a group of reverential followers, scholars, famous rabbis, heads of Yeshivot, Hassidim, men of fine deeds, as well as a large mass of people who would come to hear Torah and instruction on proper conduct from his mouth.

His pleasantness of speech, his personality which exuded wisdom, the deliberateness of his actions in every matter, the friendship which flowed out of him – all caused the Admor of Sochaczew to be revered, loved, and respected by everyone. This did not only include Hassidim of the line of Sochaczew, and not even only Hassidim. Hassidim from different factions streamed to him: some in order to clarify halacha and others to learn Torah from him and to benefit from his advice. Prominent Jews from the world of science, writers, and Jewish political leaders all came to him and were welcomed with a friendly countenance and a good heart which were characteristic of him.

The Torah of the house of study of his grandfather, his learning acquired during his tenure in Wyszogrod, his depth of knowledge in the works of Hassidism and Kabbalah, his constant contact with scholars and people of all walks of life, his experiences from his travel through the lands of Europe, his meetings with Jewish leaders – all of these left their mark on his variegated personality. His discourses were noted for their broad horizons, widespread grasp, and exalted ideas.

From among the large group of people with whom he was in contact, there were those who met in council with him for long hours at set times. These included various Admorim whom he met in his visits to the healing spas. There, amidst the beautiful scenery, where there was no community of followers to disturb them, one-on-one discussions took place on the secrets of Kabbalah, of which the Rabbi of Sochaczew was one of the greatest experts.

The difficulties that afflicted the Jews of Poland, the difficult economic situation, and the new decrees that were starting did not leave the Admor in difficult straits. His personal plans and his position of great influence placed him at the center of the Jewish religious leadership of Poland. He acted indirectly upon his Hassidim through his emissaries in various institutions. He was influential in many different circles, and he participated personally in delegations to the government. Some of his Hassidim were the parnassim of communities, the leaders of the Warsaw community, and representatives to the Sejm (Polish government) and Senate. Every important matter of Jewish politics was brought before him. Decisive meetings regarding the status of Orthodox Judaism took place in his home. He paid attention with patience, listened with deliberation, and made judgements cautiously.

Aside from the responsibility that he bore on his shoulders for the Jews of Poland, his strong desire for the Land of Israel was also expressed.

When he was a member of the Council of Torah Sages, he influenced the relationship of Agudas Yisrael to the Land of Israel in his famous speech "His Society is Founded on the Land"[8]. – that is to say that the foundation of "Aguda" should be upon the Land of Israel...

He visited the Land again in 5685 (1925) accompanied by an entourage of family members and a group of his close associates.

The holy places of Jerusalem, Safed the city of the Kabbalists, as well as the new settlements that were creating new life – all places were to him a wellspring of inspiration, holy enthusiasm, and a refreshing of the spirit.

He spent Purim in Tel Aviv full of happiness and rejoicing, with days filled with dances and songs of praise. He spent Passover in Jerusalem, in sanctity as it was in days of old. He spent Lag Baomer in Meron, enlightened by the light of the Kabbalah and Hassidic devotion.

The entire duration of his visit to the Land of Israel was like one long day of exaltation and joy of the heart.

He attempted to settle his children in the Land, to assist his Hassidim to fit in there, and he established the foundation of a Yeshiva in Hebron, based on the study of Torah and agricultural work. He longed to settle in the Land, to see the joy of the creativity of its builders, and to fulfil with his own body the commandment of settling in the Land of Israel.

However, he realized that he was still needed back home, for there were the masses of his Hassidim who were troubled by their lot in life, and that was the place where the majority of the Jews lived. His departure from the land that he longed for was difficult for him, however stronger than his desire was the responsibility he had to his flock, to the part of his family that still remained there, to the embattled Jewry of Poland. He returned. His students needed him – his Hassidim in the Diaspora. There were two evil tidings. There was open hatred against the Jews, evil decrees and damage to the fundamentals of faith – and there was a ban on shechita (ritual slaughter). The disaster was looming. Jewry was embattled and suffering.

The Admor participated in national councils, delegations and along with the rest of the Jewish leaders he did what he could to lighten the load, to nullify evil decrees and sweeten the verdict. He was the bearer of words of strength and encouragement to his group of Hassidim during the difficult times.

However, in the future there would be days even more difficult than these.

The danger that was impending for the Jews of Poland with the outbreak of the war placed a different responsibility on the leaders.

The Admor of Sochaczew moved from Lodz to the capital city of Warsaw, and hid in various places. There, with suffering and mortal danger, he fulfilled the commandment to learn and to teach. He gathered Yeshiva students around him who maintained the flame of Torah with great self-sacrifice, ensuring that it would not be extinguished in the darkness of the disaster. It is amazing: in the midst of these turbulent times the Admor occupied himself with the publication of the Torah novellae of his grandfather the "Avnei Nezer", namely novellae on the Tractate of Eruvin[9] which had yet to be published.

A miracle took place in Purim of 5700 (spring of 1940): the news arrived that the Admor and his family could save themselves. The government authorities in Rome were willing to give him a permit to enter Italy, which was still a neutral country in those days.

This was the beginning of salvation. However the Admor did not leave. He did not leave his students, Hassidim, and friends, who were to him like one large family. He was like a captain whose ship is in danger, but does not abandon his ship until the last of his passengers is safe. The ship was going down, however he did not leave it. He did not leave his guard, his holy work in spreading Torah and comforting his people. He did not cease publishing the novellae of his grandfather, and did not leave his friends and students.

He remained with them until his soul left in purity, on the 8th of Kislev 5703 (December 1942).

TRANSLATOR'S FOOTNOTES:

1. Famous rabbis are often known by the name of their magnum opus. Thus, Rabbi Avraham was known as the Avnei Nezer, and Rabbi Shmuel was known as the Shem Mishmuel.

2. Most probably referring to the mocking of religion due to the enlightenment (Haskala) movement.

3. These are four expressions that G-d used in promising Moses that He would take the Jewish people out of Egypt. The four cups of wine drunk at the Passover Seder are based on these four expressions.

4. Implied here is the phrase "than not keeping the commandments".

5. A minor festival that falls about month after the conclusion of Passover, on the 18th of Iyar.

6. "Even though I walk through the valley of the shadow of death, I shall fear no evil, for You are with me, your rod and your staff they comfort me."

7. A reference to the Torah prohibition of eating mixtures of milk and meat products, and the halachic queries that arise by such accidental mixtures.

8. This is a part of a biblical verse, and is a play on verse on the word "His Organization", which is in Hebrew Agudaso (or Agudato), which he used as a reference to the Agudas Yisrael movement. His meaning was "The Agudas Yisrael should be based upon the Land". Incidentally, the Agudas Yisrael movement was and still is a non-Zionistic movement. Orthodox Zionism finds its expression through the Mizrachi movement. Mizrachi and the Agudas Yisrael differ philosophically in their outlook toward Zionism.

9. Eruvin is one of the tractates of the Talmud, dealing with the laws of carrying on the Sabbath.

{79}

Reb Avrahamele Sochaczewer
by Aharon Cejtlin
Translated by Jerrold Landau

Reb Yechiel Meir Gastininer would call the Sochaczewer Rebbe nothing other than: the Torah Jew

"It is clearer to me than day", he used to say, "That just as the Torah Jew decides below, it is decided in Heaven above."

The Sochaczewer lived with Torah, breathed Torah, and simultaneously – lived with Hassidism and breathed Hassidism. This Gaon, from the mighty upholders of Torah, the author of "Eglei Tal" and "Avnei Nezer" on the Shulchan Aruch (Code of Jewish Law) was indeed one of the greatest of Polish rabbis.

Aside from his own pedigree and aside from the pedigree of his ancestry (he stemmed from the Rema and the Shach) [1] he also had the pedigree of Kock. The Kocker was his father-in-law. His father, Reb Zeev Nachum, an eminent Gaon, was a rabbi in Olkusz, and later in Biala. The father, just like the son, was both a Gemara Jew and (as the son wrote in the introduction to the father's book) a person "versed in miracles".

It was also told regarding the mother of the Sochaczewer, Dovrish as they called her, (see "Abir Haroim), the she merited to see a vision of Elijah. This should not surprise us. The Hassidic stories relate that the grandmother of Reb Michel Zloczewer, Yentl, used to open up a heaven full of angels. The angels would sing Kadosh [2], and Yentl the prophetess – as they called her – used to sing together with them. Reb Nachman's mother Feiga [3], the granddaughter of the Baal Shem Tov, Hodel's daughter, used to be called Feiga the prophetess by the Hassidim. They used to relate regarding her that she used to unify herself with the Baal Shem's soul. Hodel herself, the daughter of the Baal Shem, used to take part in her father's ascendancies and rectifications, as is told by Hassidic tradition.

The Misnagdic, anti-Hassidic learning based itself upon the statement that, since the destruction of the Holy Temple, "G-d only has the four ells of Halacha" [4] – that only Halacha remains before the Creator of the World as it were. On the other hand, Hassidic learning was all encompassing. Everything in Judaism was bound and cemented to learning (as is espoused, for example by Zhidachov and Komarno, but especially Chabad [5]) and it is thought that the Halacha itself is the universal revelation of G-dliness, like a Halacha oriented tradition. The "four ells of Halacha", are surrounded – in all worlds, and are seen through the prism of the Jewish people, the "singular nation in the land".

Reb Avrahamele Sochaczewer, just like Reb Avrahamele Czestochower, and just like virtually all or almost all of the great rabbis, was a living confirmation of the thought that I had developed in the previous discussion: the thought that Hassidism created a synthesis of Jewish values.

He was born in the year 5599 (1839) in Bendin. The Kocker – Hassidim relate – told a secret to his father, the rabbi of Biala, that he merited such a son on account of the bizarre incident. One Purim, Jews were so deeply immersed in the mitzvah of the joy of Purim, that there indeed was a moment when no Jew except for the rabbi of Biala was studying any Torah. Were it not for him, the world would have remained without a sound of Torah at that moment. It was good fortune that the rabbi of Biala did not desist from his learning even at such a time. Therefore, it was decreed in Heaven that they would send him a son would enlighten the eyes of all of Israel.

The father's diligence in Torah was transmitted to the son. Reb Avrahamele Sochaczewer fulfilled the adage "and you shall delve into it day and night" with the same dedication as his father.

He once said that, since from the moment a Jew dies until his burial, he has nothing to do – it is good that the corpse would not lie empty, but should rather recite Mishnas by heart.

Here you have the entire essence of the Sochaczewer: the exceptional learner whose "mouth does not desist from study" – literally that he cannot imagine that a Jew would desist from Torah even between death and burial; and the Rebbe, whose sense for the mystical reality is worthy of discussion, to whom the revealed and the hidden are within the same boundary; and a Jew to whom it is an obvious and self-evident matter that someone between death and burial would lie and recite Mishnas by heart.

The Sochaczewer often used to cite what his father-in-law, the Kocker once told him about the path of Hassidism and the path of learnedness. The Kocker would say that if the Baal Shem Tov was sent to earth in order to lead a new way of the worship of the Creator, it was not because that path, the Hassidic path, is higher than the path of learnedness. No. It was therefore because of the false interpretations with which one had interpreted the Torah – because of this, with our great sins, an injury came upon the Torah and a great accusation was taking place in Heaven. There was no other solution than to send the Holy Baal Shem Tov to our world, so that he would found a new way. However, aside from this, the path of drawing close to the Master of the World through learning is much greater.

We have already seen that Hassidism, in any case, at its summit, bound together the revealed and the hidden into one unit. Thus, the path of learning and the path of Hassidism indeed became one. Indeed, we can bring a proof from the Kocker himself and from the Sochaczewer himself. However, not only from them. We see this everywhere in Hassidism, from the "Toldot Yaakov Yosef", the Baal Shem Tov's direct student until Reb Tzadok HaKohen of Lublin, and from the author of the Tanya until the Ostrowicer, the last great Rebbe personality in Poland.

The Kocker's aforementioned statement was certainly a sort of a paradox. We can take it as a correct formulation of the way that Hassidism had experienced if we understand that talking about service the Creator of the World through study is what the Kocker meant by the Hassidic path of learning. The only reservation is with regard to the Baal Shem Tov. The truth is that the Baal Shem Tov's methodology did not place "service of the heart" higher than learning. It only placed more stress on "service of the heart" for the reason that the Kocker brought down. Hassidism, I repeat, was the one and only path, but this does not imply that it did not have its own dialectic.

Illustrative of the truth – the Sochaczewer searched both in learning and in Hassidism. He said the following regarding his way of learning:

There is an enlightened intellect and a dark one. If a person has novel ideas in Torah in a wonderful manner, and then finds a contradiction to his novel idea and wishes to forcefully resolve the contradiction because it would be a shame for him to lose such a wonderful didactic; he mixes the dark intellect with the enlightened one, and comes up with the resolution. In such a case, he has a personal stake, he is a stakeholder, it must be the case! My way and no other. If I want to innovate something, I would first search in every hole and in every crack in case I find some contradiction to it. Why should I come up with something that is not the truth? My nature is, that if I search for a problem in my own achievement more than in someone else's, and if I say or write to another about some innovation of mine – my sole intention thereby is: perhaps the other might find an opposing piece of evidence, and through that, I myself might clarify the matter.

From the "dark intellect", the Sochaczewer leapt to the illuminated.

The Torah Jew, the Sochaczew, was a Torah Jew with an illuminated intellect from childhood. Once, at noontime, he was reaching for cereal at the table. His father, the rabbi of Biala, asked him in jest: Nu, Avrahamel, to such a question do you also have an answer? [6]

"Now I am eating", said the youth, "we will see after eating".

"Nu?" his father reminded him later, "What do you say?"

"An answer", said Avrahamel, "Is relevant when there is a question (kashia). Now there is no more cereal (kasha). So why is an answer needed?"

During his entire later life, the Sochaczewer did not seek for any answers when there was no question.

The young genius lived in Kock for approximately six or seven years, until his father-in-law's death. Throughout his entire life, the Sochaczewer did not cease to talk about his father-in-law with enthusiasm and wonderment. Exactly like the Chidushei Harim [7] – he was struck with wonder not only about the Kocker's greatness in the revealed, in his power of Torah. The Sochaczewer possessed that power of Torah himself in his younger years. The Chidushei Harim, to whom the young genius used to travel after his father-in-law's death, said about him once, when he was taken by a touch of genius, the following words: The holy Kocker left us a beautiful inheritance; in every generation there is one who is the mirror of the generation, and they look into that mirror from Heaven. Today this young man, the Olkuszer genius, is reflecting thus.

Since one has to concern oneself with one's sustenance on the earth, it was no longer appropriate to remain in Kock. The privation increased, and the Kocker's son-in-law became the rabbi in Parczew. He was persecuted in Parczew, and it even came to the point where he was left without bread. In later years, he would relate that he did not even have a room in which he could sit and learn – he would go out to learn in a field among the stocks of corn. Even at that time – he would say with a sigh – even at that time, I grew by leaps and bounds. Where did those years go? The learning among the stocks of corn was so pleasant... if the persecutors would only know, the persecutors did such good, the persecutors would have kissed the coat tails...

There, he became acquainted with the young rabbi, the Gaon Reb Yehoshuale Kutner. The Kutner [8] was very active. Due to his greatness, he wanted to have him close by. This lasted for a long time, and his Rebbe, The Chidushei Harim, no longer had to help his persecuted student with a weekly allowance, which he used to send him from Ger. Since Krosniewice needed a rabbi, Reb Yehoshuale himself went there. He called together the householders into the Beis Midrash, went up to the bima, and made the following statement: "My masters, since you are left without a rabbi, you should know that I have engaged in Torah didactics with a certain young man. If you accept him as the rabbi of the city, your city will have a rabbi as great as the Rashba [9]. My masters, I rarely defeated this young man, and only with great help from heaven was I saved from defeat by him [10]."

The Krosniewicer householders agreed, not even knowing to whom Reb Yehoshuale was referring. Later the Kutner Gaon disclosed that he was referring to the young Parczewer rabbi, the Kocker rabbi's son-in-law. He himself, the Kutner, inscribed the authorization of the rabbinate. In it, he entitled him as: Prince of Torah.

He had no rest in Krosniewice as well. The householders stirred up trouble and complained that the rabbi "Mixes himself into too much".

He was the rabbi in Krosniewice and he also became a Rebbe there after the death of the Aleksandrer. Reb Henech was his third Rebbe. The first was the Kocker, and the second was the Chidushei Harim. After the death of the Chidushei Harim, he traveled to the Aleksandrer and became his greatest confidante. He bound himself strongly to him. When the Aleksandrer passed away, and a portion of the Hassidim cast their eyes upon him, the Krosniewicer rabbi, after a long period of deliberation, he agreed to lead the community. His own father, the rabbi of Biala, traveled to him as a Hassid to his Rebbe. After Krosniewice he went to Nasielsk, and finally to Sochaczew – the city by which he is called. It is related in the pure book of wonders, "Abir Haroim", which has a treasury of material regarding the Sochaczewer (and the Kocker), that the "Nefesh Chaya" came to Sochaczew and told the assemblage that the city must purify itself and prepare to welcome the holy Jew, who is the equal of a Torah scroll.

His light spread to the entire Poland from Sochaczew. Students from everywhere came to his Yeshiva. Chasidim streamed to him in order to be helped spiritually and physically. They told wonders regarding him.

Although the Sochaczewer conducted himself entirely differently from the Kocker, he nevertheless would on occasion utter a sigh and relate out loud a dream that he had regarding a quorum of Jews... For if the Kocker required a quorum of Jews on a roof, beyond and outside of the world, the Sochaczewer's dream regarding a quorum was entirely different. He dreamed of ten students. He sat with the ten students somewhere on an island. This was a miniature Yeshiva on an island, and he, the Sochaczewer, sat and studied Torah with them for its own sake, without any disturbance in the great silence of the island.

"If such were possible", he would say, "I would thereby bestow a good turn upon the entire world. This would be the proper rectification."

This means that one must detach oneself from the world, but only in order to help the world – to bestow a rectification upon the world. One must go away from it in order to rectify it.

That dream of a Yeshiva on an island with ten people who would rectify the world through Torah – that alone was a piece of Torah, one of the finest and most typical Torah statements of Reb Avrahamele Sochaczewer.

("The Morning Journal", July 30th, 1950)

{85}

The Rebbi's Court
M. B. Sztejn
Translated by Jerrold Landau

The Jewish community of Sochaczew and the Rebbi's Court are now, to our great sorrow, in the world of truth [11]. From both, all that remains is a gnawing sorrowful elegiac legend. The blood, which was once hot, is now congealed. The old controversies are long, long forgotten, and the excitement does not even cause any stirrings any more. Only the memories, which are etched in our minds, always grow with us; and I wish to tell you about a life that so tragically ended. I hope that I will be forgiven if I make any error in my recollections.

The Rebbe...

Many years ago, in the year 5642 (1882), Hassidim from all areas of Poland purchased a single-story, brick house in Sochaczew, close to the end of Trojanower Street for their Rabbi, Reb Avrahamele. Spread out around the house were the outlying fields, the priest's gardens with tall linden trees, the peasant's paths into the forests, and the gently flowing tributary of the Bzura – the

Sochaczew Creek. In front of the house were five broad-branched chestnut trees; which sparkled through the panes of the windows, cast green shadows in the spacious room, and guarded the gates to the yard of the house like watchmen.

This house, with its paved courtyard and former gardens, once belong to a gentile official of the post office. He did not maintain the gardens. A dog guarded him and his trees. He made sure to maintain the rooms in a nice and convenient fashion. There was an entranceway built there, and obnoxious, frivolous, noisy people used to enter there....

Reb Avrahamele was known as the rabbi of the city of Sochaczew. He was not only the Gaon (genius) and the expert teacher, but also the Rebbe. Hassidim used to flock to him since the time that he was the rabbi and Rebbe in the cities of Krosnowice and Nasielsk before he was known in Sochaczew. Rabbi Avrahamele's Hassidim were not content to have their rabbi live in the staleness and the moldiness of the communal houses near the communal Beis Midrash, above the communal mikva (ritual bath) where the previous Sochaczewer rabbis lived.

The Hassidim cast their sights upon the house of the gentile postal official. They redeemed it from him, the obnoxious, frivolous tenants, and the dog; and the house with its neglected garden, paved courtyard, five chestnut trees by the entrance – became a place of Torah and Hassidism for the rabbi, Rav Avrahamele.

The joy was great in Sochaczew when Rav Avrahamele came to the city as rabbi. Residents came out to greet him in coaches, and they accompanied him into the city with music. Children and adults were out on the streets in order to welcome the rabbi. The streets leading to Grodzisk and Zyrardow were full of people. The enthusiasm was great when Rabbi Avrahamele, dressed in long, black, silk rabbinical cloak, adorned with a graying, black, thick beard, ascended the three steps in front of his house, and with his white, delicate hand that had never before held a hammer, took up that tool in order to affix the large mezuza [12] to the door of the front entrance.

A shiver, like the sound of the rustling corn in the surrounding fields, passed through the group of people that were assembled in the street. Everyone waited with restrained breath, and when they heard the bang of the hammer, everyone felt that redemption has come. On the house with the dog and the frivolous residence, there is now affixed a mezuza with large 'shin' 'daled' 'yod' letters, and Reb Avrahamele, with a pure, holy hand, affixed it himself. The impurity no longer has a hold on that house. Holiness came to that place. The city and the Jewish hearts became purified. Jews looked at the chestnut trees in front of the house, and saw that they spread their green, elongated shadows like a canopy, hiding and protecting the holiness from evil.

Reb Avrahamele's head, adorned with his large hat, arched toward the doorway, his hands rested on the door, and there was a silence around. Everyone waited for Reb Avrahamele's blessing. Soon, he began his awesome "Blessed art Though", and a bang of the hammer broke the silence. An echo resounded in the distance. Another bang and another bang, and the mezuza was affixed to the doorpost. The crowd expressed their glee. A song broke out among the people, and the musicians of Sochaczew started playing a freilach [13]. People drank 'lechayim' [14]. Everyone stretched out their hands to Rabbi Avrahamele to wish him happiness and a long life. Arms and shoulders joined together in a dance, and it seemed as if the surrounding fields and trees were also participating in the dancing. The sun shone brightly, and the waves of the Bzura splashed joyously. The singing and music was joyous, and the dancing was enthusiastic. Reb Avrahamele, accompanied by his family, entered in the house had been furnished for him.

The Sabbaths in Sochaczew became like festivals. Each Sabbath was a different festival. Housewives baked fat, sweet kugels [15] to send to the Rebbe's Sabbath table. Simple folk along with veteran Hassidim heard words of Torah from Reb Avrahamele's mouth, worshipped at the Rebbe's Hassidic minyan (prayer group), and boasted about their Rebbe and the merit that their city of Sochaczew was blessed with. They became surer of themselves. They had where to take refuge, G-d forbid, in a time of misfortune; and who to pray on their behalf at a time of danger, or to plea for their livelihood. Indeed, one looked with greater confidence at the green meadows and forests that grew around the city, from where their livelihood was derived. People joyously hitched up their horses and wagons on Sunday [16] mornings; walking with sticks in their hands and sacks over their shoulders, bent under the heavy burden; when they were wandering around on the routes, they would cast a glance at the Rebbe's house, which filled them with faith and hope emanating from the light of the Rebbe's private room. They would hear the quiet chant of the Rebbe's Torah study, and with faith and hope in their hearts; they would ascend the steps of the Rebbe's house where the mezuza was affixed, touch the holiness with their hand, and give it a pious kiss.

They began to make a greater livelihood in the town. People set up guesthouses for Hassidim who would come from outside to visit the Rebbe on Sabbaths and festivals. Already on Thursday, they would be cooking large pots of fish and meat for the Hassidim who would certainly be coming for the Sabbath. Scampering about with red cheeks, the wives of the guesthouse owners went about, doing everything with great haste. They sampled the Sabbath victuals to see if they were missing a bit of salt or pepper, and they went out to see if the Hassidim were already arriving along the highways.

In the shops, it was also evident that Hassidim were coming. The pidyon [17] also became larger. The baker in town also felt the blessing in his bakery.

Things went well even for the tailor and the shoemaker. They had more work and more mending, for who could go around in an unkempt state. It would be embarrassing for an arriving Hassid if one of his garments or his boots would fall apart.

The most fortunate were the wagon drivers. The crack of the whips resounded like shots, and the horse's feet made a din and noise on the cobblestone. With a "viau' [18], the wagons, packed with Hassidim, traveled through the streets and the market. Velvet Hassidic caps, streimels, and silk and satin kapotes [19] glittered in the sun. A Sabbath is coming... A Sabbath is coming... and the windows of the houses sparkled. Another carriage, another covered wagon is arriving.

Later, they laid the bricks for the large, spacious Beis Midrash, and paved the courtyard with cobblestones. The walls of the Beis Midrash went up literally overnight. The lumber was set up, and the holy place was ready. The singing of the Hassidim was heard louder, the sound of the learning of the young men in the Rebbi's Yeshiva was louder, and the quiet Trojanower Street was enlivened. They were no longer bothered by the priest's gardens and the "Lustgarten" where there was a "Czemtasz" in old times. The Kohanim no longer had to go around [20].

Jealousy, Hatred, and Controversy

Those who are familiar with the history of Sochaczew are able to relate that the Jewish community of Sochaczew is older than that of Warsaw. There was a time when the Jewish dead were brought on wagons from Warsaw for burial in the Sochaczew cemetery.

The rabbinate of Sochaczew also has a rich tradition. The rabbi and well-known Gaon (sage), the author of the book "Panim Meiros" had been a rabbi on Sochaczew. We know about Reb Aryeh Leib, known as the Holy Jew, from Reb Moshele Charif, who left a will before his death stating that during times of tribulation, a quorum [21] should gather together at his grave to recite Psalms, and he stated that he would intercede before the Throne of Glory that the tribulation should pass. However, the location of his grave disappeared, and even the members of the Chevra Kadisha (burial society), were not able to find it. At a time of tribulation it became revealed, Jews prayed and were helped, and the grave disappeared again. Thus did our grandfathers relate. The old timers still thought that Reb Eliezer of Sochaczew, about who we are talking, was saved from a blood libel in Sochaczew.

In the evenings, in the anteroom of the communal Beis Midrash, the older residents would share stories that they had heard when they themselves were children. These stories would be about great rabbis, Tzadikim, and lamid-vovnikim [22] who lived in Sochaczew in an unassuming fashion and intermingled with the common folk. They, the residents, were disgruntled with the Hassidic enthusiasm, with the haughtiness and with the great racket around the Rebbi's courtyard. It happened that the Hassidim would be mocked by the common folk. They took umbrage to the noise and clamor that interfered with the sleepy, small-town stillness. The wagons and carts of the Hassidim drove too fast, the horseshoes clanged too noisily on the pavement and the Hassidim sang too loudly when they were with the Rebbe in the Beis Midrash. Quietly, so nobody should hear, they would call the Hassidic scholars "Lamdzuches", the ordinary Hassidim – "schleppers" [23] and "Hassidikes", and the unfriendliness grew. There was no longer a quorum in the synagogue... the communal Beis Midrash was vacant... a pall pervaded around the rabbi's empty dwelling over the city mikva... – thus did the talk, and they began to look upon the center of Torah and Judaism that had moved to the end of Trojanower Street as if it was not theirs, as alien...

Rabbi Avrahamele himself was not the same type of rabbi as the preceding rabbis. His door was not open for the local communal members, as was the case with the prior rabbis. One could not go to see Rabbi Avrahamele when one wanted. One had to first make a request from Rabbi Avrahamele's shamash that he be allowed in to the Rebbe. They were saddened by Rabbi Avrahamele's seclusion, which therefore made him pale in comparison to the esteem and greatness of the prior rabbis, to whom one could enter to visit whenever one wanted...

Slowly, little by little the separation grew, until the more impetuous communal members lost their tempers.

Shmuel Czundik, the horse dealer, whose house was on Trojanower Street near the Rebbi's house, woke up from his Sabbath nap one Sabbath afternoon, went out in the street, and screamed out in a loud voice against the Hassidim who were interfering with his Sabbath rest. He gestured to them and shouted that he would teach "the Hassidikes" a lesson.

The youth were also unfriendly. The Sochaczewer Rebbe's supporters were quite pious, and they wanted their children to be educated in the manner of the "courtyard". At every step, they moralized to their children, and had them educated by the youths of the Rebbe's Yeshiva, who were themselves also young and spent the entire day and night learning. The youth resented this, and found fault in the Rebbe's court. In order to antagonize the Rebbe's court, students took to learning in the communal Beis Midrash in order to demonstrate that one can also learn outside of the court. At the same time, they began to introduce Chovevei Tzion [24] and socialist ideas into the town in competition with the Rebbe's court, which held that Zionism and, even more so, socialism, were heresy and apostasy, Heaven protect us.

There were also those residents who were burning with jealousy toward the innkeepers and other Jews who made their living from the Rebbe's court. Stories, true and false, were dragged from the town to the court and from the court to the town. Jewish Sochaczew was divided into two camps, and the hatred became more and more intense...

I do not know who is guilty of the following incident. Rabbi Avrahamele was deposed as Rabbi of Sochaczew by the Russian regime. It is quite possible that the pretext for this was the law at that time regarding the exams that rabbis must pass in order to be recognized as rabbis [25].

Suddenly, Rabbi Avrahamele was called before the gubernator of Warsaw. The gubernator suggested to the rabbi that he set a timeframe as to when he would take the exam. Even though many older rabbis, who entered the rabbinate prior to this law being passed, were exempted from the exams, the gubernator requested that Rabbi Avrahamele be examined. Did the Czarist governor know anything about the conflict that Rabbi Avrahamele had in the town; was this simply an evil deed; or was this a framing or set-up by the lesser officials in town? We will never know why Rabbi Avrahamele was forced to take the exams. He boldly answered the gubernator: "I am certain of matters of the intellect. It would not take me long to learn, but I do not wish to spend the time studying a language. My time is more precious. "

Reb Avrahamele's opponents were victorious. Rabbi Avrahamele became an ex-rabbi [26]. This affected him deeply, and he wrote about it: "If I were to live in the forest, the trees would struggle with me, but not with the rabbi of Sochaczew. " The court was conducted as previously. On Fridays and eves of holidays, the streets of Sochaczew were full with Hassidim who came from outside. Shiny kapotes continued to glitter in the sun, Hassidim in caps and streimels were seen hear and there. The windowpanes in the houses glittered from the movement of the covered wagons that arrived. The noise in the town did not cease. The jealousy and hatred did not let up, but greater levels of controversy did not arise.

Furthermore, Rabbi Avrahamele's yeshiva continued to exist. Students from all areas of Poland would travel to Rabbi Avrahamele. His name as a Gaon spread through the entire world, wherever there was a Jewish community. People from all Jewish communities would ask him questions, and he became a halachic authority. The Rebbi's court remained in Sochaczew until the First World War (1914-1918).

Rabbi Avrahamele passed away in 1910. His successor was his only son, Rabbi Shmuel the Sochaczewer Rebbe. The five chestnut trees, almost at the end of Trojanower Street, continued to stand and guard the entrance to the Rebbe's court.

{92}

The Rebbe's Funeral
by David Wolrat of New York
Translated by Jerrold Landau

My town of Sochaczew, which lies between Warsaw and Lodz, is known throughout Poland on account of the great Tzadik, Reb Avrahamele of blessed memory. Hassidim from the four corners of the world would come to the Rebbe, and the court was a source of livelihood for a large portion of the residents of Sochaczew.

Since as I was a grandchild of Malka the cake baker, whose cake made it to the Rebbe's court, I had opportunity to go the Rebbe's palace every Friday. I would bring cake, and always give it over to the Rebbetzin herself.

I spent the entire Friday morning at my grandmother's, ready for the mission. I stood with outstretched hands, tight as rods, and grandmother placed the cakes one on top of the others, like boards, until they were stacked higher than my head. Thus, with obstructed eyes, did I set out on my weekly trek.

The Rebbe lived at the extreme edge of the city, on Tranower Street [27]. His house (palace) stood in a garden surrounded by a fence with barbed wire at the top. The route was a considerable distance. With numbered steps, so that no stumbling would Heaven forbid occur, I arrived in peace at the Rebbetzin's. I often encountered the Rebbetzin as she as was in the middle of reciting the Shmone Esrei [28]. Since she did not want to interrupt her prayer, I had to stand with my "rods" without uttering a peep until she finished Shmone Esrei, recited Aleinu Leshabeach [29], and spat three times. Only then did she come over to me.

The Rebbetzin was an elderly woman with a satin black hat on her head and a face as pale as milk. Two severe eyes peered out from silver spectacles. She began to lay out the cakes in a row, going through them like a general on an inspection, inspecting each cake-soldier separately with her eyes. She would cut each one in the middle, and insert her "fat" finger to touch it to see if the cake was baked well. She was never able to select enough for her liking on the first shipment.

The Rebbe would often pass through while I was standing and dealing with the Rebbetzin. He never walked but only ran. He would stop by me, pat me on my head, whisper something quietly to me, and be off. My young heart jumped with joy at that time. The rods remained paralyzed at that moment...

I recall that spring day when the Rebbe of blessed memory passed away and was brought to burial.

That spring morning, when the entire town was awakening from sleep, when it still smelled of the dampness of morning due, Jews were already going to morning services with their tallis and tefillin under their arms. The shops had just opened and the dairymen from nearby villages came to the market with dairy products. The sun had begun to warm up and the day had broken, when suddenly the sad news spread about like a bolt of lightning, "The Rebbe is on his deathbed" [30]... Jews, women, children, everyone tore out of their houses as if they had caught fire. Large groups of people congregated wherever one turns. Stores began to close. Crowds of people filled the synagogue, Beis Midrash and all of the shtibels to recite Psalms. Women with "moral" voices went to the cemetery to "pick a quarrel" [31]. The entire Sochaczew quickly became a place of prayer for the Rebbe.

The news quickly spread like a fire in a dry forest. It reached the nearby cities, and throughout the day, rabbis and Rebbes began to arrive. This went on for an entire day and night. Nobody slept that night. Tranower Street was black with Hassidim throughout the entire following morning. Nobody could enter the court. Some Jews reached the window of the room where the sick man was lying, and from there were informed of the situation...

Suddenly a deathly silence passed over everybody – "The Rebbe has requested his tallis and tefillin"... The Jew standing by the window whispered with trembling lips... Hearts began to beat faster. The congestion became greater and thicker. "They dressed him in his tallis and tefillin"... "The Rebbe is reciting the confessional" [32]... Large and small stood with outstretched hands and heads turned Heavenward. Terrible shrieks cut through the air: "Save our Tzadik!"... A sound of a shofar on a mountain peak cut through the air: "It is the time of the departure of the soul..." Everyone's hands and feet froze. Clairvoyant people fell silent. A Jew by the window declared with a face contorted by pain, and hands clutching the hairs on his head: "Blessed is the true judge!" [33] The crowd repeated with muffled voices: "Blessed is the true judge!"...

The city was enveloped in a dark grief. People were weeping as they passed by. People looked at each other silently. They cast a glance and then continued walking. Crowds of people came from all ways and paths. People came by coach, carriage and wagon. People came by foot from the Warsaw highway, from the Lewiczer highway – Misnagdim, Hassidim in satin kapotes with velvet hats, rabbis with velvet hats, Rebbes with streimels, shoes and white socks. All of the streets were black with Jews, with long beards, short beards, thick beards and thin beards. There were boys with blond "sprouts" – everyone converged on the Rebbe's court on Tranower Street. Every Jewish house turned into an inn, even though nobody was going to go to sleep. All of the Jewish houses, all of the shtibels, the Beis Midrash, the synagogue – all were full with out-of-town Hassidim.

Correspondents from the Jewish newspapers of Warsaw and Lodz arrived. The late journalist B. Joaszon and my brother Pesach "dressed up" in satin kapotes and went into the courtyard. I begged my father of blessed memory to take me as well. It took a half a night for us to reach the room where the deceased was lying. With great effort, we finally went indoors. The room was almost dark. Walls of people were standing all around. A hazy light shone from the middle and cast long shadows on the walls and the ceiling. My father lifted me up over the nearby heads, and I saw: in the very middle a small hill lay [34], dressed with a black satin kapote that the Kocker gave to his great son-in-law the Sochaczewer. A yellow, wax candle flickered at the head. Rebbes with books in their hands, weeping in the great sorrow, were half sitting, half lying on the ground around the deceased.

The next day, all those who had the merit to occupy themselves with the matter, whether with the new shrouds or with the tahara [35] had to immerse themselves before they could touch the deceased. The route from the Rebbe's court to the cemetery, though the weeping bystanders, took three quarters of an hour; for the pallbearers stopped at every step. The bier and the coffin were made from the table by which the Rebbe used to study.

The correspondent B. Joaszon had the idea that my brother should photograph the procession. I brought the apparatus. We went up to the roof of the butcher shop and set up the apparatus under the chimney so that nobody would notice us. We could see from afar how they meandered with the bier around the swarm of heads. When they drew near, some Hassidim noticed us and drove us way...

I then set out for the cemetery. There were already thousands of people there. They tore around and argued in order to approach a piece of the coffin so that they could write down their name. With great difficulty, I managed to reach an edge of a board and I wrote down the names of my parents, my brother and myself.

The sun was about to set and was sinking in the other side of the Bzura River, which flowed close by the hill of the cemetery. At nightfall, they brought the great deceased Reb Avrahamele Borensztejn of blessed memory to burial. Throughout the thirty-day mourning period (Shloshim) Hasidim stood day and night as they were erecting the canopy.

("Tag" – 1944)

The rabbi Rav Shmuel, the "Shem Mishmuel"

The Shem Mishmuel
by A. Chetzroni
Translated by Jerrold Landau
(4th of Cheshvan 5617 – 22 Tevet 5686) [36]

The Shem Mishmuel was born in Kock (5617) and spent his childhood in Parczew and Krosniewice, where his father, the Gaon was the rabbi. He learned Torah from his father. His mother, the righteous woman Sara Tzina, was the daughter of the Admor of Kock Reb Menachem Mendel of holy blessed memory. In 5634 (1874) He married the daughter of Reb Eliezer Lipman of Radomsk, the brother of the author of "Tiferet Shlomo" – an enthusiastic Kocker Hassid. He remained with his father and went with him to Nasielsk and Sochaczew. He lived in a separate house in the center of the city, and he earned his living from a wine business, even though he was not very interested in business.

After the death of his first wife, he remarried (in the year 5673 – 1903), the daughter of the Kozinczer rabbi, Reb Moshe Natan Szapiro.

After the death of his father the Gaon, he was coronated as Admor in his place, and he moved his residence to the court.

He was at a spa in Germany at the outbreak of the First World War. After much wandering, he succeeded, along with a series of other rabbis, to return to Poland. Due to the pressure of the Czarist army, he decided to remain in Lodz. He moved his family there. Thus, he was not in Sochaczew at the time of its destruction in the year 5675 (1915).

He remained in Lodz during the war years, where he led a community of his Hassidim. He directed them and encouraged them during the difficult times. He moved to Zgierz, a small town near Lodz, in the year 5679 (1902) in order to continue on without the tumult of the large industrial city.

There, he founded his Beis Midrash and settled there, despite the fact that he never ceased to make plans to return to Sochaczew.

He became ill in the year 5686 (1926). He was brought to Otwock, where he died in the 24th of Tevet, 5686. He was brought to burial in the canopy of his father in Sochaczew.

The entire Jewish world bitterly lamented he loss.

The Shem Mishmuel was the only son of his parents. (They also had a daughter, Esther, who married the Gaon Rabbi Meir Borensztejn, her father's brother, and lived in Sochaczew, where she died.) From his earliest youth, he became closely knit and bonded with his father. He was always with his father. He was seen as his student, and he revered him. Even in the later years, when he was the father of a large family, not a day went by when he was not with his father. At the time that he took over as Admor of Sochaczew after his father's death, he was seen as nothing more than an elucidator and commentator of his father's Torah.

This was not because he had a soft and mild nature. Just the opposite: he was strong in his opinions, with a sharp, independent intellect, which he did not quash before anyone. In relation to his father the Gaon, however, he was always soft and mild, a son and a student.

As well, the relationship of the father to him was extraordinary. The father related to him with honor and respect. He used to call him (not by his instruction) "My Reb Shmuel". He valued his opinion, and did not make any great or small decision without conferring with him.

Thus did they live together for 35 years, with full collaboration in all domains of life. Thus did they have one soul, one vision, and together breathed the sublime air of Kock. It often was the case that the father the Gaon, whose word was yearned for by many, found his support and refuge on the strong Kocker shoulders of his son. Therein may indeed lie the reason for the tremendous reverence of the son for the father. Who other than he knows his spiritual elevation, his greatness in Torah and fear of G-d. Even the relationship of respect between the father and the son, the Kocker grandchild – is a reflection of his boundless reverence to his Kocker father-in-law from whom he was not freed until his old age.

Even this trait – the style of Kock – accompanies his very active and spiritual life, and expresses itself in various of his books that were published after his death – the eight volumes of "Shem Mishmuel" that discuss the Torah and Hassidism as related to the weekly portions, that he used to say before of his Hassidim between the years 5670-5686 (1910-1926). These books were written with his fine and rich language, and with a warm heart – as if they were today heard from his mouth.

The chief point of his Torah: the incessant demand for completeness and unity of all parts of the soul in Divine worship; that the heart should yearn for the Creator with full zeal and feeling, and simultaneously that the brain should exert its influence to rectify the activity of the feeling, so that the purpose can be achieved – to elevate and unite with the Creator and the Torah.

He was simultaneously active in Jewish societal life. He had a clear opinion on all kinds of problems, and also on the question of Zionism. He expressed his opinions clearly and boldly. He always aspired to settle in the Land of Israel. During his youth (5651 – 1891), with the urging of his father the Gaon, he visited Israel in order to purchase land for a Hassidic colony, however the ban of selling land to Russian Jews prevented this. He had a positive attitude toward religious settlement in the Land of Israel even at the time of the Balfour Declaration. He thought about aliya to the Land of Israel even at the end of his life.

When he was coronated as Admor after his father's death, all of the Sochaczewer Hassidim gathered around him, including Gaonim such as the Kinczkewer Rabbi, Reb Yoav Yehoshua, the Ravad from Warsaw, Reb Yitzchak Fajgienbaum, and others. He presided over the way of his father – Torah conducted with Hassidism, and engrossing oneself in Halacha with enthusiasm. However, he did not bring in his own traits, his own novel ideas in the Torah of Kock – Sochaczew. With his grasp of language and his wonderful skill in expression, he strengthened Sochaczewer Hassidism. He also imprinted his mark upon Polish Hassidism prior to the First World War. His books were accepted in wide circles.

He renewed the Sochaczew Yeshiva, and placed the Gaon Reb Aryeh Tzvi Frumer (later the Rosh Yeshiva of Chachmei Lublin) as its head. He developed his father's work.

TRANSLATOR'S FOOTNOTES:

1. The Rema (Rav Moshe Isserles) was an early Polish rabbi who wrote the Ashkenazic glosses on the Shulchan Aruch. The Shach (Siftei Cohen) was one of the main commentators of the Shulchan Aruch.
2. "Holy, Holy, Holy is the L-rd of Hosts", considered being the song of the angels.
3. Reb Nachman is Reb Nachman of Bratslav, the founder of Bratslav Hassidism.
4. An 'ell' is a unit of measure. The term 'The four ells of Halacha' implies 'The narrow confines of Halacha'.
5. These are the names of three Hassidic sects. The first two are named after towns. The third, Chabad, is the acronym for Chachma, Bina, Vadaat (Knowledge, Wisdom and Understanding). Chabad Hassidism is the equivalent as what is commonly known today as Lubavitch.
6. This is a play on words: "kasha" is kasha or cereal. "kashia" is Hebrew for question.
7. One of the Rebbes of Ger.
8. Kutner must not be his last name, but rather the appellation, "The Rabbi of Kutno".
9. A well known Talmudic commentator.
10. Referring to the Talmudic discussions.
11. The 'world of truth' refers to the life beyond this world, after death.
12. A mezuza is the casing containing a parchment scroll that is affixed to the doorposts of Jewish homes in accordance with the commandment of Deuteronomy 5:9 and 11:20. The scroll contains the verses surrounding those two sections of Deuteronomy. The casing is often designed in an ornamental fashion. The outside of the scroll, and sometimes the casing, is inscribed with the letters 'shin' 'daled' 'yod', which is one of the names of G-d, and is also an acronym of 'shomer daltot yisrael' – 'The Guardian of the door posts of Israel'. The affixing of a mezuza is accompanied by the recitation of a blessing: "Blessed art Though, oh L-rd our G-d King of the universe, who sanctified us with his commandments, and commanded us to affix the mezuza.
13. The Yiddish word for joy, which also can have the connotation of a joyous round of singing and dancing.
14. 'To life'. A traditional Jewish toast.
15. A kugel is a pudding made from noodles, potatoes, or the like.
16. Sunday being the first workday.
17. Literally 'ransom'. Its connotation here is a payment to a Hassidic Rebbe for his blessing.
18. The Yiddish word for 'giddy-up'.
19. A streimel is a Hassidic fur hat, and a kapote is a Hassidic long black cloak.

20. The reference here is not clear. Apparently, the "Czmentasz" is a cemetery. Kohanim (members of the priestly tribe in Judaism), are not allowed to come in contact with a dead body, nor to enter a cemetery, and the implication here is that, prior to the erection of the new Beis Midrash, it was necessary for them to take a circuitous route to avoid entering the cemetery.
21. A quorum for Jewish prayer consists of ten males over the age of 13, and is known as a minyan.
22. There is a Jewish tradition that in every generation, there are 36 hidden specially pious people (tzadikim) in the world. Such a person is known as a 'lamed vovnik', from the Hebrew numerical equivalent of 'lamed vov', 36. The terms can be used generically for a discreet pious person.
23. A 'Lamdan' is a scholar, and the ending adds a derogatory tone to the word. The 'ke' ending of Hassidikes, also adds a derogatory tone, i. e. pesky Hassidim. A 'schlepper' translates as a hobo or a bum.
24. Chovevei Tzion was an early Zionistically oriented group in the late 18th century, founded even prior to the founding of the formal Zionist movement.
25. There were periods during the 19th century when Russia tried to impose academic standards upon Rabbis and Yeshivas.
26. Apparently, he maintained his position of Hassidic Rebbe, but lost his position as the official rabbi of Sochaczew.
27. Elsewhere, this street was spelled as Trajanower. It seems like one syllable is missing here.
28. The main part of the daily prayer service. The Shmone Esrei is recited in silent devotion.
29. Aleinu Leshabeach is a prayer recited at the conclusion of each of the three daily prayer services. The Aleinu prayer contrasts the monotheism of the Jewish people with the idolatry of the nations of the world. It contains a phrase "and they bow down to emptiness and nothingness, and pray to a G-d who does not save" – referring to the nations of the world. Some people, especially Hassidim, have a custom of spitting discretely when reciting this phrase.
30. Literally, "The Rebbe, he should live, is destroyed".
31. To beg G-d.
32. The deathbed confessional.
33. A statement made at the time of hearing of a death, acknowledging the righteousness of Divine judgement.
34. Apparently referring to the corpse.
35. Tahara means purification. Here it refers to the ritual washing ceremony that the Chevra Kadisha (Burial Society) performs on the corpse before it is placed in the coffin.
36. Nov 2 1856 – Jan 8 1926.

{103 - Yiddish} {647 - Hebrew}

SOCIAL AND SPIRITUAL LIFE

Between The Two World Wars
by M Frydman
Translated by Jerrold Landau

The Jewish life of Sochaczew was active and full of beauty. The city experienced ups and downs, as did Polish Jewry in general.

I left the city in 1927 with the stream of emigration that flowed out of the smaller towns to the city, in order to remove myself from "provincialism". I returned, and was active in communal life, and even during the days of deprivation I breathed the air of my town. Now, here I am as one of the survivors who witnessed the destruction.

Sochaczew was known as an old community, as a center of Torah and Hassidism, and anyone who had a feel for Jewish life in the country as a whole would be connected to it as well. Due to the tribulations of the time and the battles that took place on the banks of the Bzura, a portion of the population fled to Warsaw after the First World War, and settled there as well as in other places. However, Jews from other places also came to Sochaczew. The Jews slowly but surely overcame the difficulties of the destruction that came in the wake of the war, and displayed much fruitful initiative, especially in the realm of business and workmanship.

Sochaczew was surrounded by many villages, whose population depended on it for shoes and clothing, which were supplied by the Jews. The Jews also began to trade in wheat. They were the middlemen between the city and the town, and were the prime suppliers. There was a market day in the town. Those days were actually 'barter days', where the Jews sold their wares and purchased the produce of the villages. Another area was completely in Jewish hands: fruit orchards, many of whose owners were wealthy Christian landowners.

The Jewish gardeners leased the fruit orchards even during the cold days of winter. There were also cases where shoemakers, tailors and carpenters worked in their own profession during the winter, and leased out fruit orchards during the summer, even though both endeavors together did not guarantee them a comfortable livelihood...

Communal Life

Many members of the intelligentsia were among those who left the city after the First World War, and did not return. These include:

1) Alexander Zusha Frydman (the son of Yehoshua), the leader of Agudas Yisrael, an author of Torah literature, and an esteemed communal leader. He was one of the leaders of the Warsaw Ghetto, and one of its victims.

2) Ozer Warshawski (the son of Gedalia), a well known author (the author of the novel "Smugglers"). He was from the school of Y. M. Weissberg. He lost his life in a concentration camp near Paris.

3) Pinchas Graubard, a donor and patron of literature, a publisher and folklorist. He arrived in America in 1941 with a group of refugee authors and communal leaders. He died in America.

4) M. B. Stein, the son of the Rabbi of Sochaczew. He was an author, and he wrote the dramas "Erd Un Himel" ("Heaven and Earth"), "Di Churba" ("The Ruin"). He settled in Israel.

The pharmacy.

The market.

However, the communal activity did not stop. Zionist organizations were founded, with Simcha Grundwag, Berel Laufer, and Moshe Lodzer (Jakobovitz) at the helm. They also founded the first Hebrew school "Hatechia" ("The Renaissance"). Through their efforts, other assistance and support organizations were founded.

The second communal body which was established was the populist faction ("Folkistn"). Its leaders were Vove Rosenberg, Lotek Skotnitzki, and Moshe Schwartz (who moved to America). It was the umbrella organization for progressive and activist organizations, and filled a significant role in the community during the period right after the world war.

Since the workers organization was not yet founded (it only started during the 1920s), a controversy broke out between the Zionists and Folkists over control of the Jewish community. This controversy first manifested itself in the first elections of the city and community. The Folkists gained control over the library, which had been renewed and had been previously led by Zionist activists. The Folkists filled an honorable role in the spiritual life[1] of the Jews of Sochaczew.

This activity stirred up dormant forces within the Jewish community, and awakened it from its complacency. The social awakening occurred simultaneously with the economic awakening in all branches of work, artisanship and small-scale manufacturing including tailoring, shoemaking, carpentry, and hat making. The number of hired workers increased, both among the locals and outsiders. The Jewish population grew. In the civic elections of 1925 Jews accounted for half of those elected – 12 out of 24. Moshe Schwartz, the leader of the Folkists, was elected as deputy to the Polish mayor Moszikowski.

The focal point of cultural life as the library, where in particular, the youth gathered and conducted heated debates about issues of literature and culture. Speakers were invited from Warsaw. A drama group was founded under the leadership of Nachum Grundwag, which bestowed pleasure and spiritual joy to the Jews of the city, and was held in high esteem. The group was conducted without controversy, and there were no interruptions in its work. The first leader was Nachum Grundwag, a Zionist leader, followed by Simcha Cohen, Moshe Schwartz, and Yosef Muney – without any controversy.

The communal and spiritual life of the Jews grew and flourished until there was a spiritual crisis among the youth. One of the reasons for this was the lack of opportunity in the town, as well as the backwardness that still prevailed in town. There were still Jews in town whose work was an embarrassment and shame to them. The anti-Semitic climate prevented Jews from entering into communal service and official positions. Furthermore, there was a general depression to which the Jews of Sochaczew were not immune.

The time of the fourth Aliya[2] arrived. A portion of the youth decided to immigrate to the Land of Israel, however some returned since they were not able to withstand the difficulties of work and pioneering. A portion of the youth, the non-Zionist intelligentsia, and others left the town to go to larger cities or overseas, in search for an outlet for their activism and talents. All of these factors together were the root of spiritual and social decline in the city, the indifference and hopelessness.

Those who remained continued their activities and were jealous of those that left. The communal activity weakened. The library was only open for two hours each evening, but nevertheless it obtained every new book, continued on, and guarded the spark.

In 1929, the first large factory was founded in Chodakow, as well as smaller factories for the production of bricks and gunpowder. In addition, Sochaczew was an important communications terminal. However, the conditions of work were poor and difficult. There was a reawakening among the artisans, in particular on the evenings before the large fairs, which took place on the first

Tuesday of each month. Prior to the fairs, they would work through entire nights, as this was an important part of their livelihood. There was no limit to their hours of work. As morning approached they would hurry off to their prayers, and then return to work. They would eat breakfast in haste and return to work again. There would be a short break around noon for the afternoon prayers (mincha), and lunch would be merged together with supper. In the factory of Moshe Nelson, for example, where eight or ten people were employed, they would pray the mincha and maariv (evening) services at the factory itself.

There were two types of workers in the town: salaried workers, and people who worked at home ("chalopnikes"), who worked for cash and were paid for the finished product. At times, the conditions of the home-workers were more difficult than that of the salaried employees, since they would work without limit together with their wives and children.

They waited all week for the Sabbath day of rest, and they would return to work right after havdalah[3]. They hurried out to services on Sabbaths, at "Chevra Tehillim" or the house of study, they ate their meal, and returned to rest. After their rest, they returned to the house of study again until the conclusion of the Sabbath. This was the set order of life.

At the end of 1925 or the beginning of 1926, the founding meeting for workers union took place in the home of Feivel Galek. At that time I was an apprentice for Moshe Temes. How much simplicity and naivete was there at that meeting! The organizers had no idea how to conduct a professional union and how to organize it. Nevertheless the union was founded, even though it was about twenty-five years later than in other cities...

The union rented an apartment for itself from Geitin. A secretary named Wyszogrodsky came from Wyszogrod. He was a communist, who later switched affiliation to the "Bund". He lived in Woloczlok, and later died in a concentration camp. The secretary received a salary that was paid from the membership dues. The union organized not only the tailors, but also the shoemakers and workers in other fields, who were organized into separate sections. Its activities included the organization of strikes and the setting of wages. An employer had to come to the union and to reach an agreement with the professional committee who would set the acceptable tariff. After some time the employers also established a union – and the deliberations would occur between the representatives of the two bodies.

The union began to campaign for a workday of eight hours. After a difficult campaign, including a strike, the workers were victorious in 1927 – and the salary was not cut. The next day, the union sent out auditors who would check that the workday of eight hours was being respected, since the workers themselves also needed to be monitored...

The victory achieved the main objective of its time, and the union removed the possibility of extra hours of work, so that the workers would be able to enjoy the fruits of their victory. I remember that Mendel Plonski came to the union to request permission for his workers to work extra hours, since he had to pay a pressing sum of money.

Even though the establishment of the workers' union in Sochaczew was late, it was very active and vigilant. The union was at first affiliated with the communist center in Warsaw, and was subject to its influence. It conducted activities in the economic and political realms. The secretary oversaw all activities.

Alongside the union, the was an illegal communist "cell", which maintained relations with the non-Jewish left, and conducted joint activities.

At that time, Ezriel Skornik, who was a tailor and the organizer of the union, died of tuberculosis. The union arranged the funeral from its own accounts, and prevented the Chevra Kadisha from conducting a religious service. Work was stopped during the time of the funeral, and a demonstration was organized, with banners and slogans against the government. Political speeches were given at the open grave. The police then came and broke up the large gathering.

This was the first event of its kind in Sochaczew.

That year (1927), the union made preparations to celebrate May Day along with the Polish workers. The night before, they prepared banners, placards, and "flower" ribbons[4]. The youth, both the communists and Bundists, prepared for the day with all their enthusiasm, and hoped that the status of the Jews would rise in relations to the Poles. For was this not the first demonstration of the Jewish workers in the city, alongside with their non-Jewish friends!

The demonstration took place despite the rain that fell that day. After the procession through the streets, a general gathering was held. The well-known communist from Blojna, Hirsch, spoke on behalf of the Jewish workers. He inflamed the gathering, but was forced to immediately flee from the place due to the police. He eventually fled to the U.S.S.R., and died in the "purges" of 1937.

There was a recognizable faction of Bund members in the union. They invited the secretary of the union of the hide-workers in Warsaw, Berel Ambaras, to speak at the union in 1927. Afterward, a meeting of the Bund membership took place, and a local branch was established. The beginning was not straightforward, as the branch had to stand up to opposition from those further to the left, as well as from the Zionists.

I recall the following curious event, which was told in jest:

During the events of 5689 (1929) in the Land of Israel, the Bund, as is known, stood in opposition to the Zionist camp. The Bund activist Simcha Goldberg (the son of Binyamin the tinsmith) lived in Sochaczew, and they chased after him declaring that he had letters from Arabs hidden in his pockets... It is obvious that nobody took this seriously.

Aside from the workers, there were a significant number of home-workers ("chalopnikes") under the influence of the Bund. They later founded the socialist union of artisans, who played an honorable role in the town until the war of destruction.

This union, which included members of other unions, was headed for a long time by the Bundist Ziama Steiglitz. The communist Adam Kloska was also always involved in the leadership of this union. He gave much of his time to communal activities.

The Bund maintained constant contact with the P.P.S. Its leader Darber was a sympathetic leader and a friend of the Jews. He was killed in Auschwitz. Through his good offices, they were able to obtain a representative in the town, Meir Zaltzman ("Shkolak") who returned from Russia in 1905. He was the only Bundist in Sochaczew prior to 1905. They also were able to have a representative to the government health care fund – Shlomo Swiatlowski. As the Bund organization expanded its sphere of activities it rented a hall, founded a youth movement "Zukumft" ("The Future"), and a sport organization "Morgenstern" ("Morning Star"), established a library, conducted cultural activities, invited speakers from Warsaw, and began to actively turn around the sad situation of Jewish communal life. Nobody in the Bund in Sochaczew ever worked for money. The activists included Yuntel Rosen, Hershel Warshawski, Steiglitz, Simcha Goldberg, Mendel Frydman, Moshe Geier, and Chaim Pinczewski (who transferred allegiance from the communists to the Bund).

The Zionist movement also strengthened, even though some of its activities left the town. The "Yavneh" Hebrew school was founded. Representatives from the Sochaczew Mutual Benefit Society of America came for the laying of the cornerstone. The primary donors were Yisrael Keller and Tema Rabinowitz. A great celebration was organized. After several years the building of the school was completed, and teachers were brought in for the six grades. The school was granted government privileges. The language of instruction was Hebrew. The school was directed by a board of governors, and always required the assistance of the town -- the requests of the Jews were always answered positively by the P.P.S. and its leader Darber.

The "Yavneh" School. The teacher Streicher with his students.

The Beitar group of Sochaczew, Lubitz, April 5, 1931.

The municipal high school.

There was another Jewish school in Sochaczew, a religious school founded by the Aguda. This school was called "Yesodei Hatorah" for boys and "Bais Yaakov" for girls. They also invited in teachers from outside the town. These schools existed until the Holocaust.

The Zionist organization renewed its efforts under the leadership of Simcha Grundwag, who won general respect. We should also mention the organization of Revisionist Zionists[5], which was directed by Dr. Salomon. The head of the Beitar youth movement was Pinchas Bressler. Members of this movement participated in physical activities, wore uniforms, and participated in various festivities. This is my recollection of one of their events:

In 1930, the Beitar movement organized a flag dedication celebration in the synagogue, in the presence of many guests from out of the city as well as government representatives. At the critical moment of the raising of the flag, Yona Livna appeared from out of the women's section with a red banner displaying slogans against Beitar... a tumult and disruption then took place. Suspects were arrested and sent to the prison in Lewicz. This event was a topic of conversation in the town for quite some time...

The head of the Chalutz (pioneering) organization was Pinchas Weinberg (who survived the war but was killed in Sochaczew by Polish murderers as he returned from his hiding place). The Chalutz excelled in its local activities, and was held in high esteem in the town. It had its own band that played during festivities and events. It also sponsored courses in the Hebrew languages, which were taught by a teacher from Yavneh.

The Mizrachi[6] organization was quite active in town. Its heads included Izak Waldenberg and Yaakov Biderman. Its youth branch was headed by Mottel Baumhertzer and Eliahu Blumenthal.

The Jewish National Fund (Keren Kayemet Leyisrael) was quite active in town, and every organization sent a representative to its directorship. The chairman was Simcha Grundwag, and later Michael Cohen, who returned to town and was active in it until the last days. He founded the local newspaper "Sochaczewer Leben" (Sochaczew Life), which ceased publishing after a few editions due to financial difficulties and shortage of staff.

The organization of Orthodox Jewry was "Agudas Yisrael", whose membership consisted of a significant amount of the local Jewish population. They had representatives on the city council, and held the chairmanship of the community council for several years. Yosef Wolkowicz was at the helm. It conducted a great deal of activities with the youth, and founded an organization "Poale Agudas Yisrael". Aside form Yosef Wolkowicz, other activists included the brothers Mordechai (Mottel) and Yitzchak Winer (who was later the head of the community), Sheynwald (the son of Yankelel the teacher), and others.

Beit Yaakov School

There were also communist youth in Sochaczew. These were organized clandestinely, and conducted various activities. Some of the activists were imprisoned, and others fled abroad. Some transferred allegiance to the youth wing of Bund, which was also quite active. The chief activities of the Bund were in the realm of raising the quality of life and level of culture among the oppressed and impoverished masses.

It is important also to point out the role of the teachers in the Polish public schools in the spiritual and public life of the community. For example Kampelmacher was a multi-faceted personality who did not belong to any specific movement. He came to Sochaczew in the 1920s and remained there until 1936. He was assimilated, but was a man of the people who did much for the youth, primarily in the real of physical education, the organization of sports activities, choirs, reading clubs, and other such activities. He founded the Z.T.G.S. sports club.

A generation of youth grew up, who were active, cultured, and workers. (In the silk factory in the village of Chodakow, four kilometers from Sochaczew, there were more than 5,000 employees, but Jews were not accepted for employment.) Business developed. A period of economic success and communal progress came to Jewish Sochaczew. Organizations were founded, and various institutions such as banks and mutual benefits organizations were set up. A public organization called "Ogroid" was even set up – it was a para-communist organization to promote the settlement of Biro-Bidzhan[7]. There was also an organization for the supporters of the Esperanto language, a library, as well as a drama club that continued to flourish and maintain a high level of activity even though several of its members left the city.

In the final summer, the summer of 1939, we made preparations for a performance of "Noach Pandra" which had already been put on with much success in Warsaw. It wasn't to be...

Jewish students from the municipal school with the teacher Kampelmacher

The library played a special role in the development of the town, in particular among the youth. It was a center for common activity among all the different factions. It attained its height of development during the final three years prior to the war of destruction. It was a center for education and information for the youth, in a sense a university for the masses. A reading-hall was adjacent to it. Its membership grew from 40 or 50 people in 1937 to 200 in 1939.

There was a change in the administration of the library in 1937. This took place during the annual general meeting. They decided to expand the newspaper group in the reading hall (by subscribing also to "Folkszeigung", the Bund newspaper), and to make connections with book publishers. However, Avraham Cohen, who was serving as the chairman of the library, revolted... On the evening following Yom Kippur, he called a meeting with various activists – including the writer of this article, Pinchas Weinberg and Yisrael Eisman. They feared government intervention, in particular the intervention of the inimical vice-mayor (vice-starostowa) Borkowski ("Brodka"). Simcha Grundwag, Simcha Cohen, Lotek Skotnitzki, Menashe Knott, Nachum Grundwag, Michael Cohen (Avraham's brother), Yosef Muney, Hershel Warshawski, Yoel Miller, Dr. Kaplan, as well as others all participated in that stormy session. A committee was set up comprising of Lotek Skotnitzki, Menashe Knott and Mendel Frydman, who were to travel immediately to Noach Prilocki in Warsaw in order to insure, first and foremost, that the government would not close the library. Due to the intervention of Noach Prilocki and the leader of the Bund Henryk Erlich, the library was not closed.

Library committee 1925

A new general meeting took place with government permission, and in the presence of the government representative Skrent. However prior to that, a meeting of the library activists was called, with the participation of the vice mayor who announced, first and foremost, that the request for an allocation from the town was refused, and even were such a request to have been authorized, it would have been cancelled, since the Jews have enough money... He also advised, for example, that a fine should be imposed on one of the householders who was there in the library at that time, Mr. Goldman, for the crime of uncleanliness, and he would set the amount... Of course we rejected this advice and advised him that if the request would not be authorized, we would appeal to higher authorities. Later, he requested to inspect the catalog in order to advise us which books should be removed so that the Polish population would not look upon us as strangers, and that we provide a poor education for the youth... He advised us to remove the works of Gorki, Tolstoy, Rolen, Barbis, Tovim, Janowski, and others. He particularly advised us to remove all socialist and progressive books. He also advised us to remove from the list of members anyone who was not a "patriot". We were warned about the dangers of communism that was lurking within the Jewish populace, and that the government would fight against it until its annihilation...

Members of the sports club with the teacher Kampelmacher.

A flyer from the library, in Yiddish. Here is a partial translation (note, the photocopy itself is not clear, so a full translation is not possible):

Jewish People's Library and Reading Hall of Sochaczew

Today, On November 9, 1938[8], at 8:30 prompt
Come to a program
An Academic event
Marking the 20th yahrzeit of the Jewish author Mendele Mocher Seforim

Program: {details not translated}

Introduction
"Zeidene Kroin" – a song
Mendele, his life and works
{cannot make out}
"The Travels of Benjamin the Third"
"Zeidene Kroin" – the song again
Conclusion

Come give honor to the kind Mendele!!!
Come Promptly!!!
All places are 49 groszy

Notice!!! The library has moved to a larger location, 50 Staszica St. (Tilman's house), front entrance, first floor.

———

Drama club: performance of "The Mute" by D. Bergelson

We presented the results of the discussion at the general meeting. We realized that the battle was about our right to existence as Jews. Representatives of the government, including the Jewish official Mondacz were at the meeting. Menashe Knott chaired the meeting. Everyone vetoed the stand of Avraham Cohen, and blamed him for the events that took place during the previous administration. At the end of the meeting a new administration was appointed, consisting of: Lotek Skotnitzki, Menashe Knott, Yona Bressler, Yisrael Eisman, Pinia Weinberg, Mendel Frydman, Avraham Taub, Yosel Grundwag, and Shpotrik (a dental technician who arrived in Sochaczew). L. Skotnitzki was chosen as chairman, M. Frydman as vice chairman, Weinberg as secretary, and Y. Eisman as treasurer. This committee served until the end. Skotnitzki died suddenly of a heart attack in 1938. At the memorial gathering, M. Knott was chosen as a replacement.

The administrative committee rented a larger hall in the home of Hertzke Tilman. New books were purchased, a larger reading hall was opened with newspapers and works of Jewish and a few Polish authors. Contacts were made with publishing houses. New members joined. The drama club made its home in the library, and an attempt was made to found a theater group as existed in other cities. Actors were invited from Warsaw, and various plays were performed.

In 1938, the administration of the library invited the Jewish violinist Klara Mendelson, with the approval of the writers' club of Warsaw. They also invited writers to give lectures on Friday nights, with great success. The cultural activities of the library provided great enjoyment and sowed light in the lives of the youth.

In the winter of 1938, they organized an academic evening in memory of Mendele Mocher Sefarim, and on Passover a celebration of Peretz, which was the final event! Both events took place in the largest halls in the city, and were attended by a large audience. Sections of "The Travels of Benjamin the Third", were presented at the first gathering, and a thirty person choir performed under the direction of Leibel Furstenberg. At the evening in honor of Peretz, selections of his works were read, and lectures were given; however the atmosphere was already saturated with the fear of the times!

Anti-Semitism grew in the meantime. Jews were beaten in Sochaczew, and guards were placed near the Jewish shops. However, life continued, and the Jews were not subdued. The library continued it existence and development.

When the draft order was issued, we decided in an emergency meeting of the directors to pack away the books in chests and hide them in the attic. Many members were asked to help with this work. The last of the books were hidden away as the enemy fire had already begun to rain down on Sochaczew.

When I returned from Russia together with Hertzke Tilman in 1946 we went up to the attic, but there was no remnant of the thousands of books. Several torn out pages from "Antiquities" of Spinoza and "A Night in the Old Market" of Peretz were found rotting in the trash... According to the story told to us by the Poles, the Poles burned all of the books on the orders of the Nazis after the Jews were expelled from the ghetto. A bonfire was set up in the middle of the marketplace.

The two years prior to the destruction were the height of communal activity, as well as economic growth in our town. Professionals and experts, in particular Jewish doctors and lawyers came to Sochaczew from other cities. Sochaczew natives who had left returned.

With all this anti-Semitism, boycotts, shoving incidents, and hooliganism grew. Posters and placards of anti-Semites were posted on Jewish stores. The inimical "Brodka"[9] excelled in anti-Semitism; riding on his white horse, dressed in platinum[10], he instilled fear in the hearts of the Jews. The Jews were oppressed, fined, and persecuted. Work and business were forbidden on Sundays and days upon which Polish holidays fell. Jewish communal life became bogged down and permeated with difficulty. Attacks on Jews increased, particularly during the evening hours. Non-Jewish artisans began to stream into Sochaczew. The heating up of the activities of our enemies in the German government obviously strengthened the hooligans in Poland.

Even with this tense situation, it was necessary to continue activities, to encourage the Jewish population, and to strengthen ties with the portion of the Polish population that had not yet been poisoned. The P.P.S. party and its leader Darber in particular stood with the Jews in their difficulties.

Municipal building.

Two events took place in this atmosphere of terror and oppression. The final elections of both the town and the community took place. The son of Zmiaowski, a well-known Andak[11] hooligan, was the chief of the ruffians. He chased the Jews out of the line of voters, however the Jews resisted, and the number of Jewish voters was not reduced. The Bund gained proportionally in the elections. All of the Jewish factions and organizations continued their activities until the destruction. It is obligatory to note here the head activists who stood in their posts until the final moment:

General Zionist – Simcha Grundwag, Moshe Lodzer (Jakobovitz), Yoel Miller, Dr. Kaplan, Shimiontek.

Mizrachi – Yankel Biderman, Montshik, Izak Wazenberg, Blumenthal.

Agudas Yisrael – Yosef Wolkowicz, Yankel Bienczkowski, Eliezer Zusman, Yitzchak Winer.

Hechalutz – Pinia Weinberg, Shmuel Jakobovitz.

Bund – Hershel Warshawski (the brother of the writer Ozer), Yuntel Rosen, Aharon Greenberg, Simcha Goldberg, Chaim Pinczewski, Mendel Frydman.

The communist faction was disbanded in Poland, including in our town, in 1937. The professional union ceased to function, having been disbanded by the authorities after they imprisoned several of its activists during a Beitar celebration.

Simcha and Sara-Rivka Grundwag

The role of the Jews was reduced after the final elections for the civic and communal institutions. There were only three representatives in the city in accordance with the new structure of the local authority, namely: Michael Cohen the representative of the Zionists, Yosef Liksztik representing the artisans and small scale merchants, and Chaim Pinczewski representing Bund.

The final chairman of the community was Yitzchak Winer of the Aguda. The Bund representatives (who were elected for the first time) were Hershel Warshawski and Aharon Greenberg.

On September 1st, 1939 everything ended... Sochaczew was bombarded already on the first day of the war, and victims fell. On the fifth day of the war the Polish army appeared in town during its retreat, and the Germans already stood at the gate of the city. The Jews all fled. Many of the Jews of Sochaczew gave their lives in the Warsaw Ghetto.

Only very few survivors returned to Sochaczew after the flood of blood. Not one Jewish household remained intact.

The Germans and their helpers destroyed everything, uprooted everything from its roots. They slew and took possession[12]. A Jew such as Yechiel Meir Tilman, who owned ten houses in Sochaczew, did not find one corner for himself when he returned from Warsaw.

The community that acted, created, struggled, and organized its life for centuries was cut off.

We will not forget its contribution to the life of Jewry, and its memory will last forever.

Jews from Sochaczew participating in reception for Nachum Sokolow

Farewell banquet for Chaim Tempel and wife before aliyah

{180 - Yiddish} {659 - Hebrew}

The Local Theater
by Yosef Grundwag of Jerusalem
Translated by Jerrold Landau

A group of theatre dilettantes started in Sochaczew immediately following the First World War. My father, Nachum Grundwag filled the main role. He was the producer. He played roles in plays and his name drew audiences also from the surrounding towns.

However, the theatre activity in the town was not only due to his efforts, since there was a group of amateurs in the town already fifty years previously. My father, when he was still a youth, participated in performances. It is interesting to note that his first role was that of a woman, and at that time, apparently, he became enthralled with theater.

Aside from my father, the following individuals participated in performances: Moshe Schwartz, Yaakov Frydman, Vove Rosenberg, Bluma and Rachel Weinberg, Lotek Skotnitzki, Chaya Rashel Fleischman, Machla and Dina Grundwag, as well as my mother Rivka. Of course, as time went on, the cast changed, and others joined such as Bina Festman, Avraham Nashelwicz, and others. My father expended great effort, and worked with great dedication to raise the level of the amateur players, so that their names and plays would become known in the surrounding towns, which would invite them to entertain them with their plays.

Almost every performance was associated with a memorial day or a celebration. Every new play was a festive time for the community as well as the actors. They related to their roles with seriousness and dedication. The put their best efforts into their performances, in order to insure a high level of entertainment. My father's name went before him in every performance. It as sufficient to publicize that Nachum Grundwag would participate in the performance – and success was guaranteed.

The greatest success came from the performances of the productions of Peretz Hirschbein ("Nevala" – "Travesty", and "Hasadot Hayerokim" – "Green Pastures"); Sholem Asch ("Amonoteinu" – "Our Craft"); Strindberg ("Haav" – "The Father"); and Shalom Aleichem ("200 Elef" – "Two Hundred Thousand"). The following performances were also put on: "Kuni Lemel the Second" of Goldfaden; "El, Adam and Satan" – "God, Adam and Satan", and "Haalmoni" – "The Anonymous", of Gordin (March 1918); "Kreitzer's Sonata" (Passover 1922); in which I also participated by playing the role of Albert the son of the Eight. I remember that on that day tears overtook me as I took to the stage, and father showed me how to stand, which movements to make and how to speak.

On the long Saturday nights of the winter, we would conduct theatrical Melave Malka[13]evenings, in which, aside from my father and others, writers from Warsaw would lecture about topics from the fields of literature and theatre. Performances of professional actors from Warsaw would also took place.

Shortly before the Second World War, my father along with the other amateurs put on sonorous performances. He himself composed ballads, parodies, and songs and prepared them for the stage. Freda Chmiel (who currently resides in Argentina), and her husband Meir Zaltzman of blessed memory excelled in these performances.

Nachum and Rivka Grundwag

A scene from the play "Haalmoni" – "The Anonymous".

My father was the director and producer of the dramatic club of the workers "Yidishe Bina", and he performed with them "Hacheresh" – "The Deaf One" of Bergelson, which was highly successful.

Of course, there was no shortage of comical events in our town – and I will mention some of them here.

The drama club

At the time of the appearance of the Warsaw actor Jack Levi (who had mainly a classical repertoire), our community witnessed the miracle of "the resurrection of the dead". The following is what transpired.

When the actor dressed himself in the Roman toga for his role as Marc Anthony and began the well-known Shakespearean eulogy for Caesar, the "dead" Caesar suddenly came to life; he jumped up from the table and fled... Pandemonium broke out in the theater. The actor was astounded and frightened.

It was later verified that the two candles that were burning near the head of the "deceased" dripped wax onto him and burned him – therefore he got up and fled...

There was this and more.

The Zionist drama group decided to perform on Saturday night after the Sabbath, without paying attention, due to forgetfulness, that the evening was between the 17th of Tammuz and the 9th of Av[14]. Therefore, the rabbi and the Orthodox people decided to prevent the performance from taking place. The rabbi called on the Hassidim and other householders for a "holy war". Immediately after the conclusion of the evening service (maariv) at the conclusion of the Sabbath, they hurried to the "theater" and "took over" the fire-hall in which the performances were held. A lengthy dispute took place between the two sides, and a significant number of the theater goers who came to purchase tickets met in the hall ... their fathers wearing their Sabbath kapotes, and did not dare to cross the threshold of the theater.

Nevertheless, it was impossible to cancel the play after the manifold preparations. As usual, a policeman was stationed near the hall in order to investigate the goings on and to report immediately to the civic supervisor who also appeared... The Hassidim did not want to leave the hall, and explained their reasoning to explain to the supervisor in Polish "This month has three weeks". However the captain did not understand at all what they meant...

"How can this be, doesn't a month have four weeks and not three?" he asked.

Even after the conversation between the supervisor and the rabbi, they did not understand one another, and at the end the rabbi and his entourage left the hall. Of course, there was no income from that night, since most of the tickets were not sold. And from that time on, the drama group never performed during the "Three Weeks".

The third episode is as follows:

During one of the performances of the drama group in the hall near the library (in 1920), the talented actor Hermelin Malewicz performed. He stayed in our house, as was customary for that caliber of guest. After he left his suitcases and belongings in our house, he went with our family to the performance in the hall of the library. The atmosphere was festive and exalted.

The large picture of Jeremiah, entitled "By the Rivers of Babylon", that was drawn on a hanging by a talented artist from Sochaczew, added seriousness to this event, as well as a pleasant atmosphere. (For years, this hanging served as a wall for grandfather's Sukka[15]. This is what took place.

We returned home very late at night (the performances always ended a long time after midnight), and we found the windows of our house broken. The clothing of our guests were missing, as well as a plush cloth, which the "thieves" used to wrap the goods. The suspicion was that this was the work of political opponents, who wished to take revenge in this manner on the drama group, which had Zionist tendencies. The investigation and bargaining were to no avail – the clothing was not returned, and the guests who were robbed left in disappointment.

This document is in script Yiddish, and the script is not easy to make out. It is apparently some notes about the performance of "Kreitzer's Sonata". The notes give a list of the characters, and the actors that will play them. They note that there are four acts, the first three take place in Russia, and the final act in America. Between the first and last act, seven years elapse.

There was controversy in the town for several weeks regarding the cause of the "robbery".

At the time of the outbreak of the Second World War, there was a group of amateurs in Sochaczew who put on performances themselves, and also invited professional actors from Warsaw.

My father stood at their head until the bitter end. He taught the group their repertoires, encouraged them, and implanted culture and joy in the town.

A.group of activists. Standing: L Skotnitzki, M. Schwartz, V Rosenberg. Seated: P. R. Fleischman.

{664}

Sochaczew as I remember it
by Yerucham Ines
Translated by Jerrold Landau

In the country of Poland, in the vicinity of Warsaw, surrounded by clean fields and villages, lies the city of Sochaczew. As out of the darkness, the image of my birthplace Sochaczew appears before my eyes, with its Jewish inhabitants, surrounding villages, "Schlossberg" mountain rising to the north. On top of the mountain are the remnants of an old palace covered in mystery and legends, the Bzura River flows at the foot of the mountain, with its clear water covered with rays of sun – what a glorious vision I behold. People thirsting for water would come to the waters of the river that were flowing with the current, and the elderly water-drawer Kalman Yankel, walking with difficulty, laden with his pole and buckets, would draw water in both the summer and the winter for the homes of the Jews of Sochaczew.

During the warm months of the summer the townspeople would go down the slope at the edge of the road to Tarnow, near the hospital, in order to bathe in the waters of the Bzura. During the cold days of winter, days of snow and ice, the youths would gleefully skate on the river, on foot, with skates, or with handmade sleds. With the approach of Rosh Hashana, once again the banks of the Bzura teamed with the local Jews, who came for the Tashlich ceremony, in order to empty the sins of the past year into the depths of the river

Thus was the Bzura interwoven an inseparable element in the happenings of the lives of the Jews of Sochaczew.

The marketplace was in a central location in the city. The area of the marketplace was paved with large stones, and was surrounded by stores, wooden shacks and rows of merchants' stalls, primarily for merchants of fruits and vegetables. During the cold days of winter, heat would be obtained from burning wood coal in cast iron basins. In the center of the market area there was a high platform with an alarm bell on top of it, which would be used to call the firemen whenever a fire broke out.

On Tuesday, the market day in the city, the marketplace would appear very different than any other time. The marketplace and the adjacent roads would be filled with farmers from the nearby towns and with wagons laden with sacks of wheat, animals and poultry. The shouts of the villagers would be merged with the noise of the wheels of the approaching wagons, the neighing of horses, the clucking of chickens and the mooing of the cows into one thundering, deafening sound. The local merchants would circulate around, this one meticulously checking the quality of the wheat, another one examining the poultry that was for sale or the calf that was on top of a wagon. They would estimate the value and finally reach an agreement and complete the transaction.

Once a month, on the day of the large fair, the city would be filled with farmers and merchants who came from near and far, bringing all sorts of desirable merchandise, from a string to a shoelace[16]. The marketplace was full of stalls that sprouted up as mushrooms after the rain. Purchasers would mull around the crowded area, as well as people who were simply curious due to the picturesqueness of the area. There was also no shortage of jesters, magicians, fortune tellers, card diviners, puppeteers, and swindlers of various types.

The stores and artisan shops would all be quite busy on that day. The majority of the Jews of Sochaczew were merchants or artisans, and the bulk of their livelihood came from the fair days, which they eagerly awaited from one month to the next.

Zeinwil Zibola and his wife.

The market and fair days were a blessing for the city as well as for the surrounding villages, with the exception of isolated incidents perpetrated as drunks would break into the area as the marketplace was being evacuated. The villagers would bring the fruits of their labors and the fruits of their fields to the city, and would purchase provisions that were produced in the city. The merchants of Sochaczew would export grain, poultry, eggs, and vegetables that were purchased from the farmers to the capital city of Warsaw as well as other localities.

From the marketplace, the city spread out in all directions. Warsaw Street was the largest street. This street began at the bridge over the Bzura, adjacent to which stood the Christian church with its steeples and crosses, and crossed the entire city to the other side, where it joined with the highway leading to Warsaw. The second largest street was Tarnow Street, which ran from one edge of the city which bordered on fields and gardens, crossed the city by its width, passed near the area of the marketplace, and on the other side of the city passed by the railway station and the Christian and Jewish cemeteries.

There was a distance of several kilometers from the city to the train station. In order to travel that route, the people of the city, primarily the merchants, would require the services of the coachmen of Sochaczew, such as Leizer Droshkosh, Hersch Tindel and others who always stood by – in the summer with their wagons and in the winter with their sleighs – ready to transport those who were making haste to the departing train.

The homes of several dozen Jewish families surrounded the train station. These Jews obtained their livelihood from the railway. The house of Mordechai Fein was located in this area, and this house contained the synagogue for the local Jews. The pastureland of the villages Janowiec and Duranow was on the other side of the train tracks.

On Sabbaths and festivals the roads would be filled with strolling youths, as well as other Jews, who would go out bedecked in their Sabbath finery to enjoy the world around.

The memory of the deeds of the local anti-Semites also comes to my mind. I recall the wildness of the soldiers and army conscripts as they would pass through the city. I particularly have bad memories of the "Hellerchiks" named after their commander Heller and the "Poznanches" named after their city Poznan. These wild men dressed in army fatigues were expert Jew haters, and they caused the Jews of our city no small measure of suffering. I can never forget, and I still see in my mind the image of one of these hooligans in a Polish army uniform torturing my father of blessed memory, and pulling out the hairs of his beard along with the skin of his face which was dripping with blood...

The instigation of the Andaks[17] and other anti-Semites in the city also poisoned the souls of the Christian children, and I can still feel it in my flesh very well to this day. As we returned from Warsaw as refugees from the world war, having lost all of our property, we took up residence in one of the houses owned by my grandfather on the other side of the train tracks in the Christian neighborhood. On several occasions as I was going into the city to study, I had to be on guard for the youths of our neighborhood who would incite their dogs against me, and I can still remember their curses to this very day – "Jew to Palestine", or "Jew a pig is chasing you", and other such curses which hurt my young heart.

The Jewish community of Sochaczew, one of the oldest in the vicinity of Warsaw, numbered approximately 5,000 souls. Mutual benefit was well organized, charitable organizations helped the poor overcome their straits, and the commandment of caring for the sick was fulfilled with great diligence.

The synagogue and study hall were located a small distance away from the rest of the buildings of the city. The synagogue was very beautiful with its high, round dome and long glass windows with a colorful mosaic. The interior of the synagogue was also very glorious. The prayer stand and holy ark were fine crafted with engraved wood. The ark cover was woven with fine gold, and a beautiful lectern (bima) stood in the center, upon which one would ascend by steps. The bima was surrounded by small, engraved pillars. At the entrance there was a large sandbox[18] and the chair of Elijah the prophet which would be used for circumcisions. To us children, the appearance of the synagogue resembled the Holy Temple, about which we had learned in cheder.

On Sabbaths, and in particular on festivals, the synagogue would be full of worshipers, and the Rabbi would give a lecture about the significance of the day. I in particular remember the words of Rabbi Perkal of blessed memory on the second day of Shavuot (Pentecost), which according to legend was the day of the passing of David the king of Israel. On that day the synagogue was decorated in honor of the festival, and a festive atmosphere pervaded everywhere. With the dancing flames of the lit candles in the background, Rabbi Perkal preached, and proved with great enthusiasm that the time of the redemption was approaching.

The Zibola twins – Yitzchak of blessed memory and Eliahu may he live long.

The study hall which stood next to the synagogue building served as a popular place of prayer for the Jews of the city, who flocked there in great numbers. Various preachers and expositors of Zion would come to preach from the pulpit of the study hall, and their words would find paths into the hearts of the multitude of listeners, in particular of the younger generation, in whose hearts longing and dreams of the return to Zion and the redemption of the land would be awakened.

During this period, Sochaczew began to become more active in organized communal life, and culture began to sprout up; cultural organizations began to have activities, and politically oriented youth movements began.

When my late father made Aliya to the land in 1922, we began to receive postcards and letters from him, and I was very excited to see the square letters which were printed on the stamps and letters.

My family made Aliya to the land at the end of 1924. It was difficult to part from the rest of our family whom we left in the city, as well as our many acquaintances. Who would have imagined that this parting would be permanent ...

Everything terminated... the gravestone was placed upon the Jews of Sochaczew...

1942 was the year of suffering and destruction for the Jews of Sochaczew, the year that they were sent to the Warsaw Ghetto. The final journey of the community was complete. There was slow death from hunger, sickness and torture, as well as the tragic end in the death camps.

The Jews of Sochaczew are no longer. Entire families were wiped out without leaving a single survivor. The simple folk along with the Torah scholars, the artisans along with the property owners; innocent Jews, pure souls who conducted themselves with modesty, including my own family members of the Ines family. They stand before my eyes with a thirst for life and activity, longing for peace and good deeds – and now nothing remains except for a memory.

Everything ended. Sochaczew is empty of Jews. The work of dozens of generations was destroyed. Our Christian neighbors filled their houses with pillaged Jewish property. The murdered would no longer claim their properties... so the conscience of the Christians would be at peace. Most of the work was done by others; however they did assist with the bloodbath in some way.

When he arrived in Sochaczew after the liberation, Pinia Weinberg, may his blood be avenged, was greeted with pistol fire. His pure blood flowed onto the streets of his birthplace.

The community of Sochaczew was wiped off the face of the earth. Its charitable and cultural organizations, which were founded and nurtured with great self-sacrifice, were all destroyed. The Jews who excelled in love of their fellow Jew are no longer.

May their memory be blessed and sanctified for generations to come. Yitgadal Veyitgadash...[19]

TRANSLATOR'S FOOTNOTES:

1. The term 'chayey ruach' does not mean spiritual life in the religious sense, but rather 'life of the spirit'.

2. The fourth wave of immigration to the Land of Israel, which took place between the world wars.

3. The ceremony marking the end of the Sabbath.

4. I am not sure what the reference is here.

5. The right wing Zionist movement (the precursor the modern day Likud and Herut parties), founded by Zeev Jabotinski. The youth wing of the revisionist Zionists was called Beitar.

6. Religious Zionist organization.

7. Biro-Bidzhan is an area in eastern Siberia on the Mongolian border that was set up as a Jewish Autonomous Republic by the U.S.S.R. in an attempt to solve the Jewish national problem.

8. By coincidence, this was the night of Kristallnacht!

9. Here spelled "Broka", but the previous mention was spelled "Brodka". One is in error.

10. Perhaps a suit of armor.

11. The Andak was apparently an anti-Semitic party in Poland.

12. A very poignant Biblical reference from the book of Kings. It is an allusion to the question posed by the prophet Elijah to King Ahab after Ahab had killed Nabot in order to take over his field which he desired: "Have you slain and also taken possession?"

13. The 17th of Tammuz and 9th of Av are two summertime fast days marking the breach of the siege of Jerusalem and the destruction of the temple respectively, as well as several other tragic events in Jewish

history. The three-week period between these two fasts is a semi-mourning period in the Jewish calendar, when weddings as well as any other musical festivities are prohibited. This period is often known as the "Three Weeks".

14. A sukka is a temporary hut used during the celebration of the fall Feast of Tabernacles (Sukkot).

15. The "Tallit Gadol" or large prayer shawl, is worn primarily during prayers, while the "Tallit Kattan" or small prayer shawl, is a smaller garment worn at all times. Most Orthodox Jews wear it as an undergarment, however, some Hassidic Jews, primarily in Europe, wore it at all times on top of their shirt.

16. 'A string to a shoelace' is an expression meaning a wide variety of items. This is taken from the expression that Abraham used in the book of Genesis when refusing to take any of the booty that was offered to him by the king of Sodom after his victory in the battle against the four kings. Here its meaning is similar to the English expression "everything but the kitchen sink".

17. Andak was the name of an anti-Semitic Polish party of the time.

18. The sandbox is the sand-filled receptacle for the burying of foreskins after a circumcision.

19. Yitgadal Veyitkadash (or Yisgadal Veyisgadash), are the first two words of the Kaddish, which is a prayer said in memory of the departed, as well as on other occasions during the course of a prayer service.

{672}

Moshe Jakubowicz (1880-1943)
Translated by Jerrold Landau

One of the first, –
Of the "dreamers of the ghetto" who did not witness the redemption,
A Zionist in all of the 248 and 365[1],
Faithful and strongly dedicated, active and inspired others to action,
Upright in his manner and pure of heart,
Humble and possessing a refined soul,
Well read and pleasant at song.
One of the dear ones of the community of Sochaczew
In the period between the wars.
Went along with those going to their deaths
As his soul pined for Zion…

Y. Jakubowicz

{141}

The Destroyed Home
Moshe Szwarc (Chicago)
Translated by Jerrold Landau

From steel and iron, cold, hard and mute,
A heart beats on its own, the person – he comes!
Ch. N. Bialik

Despite the fact that my task is to describe a specific period of life in Sochaczew, I cannot let pass and not mention, at least with a few words, the great destruction.

The hand shudders and the heart is full of grief when one makes mention of the fate of the Sochaczew that I left in 1926 full with an ebullient Jewish life, and the Sochaczew to which I returned in 1949. Between those two dates lies a deep abyss, a sea filled with blood, woe, agony and destruction.

The established way of life is to forget that which the earth covers up. However, who can ever forget the destruction of an entire group of people, of a community and its brutal death.

It is hard for me to eulogize my native town, which is so beloved and familiar to me. I am bound to the Jewish life of Sochaczew with thousands of bonds. I shared in its agony and joy, and in the happiness and suffering of every Jew in the town.

Now, it is my lot to participate in the recording of the sorrowful chronicle, and the erecting of a headstone to perpetuate the memory of our destroyed Sochaczew and of the murdered martyrs;my own flesh and blood, and my fellow natives whose lives were cut off follow after me like a Satan in my grave.

Sochaczew adds a significant chapter in the colorful and unique life of the Jewish in Poland which exuded its illuminated spirit over all of the Jewish communities in the world throughout the generations, and nourished our people with the precision of Jewish tradition, with Jewish knowledge, with the work of Jewish thought and Jewish creativity.

Sochaczew symbolized, and was the synthesis of both Jewish traditional life and progressive cultural life. These were years when deep roots were planted, which assured continuity - until the great national misfortune. The survivors who remain have the sorrowful longing – a longing for those years and days, for the summer evenings of childhood;for the joyful Sabbaths and festivals. A nostalgia for home, for the alleys and streets populated by Jews who sat in their homes on summer nights with their Jewish wives from whose simple women's talk one could discern the difficult socioeconomic and political life of the Jews in the Poland that once was;a nostalgia for the dear, simple Jewish common folk who were murdered in such a brutal fashion. The city of my birth always enchanted me, and I always look back at it with affection. Wherever I am, I always recall Sochaczew, the city of my youthful ideals, the city where my dreams of youth took shape and which set me upon the intellectual path of my life.

The period between 1915-1925 can be considered to be a period of renaissance, the upswing of Jewish social, political and cultural life in Poland.

These were stormy years of wars and revolutions;years of birth pangs, of new sociopolitical orders in many countries, and the freeing of downtrodden peoples, including Poland which became independent on November 11th, 1918. All of these events left their tracks, and brought deep changes to Jewish life in Poland.

Ignoring the difficult economic situation, under both the German occupation and later the "free" Poland, Jewish life underwent a great cultural strengthening, and the political and social life pulsated. Sochaczew was not only a part of the Polish-Jewish society, but rather it stood in the foreground of the strong, pulsating life of Polish Jewry, whose actions were expressed in widespread cultural activity, including a rich civic library that contained a collection of several thousand books in Yiddish, Polish, Hebrew, and Russian;a reading hall which was filled with boys and girls each evening as they discussed various literary and political issues;lectures given by local personalities as well as reports from neighboring Warsaw about new streams in Jewish and world literature and other issues. There was also a very capable and active dramatic group, conducted at various times by the theater connoisseur Nachum Grundwag, which made a name for itself by presenting frequent dramatic performances and literary-musical evenings with programs from the Jewish classics and world literature;accompanied by song numbers from the choir of literary troupe.

This was all possible thanks to the intelligent youth, who embraced a new life, and who were distinguished in their active work that brought light, knowledge, and a new spirit and rhythm to the entire Jewish life.

Even prior to the First World War, Sochaczew had a "Jewish communal library" and a dramatic troupe that was affiliated with the library. However, with the outbreak of the war, the Jews of Sochaczew, as the Jews in many other cities and towns, were driven by the Czarist regime into Warsaw, leaving the entire endeavor, along with the entire city, destroyed.

Later, when the Germans took Warsaw in July 1915, the Jews began to return to Sochaczew. Returning home and beginning to build up the destroyed lives and destroyed homes, they quickly began to think about the life of the intellect.

The greatest worry was where to live, for there was almost no home that was not damaged;however the strong desire to improve the day to day economic life did not dampen the desire for a spiritual-societal life.

With the greatest persistence and effort, with restricted human and financial resources, the "Jewish communal library and reading hall" was opened. This quickly became the home and center of the youth who returned. Almost all of the youth of Sochaczew gathered around the library, as well as a number of the adults, representatives of the various ideologies and party affiliations. The library became more than a place where one obtains a book, it became an educational institution that concerned itself with the intellectual development of the youth, and made sure that each member or reader would read the appropriate book.

The process of cultural growth led to brighter ways, and the upswing expressed itself in a variety of cultural means. The dramatic troupe was formed in the library, and everything contributed to the integrated composition of the general Jewish life in Sochaczew.

The dramatic troupe undertook great tasks from the beginning, and left its mark on all areas of Jewish life, which spurred it on to its future successes. The task of the dramatic group was to perform Jewish theatrical productions and the best of Jewish drama, to improve and enrich the city culture center, and thereby to fulfil the intellectual needs and longings of the Jewish population.

In a very short time, the dramatic troupe grew into one of the finest cultural institutions in Poland. By 1926, through their activities, they were recognized both for their artistic style, with their high cultural level and their breadth of repertoire.

The Sochaczew library and dramatic troupe were known in many cities in Poland, and their performances were in high demand in the neighboring towns such as Bialynin, Grodzisk, Wyszogrod, Lubowiec and others.

When this book is completed, those who lived in Sochaczew at that time, and now live throughout the world will surely relive those fine days of festive success of the artistic performance of Yaakov Gordon's "The Unknown", "God, Man and the Devil", "Kreizer Sonata", and the "Stranger"; Peretz Hirschbein's "The Carcass";"The Mute" by A. Weiter;"The Family" by Nambergen;Shalom Aleichem's "Scattered and Spread", "Mazel Tov", and "Agents"; "Yankel the Smith" by David Pinski; "Return" by Shalom Asch;as well as other single act dramatic performances, short artistic evenings, choir recitals, which brought a great deal of spirit and festivity to the Jewish street.

The Jewish cultural activists in Sochaczew would mark with great honor and holiness the yahrzeits (anniversary of the death) of the deceased Jewish classical writers. The yahrzeits were marked each year with great activity and intellectually stimulating programs, performed by esteemed writers from Warsaw, who introduced the liberal Jewish masses to their creations.

Aside from the library which was not affiliated with any party, there were also, of course, circles of the Zionists, Folkists, and Workers, who conducted liberal, variegated cultural and political publicity work.

We went through various episodes perpetrated by anti-Semitic characters from Poland of the time. One of them is worth mentioning – it is connected with the later leader of the Bund, the writer and orator A. Lutwak.

He was invited by the library to give a lecture about Y. L. Peretz. It was necessary, as always, to obtain an appropriate permit for this. As was usual, on that Sabbath evening an hour prior to the lecture, representatives of the police arrived with an ordinance in the name of the starosta (mayor) stating that the speaker must deliver his lecture only in the Polish language, and not in Yiddish. All explanations did not help, and the writer of these lines, as the chairman of the library and representative of the Jewish community, signed a paper that he took upon himself the entire responsibility toward the Polish authorities for not following a police ordinance.

This matter was clarified by the education ministry, and later lectures in Yiddish took place without interference.

To my great pain, the majority of those who led and participated in the development of Jewish social and cultural life in Sochaczew were among those murdered. With great awe and respect, I wish to mention here the names of Simcha Grundwag, Nachum Grundwag, Machla Grundwag-Szwercer, Bluma Wajnberg, Chaya Flejszman, Chwacza Lefkowicz, Bina Festman, Simcha Kan, Yosef Muney and Yosef Luksztyk, as well as others whose names I no longer remember.

Let us here also mention with respect Yosef Leib, better known as Lutek Skotnicki, who died before the last war. For the entire time, even after I left Sochaczew in 1926, he stood at the foreground of Jewish social, political and cultural life in Sochaczew, and brought a great energy to the struggle against anti-Semitism since the rise of Polish until his sudden death.

With awe, respect, grief and agony, I wish to also mention here the name of Vove Rozenberg, who died in New York on May 14th, 1953. The deceased, with his intelligence, energy, and deep proficiency in literature and theater, played a great part in the development of the life of the spirit in the city. (He prepared to participate in this book, but with his death, his life and his plans were torn apart.)

With grief and agony, I wish to also mention here an important activist from that time, whose young life was also suddenly cut off – Aharon Friedman, who died in Jerusalem on the eve of Yom Kippur, 1953.

With grief and nostalgia, I wish to mention Eliezer Meir Libert, the former president of the Chicago Sochaczew Mutual Benefit Society for 28 years, who died on July 20th, 1956. His death deeply affected all of our fellow natives. He excelled in bringing assistance to all Sochaczewers who were in need.

Of those who remain alive, we should mention:Yaakov Friedman of Schunat Borochov, Rachel Weinberg-Levanon of Tel Aviv, Hershel Kac of Los Angeles, and Moshe Szwarc of Chicago.

{146}

The Sprouting of the New Poland

On November 11th, 1918, Poland proclaimed itself as an independent kingdom. Along with the celebrations and liberation came a wave of pogroms. Jewish blood flowed; they cut beards, threw Jews off of trains. The illusion of a happy Poland, for which we had dreamed of and placed so much hope, trickled away. The previous anti-Semitism became stronger in all of its manifestations. The way things turned out in the new Poland became a great disappointment to the Jewish youth of Sochaczew, as throughout Poland.

However, with the birth of an independent Poland, a change came in the history of the Jews in Poland. There was an awakening of activity in all Jewish political and national streams in the land. This brought a new birth and life to the entire political and social life in Sochaczew, which was not left behind. That era marked the complete end of the previous situation of apathetic-congealed Jewish life, and the Sochaczew Jewish community began to take up the struggle, and faced all of the problems that went around in life, as they struggled for the rights for Jews as citizens in the new Poland.

Sochaczew demonstrated with honor that it was an integral part of the colorful Polish Jewry in all domains of political, social and cultural life.

Jewish civic council members as part of a delegation to greet the president of Poland.

{148}

The Social Makeup

Of the approximately 800 Jewish families who lived in Sochaczew at that time, most were artisans, tradesman, small shopkeepers, wheat handlers, or people without definite occupations. Sochaczew, like most towns of Poland, did not have any specialized industry. Most of the tradesmen were tailors, shoemakers, butchers, wagon drivers, boot makers[1], metal workers, horse drawn cab drivers, porters, etc.

There were also a small number of well to do people who conducted business in forestry and wood products, who were large scale grain businessmen, and who were involved in various other businesses. However, most of the merchants struggled for their economic existence under the yoke of high taxes and significant restrictions in business.

There were also a small number of people involved in other trades. However the majority were involved in the above mentioned businesses, and later organized themselves into a professional organization. That group, even though it was small in number, soon began to play an important role in the social, economic and political life. Aside from being active in political training, they also succeeded in working for better economic conditions for the workers.

The tradesman also conducted activities to the best of their ability, and formed a handworker's union.

There was also a societal cassa in town, where the artisans and small businessmen could obtain a loan in order to lighten their difficult lives.

The handworker's union also played a political role in both Jewish and civic life.

The Jews of Sochaczew took a significant interest in the general political life of the country and in the situation of the civic communal economy. They demonstrated political maturity and unity at the time of the elections for the civic council.

Even at the beginning of the 20thcentury, the Jews of Sochaczew formed a coalition with the Polish Socialist Party (P. P. S), elected a Jewish vice mayor, and thereby wrote an important page in the history of the Jews in Poland, in particular with regard to the militancy, might and struggle for equal rights. With their unified power, at that time they were able to elect a progressive mayor, who defeated the candidate of the reactionaries. The anti-Semites could not bear this situation, and therefore they threatened to toss the provisional vice mayor, who was indeed the writer of these lines, into water in a sack if he would not immediately resign. However, they did not carry through. He remained at his post as a proud Jew and a Polish citizen with full rights as he continued with the struggle for Jewish rights until his immigration to America.

The Sochaczew population at that time was made up of 60% Jews and 40% Christians. The Jews of Sochaczew played a progressive role in the sociopolitical life. Until the time that I left Sochaczew, they were united in all civic elections, and as a result of their unity, there were 14 Jewish councilors out of a total of 24. They came from the entire spectrum of the Jewish social spectrum – Zionists, the handworker's union, the Folkists and Bund. They blocked the anti-Semitic plans to undermine Jewish business in the upper areas of the city and to expel the Jewish wagon and carriage drivers from the market, in which Jewish families earned their livelihood for generations. Later, these anti-Semitic plans, through various geographical machinations, arranged for all areas of the city to have a majority of Christian residents, and therefore, the number of Jewish votes, and correspondingly, the number of Jewish councilors, was reduced.

I should mention here with honor the long-time Jewish activist of Sochaczew, Simcha Grundwag. Aside from his activities in other areas of the city, he especially excelled in his work for the city council, as a long-serving councilor, in his day to day struggle against the Polish reactionaries and anti-Semites in order to promote the interests of the Jews of Sochaczew.

{150}

The Elections for the Jewish Community

Of the 652 cities and towns in Poland, Sochaczew excelled greatly in the area of establishing an organized official Jewish life.

When the ordinance was issued calling for elections for the position of chairman of the Jewish community, the entire Jewish political and communal spectrum began preparing for the historic day with their entire partisan might.

The internal Jewish life in Sochaczew, just like in all other cities, changed greatly after the independence of Poland. Official Jewish life used to be dominated by a small number of wealthy people, "fine" and "lovely" Jews [2], parnassim (communal servants) and leaders. These "leaders"of the Jewish community were for the most part removed from Jewish life and did not feel for the lot of the poor Jewish masses.

The entire work was in matters of kashruth (Jewish dietary laws), synagogue, the Beis Midrash, the mikva (ritual bath), ritual slaughterers, etc. The entire agenda was out of date and obsolete. The common folk and the tradesmen did not have any respect or reverence for the powers.

Therefore, with happiness, elections took place understandably to reorganize Jewish life under the name of "the religious Jewish community". According to the election ordinance, Sochaczew must appoint four heads of the community. The Rabbi of the community, who at that time was Reb Yehoshua Prekal, was automatically a representative to the communal council.

Those who lived in Sochaczew at the time and will read these lines will surely remember those days of the zealous election campaign. The Aguda[3] with the assistance of the rabbi conducted an intensive election campaign against all the other parties; the tradesmen and the Folkists wanted to free themselves from the hegemony of previous "leaders" and wished to elect a number of representatives who would concern themselves with the needs of the broad populist masses. Officially, three parties ran – the Aguda, the Zionists and the Folkist party. Although the latter was small in number, it had a strong following from the handworkers, workers and all those who wished to bring a radical change to Jewish life.

After a long and intensive election campaign, an action that initiated a new upswing in Jewish political, religious and cultural life, both the Zionists and the Folkist party were victorious. Despite the fact that the Aguda expected to elect no fewer than all four candidates, they barely elected two. The Zionists elected one representative, as did the Folkist party.

The Joint [4] kitchen in its activities after the First World War – distributing food to children of the city.

The results of the election initiated a new chapter in the history of Jewish life in Sochaczew. The two progressive representatives were a significant factor and an important power in the life of Sochaczew Jewry, and they expanded their activities beyond the realm of purely religious matters. The meetings and deliberations were open, and always drew a large audience. The communal office became a veritable open populist tribunal, where discussions took place on important political, national and world matters. The communal committee became a true reflection of the Jewish community of Sochaczew, and acted in a serious manner, with its full authority, against every challenge to the Jewry.

In the first place, the Jews of Sochaczew felt that their lives had taken on a new form. The social and economic situation began to be reflected in the meetings of the communal organization.

Around the years of 1924-1925, Poland became entangled in a difficult crisis. The workers and small businessmen made up a greater portion of the population than previously. The Grabowski "wagon" removed a bit of the poverty from the impoverished Jewish handworkers and storeowners[5]. Under these difficult conditions, the duties of the communal committee became more serious. They often had to intervene with the tax office for the benefit of a number of Jews, and were often successful in saving them from complete ruin.

Thus did the community go about its activities, always placing great importance upon the economic situation of the artisans and small businessmen, and their poverty.

The poorer segments of Sochaczew Jewry, whose numbers increased during the crisis and who were in need of assistance, were helped by the communal organization in various ways in a fine, modest fashion. The imposition of the Jewish communal tax affected the economic situation of each individual, and this was often the cause of a struggle with the representatives of the Aguda.

This was the picture of Jewish life in Sochaczew when I left in February 1926. I visited Sochaczew in 1949, and my heart bled profusely upon witnessing the great destruction.

Sochaczew remains as a corner of light in the soul of every Sochaczewite. The beginnings of my generation were not lost. Those who were carried by fate to all corners of the world carry on the beautiful traditions of Sochaczew – some have participated in the founding of the State of Israel, and others struggle for a nicer and more just world.

TRANSLATOR'S FOOTNOTES:

1. A 'kamash' is a low-laced boot or gaiter.
2. A form of sarcasm, denoting people whose main claim to power was their financial standing.
3. Referring to the Orthodox group Agudas Yisrael, often known as 'the Aguda'.
4. The Joint Distribution Committee, a worldwide Jewish organization to take care of poor and oppressed Jews. This organization is often referred to as the "Joint".
5. I am not sure of the meaning of this sentence.

{154}

Organized Institutions
by Sh. Swiatlowski
Translated by Jerrold Landau

Sochaczew, like all Jewish cities and towns in Poland, had an entire series of organizations that bore the character of a type of self-help. These institutions were headed by the poor workers – "the masses". I wish to mention here the most senior organization, "Linat Tzedek", which was founded by such Jews as Daniel the shoemaker from the Moszenberg family, as well as his brother Yosef Yonah the jester and Hersch Kluska, both shoemakers; Moshe Aharon Moszenberg (nicknamed Fatom) the bearer of a trade; Shalom Zelmanowicz, also a shoemaker by trade; and other working men, tradesmen and artisans.

The first Siyum Hasefer [1] which the Linat Tzedek organization conducted with solemnity, when people accompanied the Torah through the entire city to the synagogue, will remain in the memories of Sochaczew Jews for a very long time. Zelig Kluska, a Jew from among the poor of Sochaczew, blew oil from his mouth with a large tin pan, which he carried with great solemnity. The oil was ignited and singed Zelig's beard. He barely noticed that he was being burnt...

The Linat Tzedek organization organized a great deal of assistance for the poor of Sochaczew. The members of the organization went out to "Linatan" – that is to say, spending the night with the ill and concerning themselves with all of their needs, from prescriptions to bedding. We must not forget the conditions in which the Sochaczew poor lived – mainly in attic rooms or in damp cellars. The "Linatnikes" went to those places to offer assistance to the ill.

The Hachnasat Orchim, Bikur Cholim, Hachnasat Kalah, and others offered assistance in different realms [2], whose sole aim was mutual assistance. Their organizers were the poorest people in town[3].

The Jews were not able to demonstrate their initiative everywhere. The upbringing of the poorer children was on a very low level. The premises of the Chevra Kadisha was given to the poor children, where the teacher Moshe Kiszka was located. The teacher of the Talmud Torah had to collect the tuition for them by himself. The students went around with torn clothing and barefoot. More significantly, the visors of their hats were torn... This happened because the teacher Moshe Itche used to figure out how to pull down the visor over the eyes of the students when they complained, saving thereby the gift of the hand [4].

{155}

The First Professional Union

The First World War brought a great destruction, and the poverty in the town increased.

The German army approached the villages of the Bzura at the end of 1914, and the front settled in near the town. Natan David the teacher was killed, and the Russians hanged three Jews: Yosef the teacher (Kacew), and Simcha Yehuda and Aryeh Leib Sznajder. The survivors fled naked and barefoot in the middle of the winter to Warsaw. Jewish Sochaczew ceased to exist.

The battles between the Russians and the Germans continued for eight months. The larger portion of the town was destroyed, and the Germans finally took Sochaczew in June 1915. Later, the German army entered Warsaw. Jews returned to their birth town, mostly the poor and the middle class. On the other hand, the richest families such as the Rechtmans, Graubards, Engelmans, Warszawskis and others remained in Warsaw or Lodz. They returned to Sochaczew only at the end of the war. The rabbi's family remained in Lodz. The town returned to life. The ruins were cleared away, and new houses were built. The appearance of Sochaczew Jews also changed. Jews began to appear in European clothing. Social life also renewed itself, and took on an entirely different character than what was before the war. A library was created, the first cultural institution in our town. The first dramatic club was founded. A struggle between the parties for hegemony began.

A professional movement also began in parallel with the cultural work of the library. The first professional union was set up in the Linat Tzedek headquarters in 1925. Feivel Galek was elected as chairman, who was the publicist [5] of the group. A second Orthodox young man was elected as secretary. The first general meeting elected an initiative group of ten members, including myself. After the "initiation" [6] of the chairman Feivel Galek, in which the "Bund" did not permit worshipping[7], a majority decision was taken to affiliate with the central professional union in Warsaw, located on Bracka 11 (The central organization of the elected Communist professional union). After a strong clap on the podium by the blind Itche to inform the gathering that it is time to conduct the Mincha service, the founding meeting took its decision...

{156}

The First Strike

The central organization decided to declare a strike on account of the fact that an employer, Mendel Plonski, refused to give work to the member Adam Kluska, who worked as a home manufacturer. I warned that the strike would fail, because it is after the season, however the central organization took interest in a political effect, and decided to strike.

The strike was impressive. Everyone except for one person participated in the strike. However, the end was sad. Due to a provocation, the authorities dissolved the Communist central, arrested a large majority of the members, and confiscated the entire archives. The police quickly threw themselves onto all of the branches in the country, including the branch in Sochaczew. Arrests and inquisitions began. This caused the employers in our town to become brazen. They organized themselves and declared a lockout; nobody was allowed into work. An oppressive mood overtook the workers in town. The strike failed terribly. The organization was dissolved by the police and the chief organizers, myself included, were placed under police supervision, which caused various other difficulties.

Some time later, around 1926, Yechiel Meir Zalcman (Szkolak[8]) appeared in Sochaczew. He had taken part in the revolutionary movement in Sochaczew in 1905. He was in Russia during the revolution of 1917, and later came to Sochaczew, where he stood at the head of the worker's movement. He called a meeting, and we decided to renew the professional activities. He proposed that we should affiliate with the Bundist headquarters. The motion was accepted with a majority of votes, and shortly after the first actions to organize anew the professional movement in our city, the headquarters sent its representative, the member Berl Ambaras [9] (Berl Szteper), who organized the activities of our union.

The movement developed very well. For the elections to the town council, we succeeded in including one of our members, thanks to our member Moshe Szwarc, who was held in high esteem. Our councilman was indeed our member Zalcman. This further enhanced the esteem of our professional union. We elected two councilmen in the elections for the regional sick fund: Yechiel Meir Piernik and the writer of these memoirs. Later, I was elected to the search committee, where I worked for five years until the liquidation of the mutual benefit organization by the Sanacia regime in Poland.

Our representatives to the sick fund greatly assisted the poor Jewish people of the town, and we struggled to make sure that there would be a Jewish doctor and feldscher [10] in town.

As I have already mentioned, Sochaczew was able to sustain various organizations that were involved in mutual assistance. These organizations had a philanthropic character. After the First World War, in the renovated Sochaczew, new mutual assistance organizations and cooperative activities were established. Together with the economic boycott policies of the anti-Semitic Polish regime, which did everything to destroy Jewish livelihood in the towns, the mutual assistance in Sochaczew strengthened. Thanks to the effort and energy of Yaakov Benczkowski (Yankel Trepiasz), a cooperative people's bank (Bank Lodowy) was founded in Sochaczew. It assisted several hundred families of the Sochaczew middle class and poor to save themselves from going under.

I should also mention the charitable fund that was led by Yechiel Meir Tylman. His work was done with selflessness. More than one poor handworker or poor merchant was saved with money from this fund.

Thus did the simple "townsfolk" Jewish of Sochaczew conduct their economic lives, helping each other and being active for the benefit of the public, until the Hitlerist murderous hand fell upon them.

TRANSLATOR'S FOOTNOTES:
1. Festivities upon conclusion of the writing of a Torah scroll.
2. Hachnasat Orchim – taking care of guests. Bikur Cholim – visiting the sick. Hachnasat Kalah – taking care of brides and wedding needs, primarily for the poor.
3. I am not sure if this means that their beneficiaries were the poorest people in town, or more likely, in a somewhat exaggerating statement, is indicating that the activists in these organizations come from the poorer or working class strata of society.
4. I suspect the 'gift of the hand' is a euphemism for a spanking.
5. The term used here is 'baal koreh', literally the person who reads the Torah. I expect that here, it means the publicist.
6. Literally "justification"
7. This is very cryptic. The Bund is an extreme left wing socialist movement, which is noted to be very anti-religious. My guess is that there was some religious controversy here between the Orthodox members and the left leaning members as to the proceedings at the initiation ceremony. From the next sentence, it is obvious that one of the set prayer times (Mincha – the afternoon service) fell during the meeting time, and a controversy arose as to whether to allow a break for that purpose.
8. This word means 'quilter'. The members of such a socialist organization would often be referred to by their professions.
9. Ambaras might mean 'the warehouse worker'.
10. A feldscher is an old time barber surgeon – a type of medic.

{158 - Yiddish} {669 - Hebrew}

The Birthpangs of Zionism in Sochaczew
by Sh. Grundwag
Translated by Jerrold Landau

Introduction

In my memoirs about the awakening and growth of Zionism in our town, I will try to elaborate in depth about the persecutions and methods employed by the Hassidim under the influence of the "Courtyard of Sochaczew" in their battle against the movement of national renaissance during that period. They published an edict, signed by the Rabbis of Gur, Alexander, Amshenov and others – that declared an excommunication and ban on Zionism in all of their respective places.

Later I will deal with the various personalities from both camps, as well as the relation of the Czarist government to us. I will deal with in particular the failures and victories in the difficult arenas of cultural life, nationalistic and religious life, and national political life.

A Center of Haskala

Years ago there was in our city, similar to many other towns, a small club of enlightened and progressive Jews, which included Sh. Gelman, G. Lichtenstein, Y. M. Grundwag, G. Warshawski, M. Festman, A. Rosenfeld, K. Welman, as well as the author of these words. This club met in the home of Y. M. Grundwag, where there was a library that contained daily newspapers and periodicals in Yiddish, Hebrew and Polish. These included "Hamagid", "Hamelitz", and "Hatzfira". During our meetings, we read the news, and conducted debates about the current events.

These meetings and deliberations raised the national consciousness of the participants, and due to the influence of Pinsker's "Auto-Emancipation" and Herzl's "The Jewish State", the members of the group began to regard Zionism as the ultimate and only answer to the problems of the Jews and the tribulations of exile. As a result, the first official Zionist meeting took place.

At that time there lived in our city a great Talmudist who was an expert in Bible and grammar, by the name of Reb Yehoshua of blessed memory (the only son of Rabbi Elazarel, the Rabbi of our city). He had a deep connection to national issues. He requested that the entire group of maskilim[1] should gather in his house, and, secretly, the first Zionist meeting would take place. Other honorable people were also invited to this meeting, such as Reb Leib Greenberg, Reb Hersch Frydman (the mohel – ritual circumciser), Reb Menashe Rabinovitz, and Reb Godel the teacher. Most of those invited were suspected as being apikorsim[2].

On the evening when this gathering was supposed to take place, the famous nationalistic speaker Y. Weintraub was staying over at our house as a guest, as he was invited to a wedding in the Rebbe's courtyard. Due to the efforts of M. Festman, he was able to participate in our meeting. At that meeting, he, along with K. Welman and the writer of these lines, laid the base for theoretical and political Zionism.

Thus was the Zionist movement founded in our city. It numbered 15 members, and was headed by a committee.

The First Zionist Organization

In order to provide an opportunity for the Zionist organization that was founded at that time to continue, and to spread the Zionist idea in wider circles, a Zionistic prayer hall was founded by the name of "Chevra Bnei Zion Sochaczew". This prayer hall was in the home of Gotteskind, a teacher of children, who gave over his schoolroom for this purpose for no fee. Public prayers took place there each Sabbath and festival, Bible and Jewish history were studied, and Zionist and general Jewish newspapers were read. Lectures on current events took place on every day of school vacation, in order to emphasize the nationalistic idea. Due to systematic public relations activities, the numbers of members of the organization grew. Reb Chaim Mishrowitzer, Reb Sh. N. Warshawski, Reb Meir Nashelevitz, Reb A. L. Shemiantek, Reb Meir Kan, and Reb Ben-Zion Kroin all joined. The group of supporters grew. At that time, the Zionist organization moved to a larger hall, in the home of the chairman Reb Sh. Gelman.

With the move toward organized Zionist activity, and with the importance attached to unifying all of the Zionist organizations into one world Zionist federation for the purpose of political Zionism, the committee decided to send three representatives – including this writer as secretary – charged with the mission to formalize our affiliation with the central Zionist organization of Warsaw. This organization was located on 3 Czapala Street (in a four by four room – i.e. a tiny room), and was headed at the time by: the lawyer Jasinowski, Dr. T. Hindes, N. Sokolow, A. Podlishewski, Lewita (the father of L. Lewita), and Dr. Z. Bichowski. A central committee had not yet been established. Congress Poland was at that time divided into districts, each one with a separate delegate. We gave our accounting of the founding of our organization and its activities to the above mentioned representatives, and indicated our willingness to participate in the regional office. They accepted our notice with great satisfaction, and promised their spiritual and judicial help in our Zionist activities.

They fulfilled their promise, and after a short time the well-known nationalistic orator Korotkin visited us. He presented convincing explanatory lectures about Zionism in the city's Beis Midrash, and inspired enthusiasm among the listeners. 400 shekels (tokens of membership in the Zionist organization) were sold on the spot. He presented a special presentation in our own hall, specifically for our members, and this inspired a reorganization of the groups and the election of a formal committee. This writer served as the chairman, M. Festman served as secretary, and A. Rosenfeld as the treasurer. Committees for publicity, finance, culture and education were also elected.

The new committee conducted its activities from the outset with the inspiration of the words of Herzl, that "Zionism involves a return to Judaism prior to a return to the land of the Jews". The committee did not see for itself the possibility of effective Zionist activity without the founding of a school which would educate the younger generation in the nationalistic spirit, ingrain in them an appreciation of the richness of our nation, awaken a love for the Hebrew language, etc. After much effort, the committee opened an elementary school, headed by the noted Biblical scholar G. Warshawski.

It is not easy to describe the persecutions that accompanied the opening of such a school in those days. The outcry of the veteran teachers reached to the hearts of the heavens... and most of the community raised a furor until word reached the courtyard of the Rebbe, from where the "bomb" against Zionism in general and the local Zionists in particular was issued.

(The above was the first of a series of articles that appeared in the newspaper "Sochaczewer Shtima". The rest of the issues were lost.)

A group of girls from Sochaczew.

TRANSLATOR'S FOOTNOTES:

1. Maskil (plural maskilim), is literally an well-educated person, but the connotation here is to an adherent of the Haskalah movement, which was the movement prevalent in Jewish eastern Europe of the 19th century which was marked by the trend toward greater secular education and involvement, and a move away from tradition and strict Orthodoxy. Many maskilim would have rejected Orthodoxy outright, while others would have maintained it and blended it in with the modernity of the day.

2. An Apikoros is a Jewish heretic, freethinker, or non-believer. Colloquially, it could also refer in the current context to someone who maintained a degree of Orthodox practice, while simultaneously holding haskala type views. The word literally derives from the Greek philosopher Epicurus, whose motto was that one should enjoy this world, as there is no hereafter. This term is used throughout Jewish religious literature as a halachic term with a formal definition, however it is also colloquially used as a term of denigration for people who are swerving off the path of tradition.

{164}

The Pioneers of the Hebrew School
Yaakov Frydman
Translated by Jerrold Landau

The Cheder Metukan[1] in Sochaczew had little that differentiated it from the old-time cheder. It had the same order, the same table, and the students sit around the table – with their books – and the teacher – the Rebbe, sits at the head. Or he wanders around the table, studying with the children, and always stands beside a second student and asks him something; or he orders him to recite himself... The difference between the old cheder and the Cheder Metukan is that in the Cheder Metukan they studied "Hebrew in Hebrew" [2], everything in the Holy Tongue [3], more Bible [4], etc...

The teacher (Melamed), who was already called "Lehrer", would from time to time still pinch a student there who was getting comfortable; or yank at his ear, so hard that the student thought that his ear remained in the hand of the teacher; or from time to time would utter a curse just like the old Rebbe. Just like the Rebbe-Melamed, the "Lehrer" would also die for a coin, until he would receive the tuition, Rebbe-gelt (money). His situation was somewhat worse, for he had somewhat fewer students than the simple Melamed. Children of Zionist parents, who wished to fulfill the commandment of Zionism with their entire will, studied in the Cheder Metukan. And how many such families were there in the city? And if there were not one such crazy person given over to this idea who would be the first to bring their children as a sacrifice to the Holy Tongue, the Cheder Metukan would not have been born. In our town, this person was Simcha Grundwag. He was the first one who, with his iron will, created the Cheder Metukan and later the Hebrew School. Thus through the course of several years, a generation of Hebrew speaking children and youth appeared. In later times, after the First World War, the Hebrew School enlarged, and the "Yavneh" School was created.

When we mention the revival of the Hebrew language, it is our duty to mention the idealistic teachers who sacrificed themselves for the language, who went hungry, suffered, and struggled for their existence, perhaps even with more difficulty than the Melamed in the city. They were called heretics and apostates. They were persecuted from all corners. Let us make mention of these idealistic teachers.

{165}

Gedalya Warszawski

He was born in 1867 and died in 1908.

He was the son of a wheat merchant. He stood out from all of his brothers. He joined the Zionist movement already in Herzl's time. He was given over to Zionist activity with his heart and soul. He understood that Zionism implies the revival of the Hebrew language, and he started teaching a group of children with the "Hebrew in Hebrew" methodology. I still remember today the names of the parents to whom he was the first teacher of their children. These were the children of the teacher Gedalya Warszawski – Shlomo and Ozer, the children of his brothers Shlomo and Nachum, and the children of Nachum Grundwag, Hertzke Graubard and Yitzchak Warszawski.

These Hebrew studies continued until the Russian-Japanese war [5]. Warszawski went away to London, and occupied himself there with the spreading of the Hebrew language. He reopened his cheder when he returned to Sochaczew from London, and called it by the same name – The School of Ivrit Belvrit of Gedalya Warszawski. However he became ill, and he died a short time later at the age of 39.

His death resulted in a rupture of Hebrew education, for there were not enough new young powers who were able to continue his Hebrew education. The period of the Cheder Metukan came later.

The Teacher Patalowski

He was tall and thin with large eyes that looked through strong concave glasses with a great deal of goodness. He was a family man with several children. He lived in room that served as both his residence and his cheder for teaching. It was not for naught that he was always upset and very angry – only during the times that he studied with the students. His constant agitation was due to several reasons: he had a difficult life, he did not have an assured existence, he worried about his income that was not received on time, and perhaps this was the reason that he wished that the students would absorb the Hebrew words and expression quicker and in greater quantity. He wanted the children to think only in Hebrew. He wished that the language should go hand in hand with the Zionist movement, and this was no light matter. Perhaps this was the reason that he could not remove himself from the old teaching customs – a strong pinch, a tug on the ear, or he would even honor the students with a blow over the hands, which would bring tears to the eyes. It is possible that he had to do this, that he had a need for this. His thoughts, feelings and devotions could not resist the far off, so that if he saw that some student is not progressing – he wished that the student would feel "as far off as he" – – –

Thus did the teacher Patalowski bear the heavy yoke for years, until he obtained a second place with more income in a second city.

Prior to his taking leave of Sochaczew, the thought was hatched to open up a modern school with modern arrangement and with a set curriculum. The "Hatikva" School was founded, with a certain amount of students who already knew Hebrew. The assistant of the teacher Patalowski became the head of the school.

{166}

Plucer

The new teacher took over a great deal from his Rebbe: being upset and beating the students. He did not think at all about the fact that the student was still a young lad, and that he should conduct himself entirely differently. Perhaps that was the reason that his state of health deteriorated. He coughed constantly and did not eat to satiation. He almost did not eat at all, but he was full of flaming fire. His Zionist speeches were inspiring, and the youth drank his words with thirst. The students also liked him very much, for he sacrificed for the existence of the school.

He conducted the studies for several years in that manner, until the school enlarged and they had to engage another teacher or two. He could not manage with the new teachers, for his hot temperament made it difficult for him to get along with people. He left the city.

He had many difficult years. He lived in a small room in an attic near the school, large enough for one person. He went hungry more than once, which caused his illness to worsen.

Later we heard that he was lying in critical condition in the Jewish hospital in Warsaw. Some of our friends visited him. Finally the news came that he was dying. We went to Warsaw, and found him already dead. Thus died the young temperamental Hebrew teacher who sacrificed his life for the Holy Tongue.

During the time of the interruption, the aforementioned wealthy families, Rechtman and Graubard, brought in a private teacher who, with the permission of those families who hired him, took on a few other children from the city, and further spread the Hebrew language. This was the teacher:

{167}

Aharon Rumianek

He was a Lithuanian Jew who knew Bible, Hebrew, and other subjects very well. The two aforementioned families put him up in their courtyard. All of the students in their courtyard studied with him, and also a few of the neighbors, such as Dawidowicz and others. Later Rumianek formed a group with whom he studied Ein Yaakov [6]in the Beis Midrash, and also established a group of Zionists to study Bible in the Beis Midrash. Because of him, the first scandal broke out between the observant Jews and Zionists who interpreted his words, which injured the honor of the observant Jews.

Moshel Grodzisker

He was a simple Jew, a Melamed like the other Melamdim, but with a different methodology. He wished to educate his students only with the Hebrew language. Moshel Grodzisker had his students. I still remember the names of some of them, like: David Wolrat, Shaya Rozenfeld, Pinka Kohen, Shmelke... Katriels, Ozer Warszawski, Graubard and Yaakov Szuster.

Aside from these, there were a few other teachers of children in the city – some who taught Talmud and others who taught Bible to the children.

{168}

Hashomer Hatzair
by Yaakov Frydman
Translated by Jerrold Landau

After the great suffering of the First World War, a new, free life began. The four years were marked with blood and destruction, and the future was seen as if through a fog. Nobody knew how and with what to begin, until Zionism arrived and opened up new perspectives. The Zionist work called and placed its demands. The young and old followed after the call, and a ray of new life appeared. The call was to go together and confide, for the word "Land of Israel" resonated deep in the Jewish heart, and the new word "Chalutz" (pioneer) attracted us to our Land, to a new life and future. The movement took off, and the nationalist youth especially threw themselves with their fiery temperaments into the arms of Zionism.

The situation of the children of age 12-16, mainly cheder youth, brought me to the realization that something must be done about the situation. However, it was not so simple. The children were not of one makeup, but rather came from various families, observant and secular, and one must earn their trust as well as their interest. We had to find the proper language and appropriate movement.

I organized a small group of children under the name "Pirchei Zion". After a certain period of time, I saw that this was not succeeding in attracting the children, especially the Orthodox children. However, I took a new step, rented a room and began to invite the children together, and systematically declared the purpose. Some of them were content with such a small movement, and others began demand a purpose, a program, for the program of "Pirchei Zion" was too weak. Then I found it necessary to connect with Zelig Wajsman of blessed memory of Warsaw, who at the time was the leader of Hashomer Hatzair. He advised me to adopt the program of Hashomer Hatzair for the children. The small group revived, and had an effect on the large number of new children who joined with the agreement of their parents. This was a very great step forward, bringing girls and boys together in one room where the conducted various sporting exercises and Hashomer style scouting activities, with a special emblem and uniform. The parents trusted me very much with their children. The movement organized itself very smoothly in accordance with the program, as a troupe divided into twelve tribes, with each tribe having its own emblem and leader. We began to learn the history of Zionism and the Land of Israel.

From time to time, the parents were invited into the headquarters of the Hashomer Hatzair, so that they could see with what their children were occupied, and how seriously they were enveloped in the new youth movement. They liked the regimen to which everyone submitted themselves, and all of the regulations. If a conflict broke out between parents and children, the parents turned to me – and everything was straightened out.

From time to time, Hashomer evenings were organized, which made a good impression. The income went to the national fund.

The first Lag Baomer expedition left a strong impression upon the Jewish population of the city. They saw for the first time in Sochaczew how their children marched under the national banner, like scouts with all of their details, through the streets of the city and out of the city into a fresh forest, to spend the day not only with "bows and arrows", but with pride and joy in the fresh air and open field. At night, when the expedition returned to the city, everyone was waiting for them, and looked for them with satisfaction. When we returned to the Zionist headquarters from where the picture of Dr. Herzl was hanging in honor of the expedition, everyone paused, and the young heads made an arc around the great Zionist leader. This had a great reverberation with the Jewish population, who perhaps witnessed this for the first time.

Keren Kayemet activists with Aharon Freidman of Jerusalem during the time of his visit to Sochaczew in 1937. The inscription on the photo reads: "In memory of the visit of Aharon Ish-Shalom from the Land of Israel on the days of 12-30 Tishrei 5698. The Activists of the Keren Kayemet LeYisrael in Sochaczew.

After the expedition, other children, young and old, came to us.

The development of Hashomer Hatzair, the first youth organization in Sochaczew, brought great benefit to the nationalist movement, and brought much life into the Jewish home. The parents assisted, with the hope that this would help them realize their plans to go to the land of Israel. However, only a small number merited doing that.

The Hashomer Hatzair in our city wrote a fine chapter of history during its short period of existence, until my leaving for the Land of Israel at the end of 1920. In order to commemorate my taking leave of the children on the final day before my departure, I photographed them – and this photograph remains as my only memento of all of them. They gave me the first emblem of the troupe and the banner as a memento, and to guard until they themselves would come to the Land of Israel, as well as a private small gift. They could not take leave of me, and the fair member Chaim Krongold, who became the leader after the departure of Zelig Wajsman to the Land of Israel, found it necessary to accompany my wife and I to the Polish border, in recognition of my service to Hashomer Hatzair in our city.

Thus ended a fine chapter in the life of our young children, who were later murdered by the murderous Hitlerism.

Hashomer Hatzair in Sochaczew.

{173}

The Worker's Movement
by A. Sztszafa of Paris
Translated by Jerrold Landau

I came to work in Sochaczew in the year 1926. A short time later, I founded a Communist circle along with Betzalel Jakubowicz, David Skornik, Yehoshua Skornik, Shaul Diamant, Gershon Peperkowicz, Chaim Meir Kalabielski, and others.

Later, two professional unions, of shoemakers and tailors, were founded. Berl Brzozowski (Sztivniak) [7]was the chairman of the shoemakers, and Mordechai Knobel was the chairman of the tailors. In the beginning, we were located with Yechezkel Bornsztejn on Warszawer Street, in a not overly large room that was furnished with one table and several long benches. Later we were located at Shmuel Gitejn on Warszawer Way (near the line that went to Wyszogrod). Still later, were moved to Yidel Loksztyk on Trajanower Street.

We created a library for the professional unions under the name "Worker's Library of the Professional Unions", where the working youth borrowed and read Jewish books.

From time to time, strike actions occurred. In the year 1928, a large strike of all of the tailoring workers took place, which ended with a victory for the workers. On May 1, 1929, a large demonstration of Polish and Jewish workers took place. On the eve of May 1, there were a few arrests of Jewish and Polish workers. My wife and I were arrested, among others. We were sent by train to Lowicz at night. We spent a day there, and were freed at night.

A Communist faction existed in the above-mentioned organizations, which in fact controlled their cultural and professional activity. We also had a "Moper" (assistance for political arrests) party cell.

Adam Kluska, Beniek Jablonka (the shingle maker's brother-in-law from Kaluszyn), Shaul Diamant, and others were active in the above mentioned organizations.

A Bund group was also active under the leadership of Sh. Swiatlowski and Yechiel Meir Zalcman (Szkalek). They joined together with the P.P.S. during elections. Shlomo Swiatlowski was the leader of the sick fund, and Zalcman was a member of the city council.

The professional unions were dissolved in 1930, due to police persecution. However a group of enthusiasts did not give in, and continued on with this work. In the 1930s, a sporting society was founded under the name of "Sztern", which was first located in the house of Nachum Warszawski, not far from the Magistrate. Later, it moved to the house of Zelig Izraelski on Warszawer Street. I was part of the management committee along with Yossel Grundwag and others.

We conducted cultural activities. The aforementioned workers library was given over to us. We even had a group that studied Esperanto. We often organized readings of Jewish and Polish writers and lecturers, which were well attended. We went on excursions from the city during the summer.

An especially honorable chapter in the Sochaczewer workers movement was taken by the dramatic circle, which was comprised of gifted amateur players. I will mention a few of the participants: Lipman Diamant, Aharon Kahn, Yossel Grundwag, Machla Szwarc, Shaul Diamant, Zalman Fursztenberg, Pese Fursztenberg, Aharon Grosman (from Wyszogrod), and Feiga Broder. They put on good performances. The beautiful decorations made an impression.

Our activity greatly assisted the development of the cultural level of the working youth of Sochaczew. Our readings were not only attended by the workers, who made a point of attending our performances. The entire organized Jewish community of our city loved our amateur players.

Thus did we maintain our cultural activity until the outbreak of the war in 1939.

TRANSLATOR'S FOOTNOTES:

1. Cheder Metukan is an 'improved' cheder, which employs modern pedagogical methods.
2. A Hebrew language teaching methodology (called Ivrit beIvrit) where the Hebrew language and even other subjects are taught with the language of instruction being Hebrew. This methodology is used in many present-day Hebrew schools as well.
3. A term for Hebrew. Here it is as opposed to Yiddish, which would have been the language of instruction in the older cheders.
4. Bible here refers to the Prophets and Writings (as opposed to the Chumash or Pentateuch). The study of these subjects in the traditional cheders would not be de-emphasized. Rather, after mastering Chumash, the students would have gone on to Mishna and Talmud.
5. 1905.

6. An anthology of the aggadaic (story type as opposed to legalistic) sections of the Talmud.
7. Shtivel in Yiddish is 'boots', so Sztivniak might mean the 'bootmaker'.

{175}

The First Amateur Theater
by David Wolrat
Translated by Jerrold Landau

At the beginning of the twentieth century after the period of the Sale of Joseph [1], my father returned home from America. He left with a Polish Jewish hat with a visor, and he returned with a short jacket, a hard, black men's hat, and a shaved beard.

Of all the miracles that he had seen in America and talked about, what he had seen in the New York Jewish Theater affected him the most. The stories strongly influenced my brother Pesach. Every evening, the audience of listeners grew in number, more and more. This was a daily event – every evening after work and dinner, our house with full. My father sat under the shine of a flashlight and talked. He also sang the songs that he had heard. The fantasies of the audience were awakened. People began to buzz, and theater became the source of excitement in daily conversations – until people boldly came to the idea that an amateur theatrical troupe should be created to perform a theatrical piece. After heated and sizzling debates, it was decided to perform Hertzele Meyuchas (Hertzele of Good Lineage) by Moshe Richter. My brother Pesach was nominated as director, and he put together a troupe. The biggest problem was – men, there were – but women?.... Whose respectable daughter would go out to perform in a theater...

Our relative Rivka Szwarcer was a frequent visitor to us – she was young and sweet, with a long, charming face, black hair, and a keksl [2] on the top of her head.

It did not take long for her to be overtaken with the desire to play in the theater. She girded herself in strength, and demonstrated her willingness. She ignored the scandals that took place in her home, that even led to slaps.

The roles were distributed as follows:

Hertzele Meyuchas:	Mote Pindek
Izikel his son:	Pesach Wolrat
Yankel the wagon driver:	Pinchas Rozenfeld
Teibele his daughter:	Rivka Szwarcer
Chava Leah:	Lozer Rozen [3]
Chaim Yoel:	Mordechai Hejman
Directed by:	Pesach Wolrat
Simcha Grundwag:	Prompter
Lozer Rozenfeld:	Decorations and makeup
Music:	The Rotsztejn brothers

On the Sabbath after dinner, the city was sleeping, the shutters were closed, my father was reading, my mother was tired and fell asleep. Outside it was sunny and warm, and the young people wished to go strolling in the Lustgarten [4]. I had a completely different desire on those Sabbaths. I had to accompany Pesach – we had a very important mission, since Pesach was the official "photographer" of the intelligentsia of Sochaczew. My mission as follows: to wait in the house until I was sure that father and mother were sleeping soundly. Pesach would then cautiously open the shutters to the outside, and then the windows. I then handed over to him the sizable apparatus. I then sneaked out through the window, closed the shutter, and carried the apparatus for Pesach.

We went to the Schlossbarg [5] and climbed up to the summit, where wall were standing that were marked with shots from bygone battles.

Already waiting there were: Yankel and Nachum Bombasz, the Dawidowicz brothers, Simcha and Nachum Grundwag, Simcha and Vove Rozenberg, Avraham Zylbersztejn (the jester, Pinchas Graubard, Moshe Sznajder with his girlfriend the daughter of Yosef Wolkowicz, Mote Pindek, Moshe Leder's son, Rivka Szwarcer, Gutsha Zajdendorf, Lozer and Pinchas Rozenfeld, Lozer Rozen, and several others whose names I cannot remember now.

There we began the first rehearsals of Hertzele Meyuchas. Pesach photographed the group between one scene and the next. Herman and Lutek Skotnicki stood on a neighboring hill playing Poliand [6] with the son of Pinie the rope maker.

Those rehearsals continued until late in the afternoon – when the sun already began to sparkle and reflect over the Bzura, which ran close to the hill. At that time, some of the group were sitting and others were lying on the soft grass, dreaming of the first performance.

When the stars began to appear in the deep blue sky, the group climbed down from the mountain and intermingled with the Jews who were returning from Maariv in the synagogue...

Eventually, posters began to appear on the streets. Curious young men and women stood in little groups with Parisian heads [7] – reading...

The entire Sochaczew was on wheels [8]. People could barely wait for the Saturday night when the troupe would appear in the new theater in Chaim Lezjor's place.

On Saturday morning, groups of wild people formed in front of the synagogue. They were delirious, and forgot that inside; they are already at the spitting [9]... In the community shtibel, the services were already long over...

Immediately after Havdalah, Shrege's [10] people began to line upon Trajanower Street – from Barsower Street until the Synagogue lane – all of them were streaming from Warsawer Street to the theater, where they pushed one on top of the other to purchase tickets. Inside, long rows formed. On the wall there was a portrait of the Kaiser with a number of medals on his chest. The musicians sat right by the stage, headed by Moshe Rotsztejn with his half closed tearing eyes... His face was adorned with a black trimmed beard – he played the first violin – his violin played best when he had first made Kiddush over a little 96er [11]...

Chaim Rotsztejn also had no objection to whiskey – he played the second violin. Yisrael Rotsztejn had a rosy, round face with a black, thick moustache, thick lips, and a small goatee [12] under his chin. He played the trumpet.

Tall Noach stood hunched over the bass and strummed.

At one point, Yisrael Rotsztejn stood up, and gave a signal to the orchestra. They began to play the overture. Hearts began to beat faster – the audience sprung up. A portion of the audience stood up on the benches.

In the cellar where the dressing rooms were located, everything was in a heat. It smelled like makeup. Lozer Rozenfeld applied makeup to the actors. The former young people suddenly grew older... they simply could not be recognized. I was getting in the way – passing the boots and kapotes to them – and to someone else, the whip and the cotton kaftan. Lozer Rozen, who was playing the servant girl Chava Lea, was standing in the hall, dressed in ladies shoes with high heels, with red makeup on his cheeks. On his hair he wore a long haired wig with a braid. He attempted to squeeze into the dress, and he required the help of the women. He attempted to take some steps and he fell – he was not used to these shoes...

Pesach was standing behind the scenes. He took a final glance to ensure that everything was in order. He looked through a specially prepared hole in the curtain.

The hall was full... Simcha Grundwag called the personnel to the stage. Everyone was in a fever due to nervousness. The bell was heard – a signal that the curtain was slowly opening. It was dark in the hall – it became silent and one could hear a pin drop on the ground – hearts stood still – the curtain was open, and the first words of Yankel the Wagon Driver could be heard from behind the scenes.

"Brrrrr, there is a frost today". Pinchas Rozenfeld made his debut.

The first act finished. The entire audience clapped bravo. The musicians played, the audience did not hear – a faint noise that grew louder – the bell rang – it was silent again.

During the second act, Lozer Rozen sang – "Chava Leah, good Sabbath". He begged her response. Suddenly, the soprano started. The audience gasped with laughter...

The final curtain fell, fell and rose. The audience did now want to leave. They tore toward the place of honor, for they wished to personally thank the actors who were still bowing down...

New stars appeared in the Sochaczew sky – wherever one went and wherever one stood, people talked about theater and the actors.

Sochaczew was elevated to new heights. Further performances were arranged – which included:

David's Violin: by Joseph Lateiner

The General Strike: by Herman Shtipt

Father and Mother's Problems: By Boris Thomashefsky [13] and Max Gabel.

However, the troupe lost one of its finest and most active talents. Pinchas Rozenfeld drowned while bathing in Gambin. He was fourteen years old.

The troupe made an impression not only in Sochaczew, but also in neighboring cities – where it was invited for visiting performances. I was the "kmahele" [14] of the troupe. I sang in the choir as we traveled to Lowicz – Grodzisk. Things went smoothly... Gradually, members of the group began to get married, and the period came to an end. It left behind a fresh excitement, which was taken over later by the younger group...

TRANSLATOR'S FOOTNOTES:

1. I am not sure of the reference here, but I suspect it is referring to the name of a play.

2. I am not sure of the meaning of this word. It is evidently some form of hairpiece.
3. This is a female role played by a man.
4. The public gardens (literally, Cheerful Gardens).
5. A hill in the city, as described in other articles in this book.
6. Probably a game called 'Napoleon'.

7. I am not sure of the reference here. I would guess that "Parisian heads" is a reference to sophistication and interest in culture.
8. An expression for excitement.
9. The 'aleinu' prayer at the end of services contains the phrase "And they bow down to emptiness and nothingness, and pray to a god that does not save" – referring to the idolaters. I accordance with some customs, particularly Hassidic customs, people discreetly spit when reciting this verse (immediately covering it up with their shoes). This is a play on words of the word 'nothingness' ('reik'), which can also mean 'spit'. This phrase here means "that they were already at the end of the service".
10. I am not sure what the term Shrege's refers to. It could be a personal name.
11. A reference to a type of whiskey.
12. The word used is 'fishbone'.
13. For a online biography of Boris Thomashefsky, see http://www.us-israel.org/jsource/biography/Thomashefsky.html.
14. I could not find this word in the dictionary. It appears to be of a Polish root, and probably means something to the effect of "choir director".

{186}

The Wind Orchestra

Yitzchak Wajnsztok

Translated by Jerrold Landau

The first pioneers who founded the Jewish wind orchestra in Sochaczew were a group of youth who had the strong striving and boldness to undertake such a colossal step as building up such an orchestra, not having any elementary means of doing so. At the beginning, they ran into great difficulties in obtaining the first instruments. However, they were not deterred by the difficulties, for they had a strong will and love of music. Then, the feverish work to learn how to play began.

This went on for a certain time, and then the results of the intensive work were evident. Avraham Nasielewicz and Hershel Graubard were able to play the cornet; and Hershel Oklanski and Yossel Grundwag – the baritone. Then there were successors, such as Yosef Kiejzman, Motel Groman, Sender Brot, Itche Skornik, Zawadzki, Wolf Itche Galek and others.

During the summer months, they engaged the gifted conductor H. Kumok from Warsaw, who rehearsed with the orchestra for a few months. Thanks to his intensive and diligent work, the orchestra began to appear publicly. But from whom does one obtain the money with which to purchase the necessary instruments? The members of the orchestra came upon the idea of organizing theatrical performances with their own energy, the income of which would enable them to purchase the necessary instruments. The plan came to reality. After an intensive period of effort, the orchestra developed such that it was able to perform publicly with a wide scope.

The feeling grew within the Sochaczew cultural life that there existed an orchestra. It always played between the scenes of a theatrical productions, at dance balls, etc. It represented the Zionist organization in Sochaczew with marching and playing on the streets of Warsaw at the celebration of the Balfour Declaration, and at Lag Baomer excursions.

The Orchestra.

When Nachum Sokolow visited his birthplace of Wyszogrod in 1924, the orchestra took part in the celebratory procession through the streets of Wyszogrod. That orchestra was a source of satisfaction and pride for the Jewish population of Sochaczew.

Unfortunately, due to various reasons, it could not maintain its independent existence during the final years, and it had to unwillingly disband. A few members of the orchestra played in the civic firefighters orchestra until 1939, when the anti-Semitic spirit began to be felt.

{189}

The Sochaczew Newspaper[1]

Yaakov Frydman

Translated by Jerrold Landau

Sochaczew did not stand out from other cities and towns in the country of Poland. Sochaczew also had its own newspaper for a period of time. It was a small pamphlet of four small printed pages, which was published only once every two weeks.

We do not know if the residents of Sochaczew had complaints that their newspaper was published only once every two weeks. Either they saw enough events with their own eyes, or they paid once every two weeks the few groszy which the newspaper cost. One can assume that they used their heads properly. We can rather ask why did Sochaczew, which was so close to Warsaw with its rich press, need its own newspaper at all? Would they have, Heaven forbid, felt at a loss without the newspaper? Why did they expend so much power and energy, as would be needed for such an undertaking, when Warsaw was right under their noses?

As it was, the temperamental youth of Sochaczew felt otherwise, and believed that our city must have a Yiddish newspaper.

The first edition of the "Sochaczewer Newspaper" was published on November 20th, 1936, on a Friday in Kislev [2]. It contained an editorial article with the signature "Ben Y." ("The son of Y.) and the headline: "A necessary effort". Ben Y. writes: "It was a successful idea to publish the newspaper, so that what is transpiring in our city and in the Jewish world at large will receive an appropriate reflection in the printed word."

"One must take into consideration that even in a small city, things happen that must be publicized and dealt with. Sometimes, there are things of first class significance from the Jewish society, neglectful communal leaders, or things that not infrequently cause a great shame, which are worthy of catching the interest of the Jewish population. The disinterest in these matters stems from the lowly societal life in our city, and therefore, I hope that we can improve this with this newspaper, which should make a breakthrough from the previous situation."

In general, Sochaczew with its newspaper at that time exhibited the appropriate interest in the problems of Jewry. This is shown in later articles. An article entitled "History Repeats Itself", written by "Hagiladi", dealt with the happenings in the Land of Israel; with "manufacturing in the Land of Israel"; with the demands of the nationalists and the Aguda, neither of which was willing to abandon their control. The article ends with the call: "The world should know!". A second article entitled "Present and Future" written by Yaakov Z-n, discusses the Jewish economy and specific economic condition, Zionism, the Land of Israel, etc. Further on, there is "Local matters": the merchant's union, the community, telling off somebody or another, written by Michael Kahn. There was an article by some A. B. against cooperatives, and thereafter a eulogy "by the fresh grave of Dr. Yehoshua Thon of blessed memory". The last article in the small newspaper was by S. Grundwag – "The Birthpangs of Local Zionism". This was a true piece of Jewish history in his fresh style. It is a great shame for us, the survivors of Sochaczew, as well as for Jewish history, that the article was not completed. Forty years of Zionist history in Sochaczew talks to us with the language of names, old well-known names, and pacts of blood. It will yet be told how the small town of Sochaczew, with its naivete, reacted to the large, world-wide Zionist movement, and the influence that Achad Haam, Kalisher, and Sokolov[3] had in Sochaczew.

Reb Yehoshua (Shia) Brzezinski

Grundwag's article justified the entire newspaper, and furthermore – showed clearly who were the planters of Zionist thought in Sochaczew, which led to several decades of Zionism. The newspaper carried on the same train of thought.

The second edition, which seems to be the last, is dated December 11, 1936, 27 Kislev. This edition was from Chanukah 5687 and the articles are similar to those published in the first edition. This edition also contained a continuation of S. Grundwag's article.

Sochaczew did not stand out from other cities and towns in Poland, either in religiosity, or in modern social and cultural life. The Hitlerist exterminations choked off the vibrant Jewish life.

A social activist, Menashe Knott.

TRANSLATOR'S FOOTNOTES:

1. The title of this article is actually a photocopy of the main caption of the newspaper. It reads "Sochaczewer Newspaper (Sochazczwer Caitung), Price 10 groszy, number 2, Published every 2 weeks. Sochaczew, Friday 27 Kislev 5686, December 11, 1936."
2. The date is Kislev is not given here, but from the photocopied title, it can be calculated that this was on 6 Kislev.
3. Early Zionist leaders.

{193}

Chevra Tehillim (The Society of Psalms)
By Elchanan Kac
Translated by Dr. Heather Valencia
Donated by Anthony J. Stern and Elaine Goldman

I remember the "Chevra Tehillim" from before the First World War, when, as a young boy, I went to cheder. My father was the gabay (warden) in the Chevra, and every Friday he gave me a list of the members of the Chevra, so that I could go to them to collect their weekly contributions. The money (one and a half rubles) was needed for the Rebbe who taught in the Chevra on Sabbath morning, before the morning prayers, and also before minkha (Minkha – the afternoon prayer); it was for the two shamosim (beadles) of the Chevra, Yakir Shuster and Reb Moishe Aharon the Shulklaper (the man who knocks on people's doors to remind them to come to the synagogue) and the rest for candles. The Rebbe was Reb Menashe Zimerinski of blessed memory. When he was teaching the place was always packed full with people. They even stood outside the windows. He was also a constant participant in the prayers of the Chevra, and on the Days of Awe it was his right to say Kol Nidre, Musaf and Neila (three of the five prayer services on Yom Kippur). The Chevra Tehillim was the biggest in Sochaczew, almost 60% of the inhabitants were members. The book containing the names of all the members was kept at our house. I used always to read the names and even then before the First World War there were names from 200 years previous.

The participants who prayed every Sabbath amounted to about six minyans (prayer quorums of at least 10 people) or more. They were to be seen once a year in synagogue, on Shavuot (The Feast of Weeks or Pentecost, 50 days after Passover) the anniversary of the death of King David. The synagogue was packed with people, and everyone was given the honor of reciting some psalms. And the respected members of the community were given the honor of Shir Hayichud (Literally – Song of Oneness, a series of seven responsive poems, corresponding to the seven days of the week that is said in some synagogues on festivals). Saying the first chapter of Shir Hayichud was the right of Reb Moshe Rechtman, then Reb Leibish Graubard, Reb Noach Deichus, Reb Binem Frumer, Reb Dovid Yitzchok Hamer, Reb Menashe Zimerinski etc. The Chazan sang Aanim Zemiros (The Hymn of Glory, sung at the end of the Sabbath and Festival services). We, the cheder boys went on the holiday from house to house with boxes, collecting candles for King David's yahrzeit.

Every Sabbath the Chevra members said the psalms. In the synagogue, in summer at three o'clock in the afternoon, and in the winter on Friday night at three in the morning in the Bet Midresh: precisely on time Reb Yakir Shuster called them to say the psalms.

When I was a little boy, I asked to be wakened up too, for I wanted to go with them to say psalms. My father did not wake me up, but my older brothers went with him. When I woke up on Sabbath morning, I wept because they hadn't woken me up in order to go. When I got older, I didn't have to plead, because my father used to wake me up in order to go to say the psalms.

Reb Mendl Frydman: one of the prominent community leaders.

Reb Shmuel Hacohen Zaltzman

The gaboyim (wardens) of the Chevra Tehillim were: the first warden: Reb Ezekiel Kac, second warden: Saul Fleishman, the third warden: Sholem Tzvi Soferman. The participants prayer every Sabbath, as far as I can remember, were: Reb Aba Kluska, Reb Menashe Zimerinski, Reb Moishe Berman, Reb Aharon Berman, Reb Saul Fleishman, Reb Ezekiel Kac, Reb Sholem Tzvi Sapirman, Reb Sender Biezanski, Reb Mendel Hitlmacher, Reb Yekhiel Feferkovitsh, Reb Yitzchok Erlich, Reb Tzvi Nelson, Reb Lipe Nelson, Reb Binyamin Rabinovitch, Reb Naftali Rabinovitch, Reb Moshe Levkovitz, Reb Mendl Stieglitz, Reb Berl Jakobowicz, Reb Nachshen Kefer, Reb Leibish Fleischman, Reb Leibel Taubenfeld, Reb Meyer Bzozowski, Reb Avrom Meyer Leizers, Reb Zisi Kaufman, Reb Moishe Kac, Reb Shmuel Kac, Reb Alter Berman, Reb Hertske Berman, Reb Berish Kac, Reb Avrom Kac, Reb Leibish Knott, Reb Eliezer (Leizer) Zuckerwitz, Reb Yisrael Moishe Zuckerwitz,

Reb Yitzchok Meyer Brofman, Reb Gershon Frydman, Reb Shaye (Shaykele) Frydman, Reb Berl Poznanski, Reb Shaye Poznanski, Reb Chaim Poznanski, Reb (Yaakov) Yankl Beker, Reb Shmuel Skurnik, Reb Yitzchok Grushko, Reb Yisrael Shaye Rutshteyn, Reb Leibl Zaltzman, Reb Yaakov Dovid Zaltzman, Reb Pinchas Zaltzman, Reb Eliezer Zaltzman, Reb Betzalel Zaltzman, Reb Dovid Berman, Reb Baruch Mordechai Kahan, Reb Chaim Kahan, Reb Pinchas Sheynwald, Reb Moshe Nelson, Reb Baruch Fleischman, Reb Pinchas Levin, Reb Feivish Holtzman, Reb Hershel Kluska, Reb Pinchas Beker, Reb Chaim Yorzinek, Reb Chanan Libert, Reb Eliahu Marienfeld, Reb Yisrael Wolrat, Reb Ezekiel Kezman, Reb Pinchas Blumenthal, Reb Meyer Blumenthal, Reb Zelig Gelbstein, Reb Mordechai Segal, Reb Shloyme Matsno, Reb Mayer Nashelewicz, Reb Yakir Shuster, Reb Moshe Aharon the Shulklapper, Reb Yosef Satenberg – all of blessed memory.

On the High Holidays even more people came, people from the villages too. The leaders of the prayer were Reb Hershel Biezanski and Reb Menashe Zimerinski. The one who always blew the shofar was Reb Henekh Brofman (now living in America). Of all the above named, some died before the Second World War, some went to America, and the others remained in Sochaczew until the destruction of the community.

The Chevra Tehillim was very well established in all respects. It also had a gemiles chesed fund (lending money without interest therefore "Free Loan Fund"). Every Friday one of the second gaboyim went round to collect the debts. Twice a year the accounts of the fund were calculated – during the intermediate days of Passover and the intermediate days of Sukkot. Every borrower had to pay off the rest of his debt. There were some who did not have enough to cover their debt. I remember that my father gave them money. They waited until after the meeting and took out new loans; and then they immediately paid back enough money to cover the previous loan, and they still had a few rubles left over for themselves.

Apart from the gaboyim there were also some among the participants who took interest in the poor people and they got money and helped them. And there were family men with 6-8 children, who did not even possess a groszy. Their work was hard and bitter, they lived on funds from the gemiles chesed, they borrowed on Sunday and gave it back on Tuesday, borrowed again on Wednesday and gave it back on Friday. And nevertheless the poor people lived a good family life, married off their children and had pleasure from life. The members of the Chevra saw that children did not suffer, and helped everyone. Mutual relationships were very fine. The poor man lived with hope and respect, and did not bear grudges against anyone. It was said that there was in Sochaczew only one case of tragedy.

Because of poverty: in 1880 a tailor, Reb Naftali Hirsch, a father of eight children, hanged himself because he was deeply in debt. His case was talked about for years after.

When one of the members of the Chevra Tehillim died , the Chevra members came to pray for the whole seven days, in the morning and evening. Sochaczew had a good reputation for its -support and -help for the needy.

Yisrael Meir Silberman.

Two adjacent tombstones of Silberman family.

Inscription on leftmost tombstone: Here is buried a man who died old and full of days, who did charitable and kind deeds. Our Rabbi Natan Notta the son of Akiva Moshe Zilberman of Sochaczew. Died 7 of Av 5670 (1910). May his soul be bound in the bonds of eternal life.

Inscription on rightmost tombstone: Here is buried the prominent youth Elchanan the son of Yitzchak Palet, who was cut down while in his prime. Died 12 Nisan 5688 (1928). May his soul be bound in the bonds of eternal life.

{199}

The Chevra Kadisha (Burial Society)
By Yitzchok Frydman
Translated by Dr. Heather Valencia
Donated by Anthony J. Stern and Elaine Goldman

This was one of the main organizations in every Jewish community. Not everyone was accepted as a member. One had to have great moral virtues and a good reputation. They were very special people. The fate of every deceased person was in their hands. More than once it happened that when affluent families did not want to give the Burial Society the sum which they asked for the work of burying the deceased, and there were scandals and quarrels which could last for two or three days. People were frightened of them for two reasons: firstly because they were dealing with dead people it is important to live in peace with them. And secondly, people always were wary of insulting members of the Burial Society.

Desecrated Torah scrolls are buried in 1916.

The cemetery was under their supervision, and they carried out their policy on burials. They decided the place for the grave according to the honor of the deceased or of his family. They did their work honestly, piously, and with purity, with the greatest respect, and without expectation of reward; but after such hard work, especially in winter, when they often had to stand for hours and burn wood on the place where the grave had to be dug, in order to warm up the earth so that it would be possible to dig – after this they would have a good drop of liquor. Twice a year they organized banquets.

Every Friday, a member of the Burial Society used to visit all the inhabitants of the town to collect the weekly subscriptions. They made a list of the needy, and took gifts to each one's house.

Moshe Temes Sheynwald

{201}

Life of the Spirit
By Meir Goldfarb
Translated by Dr.Heather Valencia
Donated by Anthony J. Stern and Elaine Goldman

The " Yavne"[1] school was under the supervision of the " Mizrachi" during the time when the Zionist organizations, artisans, small traders and merchants had the majority in the kehile; led by Biderman and the wardens Mantshik, Muney, Gingold, Lukshtik, they founded the school in the kehile building. At the same time the "Beys Yaakov" school for girls was founded in part of the same building.

The first director of the Yavne School was Yitzchok Shapira. In later years the building became too small for the school. So the Parents' Committee led by Yerachmiel Gersht and the technical secretary of the school Zaynvel Groinem rented more rooms for the higher classes from Hertske Tilman on Staszica Street. Then we pupils were not allowed to quarrel with the Polish schoolchildren as we had before, because all Polish school subjects were taught on the spot in the Yavne School. The teaching staff changed very frequently, and some only taught there for a short time, like the teachers Aronovich, Borenstein, Bialiskenski, Opotovska, Dr. Shapira, Aronson and others. On the other hand there were veterans who worked there at various times, among them the Hebraist Yitzchok Shapira, the Polish specialist Streicher, and the Talmudist Tzvi Drizhan, who before the war was invited to Finland as a teacher.

After finishing at the Yavne School the young people went their ways, either studying further or acquiring vocational training, and then began a struggle between the parties to attract the young people. Orchestras were created, ping-pong competitions were organized, and so on.

Some of the young people participated in various sports run by the Z.T.G.S. This was at the time the only Jewish sports club, and was led by Yoel Miller, Yisrael Ayzman and Leibel Zand.

At that time we were preparing to celebrate the fifteenth anniversary of the Sports Club. We young people founded a basketball team in order to take part in the celebrations. The young people were also active in all sorts of political youth organizations and also participated in the activities (puzzle evenings) organized by the Jewish Library. Naturally, young people also participated in the political struggle. We young people from the left wing had particular difficulties with our parents.

Hertzke Goldfarb and his family.

It was a surprise to everyone in 1939 when the Bund brought out its own list of candidates for the community elections for the first time. After a successful election campaign, the Bund succeeded in having two wardens elected, Hershel Warshawski and Aharon Greenberg. At the constituent assembly the Bund submitted as candidate for the presidency Hershel Warshawski. So the following situation had arisen in the election for the president of the kehile, Yosef Wolkowicz who had entered the elections with an independent list, had not voted for the candidate of the Agudas Yisroel, Yitzchok Winer, but for the Bundist candidate Hershel Warshawski.

Yudel Moshman

The result was four votes for the Bund and four for the Aguda. Rabbi Frekal did not want to cast the deciding vote. So it was decided to cast lots. The lot fell on Hershel Warshawski, but the provincial governor refused to ratify the election. Then, against the wishes of the Bund a pact was made between the other factions and Yitzchok Winer was elected. The provincial governor ratified his election.

The elections for the town council were another story worth telling. They took place on May 21, 1939. Anti-Semitism in Poland was then flaring up wildly. The main struggle was between the ruling party that had been recently created by the Folkist Adam Kac, "OZON", and the workers party P.P.S. But the Phalange with its anti-Semitic agitation and boycotts was also quite active.

On the evening of May 17th I was walking toward the bridge with Frimet Degenshein, Roza and Bracha Moshenberg, Yosef Goldhaft, Chaim Sheynwald, and others; we noticed that several people with sticks and buckets were standing at the house of Shimon Krakow and painting a picture on the wall of a Jew leading a pig on a rope. On the pig was written P. P. S. And under that was written "P.P.S. – zhidowow Pies. Later we met several members of the P.P.S. and of "Tur" with whom we decided to wash off the inscriptions. Then came the first incident between us and the anti-Semites who were guarding the graffiti. We had the better of them, but they continued their work nevertheless. The activists of the P.P.S. reacted appropriately.

Chaim Sheynwald – son of Reb Zalman

On May 18th Moshe Geier was arrested, and on the 19th many more people. The police were also searching for me.

On the morning of May 20th I was walking with Zalman Rosenkopf to the station to meet the representative from Warsaw, who was supposed to hold an election meeting.

The treasurer of the "Tzukunft" ("The Future"), Avrom Izralevitch was also on the train from Warsaw. After discussing the matter with the representative from Warsaw we decided that I should go and give myself up to the police.

When I arrived at the police station I met twelve detained comrades, chief among them the candidates for the town council elections, Chaim Pinczewski and Weinstein. After a whole day of examinations the group were brought to the beaten anti-Semites to see if they could recognize their attackers. It is interesting: they recognized the attackers, with the exception of two other friends and myself.

That same evening, after conducting the electoral meeting, the president of the "Culture League" Tzvi Warshawski along with the representative from Warsaw Yosef Guttgold came to the police station, and due to their intervention we were all freed. On Sunday, the 21st of May, during the day, the council elections took place in the town, and it was a festive day.

Yosef Nadelhaft – the son of Reb Naftali

You should understand that it was not without provocation that a group of "Falangists", headed by Gorski the son of a Polish merchant, fell upon the Jewish voters. However, there were no casualties. The final results of the elections were that the P.P.S. headed by a member of the "Bund", gained an absolute majority. The town became calm again after the elections. Many of the young people went to youth camps and a few took the exams at the end of the school year. In July, we were guests at "Zukunft", and the air still smelled of gunpowder. That was the time of the first mobilization. At that point, it was difficult to travel to Sochaczew.

On Sunday, September 3rd, the third day of the Nazi invasion of Poland, I went to the offices of "Zukunft" and burnt all of the lists and all the files of the archives of the "Culture League".

Three days later, the majority of the Jewish population was expelled to Warsaw. Many, myself included, were not able to reach Warsaw and remained in Blonie. On Rosh Hashana, the first Germans arrived in Blonie and took over the village. I returned to Sochaczew along with a few other young people before Yom Kippur. The Jewish quarter had been burned, the businesses plundered, and it was impossible to meet a Jew. I stayed over at Berl (Dov) Shladow's house on my first night in German occupied Sochaczew. Even the mattresses from the beds had been plundered. A few days later, more Jews returned from Warsaw, and we were informed at that time of the murder of the Gotthelf and Berg families in Warsaw.

In January, a few of us youths decided, with Zilpa Kahn in the home of Noach Deichus, to steal across the border to Bialystock. And that is what we did.

The Town Hall

TRANSLATOR'S FOOTNOTES:

1. Yavne is the name of a small town in Eretz Israel that was the first Jewish spiritual center after the destruction of the Second Temple.

{207}

The Cooperative People's Bank
By Shlomo Swiatlowski
Translated by Jerrold Landau

Sitting from right to left: Naftali Rabinowicz, Yankel Benczkowski, Hirsch Gutgiesztaldt (auditor from Warsaw), Avraham Rozenperl, Shmuel Kac. Standing from right to left: Hershel Gothelf, Aba Rejtman, Shlomo Swiatlowski, Motel Brzezonski, Manczyk, Mendel Plonski, and Yehoshua Liberman.

The rise of the economic institutions of the Jews of Sochaczew must be divided into two separate phases: 1) The Jewish economic institutions until the First World War, which were ruined, and the entire Jewish population had to emigrate and leave their possessions in G-d's custody. 2) The post war period, when the majority of the Jewish residents of Sochaczew returned to their destroyed homes, and began to rebuild the city together with the Polish population.

To the extent that my memory does not fail me, prior to 1914, there were no Jewish economic institutions in Sochaczew. This was aside from some philanthropic and charitable institutions such as "Linat Tzedek" and "Hachnasat Orchim", which conducted their activities but had almost no influence on the economic life of the city; and also aside from the small, private bank of Yechiel Meir Tylman.

The situation was entirely different in 1918, after the rise of the independent Polish government. The Jewish population of Sochaczew returned to the city, rebuilt the city, and reclaimed their destroyed economic positions.

In Warsaw, the Jewish handworkers and small-scale businessmen began to organize themselves. Under the influence of Warsaw, a "Handworkers' Union" was founded in Sochaczew, which was affiliated with the Warsaw central organization. The handworker activist Chaim Ratner stood at its head. A Handworkers' Bank was founded alongside the Handworkers' Union.

A little while later, the Socialist Workers Party founded a Socialist Handworkers Union in Sochaczew, and took the small-scale handworkers and home manufacturers into its ranks. Both of the handworker unions carried on an ideological dispute between themselves. Both were under opposing influences. However, both helped to rebuild the lives of the Jewish handworkers in Sochaczew and the economic stronghold, after the destruction that the war had caused.

The Polish chauvinism and anti-Semitism began to manifest itself in the New Poland with the politics of discrimination against the Jews in general, and against the Jewish small businessmen and handworkers in particular. A great danger stood before the Jews after the battle to retain their economic positions. The Jewish handworkers' organizations, both the Socialist one and the non-Socialist one, felt this danger, and a great wonder took place in Sochaczew – the uniting of both handworkers' groups. Thus was founded the "Jewish Cooperative People's Bank", which in effect united all of the Jewish organizations that were active in Jewish life in Sochaczew – from Agudas Yisrael and the Zionist organizations, to the Bund and Communists.

The initiator of the Jewish Cooperative People's Bank, who invested a great deal of energy in order to bring together the opposing factions to one table and create the cooperative people's bank – was Yaakov Benczkowski, a member of the Aguda in Sochaczew.

Yaakov Benczkowski, himself a handworker, owned a workshop for wooden soled shoes, called "trepes", in partnership with his brother and children. During the time of the war and shortly thereafter, when there was a leather shortage, "trepes" were a current commodity, and many Jewish families earned their living from them. Yaakov Benczkowski, however, looked a little farther: the times would return to normal, and "trepes" would have less of a use. There would be a great competition. The Polish cooperatives would become close to the government authorities, and something would have to be done so to ensure that the Jewish cooperatives would be able to compete. He made use of the esteem and trust that he had among all of the parties in order to make movement toward uniting them for the benefit of the Jewish handworkers and small businessman. From all of the small party-based banks, one large bank partnership would be formed – the "Cooperative Jewish People's Bank".

Yaakov Benczkowski's success was great. His plan was understood. They listened to him, and under the supervision of the central bank of cooperatives in Warsaw, and with an initial payment from the handworkers of Sochaczew from all sides – the Jewish Cooperative People's Bank was opened. A supervisory committee of five handworkers was founded, consisting of two Socialist handworkers, and three from "Aguda" circles. The bank began its operations. Its success was evident soon.

In the beginning, the bank gave out loans in the sum of 250 Zloty, which were to be paid back in sums of 10% of the credit, that is 25 Zloty. As time passed, the bank began to gain the confidence of the Jewish people of Sochaczew, and they entrusted it with their savings. The value of the loans was raised to the sum of 300 Zloty plus 200 Zloty of discount for promissory notes, together totaling 500 Zloty. This was a respectable sum for a handworker. It helped him to extricate himself from his financial difficulties, and left him over a reasonable sum for business capital, so that he would not have to rely on the Polish anti-Semitic banks, who would only make the existence of the Jewish worker more difficult. The Jewish handworkers and small businessmen could breathe easier. The felt that they could rely for assistance upon an institution that was concerned about them and that would support them during a time of difficulty.

The Cooperative Jewish People's Bank developed. The bank committee initiated premium savings books, with which a sum of 500 Zloty could be won twice a year. Thus did the savings in the bank grow. This gave the committee the possibility of increasing the credit to the sum of 1,000 Zloty – 500 for a loan and 500 discount.

The bank committee, however, was still not satisfied. The credit was too small to allow the Jewish handworkers to develop. The discrimination against Jewish handworkers and small businessmen became stronger. Jewish handworkers were not permitted into any open work, and the committee of the Jewish Cooperative Bank was obligated to turn to the supervisory council of the central audit committee in Warsaw to ask that they also permit the increase in the amount of credit in the form of vinkolatzia [1].

Vinkolatzia means that the handworker could purchase merchandise from the factory or the wholesaler on credit for his use throughout the entire season. This is so that he would be able to work in peace, and would not have to run to search for the little bit of merchandise that he needed for his work. The merchandise would be sent on the account of the bank, and would be distributed to the handworker in small quantities [2] in accordance to the needs of his work. The supervisory committee did not permit the vinkolatzia form of credit until then, for they were afraid of the great risk that the bank was taking upon itself.

Vinkolatzia was literally a salvation for the Jewish handworker. It enabled him to purchase larger quantities of merchandise cheaply, and the merchant or the factory would be assured of the money that was lent to the handworker. With the consent of the central audit committee, the Cooperative People's Bank of Sochaczew was able to conduct vinkolatzia transactions.

The Jewish tailors, shoemakers, and hat-makers were revived. The manufacturers and bulk merchants were able to stock merchandise throughout the entire season. The People's Bank of Sochaczew assured the entire amount. The credit was issued from the stock of the People's Bank of Sochaczew in small quantities[2], and each item of merchandise was accounted for separately. Thus was the handworker able to obtain merchandise for a cheap wholesale price. He was able to withstand the competition.

The Jewish Cooperative People's Bank existed and conducted its activity for the benefit of the Jewish handworkers and small businessman until the Hitler plague. The bank ceased to exist together with the last trace of Jewish economic life in Poland.

From right to left: Holcman, Aharon Frydman, Avraham Yitzchak Wajnberg, Avraham Yaakov Brzezowski, Elazar David Kac and Pinia Wajnberg as a child.

TRANSLATOR'S FOOTNOTES:

1. A banking term that is not in the dictionary, but is defined in the next paragraph of text. I detect the word 'collateral' in the latter part of the word.

2. Literally 'one by one'.

{213}

The Teacher of Children
Leib Fursztenberg
Translated by Jerrold Landau

It was in the schoolyard of the Powszechner[1] School. It was the major recess. The place was full with a few hundred children. Happy resounding voices were heard; people played, danced, sung, had fun, and one could see various pranks.

In one corner of the yard opposite the window of the administrative office, where the teachers rested and prepared for the second lecture, a group of children gathered together and built a type of large castle. In the meantime, two children were fighting, a Pole and a Jew. Although the Jewish child was one of those who does not let up, nevertheless… he accepted the blows, while all of the Polish friends added heat to the situation and encouraged the sheketz with shouts of "Give it to the Zyd!", "Kill him!", "Knock his teeth out", etc. We Jews stood and kept quiet, a bit from fear and a bit from timidity, and we could not help our beaten friend at all, for a statute existed in the Sochaczew school yard – if one student beats up another, no children should interfere. The sheketz became wilder, for the cries of the poor endowed him with more chutzpa[2]. He administered stronger blows to the Jewish child, and the Jewish child was already bloodied.

At that moment, a new teacher ran out of the teachers' room. He was chubby and not very tall. On his large head, which was out of proportion with his body, he had a bit of blond hair. He resembled a Christian, but with a pair of brown, Semitic, good eyes. He ran to the children quickly, broke them up, grabbed them both by the ears, and took them to the office. The Jewish child was saved from further blows and mockery from his mates. We Jewish children accompanied the teacher with thankful glances as he went back in. This was the teacher Kampelmacher.

Town activists near the municipal building

He came from a city in Galicia. He was a retired officer of the Austrian army. He was less than forty years old. He was very assimilated. He did not know Yiddish or Hebrew. He was sent by the committee of trustees to be a teacher in the Sochaczew public school.

He came at a time of disarray in the lives of the youth of Sochaczew. The "Hatechiya" Hebrew school had been liquidated, Hashomer Hatzair was dissolved, and the wind orchestra and stadium had disintegrated. It was prior to the organization of the workers organization. The only organization that existed was the library, which functioned in a weak fashion. There was a crisis due to the struggle between the Zionists and the Folkists.

Kampelmacher quickly sensed the situation. As a man with a sparkling temperament and a great deal of initiative, he realized that something must be done for the Jewish youth of Sochaczew. He approached the youth, initiated contact with them, and decided to create a non-partisan sports club. This was a new thing in Sochaczew.

However, from where does one obtain the money, for the city was impoverished? There was simply no money with which to purchase the first football[3].

He gathered together the more capable children from among the students of the Powszechner School and organized a choir in his own room (at the home of Velvel Pinczowski). He taught us a few songs in the Polish language (for he did not know Yiddish), and organized a recital on the intermediate days of Passover in the former hall of "Hatechiya". The purpose was realized. The following week, when the "teacher" was in Warsaw, he brought back the first football.

This was the beginning. We used to meet three times a week at the horse market near Mikhalski's mill to play football. None of us knew the rules of the game, including the teacher himself, for he had not received any training and had very little knowledge. He brought in Kova Gutein, who had studied in Warsaw and was one of the best players in the Warsaw club. The struggle for the maintenance of the club was now in process.

The youth of Sochaczew joined the sports club en masse. The rented rooms became too crowded, and it was not appropriate to run a club in an attic. One has to have a location. But from where would the money come? The teacher Kampelmacher had a new idea; to arrange dance evenings with a light recreational program such a choral singing, recitals, gymnastics events, or musical numbers. These evenings were given impressive names such as "A Grandiose Purim Ball", "A Chanukah Celebration", "A Dance Evening with a Jazz Orchestra from Warsaw". This was a new thing in Sochaczew. Until then, young people danced only at events in private houses or at weddings. At every meeting of the drama club, they would move aside the benches and dance.

The Women's Section of the Z.T.G.S. Editor's note, the Polish inscription on the placard reads as follows: "Z.T.G.S. Sochaczew I. Druiyna Zeniska 1923-1926".

Kampelmacher made completely new innovations. Tables for guests were set up in the finest halls of the city, which had already been decorated. There was a buffet with good food, and a good dance orchestra. The guests dressed up in evening dresses, each in accordance with their means.

In time, the club moved in to its own place. The football players already played with people from other cities, and with the local Polish clubs, who quickly began to imitate the Jew Kampelmacher. The premiere players already began to play in new football shoes and in a special club uniform – black pants and jackets with black and white stripes and an emblem: Jewish sport and touring club of Sochaczew in Yiddish, and Z.T.G. in Polish. A large mandolin orchestra was established with sixty people, conducted by the teacher who played the fiddle.

The first concert took place in Sara Ajzenman's as yet unfinished house, in rooms without windows or doors, with blankets hanging. Since it was during Chanukah, it was a little cold and we warmed up with Chanukah-punches and hot tea. The concert was successful and had positive reverberations the next morning in town.

In the summer, various activities were organized, such as: Leichtathletik[4], handball, ping-pong, gymnastics, boxing, chess, amateur photography, and touring.

The choir was well known at all of the concerts and entertainment balls in the city. It was the first organized section, and it sung songs in Yiddish, Hebrew, and Polish. The teacher, who himself did not know Yiddish and was far from Hebrew, suffered greatly to teach us the Yiddish and Hebrew version, to make the songs appropriate for Jewish holidays and celebrations.

The club grew in quick steps, and incorporated and interested almost all of the youth. Z.T.G.S. became a place for the youth of Sochaczew, where their interest could be stimulated. The teacher derived pleasure from his efforts and toil, and he always came with new plans. He intended to build our own tennis court. To this end, he obtained a plot of land behind the city from the magistrate. We went there with spades and hatchets, and flattened out the area with our own efforts. Several of the capable members built a tennis court with asphalt. Tennis rackets and balls were purchased, and the teacher was honored with the first game in Sochaczew, the first in the history of Sochaczew – on the tennis court.

The teacher set another, larger goal. He came with a plan to build our own house with a sport hall for gymnastics and entertainment evenings. We would obtain a plot from the magistrate. We had a few thousand Zloty, and the rest of the money we would have to raise from the people of Sochaczew. Due to the large sum of money that the house would cost, we suggested that the Jewish library build a Jewish culture house in cooperation with us. However, due to various personal reasons in the life of the teacher, for the first time, one of his plans did not come to fruition.

The youth of Sochaczew were musical. People loved to sing in Sochaczew. There were fine prayer leaders, and fine choirs that accompanied Cantor Shmuel Yechiel Liberman and the final Cantor Hersch Helmer. It was pleasant when Meir Nasielewicz sung. Between the two world wars, there were three wind orchestras in Sochaczew. The first was for simple music lovers. There was a second affiliated with "Hapoel", and the third was affiliated with "Beitar". This was over and above the mandolin orchestra and the choir affiliated with the sports club. Sochaczewers were active, good listeners, with a good conception of music; however they had very little knowledge of world music, of famous composers, musical works and the history of music.

It is said that foreign tourists used to come to visit the birthplace of Frederick (Fryderyk) Chopin, which, as is known, is Zelazowa Wola (6 kilometers from Sochaczew). One came a cross a notable woman from Sochaczew, and asked her if she knew how one get to the Chopin memorial. She answered "The 'szopes', the 'szopes' are not far, on Trojanower Street". She pointed to the fire station, which was known as "Di Strazhacka Szopes".

Kampelmacher taught us who Chopin was. He led us into the world of music, and imbued a love of music, fine arts and nature. He often took us to the house in which the great composer was born, and which had been converted into a small museum. In the evenings we would bring us out into the fresh air near the stream that crosses through the yard, and conduct a light discussion with us on the history of music. Even though not much changed in the house and yard of Chopin, we enjoyed visiting there often. We would sit in a circle by the willow tree, where Chopin used to sit for many hours, listening to its faint noise as he created his wonderful Polonaises and Mazurkas. We would listen to the teacher Kampelmacher relate his interesting discussions.

The holiday of the P. W. (youth organized into military cadets) was celebrated with an annual solemn parade and march-by. However, the high point of the program on that occasion was a football match between representatives of the Christian clubs with a club from another city. It happened that one day prior to the game, the foreign team decided that it was not coming. As the saying goes "Jak bida, to do Zyda" ("when in need, turn to the Jew"). They turned to the Jewish team and asked us to be the opponents. At first, we were frightened. First of all, we would be playing against a group of the best Polish football players, who had been preparing and training for this match for many weeks. We had not prepared at all. Secondly, we were afraid of being embarrassed in front of the population of Sochaczew. However, the teacher accepted the invitation, and believed in our abilities.

The football team. Z.T.G.S. Sochaczew.

On the designated Sunday, several thousand people, Jews and Christians, along with some guests from outside, gathered in the new sports place near the Kalajka. The Jews were nervous and awaited with fear the end result, which could have come with an embarrassment. The gentiles were in a good mood, and waited in crowds so that they would be able to make fun of the "Zydkes".

With pounding hearts, we played honorably. Our eleven players ran out, and were treated coldly. The Polish team was greeted with strong applause. The Polish referee, a captain in the army, blew a whistle – and the game began. A miracle happened and instead of we being on the defensive and them scoring one goal after another, we were on the offensive, and it was not long until we were in the lead by one goal. The power of our team continued, and they went over in a storm. At the intermission, the Jewish sport club was in the lead four goals to zero. The gentiles could not even score one goal against us. The Christian audience was siting with lowered heads, ashamed. They did not expect such a terrible outcome, and from whom – from a group of Jewish youth?

After the intermission, there was a change in the course of the game due to two factors. First, Yisrael Ajzenman, the best player of the team, had to leave for personal reasons. His departure weakened the playing and the morale. Secondly, the referee came to a decision that he must conduct the match in such a manner that the Jews should not, Heaven forbid, be victorious and win the cup.

Indeed, that is what happened. The referee did everything to ensure that we would not be able to shoot into the goal. The shkotzim scored five goals, legitimately and illegitimately. We were indeed defeated, but we left the playing field as the moral winners.

People talked about this football match for a very long time in Sochaczew.

The word that the teacher was leaving Sochaczew and traveling to Grodzisk was a hard blow to us. The reasons were many: Kampelmacher's greatest dream was to become the principal of a Jewish public school, where he would only teach Jewish children, and he would have the opportunity to use his capabilities and talents for Jewish children.

The second reason was that he was not accepted into the Jewish block for the city council elections, where he had always been a councilman, and always defended the Jewish people with his fine Polish. The teacher did not wish to be defeated and shamed before his Polish school colleagues. With our help, with the club, he set up a separate list. Unfortunately, the list was defeated, for we did not yet have voting rights…

The third reason was, I believe, the most important. They had two children, two sons. The eldest was Edek and the younger was Lundek. They were successful, fine intelligent children, who were raised with great love, especially by his noble wife Berta Kampelmacher.

It happened that the young Lundek took ill, and there was no salvation from the well-known doctors and professors from Warsaw. Our beloved friend gave up his young soul. The pain and sorrow of the family is hard to write about. A half of the city, Jews and Christians, took part in the funeral.

Kampelmacher left behind the sports club and everything that he had built up during that beautiful period. The majority of the youth from all strata were members of the club. Even Christians became members. The teacher was certain that he had left behind good, active deputies. He created a new management committee with the Wolwowicz brothers, the Miler brothers, the Balas brothers, Shmuel Rechtman, Reizl Brot, Chava Frajdman, Leibel Zand and above all the active and gifted Pinia Wajnberg, who was full of initiative and ideas. He organized Friday night lectures, discussions and other splendid evening events. Every Friday night, the club was full of young members and strangers. Hot discussions on various topics took place.

The Football team with the teacher Kampelmacher. Libert is on the left.

Wajnberg organized a chess and ping-pong tournament, in which many young people signed up. New sections were formed, such as a drama group, and P.W. (military cadets). L. Fursztenberg conducted the choir and the mandolin orchestra. It performed at a few large performances at the teachers' gathering in Poznan at the Land Exhibition[5], as well as in Gdynia, Kuzmir and nearby cities such as Plock, Wyszogrod, Bieliny and Grodzisk. New young powers joined the football team, and it later became the strongest football team in the city.

We had a great success with the "Little Maccabiada" in Lowicz. In 1932, the "Maccabi" of Lowicz organized a gathering of Jewish sports clubs from several cities: Kutno, Sochaczew, Skierniewice, Zyrardow, Gostynin and Lowicz.

Our Z.T.G.S. from Sochaczew represented itself finely. First of all, we all came dressed in uniform, and carrying the flag of the club. We obtained the first spot in the parade through the city.

However, these were the last fine active years of the sport club, for a decline started in 1933. Strong political organizations were set up in the city. Pinchas Wajnberg left the club and joined Hechalutz, whose aim was hachsharah for aliya to the land of Israel. The youth joined the new organization en masse. Soon after, Beitar was set up as a bourgeois movement, which also attracted a large number of youth from the club. The workers set up two sports clubs: the Bund set up "Morgenstern" and the Communists youth set up "Gwiazda".

The teacher Kampelmacher settled in Grodzisk. He set up an exemplary school for only Jewish children. In order to get over the death of his son, he devoted all of his energy, might and activity into his school. He displayed literally wonders in the organization. He built up his own school building, a sports club and a wind orchestra affiliated with the school. He was loved and appreciated by the youth of Grodzisk, just as in Sochaczew. We, his Sochaczewer students, cannot forget him. We remained in constant contact with him. We often came as guests to various celebrations of the Grodzisk school, and we also had sports competitions with the youth of Grodzisk. As well, the teacher, his wife and son came to visit us during our festivals and celebrations.

I believe that the last moments of his life, when his refined soul departed, were spent in some gas chamber in Auschwitz or Majdanek.

At the grave of Lundek, Kampelmacher's son.

TRANSLATOR'S FOOTNOTES:

1. Powszechne is public in Polish. The 'r' suffix is a Yiddish adjectival suffix.
2. Chutzpa does not translate well into English – roughly it means 'nerve', 'brazenness' or 'audacity'.
3. Soccer ball.
4. Leichtathletik – athletics. r
5. This sentence was somewhat confused, and may not be translated entirely accurately.

{227}

Rabbis of Sochaczew

Rabbis of Sochaczew
by Moshe Levanon

According to the history of the Jews in Sochaczew, it seems that the first rabbi who occupied the rabbinical seat was Reb Yonah Nachum Hakohen the son of Reb Meir Kac, a brother of the Shach (Siftei Kohen) [1] and a son-in-law of Reb Aharon Shmuel Kadynower, a student of the Gaon Reb Yaakov Tomaszower. He published his father-in-law's book "Birchat Hazevach" in the year 5423 (1669) [2].

It is written in the old ledger of the Chevra Kadisha that the rabbi, before his death, promised the city that in the event, Heaven forbid, of a time of trouble, they should come to pray at his grave, and the city would be saved. Individuals as well would be helped.

After his death, the community waited until the end of the thirty-day mourning period (Shloshim) and decided to erect a canopy over his grave. When they went out to the cemetery to accomplish this, they could not find the grave, and therefore, a canopy was not erected. Others told that some individuals merited seeing the grave and praying there. They were helped.

(See: Shem Gedolim Hechadash" paragraph 5. 8.)

Reb Moshele Charyf

In the old cemetery a grave with a very low, three-cornered stone, upon which one can barely make out the letters. This is the grave of Reb Moshele Charyf, a rabbi of the city.

He was great in Torah and in character. Jews used to pray at his grave.

(According to a tradition.)

Reb Meir the son of Reb Yitzchak Ajzensztadt

He was the grandson of a sister of the Shach (Siftei Cohen), and the author of the book "Panim Meorot". He was a rabbinical teacher in Sochaczew. He went from Sochaczew to Worms [3], and from there to other communities. His wife was the daughter of Reb Moshe from Sochaczew – probably the daughter of the aforementioned Reb Moshele Charyf. He died in the year 5504 (1704).

("Shem Hagedolim Leeretz Hagar". Paragraph 40. 14.)

Reb Aryeh Leib Charyf

When Reb Yeshayale Przedwozer and the Holy Jew left the Yeshiva of Reb Leibish Charyf, the head of the rabbinical court of Opatow (Apt) – he could no longer remain in Opatow, and he took over the rabbinical seat of Sochaczew. There he founded a large Yeshiva in which, among others, Reb Bunim of Przysucha, studied.

He was known by the name Reb Leibish Charyf. He lived in the time of the well-known Gaonim Reb Pinchas Horowitz from Frankfurt and Reb Meir Pozner, approximately in the year 5550 (1790). He was the author of the Novellae of the Mohara on Tractate Gittin [4].

("Shem Hagedolim Hechadash" 30, 17. See in "Siach Sarfei Kodesh".)

Reb Michele Magid

He was the head of the rabbinical court, a Gaon and Kabbalist. His son-in-law was the head of the Rabbinical Court of Serock (Reb Aryeh Leib). He was a holy and pure man. He was extremely meticulous. Among other things, in the summer, he was careful about mites in food [5]. Reb Leibish

Charyf would often say regarding him that if he had the power to taken on the same afflictions [6] as Reb Michele, the angels would be standing at the door. He died in the year 5588 (1838).

("Dor Dor Vedorshav" and "Siach Sarfei Kodesh".)

The Rabbi Reb Shlomo Yissachar Dov Ber

He was a son of Natan Aryeh, the judge and teacher in Hrubieszow. He was a great-grandson of the Pnei Yehoshua. They called him the Kurower rabbi. He had a strong dispute in the city. It is related in the book "Siach Sarfei Kodesh" that his disputant brought a judge into the city. On Friday, when the judge went to the ritual bath (mikva) a large crowed accompanied him with great honor. When this was told to the rabbi, he said: "It is indeed written that this is before the destruction of the Gaon". Indeed, thus it was. The judge went into the mikva, went into the bath, fainted and died.

Reb Elazarel, the later Sochaczewer rabbi, related that he studied with the Chidushei Harim in Warsaw. A Jew dressed in tattered clothing came to them and said: "There when they do not know me, it is permitted for me to say that I am a scholar. I am an expert, and I know the Even Ezer [7] by heart." The Chidushei Harim began to chat with him and saw that he was indeed an expert. The rabbi told them that the city of Sochaczew had driven him out...

The Chidushei Harim and Reb Elazarel together collected fifty dollars [8] so that he could get dressed appropriately. Later, he became the rabbi in Plonsk-Nasielsk and a teacher in Warsaw.

{229}

The Rabbi Reb Natan Frenkiel

He was a rabbi in Sochaczew. Responsa from him exist in the book "Divrei Chaim" and also in the book "Kinat Sofrim". He was also a rabbi in Staszow. His genealogy is written In the book "Tzvi Latzadik Moreh" of his grandson Reb Avraham Natan Ajzenberg (Chapter 9).

The Rabbi Reb Yaakov

He was a rabbi in Sochaczew and Sokolow. He was the father-in-law of Rabbi Yehuda Leib the son of Reb Asher Ginzberg of Vilna ("Anshei Shem", part 2, Section 10).

Reb Treitel the Rabbi

The rabbi honored his city. He did not want to take a designated salary from the community. He was a person who sufficed himself with little. They wanted to make him into a rabbi, but he did not want to accept a rabbinical seat.

(According to a tradition)

The Rabbi Reb Elazarel Hakohen the son of Reb Zeev Wolf

He was the author of the Novellae of Maharach [9], and the son-in-law of the well-known Lisser rabbi Reb Yaakov the author of Chavat Daat. In Sochaczew, he was called Reb Elazarel. The city related to him with honor and awe. He was great in Torah and Hassidism. He was from among the most important of Kocker Hassidim. He merited carrying the Kocker in his hand [10].

At first he was a rabbi in Pultusk, the in Sochaczew, and later in Plock. Then he returned to Sochaczew. All kinds of stories were told about him in Sochaczew [11].

Despite his greatness in Torah and righteousness, one could find people who impinged on his honor. Among them there was one Jew, a person imbued in Torah, even a rabbi, I still remember the man – from a deeply suffering family. The city related that this was a result of the impingement.

He died on the 21st of Cheshvan 5643 (1883) in Sochaczew. The community erected a canopy over his grave, and it was considered a great honor for a deceased person to obtain a gravesite near the canopy.

{230}
The Rebbe Reb Avrahamele Sochaczewer

Old time Hassidim relate that when news reached the Nasielsker rabbi and Hassidic leader of the time that Reb Elazarel Hakohen, the Sochaczewer rabbi, had died, his sorrow was so great and he could not find any place [12].

Standing thus by the window and looking into space, it was as if he was talking to himself – now they will call me to Sochaczew... It was indeed not long in coming, when the head of the community Reb Mendel Fromer (also a Nasielsker Hassid) accompanied by important householders went to Nasielsk with a prepared rabbinical script for Reb Avrahamel. However, he imposed some conditions: not to live in the communal house that was on top of the mikva, not to be required to be the officiant at every wedding, and that the shochtim (ritual slaughterers) must be under his supervision. He imposed numerous other conditions, to which the emissaries agreed. Nasielsk resisted, not wanting to let the rabbi go, but also not being able to prevent him from taking on the yoke of the rabbinate of Sochaczew.

The day of his arrival in Sochaczew was a festival. The honor at the reception was great. They unhitched the horses from the coach and people led him into the city. The new rabbi asked: "Is it possible that a human being should receive such honor? I have come to the conclusion that this honor is the honor of the Torah."

The new rabbi settled in his private house on Trajanower Street, which his Hassidim had purchased for him. Hassidim related the following regarding that house: the Kocker Rebbe went through Sochaczew, as he arrived from the villages of Snecemien and Luanczyn [13]. When he arrived at the house where a Russian postal official lived, he stood still and called out: a light of Torah shines out from this house, as well as some aroma of sanctification of the Divine name. (an innuendo of the four holy ones). This house, along with the city, indeed became known as a place of Torah.

The city was indeed happy with the new rabbi and greatly honored him. Jaszunski the forestry merchant sent the coach every day to take the rabbi to the synagogue to worship. The first time that the new rabbi came to worship in the synagogue, he turned to the worshippers with the following request: "I beg of you, Jews, do not take me as presumptuous, from my childhood, I have worshipped in the Sephardic style; and this synagogue worships in the Ashkenazic style, I beg of you Jews to permit me to worship in the Sephardic style [14]. Naturally, nobody objected. His word was holy.

He began to lead the city with love and simultaneously with discipline. From time to time, he sent his assistant to check the scales in the stores. He even sent him to check the fruit stalls in the market to see that they do not display fine produce on top to cover up rotten produce. He penetrated all domains of Jewish life in the city.

For various reasons, he established an early prayer service on the Sabbath (Jews called it "davening by Shkama") [15].

With time, he also founded a Yeshiva in which students from all over Poland studied. If one talked about a student, one understood that he was a Sochaczewer student of the Avnei Nezer. He simultaneously strengthened Sochaczewer Hassidism. More Hassidim came, and the city was full with the spirit of Judaism and Hassidism. Old Sochaczewer Jews talk about that era with awe and honor, and they refer to it as a "Golden era". It is necessary to point out, though, that the greater portion of the population was not happy with the strictness in Judaism.

It was once told to the rabbi that there was going to be a wedding in the city at which boys and girls were preparing to dance together after the wedding dinner. The rabbi summoned the good Yeshiva student Feivish (the shochet Reb Shmuel Yechiel's brother-in-law) and asked that he go with him to the wedding ceremony. The parents of the bride and groom found this to be a great joyous occasion – it was a big deal that the Rebbe had come to their children's joyous occasion. How taken aback were the parents when the rabbi sat down to talk and study with Feivish after the ceremony. He did not want to involve himself with the meal. Rather he sat and talked until the last of the guests, along with the band players, left the wedding hall.

Naturally, such incidents aroused ill will among a portion of the Jews. At the beginnings of the Zionist movement, he at first related to Zionism as if to an awakening of the settlement of the Land of Israel, which he held to be a great mitzvah. I still remember the shekalim [16] that were purchased by a Hassidic Jew (a Sochaczewer Hassid), and the Rebbe found out about this.

Similarly, when people began to tell various stories in a certain manner, and therefore the Zionists of Sochaczew founded a modern cheder (Hassidim called in "Cheder Mesukan") [17] – he called out in wonder: "So is it! They intend something different, not only the Land of Israel". An order then was issued not to purchase shekels.

Thus, differences of opinion between the two sides began to be formed; Reb Chaim Mordechai Wolkowicz (Yosef Wolkowicz's father), Moshe Czemiernicki and Zalman Albert were at the head of the one side. At the head of the other said were Gedalia Warszawski, Simcha Grundwag, and Aharon Rumianek – all of them Zionists. It came to be a quarrel, and even came to blows. The peace was disturbed.

It was also no easy mater to have a rabbinical judgement with the rabbi. One of the litigants merely called out a loud "Good morning, rabbi". He considered this as the borderline bribery, and would not agree to conduct the judgement. If a rabbinical judgement was indeed taking place; when the time came to issue a decision, he would wrap himself up in his tallis and shake for a few minutes so that a fear would fall upon the litigants – for he had advised everyone not to hold a rabbinical judgement. It was also not easy to come to the Rebbe in his home. An exception would be made if he were to be informed of an ill person. The Shamash (attendant) would make an announcement, even in the middle of the night. His sermons in the synagogue were also sharp. If the rabbi was going up to the Holy Ark to deliver a sermon, he rapped himself up in a tallis, shook for a few minutes and said, "And may a redeemer come unto Zion and let us say Amen". Thus did he end his sermon. This caused excitement among the Hassidim, and wonderment among the regular people.

{233}

The First Expulsion

We do not know why the local authorities sealed up the Rebbe's private Mikva and courtyard. The fact is that when Reb Avrahamele needed to go to the mikva, they released the lock and he was able to enter to immerse himself. Shortly thereafter, the authorities in Warsaw challenged him. The wealthy forestry merchant, Yitzchak Engielman, who knew Russian, went with him as a translator. The governor asked, among other things, if it was indeed written that the law of the land is the law [18]. The rabbi answered regarding this that the law is applicable when the rights of all of the citizens are equal, but if the Jews are treated as exceptions to the law, then the law is not applicable to them. (We do not know if Reb Yitzchak convinced the governor of this.) Reb Yitzchak Engielman managed to persuade the governor that he (the rabbi) was not a traitor against the government... (In truth, it was otherwise.) Therefore, he remained rabbi, but received a severe warning.

Two Jews were engaged in a bitter monetary litigation. The sum was not large, perhaps more than a hundred rubles. The lender, seeing that the borrower was denying the loan, made use of the law of that time that the court should demand an obligatory oath. The lender demanded a Torah ordained oath, that is, by utilizing a Torah scroll and a black candle. He also demanded that the administrator of the oath should not be the rabbi but rather the Tzadik (as the Christian people called him at that time). Naturally, the court demanded the oath. They informed them of this in the Rebbe's court, but Reb Avrahamele did not want to obey. His intimates began to negotiate with the lender and wanted to give him a sum of money equal to the claim, but this did not help. He demanded nothing other than an oath. He believed that if his co-litigant would swear, he would drop dead on the ground.

On the designated day of the oath, the Russian judge, his secretary and a soldier in uniform came to the synagogue to administer the oath. However the rabbi did not come. On the spot, they wrote a report to the regional council (gubernia), and a few days later, an order came regarding the upcoming resignation [19] of the rabbi. When he heard the news, Reb Avrahamele called out: "If I would have lived in the forest, the trees would fight with me".

His intimates made strong efforts to have the decree repealed. The expulsion order was repealed after strong efforts. However, the resignation order remained – and he became an ex rabbi [20]. He was the rabbi of Sochaczew from 5653 until 5651 (1883-1891). He was known as the Sochaczewer Rebbe under the name "Eglei Tal" or "Avnei Nezer" – the works that he wrote over the course of several decades. Even now, in the year 5721 (1961), one can find a new publication of the Mishna with the glosses of the Avnei Nezer, that elicits great interest in scholarly circles.

He died on the 11th of Adar 5670 (1910). From the time of his burial until the erection of the canopy, two Hassidim stood by the grave even on the Sabbath. This also occurred with respect to the grave of the first Sochaczewer rabbi, Reb Yonah Nachum Hakohen.

The city could not make peace with the departure of Reb Avrahamele from the rabbinate. He still remained as the rabbinical leader, the slaughterhouse remained under his supervision, and everything that was done took place with agreement of the Rebbe's court. This lasted for a long time. The community did not want to take on a second rabbi, and no rabbi wanted to take on the rabbinate of Sochaczew. This went on until an order came from the regional council (gubernia): If the city does not engage a rabbi, they would send in a "Kazionem" [21] rabbi. Thus it was.

{234}

The Kazioner Rabbi

Sochaczew was getting a "Kazionem" rabbi, after a long chain of glorious rabbis. First of all, the rabbi was a Lithuanian. It was difficult for him to understand how to speak to the Jews of Sochaczew, and it was also no simple matter to understand him. Therefore, he behaved like a puppy. It never happened that the puppy came to the synagogue later than he did. He was present at every wedding ceremony. The rabbi and teacher [22] conducted the ceremony, and he arranged the civil documents. They never came to the rabbi with questions of kashruth. It once occurred that a Jewish woman came to him with a question about a little bit of milk that ran under a meat pot. The rabbi did not know what the issue was. He asked her: "How much does a pot cost?" She answered, "Five groszy". He answered her, "Take five groszy, Madame and do not bother me."

He used to come to the Rebbe's table celebration and even obtained some leftovers and wine [23]. He was not able to remain for a long time in the city, and he left after a few months.

{235}

Reb Yerucham the Rabbi and Teacher

He was a quiet man who did not know how to raise his voice. In his time, he took the position of a rabbi in the city. He came to help Reb Bunem the teacher, the Kocker Hassid and great scholar. They both occupied themselves with answering questions, conducting marriages, etc.

A city must have a rabbi, and the communal leaders turned to the Rebbe to bring in a rabbi. The Rebbe turned to Reb Shmuel Turower, a scholar, important Pulawer Hassid, and a teacher of select students. Rabbi Turower was intertwined in a sharp dispute. Presently, he was having a dispute with Shmuel Yechiel the shochet of the Rebbe's court. For a long time, he would not eat meat that was slaughtered by him, even at the Rebbe's table. Furthermore, they called him "the trusted one", since he placed candles in the window when it was a Russian holiday. In Sochaczew, there was no need for a sharp dispute to flare up. The sophisticated portion of the people supported Rabbi Turower. On the other hand, the Hassidic Orthodox householders (and who at that time in Sochaczew was not Orthodox?) were against him. During that time, it occurred that young women, mothers of young children of good lineage, died [24]. The Jews of Sochaczew associated this with the sin of the dispute. Rabbi Turower himself left Sochaczew for London, where he died.

Rabbi Shmuel Yitzchak Landau

He was a grandson of Reb Wolf Strykower, and a great-grandson of the well-known Czekanower rabbi, Reb Abraham. After this, when the city was once again left without a rabbi, the "Eglei Tal" sent Shmuel Yechiel the shochet and a few other important residents to Sobota, where Reb Shmuel Yitzchak was, with a rabbinical writ. There they asked him, under orders from the Rebbe, to accept the rabbinate of Sochaczew.

Rabbi Landau left the city of Sobota, acceded to the request of his Rebbe the Eglei Tal, and arrived in Sochaczew in the year 5661 (1901). He was 26 years old at the time. I remember the rabbi very well.

No dispute occurred during his 12-year rabbinate, despite the fact that he was strict in matters pertaining to Judaism. The city honored him. He loved his fellow man greatly. "Linat Tzedek", "Hachnasat Orchim", "Bikur Cholim" [25] and other such institutions were founded under his supervision. He supported people with weekly stipends, and poor sick people with free medicine. He was the victim of a robbery. They stole his pillows. He did not want to inform the police, for it is possible that the thief was a Jew who needed the pillows to sleep upon. During that time, they honored him with being the sandek at a bris [26] (such was the custom in the city). When they brought in the child to be circumcised, the rabbi recognized the pillow upon which the child lay as his pillow. However, he did not let on that he knew. At a bris of a poor family, he used to send liquor, bread, and herring, and saw to it that those gathered washed their hands for the meal [27]. Later, someone abandoned the pillows in the rabbi's house. He sent for the man whose child had the bris and asked him to come. He requested that he no longer steal. Following that, he would secretly send that man one ruble and twenty kopecks every Thursday. His sermons excelled in Halacha, exegesis and didactics. Regular people and scholars of Sochaczew enjoyed these sermons. At the funeral of the Rebbetzin of the Avnei Nezer, the Avnei Nezer asked the rabbi to say something. Rabbi Landau delivered a eulogy. At the conclusion, the Avnei Nezer called out to him: "The local rabbi spoke well! Well spoken!" A portion of his sermons, including the eulogy that he delivered for the late Hirsch Friedman, are published in his book Chidushey Sh"Y (Shmuel Yitzchak), published by his son Rabbi Wolf Landau in Tel Aviv in the year 5760 (1960).

He left Sochaczew in the year 5671 (1911) to take over the rabbinate in Czekanow, where his holy grandfather, Reb Avraham of Czekanow, used to be the rabbi. He died on the 24th of Tamuz 5675 (1915) at the age of 40 years. It is worthwhile to read about his death in the aforementioned book of Chidushey Sh"Y.

At that time the following rabbi, Rabbi Frenkiel, was the rabbi.

{236}

The Final Sochaczewer Rabbi

After Rabbi Landau left Sochaczew, a small dispute broke out between the local residents and the family of the Rebbe's court. It was not very widespread. The city agreed in principal that the rabbinate should pass as an inheritance to the Rebbe's court. However, who should be the rabbi: the son of Reb Shmuel (The Shem Mishmuel), the current Syszogroder rabbi and final Sochaczewer rabbi Reb Dovidel, or the son-in-law of Reb Meirl Borensztejn, Reb Avrahamele's brother, the husband of Rebbetzin Hodel who was a granddaughter of the Avnei Nezer. The Shem Mishmuel wished that his son Reb Dovidel would be the rabbi, however he wanted the agreement of everybody. It is entirely possible that if Reb Meirl did not claim that the inheritance of the rabbinate should go to his son-in-law, Reb Dovidel would certainly become the rabbi. Since there was resistance from within his own family, the Shem Mishmuel presently demurred. The Sochaczewer Hassidim even wished to participate in a competition, however the Shem Mishmuel strongly prohibited it. It is interesting that Reb Meir succeeded in attracted the entire Zionist segment of the population of the city, headed by Reb Simcha Grundwag. Thus was the sole candidate, Rabbi Tzvi Frenkiel, elected. The Sochaczewer Hassidim, and the Hassidim in general, did not participate in the election.

Rabbi Frenkiel was a great scholar and expert in all aspects of Torah. He occupied himself with Torah day and night. In his youth, he studied together with the writer Mr. D. Nomberg, and they were good friends. Unfortunately, the city did not have any benefit from his learnedness and expertise. He was hard of speech, and he could not benefit the people with sermons. Therefore he acted quite cautiously with every step in the city which had, in his opinion, any connection to Judaism.

It should be stated here in praise of the Jews of Sochaczew that despite all of this, they honored him. On Shabbat Hagadol or Shabbat Shuva [28], when the rabbi delivered a sermon, the synagogue was packed with householders and Hassidim, not so much to hear the sermon as to give the rabbi honor. Even the sophisticated people related to him with honor. Some juvenile [29] dragged him out of his home by the hands, sick and weak, placed him in a car, and drove him to Warsaw, where he died in the ghetto during the years of the Nazi tribulations.

{237}

The Final Rabbi and Teacher

Reb Leibel Wolman, the son of Chana Bencjanowski (from her second husband) was a grandson of Reb Aharon Grynszpan. He was born and raised in Sochaczew. He was a friend of Reb Alexander Zisha Frydman. He picked up his fundamentals in learning from the teacher "The small Moshe Dovidl", with whom not more than four youths studied. He also absorbed Torah in the year 5674 (1914) from the Rosh Yeshiva Reb Aryeh Leib Fromer, who headed the final Yeshiva of the Shem

Mishmuel, and later in the Yeshiva of Chachmei Lublin. The rabbi and teacher Reb Leibel Wolman taught only in Sochaczew, and was accepted unanimously by all strata. The Jews of Sochaczew said that he was of their own flesh and blood, for he was locally trained. He was indeed great in Torah. He was murdered along with the Jews in the Warsaw Ghetto.

{238}

Rabbi Elazar Hakohen
M. B. Sztejn
Translated by Jerrold Landau

Reb Yehoshua, Reb Elazarel's son, lived in Sochaczew until the First World War. He describes the following story in the booklet "Eitz Avot", printed at the end of Reb Elazarel's book "Chidush Mehrech".

Reb Elazarel was a Baal Tokea[30] in Kock during the life of the Kocker Rebbe, Reb Mendel. One time near Rosh Hashanah, Reb Elazarel began to ache in his neck, and it was doubtful if he would have the power to blow the shofar. He went to the Kocker Rebbe, Reb Mendel, and complained to him.

The Kocker strongly answered him: "Is it only you and none other who can blow the shofar?".

Reb Elazarel responded: "I don't know whether or not I can".

"Hirsch!", The Kocker shouted out to his steward Reb Hirsch Parcower: "Take out my fir boots from under the bed and give them to the Baal Tokea to wear!". He said the following to Reb Elazarel:

"Wear my fir boots and go blow the shofar."

Reb Elazarel was left standing in amazement. The Rebbe was short in height and he was tall and wide boned. The Rebbe's fir boots would not go over his feet.

However, what the rabbi planned for was doomed. Reb Elazarel left the Rebbe and with some difficulty forced the Rebbe's small boots over his large feet. The Rebbe's fir boots hurt his feet until his heart clouded over. He limped with every step. He did what the Rebbe bid, and he went limping into the Rebbe's Beis Midrash, blow the shofar as the Rebbe had commanded, and his neck no longer hurt him. Thus relates Reb Yehoshua the Rebbe's son.

If one does not look at the story, it is evident that it is very characteristic of Reb Elazarel's entire life.

He was born in Warsaw to a father who was a manufacturer and merchant, Reb Wolf Lajpcykier, who had the merit of being a Parnas (communal administrator) in Warsaw. In his father's home, Reb Elazarel was raised in a broad, mercantile, wealthy environment, and nothing was too expensive for Reb Elazarel. His father hired the best teachers from outside of Warsaw for his son.

When Reb Elazarel came of age, his father made a match for him with the family of the great Gaon and halachic decisor from that era, Reb Yaakov the Lisser Rav[31], the author of many erudite halachic books and Lisser Rav.

So that he would be able to study as a married man with the Lisser Rav, the wealthy Wolf Lajpcykier invited the bride, Breindel the daughter of the Lisser Rav to him in Warsaw, and sent Reb Elazarel to study in Lissa with the Lisser Rav.

Reb Elazarel's grave canopy among other graves in the Sochaczew cemetery.

As he did previously in Warsaw, he sat day and night in the Yeshiva of the Lisser Rav and studied; he studied and succeeded. He became an expert in Talmud and halachic decisions. Everyone who came into the home of the Lisser Rav could not stop wondering at him. Thus did he continue to study after his wedding with the daughter of the Lisser Rav as a young man under parental support (kest). Already at that time, he merited being chosen as the judge of Lissa. The story went as follows:

Once, the Lisser Rav issued a decision regarding a question, and later realized himself that he had erred; that his decision was not in accordance with the law. The Lisser judge saw this as a sign from Heaven; from Heaven he was made to err, and they did not want him to decide questions any more. He called together the heads of the community of Lissa, and said to them as follows:

"Chose another rabbi for yourselves, I can no longer serve as the rabbi."

"What does this mean? For what sin? If the rabbi does not earn enough from the rabbinate, we will gladly add to the amount", they retorted.

The Lisser Rav answered the communal leaders as follows:

"I erred in a decision, and I will no longer accept any questions to decide upon, for how can I be the rabbi of Lissa? Search for a different rabbi who is able to decide upon questions."

The Lissa communal heads answered:

"To decide upon questions, one must engage a judge, and the rabbi can continue on as a rabbi."

The Lisser Rav agreed. The city engaged a judge to decide upon questions, and the judge was the rabbi's son-in-law Reb Elazarel.

Reb Elazarel did not remain in Lissa for long. The time of kest (support) from the Lisser Rav ended, and Reb Elazarel did not wish to remain in Lissa, living in difficulty and dependent on the goodwill of the community. His father's wealth awaited him in Warsaw, and he preferred to be a wealthy householder in Warsaw, giving out with a generous hand, to being the judge in Lissa.

When Reb Wolf Lajpcykier, the wealthy manufacturer and merchant, found out that his son was thinking about returning to Warsaw, he furnished a house for him in regal fashion and opened a silk warehouse for him, so that he would be able to maintain himself on his own and would not have to come to his own father in need.

Reb Elazarel returned to Warsaw with great honor. Being such a great scholar and the son of the wealthy Reb Wolf Lajpcykier, no honor was lacking for him in Warsaw. Both the Hassidim and Misnagdim of Warsaw had respect for the Lisser Rav's son-in-law, and Reb Elazarels's wealthy house became a warm home for scholars and Hassidim.

Rabbis and Gaonim who came through Warsaw saw it as their duty to be with Reb Elazarel, and his name became known among rabbis and scholars. He became an important person in Przysucha with Reb Binem. After the Rebbe's death, he became a householder in Kock, with Reb Mendel the Kocker. One time, when Reb Mendel Kocker was not feeling well at the table celebration (tisch) for Shabbat, Reb Elazarel took him by the hand and led him to his own private room.

Reb Elazarel became a central figure in Warsaw as well. The heads of the community of Warsaw suggested that he become the Parnas of the place of his father Reb Wolf Lajpcykier, who was still an elder at that time. However, Reb Elazarel did not want to be a communal activist, which would take away time from his learning. Similarly, he also did not want to submit his candidacy as a rabbi in Warsaw during this time of the great dispute between Hassidim and Misnagdim regarding the rabbinical seat in Warsaw. The Hassidic candidate was the brother-in-law of the Kocker Rebbe, the Gaon and future Gerrer Rebbe, Reb Itche Meir. The Misnagdic candidate was Reb Yankele Gesundheit, the future Warsaw rabbi. Reb Elazarel's candidacy as a Kocker Hassid and son of a Parnas of Warsaw had every chance of being accepted by both the Hassidim and Misnagdim. However, he did not want to remove the "narrow boots" and enter into a dispute. Therefore, he declined to submit his candidacy as the rabbi of Warsaw.

However, he had to put on the "narrow boots" for many bad conditions. The choice was not in his hands, and he was forced to put them on.

His father Reb Wolf Lajpcykier went the way of all the living, and left his son Reb Elazarel an inheritance of 150,000 rubles (a large sum in those days). This inheritance gave Reb Elazarel the possibility of becoming a larger building contractor, and he undertook via competition to build the Warsaw Citadel for the Russian regime.

The undertaking of such a large-scale project for the Russian regime seemed to everyone to be a stroke of luck. However, the Russian regime told him to send non-salaried workers from Russia for free. Reb Elazarel had to hire workers in Warsaw and pay them from his own account. At the end, he came out of the "large undertaking" as a large poor person. The inheritance from his father was lost to him, and he was left in debt.

He had to take on a rabbinical position in order to sustain his household. It was not to be in Warsaw, but rather where something was available. Thus, he became a rabbi in Makowa, later in Pultulsk, and in the year 5610 (1850) he became the rabbi of Sochaczew.

Walking in the "narrow boots" was painful, and even bound up with greater agony than he had ever lived through. And who was so guarded as Reb Elazarel? Being rabbi in a city meant that he would be the opinion maker of the city. The city had to obey him in every matter, and his words were decisions about which nobody could even question. In what type of city would a rabbi at that time have no opponents? And what rabbi in that era did not have to endure shame and friction from the heads of the community?

Reb Elazarel, as much as was possible, exchanged the "narrow boots" and sought out ones that were mainly still narrower. From Sochaczew, he went to Plock, and again to Makowa. From Makowa, again to Pultusk, and from Pultusk, he came in the year 5630 (1870) a second time to Sochaczew.

He was always wandering. His lot, which the Kocker Rebbe Reb Mendel decreed on him that Rosh Hashanah to wear specifically the narrow boots and blow the shofar, remained with him for his entire life...

Reb Elazarel's final rabbinical position was in Sochaczew. During his first tenure as rabbi, the good earth of Sochaczew claimed his 12 year old genius son Efraimel in the year 5612 (1852) during the cholera epidemic.

The Rebbetzin Breindele could never forget Sochaczew during all of Reb Elazarel's rabbinical tenures, where her Efraimel had died. She returned there in the last years of her life to be near her son in the Sochaczew cemetery.

Reb Elazarel died in Sochaczew in the year 5642 (1882). The Sochaczew community erected a canopy over his grave, not far from the Bzura.

During times of tribulation, the Jews of Sochaczew would pray over his grave, and the peaceful Bzura more than once heard heart-rending cries from his canopy.

{244}

My Father of blessed memory
Zeev Wolf Yechiel Landau
The publisher of the book "Responsa of Sh. Y." [32]
Translated by Jerrold Landau

The writer of these lines is the son of Rabbi Shmuel Yitzchak Landau of blessed memory, who was the rabbi of Sochaczew between the years 5661-5672 (1901-1912).

Peace reigned in the city during the time of his rabbinate, and all segments of the population related to him with respect. He excelled in his fine character traits and in his truth and simplicity with his relations with everybody, whether great or small.

He also excelled in the philanthropic domain. Aside from his activity on behalf of the Yeshiva in which he gave a lesson, he founded the "Hachnasat Orchim" ("Society for Taking Care of Visitors") under the direction of Avraham Chaim Kuper, Leibush Keller, Meir Dajchus and David Lichtensztajn. He also founded the "Chevrat Linat Tzedek", which would sent volunteers to protect and help poor sick people. Father of blessed memory used to also give out notes to obtain medicine from the pharmacy, and he would send sick people to the doctor without a fee. The feldschers [33] Skotnicki and Leibush Feldscher used to also visit sick people without taking a fee. I remember that Moshe Engielman, Henech Zajonc and Shlomo Grodzisker – all now have passed away – used to collect money together with father for the needed expenses.

Father of blessed memory was beloved by everyone, including by the members of the Chevra Mishnayot (the Mishna study group) and Chevrat Tehillim (the group of reciters of Psalms). It is worthwhile to mention the image of the Shamash (sexton) of the Chevrat Tehilim, H. Jakir, a shoemaker who used to awaken the Jews to recite Psalms. "My beloved people, I wish to tell you something: the clock has already stuck three, and it already time to recite Psalms". These words were sweet and heartfelt, and the Jews would get up and go to recite Psalms.

Once on a winter night, Reb Jakir fell down in deep snow, and he was unable to move from there. He was already elderly by then. Suddenly a handsome Jew appeared near him, and bade him to stand up and continue to call the Jews to recite Psalms. He immediately disappeared. Reb Jakir used to say that it was King David [34]...

The sounds of Torah and sounds of Psalms were heard in Sochaczew until morning.

Reb Hershel Brzezinski.

I wish to make mention here of the Talmud Torah, with its Gabbai (trustee) Reb Baruch Najman and teacher Reb Moshe Itche. From the beginning of the month of Elul, they would come with the students to recite Psalms in the Beis Midrash every morning; and then they would partake of cookies and candy. Father of blessed memory was the examiner who examined the students. He used to take interest in every child separately, and he concerned himself at the beginning of the winter with the providing of boots and warm clothing for them. The melamed (teacher) also used to study with his students with great love and dedication for every child, as did the other melamdim Reb Yankel Melamed and Reb Yeshayahu Yonah.

Who does not remember the elderly Reb Binem Melamed, who used to occupy himself with raising money for the Land of Israel? He was always studying. His wife had a stall in the market, and did business with bags. Thereby she provided for her home.

I wish to also mention here the mohel of the city, Hirsch Frydman, who would go to the surrounding village in order to circumcise children. He did not ask for wages, and he would not even take money for his expenses.

Our gabbai (synagogue trustee) Reb Hershel Brzezinski would check the eruv [35] with dedication, to ensure that it was in order.

All of these personalities are individuals within the precious human mosaic of old Sochaczew.

TRANSLATOR'S FOOTNOTES:

1. The Shach is a well-known commentator on the Code of Jewish Law (Shulchan Aruch). The commentaries of the Shach and the Taz appear prominently on the main folios of most printed editions of the Shulchan Aruch.
2. There is a mismatch of dates here. 5423 would correspond to 1663.
3. Spelled in its Jewish form her "Vermaiza". Worms is a city in the Rhineland area of Germany, and is known as the city of the famed Biblical and Talmudic commentator, Rashi.
4. Gittin is the Talmudic tractate dealing with the laws of divorce.
5. Mites are forbidden to be eaten, and one must be careful of infestations in otherwise kosher food.
6. Self afflictions and denials for the purpose of enhancing one's spirituality.
7. One of the four sections of the Code of Jewish Law, dealing with marital laws.
8. A dollar is not the Polish (or Russian for that matter) unit of currency, and is apparently used here as a generic term for a unit of money.
9. The acronym of his name Moreinu Harav Elazar HaKohen.
10. Possibly meaning "to walk hand in hand with the Kocker".
11. This implies stories of works of wonder.
12. I.e. he was at a loss.
13. I could not identify these villages.
14. Sephardic style (Nusach Sephard) does not refer to the true North African and Middle Eastern Sephardic prayer style, but rather to an adaptation thereof that is used by Hassidim. European Misnagdim use the Ashkenazic prayer rite.
15. A Hashkama Minyan (early prayer quorum) refers to a Shacharit service conducted at the time of sunrise, considered the most propitious time for this service (albeit the service is valid for the first three hours of daylight). The colloquial name for this given here is obviously a play on words.
16. Tokens of membership in the Zionist organization.
17. This is a play on words. Cheder Metukan is "Modern Cheder". Cheder Mesukan is "Dangerous Cheder". h
18. There is a Jewish law that states that the law of the land is the law (known as Dina Demalchuta Dina).
19. Seemingly a forced resignation.
20. I assume that this means that he formally relinquished his position of rabbi of the city. He obviously stayed on as Admor.

21. This term means "commonplace". The implication here is seemingly to a government appointed rabbi.
22. Here seemingly referring to Reb Avrahamele.
23. It is a custom at gatherings around an Admor for the people to eat the leftovers (sherayim) of the Rebbe.
24. This implies that there seemed to be a spate of untimely deaths, probably due to illness. r
25. These are the name of various charitable institutions.
26. A sandek is the man upon whose lap the bris takes place.
27. A bris ceremony is supposed to be followed by a celebratory meal. A poor family would have difficulty in affording this.
28. Shabbat Hagadol is the Sabbath before Passover. Shabbat Shuva is the Sabbath between Rosh Hashanah and Yom Kippur. On both of these Sabbaths, it is customary for the rabbi to deliver a major address about the upcoming festival.
29. Obviously referring to a young Nazi.
30. The man who blows the shofar for the congregation in the synagogue on Rosh Hashanah.
31. The rabbi of Lissa.
32. The Sh. Y. is the acronym of the author's father, about whom this article is written.
33. A feldscher is a 'barber surgeon', which would mean a medic or an amateur doctor.
34. King David is considered to be the prime author of the book of Psalms (although various chapters in the book are attributed to other authors).
35. On the Sabbath, it is prohibited from carrying objects from a public domain to a private domain and vice versa, and also from carrying objects within a public domain. (The technical halachic detail of this law is beyond the scope of a footnote). Under circumstances where this prohibition is of rabbinic rather than Torah origin (which for practical purposes includes most circumstances), an entire area can be halachically converted into a private domain by the construction of an eruv (Sabbath boundary – literally 'intermingling' of domains). Today, most cities and towns with a reasonable sized Jewish community have an eruv.

Sochaczevers - Their Role in Cultural and Spiritual Life

Alexander Zisha Frydman

{249}

Alexander Zisha Frydman
M. B. Sztejn
Translated by Jerrold Landau

In the final years prior to the Hitlerian war, Alexander Zisha Frydman did not belong to Sochaczew alone. As the general secretary of Agudas Yisrael in Poland, he belonged to all of Polish Jewry.

His grandfather Friman Hirsch Frydman was one of the notable activists in Sochaczew. Alexander Zisha's childhood and youth were spent in Sochaczew. He was a student of the Sochaczew Yeshiva that was run by Reb Avrahamele Sochaczewer.

Already as a youth, Zisha Frydman (as he was called at that time) showed great capabilities in learning. Not one Sochaczewer alive today can still remember his youthful voice, which was heard in the large Beis Midrash of the Sochaczewer Rebbe from morning until late at night. From that period of Zisha Frydman's life, Dr. Hillel Zajdman in Morning Journal brings down the following episode:

"In Warsaw there was a well to do Jew, a homeowner and a merchant, who imported watches from Switzerland. His name was Meir Yoel Szwarcsztajn. He came upon an idea as to how to infuse the youths with a desire to learn. He would examine them, and if the student did well on the exam – for that Jew was himself a scholar – he would receive a "prize": an authentic Swiss watch. The greatest geniuses would get the best watches.

Zisha Frydman's watch, which he received at the time of his Bar Mitzvah, still ran – as he showed me – when he was in his forties."

His illustrious youthful years in Sochaczew accompanied and lit up Alexander Zisha Frydman's political activities in Warsaw. Dr. Hillel Zajdman further relates:

"In all his days, when he was extremely busy, he not only knew how to learn, but he learned in a scholarly manner. He studied not only Talmud, but also Tanach (Bible). He had rabbinical ordination, but he did not wish to serve as a rabbi, even though he had all of the qualifications for that.

His Torah novellae[1], published in "Degel Torah", that was issued in Warsaw during the 1920s by Rabbi Menachem Kasher (the author of "Torah Shleima"), were recognized by scholars. His book "Kesef Mezukak"[2] – as the well-known Warsaw banker and philanthropist Refael Szereszewski referred to him – was both pedagogical and scholarly. His collections under the name "The Torah Well" were not only obscure "items", but even more so, they were full of breadth and sharpness.

He loved Hebrew. He was the pioneer of the Hebrew press of Agudas Yisrael in Poland. He was the founder and editor of the "Digleinu" ("Our Flag") newspaper, and later of "Darcheinu" ("Our Way"), which were published in Warsaw.

His articles in "Yid" and in "Yiddishen Tagblatt" in Warsaw were full of temperament and logic. His style was fine and clear.

Zisha Frydman was the greatest organizer. As general secretary of Agudas Yisrael in Poland, he was responsible for the significant growth of that organization during the latter years. He put in much energy to this."

Alexander Zisha Frydman, the great organizer who was responsible for the growth of Agudas Yisrael in Poland, the general secretary of Agudas Yisrael, was more of a populist activist than a political activist. He left "the politics" for others, and primarily involved himself with education. He was the executive director of the "Chorev" religious educational organization. This was a continuation of his years of Yeshiva in Sochaczew. He was appointed over the "clothers of the naked"[3] of the Yeshiva students. This is what he was involved with when the misfortune of Jewry, the Nazi invasion of Poland, took place. As Dr. Hillel Zajdman relates:

"The war came, and then Zisha Frydman showed his true colors. Already from the very beginning, the greatest victims were the Orthodox Jews, and especially the rabbis, educators, scholars and Yeshiva students (why this was so – we will leave for another time – Z. [4]). Zisha Frydman heard the heavenly voice: "Woe to humanity for the disgrace of Torah"[5] . He was the constant intercessor for those categories of wronged, neglected, forlorn people. He never ceased to make the rounds to all of the committees, assistance organizations, communal institutions, the "Joint", etc., saying: "Woe to the generation in which you are the communal leader, for you do not understand the agony of the scholars"[6]. They did pay attention to him, either because of his sincerity, or because, as they knew, he was the representative of religious Jewry. Later, everyone recognized him as the leader of religious Jewry, despite the fact that he did not want to take on any official position.

In 1940, he was invited to be a member of the communal committee: he declined. Later, Adam Czernikow, the communal leader, begged him many times to take a seat on the communal council. On can surmise that he tried to encourage him with, aside from the salary of 1,000 zloty a month, a set of benefits and a certain level of security. He never agreed. He was committed solely to the work.

This activity, which he undertook for a few zlotys to cover his basic needs, grew into a grandiose, multi-branched assistance effort, with many public kitchens, schools that served as secret Talmud Torahs[7], Yeshivas, Beis Yaakov courses for girls[8], classes and libraries."

He was in his prime when the Nazi murderers entered Poland. From among the Jewish political activists, who did not make haste to save their own skins and leave the Jewish masses to their fate, Alexander Zisha Frydman remained at that unfortunate time in his position, and together with those that remained, bore the Jewish fate in the ghetto.

"Alexander Zisha Frydman became a shoemaker in the "Shop" of the German firm "Schultz" on Nowolifia 44-46. The foreman was Mr. Avraham Hendel. Many rabbis, rebbes and scholars were employed there. He resided in the dwelling of Mr. Yosef Krel (junior) on Nowolifia 59. He worked in the workshop for an entire day or an entire night, twelve hours straight. I visited him there. He was sitting in good company: Moshe Betzalel (the brother of Alter, the Gerrer Rebbe); the Piaseczener Rebbe Reb Kalonymus Szapira; the Sosnowiecer Rebbe Rabbi David Halbersztadt; Rabbi Alter; the Rapaport brothers – Mendele, Simcha, Aharon and Yaakov from Bielec. They would remove nails from old shoes and study Mishna from a book that was lying on the knees under the tabletop. Reb Zisha Frydman recited the Mishnas to those gathered around. They were studying the Mishnas from the Order of Moed[9]. In the evening when they came home from work, he taught an in-depth class in Talmud discreetly to youths. He also taught a chapter of Bible from the book of Jeremiah. Thus did one live, between fear and hope, as one drew strength from the Torah, "from the eternal wellspring". Zisha Frydman completed his book on commentaries on Torah and the Bible, called "Even Haezel". He showed me several thoughts that actually came to him at the workshop. I now understood how Rabbi Yochanan Hasandlar was able to be a shoemaker and a Talmudic sage simultaneously...[10]"

At the end, he drank from the bitter well. He alone remained from his family. In the despair, he elevated himself and wrote a poem.

"He was very deeply pained. He remained alive alone. He lost his entire family: his wife and his beautiful daughter, who was born 11 years after his marriage and who was 13 years old. A splendid child, raised in the manner that an educator such as Zisha Frydman was capable. He wrote a Hebrew poem, in which he lamented his beloved child. He showed it to me. In it he wrote that he does not know what to request, whether she should come back or whether she should be no longer alive: that she should have an easy death and not have to suffer any torture."

The Nazi murderers could not break him. Steadfast like an oak tree, he withstood all of the tribulations. He fulfilled his task, which was indeed a part of him – to help Jews. But who could he help, for soon there was nobody to help, for those who remained alive had to live underground in order to avoid the danger that hung over them like a sword over the head, and the sword could drop at any moment. Hidden in bunkers, they studied Torah in the modern language, as Dr. Hillel Zajdman relates:

"In the Warsaw ghetto, there existed a combination: Yeshiva-bunkers.

'Bunker', which for the Germans connoted a nest with machine guns from where one shoots, in the ghetto connoted – an underground cave where Jews hid from the Nazi slaughter. Often the bunkers were equipped with various amenities: running water, electric light, and gas; and when students studied in such a bunker with great rabbis, it would be called – Yeshiva-bunker. There were many of these in the Warsaw ghetto.

From where did they obtain their food? How could they sustain themselves with the stocks?

A new factor entered into the picture, Zisha Frydman. He was certainly one of the finest august personalities, not only in his own personal history, but also in the general history of Warsaw Jewry.

Zisha Frydman, already without his family, working as a "shoemaker" in Schultz' "shop", ran around all day – and it was indeed a danger at that time to go around in the streets – knocking on all the doors and collecting food for the underground (literally) Yeshivas.

The task was a difficult one, for during that time now, unlike now, people did not only keep their daily provisions on hand. No, that was not sufficient. People had to put aside "stocks", and who knows for how long? The longer the better, for one has to have enough provisions to hold one over until the end, i.e. until the day of liberation (they did not yet know that bombs would eventually be thrown into the cellars).

Zisha Frydman found for this task men who had an understanding of Torah and the concept of the sanctification of the Divine name. His confidantes included: Avraham Gefner, the president of the Central Jewish Merchant's Union prior to the war, and today the director of the food office of the Judenrat; Yitzchak Giterman and David Goszik, the dedicated director of the Joint (it was no simple matter at that time to be a director of the Joint... today it is much simpler. They helped him warmly, and provided the needed sums and large reserves of food.

Frydman also provided food for the rabbis who studied with the students in the Yeshivas. The following Torah luminaries were in Warsaw at the time: Rabbi Menachem Zemba; Rabbi Ari Fromer, the former rabbi of Kozieglowy and later the Rosh Yeshiva[11] of Lublin; Rabbi Ari Leib Landau, the Kalibieler rabbi and also a Rosh Yeshiva in Lublin.

Reb Yehoshua (Shea) Frydman and his wife, the parents of Alexander Zisha Frydman.

Thus did hundreds of Yeshiva students sit in bunkers, studying day and night in depths and innovating thoughts of Torah. The rabbis gave classes and lectures, and conducted the learning.

Above ground, in the "legal" world, the Nazi murderers raged about, carrying on with frightful cruelty; while underneath, below the ground, Jews sat immersing themselves in Torah, as they lived in the netherworld full of refinement, displaying the epitome of spiritual strength.

The regime of the deepest darkness reigned above, and the light of the sanctification of the Divine name – through life – went on beneath the ground. The voice of Torah rose from the deepest depths.

I was in those Yeshiva-bunkers more than once. In the first place, when I came inside from the street, where the Nazi beast lurked in every corner, it brought to mind images of ancient times: of Rabbi Shimon Bar Yochai, who studied Torah in a cave, which was also a Yeshiva-bunker [12]; of the Marranos in Spain, who also served G-d from their hiding places, and whose light still shines to this day.

Thus should the light from the Yeshiva-bunkers of the Warsaw ghetto shine.

Heaven and the abyss merged together.

Between them fluttered the soul of the nation. The light from "down there" is their legacy.

In our own precious legacy, we must preserve the light from this legacy."

Zisha Frydman was active in the Warsaw ghetto until 1943. He was a member of the resistance committee. At that time the murderers deported him from Warsaw to the Trawniki labor camp near Lublin. In one of the "selections", he was sent in the known direction.

May his memory be honored!

May his soul be bound in the bonds of eternal life.

TRANSLATOR'S FOOTNOTES:

1. A Torah novella (in Hebrew, a chidush – an innovation) is a reference to a novel Torah thought.
2. Refined Silver. Books of Torah thoughts often are entitled by the nickname of the author.
3. A reference to the daily morning blessing, thanking G-d for clothing the naked (i.e. providing humans with clothing). Here it apparently refers to teachers, who spiritually "clothe" the spiritually "naked" young students with the "clothing" of Torah.
4. Z. is evidently the initial of the interjector of this comment into the text. It must stand for Zajdman, the author of the quoted text.
5. A "heavenly voice" here is literally a "bat kol" ("a daughter of a voice") which is a term used in Talmudic literature for a message from Heaven after the termination of the period of Jewish prophecy. The quote here comes from the sixth chapter of Pirke Avot (The tractate of The Chapters of the Fathers).
6. A quote from the Talmudic tractate of Brachot, chapter 4, rebuking a communal leader whom did not realize the dire straits that the scholars lived in.
7. Torah oriented schools.
8. Orthodox girl's schools are often given the name "Beis Yaakov".
9. Mishna is divided in to six Orders (Sedorim), and each Order is subdivided into tractates. Moed (Festivals) is the second Order of Mishna, dealing with the laws of the Sabbath and festivals.
10. Rabbi Yochanan Hasandlar (literally, Rabbi Yochanan the Shoemaker) was a talmudic sage who was a shoemaker by profession. Many well-known Talmudic sages earned their livelihood from their own professions.
11. A head of a Yeshiva.

12. According to the Talmud, Rabbi Shimon Bar Yochai spent thirteen years studying Torah in a cave with his son, hiding from Roman persecution. They were sustained by the fruit of a carob tree.

{257}

Ozer Warszawski

Lea Kenig

Translated by Jerrold Landau

Ozer Warszawski

A.

When we are to talk about Ozer Warszawski the artist, we must gird ourselves with strength and forget about his tragic end: We have sufficient self-esteem – and we are guilty towards our literature – not recognizing our own artists, when they fall like martyrs.

I am also certain that Ozer Warszawski would himself have had it thus.

I see Warszawski's slender, elastic figure; his pale, half-boned face, as he talks, standing over an aperitif in the café on Montparnasse:

"Go, forget it. don't even mention it... if you want to draw me – draw; if you want to paint my portrait – paint... make a good thing, but without the olive oil embellishments about holy martyrs. I have a good face for a holy Antony, or Reb Nachman...However, be careful not to fall into artificial falsehood, in poses... in "composition"... Make a good portrait, if you can. A human face is indeed a world with form, with lines. And a martyr's wreath around the skull can have a theatrical effect, and can spoil a good portrait of a person.

... Do not speak about my end. I have completely disappeared, as one who disappears in a thick, English fog. I am like one who became lost afar in a strange place, one does not know where, far from myself and friends. It is better thus, I wish to die only where one sees them die, however I have disappeared and am lost – I believe that they will not return... Therefore one does not know if one should sit Shiva [1] for them.

The immortality of those who disappeared and who are lost. Perhaps the only immortality..."

B.

Ozer Warszawski is – and will remain – a lonely figure in our literature. A one of a kind in many important details:

He appeared to us not like most of the Jewish writers, with "first steps", with sketches, with short, promising narratives and songs; He appeared suddenly, was quickly noted and became well known in our literature with a large work, with a large novel. And this is a rarity. I cannot mention whom of our older and younger Jewish writers and poets showed such maturity, such a thorough entry into our literature.

He probably also wrote before the publication of his "Smugglers"; perhaps he also published something, but nobody heard of his first steps. Suddenly a Jewish novel was published in Warsaw – a large one, a robust one, a new novel – and Ozer Warszawski became famous. Ozer Warszawski became a figure in our literature. (Already the mere sound of the name Ozer Warszawski implied something ready, something mature, although he was in his early twenties when he wrote the novel.) Naturally, we will all greatly rejoice when as yet undiscovered, important writing of his will be found. He would always experiment in his writings during his later years; however from 1920 until today, we know him especially as the author of "Smugglers".

We certainly know that he wrote a fine number of works after that novel. He wrote a large work "Harvest Time", and a couple of essays. We also remember the brief period when he was involved with the Imaginist-Expressionist group "Chaliastra" [2]. We know and also love the "Parisian", the esthetic naturalist Ozer Warszawski. However his life's work, his unique work is, as far as we can see, the novel, the truthful, large novel "Smugglers".

C.

A unique person.

A writer, who was suddenly exposed with a great artistic work, and just as suddenly stopped writing.

"Oh, Ozer Warszawski has a great talent", said his writer colleagues among themselves, "However he has ceased to write. Now he creates nothing"...

Even though it was completely and only through the guilt of the successful author that the time came that he ceased writing, one need not search for the true reasons of the silencing in the general socialist and nationalist underground[3].

And this I now wish to note. It is a great trait that many writers do not cease to write and are able to repeat their initial success, so that they can earn their living. It is most certainly the case that many writers – in all literatures – lament greatly when they cease writing, when they in truth have nothing more to say. The true strength of a writer is perhaps to overcome the "drive" to "create" over and over again.

It is obvious that "working" is a great thing, but more regarding quality than quantity... and I must admit a difficulty: My love and respect for Warszawski increased, despite, or rather because I knew that he stopped writing. In his "cessation of writing" we can hear the artistic honesty that says: Rather than staying on and repeating, it is best to maintain the former honorary position, a city in the east.

I have long ago come to the conclusion that a true good writer can be recognized more from what he doesn't write than from what he does write. I often regret the famous national chief poets and writers: in their youth they are very pleasant and spontaneously creative.

D.

In our literature, Ozer Warszawski is the only one, it appears, who came out with a book that immediately placed him among the first ranking storytellers of our time. This book – "Smugglers" – remained his unique book.

Why?

Is this, which one calls "talent", such a thing that can suddenly appear like a flash and just as suddenly be extinguished?

Was it Warszawski's illness that prevented him from continuing to write? Gorky's attack of blurry vision did not hinder him from write for long. (Incidentally, he, Gorky, wrote his best book "Memoirs" in the latter, mature years of his life).

Is then an illness not a stimulus for artistic work? Would, for example, Marcel Praust have written his major work had it not been for his asthma?

So why did Warszawski stop writing? Why do we know him only by his "Smugglers"?

Is Y. M. Weisenberg[4], who "discovered" Warszawski correct when he used to angrily claim that Ozer stopped writing because he was away from Poland, and yet (or, it seems like it was only?...) he developed and grew artistically on foreign soil. One can perhaps say that most of our poets and artists wander from land to land together with their masses of readers, that is to say, that their territory wanders with them. And who of us does not thank G-d now, that such a large number of Polish Jews with their poets left their Polish home in the years between the two world wars?

"Paris harmed Warszawski." – When I heard this from Weisenberg, I had a thought that would he, the artist Weisenberg, not be harmed at all if he had spent a few years in Paris, if he had seen Jewish Poland from afar for a period of time...

E.

Ozer Warszawski's three part novel "Smugglers" was published in 1920 – that is in the time when the crisis that led to the Second World War began to become apparent in Europe; and our Jewish literature, just as other world nationalities in general, began to strongly feel the internal, terrible crisis, from which we are not free of until today. The new platonic idealism of the European intelligentsia after the First World War began to evaporate and the economic, nationalist and ideological contradictions and conflicts, which almost destroyed Europe and European Jewry during the Second World War, began to be seen.

The luster of the center of Warsaw was removed with Peretz' death[5] . The great literary center was slowly drained and became impoverished. Almost everyone dispersed, and the only one left was the somewhat primitive, great artist Weisenberg (the others, even Nomberg [6] who used to be in Warsaw were living by now outside of Poland). Warszawski was too young and too fine an artist to remain only with Weisenberg; and when the rift in the "Chaliastra" came – Uri Zvi Greenberg[7] went to the Land of Israel and Markish[8] went to Russia – Warszawski remained alone in Paris. He was perhaps too fine and too artistically Bohemian to relocate to the America of that time.

F.

And the main thing: when Warszawski's realistic-animalistic novel was published, the end of the realists had already begun – the earlier Maskil-satirical and later artistic – era in our literature. It is true that at approximately that time, the robust realistic storytellers Y. Y. Zinger and A. M. Fuchs appeared, and that theme led to Shalom Ash's Kiddush Hashem [9] themes and Opatoshu's[10] Polish forests (not for naught did the realist Weisenberg begin at that time to incite rebellion against Ash and Opatoshu). That short period, when we began to enjoy the "healthy Jews" in the Jewish literature (and with "Rayach Hasadeh"[11] in Hebrew literature), came to an end unnoticeably. The tendency to display our lives – for us and for other people – as it was, without the perfume and the apologetics, was replaced with a tendency to search for and display positive words. And not only because bad times had begun to appear, but rather because we began to idealize and publicize our accomplishments: we indeed already had a literature, a new Russia, a Balfour Declaration...

We began to rejoice greatly with Shalom Aleichem, but primarily because of his optimism. Through him, we idealized the "masses". Not for naught was Shalom Aleichem so "idealized" in Russia, where a proletariat socialist, that is a romantic realism, began to dominate – and still dominates to this day. And the young Warszawski was absolutely a realist. And he had the "misfortune" to be taken with becoming a writer and artist caught between two spirits of the times, when our literature suddenly came to the cross-paths.

After "Smugglers" he attempted to rescue his artistry in an expressionist realism, which was revolutionary at that time. However, finally, he presently split off into proletariat art from one side, and into various romantic and ideological meandering and searching from the other side. Warszawski was perhaps too honest in his artistry (in other words, his sincerity was a weakness) – and he remained alone and "lost" in Paris.

G.

Nevertheless, if Ozer Warszawski is a lonely and tragic figure in our literature, his "unique" work "Smugglers" is not from the rare works that are relics from an earlier era, or first sprouting of an era, which must first come. Warszawski's novel is not a work of an isolated existentialist artist. Just the opposite, the novel "Smugglers" is as we say a parent of our literature: the personalities and characters – often a little too silhouetted – that we find in Warszawski's book are not at all strange to us. We have already met their kin, their flesh-and-blood relatives, brothers and sisters, in the first stories of Shalom Aleichem and Weisenberg.

... Warszawski's "Smugglers" is a continuation of our literature, not an isolated artistic phenomenon. Warszawski stems more from Weisenberg than from Ash's "Shtetl". And perhaps even a breath from Mendele's influence – which is natural and healthy – can be noted in Warszawski's novel.

Warszawski is poetic and lyric in spots, like Ash; not as plastic as Weisenberg, but therefore picturesque. He was more colorful than plastic.

That which mainly distinguishes him from the earlier Ash and Weisenberg is his strong inclination to the grotesque, which brings him nearer to the expressionists, who were at that time modern.

In comparison to him, Weisenberg was classic and academic, and Ash – idealistic. Warszawski had a strong tendency to the picturesque grotesque, and his protagonists were very animalistic and sexual, unlike those of other Jewish writers.

Ash flirted with his sexualism; Weisenberg presents the women as sober and hard. In Warszawski's "Smugglers" sexuality rages. Often, he presents the impression of an orgy of passionate, provocative bodies; To him, men are primarily animals who tear and fight for women and bread, although they can also be fine and romantic, as when he depicts, for example, the awakening of true love between Pantel's son Mendel and the prostitute Natshke.

Often one feels oneself in the infuriating calm depicting the announcement of the later, meandering, refined artist Warszawski.

H.

However the news that surprised and delighted when the book appeared, was that it was not a novel from the far or recent Jewish past, but a great and wide canvas of the Jewish-Polish present of that era.

The modernity of the new novel "Smugglers" was very surprising news; Warszawski had wildly and vehemently opened the door of our literature to the truth, which had closed after the death of Mendele and Shalom Aleichem. Most of the young artists of that time – and not only from our literature – published with portraits, sketches, narratives and even novels from their childhood memories and experiences from the recent past. Almost all of our best storytellers did not touch the present and the nearby surroundings. It is possible, and such would have been natural and perhaps even artistically correct, to write with the necessary perspective. Thus our literature often gives the impression of being a literature of historical themes, a literature based on memories, particularly from recent times. Our artists and poets, with a few exceptions would be afraid to touch our tragic and often loathsome reality. On occasion a new writer appears, and with great boldness describes upon a giant canvass the life in a Polish-Jewish Shtetl, perhaps the entire Jewish life in Poland during the German occupation of the First World War.

A young, as yet unknown writer should come with such great pictures of the present day life which he himself lived through!

That was the novelty and pleasant surprise of that novel: it was not related to the distant past, but rather it was a great artistic and social canvas of the experiences of the realities of Jewish Poland at the time of the German occupation. It was not a documentary novel – in 1920, that type of thing, apparently, was not known.

Already at that time in our literature, greater novels were known that described the realities of that time, of vivid depictions and characters of the region: Nomberg already gave us "Fligelman" ("Wing Man"), Berglas – "Arom Wokzol" ("Around the Station"), and "Noch Alemen" ("After Everything"), Ash – his novel "Meri", Weisenberg his "Shtetl", Reisen and others already sketched various modern issues externalities, teachers and various lively experiences. If a great novel about experiences of a national and social drama – from a young, still unknown writer, and a first book – this is what the happy surprise was. And it was a book that did not fear portraying the true face of a Jewish Polish Shtetl at the time of the First World War.

It was the time when we still were afraid to portray the true, realistic pictures of Jewish life, it was the time when we were still healthy, or considered healthy as a people. One can say that it was the time when our eyes were still not blinded by the true and false tears of destruction like in the present.

I.

Reading Ozer Warszawski's "Smugglers" again, I got the impression that this book is still timely. Most books become watered down and faded with time. They become difficult to read, even though they were very interesting when they were published. Warszawski's books is, as we say, beyond time, despite the fact that it was published more than thirty years ago. And what a period of thirty years this was for all people, for the Jewish people.. for tormented Polish Jewry.

When we read Warszawski's book in the present, we quickly get the feeling that we have come to a new terrible tragedy with frightening freshness, almost like it is in the present. Therefore I believe that Warszawski's "Smugglers" will remain as a novel in Jewish literary history.

The coming history for the once great, healthy and creative Polish Jewry ("Vos far a min gezuntenish" [12] – as Warszawski used to write) must be read and reread in Warszawski's "Smugglers". And even the Jeremiah[13] of the destruction of Polish Jewry during the Second World War can be read in Warszawski's unique book.

In our literature, it seems that there aren't such artistic works that reflect upon Polish Jewish life during the First World War under the Germans. (And it seems to me that in the general war literature, Warszawski's "Smugglers" should take an important and unique place, and it should be translated into other languages.)

In the book, we see the degradation and demoralization that war brings into the life of the civilian population. We see a picture of decline and degradation of the Polish-Jewish Shtetl during the time of the First World War, when even proper people had to take to smuggling and liquor production in order to save themselves and their children from hunger, and when with our primitive healthy popular energy with which Polish Jewry was so rich, we created such a life-wisdom as "The kosher groszy should atone for the treif[14] ruble"!

"What is it with health" – and in the full-blooded curses, animalistic coarseness of Warszawski's wagon drivers and smugglers, we painfully feel the despair and oppression of the exile.

Ozer Warszawski's "Smugglers" is not only a grotesque Rubenesque [15] orgy of struggling, wild sexual passion from half-primitive youth in their struggle for death and life. A continuing respect for "humanity" and "Judaism" glistens like a light fog over the smugglers, their wives and "mistresses"[16].

The naturalist-animalist Warszawski is also a fine sophisticated poet and he knows how to tell about Arele the quartermaster, who saved seventeen Jews from being shot, placing a patch over the army cloak of the "commandant". One feels such sharp bitterness in that work, the bitterness of a young painter and poet who saw and survived a raw, naked life of humans who were half animal.

This was a bitterness of despair that he certainly could not free himself of during his own Parisian years, and which perhaps prompted him: what to write? Was that then the hope of that type of person?

J.

Pantel – one of the prime heroes in Warszawski's "Smugglers" who is somewhat blurred and party formless – a type of a Jewish Taras Bulba [17] , utters "prophecies" about when the war (don't forget, the First World War) will end, his "pshiatsheles" smugglers are afraid that they will have to take their peaceful "kosher" groszy: -- "I, Pantel, I say: now the true smuggling will be begin .. the kosher".

Pantel's prophecy came true. And afterwards like...

I stated that Warszawski's "Smugglers" has now taken on a new freshness; and I will give over its meaning.

Perhaps on account of the time, the over thirty years that have elapsed since the novel was published, a new edition of the book should appear.

The bitter tragedy is: when we read "Smugglers" in the present, it presents the effect to us as an ideal Polish-Jewish life during the First World War.

The German occupation of Jewish Poland was at that time so humane and so ideal in comparison with the German occupation during the recent Second World War.

Now, the lot of Polish Jewry during the first World War – and its lot during the recent Second World War!...

The final quarter century has refreshed Warszawski's "Smugglers": a brutally realistic novel was turned into an ideal. And Ozer Warszawski, the fine poet and painter of the "Smugglers", who left Poland and celebrated the exile in Paris, was not spared the lot of Polish Jewry, and was killed like them and along with them.

"Speak not of this, good brother... keep quiet about this, be mute and do not even ask if I have another song"...

("The Golden Chain", number 14)

Gedalya Warszawski – the father of Ozer Warszawski.

TRANSLATOR'S FOOTNOTES:

1. The seven day Jewish mourning period for close relatives.
2. In Polish 'Halastra' is a mob.
3. This sentence is quite cryptic.
4. Y. M. Weisenberg was a Yiddish novelist from Poland (1878-1938). Note: for author's names, I have used the name by which they are generally known, rather than the Polish version. For some of the authors mentioned, the Polish version would be as follows: Weisenberg – Wajsenberg, Peretz – Perec, Fuchs – Fuks, Ash – Asz, Greenberg – Grynberg, Markish – Markisz.
5. Yitzchak Leib Peretz was a prominent Yiddish writer who lived from 1852-1915.
6. Hersh David Nomberg was a Yiddish writer who lived from 1876-1927. The following article about Nomberg appears in the Radomsko Yizkor book, translated on the JewishGen website: http://www.jewishgen.org/yizkor/Radomsko/rad274.html.

7. Uri Zvi Greenberg, born in Lvov, was a well-known Yiddish write who lived from 1896-1981. A brief biography of Greenberg can be seen at http://www.us-israel.org/jsource/biography/uzgreenberg.html.

8. Peretz Markish, a Yiddish poet, was born in Volhynia and lived in the Soviet Union (1895-1952). See the following article on him, published on the JewishGen site: http://www.jewishgen.org/yizkor/Radomsko/rad274.html. He was murdered in Stalin's purges. Incidentally, when I was a young child attending the Hillel Academy Day School in Ottawa, perhaps in grade 4 (approx. 1970), I distinctly recall a school assembly where we were addressed by his widow, Esther Markish.

9. Kiddush Hashem is sanctification of the Divine Name, often referring to Jewish martyrdom. Shalom (or Sholem) Ash was a Polish born (Kutno) American Yiddish novelist and playwright (1880-1957).

10. Yosef Opatoshu, 1886-1954. Yiddish writer, born Yosef Opatowski in Poland.

11. The aroma of the field – from the Bible a reference to the aroma of the field on Esau's garments that were worn by Jacob when he went to receive the blessing from Isaac.

12. Does not translate well – it means something like "What is it with health", or "What's the business with health".

13. The prophet Jeremiah foretold the destruction of the temple.

14. Treif is non-kosher.

15. Probably a reference to the artist Rubens.

16. Literally – 'bride shikses' i.e. 'bride gentile women'.

17. Taras Bulba and Other Tales is the title of a book by Nikolai Vasilievich Gogol. For an excerpt on line, see http://www.worldwideschool.org/library/books/lit/shortstories/TarasBulbaandOtherTales/chap12.html.

{268}

Biographical Notes
Melech Rawicz
Translated by Jerrold Landau

The first name that rang through all the revived continents and isles of the Jewish literary world after the standstill of the First World War – was the name Ozer Warszawski, and the first great work was his "Smugglers". This was a completely new name at that time, and its bearer was scarcely twenty-something years old. The realists took the matter as it was – it was a time of smuggling during the German occupation, from Poland to western Russia, and this made an imprint on the literature. Such was natural. The idealists interpreted it with idealistic noses. It was not only a time of smuggling, it was a pathetic time, it was also a time of great upheaval in Europe, a time of preparation for great revolutions, a time of great transition and great premonitions, and then the Jewish people come out, a people with seven faces – all kinds of ideals are established – and the people reveals itself with an eighth face, which is not its real face, it reveals itself as the people of the smugglers. However, this was not the fault of Warszawski, but rather of those who silenced the seven faces, and not the fault of he who disclosed the eighth face. He was a naturalist artist and he performed his duty. He certainly cannot do the job of others.

Itche Meir Weisenberg (Wajsenberg) initiated Warszawski into literature. And he has was forever so proud of him, such that Warszawski would not have had his fortuitous discovery had he not been the messenger, the secretary who inscribed his – Weisenberg's – work. Weisenberg enjoyed discovering talent, and he also had a talent to discover talent – mainly prose talent – (Shimon Horonczyk was also his discovery). However, he also enjoyed reminding the world that he was the one who discovered the talent. He generally held the accounts for the talent that he discovered before the eyes of Jewish literature. He did not allow the accounts to be paid once and for all, and he did not, like a gentleman, return it to their pocketbooks. Rather, all of his talent and the talent of others praised him, recalled to him, and fell on their knees before him, in the manner that Columbus holds before the world his accounts for the discovery of America, so that one could say to him one fine day: Take America back, and take back your accounts! – Thus did he hold his accounts before the Jewish literary world. Thus did he even moreso hold them up before the uncovered talent themselves, so that he acted literally despotic. He would correct their work, control their friendships, upwind their friendships, their sympathizers, their conclusions, and he imposed upon them the orthography of his native town Zelichow. A short time after his great success, Warszawski left Warsaw and went to western Europe. A document scrambler also played a role, or perhaps a scrambler of military certificates, however the chief role was played by Weisenberg. I often observed encounters between Warszawski and Weisenberg. Warszawski appeared thin, delicate blond, and white complexioned. He was a calm speaker, and did not like to speak about high matters. Weisenberg was exactly the opposite. When Ozer noticed Weisenberg, he would appear even more thin, delicate, blond and pale, and would become even quieter. His face changed color. It was somewhat like a delicate genius before his coarse, youthful father, which implies that the genius must sit over books and the young lad realizes that he can also know about this. If the discoverer would enter the club, the discoverer would look around at all sides to see that there is no possibility of escaping. However, when speaking to others, Warszawski would boast about his Rebbe to the heavens.

After his great success with "Smugglers", Warszawski never again found literary appropriateness. At that time, one could not place almost the entirety of Yiddish literature on his left shoulder. One turned to the right, the other to the left, and there was no other set path – and the European Bohemian life meandered and turned – and whomever would come from Paris to Warsaw – after the year 1924 – would hold it his duty to inform someone or another that not all was straight with Warszawski. One would tell of his excessive romances with Parisian women, another would assert that it was bad luck, and a third would say that he held literary to the Bohemian principle of doing nothing – and work for Warszawski became very scarce, until it completely ceased. – I met him a few times in Paris. He had become even thinner, paler and quieter – He would often make motions of despair with his thin hands, displaying a silent cynicism. However, there was never any lewdness. I would always take leave of him with the belief that a good director could revive him and bring him a great work. The material was indeed in him. During all the years of silence he read a great deal, learnt a great deal, and observed a great deal. He was only lacking internal organization and external stimulation.

{271}

Shmuel Lehman of blessed memory
the Lamed Vovnik [1] of the Jewish People

Yeshaya Trunk

Dedicated to the Memory of:
Bernice Phyllis (Mann) Knee (nee Mittleman)
Beloved Sister of Sandra Mittleman Robinson,
Granddaughter of Sochotzover Society Member Charles Miller

Translated by Jerrold Landau

Shmuel Lehman belonged to the group of Divinely blessed "Crazies for one thing", thanks to whom things which nobody looks upon them and which lie upon the street "as a stone that nobody turns over" are gathered together for generations and preserved in treasuries.

For his entire life, which was filled with hardship and need, he renounced the pleasures of this world literally as an ascetic. That wonderful fanatic of Jewish folklore traveled around Jewish cities and towns, climbed around the attics of shtibels, cellars and hideouts in Stawki, Dzikow and Szmatsze and Warsaw. He did not tire of jotting down in hundreds of notebooks, with his cut off, almost illegible handwriting, Jewish folktales, folksongs (mainly about thieves), proverbs, anecdotes, etc.

That, which for the nations of the world is done by government scientific institutions with costly expeditions, is done for us by individuals such as Shmuel Lehman. He forsook all of his own concerns, and expended his entire means, including his wife's dowry, in his travels over the Polish provinces. (He and his wife came from Jewish families of means.) How often did Shmuel Lehman have to pay another ruble or more for somebody to sing a song, or tell over a story or for some chaps, -- "good brothers: from the Stawki alleys to put out a bottle of liquor and a snack. That Don Quixote of Jewish folklore (externally, he looked like the beloved Don Quixote) performed his holy work quietly and modestly for decades.

That oddball, who paid rubles for songs and stories, was very popular among the Jewish poor in Stawki and Szmatsze. They called him "The sucker in a man's hat".

Later, when Shmuel Lehman had already become impoverished and was not able to pay rubles for songs, they often would, with a mocking chuckle, forego the payment, and not bother with the sucker games. They would even pull the sucker's hat over his brow in a good-brotherly manner.

Shmuel Lehman had no professional education in the subject of folklore. Rather, he possessed an extraordinary feeling for Jewish folklore. With his sharp, pointed nose, he would always discover in the attics or cellars a new song or perhaps a tenth variant of a folksong or folktale that was already known to him. He had his own system of recording melodies, since he had no formal training in music. Shmuel Lehman did his work himself, without public displays, without having the minutest support of the official Jewish community in Warsaw. Here I will tell the secret, that the 30th jubilee of his activity in 1932 was noted in Poland thanks to the private initiative of a small group of his friends and fans.

As a result, Shmuel Lehman collected an immense treasury (dozens of notebooks) of written Jewish folklore, of which only a few were permitted to see the light of day: "Work and Freedom", 1921, "Robber's Songs", 1928, "By Us Jews" (Together with Professor Graubard), "Jewish Proverbs,

Smalltalk, Manners of Speech, and Nicknames in Lands, Regions, Cities and Towns" (Together with N. Prilucki) – in Prilucki's anthologies "Of the European War", anthology "Life", etc.

It is one of the tragic paradoxes of our Jewish life that the collecting work of Shmuel Lehman received material support for the first time in the Warsaw Ghetto, under the auspices of the general activities to save Jewish creative intelligence. Dr. Emanuel Ringelblum and Yitzchak Guterman of blessed memories took special interest in his work. In the era of destruction and doom, the need to preserve – if not the enthusiastic bearers of Jewish folklore – then at least a portion of their treasures, was understood.

Aside from this, unlimited possibilities of work opened up for Shmuel Lehman, for in the Warsaw Ghetto, there was a true gathering of people from all of the provinces of Poland – fleeing or driven out of hundreds of cities and towns. The refuge points were a well from which Shmuel Lehman was able to draw in abundance.

I wonder how Lehman wandered around with his notebook through the starving refugees and searched there – in the sea of human desolation and need – the new tragic folklore, the new frightening ghetto songs, stories and ghetto anecdotes. The role of "The sucker in a men's hat" in a new and tragic situation was certainly nothing to envy. Those people whom fate designated for certain death in terrible need and pain certainly did not have it in their minds to sing ghetto songs for that oddball. His sensitive heart had to cramp and sigh at the appearance of those human laments. All of them were gathered here, in hell of Warsaw, all of his previous "clients" from Jewish cities and towns – the girls with their love songs, the elders from whose mouth he first recorded the wonderful stories of Elijah the prophet and the spellbound Poretz (landowner). However, in the consciousness of his historical mission, that Divinely blessed fanatic stood with a sealed heart and sealed lips, and recorded the song of the depths.

Together with Shmuel Lehman (who had the merit of dying a natural death in the Warsaw ghetto on October 23, 1941), what was perhaps one of the richest collections of Jewish folklore also perished. Its loss is incalculable – the fruit of over forty years of dedicated, superhuman work.

Regarding his death in the Warsaw ghetto, Emanuel Ringelblum writes the following in his notebook of October 1941:

"On October 23rd, Shmuel Lehman died. He worked up to the last moment, collecting a great deal of wartime folklore. The representatives of Jewish Warsaw were present at the funeral. Characteristically, his funeral took place at the same time as the funeral of one of his heroes, Berl Khazer, who told him many stories. Berl's funeral was a large one, like Lehman's. The chairman Czernikow, to whom we turned for a free plot, unfortunately did not know who Lehman was. He lies in the literary alley, near Y. M. Weissenberg.

TRANSLATOR'S FOOTNOTES:
1. In Jewish tradition, there are 36 hidden righteous people in every generation. These are termed in Yiddish 'lamed vovniks' – from the numeric value of the letters lamed vov, which is 36.

{274}

Pinchas Graubard
Y. Frydman
Translated by Jerrold Landau

He was the son of Leibish Graubard, a rich homeowner of Sochaczew. In his younger years, at the time of the revolution of 1905, he was a member of Poale Zion, and he organized a strike of all of the Jewish maids in Sochaczew. The Russian gendarmes began to persecute him, and he had to flee to Belgium. After tribulations in the foreign country, he returned home.

In 1910, he traveled to the Land of Israel and returned from there. He published a book: "Regarding the Ways of the Land of Israel". He joined forces with Noach Prilucki and Sh. Anszki, and they began to collect Jewish folklore.

After the First World War, he became a patron in Warsaw. He supported Jewish writers and helped many of them to publish their books. Thanks to him, Jewish writers published books that would have otherwise become lost.

After the outbreak of the Second World War, he fled from Warsaw to Vilna, and from there to America.

In his letter from New York, he describes his disappointment with life. He did not see there the beautiful, rich Jewish life that he had seen in Poland. He saw how they would throw pictures of parents with beards and peyos out of the window[1] , or store them in the attic. He saw Jewish books lying around in the rubbish, etc.

Life in America broke him. After a brief illness, he passed away in New York at the age of 58, on December 23, 1953.

{276}

Pinchas Graubard
A. Alemi
Translated by Jerrold Landau

Pinchas Graubard.

The death of a close person, a friend or a relative, inspires in us not only sad feelings, but also – as strange as it may sound – happy thoughts. We focus not only on the unavoidable end, but illuminating memories of long ago are awakened in us, of youth, happenings, plans, events, and dreams.

Such illuminating dreams of youth were aroused in me by the death of my childhood friend Pinchas Graubard, the folklorist, the close collaborator of Sh Anszkin[2], the former book publisher and supporter of literature – in the "green" years of our youth, and of modern Yiddish literature.

Pinchas Graubard was still a youth when he came to Warsaw from nearby Sochaczew – and he came not only with enthusiasm for Yiddish literature and its creation, but also – with money... He received[3] money from his father, the well-to-do businessman and wood merchant, and with that money, he helped in the publication of journals, festival pages, and books, or he simply directly supported a needy young Yiddish poet...

Graubard took an interest in Jewish folklore, and he organized a group of folklore collectors, under the influence and leadership of Noach Prilucki. Aside from Graubard, the members of the group included Shmuel Leman, Miriam Chmielnicki, Yehoshua Perla, Sara Kornbajser (later Perla's wife) and the writer of these lines.

We traveled about through Jewish cities and towns, as well as through the streets and alleys of Warsaw itself, collecting and recording from the sources of such information – from the mouths of the masses. People looked upon as fools[4] : why would older youths be involved in this! ... Jewish young men and women, Hassidim and Misnagdim[5], old men and women, and, on the other hand, underworld characters, pickpockets, bearers of knives[6], and prostitutes. They would often shrug their shoulders, but they would give in to the naïve "milkers', as Prilucki called this, often for the price of a few rubles.

People sang for us, told us stories and jokes, sprinkled us with proverbs, charms of exorcism, and "Zabobones"[7]. Old Jewesses, including my grandmother Chaya, my father's mother, recited techines for us,[8] including "Got Fun Avraham" – and we recorded.

Jewish folklore – the collection of folk treasuries – was a new field of knowledge. It quickly became the most popular activity in the Jewish cultural world, not only at the edges of the Czarist Empire, but also in Moscow and Petersburg. Marek and Ginzberg had already compiled an anthology of Jewish folklore. Ignace Bernsztejn in Warsaw did the same. Now, Noach Prilucki and Sh. Anszkin became involved in this endeavor, as did Peretz and H. D. Nomberg. Prilucki made this into an organized movement. He conducted lectures for us on the folklore of the Jews and of other peoples, about the importance of collecting, and also about methodologies of collecting.

However, a rift arose between Prilucki and the group of collectors – with regards to heaven (h i m l) [9]... Prilucki would talk to us and write exactly "as the people talk". Not, for example "d o s, v o s, v e r", but rather "d o e s, v o e, v e i o", etc. The problem was that Noach was a Volhyner[10], and in his region, they would say "i m l un h e r t" rather than "himel un erd". He would also hear it as "i m e l" in Poland... he would correct our material, and when he saw "h i m e l", he would erase it and replace it with "i m e l".. In truth, Polish Jews, in particular those from Warsaw, do not say either "h i m e l", or "i m e l", but rather – "h i m u"...

We protested against Prilucki's "i m e l". We wanted only "h i m e l", but Prilucki was stubborn and did not want to give in. Later, other conflicts started. Finally the group fell apart. Shmuel Leman went off on his own[11]. Graubard also went off on his own and specialized in the songs of robbers.

Reb Hirsch (Shalom Zvi) Friedman

Later, he teamed up with S. Anszkin and they became faithful collaborators, companions, and part time patrons. Perla and myself remained with Noach.

In the summer of 1911, Pinchas Graubard had a new plan: to establish a pioneering group and to travel to the Land of Israel to plough and sow… For us, it was a pity to leave behind the "Moment"[12]. I had taken my first steps into journalism – and it was only a few months, since November 10th, 1910, that the first issue of "Moment" was published.

However, the idea of traveling, especially to the land of Israel, did not leave me be. I helped Graubard to put the group together. Members included the journalist Y. Y. Trawka, the young poet A. Y. Krawski, the young storyteller Yosef Rozenfeld (from Radom), and a few others whose names I no longer remember. "Moment" informed its readership that its collaborator – that is myself – is traveling to the Land of Israel and will write about the Holy Land from there.

We set out – with empty pocketbooks, without documents, without a plan, but we depended on our overseer and patron Graubard… It was evening. At every station where the train stopped, we were greeted by groups of young people, particularly girls, with flowers. We sang "Hatikva"[13], we shouted, we were boisterous. At one station, I believe it was in Grodzisk, two particularly beautiful girls, sisters, came forth with flowers. Trawka (who later became a resident of the Land of Israel and the publisher of the large Hebrew Encyclopedia) grabbed me by the cape:

"Come, let us descend, let us go meet the delegation!" … We jumped off the train, greeted the young people, but I could not take my eyes of the two sisters… The group sang. We felt like heroes. We forgot about the train, Graubard, the Land of Israel… The whistle of the train brought us back to reality… But the thick smoke of the train was no longer there… We would have to wait for the next train, but the next train goes in the other direction, to Warsaw. That is to say, we traveled back to Warsaw…

I thought of a justification. Zvi Prilucki, the editor of "Moment" was furious: The readers have been misled!… The anti-Semitic Polish newspaper "Goniec" published a sensation: "Zionism is bankrupt. As a sign of this, two of the collaborators of "Moment", who set out with a group to the Land of Israel, had regrets in the midst of the journey and returned to Warsaw..."

Oh, the recklessness of youth! At that time, we were only youths of 16 and 18...

Pinchas Graubard returned from the Land of Israel a year later –with great plans, but America was sweet for me at that time, and it was the eve of the First World War[14]. Between the two world wars, Pinchas Graubard became a very well to do man. He founded a book publishing house, and published the large anthology of folklore "Bei Unz Yidden" ("By We Jews") that was edited by M. Wanwild (Sh. L. Kawe), a book on his reports from the Land of Israel, and a series of works by older and younger writers. However, folklore remained his greatest interest, and he had great plans about a grandiose publishing house that would form a literary bridge between Warsaw, New York, Buenos Aires...

My final meeting with Pinchas Graubard was at Mordechai Dancys' funeral. We shared memories of times gone by. We talked about our friend from our youth Y. Y. Trawka who came to America from Israel on behalf of his Hebrew Encyclopedia, and dropped dead in Montreal. We discussed the Warsaw of times gone by that swims around in the shadow of death, the so close but yet so distant years of youth, the few youths who left for the Land of Israel before the First World War to plough and sow... Above else, Graubard had grandiose plans, plans, plans.

("Tag Morgenjournal", January 11, 1953.)

TRANSLATOR'S FOOTNOTES:

1. An metaphor for abandoning Jewish tradition.
2. In the previous article, this name was spelled as Anszki.
3. The word used here means more than 'received'. It actually means he 'pulled out' or 'dragged out'. The connotation is not one of conniving, but rather it seems of making use of nagging or pleading to convince his father to give money to this cause.
4. The word here 'mishegoim', has a somewhat endearing connotation here.
5. Opponents of Hassidism.
6. There is a term here 'marevichers'. I am not sure what it means, but it is surely some type of unsavory character.
7. I am not sure what the term 'zabobenes' means.
8. Techine (literally, supplication), is an informal Yiddish prayer, passed down from generation to generation, often recited by women at significant occasions, such as at the time of the lighting of the candles before the Sabbath and festivals. 'Got Fun Avraham' ("G-d of Abraham") is a well-known techine recited at the conclusion of the Sabbath. Its is one of the few techines still popular, and is published in various modern prayer books, including ArtScroll.
9. The reference here is to differences of opinion on the spelling of Yiddish words. I will spell out the Yiddish words in this paragraph (in parentheses) as best I can, using 'a' for aleph with a patach, 'o' for aleph with a kometz', and 'e' for ayin, and 'i' for yod . There are different ways of spelling Yiddish words – the formal manner and the more colloquial manner. "Himel un erd" means heaven and earth. For those who are not familiar with the nuances of Yiddish spelling and letters, all that is important here is the theme – the group had a disagreement over exact vs. colloquial Yiddish spelling.
10. From the Volhynia region of Ukraine.

11. The Yiddish expression here is "made the Sabbath for himself".
12. There seems to be a play on words here with the name of the periodical "Moment". There is also the implied meaning of "missing the moment".
13. The Zionist anthem, later the national anthem of the State of Israel.
14. There is a play on words here, with the Hebrew word 'erev' (the Hebrew word is used instead of Yiddish). It means both 'sweet' and 'eve' in different contexts and with different vocalizations.

{280}

Wolf (Vove) Rozenberg

Moshe Szwarc of Chicago

Dedicated to the Memory of:

Bernice Phyllis (Mann) Knee (nee Mittleman)
Beloved Sister of Sandra Mittleman Robinson,
Granddaughter of Sochotzover Society Member Charles Miller

Translated by Jerrold Landau

It is impossible to mention Sochaczew, particularly during the period from 1915 until the beginning of the 1920s, without bringing to light the bright personality that was Vove Rozenberg, who embodied the Polish-Jewish people-intelligentsia. He was characteristic of colorful Polish Jewry.

He did not get caught up in the stream of assimilation. He remained tightly bound to the Jewish people, through Yiddish literature, Yiddish song and Yiddish culture until the last day of his life.

As a close friend of Vove Rozenberg, and incidentally one of the few left of our generation, it is known to me that Vove dreamed and created great plans for many years about perpetuating Sochaczew in the form of a Yizkor book.

He was born in the year 1892 in Sochaczew into an observant, Hassidic household. His father was the eminent Gerrer Hassid Reb Hershel Shochet. He spent his childhood years in the traditional Hassidic home. As an older child, he studied in Yeshiva and became imbued with the Talmudic and old-Hebraic wellspring. Already in his youth, he tore himself away from his home and lived in Warsaw where he was able to become familiar with classical Jewish literature and with world literature. He entered into the circle of Jewish artists, writers and intelligentsia. He began writing Yiddish songs in those days. He became a confidante of Y. L. Peretz and a close friend of Noach Prilucki. He made a name for himself in the Jewish cultural society of Warsaw.

In 1915, when the German army took Warsaw, the Jews who were driven out from the surrounding towns began to return home. The Jews of Sochaczew also returned. Together with the reestablishment of economic life, they began to build the cultural and societal life.

Vove Rozenberg also returned to Sochaczew for a time at that time. He occupied himself with law even though he had not graduated as a lawyer. He was one of the pillars and leaders of political and societal life. His spiritual influence spread over those who were around him, and planted deep roots in several generations.

He went back to Warsaw a few years later, where he was together with the Jewish writers and activists Sh. Stopnicki, H. D. Nomberg, Noach Prilucki, Shlomo Mendelson, and others in the national leadership of the newly created Folks-Party. He visited a number of Jewish communities in Poland on their behalf.

At that time, he held a responsible position with the Joint, which was conducting a large-scale assistance action in Poland.

In 1924, he left Poland and traveled to America for the second time, for he had spent a short time there in the year 1910. This time, he went with his wife Bronka. He became a temporary resident, and settled in New York. He embarked on the difficult path of becoming used to a new way of life and conditions. The disappointment was heavy. He always felt the pain of pining for the former life. He also found difficulties in establishing himself economically.

However, he never was passive to the current problems, and he was always closely bound with Jewish and general life. He lived through this trial and the swift flow of world events with might and life. Despite the fact that his Jewish world outlook was to a large extent conservative, restrained and with an unrealistic hope of witnessing the grand, historical happenings and changes in the world order – he did not become involved in any political party or group during his years in America, aside from cultural work. He always stood at the side of the oppressed and suffering people.

He was a sincere and sensitive person. The Hitlerian destruction, which also killed his relatives in Poland, had a terrible effect upon him, and left deep wounds upon his heart and soul, until the cruel death overtook him at the age of 61.

Vove died in New York in 1953 after a long and difficult illness. Three years later, his wife also went off to eternity, leaving behind their only daughter Nina.

Elchanan (Chuna) Libert with his wife.

Moshe Yakovitz

{674}

PERSONALITIES

Reb Alexander Zisha Frydman
by Dr. Hillel Zeidman
Translated by Jerrold Landau

The Environment

Reb Alexander Zisha Frydman, the general secretary of Agudas Yisrael in Poland, was a central personality in Orthodox Judaism not only because of his official position, but also because of his personal strengths, his abilities, activities, and accomplishments.

He was the nurturer of the Polish style of Agudas Yisrael. He nurtured the movement and grew with it; he influenced it and was influenced by it. He was an inseparable part of it. Therefore, anyone who wishes to evaluate the man must peer into the movement and the environment in which he lived and worked, into the Polish style of Agudas Yisrael.

What is meant by "the Polish style"? Just as Orthodox Judaism in the lands of the west took upon the motto of Rabbi Samson Rafael Hirsch "Torah with the way of the world", which refers to Judaism that is faithful to the Torah according to the exact definitions of the code of Jewish Law, while at the same time – being knowledgeable in the vernacular, in culture, in the way of life, and the culture of Western Europe – in the same manner, the way of the Aguda in Poland, just as the way of Orthodox Judaism in general in that country, was Torah alone without any mixture, not only exacting in the fulfillment of the commandments, but encompassing all expressions of life, all the manners of man, all its manifestations, with all 365 sinews and 248 bones[1].

The "Polish style" – as strange as it sounds – was different from Poland, from the nation in which the Jews dwelled. It was completely different, with no compromise. "In their ways you shall not go"[2] encompasses all facets of life. It was sufficient for a Pole to do something – even something that was permitted by Jewish law – and the stamp of "goy" (gentile) was placed upon the deed, and it became completely invalidated.

What was the difference between Orthodox Judaism in Western Europe and in Eastern Europe? The Judaism in the west restricted its orthodoxy to a narrow sector, and placed a still narrow boundary on its "Aguda". However in Poland, Orthodox Judaism was quite widespread, and the Aguda bore its crown and its manner of conducting itself in the world. An Orthodox Jew refers to everything: education; and political activity, whether worldwide, national or local – therefore, there were Orthodox representatives in the legal systems of the towns and communities; in economy – and therefore cooperatives, banks and economic institutions of various types were established; in propaganda and public relations – and therefore there were factional newspapers, daily, weekly, and periodical; and especially with regards to the settlement of the Land of Israel, in that it should be built up in accordance with Torah and tradition. In reality, there was not one area in which the Aguda did not exert its power, in which it did not try to penetrate and exert the influence of its spirit.

Therefore, the Polish Aguda was active in the midst of the Jewish community at the time in which the Judaism of the west was straddling two paths, so to speak, separating the Jewish path from the general path.

Zisha Frydman gained his prominence in this environment, and became the spokesman of Agudas Yisrael. He reached that position directly from the Beis Midrash and the Hassidic Shtibel. He absorbed full influence from both the Beis Midrash and the Shtibel. He was not a dry scholar, and not a fanatical Hassid. His soul bore the successful mixtures of both influences, of scholarship and Hassidism. He was complete in everything. He probed to the depth of maters and did not satisfy himself with superficial discussion. Everyone who knew him knew his depth.

His Roots

Alexander Zisha Frydman was born in Sochaczew, Poland on the 11th of Av, 5657 (1897). One of his sisters, who was a teacher in the Beis Yaakov school, is today the wife of Reb Avraham Mokotowski of Jerusalem. His parents, like most of the Jews of Poland, earned their livelihood through the sweat of their brow, but did not hesitate in denying food to their mouths in order to give their son a fitting Torah education. They did not resist even the most expensive teacher, as long as their son would draw Torah from his well.

Reb Alexander Zisha's father, Reb Aharon Yehoshua Frydman, was the Shamash in the synagogue of Sochaczew, and earned his livelihood with great difficulty. His wife assisted him in his livelihood. He traveled to various fairs with his merchandise. When Zisha was three years old, he knew the entire book of Genesis off by heart. He moved from teacher to teacher for several years. When he was nine years old, the teacher came to his father and said: "There is nothing more your son can learn from me. I advise you to enroll him in the Yeshiva of the Admor of Sochaczew." His father did not want to do so out of fear of the evil eye. He heard that three of the rich men of the city, fathers of good children of Bar Mitzvah age, hired a teacher who was an erudite sage from a different town, and paid him generously at the rate of three rubles per week, a large sum in those days, with the condition that he would only teach those three children. Reb Zisha's father went to one of them and said to him: "It is my desire that my son shall also learn with your children". He was happy with the request, and said, "Certainly, certainly". However Reb Yehoshua Aharon would not agree unless they would accept the complete tuition from him, at the rate they were paying. They said to him "No! If you wish, we will pay you three rubles a week so that your son will join up with our children. It is given to you!" He answered: "I will pay one ruble a week, for this is the entire amount that I earn from being a Shamash." From then on, he earned his livelihood only from the meager earnings of his wife (Reb Zisha's parents merited to live at the end of their lives in Jerusalem, and died there).

At his Bar Mitzvah feast, Reb Zisha gave a lecture that was wondrous in its depth and breadth. All of the residents of the town stood at the doors and windows of his house, since there was no room inside. The Rebbe of Sochaczew and other great rabbis participated in the Bar Mitzvah celebrations of that genius. Reb Zisha studied in the Yeshiva of Sochaczew until the outbreak of the First World War. In the year 5674 (1914) the entire family fled to Warsaw.

In the summer of 5674, he became engaged to a girl from a small town near Sochaczew called Jalowa. His bride was the only daughter of her father, who was a simple man without wealth. However, the mother of the bride was known in the entire area as one of the great righteous people, with regard to her fear of heaven and generosity. This righteous woman would give all that her husband earned to the poor and scholars. Her daughter of blessed memory became the wife of Reb Zisha.

In Warsaw, Reb Zisha became close to Rabbi Baruch Gelbart, a great scholar, and author of books. He wished to benefit all of his students with his munificence. However, Reb Zisha refused to derive any benefit except from his Torah knowledge. There, he also became close to Dr. Emanuel Carlebach, who lived in Warsaw during the German occupation and organized classes in Jewish wisdom for the best students. Reb Zisha also studied with him and excelled in his studies.

Reb Zisha's father was a Chasid of Amshenov[3]. So was his son. However, later when he studied in the Yeshiva of Sochaczew, he became close to the Rebbe. The youth was very diligent and caught on to his subjects very deeply and quickly. He became known as a genius. However his personality was very discreet. Calm and refinement exuded from his face, and anyone who saw him and knew him was jealous of his parents, that they produced such a splendid offspring. He was a refined and wholesome young man. He was an excellent Torah reader, and a fitting prayer leader with a sweet voice. On the High Holy Days as he led services, he moved the worshippers with the feeling of his prayers and the sweetness of his melodies.

There used to be a well-to-do and scholarly merchant in Warsaw, Meir Yoel Swarcsztejn. He was a clock merchant, and he loved to test the young men who studied Torah. Anyone who knew 50 pages of Talmud off by heart won a prize from Reb Meir Yoel – a valuable watch. Zisha Frydman won this prize when he reached the age of Bar Mitzvah. He carefully guarded this watch until his last day.

Zisha Frydman was young when he became active in the Aguda. It was natural, due to his young age, that he turned his attention to the Agudas Yisrael Youth. He had three important traits that were all of great benefit to Aguda: he was a speaker, a writer, and an organizer. He gave over all his skills to the movement. It is no wonder that he moved up in the organizational ladder with the speed of lightning. He established the Agudas Yisrael Youth organization, which to a large degree bore the main yoke of its parent organization, the Aguda. There were no finer days for Agudas Yisrael Youth as the days at the beginning of his activity. However, after he spread his wings to other endeavors and was no longer able to restrict himself to the four ells of this organization, he remained the captain and leader in the eyes of the myriads of youth, who took pride in him. The years of his activity in Agudas Yisrael Youth were years of unusual flourishing and growth of that organization. All high thinkers, idealists, people of action, dreamers and strugglers gathered around it. Its publication "Digleinu" overflowed with ideas like a volcano. It was full of thrill, strong influence and power. It influenced the thoughts of the Orthodox youth and watered the treasuries of their minds. Alexander Zisha Frydman was the editor of the publication, and he astounded his readers with the clarity of his language, the fertility of his style and his lightning-like ideas. He educated activists and counselors of Agudas Yisrael Youth and prepared them for activity. Through this, he extended his influence upon the Agudas Yisrael Youth for a long time after he moved to another section of the front – to Agudas Yisrael, to the adults.

He appeared in the year 5679 (1919) in the first national convention of the Aguda and inspired his audience with his speech. At that time, he was asked to serve as the secretary of the central Aguda organization, then called "Shlomei Emunei Yisrael" ("Those at Peace with the Faith of Israel").

The leaders of Agudas Yisrael removed him completely from Agudas Yisrael Youth. They had long awaited a man such as him. In 5685 (1925) he was appointed as the general secretary of Agudas Yisrael in Poland, a position that he held until his last day. In the central offices of Aguda, Zisha Frydman was like a river of water in an arid desert. He introduced an organized administration, for prior to that time, they did not relate to that idea with proper seriousness. He conducted steady and organized correspondence. He established contact with hundreds of branches throughout the country, and with the sister Aguda organizations in other countries. He established protocols for meetings, introduced orderly record keeping, set up a schedule for meetings, and his own schedule – all with wonderful exactness, order, and regimen. He did this without negligence, and without accepting the "I don't care" that was often the manner of the masses, even of honorable people, who concern themselves only with large and important matters and ignore the small details and the day to day order. Reb Zisha Frydman was concerned with the larger matters, while not neglecting the small matters. Even though he was the leader, he was not repulsed by the task of administrator, and he was an exemplary record keeper. The former Senator Refael Szereszawski, the well-known banker from Warsaw, praised him greatly as a record keeper and accountant.

Even though he was an expert factional activist, faithful to the official line, diplomacy and propaganda – he was not afflicted with the typical empty factional formality. He was a scholar, full of understanding. He behaved as a scholar in his manners, traits, words, way of thinking and way of life. He was seriously, and dedicated and straightforward in his actions. He did not carry himself haughtily. He was always "one of us". He was a friend to all Hassidic youth, to every Yeshiva student. He understood their needs, aspirations, requests and concerns.

The Communal Administrator

Reb Zisha Frydman was a revolutionary by nature. He was quiet and modest, he had no desire to shake up the existing institutions and he did not aspire to an uncalled for revolution. Nevertheless, the essence of his appearance in the national arena in the communal council of Warsaw, which served as a sort of miniature Jewish parliament, introduced a spirit of popular Judaism, a stormy and lively spirit, into the Jewish community of Warsaw. Prior to that time, there was almost no place for such a spirit in that prestigious institution.

From the days of Shmuel Zawitkower, the rich Aguda person at the time of Reb Shlomo Eiger, the son of the Gaon Rabbi Akiva Eiger the Rabbi of Poznan, until Gavriel Eizenman the owner of the metal works and son-in-law of the wealthy Hassid Reb Yishayahu Priwes and son of Reb Elazar, the leaders of the Orthodox community came from the elders of the well-to-do people, who looked after large estates, owned successful businesses whose dealings were spread all over the world, great scholars who had a place among the patrons and important men of the city, relatives and in-laws of rabbis and Gaonim. All of them were administrators, and many families were dependent on their works and good graces. They gave charity both secretly and publicly. The Rebbes' courtyards, public institutions, and charity for the poor were conducted upon their shoulders and with their money. They ruled over the entire holy community, which was borne by them. Even their external features demonstrated their special importance. They had a patriarchal visage, and serious expression of strength blended with somberness. They had wise eyes, full grown beards. On Sabbaths and festivals, they were attired in silk kapotes (cloaks), expensive streimels. On weekdays, they wore special bekishes (long jackets) known as "Privisovkes". There was always a festive air about them, exuding honor. All were connected with each other through family connections and common business interests, even though there were disputes on occasion. This was to protect their governance and rights from an invasion of "foreigners". Such was the way of the "dozors" (members of the communal council) from Warsaw.

In the period between the two world wars, the splendor of the well placed lessened significantly, the situation of the masses worsened, and their position declined on the street. When the first democratic elections for the Warsaw community took place in 1926, the traditional leaders were no longer the only ones fit for leadership. Nevertheless, a few of the remnants of such well placed people still honored themselves with the front places in the lists of those standing for election in the Agudas Yisrael party (except for Rabbi Yitzchak Meir Lewin, who, as the chairman of Agudas Yisrael, and the son-in-law of the Rebbe of Gur, took first place in the list). Reb Zisha Frydman, even though he was already well-known throughout Poland, was pushed to the sixteenth place – after the honorable people who held their customary positions.. However the Aguda won the elections and gained fifteen mandates. After three of the administrators were appointed to the governing council – Frydman also came in as a member of the council or an administrator.

Then the revolution began. This young man, who did not have a fancy house, who was not rich nor the son of rich people, who was not well connected, was not from a well connected family, and did not have business with the "leviathans" – suddenly reached the highest rung of the Orthodox administrators, after Reb Yitzchak Meir Lewin who was the official leader. All of well-to-do leaders and scholars gave way to him and became "backbenchers", who applauded the brilliant speeches of that young man, who had no connections and no wealth.

The communal council was always a battle arena between the various factions. Since no faction had an absolute majority, no group was able to impose its way upon other groups. There were two main factions – the Aguda and the Zionists – to which the smaller groups joined up. The first communal council of new Poland, which was elected in Warsaw in 1926, was divided up as follows: Aguda – 15 seats, the Zionist umbrella – 11, Mizrachi – 5, Bund – 5, the Aguda from the Praga suburb of Warsaw – 2 (one of them was Rabbi Menachem Zemba, the Torah sage who was also an iron merchant, and later was appointed as a rabbi in Warsaw), the Folkists (the populist party) – 3, the Hassidim of Grodzisk – 1. Through various maneuvers, an agreement was reached that Mr. Heshel Farbsztejn, the head of Mizrachi, be the head of the communal government, and Mr. Eliahu Kirszbraun of Agudas Yisrael be the chairman of the communal council. The representative to the Sejm was determined in accordance with this agreement[4]. In the elections of 1930, Reb Eliahu Mazur was chosen as the head of the communal government, and Reb Yaakov Trukenheim as the chairman of the communal council.

The communal council was the public arena where various factions disputed their ideas. Even though the jurisdiction of the Warsaw community was restricted by the government, and the community was only responsible to adjudicate in religious affairs of the community, all issues of Jewish life, and indeed many issues outside of Jewish life, were deliberated upon by the representatives of the various factions at the communal council. Even "an advisory against General Franco of Spain, and support for his opponents", was brought before the council by Bund and the left leaning Poale Zion[5]. Reb Zisha Frydman was the prime spokesman of the Orthodox coalition for all problems of the era. Rabbi Yitzchak Meir Lewin outlined the sphere of activity, and used to request the right to speak on fundamental and pragmatic problems. Reb Zisha Frydman was the spokesman of Aguda in all other matters. He was chosen as a communal administrator (Parnas) also in all other subsequent elections (in 1930 and in 1936). His renown as one of the best spokesman of the Jews of Poland spread very quickly.

Alexander Zisha Frydman and his family.

The Orator

Reb Zisha Frydman was a wonderful orator. His voice was sweet and strong, simultaneously preachy and stormy. He was not an improviser, and he did not speak everything that came to his mind. He felt that he was fulfilling a mission when he appeared in the name of Orthodox Judaism, and therefore he prepared himself with all his power. He prepared his speeches in advance, line by line and thought by thought, every idea in its correct place. When he stood on the podium, he did not intermingle one idea with another, and he did not speak in flowery language. He concerned himself with the content no less than the form. He always spoke about the heart of the topic, concisely and briefly. In the community, he did not attempt to be "lustrous", but rather to be decisive and topical. He did not deliberate on a point for a length of time, but rather he quickly came to the heart of the point. He consciously curbed his talents as an orator.

On the other hand, at meetings of the masses, he permitted himself to digress from the dry, factual style. Even there, he did not sacrifice the content, but he did not refrain from using a pleasing rhetorical style, and he would spice his lecture with side points, words of our sages or Hassidic sayings, for the most part based upon a verse of the Torah, specifically a verse from the current weekly Torah portion[6]. His methodology was so successful, so smooth, so pleasing, that is seemed as if the weekly Torah portion was directly related to the issue that was being discussed at the time. His words made a deep impression, and his enthusiastic audience would go over his words for weeks or months after the speech, deriving enjoyment and absorbing them. There were occasions when his words were remembered after many years. He was blessed with the ability of explaining his ideas in the simplest fashion, so that they would be understandable to the majority of people. He never spoke about "the ideology of Aguda". He never spoke about the mounds of minutia of the "program". He drew from the well. His words were based on the Torah, and were based upon reality, the day to day lives of the masses of Jews, their burdens, needs, problems, and concerns. His speeches at the central Aguda conventions, from the first one in Vienna until the final one in Marienbad prior to the outbreak of the Second World War, where works of art in their content and style, and left an unforgettable impression upon the audience. He inspired the masses and even the

Orthodox leaders, not because of the magic of his speaking style, but rather because everyone who heard him felt that the words were coming out from a pure soul, from the warm heart of a Hassidic Jew, a scholar, and a fearer of Heaven. They felt that "These words are like the heavens".

The Educator

Reb Zisha was an educator by nature, and he dedicated the best of his efforts and time to education. Even as he was serving as a captain, he saw it as an educational endeavor. When the Aguda won a victory in the Sejm elections, Reb Zisha said: "Even more than I am happy with the number of mandates we received, I am even more happy with the educational influence that will be the result of the elections. A boy student of Yesodei Hatorah or a girl student of Beis Yaakov will feel that they are not alone, they will feel that a quarter of a million Jews affiliate with Aguda and give their voice to it. What an educational influence!" When a meeting of the action committee of Agudas Yisrael was deliberating about the representation of Aguda to the parliament (Sejm), and weighted the appropriateness of every candidate for the task, Zisha Frydman found a completely different line of reasoning from the accepted one. He said: "We require a representative who will appear before the parliament in the style of the rabbis, with a bear, peyos, a kippa on his head and a waistband[7] around his waist, so that we ourselves can see who is fitting for honor in the Jewish community. When the youth see that the representative who appears before ministers and presents himself before the statesmen is a Torah scholar, an author of Halachic and Aggadaic works (he was speaking about Rabbi Aharon Lewin of Rzeszow, may G-d avenge his blood), what a great educational example this will be!"

He was the life spirit in all areas of educational and religious life in Poland. He was the general principal of Chorev, of the Yesodei Hatorah school network, of Talmud Torah, of cheders and elementary schools. He stood at the helm of Keren Hatorah, the financial institution that supported religious Jewish education. He was a member of the board of directors of Beis Yaakov and the Beis Yaakov Seminary in Krakow. He was the founder of a seminary for Orthodox educators in Warsaw located on 6 Twarda St.. This institution raised the status and honor of Jewish educators, raising them up from their poor status. From that time, they were referred to as "educators", which was a term more fitting to their task. He was not satisfied with administration, for he also involved himself directly with education. He lectured at the "Teacher's Seminary " of Warsaw, and gave summer courses for Beis Yaakov teachers near Krakow. He authored books on teaching, such as a book on the Shmoneh Esrei[8], a book on education called "Kesef Mezukak" ("Refined Silver"), and others. Even when he was involved in political activity as the general secretary of Agudas Yisrael, the prime purpose of all these activities – spreading Torah – never left his mind.

In Agudas Yisrael

Reb Zisha Frydman was one of the founders of all branches of the movement which sprouted from the large tree of Agudas Yisrael: Agudas Yisrael Youth, Poale Agudas Yisrael, Agudas Yisrael Girls, Beis Yaakov, Yesodei Hatorah, various newspapers, etc. As was mentioned above, he started by founding Agudas Yisrael Youth. When the Orthodox workers stumbled upon difficulties in obtaining work even in the factories and businesses that were owned by Orthodox people, and the realities dictated the need for the founding of an organization to protect the rights of the Orthodox workers, Reb Zisha Frydman was numbered among the ideologues and founders of Poale Aguda[9]. Along with

Yehuda Leib Orlian, Leibel Frum, Falik Lendenberg, Avraham Mordechai Rogowi may his blood be avenged, and others, he set up the foundation of this movement, which was based on the social justice of the prophets, with the aim to oppose the improper behavior of the rich Orthodox business owners against their workers, behavior which was directly opposed to the laws of the Torah and Jewish ethics.

However when the youth and the workers desired to stand on their own and no longer be dependent on the table of Aguda, Reb Zisha dissociated himself and dedicated himself completely to his work in the Aguda center and in the centers of education. He was dedicated and faithful to the line of the mother movement, and he labored to strengthen this line. However, when the youths struggled to strengthen the connection to the Land of Israel, and desired activities in the realm of hachsharah and aliya, Reb Zisha supported them, for he valued greatly setting up connections in the Land of Israel. His opinion crystallized further after his visit to the Land in the year 5684 (1924), as part of an Aguda mission headed by Rabbi Yitzchak Meir Lewin. He had words of criticism against some of the things that were taking place in the Holy Land. "Light and darkness are intermingled there" – he said as he expressed his opinions – "However the shadows do not darken the light". He turned to the Orthodox masses in Poland and called for a strengthening of hachsharah activities, aliya, and concrete assistance for the building of the Land.

According to his brother-in-law Reb Avraham Mokotowski, Reb Zisha desired to settle in the Land, however he was forced to return to Poland on account of the many duties where were waiting for him regarding Diaspora Judaism.

This was his relationship toward Poale Agudas Yisrael, even though he had no organizational connections with it and on occasion had differences of opinion with its leadership, they found support from him when then needed it. He extended a great deal of assistance to the Agudas Yisrael Girls' organization, which was mainly concerned with educational and cultural matters. He worked together with Rabbi Eliezer Gershon Friedenson, the editor of "Beis Yaakov"; Yehuda Leib Orlian, the main principal; Nota Yerucham Berliner of Lodz, the principal of the Beis Yaakov Seminary; Senator Moshe Deutscher of Krakow; Asher Shapira; Meir Heinter; and others. He gave of his energies and organizational prowess to develop this organization, whose members were for the most part alumnae of Beis Yaakov.

The Writer

Reb Zisha founded and edited the first Hebrew language Aguda publication, "Digleinu", which served as a guide for the young members of Aguda, and raised a generation of young writers. "Digleinu" was published in the years 1919-1924, and again in 1930-1931. In the years 1936-1938, Reb Zisha Frydman published a weekly "Darcheinu". This served as the main periodical of the Polish Aguda. He displayed wisdom and expertise as an editor.

However, journalism was not his profession, but served only as an educational tool. He did not write for the sake of writing, but rather to influence, explain and educate. He only wrote when he had something to say, as the "occasional scholar", that is to say: the scholar who is only a scholar when he wishes to be a scholar, and is not compelled to be a scholar, thus, he was not compelled to write[10]. Indeed, he always said his piece in a clear, bright, orderly fashion, and his pieces were filled with logical and convincing ideas. His writing, as his oration, expressed his personal traits: clearness of intellect, straightforward logic, seriousness, and speaking on the topic. He expressed these traits also in battles, not with anger but rather with calm. "The words of the wise are heard with calm"[11]. He did not struggle to be the victor, but rather to convince, not to make an impression, but rather to explain and educate, not to hurt the disputant with harsh language, but rather to set the matter straight. He weighed his words with the scales of his thoughts and with the influence of the Torah with which he was infused, since he never ceased his study. Even when he was very busy with organizational and political affairs, he set aside at least three hours each day to study Talmud, Halachic decisions and Bible. He never made use of political jargon, but rather well-understood words. Everything that he said was drawn from the well, from the never failing spring of the words of our sages of blessed memory.

Despite the flurry of political activity with which he was involved, he conducted his studies not merely to fulfill his obligation, but also to produce novel commentaries on the tractates of Gittin, Kiddushin, and Yoma[12], along with commentaries on various topics.

He worked quietly on a commentary on the prayer book (Siddur). He also published a collection of Halachic responsa, which contained an exchange of views with the Gaon Rabbi Menachem Zemba, may his blood be avenged. The Gaon Rabbi Yaakov Meir Biderman of holy blessed memory greatly praised the novellae of Reb Zisha.

He edited and published a collection of commentaries and ideas on the Chumash in Yiddish, called "Der Tora Kval" ("The Well of Torah"). This was one of the more successful compendiums. He also authored several practical books for religious schools, such as "Kesef Mezukak", "Yiddish Loshen" ("The Yiddish Language"), a textbook on the Shmoneh Esrei prayer, and he published pedagogic ideas and articles in the "Beis Yaakov" monthly. People are surprised to hear that he also authored poems in the Hebrew language, one of them "Bnei Papunia", was his first poem which was published in 1919 in "Yid", the Yiddish weekly of Warsaw. It received wide acclaim from the public, and was enthusiastically received in all circles.

He wrote the books: "A Call to the Jewish Woman" (5681 – 1921), and "Kesef Mezukak" on Talmudic principles (5683 –1923).

In 1939, he was about to publish a book on his Torah novellae, which he complied in the fortieth year of his life (5697 – 1937). However he was not able to complete this task, for the German enemy put an end to all dreams and plans.

His dedication to work and diligence were literally phenomenal. He worked on all sorts of political, organizational, and literary activities. He was diligent in Torah and work. He edited and wrote. This diligent man, who spent almost all of his time in practical, dry matters, also found some quiet time for poetry, a time of melody for his beautiful soul.

During the Holocaust

The days of storm and destruction, which came like a thief upon Polish Jewry at the time of the German conquest, brought up from the treasure chest of the soul of Reb Zisha strong powers, and placed him as the leader of Orthodox Judaism in Poland. There are people who are broken from tribulations, and there are others who strengthen themselves and raise themselves through difficulties. Reb Zisha Frydman was of the second type. He was raised up in tribulation, and he reached the heights of humanity and Judaism.

On November 20, 1939, he was imprisoned along with 21 other activists as "guarantors". They were imprisoned in jail for one week, and then freed. I still remember that I waited for Zisha Frydman at the entrance to the jail on Danilowiczoska Street. He was freed toward evening, and ran as quick as an arrow to his home in order to fulfill the commandment of tefillin before nightfall[13]. He did not have tefillin in jail, and this fact literally tortured him. He told me that he never experienced such joy in putting on the tefillin as he did the day that he left prison.

During the early days of occupation, in 1940, when the Joint[14] began its activities, and the chairman of the Judenrat, Adam Czernikow worked zealously to ease the situation of the Jews, Frydman served as the representative attorney and solicitor for Orthodox Jewry, who fell as the first victim to the tragic circumstances. Rabbis, scholars, Yeshiva students, teachers of Beis Yaakov, religious teachers, and Orthodox Jews in general, suffered in a disproportionate manner from the Germans, and were also deprived by the Jewish assistance organizations, which were headed only by secular Jewish activists. Reb Zisha Frydman was the only representative of Agudas Yisrael, or Orthodox Judaism, on the communal council that worked with the Joint, and he solicited, and demanded with steadfastness and strength of heart. He called into the ears of the directors of the assistance organizations: "Woe to humanity for the disgrace of Torah"[15]. Thanks to his efforts and diligence, the denial was somewhat rectified. With the assistance of his friends Eliezer Gershon Friedenson, Avraham Mordechai Rogowi, Yoel Ungar, Avraham Meir Krongard, David Shafran, and Yosef Moshe Haber, the head of the community of Kalisz who lived in Warsaw at that time, he set up a network of soup kitchens and assistance organizations for religious Jews. In November 1939, he founded, along with Rabbi Yitzchak Meir Lewin, a large public soup kitchen in the hall of Beis Yaakov on 37 Banlawki St., which was directed by the teachers Bochner-Szteiner, Erlich, and Rabicz. Later, other soup kitchens were added, which were directed by Aguda activists, including the young activists. There, Aguda writers found refuge and sustenance (they were also assisted by the Writers' Union on 13 Tlumacza St.). Thanks to the assistance of David Gozik, the director of the Joint, Reb Zisha received specific sums from a special fund to support men of spirit, which made it possible to maintain soup kitchens in order to ease the straits of the Orthodox needy, especially rabbis, Orthodox activists, clergy, heads of Yeshivas, and scholars.

Even in the darkness of the ghetto, the prime aim of Reb Zisha – education – was not removed from his sight. With the support money that was given by the Joint to scholars and religious teachers, Reb Zisha organized large network of underground Orthodox schools. These were Yesodei Hatorah for boys, Beis Yaakov for girls, elementary Yeshivas, and three advanced Yeshivas. Thousands of students and hundreds of teachers found refuge in these educational institutions, which were conducted under the guise of "soup kitchens" (the schools did indeed provide meals to the children), playgroups, or health organizations. When the Germans permitted the Judenrat to conduct schools in 1941, the Orthodox educational schools rose from the underground to the light of day and were strengthened by Adam Czernikow, the head of the Warsaw community, who behaved with gratitude and deep reverence toward Frydman. In February 1942, Czernikow established an independent religious council to deal with the religious needs of the population. The Judenrat, which was a staunchly secular organization, did not deal with such matters. Reb Zisha Frydman was appointed as the chairman of the religious council, and was recognized as the head of religious Judaism not only because of his position, but also thanks to his personality and activities, which inspired respect and support.

Extermination

Until July 22, 1942, the eve of Tisha Beov 5702, the day of the beginning of the liquidation of the Warsaw Ghetto, the Jews of Warsaw displayed a wondrous life force despite the oppression, torture, suffering, tribulations, epidemics, death, and fear. The Germans did not defeat the Jews with their oppression, and the Jewish community displayed great powers of adaptivity to the bitter conditions. The belief in a better future and the faith that the sun will yet shine for them strengthened and supported them in their distress. However on July 1942, when the expulsions to the death camps began, the Germans liquidated the Jewish assistance organizations and closed the schools. The ground was pulled from under Zisha Frydman's feet. The only remaining places of refuge for the remnants of the Jewish community in Warsaw were the workshops, called "shop", where they were able to work under German supervision. However, for the Orthodox Jews without any means, it was as difficult as splitting the Red Sea to enter such a workshop. Frydman turned to the "shop" of Schultz, on 44-46 Nowolipia St., which was directed by Mr. Avraham Hendel, a religious Jew who lives today in Tel Aviv. In this "shop", many Orthodox Jews found work, including well known rabbis and rebbes, such as Reb Moshe Betzalel Alter the brother of the Gerrer Rebbe, Rabbi Kalonymus Szapira the rabbi of Piaseczno and author of "Chovat Hatalmidim", Rabbi David Halberstam the rabbi of Sosnowiec and the brother-in-law of the rabbi of Radomsk, Rabbi Avraham Alter the rabbi of Pawianiec, Rabbi Y. Sender of Poznan (Posen), the brothers Simcha and Aharon Rappaport who were industrialists from Bielec, Yaakov Radzinski one of the Mizrachi activists, and others. Frydman was accepted after many pleas to the director of the Schultz "shop". In those days, this was considered to be a means of saving one's life. Finally, the director honored him and invited him to eat at his table on Sabbaths and festivals. Reb Zisha Frydman worked twelve hours a day fixing boots and shoes. During work hours, he studied chapters of Mishnah, Midrash and bible off by heart with his co-workers.

He remained alone and bereaved in his life. His wife and only daughter, who was thirteen years old and had been born after eighteen years of marriage, an intelligent and darling girl, who was educated by her father, as well as his father-in-law and mother-in-law who had been with him at that time, were all sent off to be exterminated. The woeful poem that Frydman wrote about the loss of his families still rings in my ears.

The study of Torah was his source of strength during those days of destruction.

Frydman obtained a Paraguayan passport in 1943 through the efforts of Reb Chaim Yisrael Eiz, of Zurich, Switzerland. However the passport did him no good. Frydman was sent along with the Senator Yaakov Trukenheim to the Trawniki death camp in the Lublin region. He was murdered by the German murderers in November 1943.

TRANSLATOR'S FOOTNOTES:

1. According to rabbinic tradition, a human body has 248 bones and 365 sinews.

2. A reference from the Torah enjoining the Jewish people not to follow the path of idol worshippers.

3. The Amshenover Hassidic group exists today, and is centered in Jerusalem.

4. This statement is a somewhat cryptic, but I would guess that these two people were chosen to be the official Jewish representatives to the Sejm (Polish parliament).

5. Generalissimo Francisco Franco was, of course, an extreme right wing fascist who ruled Spain from the 1930s, through the war, until his death in the late 1970s. The Bund is an extreme left wing, secular, non-Zionist faction, and Poale Zion was a left leaning Zionist faction.

6. The Torah is divided into 54 portions, one of which is read each Sabbath. A Jewish year has anywhere either 50/51 or 54/55 Sabbaths, depending upon whether the year is a leap year (which occurs seven times in nineteen years, and is intercalated with an additional lunar month). In addition, if a Sabbath coincides with a major festival (and this must happen at least twice a year due to Passover and Sukkot, but can occur as much as five times in a year depending on how the calendar falls out), the regular portion is not read. Thus, there are certain portions, which are doubled up to insure that the Torah reading cycle finishes at the appropriate time, on Simchat Torah.

7. A 'gartel' or 'avnet' is a waistband worn primarily by Hassidic Jews at religious occasions.

8. The Shmoneh Esrei (literally 'eighteen', referring to eighteen benedictions), is the central part of all prayer services. It actually consists of nineteen benedictions on weekdays, as an extra benediction was added in the first century C.E. On Sabbaths and festivals, it consists of seven benedictions, however it retains the name 'Shmoneh Esrei'. It is also referred to as the 'Amida' (i.e. 'standing' – standing prayer).

9. Agudas Yisrael Worker's faction. This movement still exists, and has often had a small representation in the Israeli Knesset. It tends to have a somewhat more worldly outlook, and is more Zionistically inclined than its parent organization, and is more. Two Kibbutzim in Israel, Chafetz Chaim and Shaalvim, are affiliated with Poale Agudas Yisrael.

10. "An occasional scholar", is literally "a scholar when he wants to be". It is an idiomatic expression that is not directly translatable into English.

11. A quote from the Book of Proverbs.

12. These are three tractates of the Talmud: Gittin dealing with the laws of divorce, Kiddushin dealing with the laws of marriage, and Yoma dealing with the laws of Yom Kippur. 13. Tefillin (phylacteries) are two black boxes containing sections of the Torah, which are bound to the arms of a Jewish male during morning prayers, in fulfillment of a biblical injunction. The commandment is generally fulfilled during the time of the morning prayers, but if that was not possible, it can be fulfilled at all times of the day, but not after nightfall.

14. The Joint Distribution Committee.

15. A quote from the Mishnaic tractate Pirke Avot ("Ethics of the Fathers"), dealing with moral adages.

{686}

A Shining Personality – Reb Zishe

by Pesia Shorashewski

Translated by Jerrold Landau

Approximately two weeks before the war, I went to one of the greatest of the Baale-Mussar[1] (who now resides in America), in order to take counsel from him and to hear his opinions about various problems that arose with regard to the education of our daughters. I saw that he was about to stop his work (he was writing a letter to someone), and I requested that he complete it so as not to disturb him. I glanced at his letter without his knowledge, and I was astounded: How could this be described thus? And who is it that was writing? One of the greatest of the Baale-Mussar, who weighs out each word, and who restrains his mouth from exaggeration?

It was difficult for me to restrain myself. I asked him to explain the situation, and he said: "What indeed is your question? Do you wish to know why I use such a description for such and such a Jew? I will answer you: the Jewish world refers to him as that." Who is the world? – I did not understand. Then he said to me: "You should know that of all the nations of the world, the Jews are the least descriptive. With us, the sense of smell is well developed. The nation of Israel senses and feels its great people. The intuition of the collective Jewish soul is always correct. I will give you two examples and you will understand. The Rambam (Maimonides) wrote a book that every Jewish scholar uses. He called his book the 'Mishne Torah' ('Repetition of the Torah'). The Jewish spirit evaluated, with all due reverence to the Rambam and his book, that this name is an exaggeration. Thus it was not accepted. Everyone Jew refers to the book as the Rambam[2].

The holy Shela, a great Kabbalist, bestowed upon the Jewish people a very important work and called it 'Shnei Luchot Habrit' ('The Two Tablets of the Covenant'). Once again, despite all the recognition and honor due to one of the giants of true wisdom, this name was not accepted in its full form, but only in its abbreviated form Shela, and not more than that. The nation of Israel is extremely sensitive, meticulous, and exacting, giving their due to those who exalt themselves... If the Jews use a specific description, you should not consider this to be an exaggeration, for our nation coronates those who are worthy of coronation, and shoots right on the mark."

When I wish now to write on paper a brief description of the personality of Alexander Zishe Frydman, I remember these things. They still beat upon my ears. The collective Jewish soul does not err... It always makes the appropriate judgements... it does not exaggerate in its descriptions... It cloaks itself in the cloak that fits...

If you were to meet him, you could not say anything other than: Reb Zishe. This is not because of familiarity, and not because this was the accepted custom. It was simply because "the knowledge of his countenance answered for him". His face was glowing, his high forehead slightly wrinkled, his eyes were deep-set, exuding fundamental Jewish wisdom, and particularly his polite behavior toward every man would convince you. You would realize that you are standing before a sage in the full sense of the word. You would nod your head due to deep-seated respect, and you would not be able to refer to him in any other way than Reb Zishe. It is interesting that even people who would speak to him in Polish would start off by saying: "Reb Zishe, what do you say?" I pointed out to Dr. Ringelblum (the well-known historian, the head of the Z.T.A.S., which is affiliated with the Joint), that it was not nice to say in Polish: "Reb Zishe". He contradicted me and said: "There is no other way, since according to my opinion, he is a true sage with respect to his wisdom, his way of thinking, his breadth of knowledge, and primarily his pureness of heart." Dr. Ringelblum continued: "according to me, he is the yardstick of pure hearted communal activity...".

I heard a great deal about Reb Zishe Frydman in our house. My father of blessed memory explained to me that he was one of the shining stars of the Yeshiva of Sochaczew. It was also possible to discern this matter from his pure, full and overflowing language that he used with reference to the sages and halachic decisors in his articles in "Digleinu", and later in "Darcheinu" (Agudas Yisrael monthly publications). When it was pointed out to him that his manner of speaking in Yiddish was simpler, and more understandable and acceptable to the people (he was one of the best orators of Agudas Yisrael), he answered simply: "On the contrary. With me, the language of the Torah is the natural language, in which I was educated and raised." He was among the first editors (in the latter period of Agudas Yisrael), who published monthly publications and manuscripts in Hebrew. "Our manner of speaking will remove in no small manner the ignorance from among us." He was among the zealous fighters against boorishness and empty-headedness. "A bookshelf is not only a nice piece of furniture in our quarters. We have to concern ourselves that our souls should be furnished with our libraries", was an adage that was frequently on his lips…

I met him for the first time in 5684 (1924). He was at that time a candidate to head the "Beis Yaakov" seminaries after the death of Sara Schenirer may she rest in peace[3]. We heard our first lesson from him, on the first chapter of the book of Psalms. We were enchanted by his methodology of explanation and his clear language. I still remember the manner in which he expounded the end of the chapter "G-d knows the paths of the righteous, and he destroys the paths of the wicked." He explained that 'knowing' has the meaning of 'cleaving'. By cleaving to G-d, we remain in life. Life distant from G-d causes destruction in a clear fashion – based on the verse "And thou who cleave to the L-rd your G-d are all alive today"[4]. Jews who tie themselves to the name of G-d will remain eternally.

We realized at that time that he was more fitting than any other scholar to direct the network of girls' schools – and we would not merit that he would remain our principal. There was another reason as well. He was not able to direct his energies to one endeavor, even though it was a very important endeavor. For his calling was to remove the stumbling blocks from the organizational bodies of Orthodox Judaism. He was not only the chief secretary of Agudas Yisrael, but he was also its living spirit, and the prime mover of the entire movement. Every city and town requested that Reb Zishe Frydman should visit, for he knew how to organize appropriate activities. His encouraging words, spiced with appropriate words of our sages, were of great influence. His visit in any town would turn into a large rally for Orthodox Judaism. He was one of the chief architects who nurtured and developed Agudas Yisrael. As a true leader with no airs about him, he realized that without the youth there would be no future for the nation. He gave himself over in particular to the Orthodox youth, and attempted to forge a bridge between the older and younger generations, to remove the natural and artificial friction from between them… He organized activities for the youth of Agudas Yisrael, and Poale Agudas Yisrael. The purpose of these activities was to raise their spirits, to refine their character traits, and to prepare them for the honorable title of 'a member of the people of Israel'. He did not have the idea of factionalism, of separation of an elite group from the people of Israel. His concept was for the entire people of Israel with the spirit of the Torah. He recognized no other master other than the authority of Torah. He understood that the holy powers of Judaism are nurtured in the creative workshops of our nation, that is in the elementary schools (cheders) and Yeshivot. He expended much of his energy in improving the lot of the students and teachers. He fought against the widely accepted yet incorrect concept that the identifying mark of a teacher was his inability to be successful in any other endeavor. On the contrary, he was wary of such teachers. Someone who teaches Torah to children in school, aside from having fine personal character, must know his profession, since he is responsible for influencing and inculcating. He gave himself over, along with the elder Avraham Feldfevel and Rabbi Yosef Begun (may G-d avenge his blood), to establish a teachers' seminary. When the Polish government issued decrees against the cheders and attempted to put an end to them under the pretext that the lack of secular education distorts the tender spirit of the youth, he participated along with the Chofetz Chaim of holy blessed memory[5], and Rabbi Eliahu Kirshborn of blessed memory (a representative to the Sejm) in a delegation to the prime minister Barter, and they were successful in averting this decree…

Rabbi Zishe Frydman set the wonderful curriculum for the "Chorev" cheders where secular subjects were included. He was the principal of "Chorev", and the overseer of the seminary for educators. Just as the center of the Bais Yaakov network was Krakow, the center of the Chorev network was Warsaw.

His lectures in the community of Warsaw (he was a parnas of Agudas Yisrael there) always excelled in courageous explanations to support fundamental religious education. Aside from his communal work, he occupied himself in learning. "My prime pleasure is when I immerse myself in the ocean of Talmud", Reb Zishe used to say. He made his nights as days, and learned without interruption. "I am very sorry that not everyone can appreciate and know the pleasure and spiritual satisfaction that is the lot of a Jew who learns Gemara", he said to Giterman (the head of the Joint), when he asked him why he is always studying.

Prior to the war, his five-volume anthology "The Wellspring of Torah" ("Torah Kval" in Yiddish) was published. Those who were in the know would acknowledge that, of all anthologies, his was the most fundamental and exact.

His entire personality was a combination of Torah and Hassidism. In him was intertwined in an extraordinary manner the essence of the Gaon of Vilna, accompanied by Rabbi Yisrael Baal Shem Tov[6]. This exalted blend of Torah and goodness, for his channels of grace drew from the overflowing and ever-flowing wellspring of Torah. The Torah was the candle before him. The Rabbi did not start or continue with any endeavor without consulting the great sages of the generation.

Rabbi Pinchas Warshawiak (the brother-in-law of the Gerrer Rebbe) testified about him that all of his actions were links in the chain of the service of G-d. I had already heard these words after the war started, after the Nazis had conquered Warsaw. Thus, even in the most difficult of times he remained faithful to his spirit and to himself. His behavior during the great tragedy of our people was notable, and is worthy of elaboration.

It was already known that the Germans had hatched the plan to annihilate the Jews, and they were interested in appointing Jews who would help bring their plans to fruition. They organized a council of elders for this purpose[7]. Warsaw also had such a council of elders, which was chaired by the engineer Czerniakow. At the outset of its duties, Czerniakow invited Zishe Frydman to be part of that council. Reb Zishe refused to accept this 'honor' and reasoned with him. "It is impossible to meet with those defiled people, whose every word is blasphemy, and their face lacks the image of G-d. And if it is not possible for me to help the Jews, why do I need this honor?". He added "I was accustomed to try to be the highest part of the door, that no other person could approach."[8] Czerniakow interrupted: "But, your life would be assured. If you love your nation, you should give yourself over to our work." (The engineer himself did not realize at that time that the entire council was just a net for the evil ones.) Reb Zishe answered: "First of all, as a believing Jew, I recite every day: 'in Your hand do I commit my soul'[9] ... Secondly, according to my judgement, my life would be even more in danger." He did not accept the position, but rather he expended all his energy in assisting and saving fellow Jews. He represented Orthodox Judaism on the Joint and the Z.T.A.S. (The latter are the Polish initials for the Jewish Organization of Social Work.) Through his efforts, cheders, Yeshivot, Bais Yaakov schools, and kosher kitchens were established, and he supported them. Aside from this, he took personal concern in the lot of every Torah scholar. I sometimes would see in his house (on Pinska 44) long lines of Jews who were waiting for support. For the most part, the people waiting in line were suffering great tribulation, in particular due to the conditions of that time. Their eyes were sorrowful, and they revealed secrets that weighed them down. However, I was astonished that each one waxed great in his praise, as they would say: "The situation is very bad, with fear, hunger, and all sorts of troubles, however G-d did not forsake us, for he provided a man, Reb Zishe Frydman, who concerns himself with every suffering Jew."

If a Yeshiva student did not receive his support (this was prior to the setting up of workshops, and aside from collective support, there was also private support), Reb Zishe would bring him to his house. He would apologize to his wife: "Perhaps he took ill, and I am required to look after him, for that is the way of the Torah." Starwinski, the treasurer of the J.T.A.S. said of him at that time: "I am astonished. Every representative has against himself complaints and claims. The youths request their dismissal, and are suspicious of honorable people. Only with regard to Zishe Frydman do I receive letters of praise." Dr. Ringelblum was correct when he called him "The yardstick of pure hearted communal activity..."

I was aware that with regard to his own household, he lived quit austerely. He answered me with his own explanation: "How can I behave otherwise. If it is a time of trouble for Jacob, can I be saved from it?"[10] It was amazing. He held the power of the entire community of Orthodox Judaism in an unofficial capacity, he stood on his guard post, and did not move from it. In the morning he occupied himself with assistance, in the evenings, he participated in meetings and gatherings, and learned the daily page of Talmud with the youth.

When a historian of the underground examines documents about the establishment of the Jewish underground, he would be able to write a great deal about the participation of Alexander Zishe Frydman. In general, he took a stand, he helped others, and he always entertained people with words of our sages, stories of a Rebbe, or a lighthearted word. At times he apologized to me with a gloomy face, and said: "Perhaps this is not correct... however my heart tells me that difficult days are coming. We require faith as strong as a rock, and G-d forbid we should not weaken, however", he said in a low voice, " it is worse for those who do not see the finger of G-d in the tragedies".

The gloomy days approached as speedily as lightning. Aktions began. The support was cut off. Those who required support were sent to Treblinka. Reb Zishe, as a faithful friend of Hendel (we will speak about the influence of Reb A. Hendel later) entered together with the family of the Gerrer Rebbe and other rabbis into Hendel's workshop. (Schultz was the director. Reb Avraham Hendel was his supervisor) and worked there as a shoemaker. I often saw him occupied with his work, removing nails from torn shoes, putting patches on the tears, humming during his work: "It once happened that two of them were running up the ramp to the altar together, and one of them pushed aside the other" (from Tractate Yoma Chapter 2, Mishna 2). I asked him: "Reb Zishe, we are all relaxing" (We only worked when we received the watchword "Achtung" from Mr. A. Hendel, which implied that the enemy was coming near.) "Therefore, why are you working, what is the explanation for this diligence?" He answered me calmly: "I am not working for the good of the defiled ones, I only want that those weaker than me should be able to take it easier."

After that week (January 22, 1943), I was frightened by the terrible news. His wife, his only daughter, his son-in-law and daughter-in-law were all taken in one day, on a Friday prior to candle lighting time, to Treblinka. How can we be comforted, what can we say? Is it possible to comfort the forlorn and bereaved father, in particular when the father is Reb Zishe Frydman, who mourns not only for his own tragedy but also for the tragedy of his entire people? I could not go to him, it was impossible... I went into the workshop and was astounded. I did not recognize him. His face was as the face of a corpse, with only the eyes sparkling and revealing the secret, eyes that had not closed for a long time ... He was humming quietly: "Rabbi Yehuda says, lest his wife die... for it says 'and he shall atone for himself and his household' ... his household is his family" (a quote from Tractate Yoma). Instead of comforting him, I began to weep, and then Reb Zishe said to me: "Do not weep, for this is destructive, and the Torah forbids this. I only pray that these souls which are dear to me, which are beloved to me more than my own soul, should be the last victims, and no other Jewish father should know of my tribulations. However I want to show you" – with trembling hands he showed me two poems (prior to this time he had published poems). I only managed to read one poem, in which a bereaved father mourns for his only daughter – "I educated her in Torah, and I trained her in good deeds. If I did not merit to bring her to the marriage canopy, in the manner of most Jews, parents of Israel, – – – – let it be brought near to Heaven, the marriage ceremony that did not take place ... the marriage canopy should be spread out between the Divine Presence and the community of Israel." I became choked with tears. I felt as if I would shortly faint. As if in a dream, I heard his voice, hoarse from the troubles – "I have another delightful child. I have a handwritten manuscript, a commentary on the Torah. I have completed Genesis, Exodus, Leviticus and Numbers. I hope that I will merit to complete Deuteronomy in the Land of Israel. Words that are stated in the Land of Israel are more important. Our sages have said that the Torah of the Land of Israel does not compare to the Torah of outside the land. I will come to you, I will see your husband, we will enjoy." I left him stirred up and in turmoil, and without thinking I proclaimed in a loud voice: "Who is like Your nation of Israel, a singular nation in the world"[11]. What fineness in a time of distress! What a superhuman power!

I never saw him again after that day. On the seventh day of Passover 5703 (1943), we were transferred to Majdanek (in the third aktion which liquidated the Warsaw Ghetto). With great luck, Hendel succeeded in moving Schultz's factory to Trawniki (near Lublin), and we were able to work there for about eight more months. This factory was liquidated after eight months. A few people who were moved to Majdanek related: "of all the Jews in Trawniki (there were 10,000), we remember one Jew. We don't know his family name, but everyone called him Reb Zishe. He helped everyone, and shared the crumbs of his bread with his fellow. He stood up before the oppressors on behalf of any Jew. There he sanctified the name of G-d"[12].

Explanations were superfluous. I already understood the end. I told the people who related this the following: "You should know that all his life he taught how to live, and therefore he surely knew how to die."" The words of the Ramchal[13] in his wonderful poem "Shimshon" are appropriate: "For if I lost my spirit, I did not lose my heart – no, I did not lose my munificent spirit, it has supported me from earliest days!..."

His parents and his family (who currently live in Israel) remain in great sorrow. It is tragic for the loss, and there are no words of comfort for the sorrow of the public. Perhaps his parents and all of Jewry who mourn the destruction can find comfort from his commentary: "G-d knows the way of the righteous, by cleaving with the living G-d, one finds life". This way, and no other way, was the essence of the life of Reb Zishe.

A note: many in Israel are his students, his admirers, and people who knew him. They should feel duty bound to collect all of his essays and publications and to publish them in a special anthology. In such a way, we could perpetuate his unforgettable name, and we will be able to educate, and make known to our young generation the glorious personality that was Reb Alexander Zishe Frydman.

TRANSLATOR'S FOOTNOTES:

1. Mussar (literally, chastisement or lessons), refers to the field of study of religious character and ethical refinement. A Baal-Mussar (literally, a master of Mussar), is a person devoted to the study and practice of Mussar. This field of Jewish religious thought was popularized by the famous Rabbi Yisrael Salanter of Salantai, Lithuania, who lived in the late 18th and early 19th centuries.

2. The Rambam wrote the Mishne Torah as a summary of the entire corpus of Torah Law. Mishne Torah means 'repetition of the Torah' or 'summary of the Torah'. This book is not generally referred to by that name, but rather as 'Yad Hachazaka' (a numerical play on the word Yad 'hand', which adds up to a numerical value of 14, which corresponds to the number of volumes of the set), or more often just as 'the Rambam'. This work was subject to controversy in its day due to its claim of being the latest complete authority on Jewish Law, but now is accepted universally (although it is now accompanied by numerous commentaries and glosses that describe alternate opinions and record disagreements).

3. Beis Yaakov is a network of orthodox girls' schools, under the direction of the Agudas Yisrael movement. These schools are still prevalent today. This network was founded by Sara Schenirer.

4. Deuteronomy chapter 4, verse 4.

5. The Chofetz Chaim (literally, he who desires life, which was the title of his magnum opus on the laws of the prohibitions of slander), Rabbi Yisrael Kagan, was one of the acknowledged leaders of Orthodox Judaism. He died in 1933, well into his 90s. His works are considered basic texts of religious study to this day.

6. The Gaon of Vilna was a leader of misnagdic (non-Hassidic) orthodoxy, and the Baal Shem Tov was the founder of Hassidism.

7. Apparently a reference to the judenrat, a Nazi-appointed Jewish council.

8. Seemingly an idiom for his utmost of devotion in public service.

9. A quote from the 'Adon Olam' prayer.

10. A twisting of a biblical verse (Jeremiah 30, 7) : "It is a time of trouble for Jacob (i.e. the Jewish people), and they will be saved from it."

11. A quote from the Sabbath afternoon prayers.

12. Sanctifying the name of G-d here refers to dying a martyr's death.

13. Ramchal is the acronym for Rabbi Moshe Chaim Luzatto, a very famous 17th century Italian Rabbi who wrote several important works.

{289 - Yiddish} {692 - Hebrew}

Simcha Grundwag

by Y. Frydman

Translated by Jerrold Landau

The final word that came to us in the Land of Israel from the Warsaw Ghetto was very short.

"Father is no longer alive…"

Yes, this was the end of a family that sacrificed everything for the community, for Zionism, and did not merit making aliya to the Land that was dear to their souls.

This is a description of Simcha Grundwag, 40-50 years ago.

To him, the good of the public was more important than anything else, even than his livelihood and family. He was dedicated to the needs of the public from morning to evening. The family suffered from many tribulations, but he did not retreat. He only saw one path for himself, lined with flowers and sprinkled with light – and that was the path that led to Zion, from the day that he heard the decree of Herzl until the time of the ghetto, and he did not flinch from that path.

This was the way it was.

Where was he not active as a communal activist? In every place, the good of the community demanded this. He never asked his friends, in whose name he appeared.

He presented himself as a democrat, but he acted with strength. For years, he ruled with force, but it was always filled with faith. He was the chairman of the Zionist organization and the Jewish National Fund for decades, and in later years, also of Bnot Zion. He founded a library at the outset of the founding of the Zionist organization in Sochaczew, and he served as its chairman. He guided it until it became the public "Jewish Library" of Sochaczew. He represented the community, founded an elementary school that would teach Hebrew in Hebrew that later became "The Hebrew School", and he always covered its deficit, as well as the deficit of the synagogue. He was not absent from any place that there was communal activity.

The older Zionists, who joined Zionism along with him, almost abandoned it later. He pushed them off, "In any case – there is me". Even the youth was under his influence. Each Sabbath, he gave a lecture on history or Zionism, and he educated a generation of young Zionists. In the later years, they took the Zionist activities into their own hands, without agreeing with the ideas and methodology of their teacher. He often became angry, but he retracted when they promised him that it was for the good of the land of Israel. He could not remain indifferent, and see how the "youth" conduct matters, without requiring his assistance…

Decades passed, and Simcha Grundwag remained a communal activist, an enthusiastic Zionist, leading communal activities in the manner of the era, with the Land of Israel being the object of his love. He lent support, made demands upon the youth, gave lectures, raised the level of national consciousness and knowledge, and educated a Zionistic generation that it should be fitting for the Land of Israel. He stood at the helm of all the battles against the Rebbe's court, which fought against Zionism.

His entire life was given to the Land of Israel, yet he never merited in seeing the Promised Land. His met a cruel death at the hands of the Nazi murderers in the Warsaw Ghetto.

I must also mention his son Nachum. We don't know what his end was. He followed a different path. He left communal affairs to his father, and he himself turned to the theater. He made his livelihood in a variety of ways – he worked in his father's store and he was a wagon driver, anything so as not to be dependent on anyone else; however he never moved from the stage. Thanks to him, a dramatic troupe was founded; the income of which was donated to communal matters.

He was often asked: "Nachum, come to The Land of Israel. With your talents and sense of humor, you will find your place in the Israeli theater." However he also did not merit, but he did send his son to the land of hope, expecting to follow after him after he got settled…

This was the bitter fate of the Grundwag family.

Simcha Grundwag gave himself over to the Land of Israel, and gave his life in the ghetto. Even his son did not make aliya to the Land, only his grandson.

His letters to his grandson and great-grandson, and also to me, are filled with reverence and love for the land, and every one of them concluded with the words. "Oh, that I may merit to see you in the Land"…

Reb Chanoch (Henech) Zaonz and his wife.

{p. 696}

{285}

Frejman Hirsch (Shalom Tzvi Frejdman)

Yaakov Frejdman

Translated by Jerrold Landau

A.

The name Frejman Hirsch, as people in Sochaczew called him, has a strange resonance. A name that resembles the family name (his name was really Hirsch Frejdman), as indeed Frejman Hirsch was himself so rare.

Externally, he was very ordinary. He was of average height, with a pious face and a small, pointed noise, with a grayish white beard. He was an Amshinover (Myszynow) Hassid.

In a grocery store that had a strange outward appearance, Frejman Hirsch sold, aside from groceries, pharmaceutical items and various "grandmotherly" medicines and herbs for various illnesses. Gentiles would gather these for him in their fields. He himself would also drink of them. Once someone saw a weeping woman running, with broken hands, into Frejman Hirsch's store, asking that he should mercifully give her a cure. Frejman Hirsch took out ingredients from his stuffed jars, and mixed up medicines with each other.

And what was Frejman Hirsch not? He was a prayer leader, a mohel (circumcisor), a gabbai (trustee) of the Chevra Kadisha (Burial Society), a chief activist, a shofar blower – and all of these "positions" were not outward positions and ordinary positions, but rather it was as if he was born into them…

He was the mohel of the city for forty some years, for the rich and the poor. Nothing held him back from going out to circumcise a child. He would leave his business. There might have been a snow or a frost, a storm or a rainfall – but the city mohel went to do the mitzvah.

Frejman Hirsch was not a special cantor. He served for decades as the prayer leader for Shacharit [1] in the synagogue and the Beis Midrash. He gladly held both positions, especially on the High Holy Days. He divided them up as follows: On the first day, he led Shacharit and blew the shofar in the synagogue – and lead Musaf in the Beis Midrash. On the second day, he did the opposite. He was also the city visitor [2]. Summer and winter, day and night, they would call him and he would come.

He became very busy when someone died in the city, when Moshe Aharon Shulklapper gave two knocks on the doors with his wooden hammer as a sign that someone has died in the city. Then Frejman Hirsch's work began. As the gabbai of the Chevra Kadisha he went out to the cemetery to designate the gravesite, and right after that he became the chief of those who occupy themselves with the deceased. When everything was ready, he performed the tahara [3] along with the other members of the Chevra Kadisha, and after that he laid the deceased into the grave. Who continues to talk when a city resident came in carrying a deceased person, or when there was indeed a met mitzvah [4] in the city?

As people used to relate, he had a dream one dark night that someone knocked on his window and informed him that a met mitzvah was lying on the Borisower Street. He sprung up out of bed, got dressed, lit his lantern, and set out directly for Borisower Street. Suddenly he noticed that there was somebody else going about with a lantern. That person was also a member of the Chevra Kadisha and had the same dream. They decided to look for him, and found him on the bridge of Borisower Street. Frejman Hirsch was the first to arrive on the bridge and find the corpse. He waited for the second to come, and both of them carried the corpse on their shoulders and brought it to the tahara room of the cemetery…

Frejman Hirsch stood out from all of the Chevra Kadisha members in that he did not enjoy "the cup" [5]. He was not a "drinking" gabbai of the Chevra Kadisha. Even on the 7th of Adar, the celebration day of the Chevra Kadisha, he did not drink a great deal of strong drink. He only did so on Sabbaths and Festivals after the fish [6] His greatest pleasure was on Simchat Torah, when as gabbai of the Chevra Kadisha, he distributed red apples with candles to all of the children for their flags [7]. At that time, hundreds of children would come to him. He did not get tired during the distribution, and he himself took part in the children's joy. For him, that was the reward for his dedicated work…

Popularity was the central foundation of Frejman Hirsch's activities. Indeed, as the ideal popular activist, he never became involved in controversies. However, he once did become entwined in a dispute, and it was actually with the Sochaczewer court [8]. The story goes as follows:

Reb Mendel Frejdman with his children.

The Zionist prayer group (minyan), that was held in Shmuel Nelson's house, wrote a Torah scroll. Frejman Hirsch was invited to come to the completion ceremony of the Torah scroll. Hirsch Frejman and his son Mendel did not decline to purchase a letter. They went to rejoice with the Torah along with all of the local Zionists and other Jews of the city. When they arrived home, a shekel [9] could be found in their wallets...

The incident of the shekel came to the Rebbe's court, and they could not forgive Frejdman Hirsch for his sin of the "shekel" [10]. When, as was the custom of the gabbai of the Chevra Kadisha, he went to the Rebbe's court each year on Simchat Torah to bring cake, red apples and very large twisted candles that were specially ordered from Warsaw, the members of the court did not permit Frejman Hirsch and his family to sit down at the table; so it was that in return for his faithfulness and honor to the elder Reb Avrahamele, he received a great reprimand from the court.

The silent controversy between the court and Frejman Hirsch lasted for years. The court asked his forgiveness when a relative of the court died and they had to come to the Chevra Kadisha to bury him. The negotiations lasted for three days, and thanks to the festival that took place in the interim, the matter ended.

He left behind a will that the sack that is laid under his head in the grave should, instead of earth, be filled with his receipts that he collected throughout all of the years from various Yeshivas and other charities, including Yeshivas from the Land of Israel; and that his circumcision knife and the small shofar that he blew every year should be placed near his head. The will was fulfilled. The entire Jewish population took part in his funeral, old and young, including children. The casket was placed in front of the Holy Ark, and the rabbi of the city, Rabbi Landau, eulogized him.

Such were the old time populist activists, dedicated with life and soul.

TRANSLATOR'S FOOTNOTES:

1. Shacharit is the daily morning prayer, and the first part of the prayer service on Sabbaths and festivals (when the Musaf service is added on afterwards). Here it refers to the elongated, complex, High Holy Day prayers.
2. I suspect that it means here the visitor of the sick.
3. This refers to the ritual purification and washing ceremony (tahara) that takes place with a corpse before it is placed in the casket for burial.
4. A met mitzvah (literally, a deceased person of a commandment) refers to a dead person who leaves behind no relatives or friends who would occupy themselves with the burial. In such a case, it is a commandment for the community to drop everything and arrange for the burial.
5. I.e. an alcoholic drink. In many places, it was a custom for the Chevra Kadisha members to wish each other well with a shot of whiskey (lechayim) after conducting a tahara.
6. It is customary to have a fish appetizer before a meat course on Shabbat and festivals. These are often differentiated with a drink.
7. On Simchat Torah, seven circuits are made around the synagogue with all of the Torah scrolls. Children accompany these circuits with flags, and in some places these flags are decorated with apples and candles.
8. The Hassidic court of the Sochaczewer Rebbe.
9. A shekel is an ancient Jewish coin, as well as the currency of the State of Israel. In this context, it refers to a token of membership in the Zionist movement.
10. As was standard, the Hassidic courts were opposed to the Zionist movement.

"Hatechia" Hebrew school.

{292}

Reb Menashe Czemerynski

Elchanan Kac

Translated by Jerrold Landau

The rabbi of the Chevra Tehillim, Reb Menashe Czemerynski of blessed memory, was a scholar, an advisor, a Gabbai (trustee) of the Chevra Kadisha, and a "visitor" [1]. He never took any money for these activities, but rather did them only for the sake of the mitzvah. If someone was up for conscription, they would go to him for advice about what to do. If someone became ill, somebody would come to request that Reb Menashe visit the sick person. The next day, somebody would come to tell him how the sick person is feeling, and to ask him what should they give him to eat. Whatever Reb Menashe said, they did.

I studied with Reb Moshe Czemerynski before the First World War. I remember how weeping women would come to him, announcing that their husband or someone else in the family was seriously ill. They would beg him: Reb Menashele, come quickly. He scolded them, "You should not call me Reb Menashele, my name is Reb Menashe [2]". Go say that I am coming soon. When Reb Menashe came, he listened to the sick person, administered cupping glasses [3] and ointments, and prescribed what the sick person should eat. If someone came to call him to a sick person while he was in the midst of eating, he would leave his food and go to the sick person. If someone came to call him to a sick person in the middle of the night, even if that person lived in an attic or a cellar, he went immediately. He never declined to go. During that time, he was the leader of the city, and also of the Chevra Kadisha, and the Shamashim (administrators) would come to ask him what to do. People would also come to consult with him for a religious lawsuit or adjudication. Both sides would agree to whatever Reb Menashe decided. People had only respect for whatever he would say.

There was no dying person for whom Reb Menashe was not present at the time of the departure of the soul, reciting the deathbed confession. If somebody was dying, even in the middle of the night, Reb Menashe immediately sent a Shamash (administrator) of the Chevra Kadisha to inform Reb Moshe Aharon Shulklapper [5] that the next morning at dawn, he must make two knocks on the doors. (It was a custom in our city that the Shamash, the Shulklapper, who used to knock on the doors of the homes [4] at 5:00 a.m. with three knocks. On Fridays, he did this twice, in the morning, and in the afternoon prior to candle lighting. And if somebody had died in the city, he would give two knocks. If two knocks were heard in the morning, they would ask the Shulklapper, Reb Moshe Aharon, who has died?).

Where today can we find such people, who do everything for the sake of the mitzvah?

Mrs. Tchipa Kac with her children.

The Tempel family.

TRANSLATOR'S FOOTNOTES:

1. A visitor of the sick.
2. The 'le' ending on a name is a Yiddish diminutive.
3. A remedy that is used to draw blood closer to the skin.
4. Literally 'shops' or 'stores', but I believe that 'homes' is meant here.
5. Shulklapper is the person who knocks on people's doors to awaken them to attend the morning prayers at the synagogue. See other articles in this book on Moshe Aharon Shulklapper.

{295}

Communal Activists of Sochaczew
Reb Zalman the "Visitor"
Shlomo Swiatlowski of Tel Aviv
Translated by Jerrold Landau

Reb Zalman Albert (the "visitor"

A.

Zalman Albert (Zalman Ajzenhendler [1]) had an iron shop on Warszawer Street, in the house of Chana Tzirel Flajszman. There was a small locksmith workshop in his small store. During his free moments, when there were no customers, Reb Zalman repaired locks and fixed keys, or he looked into a medical book.

Zalman Albert was a "visitor" ("mevaker"). He was considered to be knowledgeable in the field of medicine, and he was active in the "Sick Visiting" ("Bikur Cholim") society. After the founding of the "Linat Tzedek" society, Reb Zalman became the heart and brain of the institution.

We lived in the same courtyard as him. My father was laid up in bed for a long time, and Reb Zalman would often visit us; that dear Jew is etched in my memory. Later I was a frequent visitor in his home, and I saw his activity from up close.

I do not know how much he really was an expert in medicine... but that he wished to help people with his heart and soul is clear to me beyond doubt. I remind myself: it was a day of a fair in the town, and Reb Zalman was standing in his workshop and filing keys. There were a few customers in the store. Suddenly, a woman broke out in a cry: "Reb Zalman, please save! My father-in-law was stricken with a heart attack."

"Where does he live", asked Reb Zalman.

"At the house of Simcha the furrier in the room in the attic, which is found on Shul Gasse", answered the desperate woman.

Reb Zalman quickly wrote down the address and ordered the woman: "Run home quickly, and I am coming immediately with Skotnicki".

For Reb Zalman, the store, the keys and the locks did not exist any more. His wife Tauba Lea was already in the store, and Reb Zalman ran to Moshe Skotnicki. However Skotnicki had left for a village to tend to a sick person. Reb Zalman did not hesitate. In one breath he was already at the Linat Tzedek society, where he grabbed a few medications and a thermometer, and then he went immediately to the sick man. His suggestive and psychological approach to the ill person often was more helpful than the best medicines. He did not ask the sick man about the heart attack itself, the reason that he came, in order not to frighten him further. Like an experienced, long-time experienced tender to the sick, he turned with a friendly glance toward the sick man: "A good morning to you, Reb Yisrael, you most certainly ate something that was not good for you. We will soon see, show me your tongue!"

He put in the thermometer and took the pulse with his hand: "It is nothing, with G-d's help, everything will be fine, a little corruption that stimulated the heart. I am writing a prescription for you." Then he turned to the sick man's wife: -- "Go immediately to get the medicine from Reb Hirsch Frejdman."

The woman said to Reb Zalman in a pleasant tone: "Do not be upset, I do not wish to be embarrassed before you, but unfortunately there is no means here with which to purchase the medicine."

"Come with me immediately", Reb Zalman requested of the woman with a loving tone. "I say, do not be ashamed that one must save the sick man and also give him something good to eat." Reb Zalman did not go home before everything was taken care of for the sick man.

Epidemics of smallpox and scarlet fever broke out in the town. People would avoid going to neighbors. Reb Zalman did not lock himself away from any danger, even though he had a large family with young children. He was not concerned that he might bring the infections diseases home. He was on his feet day and night saving people. He took part in various consultations [2]. He even studied Latin, and with time he was able to write down various prescriptions. The pharmacists trusted the "visitor". The pharmacists gave medicine to anyone who brought in a prescription with Reb Zalman's signature. With the shortage of doctors at that time, Reb Zalman's practice of medicine saved many people from death.

TRANSLATOR'S FOOTNOTES:

1. Ajzenhandler means "handler of iron", referring to his profession. It was common to nickname a person after his profession.
2. I am not sure of the meaning of the word here. The Yiddish is "consoliums".

{298}

Reb Hershel Kluska of blessed memory
Shlomo Swiatlowski
Translated by Jerrold Landau

The unique personality of Reb Hershel Kluska is to be reckoned among the Sochaczew personalities who were active in various social institutions in the city.

As far as I remember, I recall Reb Hershel as one of the chief activists, perhaps the founder of Linat Hatzedek.

The masses of poor people of Sochaczew, as in all Jewish towns of Poland, lived in extremely crowded alleyways and in unsanitary dwellings. On the non-infrequent occasions when an epidemic would break out in the city, the first victims were from those crowded places. At such times, the Jewish poor saw Linat Hatzedek as a place of salvation. Those darkened alleyways were nests of various illnesses not only at times of epidemics, but also in "quiet" times – and Linat Hatzedek always had what to do. The chief task of the Linat Hatzedek society was to distribute free medicine to those who did not have enough money to have their prescriptions filled at a pharmacy. Equally important was going at night to those severely ill. Reb Hershel Kluska was extremely dedicated in this realm. He would go at night to dangerous places, bringing help and a good, warm word to the ill.

Helping the needy was his ideal. It is no wonder that they treated him with trust and respect.

In later years, the headquarters of Linat Hatzedek was established in Warsaw. It undertook financial activities to support its departments throughout Poland, including the department in Sochaczew. At that time, the "fine Jews" of the city first came to the fore, those who pushed to the side the former idealists and founders. However, Reb Hershel was not taken aback by them. On the contrary, he was happy that the institution had become a center for the assistance of the ill poor people. Reb Hershel held that medicine was not enough. He tried to actualize that which he thought was necessary. He founded a philanthropic society by the name "Ezrat Cholim Laaniyim" (Assistance for the Ill of the Poor), in which he invested a piece of his warm, Jewish heart and idealistic soul. He worked for that organization until his last breath – that is until his murder by the Nazis, may their name be erased.

Reb Hershel Kluska, one of the unique people, served properly, and the surviving Jews of Sochaczew will never forget him.

I should also mention here the names of Galek, Baruch Goldsztejn, Berl Brzozowski, Hertzke Brojtman, and others who created a premises, and purchased a new inventory of beds and bedding, and generally helped the refugees with whom they became acquainted.

Among the Sochaczew activists who were killed, we must also mention Reb Mottel Biezanski, the son of Reb Eliahu Moshe Biezanski who in their time served as chairmen of the cooperative people's bank in Sochaczew from the years 1934-1935-1936 until the outbreak of the Second World War, and who financed the bank almost completely through their own resources. This was a help for hundreds of poor Jewish families who struggled bitterly with economic terror from the anti-Semitic regime.

Men of the People
by Y. F.
Translated by Jerrold Landau

Years went by, but in the eyes of my mind the personalities and characters of our city are still clear. They implanted light into our lives during the course of their pure lifetimes, and conducted faithful and diligent work daily for the benefit of the public.

These are the modest communal activities, men of stature, who did everything for the sake of the mitzvah, without any pride and arrogance, and hurting anyone. They added their own imprint into our beautiful communal life.

A.

Freiman Hirsch (Shalom Tzvi) Frydman

The name Freiman Hirsch, as he was known in Sochaczew, had a strange ring to it. It was a very uncommon name. Even he himself was somewhat of an enigma, not fully understood. Externally, he was extremely straightforward. He was of average height, with a shriveled face, an ardent Hassid, however very sharp and drawn out. He was not an outstanding scholar, and as every Hassid, he went daily to the prayer service, returned home, ate breakfast, and went to his store and business – he purchased butter and cheese from the farmers, and sold baked goods and food. Nevertheless, he was well known and prominent in all areas of life in Sochaczew, and even his dingy store was not as simple as it apparently appeared.

In his general store he also sold various medications, 'segulot'[1] and herbs for various ailments. The gentiles in the villages would gather them for him, and he would dry them himself. Not infrequently would a weeping Jewess hurry to the store of Freiman Hirsch, with clasped hands, to request a remedy for a sick person. He would search through the full boxes and mix up a potion, as an alchemist who had found the secret to eternal life...

What did he not do? He was a prayer leader, a mohel (ritual circumciser), a trustee (Gabbai) of the Chevra Kadisha (burial society), and the blower of the shofar on Rosh Hashana. It seemed as if he was born to serve in all of these roles.

He served as the mohel of the town for forty-five years. Almost every newborn Jewish boy in Sochaczew was circumcised by him, rich and poor alike. Neither frost nor a snowstorm would stop him – for he was the mohel of the city.

He was not an extraordinary cantor, but nevertheless he served as a prayer leader for dozens of years. On the high holydays, he was in demand at both the Beis Midrash and the synagogue. To satisfy both, he would divide up his prayers. He would conduct the morning service and shofar blowing in the synagogue, and then conduct the mussaf service at the Beis Midrash. This was on the first day – and on the second day, he would do the reverse.

The high point of his communal service took place in the event of a death. After Aharon Shulklapper announced a death with two bangs of his wooden hammer, Freiman Hirsch would hurry over to the cemetery, choose an appropriate plot, and begin to occupy himself with the ritual preparations of the body (taharah), the dressing of the body in shrouds. He would lead the funeral procession and place the coffin into the grave. If a Jew from the village arrived with his 'dead', or if there was a 'meit mitzvah'[2], he would be the first among those who would busy themselves with the preparations.

He once related the following incident:

In one dark night he heard in a dream that they were knocking at his window to inform him that a 'meit mitzvah' was to be found on the route to Boristow. He arose from his bed, got dressed, lit his torch and went to search for the corpse. Suddenly, he recognized a Jew who was coming to greet him, also with a torch in his hand. Freiman Hirsch asked him where he was going, and he related that he also had a similar dream. Both of them carried the corpse on their shoulders and brought him to the taharah room[3] in the cemetery.

Freiman Hirsch was 'one of a kind' among the members of the Chevra Kadisha, for he was not inclined to take a 'drink'. He was a 'dry Gabbai'. [4] Even on the 7th of Adar, the festival of the Chevra Kadisha, he did not drink any strong drinks. [5] His greatest joy would be on Simchas Torah when, in his capacity of the Gabbai of the Chevra Kadisha, he would distribute candles and red apples to all of the children of the city so that they can place them on their flags. The children would come to him, and he would ensure that they were well taken care of, and rejoice with them.

This noble communal activist, who never entered into a controversy with anybody, was ultimately caught up in a controversy with the Sochaczew Hassidic courtyard. This is what transpired:

The Zionist "minyan" (prayer group) in the home of Shmuel Nelson commissioned a Torah scroll to be written, and he was invited to the celebration marking the conclusion of the writing of the Torah scroll, and was honored with the inscribing of one of the final letters [6]. He and his son Mendel responded to the invitation, purchased a letter, and attended the festivities along with all of the Zionists of the city. When he returned, he had a 'shekel' (membership to the Zionist organization) in his pocket.

The issue of the 'shekel' reached the Hassidic courtyard – and they would not forgive him for this 'transgression'. When he came, as he did every year in his capacity of Gabbai of the Chevra Kadisha, to the table of the Rebbe to bring him a cake, red apples, and a large 'havdalah' candle, the members of the court would not permit him to enter.

The controversy between the Hassidic court and the Chevra Kadisha lasted for several years, and they were not appeased until one of the members of the Hassidic court died, and required the services of the Chevra Kadisha.

To the simple masses of Sochaczew, Freiman Hirsch was the paramount communal activist for all his days, the Gabbai of the Chevra Kadisha, a prayer leader, a mohel – he was beloved and accepted by everyone.

He left a will which requested, among everything else, that the sack which is placed at the head of the grave should be filled not with earth, but rather with the charitable receipts that he acquired throughout the years from his donations to various Yeshivot and charities, along with his circumcision knife. On the other side, he requested that his small shofar be placed in the grave with him...

B.

Moshe Aharon "Shulklapper"

Each day, each morning, even during snowstorms and deep cold, the town would hear the twice a day his knocks that summoned people to the synagogue: morning and evening.

In the winter, before daybreak, in the dark and with the roads covered with snow, he would trek a path through the roads in order to fulfill his holy duty. He was also the first to inform people of bad news with the knocks of his wooden hammer. If someone died, and two knocks were heard at the door, the people in the house would tremble. They would open the door and ask:

"Moshe Aharon, who passed away?"

As the knocks of his hammer were heard, and the echo was heard in all houses, Jews would begin to appear on the streets, with their prayer shawls under their shoulders, hurrying to their prayers...

He was small in stature, and had a small beard. He walked with difficulty, but he nevertheless was able to make his rounds to all of the houses of the town.

Year after year, for dozens of years, he faithfully knocked on the doors of the Jews.

C.

Meir Binyamin

Whenever Meir Binyamin would go forth on the streets dressed in his black kapote[7] and girded with his belt (gartel); it was a sign that a Jew had passed away.

In such an event he would drink a cup of 90% strength liquor, in order to fortify himself so he could maintain his vigilance until after the burial. Then he hurried to the Chevra Kadisha and informed Moshe Aharon Shulklapper, so that they could determine the location of the grave. He did not rest for one minute. He prepared wood for the coffin of a 'meit mitzvah'. Close to the time of the funeral, he would pass through the main streets, stand at set places, put his right hand to his beard and chin, and shout in a loud voice: "meit mitzvah!" This was in order to urge people to come to the funeral. Then he would continue on his way. This was a sign that everything was already prepared, and it was time to come to pay final respects to the deceased. On a day such as that he proved his value, diligence and dedication. At the time of the funeral he took hold of the round charity chest, which was locked with a small locked and inscribed with a note saying "Charity saves from death" – this box was one of the main sources of income for the Chevra Kadisha.

After the funeral the members of the Chevra Kadisha would gather together to drink "lechayim" according to the custom. Meir Binyamin would then exaggerate a bit, his lips would redden, and he would tell stories on the topic of funerals and burials, as if he was taking pride in "everything was done by Meir Binyamin"... and therefore he was given the nickname "Hakol Meir Binyamin" [8].

In our eyes, to us children, we regarded the members of the Chevra Kadisha as adults who were not afraid of corpses, and he, Meir Binyamin, excelled above them all: for is it no small matter that he would go alone into the cemetery at night without being afraid...

Once I obtained a few five and ten kopeck Russian coins which were from Meir Binyamin, who was saved from a shelling attack during the First World War.

Many families remained in the city even though the front was coming dangerously close, and the destruction was increasing in the city. Stores did not open. People would remain locked up in their homes. It was also impossible to bury the dead, since the cemetery was in the area of the front. Therefore, it was decided to bury them behind the Beis Midrash, which protected against bullet bombardments. One day there were a few dead, including two gentiles. Just as the graves were being sealed, a rain of bullets began. We ran for cover. Shells fell before us, and one brushed against the clothing of Meir Binyamin, burning a hole and causing the coins in his pocket to fall out, however he himself was not harmed.

Indeed, he was a fine Jew – "Everything by Meir Binyamin".

Pesach Wolert and his family at his father's grave (name on grave is Yisrael the son of Chaim, died 27 Iyar 5671 – 1911.)

TRANSLATOR'S FOOTNOTES:

1. Segulot here refer to various remedies with Talmudic, Kabalistic or mystical sources.

2. Literally a 'dead person for which there is a mitzvah – commandment'. This refers to a dead person who has

nobody to look after his/her funeral preparations. This would often be the case for an indigent or a transient. In its most extreme connotation, it refers to an abandoned corpse. In such a case, it is considered a paramount mitzvah (commandment) for any person who can to drop all other activities and occupy him/herself with the preparation of the body for burial.

3. The 'taharah', is the ritual preparation of a body prior to burial. It involves a set ceremony of washing the corpse, dressing it with the shrouds, and placing it in a coffin in the prescribed manner. The entire procedure takes approximately an hour, and requires several members of the Chevra Kadisha to perform it properly. The taharah room is a room in a Jewish funeral home or cemetery where these taharah preparations take place.

4. Often, after performing a taharah, the participants would take a shot of liquor and toast each other 'lechayim', wishing each other a long life.

5. Chevra Kadisha members generally observe the 7th of Adar (one week prior to Purim), as a fast day, in order to atone for any disrespect for the dead that may have occurred during the performance of their duties. On the night following the fast, the annual Chevra Kadisha banquet takes place. This is generally a very sumptuous meal, accompanied by speeches and words of encouragement for the members to continue in their holy work. While most Chevra Kadishas observe this fast on the 7th of Adar (which is the anniversary of the death of Moses), others observe this fast on the 15th of Kislev.

6. At the conclusion of the writing of a Torah scroll, several letters are left blank, and at the festivities that take place at the dedication, various people are honored with the filling in of these letters. Thus, these people participate in the mitzvah of writing a Torah scroll (one of the 613 commandments of the Torah). Often, the honor of writing these final letters is sold, and thereby funds are raised for the payment for the Torah scroll.

7. An overcoat often worn by Hassidic Jews. The belt here refers to the 'gartel' generally worn by Hassidic Jews during prayer.

8. Everything by Meir Binyamin.

{700}

My Parents' Home
by Shlomo Frydman

When I come to write about my parents' home and notes about the personality, deeds, and communal activities of my revered father of blessed memory, I must preface my remarks with a reference to my grandfather Reb Shlomo Frydman of blessed memory, or as he was known Reb Shlomo Grodzisker, due to his being a Hassid of Grodzisk. His wife, Grandmother Taube was from a long line of Sochaczew natives. My father related that in his youth, grandfather used to travel to the Admor Rabbi Elimelech of Grodzisk of holy blessed memory along with the Admor Rabbi Meir Yechiel of Ostrowiec of holy blessed memory. Once my father was together with the Admor of Ostrowiec and introduced himself as the son of Reb Shlomo Grodzisker. The Rabbi honored my father greatly and spoke highly of my grandfather, his friend of his youth.

My grandfather ate "kest"[14] with his father-in-law for many years, more years than was customary in those days. He had the opportunity to occupy himself in Torah day and night and to busy himself greatly with the commandments and good deeds. He was known as an expert scholar, and I heard from grandmother that he used to give one tenth of his earnings to the poor. He was active in all of the charitable organizations that existed in the city, and he was also one of the chief activists and trustees of the Chevra Kadisha (Burial Society), along with Reb Freiman Hirsch Frydman of blessed memory and Reb Menashe Zimerinski of blessed memory. We should take not that the Chevra Kadisha of Sochaczew, as was the case in other cities in those days, was composed of the most honorable householders of the city. Hassidim as well as Misnagdim (non-Hassidim) participated together in this true form of kindness. Membership in the Chevra Kadisha was passed down as a legacy from father to son, and it was registered in the annals of the Chevra that when my grandfather and Reb Freiman Hirsch passed on, their places were taken by my father and Reb Mendel Frydman of blessed memory, the eldest son of Reb Freiman Hirsch, and they became the chief activists. This position did not only include the final act of kindness (i.e. funeral arrangements), but also included helping and visiting the sick. Sometimes they would spend entire nights at the bedside of a sick person, taking care of him. This would ease the burden on the household of the sick, since every sick person was able to rest in his own home.

In the atmosphere of Torah and Hassidism, fear of Heaven and the doing of good deeds which pervaded the home of my grandfather, two sons were brought up and educated: my father Yechiel, the eldest, who was born in 5640 (1880), and my uncle Tzvi (Hershel) may G-d avenge his blood.

In order to complete the description of my parents' home, I also must mention the household of my mother Sara Lea of blessed memory, who was the daughter of Reb Menachem Zeev Levin of blessed memory, or, as he used to be called: Reb Velvel the scribe of the forests. He was a precious Jew, a scholar, and a Hassid – apparently at the end of his days he traveled to the Admor Reb Avrahamele of Sochaczew of holy blessed memory – however he was also more progressive, in particular due to his contacts with the Polish estate owners, with whom he had business dealings due to his work in the forests. At the time that he married my mother, he worked in the forests of Mludzyn near Sochaczew. My mother was educated with a progressive education in Wola Solecka. She knew German in addition to Polish, and dressed in modern fashion. At first they used to whisper about her in the women's area of the synagogue, and say that Taube – meaning my grandmother – had gotten a German daughter-in-law, since at that time before the First World War, it was not customary for a woman to appear in the synagogue with a hat and gloves. However, they soon realized that she was modest and particular about both the easy and difficult laws, and they began to treat her with respect.

Reb Yechiel Frydman and his wife Sara Lea

My grandfather died before his time. He was the victim of an accident. This occurred on the last day of Passover when he returned from a gathering of friends in the Grodziski Shtibel, he stumbled and tripped on the stairs, wounded himself in the head, and passed away that very day. Grandmother moved in to live with us. My father was a man of means. He was in the liquor trade and was quite prosperous. After the death of my grandfather, father continued after him to be active in all of the organizations that my grandfather was a member of.

When the war broke out in 1914 and all of the Jews of Sochaczew moved to Warsaw, there was much activity in the area of mutual assistance among the refugees of Sochaczew. As a man of means, father gave himself over greatly to his communal endeavors, in particular after he arrived in Warsaw. There were at that time two children at home, my sister Gishe of blessed memory who was born in 5668 (1908), and myself, who was born in 5672 (1912).

After the Germans captured Warsaw in 1915, we returned to Sochaczew. Our house as well as the store in the home of Reb Shlomo Lewkowicz of blessed memory was destroyed. Grandmother's house on Warsawska Street, which she received as an inheritance from her father, was also destroyed. We moved to live in the home of Reb Yosef Welkowicz and Reb Shabtai Rotstein of blessed memory, one of the few homes that remained standing. We reopened our liquor store, as well as a hotel. The headquarters of the military governor of the city also was in that house. As a result of who our neighbor was, my father was called upon to intercede before the governing authorities for communal as well as private matters. Even though such intercessions incurred significant costs for my father in the form of bribes and other such costs, he did not want to receive anything in return, and always said that the good deed would be even greater in that way.

Everything that was mentioned above was from hearsay, things that I heard told in our house on various occasions. From hereon in, I will relate matters as I myself witnessed.

After Poland attained independence in 1918, the Jewish community organized on a legal basis according to the military command. At first, the regional government appointed representatives, and granted the community specific autonomous rights, and charged it with organizing communal life in the city. My father was the first deputy on the list of representatives. After the frightful incident which took place with Reb Meir Eizman of blessed memory (15 Elul 5679, September 1919), my father took his place on the communal council.

Thus was the tragedy: during the time of the sitting of the communal council in the home of the rabbi of the city Rabbi Tzvi Prekal of blessed memory, a drunken Polish soldier burst into the home, and Reb Meir Eizman, as usual, was the first to take a stand against him, due to his desire to push the soldier away in order to protect those gathered. He was stabbed to death. Reb Meir Eizman, may G-d avenge his blood, was a strong fighter for Jewish interests, a man of imposing height and great wisdom, a noble and sweet soul – he fell in the line of duty.

My father accepted his position with great pain, due to the tragic situation, in particular because my father and Reb Meir Eizman were always the closest of friends. My father was chosen as the treasurer of the council. The meetings took place at our home, for the council did not have its own office yet, and we had a large and ample home. At that time we lived in the home of Reb Motel Pinczewski of blessed memory. My father spent much time and energy as a member of the communal council, at times to the detriment of his own private activities. He did this all without expectation of reward. Actually, this was the way of most of the communal activists in Poland, who conducted their work with idealism and communal responsibility.

In the first elections for the communal council, which took place at a time of battles between the different factions, my father was not elected to the communal council, and nearly all of the former members were not elected. My father belonged to "Mizrachi", and they did not have much power in the city. The leadership of the council was divided between the Aguda, the Zionists, and the national democrats (Folkists) – with the greatest representation going to the Aguda.

My father was active on many philanthropic organizations, and in particular he spent much time on behalf of the Talmud Torah, with the aim of supporting impoverished students so that they would be able to continue with their studies. He held scholars in high regard, and he never missed the class given by Rabbi Prekal in Gemara each evening in the Beis Medrash. Along with this, he was one of those who came early each morning for the daily prayers in the Bais Medrash, which included, of course, the recitation of several chapters of Psalms, Maamadot[15], and the learning of Mishna.

Several customs of our home are particularly etched upon my mind. These include the preparation of a large vat of boiling water each eve of the Sabbath for tea. Father would set up the oven, and fill it with coals of varying sizes so that it would retain its heat for the entire Sabbath. On Sabbath mornings on their way to the synagogue, dozens of locals would come into our house for a hot drink, and father would serve tea to the guests himself. There were always poor people at our table. On Sabbaths and festivals in particular, father would bring guests home from the synagogue. The Sabbath and festival atmosphere was special, we would welcome the Sabbath queen with feelings of holiness; On Passover the house was converted into a miniature kingdom, and we all had the feeling of being actually freemen. We drew strength from this atmosphere of holiness, which sustained us throughout the mundane week.

Our large home was an eating hall – literally a hall. At times, the wedding of friends would take place at our home, or even the weddings of any Jew whose home was not big enough, and who were not well to do enough to rent a hall. My mother would spread out her nicest tablecloth, and set up a table with the nicest dishes, in order to enhance the joyous occasion.

My mother was a faithful partner to my father in all of his communal activities, and she certainly was not begrudging of guests. Friends of my sister used to come into our house to prepare their lessons, and mother would help them. Not infrequently, the girls would dance. Mother was a wonderful personality, upright, and always prepared to help her fellow. She maintained good and friendly relations with all of her neighbors. Her refined and noble personality always stands before my eyes. Several of her conversations on specific occasions are etched in my memory, how she explained to me the duty of people to be good and upright. To our distress, she was taken from us before her time, on the 11th of Sivan 5686 (1926). She called out: "Shlomo my son!", closed her eyes and returned her pure soul.

After mother's passing, father's health deteriorated, and he began to suffer from heart troubles. His economic situation also deteriorated. The government confiscated the permit of operating a liquor store. This was in the wake of unofficial restrictions against the Jews. Father did not give up easily, and engaged in litigation with the authorities for several years, as we supported ourselves on his savings.

My father remarried after about a year. He married a woman of good lineage from Grodzisk, by the name of Nicha, may G-d avenge her soul. She had been divorced from her first husband, since she did not bear children from him. My father had a daughter with her, Yehudit, may G-d avenge her blood. She was a beautiful girl, with both intellectual and physical strength. When my father did not receive the permit in return after years of litigation, he opened a large general store. In the first years, the business prospered, however as father's health weakened further over the years, the business weakened as well. Due to his poor health, he had to give up his activities on many philanthropic organizations, however he did not give up his work for the Talmud Torah, as he remained its treasurer until the outbreak of the war. He also remained active in the charitable organization of Reb Yechiel Meir Tilman of blessed memory.

In one area, father did not give in at all to his weakness and illness: when they would call him to a sickbed, even in the middle of the night, he would get up and get dressed in haste, and it was hard to believe that this man was dangerously ill. On occasion, he would spend the entire night at the sickbed, and any urging from his family or warnings from the doctors that this behavior was dangerous were ignored. He would always answer that he is sure that this would not harm him.

He was an active member of the Mizrachi movement, and was given over to the idea of the Land of Israel. However, with regard to education, he gave full support to the education of Agudas Yisrael. Therefore, he sent me to the school of Agudas Yisrael. When his friends would ask him: "why is it so, for in this city there are Zionist and Mizrachi schools?", he would answer that with regard to the education of children, there is no compromise, and if my son were to study in the Aguda schools, I still believe that I can be a good Mizrachist. Even when I later joined the Agudas Yisrael youth organizations and in time became one of their activists in the city, he did not bother me. On the contrary, I knew that my father was satisfied with this. Even when my sister joined the Agudas Yisrael girls group, he was very happy. On the other hand, he did not bother my sister when she joined the Z.T.G.S. club, founded by the teacher Kampelmacher, after finishing school.

He never interfered with my reading of books, even if the books were progressive He always did try to influence our activities and behavior, but in a very educational manner.

My father had a very pleasant blend of consistency and caution on the one hand – but on the other hand he had a great understanding of the spirit of the young generation. He was one of the close Hassidim of the Admor Rabbi Yisrael Shapira of holy blessed memory of Grodzisk, and he was one of the faithful friends and close associates of the local Rabbi Prekal of holy blessed memory, even though he did not agree with his outlook. Rabbi Prekal was known as an extreme Agudist, but my father admired him because of his greatness in Torah, his fear of Heaven, and his zealousness. My father implanted a great love of the Land of Israel in his son. My sister immigrated to Israel as a "Chalutza" (Pioneer) together with 34 girls who were leaders of Bnos Agudas Yisrael in 1935. (She died on the 8th of Cheshvan 5718 – 1958 in Jerusalem.) He desired to immigrate to Israel himself, and after I was about to go at the end of September, 1939, he was certain that his dream was about to become reality.

With the outbreak of the Second World War in September, 1939, we left the city together with all of the other Jews, and fled to Warsaw. There we suffered all of the tribulations of the bombardment for the duration of four weeks. After Warsaw surrendered, we did not return to Sochaczew since our house and store were destroyed. We went to live in Grodzisk at the home of my stepmother.

At the end of 1940 a cruel decree was issued that all of the Jews who lived in a radius of 80 kilometers of Warsaw were to be deported to the Warsaw ghetto. This was the final tribulation that he suffered in its entirety.

As soon as we arrived in Warsaw he took to his bed, and his heart troubles became worse. In the final months, he also suffered from severe asthma. Nevertheless he took great interest, and always inquired about the well being of his friends, and I was forced hide from him many things and not to tell the truth. Thus did I hide from him the news of the death of our friend Reb Yehoshua Goldstein of blessed memory, the son-in-law of Reb Freiman Hirsch, and of Rabbi Prekal of blessed memory. This was a difficult time from all aspects, the hunger increased – although I tried with all my might to make up for my father's lack of food. His situation was very severe in his final weeks, and I was forced to occupy myself in the day with all sorts of labor in order to earn the livelihood for the day, and at night I would stay beside his sickbed. I should also point out the great dedication of my stepmother. She sold all of her valuable jewelry in order to fill his needs, and she served my father with dedication until his final moments. The natives of Sochaczew also repaid him for all of his good deeds, and visited him constantly. I should mention in particular Reb Alexander Zishe Frydman, may G-d avenge his soul. Despite all his difficulties, as he was one of the chief activists of the Warsaw ghetto, he always found time to visit my father. My father accepted his fate with complete acceptance of the Divine will, however his heart ached for his family and for the lot of the Jewish people. He always expressed his happiness that he had passed his sixtieth year, and therefore had no taint of the death of 'karet'[16].

He had only one request on his lips, that they take care of him after his death just as during his life he took care of the Jews of Sochaczew who passed away. He requested that Zishe Frydman acquire a grave for him according to the law. They all promised him this, and fulfilled their promise, and were perhaps even jealous of him since he had the merit to go to his death in a normal fashion, lying on his bed surrounded by family members and friends, who accompanied him on his final journey.

On the 16th of Sivan 5702 (June 1942) he gave up his pure soul. This was a terrible and cruel time in the Warsaw ghetto, with dozens of people dying daily on the streets of hunger. Hundreds died of epidemics, due to the unsanitary living conditions. According to the statistics, 500 people died daily. Due to this, they would bury ten people in one grave.

All of the Sochaczew natives who found out about the death of my father came to the funeral. The members of the Chevra Kadisha of Sochaczew, accompanied by the head activist Reb Aharon Eliezer Zimerinski may G-d avenge his soul, occupied themselves with his funeral preparations. Thanks to the efforts of Reb Zishe Frydman, he received a grave for himself, and Reb Zishe delivered a eulogy upon his death. His words are still etched upon my memory as he expressed all of the agony, grief and pain that came forth from his heart – perhaps he was not only eulogizing my father, but also all of the Jews of Sochaczew who were murdered and killed in sanctification of the Divine name, and of all those whose hearts were torn due to this great and frightful tragedy. Perhaps he was also eulogizing at that time his own family and his own lot.

Even though these words are written with agony upon my heart, they serve as a monument to the memory of my parents' home, as well as a monument to all of the families of Sochaczew, who were similar to my own parents' family. Thus were the memories of my parents' home.

From these memories, I drew the strength to bear all of the pains, sufferings and oppression that overtook me in the work camps and the death camps. From this home I received my traditional foundation, not to worship idols during any of the vicissitudes of the times[17], and in this is hidden the ultimate victory of the people of Israel despite all of its martyrdom.

May their souls be bound in the bounds of life, and may their memories be blessed forever.

{706}

My Father of Blessed Memory (Avraham Rechtman)
by Yaakov Tzidkoni [18]
Translated by Jerrold Landau

As I bring forth various notes about the personality of my father of blessed memory, I do so for two reasons: to erect for him a monument for generations to come in lieu of his tombstone which was destroyed by the impure ones, as well as to describe the personality of a resident of Sochaczew – a lay Jew, a merchant and an important person among his people, who represents a complete example of Jews of his type and status.

He was born in Zichorzyn, a village on the Wisla River in Congress Poland. His mother Malka bore five sons and two daughters and raised them all to the marriage canopy and good deeds. His father Reb David was a scholarly and G-d fearing Jew. He was a merchant of forest products and a contractor – he provided wood to the Russian army.

Father spent his youth in the forests of Poland that surrounded villages, fruit orchards and wild fields. From there he gained his love of nature and understanding of the life, language, customs, and business practices of villagers. This familiarity with the ways of the villagers stood father in good stead during the long period when he did business with them.

When he reached the age of majority, and the time for induction into the army drew near, he did not pay attention to the urging and advice of friends and relatives to get out of the obligation of the draft by means of bribery or inflicting an injury upon his body.

Father brought back three things from the army: his musical instruments, his army hat, and his love of black bread … he would eat certain amounts of it on certain days, enjoying it as he brought back many memories into the heart and fewer memories in words about his period of army service. After he married my mother, he settled in Sochaczew, and father opened up a store that sold metal implements. Father was diligent at his work. Due to his diligence and expertise, he was able to serve several customers simultaneously. Only on rare occasions, particularly during the annual fairs, did he request mother's help. In the morning when he opened the store, even before the first customers would arrive, he would invite neighboring shopkeepers and passers by from among his acquaintances that would be returning from the early morning prayers for a cup of tea. As they drunk their tea they would discuss politics, business, and their discussions would even border on gossip.

Approximately once a month father would travel to Warsaw to purchase merchandise from the wholesalers, as well as clothing and shoes for the family. He knew the measurements and numbers off by heart, and there was never an occasion where the item he purchased did not fit the person for whom it was intended.

He was a modest and discreet person. He was well mannered and very polite, he fulfilled his obligations to the community, and supported the charitable organizations of the city, but he did not participate in communal leadership. Nevertheless, he fulfilled two public roles during the many years that he lived in the city: he served as the trustee (Gabbai) of the "minyan"[19] that took place in the home of his brother Moshe, and he established a parents organization in the "Techiya" school where his two sons learned. He filled these roles diligently, with exactness and love. The special room in which the minyan took place was always clean, well furnished, and the ark cover (parochet) and Torah covers were always beautiful and well decorated. Candles for light and wine for Kiddush and Havdala were always available[20]. He insured that there was extra light on Simchat Torah, decorations of vegetation on Shavuot, mats so that one could sit on the floor on Tisha Beov, and other such necessities. A semblance of pride was recognizable on his face as he stood by the Torah on Sabbaths and festivals, on his one side the reader of the Torah and on his other side the Cantor, as he called up people to the Torah. Once a year – according to my recollection on Simchat Torah – the members of the minyan would chose the Gabbai for the following year. Since father was the only candidate, he was always elected. This election cost him a "Kiddush", which took place in our house. The attendant banged on the table and announced that the Gabbai invites everyone to a Kiddush that would take place in our house. The tables were already set in our house – for the results of the election were assured – and the menu consisted of smoked fish, egg cakes, whiskey, wine and cookies. Everyone raised their glasses and wished "lechaim"[21], and that we should all merit to return next year and choose the host of the Kiddush as Gabbai again.

Father was very devoted to his family, and therefore he was very beloved by the family. His brothers and brothers-in-law would take counsel from him about business matters, marriage prospects, and other such matters. When one of his brothers was sick in the hospital, he stood by the sickbed day and night. When a niece of his fled out of the country to go to her beloved against the wishes of her parents, father followed after her. He succeeded in determining their hiding place, and in convincing them to return to her parents' home and to celebrate their marriage, and he succeeded in convincing his brother that he should agree to this marriage. This difficult lightning operation won father admiration. This event took place close to the outbreak of the First World War, and as a result of the war, the Sochaczew branch was cut off from the Rechtman family[22].

Reb Avraham Rechtman of blessed memory

{708}

The Courtyard of Moshe Rechtman
by Yaakov Tzidkoni
Translated by Jerrold Landau

I have heard and read about the court of kings, I have passed through the threshold of a Polish poretz (squire), I have peered into the court of a Tzadik, and I knew a very different type of courtyard, for I grew up there.

The courtyard of Uncle Moshe was a courtyard in the simple meaning of the word, as well as a description of a way of life, of an approach to life. The front yard of the house was 25 meters long. A heavy iron gate was at the opening, and it was always open. On both sides of the entrance there were long benches, upon which people were seated at all hours of the day, and in particular during the evenings. The entrance to the courtyard had a wooden floor, and there were entrances into the two dwellings that shared the courtyard: that of Moshe Rechtman and Leibish Graubard. These entrances were only used at times when honorable guests were received, or when there was a family celebration. Uncle Moshe's house was very spacious, and included a Sukkah. For the festival of Sukkot they would retract the roof by pulling a rope, and they would place 'schach'[23] upon it. The house also contained an office and a prayer hall.

The technologically advanced devices that I noticed in particular were electric bells that were run by batteries and a press for copying handwritten letters. I was awed by the large shiny black grand piano and the heavy iron trunk that was two stories high.

From among the residents of the dwelling I remember in particular a captain of the Russian army and "the little Leibishel", the wagon driver who owned the carriage that took people to and from the train station. He was short, "the shortest" in the town, in contrast to "tall Noach", who was extremely tall. When the two of them would appear in the street, people would say: "it is a short Friday and a long Sabbath"[24]. He was a pleasant and good-hearted Jew. We children were more interested in the back part of the building. There was the farm, with the cow-stall, the dove cages, various sheds, the laundry, and the ice cellar. From there was also the entrance to the cultivated fruit orchard that occupied a large area.

Uncle Moshe was the rich man of the town, the "gentleman". The gentiles called him "Pania Dzedziczo" – "Our master the poretz", and kissed his hand. He conducted business dealings with the Russian governing authorities. His business was in the cultivation of government forests. The work in one forest would last for a few years. A mechanical sawmill operated next to his house. My uncle hired many non-Jewish workers, including woodchoppers, wagon drivers, sawmill operators, and shippers who shipped the wood along the Wisla to Danzig. The only Jewish employee was a family member who was in charge of accounting, who was honest and astute, and was known as "der Schreiber".

Whey my uncle was asked on occasion why he does not hire a professional accountant, he would answer with a smile that if he did so, one would come to the conclusion that the business was operating at a deficit … Uncle would drive in his magnificent two wheeled carriage to the neighboring village for business purposes, or outside of the city for a vacation. He took with him a double-barreled hunters' revolver on every trip. He was very proud of his gun, for he was the only Jew in town with a permit to own a gun. It generally rested in the bedroom, above his bed.

In one wing of the house there were rooms specifically for guests. Just as Uncle knew how to entertain high-ranking government officials or captains, he also knew how to host a scholar or Rabbi who was passing through as a guest. He always supported the household of the rabbi Reb Avrahamele (Borenstein) and the Yeshiva. Due to this activity, he was given a decorative ornament, and was appointed as "a merchant of first rank". If a youth was conscripted to the army, he would be freed, and the completed permit of exemption ("white card") would be brought to his home. On the following Sabbath there would be a Kiddush in the minyan, a party in the home, and wishes of "Mazel Tov" would be bestowed upon the family on the occasion of the "freeing" of their son.

Once a year Uncle would travel with his wife for a vacation at a spa in Czechoslovakia or Germany.

When my uncle married off his son Baruch, he invited to the wedding various different bands and jesters from amongst the best in the land. There were hundreds of guests. All of them were put up in a large hotel for the entire seven days of festivities. An individual servant was put at the disposal of each guest. Each of the "Sheva Brachot"[25] was like a wedding feast, replete with bands, wine, dancing, music, jesters, etc. For a long time thereafter, the family would talk about this celebration, and they never tired of telling about it over and over again, until another event came in contrast to it …

Afterwards, a period of difficulties and tragedies affected the household, such as Uncle's illness; the fleeing of his daughter Rivka to her beloved out of the country; and her death one year later in her parents' home during childbirth; the refusal of the young son Pinchas Eliahu to marry his stepsister Chana; and other such things. Added to this were, of course, the tribulations of the war.

TRANSLATOR'S FOOTNOTES:

14. "Kest" is room and board, and refers to the custom of young Torah scholars being supported by their in-laws after their marriage for a certain period to enable him to continue his Torah studies.

15. Maamadot are sections of Bible and Talmud that are recited on a daily rotating basis in lieu of the sacrifices that were mandated to be offered when the Temple stood. The custom of reciting Maamadot is not widely followed today.

16. 'Karet' (literally being cut off), is a death sentence outlined in the Torah for various sins, which is not given over to the execution by a court of law. Thus, it is death by divine visitation (often referred to ad excision). There is much debate in the Talmud as to what exactly this means, since, of course it is impossible to discern if a person has lived out his divinely allotted life span or not. According to most, if not all opinions, if one has passed his sixtieth year, one is out of the category of those punished by 'karet'. This does not mean that if one dies before one's sixtieth year one has been punished by 'karet', as human beings cannot make that determination. It only means that if one passes ones sixtieth year, one can know definitively that one has not been afflicted by 'karet', at least for sins that one has committed prior to that time (i.e. it offers no guarantee about the future).

17. Here, 'not to worship idols', means not to abandon one's Jewish faith.

18. Tzidkoni is a Hebraicized version of the Yiddish Rechtman. Both mean 'righteous person'.

19. Minyan is literally a 'prayer quorum', and here means a small informal prayer group.

20. Kiddush is the prayer over wine that welcomes the Sabbath or festival. It is recited both at the evening near the commencement of the holy day and in shorter form in the morning. Havdala is the prayer over wine that signifies the end of the Sabbath or festival. Kiddush can also have the meaning of a Sabbath of festival morning snack after the prayers. This is due to the fact that the Kiddush prayer is recited prior to such a snack. This word has this meaning when it appears a few sentences further on.

21. Literally "to life", a toast upon drinking wine or whiskey.

22. It is not clear what the subject of the second part of the sentence is, i.e. was it this event that caused the branch of the family to be cut off, or was it the war? Although the former is more likely from the syntax of the sentence, the latter is more likely in actual meaning. My suspicion is that the intent is that after the war, the family did not return to Sochaczew, and thus were 'cut off' from the city from that point.

23. 'Schach' is the flimsy foliage covering that is used to cover the Sukka (tabernacle) that is mandated by the Torah to be used for the duration of the Sukkot holiday.

24. A reference to winter Sabbaths, when Friday is 'short' because the Sabbath starts early.

25. Literally 'seven blessings', the celebrations that follow for a week after a wedding.

{710}

Bernard Kampelmacher – the Teacher of our City
by Yisrael Rozen
Translated by Jerrold Landau

This name arouses countless memories and sentiments in the hearts of those who grew up and came of age in Sochaczew during the period between the two world wars.

When I bring his image, full of grace and charm, into my mind, it is as if I see before my eyes Pestalozzi – the originator of educational reform in the world, or the illustrious educator Janusz

Korczac – for in our city he filled, without any doubt, the role and mission that Pestalozzi or Korczac filled with their own students. There is no exaggeration in this comparison; on the contrary: – Pestalozzi left as a legacy guidebooks for teachers and educators in the field of pedagogy and child psychology; Korczac also left books in the field of education, as well as students who were educated within the walls of his institution "The Republicat of the Students" near Warsaw. Kampelmacher did not leave any books after him, but only students. These students were not only educated and guided by him within the walls of the school. Kampelmacher educated all of the youth in our city, including those to whom he had no legal or moral obligation, and certainly not at the request of their parents.

His activities were great. He understood and realized well that in Sochaczew of 1924-1925 he would not succeed in gathering around him the youth from the traditional and Orthodox households, and to bring boys and girls under one roof, to occupy them with sport, games, group activities, parties, dancing, singing, music and excursions. Therefore, he planted the ideas into the hearts of the fathers and mothers, he worked hard and waited with patience, energy, effort and understanding – until he won over the hearts not only of the youth, but also of the parents.

He simply convinced the parents, and it is possible to say that he educated them, with his personal charm and grace and the pleasantness of his manner. He knew how to find an approach to all of the Jews in the city, to the youth, the elderly, those with the thick beards, to the Hassidim, and even to the Rabbi of the city. He knew and held in esteem the Rabbi of the city, and I know that this esteem was mutual, that is to say that the Rabbi also held this "assimilationist" in esteem.

Even though Kampelmacher was a free thinker, and worked on the Sabbath as a teacher in the public school, to his credit it can be said that he – the assimilationist so to speak – never attempted to remove Jews or Jewish youth away from their religion, or to distance them from their foundations. All that he wished was to bring light, joy of life, progress, culture and good manners to the city. He never mocked the way of life of the city in those years, he did not mock the kapote or the sheitel[1], even though he himself was very far from these things, and he was wise enough to find a common language with the Orthodox and those that occupied the seats of the study hall, to win them over, to sympathize with them and hold them in esteem. Therefore he was able to act among the youth without opposition from the parents and the Orthodox groups, and he even had their agreement. He was concerned that the summer camp of the city, to which dozens of children and councilors went during the summer, would have Kosher food for the children. Furthermore, he even concerned himself that the children should have the opportunity to say their morning prayers! I happened to be at the camp on one occasion, when I came there with a group of councilors, and I saw Kampelmacher ask one child from an Orthodox home if he had already recited his prayers. When the child answered negatively, Kampelmacher ordered another youth to lend him his phylacteries...[2]

Reb Yankel Kavel and family

Eliahu Posnanski and his wife

{309 - Yiddish} {712 - Hebrew}

The Woman Chaikel the Wagon Driver
by Leib Fursztenberg

She was a unique "wagon driver" in Poland. She was not tall, not powerful, but she did have a strong personality. Her face was tanned, she had the blue eyes of a warm-hearted Jew, of a merciful mother.

She was honored in the city... Jews as strong as oaks, who were wagon drivers for generations, who were expert horsemen, all gave her honor.

Chaikel did not only know how to drive horses along the entire journey to Warsaw, but she also knew how to handle any problem which would arise, such as when a wheel of a laden wagon would break, when a horse would take ill. Everyone knew to consult her on such occasions. She would roll up the sleeves of her man's coat that she wore all the time and take care of the horse properly. Even the veterinarians would not have as much expertise as she did. If anyone had to purchase or trade a horse, they would ask for her advice. She did not accept any brokerage fees. On the contrary, she was always willing to help a poor and hard pressed wagon driver, using the money that she collected from others.

It was a great wonder that this woman, who spent most of her days with horses and stables, also knew how to care for a sick person with no less expertise than the local medic. If anyone took ill in a house where they were too poor to pay for a doctor, they would summon Chaikel. She knew how to look after cases of dislocated legs, to set up cupping glasses, and to prescribe pills for various illnesses. On many occasions a woman would come to her with a baby suffering from some complaint, and she would care for the baby with her strong and bony hands with gentleness and delicacy

Her husband Moshko was a blacksmith. He was shorter than her, powerful, and had strong hands. He was not the chief influence in the household, and he did not interfere too much in the affairs of wagon driving. He was immersed in his blacksmith profession. In the same manner that she was able to be master over the strongest of horses, the head of her household was subservient and pitiful as well.

Even the gentiles loved him. He knew the trade of horse shoeing. He also knew how to fix the wheel of a wagon. They referred to him as Pania Moshko. In the small synagogue (shtibel) in which he worshiped together with butchers and blacksmiths, they called him to the Torah by his name: Reb Moshe the son of Shmuel the Cohen. There, at the shtibel, he set his eyes on the Torah reader, a young single man by the name of Feivel, and chose him as his son-in-law, a husband for his eldest daughter. If he himself was not an expert in the strange letters, at least his son-in-law should be learned. When he explained this to his wife Chaikel, she had no trouble understanding – especially with regard to such a learned young man. They sold their saddle and their wagon, took out loans, put together a dowry, rented and furnished a dwelling, and arranged a wedding according to tradition. The entire town was invited to the wedding. Nobody would have thought of declining an invitation to participate in these festivities in their small house which was adjacent to the blacksmith shop and the horse stables. And if there was not enough room – they would partake of the feast in a limited fashion. However, she rented out the largest hall in the city for the marriage of her daughter, the fire hall, and invited not only their colleagues, the blacksmiths and wagon drivers, but all of the honorable Jews of the city, in addition to the honorable gentiles, including the mayor.

They feasted, danced and rejoiced until daybreak.

What did she not do for her children? When a Gymnasia (high school) was established in Sochaczew, their youngest daughter was one of the first students to enroll.

She had different plans for the youngest and only son, Chaim Nissan.

Furthermore... She – not her husband – was perhaps the only woman in Poland to be a follower of a Hassidic Rabbi. She chose a very modest Rabbi, in the suburbs of Warsaw – the Rabbi of Grochow. She extended honor and love to him. On all of her trips to Warsaw she never neglected to bring him a gift. Every summer, the Rabbi of Grochow would come to stay at her house, which was between the blacksmith shop and the horse stables. During that time, she glowed with joy and contentment, in particular on Sabbath eves when her husband would sit next to the Rabbi dressed in a silken kapote. All of the artisans, and Jews in general, would stop by. The Rabbi would say words of Torah, and they would sing Hassidic melodies until a late hour in the evening. She would be dressed in her Sabbath finery, all washed up from her weekday work, and would stand at the side brimming with joy – for was she not acquiring mitzvot and doing good deeds...

She was full of vim and vigor. In addition to the stables and the blacksmith shop, she also operated a coal and wood warehouse. In the years prior to the war of annihilation, she set up a building and a wall – after much effort and difficulty – on her own lot. She presented her case before the lawyers and judges with her broken Polish, and her various documents and permits were all hidden in the folds of her dress, and she became master of her establishment. However... September 1939 came.

Sochaczew was judenrein[3] by the third day of the war. The demilitarized city was bombarded for an entire day, with the first bombs damaging the synagogue. The Jews fled in confusion to Warsaw. They left everything behind. Even the elderly and the young went on foot, and only very few were able to travel in wagons, which were very expensive. By evening, the city was empty of Jews.

The last wagon was that of Chaikel. She stood alone by her large wagon and loaded packages, bags full of belongings, pillows, vessels – the last "property" of the Jews of Sochaczew. The wagon moved and ploughed along like a giant. She worked with her callused hands. She wore heavy boots on her feet, and arranged all of the packages so there would always be room for one more package. She did not request any payment. She took the reins with great skill and directed the laden wagon along the road to Warsaw. The road was overflowing with thousands of refugees. There was confusion and screams from all corners. Near a stone, at the edge of the road, behind a tree – was sitting one of the most honorable women of Sochaczew. Paralyzed, she was screaming and cursing as to why she had been left behind. A leading Jew acquired a small wagon, and harnessed himself in, leaving his son and his wife (a teacher at "Yavneh") stranded. And here were walking three elderly people. They had only traveled one kilometer, and they did not have any more energy to continue. They were praying for an easy end...

Chaikel passed by them, and recognized them. She quickly jumped down, and placed the three distressed people in her wagon. She continued herself on foot. However, she never made it to Warsaw.

By morning, the large crowd had reached Bielany. The route to Warsaw was closed, guarded by the army, for the route was reserved for the retreating army. The crowd turned to cross the Wiskit, confused and perplexed. With sunrise, the Germans resumed their murderous attacks. They flew over the heads of the people and mowed them down. The people abandoned the remainder of their property and fled for their lives. However, nobody was killed.

Only Chaikel did not escape.

She did not abandon the belongings of the persecuted and pursued Jews of Sochaczew which had been given over to her safekeeping. She tried to salvage whatever she could. She was not afraid of the soldiers who sealed off the main route to Warsaw. She knew all the roads and routes very well – and she managed to reach the town of Pruszkow.

There she was afflicted with a terrible tragedy. Her horses fell, and without them she was like a body without a soul. Even then she did not abandon the belongings. With extraordinary strength, and with the help of the Jews of Pruszkow, she gathered all of the packages, bags, and containers and put them in the local mikva (ritual bath).

With her last energy, she reached Warsaw on Friday, with the whip in her hands – that was all that was left.

At the end of the war the survivors of Sochaczew went with haste to Pruszkow, and were able to retrieve the remnants of their belongings which were miraculously preserved in the mikva.

We do not know where, in which furnaces, did the family of Chaikel perish. They perished in the great bloodbath of the Warsaw Ghetto.

The blacksmith shop, the stables, and their poor house – all were wiped off the face of the earth of Sochaczew. Not one remnant remained of the lives which pined, walked, suffered, and which was full of both pain and joy. A marketplace now exists in this location. A clean marketplace – as if there never was anything there...

One memory lives. The two story house on Warsawska street, which Chaikel had built in its time, and Christians are now living there. A sign is hung upon it – a small metal plate with the following Polish inscription, in Latin letters:

"Chaikel Karo, her husband and children – may G-d avenge their deaths, and may they be remembered for good."

They were cut off from the foundation stone of our people, the good and heartwarming, from which all of the Jews of Sochaczew were hewn.

TRANSLATOR'S FOOTNOTES:

1. A non-Hassid (literally an opponent of Hassidism)
2. Phylacteries (Hebrew tefilin), are black leather boxes with straps which contain pieces of parchment with biblical quotations about the fundamentals of Jewish faith. They are worn by Jewish males on their arm and head during weekday morning prayers, in keeping with a biblical commandment.

3. German for 'Jew free', a Nazi expression for a location that had been emptied of its Jews.

{336 - Yiddish} {716 - Hebrew}

{300}

Happenings Herein
Yaakov Frydman
Translated by Jerrold Landau

I was born and raised in Sochaczew. I left the city permanently when I was 26 years old.

The old Jewish community of Sochaczew is on the Warsaw-Posen (Poznan) highway, 48 verst[1] from Warsaw. The Jewish population was 1,200 families, numbering about 5,000 souls. When combined with the Christian population, which was smaller than the Jewish population, the total population was 7-8,000 souls.

Like all Jewish towns, Sochaczew had its homeowners, working people, merchants, shopkeepers, artisans, clergymen, communal activists, partisan and non-partisan youth, socialist and Zionist parties, and benefit institutions.

Sochaczew was completely destroyed during the time of the First World War. The town was situated on the front lines on the Bzura for nine months. During that time, Sochaczew was destroyed, and there were many victims.

After the war, I and some other young people no longer saw our future in Sochaczew. We came to the conclusion that the future of our people was only in the Land of Israel. We, young healthy people must part with the exile and go to build out our own fatherland. We left Sochaczew.

It was difficult for us to take leave of the town, in which every stone left behind was near to us. Even the cold graves spoke to us. The ruins of Sochaczew told stories of a previous life, of our beloved people and their lives there. We left with heavy hearts.

During the time of the Second World War, we received news from Sochaczew in the Land of Israel. Together with other cities and towns, Jewish Sochaczew, which had been rebuilt, was cruelly annihilated by the Nazis. Various images and happenings from the past swim around in my memory.

{301}

A.

Moshe Aharon Shulklaper[2]
Yaakov Frydman
Translated by Jerrold Landau

Already before daybreak, the footsteps of Moshe Aharon Shulklaper, with his heavy boots, could be heard on the Shul Gasse (Synagogue Street). With his communally owned wooden hammer in his hand, he went around waking up the Sochaczew community to the service of the Creator.

Moshe Aharon Shulklaper gave one knock on a closed shutter. At the second and third knock, the sweet sleep departed from the eyes, and the newly dawned day began in Sochaczew.

It was a custom in the town (and I believe also in other towns) that the shulklaper gave three knocks with a wooden, communally owned, hammer on every normal day: one, two, three. If someone died during the night, Heaven forbid, and there was a "misfortune" in the town, the shulklaper would only give two knocks. The third silent knock would be left hanging with shivering and terror, and instilled a mood that, like a dark Satan, smelled of death, with the "good earth", the tahara water, and a funeral[3] . A sigh issued forth from the lips, and tears trickled from the eyes...

The fate of each newly dawned day lay in Moshe Aharon Shulklaper's hand, with the wooden hammer. Its joy and its sorrow, the joyful arrival of a day or the cursing of one's day of birth[4]. He was the announcer of fortune and misfortune. With his third knock on the shutter with the communal hammer, all trembling departed...

Moshe Aharon Shulklaper's mission did not end with his announcing of a good or bad day. He had one more important duty – to announce the arrival of the Sabbath.

The Friday market in Sochaczew was lively and effervescent. The shopkeepers bustled about in their stores from early morning. The businessmen with the pushcarts – the pushcarts with fruit, and the cheap clothing dealers – all put out their racks with ready made clothing, overcoats, rags, and suits for the peasants of the vicinity who came with their wagons into the city. Soon, the market glistened with the various colored cloths of the peasants. Horses neighed, cows and goats bleated, hens quacked and roosters crowed. Among all the hoo-ha, Jewish men and women examined the bellies of the fowl for the Sabbath, purchased butter, cheese, eggs and other merchandise – bushels of wheat, a basket of plums, a sack of apples, pears. The rushing and tumult from the market to the stores, from the market to the pushcarts and to the taverns, and from the taverns to the market was such that one sounded blended in with the next sound. Jewish voices were intermixed with gentile voices. People paid, shook hands and said "na zgoda" – agreement...

Like a downpour in the middle of a bright day, Moshe Aharon Shulklaper suddenly intruded as the sun began to incline towards the west, and began to knock with his wooden hammer on the door of the open stores, and the marketplace began to move about. Everything went into ferment. The words and the mouths became silent. The buzzing and the voices became hushed, and business ceased. Quickly, the movement of the hands of the buyers and sellers stopped. The storekeeper saw to it that the customer should leave the store even faster; that he should pay even faster, take what he needs and go to from whence he had come. A rush began near the stalls and the pushcarts. Merchandise was torn from the peasant's hand. People took packages and carried them off. The peasants who were previously doing business remained standing dreamily. They did not understand what had suddenly happened, why their customers had suddenly been blown away – why he no longer laughed, no longer smiled, and remained ice cold in the middle of business.

Moshe Aharon Shulklaper's knocking with the communal hammer receded, and people began closing the outer doors of the stores, tying the chains, locking the bolts and putting away the keys. At the stalls, hammers made shambles of what had been erected in the morning. Like magic, the market became an ex-market. As if from under the ground, the street cleaner with his large broom sprouted up, and swept the large, emptied market. The Sabbath was approaching with silent angelic steps. Moshe Aharon Shulklaper had announced its advent, just as he announced the advent of the day during the week. The market of Sochaczew took on a different appearance... Soon, the Sabbath candles would be glistening in a golden fashion from the Jewish windows in the market. The Sabbath hymns would be heard from the homes; and at 3:00 a.m., when the city was still sleeping with its restful Friday night slumber, Yakir Szuster would wake up, go through the town darkness, and call out with his high clear voice:

> Listen my dear people,
> What I wish to tell you
> The clock has already struck three
> It is already time to recite Psalms.

{304}

B.

Reb Meir Binyamin
Yaakov Frydman
Translated by Jerrold Landau

Meir Binyamin was a known personality in Sochaczew. When Meir Binyamin strolled along the streets wearing his black kapote, with his gartel[5] wrapped around, everyone knew: there is a dead body.

In such a case, he first made a great "lechayim"[6] , so as not to be afraid of the corpse. Then he speedily went away with all of the members of the Chevra Kadisha (burial society) in order to designate the place for the grave. Meir Binyamin did not take council. He measured the wood for the coffin of the "meit mitzvah"[7] , and cut the boards. He took a walk through the main streets and stopped at certain places, took his little beard together with his chin in the right hand, took hold of his elbow with his left hand, and called out with a healthy soprano shout: "Meit mitzvah!". With that he convinced everyone that he had already taken care of everything, that everything was ready, and now it was time to give the final honors to the deceased. At the funeral he took hold of the round metal charity box and unlocked it with a small key. It contained a note "charity saves from death". This was one of the main sources of income of the Chevra Kadisha.

After the funeral, the chief members of the Chevra Kadisha gathered together and first made the proper lechayim toast. If Meir Binyamin lost track of the number of cups, his cheeks would become a bit red and he would begin to tell about larger funerals, and his words were: "everything was Meir Binyamin"! "If it was not for me, the funeral would still not have taken place.", and he laughed tipsily… Therefore, he was known in town as "altz Meir Binyamin" ("Everything was Meir Binyamin").

For us children, all of the members of the Chevra Kadisha were great heroes, for they had no fear of corpses. However, in our eyes Meir Binyamin was over everyone, for wow, "he goes alone to the cemetery at night and has no fear".

In fact, I was once with him, and I still have today a few silver Russian 5 and 10 kopeck coins, thanks to him, Meir Binyamin, who was saved from a shrapnel injury during the First World War.

In that time, many families did not take into account the danger that threatened us due to the front that was approaching Sochaczew, and remained in the city. In the meantime, the destruction in Sochaczew increased with each passing day. Shops were locked, and nobody had seen anyone on the streets for months. Corpses lay around, for burial in the cemetery was impossible due to the trenches that were there. It was decided to bury the dead behind the synagogue and the Beis

Midrash, where one had to protect oneself from the bullets. One day there were a few deaths, including two Christians. When the burial ended, a terrible volley of shooting began. We ran to hide. A piece of shrapnel went by us, ruffled the clothes of Meir Binyamin and singed him. The money in his pocket melted, but he was saved.

Indeed "altz Meir Binyamin".

TRANSLATOR'S FOOTNOTES:

1. A verst is an old Russian unit of distance.
2. A shulklaper (Synagogue knocker) is the man whose job it is to knock on the doors of the people early in the morning to awaken them to attend the synagogue. It is not a last name here, but a description of the person by his job.
3. The "good earth" seemingly refers to a cemetery. A "tahara" is the ritual purification of a corpse prior to burial. Tahara water refers to the water used during the ritual purification.
4. "Cursing one's day of birth" is a reference to a sorrowful event from the book of Job (chapter 3).
5. A ritual belt worn by Hassidim.
6. A toast over a drink.
7. Literally "the dead of the mitzvah", or the "dead of the commandment", referring to a dead person who either has nobody to look after his remains, or whose family is too poor to do so, and it falls upon the community as a "commandment" to look after the person's remains. Looking after the remains of a "met mitzvah" is considered so urgent so as to displace almost all other religious obligations.

{306}

C.

Avraham Meir Lejzers

Translated by Jerrold Landau

He was the partner of Meir Binyamin. His major source of livelihood was also … death. He was the opposite of his partner. He was silent, calm, and to his work with a slow gait. He drunk more liquor than his partner, but he retained his equilibrium, knowing what he was doing, and this was without noise.

He had a hoary head, and was of average height. He was a tailor all his life, and he mainly sewed shrouds [1].

As soon as Meir Binyamin would inform him that so and so had died, he would immediately go and take the measurements of the corpse, in order to ascertain how much white linen was needed. Nobody would see him on the street until he finished the clothes. It was late, just prior to the deceased been taken away, when he was first seen on the street. He fulfilled all of the errands of the members of the Chevra Kadisha who conducted the burial.

He drew the measurements of the casket in the anteroom of the synagogue, and waited until the members of the Chevra Kadisha arrived to cut the boards. Later, he took them to the cemetery and made sure that they fit the grave. Then he returned to town and informed everyone that the grave was ready. Following that, Meir Binyamin's job began, which was to call together the Jews to come to perform the commandment of burial.

{307}
D.

Chaikel Baal Agala (Chaikel the Wagon Driver)
Translated by Jerrold Landau

There were many Jewish women in Sochaczew who honestly earned the title "woman of valor". They excelled in various domains. One could find them in all strata of society. Not all of them were appreciated appropriately. That is the way it was; such should it be. First now, when I cast a glance back at that former life, I see how great was the role of the Jewish woman in upholding the existence of our people and the purity of Jewish family life.

The Sochaczewer woman of valor about whom I wish to mention here came from a family of wagon drivers. They called her "Chaikel Baal Agala" (Chaikel the Wagon Driver". She was the daughter of Chaim Nissan the wagon driver. Chaim Nissan was a simple Jew who had his commandments (mitzvas) that he upheld with the greatest of exactitude. One of them was providing Jewish soldiers with a kosher Passover.

In the Russian times, there were two companies of soldiers stationed in Sochaczew. There were Jews from Russia among them; and Chaim Nissan's mitzvah was to ensure prior to Passover that the Jewish soldiers would be freed for the festival. He gave them a room in his small house for the entire festival, and provided them with kosher food.

His daughter Chaikel possessed elements of her father's soul. She helped her father, and they used to drive the wagon two or three times a week to bring merchandise. When his father did not feel well, she would travel herself to Warsaw. Therefore, they called her "Chaikel the Wagon Driver". She was not embarrassed of the name. All of the wagon drivers gave her honor when she took it upon herself to heal a horse – literally like a doctor…

She got married to a man who later became a blacksmith, and she also helped him with his work. The street resounded, as she snapped the horseshoes onto the horse's feet, and the horse stood as if it had respect for her…

If someone's horse would take ill, whether owned by a Jew or a Christian, they would call Chaikel. They did not pay for her work; she did it all as a good deed (mitzvah). The same thing happened also when a horse gave birth. Chaikel was a resolute, tall woman. Her footsteps and her voice could be heard from far. It was interesting to see her going to examine or heal a horse. She rolled up her sleeve, stuck her hand into the body of the horse, took out from there what was superfluous, and administered medicine. She also made operations on horses. With her small, sharp knife, she would cut away wild flesh and pour salt upon the wound, or she would release blood. She did everything with precision, as if she was a veterinarian. The local wagon drivers extended honor to her. Her name was also known among the coachmen of Warsaw.

When the First World War broke out, the Sochaczewers fled to Warsaw. Chaikel was among them. The refugees from Sochaczew were billeted with residents of Warsaw, and Chaikel and her family were sent to the home of them Grochower [2] Rabbi. This honor had a great influence on her. She became a Hassid of Piaseczna. The wagon drivers of Warsaw gave her honor for this as well, in that she was found in such a house, as well as for her knowledge in healing horses. When a horse became ill, they would not bring it to Chaikel, but they would rather send her a horse cab with two emissaries, and bring her to the town where the horse was found. The wagon drivers looked on with great curiosity to see how that women healed a horse. When she arrived, all were prepared to help her. She never wanted to take any money for her work.

She returned to Sochaczew with her family after the war, and again began to ply her trade as before the war. Each week prior to the Sabbath, she would travel to Warsaw to visit the Grochower Rebbe and present to him all good things...

TRANSLATOR'S FOOTNOTES:
1. This refers to the burial shrouds that are used to dress up a body prior to burial.
2. Grochow is the name of several towns in Poland. One of them is 4.2 kilometers from Warsaw (i.e. a suburb of Warsaw) according to JewishGen's Shtetlseeker. I expect that is what this is referring to.

The Knott family.

{320}

Common Happenings and Memories

Anski-Questionnaire
Yaakov Frydman
Translated by Jerrold Landau

In the year 1913, 5603 [1], Sh. Anski sent a questionnaire to all of the Jewish communities with the name: A local historical program, sent by Sh. Anski, with the assistance of A. Yudiki, via the Jewish ethnographic expedition through the name of Baron Naftali Hertz Gincburg. (This is the same as the "Jewish Historical Ethnographic Society".) The purpose was to collect material from the Jewish communities and their lives, so that the consolidated material can later be published for future historians.

However, fate was different. It did not take into account the good will of Sh. Anski and the material assistance of Baron Gincburg. The First World War broke out and destroyed the hundreds of years of collected spiritual (and physical) treasuries of material. The entire undertaking was driven into the ground due to the wartime conditions and Anski's death.

Thus was lost the very valuable material that was certainly collected also from other Jewish communities. Who knows if this was the only material that has disappeared? During the time of the First World War, I guarded the collected material throughout all the places of my wandering, so that it would not be lost. (I guarded it for another 35 years in the Land of Israel, until the bitter lot that took place during the Second World War – after the Nazi-Hitlerian murder of the Jews, so that a historical chapter about a small town in Poland will be published, in order to perpetuate the name and the life – the Jewish life of our city of Sochaczew.

There were 166 questions in the questionnaire. There were answers to 70 questions. Beside every question the number was noted, as in the questionnaire. I will now give it over in printing, as it was written 44 years ago, with minor improvements.

Question: What euphemisms were there in your city?

Answer: Sochaczew Persians, Sochaczewer Tatars, Czechmeloch, Ra-Sochaczew.

Question: For how long was there a community in Sochaczew [2]?

Answer: For 500-800 years

Question: How many synagogues are there in your city?

Answer: One synagogue, the communal Beis Midrash, and the Rebbe's Beis Midrash.

Question: When was each of them built, and who built them?

Answer: The synagogue was built in the year 5620 / 1860. It was built by the community. The other Beis Midrashes were built later.

Question: Which ones are communal, which ones are Hassidic, and from which Hassidim?

Answer: The synagogue is for the community, the greater portion of them being Misnagdim. The same with the communal Beis Midrash. Hassidim have their own various shtibels and minyans [3]. The Rebbe's Beis Midrash belongs to the Sochaczewer Rebbe and his Hassidim.

Question: What stories and legends exist regarding the old synagogues?
Answer: At night, the dead come to worship in the synagogue. When the shamash opens the synagogue early in the morning, he makes two knocks on the door – a signal that the dead must leave...

Question: Which of the synagogues had burnt down?
Answer: The old city synagogue burnt down in the year 5619 / 1859.

Question: How did the burnt down synagogue look, and what types of illustrations and holy objects were burnt there?
Answer: Four Torah scrolls were burnt, along with the Holy Ark, and the rest of the holy objects that were found there.

Question: Are there old castles, towers and palaces, whole or in ruins?
Answer: There is an old, destroyed castle that stands atop a hill. It is called the "Schloss-berg" [4] in the city and the entire region. Now there is only the hill, and the ruins are destroyed.

Question: Who lives, or who used to live in the castle?
Answer: It is said that a Polish count used to live in the destroyed castle. Some say that a Polish king lived there. I heard from Reb Yisrael Sofer, an old man, that when he was still a child he heard it said that a great priest, an archbishop, lived in the old city. He once went up to the Schloss-berg and said that his grandfather's grandfather's great-grandfather once lived in the castle. It was further said that a king once lived there. Also – a Mazowian duke.

Question: What historical memories and legends are bound up with those buildings?
Answer: it is said to this day that there are buried palaces on the mountain upon which the castle stands, and there one can find many treasures with gold. It is said that years ago, many people dug on the mountain and found gold.

Question: How many cemeteries do you have?
Answer: Three cemeteries that are all next to each other.

Question: When did they stop burying in the old cemetery?
Answer: With the first one, it is not known. With the second one, they stopped burying about 40 years ago.

Question: Please write how you obtained the new cemetery?
Answer: The third cemetery, that is the last one (as stated previously), was negotiated for with the poretz, the owner of the baths, by the former old rabbi. The poretz sold the place with good will to the community. After the purchase, the rabbi with the Jews of the town made seven circuits with the Torah scrolls around the purchased area of the baths and sanctified it as a cemetery.

Question: Are there any graves about which legends circulate?
Question: The Shach's brother[5], (the former local rabbi) said during his lifetime that "whomever will come to my grave will be helped". After his death, many people went discretely to his grave, so that nobody else would know... When someone stole into the cemetery and went to the grave to pour out his heart – he did not find the grave anymore. It had disappeared. There is also a second version.

Question: Write about all the old gravestones of known people of old.
Answer: It is not possible to read the gravestones in the first two cemeteries. The majority of the

gravestones are small, low stones that have almost sunk into the ground. The script is almost obliterated.

Question: Are there presently or were there special Jewish industries (such as tallis makers, chandelier makers)?
Answer: Years ago there were, today there is not.

Question: Do any old ledgers of the community, Chevra Kadisha (burial society), Chevra Mishnayos (Mishna study groups), Chevra Shas (Talmud study groups), Chevra Tehillim (Psalm reciting groups), etc., exist?
Answer: The ledger of the Chevra Kadisha remains.

Question: Do any old time objects remain in the synagogues or with the residents (such as ark covers, Torah crowns, Torah pointers, spice boxes, objects with Yiddish inscriptions, etc?)
Answer: One resident had a Torah pointer with a tas [5]. One of the groups has another pointer. In the old synagogue, one can find today an old Chair of Elijah [6] that is over 100 years old, from the time when they used to circumcise the children in the synagogue.

Question: Did your city ever have a great rabbi, a Gaon, or a great Yeshiva head?
Answer: There were several rabbis who were Gaonim (Rabbi Elazar Tzvi Charlup of blessed memory, Reb Moshele Charyf of blessed memory, Reb Leibish of blessed memory, the head of the rabbinical court of Apta – Sochaczew, Reb Nachum Rapoport the brother of the Shach, Reb Nachum Gincburg, Reb Elazarl Kohenof blessed memory, Reb Avrahamele Bornsztejn.)

Question: Did your city every have a great Tzadik, an especially good Jew? From what lineage was he, and whose student was he?
Answer: The Tzadik and fine Jew the Admor Reb Avrahamele Bornsztejn was there. He was a son-in-law and student of the Kocker Rebbe, Rabbi Menachem Mendel of Kock. Today his son Reb Shmuel (of blessed memory [7]) lives in Sochaczew?

Question: Does his portrait exist?
Answer: The portrait of Reb Avrahamele Bornsztejn exists, drawn by the local artist Lozer of Alasz (Rozenfeld).

Question: Can you write about his appearance, character and way of life?
Answer: Rabbi Avrahamele Bornsztejn, short and with a splendid countenance, his eyes almost always closed. He talked very fast, such that only very few could understand him. He was always very happy with other Jews. He never differentiated between a rich person and a poor person. He gave Tzedaka with a full hand. He sat and learned day and night. He wrote responsa and led a Yeshiva. For him, eating and sleeping were limited to the necessities of life. Many stories were told about him. Of them, two characteristic episodes stood out: When he was still a lad and came home from Yeshiva, his mother gave him a roll and butter to eat. He was expected to spread button on the roll. However, he ate the roll and left the butter behind. His mother asked him, "Why is this? Why do you not spread butter on the roll?" He answered: "You want me to take the time to cut the roll and to spread the butter? This is too much neglect of Torah."

Even when he was older and already a rabbi, he slept very little. If he lay down for a few minutes, he would quickly get up, wash his hands, and say, "Mne... mne. So long to sleep" [8] In truth, he had not slept for more than a minute.

He worshipped early and did not tarry long during his prayers. He was a genuine rabbinical personality from the old world.

Question: Do any of his grandchildren remain? Their names?
Answer: His son and grandson are well-known rabbis.

Question: Did they leave behind any published books?
Answer: Yes. Reb Elazarl left behind "The Novellae of Maharach" (The Novellae of Rabbi Elazar HaKohen), and from Reb Avrahamele – "Eglei Tal" and "Avnei Nezer".

Question: Do any of their manuscripts remain?
Answer: Yes, many manuscripts remain from Reb Elazarl and Reb Avrahamel.

Question: Is there any Tzadik with you presently? What is his lineage?
Answer: Reb Shmuel Bornsztejn may he live long, is the son of Reb Avrahamel and the grandson of the Kocker Rebbe.

Question: Did you have or do you now have any well-known Jewish wealthy people.
Answer: Yes, there were and there is now.

Question: Did they play or do they now play a Jewish role?
Answer: Yes.

Question: Did you have a well-known cantor, musician, jester, joker, etc.?
Answer: There was Avrahamele the jester.

Question: did you ever have an informer in the city (a city-informer)? What can you say about him?
Answer: Yes, there was one, Menashe Freund. In his younger years, he was an inspector. At the time he forced Jews into poverty. He took what he could from them. He informed on them, and those who were arrested were warned by him that he would inflict strong penalties. Many died through him. Later, he turned over a new leaf, and he began to do good for the local Jews. He expended much money for the city. It is further told that in his old age, he would seclude himself in a room, where he would worship. They buried him near fence of the cemetery.

Question: Do you know the reasons behind any incidents of apostasy?
Answer: One instance was due to family reasons. They treated him very badly, not wanting to give him food and clothing. He turned away from the family, and to anger them, he converted to the Catholic faith. Another converted to the Praboslavic faith. A third converted with his entire family to the Catholic faith.

Question: Are there any recent cases of apostasy? How many in the last few years?
Answer: In the last few years there were no cases of apostasy.

Question: Do you know of any cases where apostates returned to Judaism?
Yes: From among the last two, one of them went to live in Krakow. He became a Jew once again. One of the aforementioned left behind a large family. The mother still lives. It is told that every Friday, she makes a clean cloth for the Sabbath...

Question: Did it ever happen that an apostate was beaten or murdered?
Answer: The person who converted to the Praboslavic faith was found murdered. Nobody knows who did it.

Question: Do you ever find bones when you dig in the earth?
Answer: We find them in many places. A few years ago we found an entire human skeleton buried in the earth.

Question: Are any special days of penitence or fast days observed from the old times, such as the 20th of Sivan, etc. [9]?
Answer: A fast day was declared during a time of illness, but it is no longer observed.

Question: Did your city have a connection with the Polish revolution?

Answer: Yes.

Question: Were there Jewish Miecznikes, who took part in the revolution? What type of sentence did they receive?

Answer: There were two men. One was captured and sentenced to hanging. One night, his father stole him out of jail and sent him out of the country. The second one is still alive. He is called Binyamele "Crower". His signal for the Polish revolution was to "crow like a hen". When he was saved from death, he gave the sign: "To the earth with a pair of pants".

Question: Do you know any stories that were spread regarding Napoleon's war?

Answer: Napoleon was in the city. The rabbi's assistant looked out of the window in order to see him, which was not permitted. The rabbi shouted out: "Baruch, where are you?" At that moment, Napoleon ordered a cannon to be shot. The cannonball went straight through the open window. A Hungarian Franciscan soldier went into the house of a Jew and found a barrel of sauerkraut. He started to eat with his mouth straight in the barrel – and he suddenly died. They found a great deal of money on him, and the family became wealthy for the rest of their days.

Question: Was there ever a blood libel with you?

Answer: In a local church, a box with the inscription was found: "Blood for Jews for Passover", and immediately spread a rumor that Jews murdered a Christian child.

Question: Did things quickly calm down, or was there a trial?

Answer: The Jews immediately turned to the governor and ask that he conduct an investigation. After that investigation, he destroyed that box and there was no trial. This happened many years ago.

Question: Did you ever have epidemics? Are there people who remember them?

Answer: There was an epidemic about 60 years ago. Many people remember the epidemic that took place 20 years ago.

Question: Who among you is occupied with communal matters (who builds baths and mikvas, and makes sure that there is a pharmacist and a physician in town)?

Answer: The city counselors. Also private activists.

Question: To which Rebbes do the Hassidim in your city affiliate with?

Answer: Amshenover (Myszonower), Gerrer, Grodzisker, Aleksandrower, and the local Sochaczewers.

Question: Were there ever disputes between the Hassidim and Misnagdim in your city?

Answer: Yes.

Question: Did the Misnagdim ever excommunicate the Hassidim?

Answer: No.

Question: Were there ever fistfights and court cases between Hassidim and Misnagdim?

Answer: Yes, there were fistfights and court cases. Twelve years ago and two years ago.

Question: Do any documents and manuscripts about them remain?

Answer: It is unknown.

Question: Do you know of any disputes between the Orthodox and the non-believers (Apikorsim)?

Answer: There were disputes between the Orthodox and the Zionists.

Question: What Jewish groups are there today? How old are they?

Answer: There is the Chevra Kadisha, the Talmud Torah group, Bikur Cholim (Visiting the sick), Hachnasas Kala (Providing for brides), Linat Hatzedek (Providing for shelter for the poor), the Tehillim group, the Bachurim (Young men) group, Hachanasat Orchim (providing for guests), and the Tailors

Question: What types of parties existed in 1905?

Answer: The P.P.S. and Poale Zion.

Question: Did you have strikes? By which group of workers?

Answer: No.

Question: How many craftsmen do you have? In which crafts, and how many are in each craft?

Answer: Weavers, blacksmiths, bookbinders, clockmakers, general merchants, tailors, shoemakes, carpenters, stitchers, hat makers. 3 weavers, 2 blacksmiths, 3 bookbinders, 6 clockmakers and rope makers. (We don't know the numbers of the other professions.)

Question: Do you have factories? What types?

Answer: Of artificial silk.

Question: Do Jewish workers work there? How many?

Answer: There is not one Jewish employee.

Question: Are there any very old people with you? What are their names?

Answer: Shamai Jakubowicz is 102, Zilpe Nasielewicz is 105.

Question: Do you have any women who are farsprechers [10], ritual bath attendants, and wailers [11].

Answer: Yes, only ritual bath attendants and wailers.

Question: Their names?

Answer: Eidel Pesse, Bine Gittel Szmejser, Miriam Sochaczewski.

Question: What is the prime industry in town?

Answer: Colonial shops, manufacturing, leather and grain.

Question: Is the Jewish community in your town rich or poor?

Answer: Poor.

Question: Is there strong emigration to America? The reasons? How many traveled? To where?

Answer: It is very strong. It is due to family poverty, not enough sources of livelihood, conscription, etc. We estimate that 200-300 families have gone. They went to Chicago, Baltimore, California, Colorado, Toronto, Canada and other places and countries.

{330}

In Those Days
by Pinchas Graubard
Translated by Jerrold Landau

Small things, nice things. However, they create the tone of our lives. They are the air that we breathe. I wish to discuss them.

We conducted a strike of the maids in our small, beloved Sochaczew. In the larger cities, one had the pleasure of inciting the factories and workshops, when the proletariat was thrown out of work by the thousands in the towns due to political or economic conditions. What type of members of the proletariat did we have in our town? Very few, a few tailors, shoemakers, carpenters, furriers, and shingle makers. We agitated them with great fear and trepidation that they shouldn't slip away from our hands...

In general, we agitated and worked with anyone who had the minutest connection to the proletariat. At times, we crossed the border and dragged in the Poale Zion working youth, children of families of householders, who had no connection to the proletariat.

It was even a bit difficult with the maid girls. At first, we had to spend a long time convincing them that they are people who are equal with everyone, and they must absolutely struggle for a better life – which for them was something that they could not completely understand. Secondly, the householders [12]made noises and issued warnings throughout the entire town, pointed fingers at the long beards and shouted: "You are already crawling to the maid girls, this is not the way it should be! You want to turn them into Socialist leaders! Otherwise you are not worthwhile. We want to show you, youngsters, what you are saying. Thank G-d that there are still police in town!"

Yes, there were indeed police in town, but our duty is to struggle with you. Therefore, we do not out-shout you, but we will continue on with the strike. The town householders sprung up from their skin, and one of them even received a few fiery blows. Regarding the blows, a relative of mine even got involved – a particularly pious Jew who had once tore the hair from his head when he saw with his sharp eyes how Gedalya Warszawski, the father of the writer Ozer Warszawski, extended his hands to a girl...

That relative began to pester us greatly. He scratched the bones with threats and informing on us... We gathered together and tried him. The verdict was almost unanimous, we would break his bones but good.

The leader of our small "group of troublemakers" ("Baiuvka") was named "Omnibus". He was crowned with that bizarre name because he was thick and chubby, and he always moved with difficulty. As he walked, he would sway to the right and the left, like a veritable omnibus. Now he had to issue the verdict. Coldly and calmly, he shook his head and muttered:

"Nu, you can leave him alone already, it will be good..."

On a dark night, he with a few other Baivuka members accosted that relative in his house, took him house into the deathly stillness of the Kaze Alley, and indeed carried out the verdict appropriately. The relative made a commotion, and the group ran away.

We had intended that this would be the end of the threats and accusations, but we were mistaken. After this relative had received his beating on the Kaze Alley, he gathered together a group of Jews and fell upon our two friends and beat them until the point of fainting. One of the two indeed later died from his beatings.

We again gathered together and conducted a trial. Since one of the beaters, Aharon B. excelled with his cruelty, we sentenced him to the extreme penalty: shooting.

One of our "tribunal" led the evening meeting in a small attic room which was the dwelling of one of our members, a bag maker who owned his own small workshop, and died from hunger ten times a day. The attic room was dirty and squalid. A bag machine was on the table, and close by was a spinning wheel with thread. The children slept on the dirty beds. They had pale, dirty faces with closed eyes, sniffling noses and disheveled hair. They slept in small groups, half covered in rags, as in Rejzen's song: "Hands and feet twisted together".

The mother was spread out on a crate, taking a nap… The windows of the attic room were stuffed with pillows and covered with newspapers. A small kerosene lamp was burning on the table, with two smoky tips with wicks, spreading a yellow, murky light, mixed with smoke and fumes. We sat down together with the bag maker and thought about the means how we could carry out this harsh verdict against Aharon B.

Suddenly, the bag maker's wife woke up. She opened her eyes and saw the faces of us conspirators around the murky light of the smoky lamp.

"What is this?" she said as she uttered as she stood up in the middle of the room, "What are these plans, I ask you?" She ran over to her husband and shook him by the shoulders:

"Shlimazel [13], a disaster and a plague to you in your bones, who has come here? What type of business do you have with them? You are, so to speak, a householder, a manufacturer, a bag maker who works for himself, as I say. And they are strikers, Siberniks [14], Socialists, who would not even put a finger in cold water for you. They wouldn't strike for you, and would not help you even if you were dying of hunger in front of their eyes."

She cleared her throat with a harsh rasp and continued her rant, "Do you want to be thrown in jail with them in Austrog? Do you not care about your wife and children? A fire will burn you all! Get out of here! You must leave now! Out! Out!"

Suddenly, she lifted up both hands, threw her head back, and began to shout at the top of her lungs:

"Gevald, gevald, gevald!" [15]

The children were suddenly woken up from their sleep and began to cry. The bag maker's wife took the barrel of water, and let it loose in a torrent in the room with her full might. The "tribunal" disbanded and fled…

2

The police would come to us with some frequency. The did not leave us alone. We also did not leave them alone. We caused them much work and worry. Something happened almost every day. Here a little strike, there a covert gathering. Sometimes someone broke the bones of an informer but good. Sometimes we disarmed a policeman, and sometimes there was a report from us of a revolution. Above all, we often afflicted the town with freshly issued proclamations.

The police would come to us together with the local gendarmes. Earlier, several Christians who belonged to the Social Democratic organization were arrested. After that, they turned to us. We must admit that both the police and the gendarmes acted with great energy. Among the gendarmes there was one small gendarme with squinting eyes and an acute nose that was able to pick up any smell. That person had a strong desire to follow anyone. He could smell better than a dog. He stuck his sharp nose everywhere and searched with his eyes. He followed after people like a Satan. You might be going along, lost in thought on a side street, or in a wide field that borders upon the street, feeling at ease. The white clouds in the clear blue sky speak of eternal joy. The wind caresses the back like a soft, warm hand, reminding one of forgotten moments of childhood – suddenly, instinctively, you turn the head around, and he is there! That gendarme with the sharp nose and squinty eyes...

You had to protect yourself from him. When you left the house, you had to look around well on all sides, looking for the short gendarme. You could not always protect yourself from him. Suddenly, I met him face to face. His eyes danced with shock. He suddenly went still as a stone, like someone beaten to the ground. Meanwhile, I sneaked into a yard and hid in a nook. Through a crack, a hole, I saw my gendarme running around like someone who was poisoned, not knowing where to look for me. I knew that this game would get dangerous, and he would eventually report on me. A few hours later, I found a safe corner below the city, and at night, Baruch Ber, a strong youth with wide shoulders, carried me to Grodzisk via Blonie.

This was the beginning of a journey to the border. I felt very sorry about my native piece of land, and I felt as if someone had delivered a sharp blow to my past, with all of the beloved personalities that were bound up in it.

Baruch Ber drove the horse. We drove fast. However, we arrived in Blonie at the exact moment when the P.P.S. was conducting a raid on the post office.

"We find ourselves, it seems in a difficult situation, what do you mean?" Baruch Ber uttered as he honored the horse with hot blows. A few minutes later we found ourselves far away and safe from the danger.

The next morning, I bid a heartfelt farewell to the wide-boned Baruch Ber, and traveled into a forest. There it would certainly be good and peaceful to stay. It was a distinguished hiding place.

However, the stillness made me nervous. The tall, silent pines reminded me of the reason I was hiding. In my imagination I saw my friends, the short gendarme, the attic room, Omnibus, my relative who was beaten soundly in the bones, and my heart felt great pressure. I pined for my friends, for the mischievous youths, and for our societal work.

I did not remain in hiding, but rather set out for Czestochowa. I had friends there. There, I met Avraham Wijewiorka for the first time, who stood in our ranks at that time.

I was also not able to remain in Czestochowa. The meeting, in which I took part, was surrounded by the police. I and a few other friends wished to escape. I was not able to remain any longer in Czestochowa, and I returned to the forest.

I decided to remain in the forest for a long time, until the arrests of our friends would cease. Indeed, the forest was also a jail for me, albeit there were no jail guards.

The emptiness tormented me, until an uncle of mine arrived to transport me to the border.

We arrived in Lodz. The city was teaming with Cossacks, police patrols and spies. The people went around with thick heads [16], and everyone was looking over their shoulders. It seemed as if the city was besieged with enemies.

My uncle shouted out:

"You go on ahead. He called me a pale one. It is not good when we go together. See how many Cossacks..."

Fear overtook him when he accompanied me a little farther. He went and trembled.

3

In Lodz I met up with an acquaintance Yoel Wosk, and bid farewell to my uncle. Yoel Wosky was a mobile, joyous Jew. He loved a joke and a prank, and when needed – he could walk around like a young, spoiled child.

I traveled with Yoel Wosky to Wloclawek and from there by horse to Lipna until Dobrzyn. The journey lasted an entire night. The horses refused to go. Yoel did not do anything about it. He was in the wagon and passed the night singing a popular song of Zunzer.

He had a weakness for me, probably because I had helped him at times in his mischief and pranks. In Dobrzyn I put on a suit, purchased a hat, and for the first time took off the long kapote with the small Hassidic cap.

Yoel bought me a "fulpasik", a type of temporary border pass of that era. I took leave of him, and set out from Dobrzyn to Golub, at that time a German town that shocked me greatly with its vanity and earthiness. Dobrzyn and Golub, two neighboring towns, two symbols – one for its lack of beauty and laziness, and the other for its culture. The culture attracted me, but my heart was yearning for that time… With the "fulpasik" in my pocket, I set out for Berlin and from there to Antwerp.

I began thinking of a purpose and a bright future. I had spent some time in Belgium, and suddenly the bag maker from my town arrived. He was the one whose wife with her hysterical shouts had broken up our "tribunal". The bag maker traveled to America. The hysterical wife and the hungry children had somehow caused him to abandon his Poale Zion ideals, and he traveled to seek livelihood in the land of dollars.

"What do you hear from home?"

"What can one hear? It is quiet."

"Quiet".

"Yes, the short gendarme no longer sniffs in the streets, the police no longer conduct searches, the householders stopped informing… there was a tumult, and now the tumult is over."

Perhaps indeed I should travel home… That thought suddenly caught hold of me, as if under duress… I thought and thought, and traveled from Belgium, from that land where I was simultaneously light and serious, like an old, true revolutionary, where I swayed to and fro on the wagon, rode horses, toured museums, heard various revolutionary speeches and attempted to become part of the proletariat.

When I once again saw my town, it seemed to have changed. It was poor and downtrodden. Poor houses, poor people, a poor sky and a poor son. Everything there was small, mundane, lonely…

Our organization had been cut down. In the streets the loafers were singing beneath the hearty laughter of the householders:

"We have already killed all of the strikers."

"We have no more fear of the strikers."

"We are free to study the Torah…"

The meager remnants of the organization were led by one of the beaten members, an ill and broken person.

I went through a deep crisis. My hands were helpless and I went around as if not in this world…

The crisis ameliorated somewhat when suddenly news broke out in town about dark tribulations. A group of hired drunks were to come and make a pogrom.

We organized a self defense group. The local S.D. promised us help. The Warsaw Poale Zion organization sent us the member Nemerin with a few other members. The brought weapons. During the day, when the community was generally uncomfortable as they awaited the pogromchiks with terror, we called a mass meeting specifically with the rabbi in the Beis Midrash. Many householders came. Nemerin delivered a sharp lecture. He spoke about the reasons that instigated the pogroms, and about Poale Zion, which educates the Jewish workers and awakens might and self sacrifice. "Gone are the times", he proclaimed, "when a Jewish worker would go around with an upright back and his head held high, and would call for the button of a policeman and the pointed moustache of a gendarme... The Jewish workers have grown up, and know how to stand up against all pogromchiks and their protectors in high places. No more fear, no more cowardice, only belief in the power of the Jewish worker!"

The householders who were standing in the Beis Midrash and who heard those words were now not smiling mockingly, as used to be their habit. They stood with their heads down, terrified and forlorn, seeking the protection of the workers, of the treif [17] strikers, the accursed Poale Zion...

The Pogromchiks did not come, and no pogrom took place. The collected arms were hidden away, and the town was calm.

Avraham Lewkowicz (Kaiser) and his wife Esther

TRANSLATOR'S FOOTNOTES:

1. The English and Hebrew years do not match here. 1913 would be 5673.
2. The implication being a Jewish community.
3. It is evident that the responder did not count the smaller shtibels in his response to the earlier question.
4. Castle Mountain.
5. The Shach, acronym for Siftei Cohen, is one of the prime commentators on the Shulchan Aruch, the Code of Jewish Law
6. A chair used during circumcision ceremonies
7. In parentheses, seemingly added by the editor.
8. I am unsure as to what the expression mne is referring to. It may be a fragment of a word.
9. The 20th of Sivan was often observed as a fast day in memory of the Crusades and the Chmielnicki pogroms. Its observance has fallen into disuse – probably on account of these events having been overshadowed by the Holocaust.
10. Women who assist other women with prayers in the women's section of the synagogue.
11. Women who lead the lamentation at funerals.
12. Literally children of 'balebatish' families. – i.e. children of householders – people who owned their own houses in this context. It would roughly be equivalent to our concept of the middle class, as opposed to the working class.
13. A term used for a person of ill luck – with a mildly derogatory connotation.
14. I suspect that this is a term for people who are liable to be deported to Siberia.
15. An expression used in case of emergency or danger. 15r
16. The implication here is somewhat derogatory – the English term 'dense' might fit.
17. The word 'treif means non-Kosher, usually in its literal sense, here in its figurative sense.

The Lamed-Vavnik[1]
by M. B. Sztejn
Translated by Jerrold Landau

From the death of the Lamed Vavnik one could learn about his life. Aside from the rabbi, there was in Sochaczew one other Lamed Vavnik, who protected the city.

The key to those hidden people in whose merit the world exists is guarded under the Divine Throne, and only G-d himself knows the secret. Their power is exceedingly great. There is no reason to talk about them during their lifetimes. As is the case with everything that is hidden – the more that it is hidden the greater it is. The matter only becomes revealed after the death of such a person. Such was the case with Yakir the shoemaker.

His countenance shone with the Divine shadow. He was pale and sublime – like a precious stone. He had a long, wide beard that flowed over his cloak. It was a silvery beard. Yakir Shuster the shoemaker, to whom nobody paid attention, had a special merit … For on Sabbath evenings after the candles had gone out and the city was enveloped in a deep slumber – Yakir Shuster was awake and called out in a soft voice, saturated with pleading, to the Jews of Sochaczew to recite Psalms.

He did not awaken anyone from their sleep, heaven forbid, and even more so not on the Sabbath, for he would not even hurt a fly on the wall. He only requested that people arise for the recitation of Psalms, and his soft voice trilled:

Please hearken my beloved people

What I say to you:

The Clock has already struck three

And the time to recite Psalms has arrived.

His voice was heard from one end of the city to the other end. He did not only awaken the Jews, but also the gentiles. He awakened the fields and forests, and no gentile, including the priest and the administrator, was brazen enough to chastise him for waking up people in the middle of the nights. They disappeared before his silken voice. This was only because King David himself accompanied him and protected him[2].

Thus was his custom year after year – in the summer and winter, in the deep snow, violent storms, and the freezing cold, he would go out on Friday evenings to call the people for the recitation of Psalms – and his voice would fill the empty space of the Beis Midrash. When the Sabbath morning prayers began, the simple folk, tailors and shoemakers, had already concluded the recitation of the verses of the sweet singer of Israel[3], and their voice had opened up the gates of mercy.

As things came to pass, the hand of Esau overpowered the voice of Jacob[4], and on Tisha Beav, the day that is marked by disaster, the gentiles were inspired to conduct a battle, and a commotion started in the city. A notice was posted near the citadel by the gentiles calling the Jews to battle. The Jews stood, men and women, weeping and praying for an annulment of the evil decree. Only one person – Yakir the shoemaker – did not move from his shoemaker's stool. He did not raise his bright eyes, and he banged nail after nail into the hard soles. People passed by him and pierced him with their gaze.

However what did it matter to him? He had no children who would be fitting to conscript for the battle, and he himself was already old.

Yakir the shoemaker did not answer. He sat as if mute nailing nails into the hard soles, and his bright eyes that sparked as the stars were gazing down. For what comfort was there in the mouth of the shoemaker for the distraught people who were first to turn over their dear ones to the hands of Esau?

Reb Leib Zawadski, the founder of the Bible study society, and his wife Frimet.

{338 - Yiddish} {718 - Hebrew}

Did He Not Promise You...
By Moshe Levanon
Translated by Jerrold Landau

Many years ago there was in Sochaczew a water-drawer by the name of Kalman Yankel.

There were several water-drawers in the town who drew water from the Bzura. In the summer they would be dripping with moisture, and in the winter they were covered with furs which froze like ice.

However, none of them had pails similar to those of Kalman Yankel. His pails were tied to a heavy pole, and they looked like large casks. He dragged them along with an erect posture, looking in front of him with protruding reddish eyelashes surrounding his eyes, as if he accepted upon himself his burden to atone for some sin that he had transgressed, and not for the porting of water or any other such matter[5].

He never knew how many times he dragged pails of water, and to which houses. When he was asked how many times he dragged water, he became perplexed and answered with difficulty:

"More than five."

It seems as if he dragged ten, and at times even twenty, in one session.

He never requested any payment for the porting of water. This was not his job, but that of his wife Freda. She kept the accounts, and therefore, as she was wont, she talked disparagingly about him, and told about her difficult life with him as she took what was owed to her.

Summer and winter, at dawn, as people were reciting the Shema[6], Kalman Yankel took the large pails, tied them to his pole, kissed his mezuzah and went down to the river. He filled them with water and returned to the city. Then he would go back, without tiring, without resting, and without uttering a word from his mouth. The impression was given that he would be forever going to the river to draw water; however suddenly, he removed the pole and pails from his shoulder, and returned again to the river not in order to draw water, but to fish with a fishing rod that was in his hand.

Nobody ever knew if Kalman Yankel ever caught a fish. And what about Freda? Perhaps she knew and perhaps she did not. It was clear that he did not sell any fish. He would stand at the riverbank until evening, with the fishing rod in his hand, looking at the water. Close to sundown he would go the Beis Midrash for the mincha and maariv prayers.

In the Beis Midrash he never moved far away from the group that sat at the end of the table that was next to the door, beside the two large heating ovens. From there, with his hands down, he stared at the Holy Ark, and did not move. He only nodded his head, as if he was agreeing with the words of somebody – but that was all. He did not answer "Amen" or "Barchu"[7]. He would stand at that edge of the table also on festivals during the prayers, with his clean prayer shawl hanging from him. His hands were always down, as they were when he was drawing water. Without moving he stood and gazed.

He was never honored with an "Aliya"[8] to the Torah. They did not know if he would know the blessings to make over the Torah – and they did not want to embarrass him. However, once a year, on Simchas Torah, he was honored with a "Hakafa"[9]. He would make the circuit quietly, with the scroll in his hand, without opening his mouth, as if deep in thought. He did not sing, he did not dance, and he did not rejoice with the Torah scroll, he just gazed ahead –

They knew him well in the city. "Mothers would warn their lazy children – "You will turn out like Kalman Yankel". Storekeepers would insult each other by saying – "All you are is a Kalman Yankel". He went through his life as "Kalman Yankel", and nobody ever told stories about him, except for the following incident that took place with him:

In a hot day in the month of Tammuz[10], around noon, he stood as usual by the river with his fishing rod in his hand. A carriage approached the river, and a merchant came out, undressed, and entered the water to bathe. Kalman Yankel did not pay attention, and certainly did not speak to the stranger. Perhaps he did not even notice. The stranger bathed, came out from the river, got dressed – and left just as he had arrived, and silence again enveloped the area of the river. Kalman Yankel continued to gaze forward.

Suddenly his rod started to be dragged downward, along with the float and the bait. Kalman Yankel was not concerned. He saw this as a sign that a fish was being sent to him from Heaven. He raised his rod, removed the silver fish from it, and placed it in the basket that was next to him. He then noticed a paper bag that was next to his basket. He deliberated as to whether to pick it up or not. He was not overly excited, however his curiosity was piqued and he picked it up. It was not a small bag, but rather a substantial one, filled with gold and silver coins.

"Dead heads" – he thought, and they should be buried. He dug a pit, placed the treasure inside, and put a branch on top of it so that he would be able to recognize the burial place.

A short time thereafter the carriage returned, and the desperate merchant came out. This was the place that he had bathed, and he had lost his treasure of coins. He searched and searched, and looked at Kalman Yankel.

"I have lost a large sum of money, silver and gold coins, and I am distraught."

Money? Kalman Yankel did not see coins, but rather heads. He found dead heads and buried them.

"Where?" He pointed to the branch that was placed in the earth.

The merchant leaped to the place, and exposed his lost treasure. With great joy he turned to Kalman Yankel.

"Fellow Jew, you have saved me". He took a handful of gold coins and gave them to him. "Take! Take! You have saved an entire family, take the wages for your efforts!"

"Heads, dead heads, what do I need them for?" – He said.

The merchant forced the money into his hands and said:

"Take! This is not theft, Heaven forbid. This is the commandment of returning a lost object."

"But not dead heads"...

The merchant looked at him as if he was looking at a madman. He then went to Reb Elazarel, related the incident to him, and left him money for charity.

The Rabbi took the money. There was no shortage of poor and needy people in town. However the incident itself was mysterious to him, but he did not talk about it.

In the evening, after the evening services (maariv), Kalman Yankel hurried to the Rabbi and told him that:

"Immediately after he returned home from the evening prayers, his wife came after him with an axe as if to murder him. He barely escaped."

The Rabbi sent his assistant and called Freda.

"Is such a thing possible? Did you approach him with an axe in your hand? Did you wish to murder your husband? A Jewish woman..."

"Rabbi, I don't have the strength to continue on with my difficult and impoverished life with him. I cannot continue on. If G-d had sent him a treasure, was it not befitting for him? He did not wish to keep the handful of gold coins that the merchant gave him. No, I don't want a husband such as this..."

The Rabbi explained to her the greatness of the commandment of returning a lost object. Kalman Yankel stood up to the trial. He did not wish to take any reward in return for the commandment (mitzvah). His reward would be great in the true world[11], after 120 years.

"However, what benefit do I get from his mitzvah? Why is my life in such straits?"

"Freda, you are correct. I decree that you should promise Freda one half of your reward in the world to come. She suffers along with you."

"Oh Rabbi" – the man trembled.

The Rabbi remained seated in his place. Kalman Yankel was not a simple person. He understood the greatness of his reward in the world to come.

The Rabbi stood up, approached Kalman Yankel and said:

"Tell me, who are you?"

As if he was forced to give up everything dear to him, he answered:

"Rabbi, let it be as you decided – I grant one half of my reward in the world to come to Freda".

He hurried to leave.

Rabbi Elazarel was lost in thought. If Kalman Yankel does not wish to reveal whom he is, he should not be forced.

However, the entire town found out about the incident, and they began to look upon him in a different light. They no longer mocked him, and the women would console Freda for her acceptance of her bitter lot in life:

"Did he not promise you, after 120 years".

TRANSLATOR'S FOOTNOTES:

1. Lamed Vav is the number 36. According to legend, in every generation, there are 36 extra-special righteous people, whose righteousness is a greatly kept secret from others. A Lamed Vavnik is a term referring to such a person. Here, the connotation is a righteous person who was not fully appreciated during his lifetime.
2. King David was the author of the book of Psalms.
3. A reference to King David.
4. A reference from the book of Genesis from the statement that Isaac made upon feeling Jacob's disguise when he came to his father to receive the blessing that was intended for his brother Esau. In this context, the phrase 'the voice of Jacob' refers to the prayers of the Jewish people, and 'the hands of Esau' refers to the violence of the gentiles.
5. The final phrase of this sentence does not appear to fit in to the context.
6. A portion of the morning prayers.
7. Various congregational responses during communal prayer.
8. On every occasion of public reading of the Torah (Sabbaths and Festivals, Monday and Thursday mornings, fast days and the New Moon), several men, the number depending on the occasion, are called up in succession to participate in the reading of the Torah. These men recite a blessing upon being called up. This procedure is called an "Aliya".
9. On Simchas Torah, seven festive circuits are made around the synagogue with all the Torah scrolls. Each circuit is called a "Hakafa".
10. The Hebrew month spanning anywhere from mid June to early August.
11. This refers to the reward in the Hereafter. 120 years refers to the fullest possible expected human lifespan (the number of years of Moses' life), and "after 120 years" is a term that a person uses to describe the time period after his death, without bringing on the "evil eye" by explicitly referring to his own death.

{342}

From the Book "Poland"
by Y. Y. Trunk

Dedicated to the Memory of:

Bernice Phyllis (Mann) Knee (nee Mittleman)
Beloved Sister of Sandra Mittleman Robinson,
Granddaughter of Sochotzover Society Member Charles Miller

Translated by Jerrold Landau

The two greatest Torah families in Poland were becoming linked by marriages. Righteous people in the Garden of Eden are drinking a toast. A postal coach is traveling through the marshes between Lowicz and Sochaczew. This is Uncle Yankel's victory. In an inn in Lowicz, Uncle Yankel makes sounds, and all are in bad luck. Jews push Yerachmiel into the coach. Uncle Yankel is as silent as a lamb. It is the fields at Purim time. Postal trumpets in the end of winter streets. Go, for it is only for a wedding. Uncle Yankel is again silent as a lamb. The Sochaczew marshes and the Sochaczew market. In-laws are traveling!

I was again in Lodz for the second winter. I still attended the cheder of Reb Aharon. I traveled home with the large cart of merchandise for the Wislickis. They discussed: the following winter, I would be given over to a teacher of Gemara. This filled me with pride. In Kutno, Aunt Itka was getting divorced from Berish.

We all traveled to a wedding at Purim time. Uncle Yitzchak, my aunt's brother – who self-assuredly held himself out as a genius – was getting married in Sochaczew. The bride was a granddaughter of the famous Sochaczewer Gaon Reb Avrahamele. It was said that this match was connecting two of the greatest and most well known Torah families in Poland. Reb Yehoshuale and Reb Avrahamele Sochaczewer. Indeed, the groom was a grandson of Reb Yitzchak Waworker and the bride a granddaughter of the Kocker. Old Hassidim said that the heavenly hosts are rejoicing with such a match. The Tzadikim in the Garden of Eden are being given cups with wine that has been kept [1] in order to drink Lechayim.

People were indeed preparing for such an important wedding. Preparations were being made in all of the Rebbe's courts in Poland to travel to the "Sochaczewer wedding". Reb Avrahamele was the greatest prince of Torah in Poland – a son-in-law of the Kocker, and a Rebbe of Hassidim.

We traveled by train from Lodz to Lowicz. Sochaczew was a small, remote town. A hicktown between marshes. No train went through it. One had to travel by covered wagon. That "extra post" also traveled in those marshes between Lowicz and Sochaczew. A large, yellow crate with a drawn Russian eagle, and with strange, tall wheels that knocked and moaned as they moved. From afar we heard that the "extra post" is traveling here. The wagon drivers of the "post" wore strange, circular hats. They also wore red, folded ropes from which hung twisted, brass trumpets. The coachmen blew these trumpets in the middle of the way, as they were going through Sochaczew. They blew strange, old-fashioned tunes that could be heard sharply and strangely from afar. When the "extra posts" went straight through a forest and the coachmen blew, the forest reverberated with loud, sharp echoes. Sochaczew was such a far-off hicktown that when one checked with the coachmen in Poland, one completely forgot about the old, yellow coach that was dragged through the marshes between Lowicz and Sochaczew. I did not know how Uncle Yankel in Kutno persuaded everybody to travel to Sochaczew not in an ordinary Jewish wagon, but rather in such a strange old-fashioned coach.

Enough – Uncle Yankel persuaded. When we were about to travel to Lowicz in the train and stay in some inn behind the train, the entire Kutno family was already there. Uncle Yankel was very occupied with his son-in-law Yerachmiel, and argued with him. In a different room for men, Grandfather Reb Moshel sat around the table in a place of honor, dressed in a rabbinical raccoon fur and a sable kolpak on his head. He held the rabbinical scepter in his hand with the thought that as he was sitting in the Lowicz inn, he was really in Sochaczew at the wedding. The groom Yitzchak with the disheveled peyos of a genius sat next to him. He wore a large velvet hat and a new raccoon fur that gave him the proud aura of a rabbinical genius. All sorts of Jews of Lowicz – who were not connected to the relatives – wearing weekday hats, pushed themselves among the Kutno in-laws. The Jews approached the grandfather Reb Moshel and gave him a greeting. The wives from Kutno were sitting in another room, drinking tea. Yaakov Comber, Hershel Najman's son-in-law and the new assistant of the grandfather Reb Moshel, pushed among them and called out hoarsely. He was a small, lively, dark Jew with a pear of burning, passionate eyes.

In the meantime, we heard from the outside the old-fashioned blaring of trumpets and the screeching of wheels. Uncle Yankel sprung out of his place, ran to the wives, and called out loudly and triumphantly,

– The post!

Indeed, the two old-fashioned, yellow crates stood outside. Moustached gentiles wearing strange leather hats sat on the upper deck. The trumpets were tied up on the ropes, and long whips were in their hands. The gentiles cracked the whips, and thereby drove the passengers to the inn. We all went in. Uncle Yankel was in a festive mood, as if the coaches were his own. He battled with Yerachmiel even outside the coach. The steps of the coach were high, and entering was not simple. One could indeed hear shouting and laughter from the front of the coach, where the women were supposed to travel. The poor women could not ascend the coach. The shamash Yaakov Comber – even though he was dressed in a velvet jacket, a yarmulke and a Hassidic belt (gartel) wound around – stood near the wives and made all sorts of ambiguous jokes at the expense of the wives, who did not know how to descend from the yellow coach. He did the same near the men. This was very difficult for the elderly Jews, even though Uncle Yankel was standing near the steps shouting, and calling everyone a shlimazel [2]. When it came the turn of Yerachmiel, he unfortunately began to sigh loudly. He held on to his stomach with his hands, and was not even able to place one foot on the step. His wife Ratza cursed him from the women's coach. Uncle Yankel fumed and called unlucky Yerachmiel all sort of names. It did not work. At first, a few Jews of Lowicz who did not know him took Yerachmiel by the hands and dragged him onto the coach. Yerachmiel sighed loudly, and Uncle Yankel ranted and called cursed by the steps. When Uncle Yankel's turn finally came to go down the steps, he also was not able to reach the first step. Uncle Yankel suddenly became silent and coughed strongly. It did not help. The same Jews of Lowicz had to take him, Uncle Yankel, by the hands and pull him on the coach.

When all of the relatives were already sitting around, the old, yellow coaches quickly set out. The place shook, and all of the passengers fell one on top of the other. Uncle Yankel no longer shouted. The coaches sighed and shook, and it seemed as if all of Lowicz was shaking along with them. The wagon driver on the seat shouted "Na Bak!" and cracked the whips. Finally, the coaches passed the last houses of Lowicz, and continued on into the fields.

It was Purim time. The fields were still covered with deep snow. The roads that lead to Sochaczew, however, do not like snow. It was one long terrible bog full of pits and potholes. The mud percolated up and splattered under the tall, groaning wheels of the two coaches. Black crows flew and cawed over the white fields. The relatives inside the coaches merged into a cluster, and they had to maintain themselves without leaving anything, for life was not certain. The grandfather Reb Moshel even had an idea to discuss a matter of learning with the groom, however it was completely impossible to do the simplest thing – and speaking was impossible, even if one shouted loudly. Suddenly an unexpectedly, we heard a loud blast of trumpets. Both gentiles on the deck trumpeted loudly in the middle of the empty, snowy fields.

Poor Yerachmiel was sitting, stuffed between the relatives, holding tightly to his own stomach. All of his own frailties began to speak things. Yerachmiel was greatly startled by the sudden loud trumpet blast. He went to Uncle Yankel and whispered in his ear that they must – no more and no less – stop the coach in the middle of the marsh, since he has to make…

Uncle Yankel became red with anger.

"Go travel with a fool to a wedding" – he shouted in the middle of the shaking clump of relatives.

The grandfather Reb Moshel decided: it's no use. We cannot let a Jew transgress such a great sin as, "do not defile yourself" [3].

With great anguish and torment, he barely succeeded in informing the gentile on the deck that he must stop the coach. The coach finally stopped. The coach with the woman also stopped. It seemed as if the deep mud in which the yellow spattered coaches made their way through with difficulty – also rested. The crows cawed wildly over the snowy fields. When the doors of the coach opened, the fresh, end-of-winter air rushed in. All of the Jews in the coach had to help Yerachmiel descend. Yerachmiel went deep into the mud. Finally, they finally pulled Yerachmiel back onto the coach with great effort. When the gentile cracked his whip and tried to urge on the horses, it became clear that Uncle Yankel also had to relieve himself. They once again told the gentile that he had to wait. The difficult labor began, getting Uncle Yankel off and returning him to the coach.

Thus did we finally approach the first houses of Sochaczew, weary and broken. Then the real mud started. The town was completely swimming in mud. When our coaches noisily role between the small, wooden houses, it seemed that Sochaczew awoke from its lethargy. All of the windows opened. Various heads of women in sleeping caps and men in yarmulkes peered out of windows. Women called out to each other from several windows, announcing that the Kutner relatives. The gentiles on the deck began again to blow the trumpets. Thus did we travel through the Sochaczew market with noise and bellowing.

The market square was full of mud, in which gentiles and Jews trampled around. Jews stood together with farmers in front of the stores and chatted. All of them looked at the Kutner relatives. Our coaches traveled between the unhitched wagons of the farmers, which stood there almost sunken into the mud of Sochaczew. The horses of the farmers stood tied to the wagons, heartily munching on hay and fodder. Cows stood in the midst of the mud, looking foolishly upon the moving coaches and chewing their cud. A few goats wandered around the mud of the Sochaczew market, sticking their bearded heads into the doors of Jewish stores, as if they were seeking something. Finally, our coaches stopped. We were all slowly sent out to various Jews. Tired and pained from the long, difficult journey from Lowicz to Sochaczew, I immediately fell into a bed and slept like a corpse.

A wedding in Sochaczew. Go to it! A desert before a sinning body. They take me back to the Gemaras. Yaakov Comber is joining up with the Rebbetzin Tzina.

Sochaczew maintained the Kocker customs as much as possible. In the Kocker "court" a wedding never took place at night, as it did for all Jews, but rather in the midst of the day. Kocker children who were getting married often waited long hours until the Kocker came out of his little room to the chupa. It was not so sharp in Sochaczew, however, the Kocker custom of conducting a wedding during the day was kept with full strictness in Sochaczew. Therefore, there were no music players in Sochaczew, despite the fact that – alas – one must have musicians at a wedding. The musicians cursed the years. Hassidim pushed them aside like hand towels. As soon as they began to play, Reb Shmuel would call out: "Go away", and Reb Avrahamele would start talking about learning with someone at the table. The jester – who had to be engaged at a Sochaczew wedding like an unavoidable misfortune – as soon as he opened his mouth, the Hassidim began to make a racket. Reb Avrahamele held that this was a denigration of Torah, and Reb Shmuel shouted out: "Enough"!. The rhymes literally remained sunken on the tongue of the unfortunate jester. He was pushed into a corner, and he was almost squeezed between the crowd of Hassidim, who had gathered around the table to hear Reb Avrahamele's words of Torah.

Thus did the wedding of Uncle Yankel take place in the middle of the day. It took place in the courtyard of Reb Avrahamele's Beis Midrash, in the midst of the veritable Sochaczew mud. Reb Shmuel's daughters were petite, dark, and pretty. Frumet, Uncle Yitzchak's [4] bride, was the prettiest in my opinion. She was petite and plump, with enthusiastic, laughing eyes. She did not wear a white wedding dress to the wedding. In Kock it was felt that women should not wear white dresses, as the ministering angels. This was restricted to the greatest Hassidim. Therefore, I recall, the bride Frumet was dressed in a yellow dress with a tam on the head and a yellow kerchief. All of the relatives in the impressive group of Hassidim stood in the mud around the chupa. The women stood a bit farther away, at the edge of the court, for those close to Reb Avrahamele must not see any woman. In the middle of the mud – when they led the bride and groom to the chupa – the musicians began to strum something, and Reb Shmuel shouted out from behind the chupa: "Enough". The musicians were afraid and desisted. The marriage ceremony began under the chupa. Quick and to the point, without any long discourses and songs, everything was in accordance with the Kocker fashion.

Since the large wedding meal was to begin in the evening, the crowd went to their hosts or to the Beis Midrash immediately after the ceremony. Reb Avrahamele went to his customary class. Reb Shmuel sat and studied. The learned people of Sochaczew took their Gemaras, or began to engage in didactics and study. People forgot that a wedding took place moments before. The day in Reb Avrahamele's Beis Midrash took on its weekday learning appearance. In Sochaczew, they did not like to dwell on wedding ceremonies. Everyone returned to the Gemara. Meir Bornsztejn discussed business matters with a wealthy Sochaczew Hassid. The grandfather Reb Moshel also sat down to learn with the groom. The dressed up female relatives wandered around like lost souls. We were all hungry. Reb Avrahamele's Sochaczew was a desert for the sinning body. Reb Avrahamele's wife, Rebbetzin Tzina, the Kocker's daughter, kept the women away from wandering around the men, so as not to disturb the Jews who were studying Torah. The men of Kutno were driven to the Gemara. The attendant of Yaakov Comber who was hungry, went to the women relatives and asked for a piece of cake. He began to chat with the woman until Rebbetzin Tzina came and cut him off. All of the female relatives began to shout at him, "Sinner, troubler of Israel, get out of here, go sit with your Gemara". Yaakov Comber lost his head, swallowed saliva, and took the deathly-hungry person into the Beis Midrash, where he sat down among learned Jews, and began to study Tractate Eruvin in a high, somewhat singsong voice.

It is the mealtime at a Sochaczewer wedding. People are engaged in didactics. The unfortunate jester! The Rebbetzin Tzina carries on with politeness toward the women.

A wedding meal in Sochaczew bears little resemblance to a normal wedding. It is simply a Rebbe's "tisch" (table celebration). The groom and Uncle Yitzchak sat in the place of honor next to Reb

Avrahamele. When Reb Avrahamele opened his mouth, a silence pervaded amongst the Hassidim. The groom was almost pushed off into a corner. The food was meager. Even this was eaten hastily. They did play around with food. The most important thing was to discuss learning. Rev Avrahamele talked quietly and very nimbly, so that one could almost grab you with his eyes. Furthermore, Reb Shmuel hurried the Hassidic waiters and urged them not to waste time, and to serve what was there. Even before people touched the food, the servers removed the plates, and then the sharp didactical lecture began. Even in the great haste, Reb Avrahamele did not sit by the table. Since he was weak, Reb Shmuel led him back to his little room. Reb Avrahamele sat by himself with his Gemara. The didactical learning continued on at the wedding celebration with the remaining great scholars.

With the women, it was literally as if they were in a desert. An unholy silence pervaded. The Rebbetzin Tzina sat at the head of the table in her sharp Kocker austere style and instilled fear in everybody. If any of the women would have even tried to open her mouth, the Kocker's daughter would have cut her off at the moment, saying that one must not have any unnecessary conversation, for Reb Avrahamele is sitting not so far away with the Torah. One must be on guard, as if from fire, to not disturb him, and it is indeed better that one not speak any foolishness. After the meal and after the grace after meals, we went to our hosts to sleep. The women had no more to do after that. This was the manner in which Rebbetzin Tzina conducted the wedding meal.

Indeed, there was one woman from among the Kutno relatives whom, when Rebbetzin Tzina saw her, she relaxed her Kocker sharpness to some degree, and even displayed modesty and sentiment. Obviously, this was only to the extent that the Kocker daughter was able to display soft heartedness and sentiment.

This was Reb Yitzchak Waworker's daughter, Grandmother Blimele.

{351}

Smugglers
by Ozer Warszawski
Translated by Jerrold Landau
Chapters from the novel

{Note from translator: this section of excerpts from the novel extends from page 351-364. Due to the difficulty in translating the literary style, and the relative unimportance to the story of Sochaczew, only the first three pages have been translated here.}

1.

Fantel Furman extended a hand, moves around under the deck, wanders from one side to the other, sits down and yawns. It is dark in the house. A week light penetrates through the two peepholes in the shutters.

"It is still very early", he stammered, rubbing his eyes and looking over the house, which was completely enveloped in a cold and darkness. Seeing the frost flowers in the house, detecting a weirdness. He called over to the second bed:

"Glika, Glika!"

"Hey what?", he grabs his wife strongly, and remains sitting with shut eyes and a wide-open mouth.

"Do you see, it is already another frost!" He points to the window and sticks both hands under his cotton undershirt in which he sleeps during the winter. He eagerly scratches his chest with the right hand, and around his shoulders with his left hand.

"What do you say?" he asks her again. She sits and rubs her closed eyelids with her moist finger.

She answers, "there is no money".

She once heard this.

"Indeed we need to buy a bit of coal, and a piece of rosy bread…"

He once again utters, "It is a frost", as if to drive something from her.

He quickly removes his hands from his undershirt, lies back down, and pulls up the blanket over his nose. His wife looks at him from the other bed. A vapor rises from her face and body.

"So, what will be? Huh?", she asks. She certainly knows that he cannot give any answer to this.

From the first room, the kitchen, a boyish voice calls out:

"Move back from here! See how it is arranged. Others don't like you, only for the shoulders.."

"Close the "Zwaratnik", Fuf,!" Answers a heavier voice.

"A cholera"…, we again hear the first, boyish voice.

"A cholera in their bones!" calls out Fantel. He has no peace during sleep.

"But what will be, what will be?", repeats Glika in the eerie quiet, "The bakery will no longer give any cherry bread. A bit of coal will burn in the kitchen…". As she repeats this, she begins to scratch both her head and her heart, grating at the sleepyhead as one grates horseradish.

Fantel was hot from lying covered up to the nose. He raises a tiny bit of the blanket, and the cold air blows over his skin. A refreshing wind blows over his entire sturdy body. He soon casts a glance over the freezing room, grabs it again over his hands, covers himself well with the blankets, and feels the refreshing warmth.

Soon, one hand started to sweat, and then the second, and then his entire body. The ends of the short, solid, dark hairs on his head and face glisten, as if covered in dew. He began to move with his short, sturdy legs. He gave them a twist, and then a stretch, exactly as would have done a horse in the meadow, and then another twist and another stretch.

"Go to hell, Fantel you thief!", shouted his wife, 'Tear apart that piece of linen that barely holds together."

But "Fantel the thief" does not hear anything now. He kicks in the bedding. He feels like a fish in the water, and perhaps he had some sort of idea… perhaps about livelihood….

"Would you like to have a new shpantzer [5]", he suddenly calls out. His voice is so tender, as only Fantel's voice can be – it was completely broken…

Since she says nothing, he also is silent and engrossed in thoughts about good things: about a better life, and a more ample livelihood.

She indeed reminds him that it is indeed the proper time to do something, and not to sit… the train gives nothing today… water and groats… and here everything is plucked, torn… one has to have laundry, footwear, coal and wood.. and one needs, and one needs…

And Fantel has prepared a complete plan… "It is not hard, G-d will help"… And he springs out of bed, not bothered a bit by the cold.

He wraps his legs with long leggings, like towels. He puts on the boots, and goes immediately to the stall, where he gives water to the horses.

2.

Koppel enters in the morning. It is cold in the room. The windowpanes are completely covered with frost. Glika looks at them and things: "it is a little bit of a dark garden" ... both of Fantel's sons lie on the wooden sleeping bench. A few burners are on in the kitchen, and a metal pot is full of water. Koppel puts on one boot and then the other. He rubs his hands together and blows into his sleeve.

"Good morning", he says. His voice in the cold room is like a barrel outside. "Aha, it is a little cold". He approaches the table that stands near the window. He pulls out his ears from under his large, plush hat, and sits down on a bench.

"Did you not go to the train?" Fantel cannot interrupt to speak in the middle of his prayers.

Fantel walks around the room, enwrapped in a yellow, squalid tallis, as it feels as if Fantel's small, cramped body sprouts with vigor.

"And there is nobody with whom", answers Koppel as he coughs. He pours a drink of liquor., "Who would indeed travel in such a chill?!"

Fantel hurries on with his prayers. He bows, spits quickly to both sides [6], whips of the tallis and tefillin, quickly rolls up his sleeve, tightens his peaked hat over the eyebrows, and takes a yarmulke out from his fur coat.

TRANSLATOR'S FOOTNOTES:

1. A reference to the Midrash that, in the World to Come, the Tzadikim will be treated with 'wine that has been kept' from the time of Creation (for an explicit reference, see the Akdamut prayer of Shavuot).
2. A half-derogatory, half-endearing term for someone of ill luck.
3. It is a violation of Jewish law to restrain oneself from ones bodily functions.
4. There may be an error here, as it was Yaakov (Yankel), who was getting married.
5. A type of clothing.
6. Some people have the custom of spitting discretely during the Aleinu prayer at the end of the morning services, as they recite the phrase, "And they bow to emptiness and nothingness, and pray to a god that does not save".

Hana Fleishman

{365}

Unkosher Merchandise
by Pinchas Graubard
A Purim Play
Translated by Jerrold Landau

{**Note from translator**: *this section is a Purim play that extends from page 365-369. A significant amount of it is written in transliterated Polish. Due to the difficulty in translating, and the relative unimportance to the story of Sochaczew, The play is about a contraband smuggler who seeks refuge in the home of another Jew, but is eventually found by the secret police. It ends with the entire cast wishing everybody a happy Purim.*}

The players of "Unkosher Merchandise"

Performance of Purim play.

{370}

The bridge over the Bzura

At the Bzura
Zvi Cohen of New York
Translated by Jerrold Landau

The lovely area of the Bzura, the corner of tones and colors, is now destroyed. However from the former principality of Lowicz until far beyond the legendary city of Sochaczew, there where the Bzura ascends from the land of the valley until the incline of the hill and winds along further to empty into the Wisla – one can see all of the footprints of the difficult battles that were fought there, and which left destruction and desolation; The principality was half destroyed and the lovely city of Sochaczew is no more. The place of Torah now remains a mound of ashes, obliterated from the earth...

Only by the Bzura remains a small wooden house, which is also half destroyed. However its walls retain some sort of a secret, and they tell a silent, holy secret...

A Jewish fisherman and his family lived in the small house. They were common people, but good, upright, and G-d fearing. The family was not large, consisting of only four people: the father and mother, and two daughters of marriageable age. The older one was Chanale and the younger was Rachele. I can still see the girls as roses. Their beauty was different. Chanale the older one was like a rose that had first opened its calyx, and its blood red, ruddy petals sprouted up... She was a slender blond, twenty-two years old, firmly built, with a refined, charming face and with a constant smile on her lips. Rachele was also like a rose, that had already closed its buds and the leaves had already wrapped around each other, as if they held a secret inside. She was also thin and firmly built, with a delicate face. She was seventeen years old, a prankster and mischievous.

The family lived calmly and peacefully until the war. The father caught fish in the Bzura early every Friday morning, brought them to the city and sold them to the Jews in honor of the Sabbath. On the other days of the week he did business in the village, and thereby supported his family.

Thus did the family live, quietly and idyllically.

Only with the outbreak war did the family encounter a misfortune. Once on a Friday morning, when the father went with the basket of fish to the city, a Cossack patrol encountered him. They were three. One of them grabbed the basket of fish from him, the second thrust his lance into him, and the third searched him, took his money, stripped off his boots, and then tossed him into the ditch. They laughed, and continued on their way…

In the afternoon, the Jews brought the corpse to his small house. A lament broke out there, and the mother and her children sat and wept around the deceased for the entire Sabbath. After nightfall, they buried him, and then sat Shiva[1] for him for the entire week. When the sorrowful week ended, the mother said to her children:

"Children, we have suffered a misfortune. This is what G-d wanted, and we cannot murmur. Help me, and I will continue to do business, catch fish, and we will earn our livelihood…"

The mother caught fish every Friday morning, and the children helped her. However, sorrow overtook the house from then on.

… It took place again on a Friday afternoon. The mother returned from the city and related what she had seen; no woman could be seen in the entire city, she stood alone in the market full of terror, all of the woman hid, fathers and mothers kept their children locked in the shops and enclosed in the cellars. Even women's dresses were cleared out of the dwellings. The previous night, they tore down the doors, took out the windows, and three Jewish girls were unfortunately killed…

Both sisters heard this, and a shiver went through their bodies, the elder more so than the younger.

When night fell, the elder did not get undressed, and remained awake on her bed. She listened to every rustling from outside. She got out of bed a few times to check the lock and bolt, and concern herself with the sounds from afar…

For the entire night, she heard the doors and windows being torn out, and the suppressed cries of woe from the women. She awoke her sister and trembled.

When the morning star came out, she and her sister went out to the river.

They sat down by the bank, and the elder sister took the younger sister's head in her lap, kissed her, and said:

"Beloved sister, you heard what mother told us yesterday about what is happening in the city. What will you do when…"

Rachele answered:

"Sister, do not ask me, it makes me so cold, a chill goes through my heart".

"And during the night sister, did you hear?"

"Oh, don't remind me, don't remind me…"

The elder continued on: "And so, beloved sister, an ocean of shame will lie upon our faces. We will no longer be able to see our reflection in the Bzura…"

"Quiet, sister!"

"But what will you do when Cossacks break through the windows…"

"Don't talk!…"

"But the Cossacks will indeed come… They murdered our father and they will fall upon us… And then… And then…"

"Sis—ter!", the younger said with a shiver, as she buried her head deeper in her sister's lap.

"Rachele!"

"What?"

"Let us... let us jump into the river, before..."

"Sister?!!"

"They are coming... They will come... And the shame will be so great..."

"But sister, you see, how the Bzura flows so prettily around the hills, and from the hills it goes on so much further, further into the Wisla. The Wisla is so pretty and large, and it flows around Warsaw. Warsaw is a pretty city, with so many gardens, theaters, and young people... It is all so pretty, and you say... Brrrr..."

"But they will come... Remember, after that you will no longer find a place. You will no longer look into the Bzura; you will no longer see your reflection in the Wisla and go to Warsaw... A world of shame will lie around you, remember that!"

"Oh G-d!"

"Be well sister!"

"Are you going?"

"Yes!"

"I also, but what about mother?"

"Let us bid her farewell, but not tell her anything."

They called their mother, fell upon her neck, and kissed her.

"Be well, mother... We are going away... We are going before they come here. We are going to preserve our honor... The world will afterwards be full of shame!"

The mother silently shed tears and said:

"Where are you going, children?"

One after the other, they slipped away from her hands, went to the river – and jumped in.

When the mother realized what had happened, that she remained alone, she looked around and said:

"And I? Where shall I remain?... Children!..."

"I will also jump in..."

Immediately, there was a voice from heaven:

"The joyous mother of children, Halleluya!"[2]

TRANSLATOR'S FOOTNOTES:

1. The seven day mourning period of immediate relatives following a death.
2. The last half verse of Psalm 113. This story of suicide in order to avoid violation is known from Jewish history. The most obvious example is the Massada story. Another instance of such a story is recorded in the elegies of Tisha Beov morning (Zechor Asher Asah, page 111 in the Authorized Kinot of Tisha Beov, Translated and annotated by Rabbi Abraham Rosenfeld), which records the Midrashic story of boatloads of youths, male and female, being transported to Rome after the destruction of the second temple. Realizing that they were being taken for purposes of immorality, the girls decided to jump overboard into the sea. The boys, realizing that the immorality being

planned for the girls was at least natural, but the immorality planned for them was unnatural, then followed suit and jumped overboard as well.

{372}

From My Experiences
by Machla Lewin-Boteler
Translated by Jerrold Landau

The meeting of the Hatechiya School lasted until 2:00 p.m. Machla Grynberg and I sat cuddled up next to each other. We were hungry, and we did not know what was going on with us. When the meeting established the school budget and the chairman announced that the meeting was over, we went home together. On the way home, she told me that she has nothing to eat at home. "Come to me", I said, "What I have we will both eat."

Seeing us both, my mother cast an angry glance at me. My mother restrained herself when she saw Machla. My mother put out the bit of food, which we greedily ate, and remained hungry. We wanted to eat more and more, and to drink something hot, but there was no more…

We both went to Simcha Grundwag to see how his child was doing. (Manya Nachum's was then ill with typhus.)

It was dark and cold on the street. There was a blizzard. The mood was quite oppressive at Simcha Grundwag's. His child was very ill. Nobody noticed Machla and I. We sat in a corner and were silent.

The elder Skotnicki entered and examined the child. He told Moshe Szwarcer and us that there was no change in the illness of the child.

Machla and I picked ourselves up and left. Nobody noticed our leaving.

I heard the loud speaking of Bracha Wolkowicz near out house. Machla and I took leave of her without saying a word, and feeling that the tears were choking her throat.

It was warm in our house. There was an iron oven in the middle of the room. Around it sat Bracha Wolkowicz, Perl Wolkowicz, Yossel Munaj and Menashe Knot. All of them wanted to hear something about the child's situation from me.

My mother passed around the potatoes that she had roasted on the iron oven, and we drank a bit of chicory water. My mother no longer looked at me angrily. She was happy that it was warm in the house, and that she had something to give to the guests.

From left to right: Aharon Frydman, Eliezer-Meir Libert, and Nachum Grundwag.

{376}

Moshe Festman
by Yaakov Frydman
Translated by Jerrold Landau

Moshe Festman

A.

Moshe Festman was a Jewish teacher who took it upon himself to teach the Jewish children – the Yiddish of a letter writer. The Orthodox segment of the city immediately announced that Festman will bring all the children to apostasy, and they waged war with him. Those who understood him did not pay attention to this, and sent their children to study in his house.

Moshe Festman always dressed cleanly, as was appropriate for a cultured man. He believed that his students should also learn esthetics from him. Thus did he teach hundreds of Jewish children to read and write.

Aside from instilling the Jewish word in Jewish children, Moshe Festman had another ideal – the Land of Israel. He was a Zionist with his heart and soul, and had an influence upon the younger generation.

His difficult material life eventually broke him. After he was severely attacked by ambush by the Hassidim, who were opponents of Zionism, he took ill. He did not rise up from bed for almost 15 years. The family became greatly impoverished, and this also affected the lives of his children.

His son, Naftali Festman

The young Chalutzim (pioneers) of Sochaczew, who obtained their education thanks to Festman, did not forget their teacher. When they set out for the Land of Israel, they went to take leave of their teacher.

It was a winter morning:

Festman lay still and melancholy in his sick bed. The Chalutzim entered his home, approached his bed, took hold of his ice-cold hand in their young hands and wished him: "Remain healthy, friend, you will yet get stronger and gain new strengths. We will see you with us there in the Land of Israel."

The sick man lay on his side, breathed with difficulty, exerted himself, and said:

"Travel in good health! Remember your task! Bring life to the Land of Israel! With your young blood and young lives, live off the land – our land – the Land of Israel. With your sweat you will moisten the thirsty soil – that it shall become fruitful… Remember on occasion, during your holy work, your old friend who struggled and toiled for you."

He exerted himself to sit up, resolutely took their hands, and continued on: "Friends, greet the Land of Israel, greet our brethren in the Land of Israel. I want to live... and be with you in the Land of Israel."

Berl Leifer

"Our... hope... has... not been lost..." [1].

He fell back upon his pillow, and tears like pearls welled up in his eyes.

That tragic scene took place in my presence, and remains etched in my memory.

TRANSLATOR'S FOOTNOTES:

1. The translation of four Hebrew words from the Israeli National Anthem, Hatikva. h

{379}

The Zionist Minyan at the Home of Reb Shmuel Nelson

by Yaakov Frydman

Dedicated to the Memory of:

Bernice Phyllis (Mann) Knee (nee Mittleman)
Beloved Sister of Sandra Mittleman Robinson,
Granddaughter of Sochotzover Society Member Charles Miller

Translated by Jerrold Landau

As soon as Dr. Herzl had proclaimed his political Zionism, a small group of people from our town of Sochacew became dedicated to the new way.

As far as I remember, these included: Yechiel Meir Grundwag and his son Simcha Grundwag, the teacher Moshe Festman, the coal dealer Meir Nasielewicz, the tailor Simcha Wymaslowski, the painter Lozer Rozenfeld, Katriel the stocking maker and Reb Shmuel Nelson.

With full ardor and great honor toward Dr. Herzl, they became involved in the new, Zionist way. The soon found strong opposition at each and every step, and they had to battle for the Zionist idea. Each one of the aforementioned people used all of their energy to bring Zionism in to each Jewish home and each Jewish heart. The Zionist fighters took upon themselves no easy job.

The idea of forming a Zionist minyan was hatched. Each Sabbath at services, they would be able to talk about Zionism without being hindered. These people were the founders. Everybody liked the idea, and they began to look for a room for the minyan. They were not able to find one house in the city that was willing to rent a room to the "Treif minyan". They also refused to give a Torah scroll to read from, lest it become invalidated...

When everyone had almost despaired of actualizing the lovely idea, suddenly Reb Shmuel Nelson announced at a meeting that he would permit a minyan to be held in his house, and he would see to it that it is not impeded. The question of a Torah scroll was also discussed. The Zionists decided to write a Torah. Thus the minyan was born, and a Torah was acquired.

The festive mood that prevailed with the Zionists celebrated the conclusion of the writing of the Torah is well remembered. Even the greatest opponents came, for they could not resist the temptation of refusing to purchase a letter of the scroll, despite the fact that it was for a Zionist minyan.

Many Orthodox Jews and even Hassidim went to the house of Shmuel Nelson, where the celebration took place. With trembling hands, they inscribed their purchased letters. They drank a good toast and took a bite of cake, and then quickly went home so nobody would know where they had been.

I still remember as now how my father came home at night. I was not yet asleep. He took a paper from his pocket and asked me what it was. I told him that it was a Zionist shekel [1]. He told me how he and Grandfather Hersh Frydman had gone to purchase a letter in the Torah scroll that was written by the Zionists. They had seen that, as venerable Jews were inscribing their letter, someone put the shekel in their pockets.

Through such means did the Zionist idea penetrate into the households of our town. Reb Shmuel Nelson did not occupy himself with any other communal maters. He ignited the Zionist fire and let it glow. When he saw that there was someone to guard it, he occupied himself with his livelihood in his store.

Reb Shmuel Nelson.

After the First World War, his son came from America for a visit to his parents. This was at Chanuka time. There was already a wide-branched Zionist youth organization in Sochaczew under the name of Hashomer Hatzair. I invited him for a visit to the premises of the Hatechiya School, and I discussed the idea of a youth organization with him. He thanked me for the honor, and Reb Shmuel Nelson invited me to his home in his name. Over a good glass of tea, the guest gave a certain sum of money for cultural purposes, and a small library was created with this money.

After some time, the entire Nelson family immigrated to America. The news reached us that his second son, Herman Nelson, occupied himself with assistance work toward his fellow natives in America, as well as for new immigrants to Israel. He was the force behind the Sochaczew "Relief" in New York. Were it not for him, the Relief would not have existed for long. It was his warm dedication and initiative that made possible the great assistance for our organization of Sochaczew Émigrés in Israel.

In America, they continued on the Zionist work, following the path of their parents – from the father's work until the founding of the State of Israel, to the son's work in America to help save his fellow natives, the refugees of Hitler's hell. Through their dedication to Israel, the father enabled the existence of a Zionist minyan several decades ago, and the son helped the State of Israel by settling new refugee immigrants who came from the camps.

Reb Shmuel Nelson died in America.

A relic from the cemetery.

{382}

Yosef Wolkowicz

by Yaakov Frydman

Translated by Jerrold Landau

Yosef Wolkowicz stemmed from an old Hassidic family. He was a parnas (communal administrator) the son of a parnas. His father, Reb Chaim Mordechai Wolkowicz was the first of the Gerrer Hassidim of the Sfas Emes, and sat at the table of the old Socaczewer, Reb Avrahamele.

He was a forestry merchant and a communal head in Sochaczew. He conducted a strong struggle against the Zionists and led the community with strength.

His son Yosef Wolkowicz was elected as the parnas by the Aguda. Despite the fact that the town did not greatly approve of him, he continued to be elected each time.

He dedicated himself to communal matters with love and life. However, he did everything according to his own will and judgement. It is interesting that the battle against him was begun by the youth of his own party, the Aguda. It was they who succeeded in making him an ex communal representative, and also an ex communal head.

He was murdered in the Warsaw Ghetto by the Nazis.

{383}

Yechiel Meir Telman

by Yaakov Frydman

Dedicated to the Memory of:
Bernice Phyllis (Mann) Knee (nee Mittleman)
Beloved Sister of Sandra Mittleman Robinson, Granddaughter of Sochotzover Society Member Charles Miller

Translated by Jerrold Landau

He stemmed from one of the oldest families in the city – and it is entirely possible that he from one of the first Jewish families in Sochaczew. He was known as being quite frugal. He himself believed that his riches came from economizing. He was an influential person, who did not desist from telling anyone the truth– each in accordance with his view. He was not afraid of doing so to Jews, and also not to gentiles. He was a representative in the city council for a certain time. If he had to attend a meeting on the night of the Sabbath, he would come dressed in a Sabbath housecoat. The gentiles resented this type of impudence from a Jew.

Despite the fact that he was known as being stingy, if a poor bride was getting married, Reb Yechiel Meir had the custom, aside from the monetary expenditure, of purchasing the tallis for the groom. It was bad when someone wanted to remove this custom from him.

With his capital, he founded a bank for the benefit of the middle class of the city. He dedicated all of his energy to this endeavor. If someone were in need of a loan, they would come to him, especially the small-scale businessmen.

He traveled to the Aleksandrow Rebbe a few times a year as his Hassid.

He was murdered by the Nazis in the Warsaw Ghetto.

TRANSLATOR'S FOOTNOTES:
1. A token of membership of the Zionist movement.

{384}

The Murder of the Regional Official Baragow
Yaakov Frydman
Translated by Jerrold Landau

This took place on an oppressively hot Tisha Beov [1] day in the year 1905. People had languid faces from fasting. Some people went about in stockings, others in flimsy shoes. Some people were on their way to services, others returning from services, as they gave a pat on their empty stomachs holding that the day will pass quickly.

They requested that my father Mendel Frejdman come to the Woyat [2] in the village of Chodakow, to discuss a matter with him. When he noticed his neighbor, who was also a representative of the Woyat, with a wagon, he decided to go with him so that he would be able to return quickly on Wednesday.

When they were a few kilometers away from the city, they suddenly heard shots coming from the ditch at the side of the street. They both sprung out of the wagon in great terror and looked at each other. At that moment a young man came out from the ditch with a revolver in his hand. He jumped into the wagon, called both of them to him, took the reins and drove the horses very fast. In great fear, my father was left standing petrified at the place, and saw what that the official's small carriage was standing at the side of the road where the shooting had taken place. As he remained standing and thinking, a second person came out of the ditch with a revolver in his hands, ran immediately to Mendel Frejdman, pointed a revolver to his mouth and asked him: "Dokad moj Spolny Uciekal?" "To where has my partner fled?" He could not speak due to his great terror, so he only showed him with his hands the direction in which the wagon had traveled. The second man began to run in that direction.

He calmed down after several minutes, and he went toward the small carriage. He saw the head of the guard Denczyk dead as a wall [3]. He asked with fear who shot him and where did they flee. Then he calmed him down, both of them went over to the ditch on the road and saw how the official Baragow was lying shot. His dog was licking up his blood and barking strongly. The guard jumped into the small carriage and set out toward the city at full speed.

Months later, father was summoned to an inquiry. It was evident that they suspected him of involvement in the murder.

Thanks to the guard who claimed that he was not there at the time of the deed, but only arrived after the shooting; and the gentile who accompanied my father who claimed that both arrived after the shooting had taken place; and also to the two terrorists who opened up their testimony and thereby saved father by stating that if there would have been another bullet in the revolver, they would have also shot the Jew, in order to ensure that no witnesses to the deed would remain and be able to present evidence that contradicted them…

Thus was father saved from death.

The Jewish population indeed mourned for the official for his good relations in the city. The Poles rejoiced, and stated with joy that: They murdered the friend of the Jews.

TRANSLATOR'S FOOTNOTES:

1. The mid-summer somber fast day that marks the destruction of the First and Second temples, and other tragedies that befell the Jewish people through the ages. There are other prohibitions on the day, including the wearing of leather shoes.
2. A regional office.
3. From the remainder of the story, it is clear that he was not dead. I believe this is a euphemism for "frozen stiff from fear".

{721}

Delights

by Y. Tz.

Translated by Jerrold Landau

Childhood games

As is the custom of all children of the earth, the Jewish children of Sochaczew used to play various games. I will list some of them here.

1. The game of buttons

This game was based on winning and losing. Two or more children would play. The game took place upon the ground. With the movement of the fingers we would bring one button close to the other, and whoever would hit the button of his friend would win it. This was played in pairs or alone.

The mothers in particular suffered from this game: for the children would pilfer any button from the house, and they also did not hesitate to remove buttons from their clothing. The varieties, types, and values of buttons were numerous, and lucky would be the player whose pockets were filled with the best types...

2. Horse and Rider

This game was played by young children in pairs. The main implement of play was a rope. Others used a thin stick or a detached branch. The rope served as a harness which was placed upon the shoulders of the child who played the role of horse. The other child who took the other end of the rope in his hand was the rider. The rider prodded the "horse" with shouts and whistles, and thus did they gallop along in pairs in the outskirts of the city.

3. Cops and Robbers

This game was a delight to the players of both roles: the robbers who are chased, and the cops who catch the robbers.

At a certain agreed upon sign, the robbers would separate from the group and flee and hide. The cops would chase after them and imprison those who did not succeed in hiding. The imprisonment was done with great fanfare, accompanied by screams and shouts of corrupted Polish and Russian swear words, as well as the tying of the hands with a rope. A stick served as a gun or sword, and they accompanied the prisoners to their jail.

4. Rolling Wheels

The implements of this game consisted of wheels and hoops made of metal or wood, as well as sticks. The children rolled the wheels, and beat them with the sticks in their hand in order to speed them up.

This game made a lot of noise and tumult in the street due to the grinding of the wheels against the stones of the street or the alleyway, as well as the beating of the wheels by the children, and the shouts of encouragement.

5. "Wars"

Older children played this game in the summer evenings, and in particular on Sabbath and festival afternoons in the public garden, in the courtyards of the marketplace, and in particular outside the town. The number of participants was variable. The participants were children who were above the age of Bar Mitzvah[12]. They were accompanied by younger children who did not go out to the "front". These served a secondary role: they were the assistants and arms-bearers of the older children. The wars took place for the most part by the throwing of rocks. When the chestnut trees ripened, the chestnuts served as missiles.

After the Germans captured the city, the war game took place in a true ambience[13]. The warriors dressed themselves up in the remnants of military gear such as belts and knapsacks, and they strung long narrow poles on their backs that served as javelins. The rubble of the destroyed houses and the trenches served as a realistic background to the game.

The participants were split into two camps and took their posts. A brave and nimble captain headed each camp.

The war took place by the throwing of stones from one camp to the other. Not infrequently, a warrior was wounded on his head or on another part of the body, and blood flowed. Wounds and dry sores were commonplace. When the stones were used up, the assistants provided new stones.

This game was accompanied by military pomp, in particular with the capturing of prisoners. At the conclusion of the game, the freeing of prisoners was accompanied by an elaborate ceremony. At first, they were exchanged one for one, and those remaining were exchanged for arms, such as javelins, knapsacks and belts.

Episodes

Translated by Jerrold Landau

{722}

Father was Sentenced to Death

It took place in 1905. Echoes of the fermentation of the revolution came to our city as well. In one episode, father of blessed memory was visiting the home of a relative and heard that the maid was insulting the mistress of the house. Her behavior angered him, and he grabbed her by the neck and removed her to behind the door.

The young maid complained to someone, and as a result, father was summoned to appear before the revolutionary court at a late hour in the evening, in a certain forest in the village of Trojanow. However, father did not answer the summons and did not appear for the judgement, because he did not take it seriously, or for some other reason. Later in the day, a special messenger brought him word of the verdict that was issued in absentia. According to him, he was sentenced to death. Pinchas Graubard, our relative, signed the verdict.

After extensive negotiations, the death sentence was commuted via a ransom sum of 100 rubles, and the letter indicating the commuting of the sentence was published in the leaflet of the revolutionary movement that appeared in our town. This small withered leaflet that contained the letter of commutation, duplicated by hectograph was kept in our family archives for many years.

{723}

The Blind Man

The image of "Meir the blind" remains in my memory as he was sitting on the porch of the house of Leibish Graubard, with his cane between his knees, winking with his blind eyes, eating the food that was served to him, with a pleased expression upon his face. The Graubard children were gathered around him serving him another course of food.

When the blind man finished eating and was satiated, those who surrounded him would test his wonderful sense of touch: they would give him a metal coin and ask him its value, and afterward, they would give banknotes of various values, and Meir would identify them without difficulty. Afterward, they would give him various pieces of textile and pieces of paper and ask him their color.

The blind man would feel the material that was given to him, "guess" the color and would not make a mistake. This was wondrous to the children. To conclude the difficult examination, the most interesting and delightful question test would be given: one of the group would turn to the blind man and say to him: "Meir, one of us will extend their hand to you in greeting, will you please identify the person". Meir held the hand that was extended to him for a few moments and said: "this is so-and-so the son of so-and-so". The surprise of the children was without bound, even though they had already proven that "Meir the blind" never makes a mistake.

{723}

The Death of the Rabbi

In my childhood they used to say that in the merit of that Tzadik I am alive. This merit happened to me by virtue of the following story: when I was a baby I became very ill, and on a Sabbath eve my sickness worsened and my father – even though he was a Misnaged[14] – ran very late in the evening to the rabbi and begged him to pray for mercy for me. The rabbi blessed me by saying: "the merit of the Sabbath will stand by the baby!". His statement took effect, apparently, as I regained my health.

When I was a small boy, father once entered into the home in a very emotional state, with the lapel of his coat ripped in "keria"[15]. After he washed his hands he related that he just so happened to have been in the lumber warehouse of my Uncle Moshe Rechtman, which borders on the house of the rabbi. Suddenly he heard the cry: "Jews, the rabbi is dying". Father jumped over the gate and therefore merited to be among the quorum of Jews who stood by the bedside of the rabbi during his final moments. All of those who were at the bedside of the deceased rent their garments in "keria".

The news of the death of the Tzadik spread very quickly throughout the city, and with my own ears I heard children saying: "The rabbi, he should live and be well, has passed away".[16]

Immediately, great preparations began to be made: people streamed into the courtyard of the rabbi and into the street. After a short time, ever increasing groups of Hassidim began to stream into the town. They would come on wagons from nearby places, and by train from farther places. It is related that the Hassidim in the larger cities hired special trains in order to come to the rabbi's funeral. Jewish stores were closed, and even the few Christian businessmen in the town closed their stores. The students of the cheder were sent home.

In the carpenter's courtyard that opened onto the street, I saw that they were preparing a new "bed".

TRANSLATOR'S FOOTNOTES:

12. 13 years of age.

13. This presumably refers to the First World War.

14. A non-Hassid (literally an opponent of Hassidism).

15. "Keria" (literally a tear) is a tear that is commanded by Jewish law to be made in a garment on the occasion of the death of a close relative. Customarily, this tear may have been made as well on the occasion of the death of a great spiritual leader.

16. Obviously, they were referring to the rabbi with their usual expression, not realizing that it no longer made sense.

{724}

A Desire which was Fulfilled

Every ring of the bell in the city that told news of a fire frightened the Jews. During the summer, many fires broke out in the surrounding villages, primarily at night. Those who were asleep would be awakened by the bell, get out of bed, and go outside and ask one another: "Where is the fire?".

Sometimes, fires broke out during the day, and then we children would follow closely what was happening around the fire. At first there would be an alarm sounded by a bell. Whoever first saw the fire or received news of it hastened to a special bell that was set up for that purpose, and would pull the rope of the bell in order to ring the bell loudly.

At the first sound of the bell, the volunteer firemen would hasten to their posts. As they were running, they would put on their capes, and fasten their belts to their loins. Afterwards, groups of horses that happened to be in the area, or happened to be in nearby stables, would be harnessed to the fire fighter's vehicles and would gallop in the direction of the fire.

Only one thing interested me of all this activity – the ringing of the bell. How jealous was I of the lucky person who merited to pull the rope and to alert the entire city. I dreamed that this honor would sometime come to me.

My dream was fulfilled in an unexpected manner: one night the members of our own household were awakened under strong moonlight to a fire in our own yard. I ran as fast as lightning into the street, emotional and excited, and I began to pull the rope of the bell in order to summon the firefighters and residents to come to help. I was trembling from emotion and fear.

{724}

Lusovniks

The youth who were in the next few weeks scheduled to go through their physical examinations in order to determine their fitness for conscription into the army of Nikolai were known by this name.

Prior to the conscription events, gentile conscripts from the neighboring villages would begin to appear in the town, and they would instill fear into the Jewish residents, particularly during the evenings. They would fill up the taverns, make noise and become boisterous. Groups of drunks would then go through the outskirts of the city, and the Jews would be wary of running into them.

It was a different situation for the groups of Jewish conscripts. Relatively, there were very few of them, a few from the town and the remainder from the neighboring villages. Their gathering place would be the house of study. I knew three things about them: they would afflict themselves, recite psalms, and at time also play practical jokes.

The Jewish conscripts attempted to lose as much weight as possible, so that the state of their health would be judged to be unfit and they would be invalidated for army service. They did this by depriving themselves of food, drink, and sleep, by smoking many cigarettes and drinking strong tea. In order to overcome the desire for sleep, they would gather in the evenings in the house of study to recite psalms.

Pairs of conscripts would go door to door in order to request money for candles, so that they would be able to light up the study hall in the nights. The residents generally responded generously to this appeal. It once happened that one of the householders did not donate sufficiently to this appeal, or insulted the honor of the conscripts in some other manner, and they would then take revenge by playing a practical joke on that person. They would remove the wooden steps from the door of the person, and in the morning the members of the household would not be able to leave their home. In other cases, they would remove the shutters from the windows, remove the nameplate, or other such thing.

{725}

Early Morning Excursions

During the spring season, in particular in the month of May, groups of older youth would organize excursion in the early hours of the morning called "maiowki". For the most part, they would go to the forest or a grove around a stream or water or a spring, several miles away from the city.

At the set time, the first people would arrive at the meeting place. A role call would take place to determine who was missing. When everyone was present, they would set out. At first they would go quietly in order not to wake up the residents who were still asleep, however as we got farther from the city, the hikers would become louder, and break out in song.

When the group reached their destination, they would sit on the ground in the shade of the trees. The day's activities would begin with a communal breakfast. They would pass the time with games, conversation and reading. The excursion would end during the afternoon, due to the necessity to dine with the family for the Sabbath or festival meal.

From right to left: Yankel Naszelewicz with his child, Lipe Nelson, Mania and Nachman Brzezinski and Keila Ringelblum

Abraham Brzezinski and the children of Shmuel Katz (Perished in Vilna)

Avraham Chazan

The Holocaust

{389 - Yiddish} {729- Hebrew}

The Martyrdom of the Elders and the Youth
by M. Rajc
Translated by Jerrold Landau

Fear already enveloped Sochaczew prior to the entry of the Germans to the city. The rumors of their cruelty instilled fear. A group of approximately two hundred youths fled the Soviet Union; others fled to Warsaw, Wiskiti, Zyradow and other places.

The Poles were aware about what the Nazis had planned for us. They hung crosses and icons on their houses at the time of the enemy invasion. The Germans poured out the first of their wrath, with terrible tortures, upon the older people and residents who had not fled, including Yisrael Goldfarb (who was a matchmaker and porter), Sara Yentel the mother of Hertzke Berman, and others. They also burned more than 100 Jewish homes, excluding those that were in proximity to Christian homes.

Those who fled Sochaczew did not find refuge anywhere. Therefore, it is no wonder that they began to return to the town after a few weeks of wandering. However, those whose houses had been burned did not return.

Even those who returned did not find shelter, as their houses had been seized by Poles. They "resided" with terrible crowding in cellars and empty huts which the town had built in its time for the poor.

With all this, refugees from other towns came to Sochaczew. In January 1940, 400 people came. The Jews of Sochaczew absorbed them, and shared their dry bread with them.

Here in Sochaczew, the situation was even worse. The town was on the main route (Warsaw-Berlin, Warsaw- Poznan) that the German oppressors and carnivores wanted. The Jews hid in large numbers in attics and homes of Christian acquaintances. All of their property was already forfeited – and soon enough they were forced again to begin their wanderings.

The local population served the murderers faithfully. Julian Prouza, who was the town secretary, was appointed by them to be mayor. This man, who was a native of Sochaczew and lived all of his life among Jews, became the chief oppressor. A special Polish police force was organized to help the conquerors, especially in the destruction of the Jews.

One day, the German guards gathered several hundred Hassidim in the market place and forced them to dance the "Mah Yafit" dance as they were attired in their Sabbath clothing, with their Kapotes and small prayer shawls[1], in order to entertain the Christians who gathered there after they came out of church. Mordechai Biezanski, Mordechai Kahn, Moshe Tilman, David Eines and others were among those who were forced to dance. After the dance, they beat them and cut their beards. The Christians enjoyed the performance of their Jewish neighbors, and after the band stopped playing, the baker Jan Zhokowski paid money from his own pocket so that they would continue to entertain the bystanders.

However, there were a few Poles who shared in the sorrow of the Jews. For example, Jan Sliwa, who owned the pharmacy, tried to help the oppressed in various ways. The survivors of Sochaczew mention his name with gratitude, and are saddened that he did not survive the war. The daughter of the Christian butcher Balcarska is also noted for good, since she had influence on the German captain Bliastshik, and attempted (even though it was for reward) to lighten the suffering of the Jews of Sochaczew. However, these type of stories are few...

A Judenrat consisting of 18 members was established in January 1940. At first the Jews of Sochaczew placed their hope in it, as if grasping at straws, that it would ease the situation of lawlessness. The members were: Yaakov Biderman, a merchant, was the chairman; Nachum Grundwag was previously the secretary of the community; Yosel Luksztik, who was previously the chairman of the workers' union; Shmuel Libert, a tailor; Monek Libert, his son, a student; Yudel Balas, a builder; Itza Gelbstein, a tailor; Yosel Muney, who was previously the secretary of the peoples' bank and a member of the town council; Shlomo Levin, Velvel Pinczewski, Pinchas Rosenkopf, David Izraelski, Yechiel Bornstein – all who had been merchants previously; and Mendel Eisenstein, who had owned an inn.

With the establishment of the Judenrat[2], the seizure of Jews on the streets for work stopped, and the Jews requested support and protection from the Judenrat.

The work included building a bridge over the Bzura, digging canals, drying marshes, and clearing the ruins of houses and the church which had been destroyed (incidentally, the church was 700 years old). The Jews also worked on enhancing the airport in Bielice, which was 8 kilometers from the city. They used stones from the cemetery monuments for this purpose. The monument of the Rabbi of Sochaczew, the monument of Rabbi Elazar, and others were destroyed at that time. The entire cemetery was destroyed.

The Ghetto

At the beginning of January 1941, when the ghetto was established, everyone was only allowed to bring three kilograms of belongings into the ghetto.

A high barbed wire fence surrounded the ghetto. It encompassed Sarna Street and it alleyways, part of Pitaszica Street, and part of Bozniczna Street with it alleyways. Life here was crowded and pressurized, full of suffering.

Not a day passed without a frightening event.

Two weddings took place in the ghetto – Hersh Gothilf and Bronia Bzozowski; and Chaim Nissan Karo with a widow from Warsaw. The latter invited guests, and the elderly instrumentalist Yisrael Rotstein played his violin. After the wedding, the Germans seized him, forced him to ascend onto a wagon, with his coat against his skin, and play his violin. This was a cold and icy day in January 1941.

At that time they brought groups of Jews into the courtyard, and forced them to strip naked and to cut down trees while they were naked. Yaakov the son of Knott, Yitzchak Zelzoko, and others were part of these groups.

The Jews sold whatever they possessed in order to sustain themselves. This was done, of course, with great danger, since the Germans prohibited any contact between the Jews and non-Jews.

At that time the Joint[3] assisted the Jews of Sochaczew. A committee was set up with Yechiel Stern, the son of the shochet (ritual slaughterer) of Lubice at its head. He was married to the daughter of Itche Meir Zisman of Sochaczew.

The Joint sent packages of clothing, food and money, which were distributed among the poor. A kitchen that distributed free meals was also set up.

The Rebbetzin Mirele Bornstein of blessed memory

The Jewish Police

The Jewish police was set up by the Judenrat in order to keep order in the ghetto and to assist in carrying out its orders as well as the orders of the Germans. The German gendarmes guarded outside the gate of the ghetto, and the Jewish police guarded inside. The following were included among the Jewish police: Binyamin Schwartz, Lipman Diament, Moshe Nabarnik, Leizer Balas, Nachman Tilman, and others. Menashe Knott, the son of the medic, was appointed as the captain.

Nightly, these young men behaved as actual policemen... in particular, they caused suffering for the Jews of Sochaczew, including Nachum Shmaltz the tailor, and Aharon Zelig Marienfeld the carpenter. The Jews had to watch out very carefully in their presence. At the end of the Germans murdered them. This took place on the evening that they ate at the table of Aharon Grossman. They chased them to the hospital, and on the journey, they beat them to unconsciousness. As they were dying, they placed them in a cellar where they died.

After a few weeks an edict was proclaimed that half of the Jews of the ghetto must go within three days to Zyradow. Pandemonium broke out. The Judenrat prepared a list of those that must go. Those who had means were able to redeem themselves at this time.

The Liquidation of the Ghetto

Later (at the end of January 1941) an edict was proclaimed that the Jews of Sochaczew must go within three days to Warsaw. Once again, severe pandemonium broke out. The Germans stirred up the fright. They murdered Menashe Knott, the captain of the Jewish police, outside of his home.

On an ice-cold day at the beginning of February 1941 the Jews uprooted themselves – by foot and on wagon – to Warsaw. Several people were transported by German drivers in return for bribes. Very few went by train for fear of beatings and torture. Everyone was allowed to take fourteen kilograms of belongings. All the rest was left ownerless.

The Jews of Sochaczew in Warsaw

Approximately 1,800 Jews of the Sochaczew ghetto arrived in Warsaw, where they were quarantined. Those who succeeded in smuggling some money or jewelry with them were able to obtain dwellings. The Warsaw Judenrat put up most of them in a "shelter".

The situation was much worse there. There was hunger, crowding, and a typhus epidemic. The first of the victims were Yosef Warshawski the son of the shochet, and Rabbi Prekal.

Some Jews managed to escape to the Aryan side. Every day people died in that process. Shimon (Chilkile) Frydman and others were shot. Their names were publicized as a warning against escaping.

The builder Yudel Balas appealed to Julian Prouza, the mayor of Sochaczew, to permit at least a few Jews to enter Sochaczew for work. He agreed to allow thirty artisans to enter. The "lucky ones" returned to Sochaczew, leaving their families in Warsaw.

Again in Sochaczew

The mayor put up those who returned in a bunk in the field, next to Stodlona Street. They lived and ate communally. They constructed bunks and repaired public buildings. Among them were the builders Yudel and Leizer Balas; the painters Eli Poznanski and his son, and Yosef Muney – who was previously a member of the town council; the tinsmith Hersch Reitman; the upholsterer Moshe Zelonka; the Klioski brothers who were shoemakers; the upholsterer Goldberg; Yaakov Marienfeld; Yoel Gelbstein; and others.

They dwelled in Sochaczew, but they did not see the city, with the exception of the roads that they traversed to and from work. They were forbidden to leave their bunk.

Those who remained in Warsaw were jealous of them. Those who were strong, as well as children, managed to make way to the villages surrounding Sochaczew. They worked with farmers who they knew in return for food. A few also joined the work camp.

After several months, the thirty were ordered to return to the Warsaw ghetto. The camp was liquidated. A few managed to hide and remain in the place. They were discovered and shot in the nearby forest. Among those shot was the upholsterer Moshe Zelonka.

Sochaczew, like other towns in the district, had become Judenrein.

Even with all the difficulties and dangers, Jews of Sochaczew left the Warsaw ghetto and fled to the forests and villages in the area of Sochaczew. Included among these were Hersch Gothilf and his wife, Goldberg the cobbler and others.

In particular, many children, whose parents were already been murdered or who had died of hunger or disease in the ghetto, were included among those who hid. They were drawn to their childhood homes. It is impossible to describe their pain and suffering. Included among these were the two children of the butcher Jakobovitz, the son of Yechiel Hirsch Reitman, the son of Hollander, the son of Beker, of Washinski, and others. Death stalked them with every step. Most of them were murdered after severe suffering. A few were saved by miracle of miracles.

After the liquidation of the ghetto, the town ordered that several pits be dug in the cemetery, where any Jew who was captured would be taken to be murdered. The Jews were no longer afraid of death – the torture and suffering instilled fear in them. A shot in the head at the bottom of the pit was considered an easy death for Jewish children, since others were murdered with great cruelty. Moshe Biezanski, for example, was tied to a tree, his eyes were put out with a hot metal rod, his tongue was cut out, and they left his dying body for the dogs who tore him to pieces...

The hunger also claimed many victims, such as the case of the shoemaker, the son of Yaakov David the water-drawer. After the murderers stripped him naked, he arrived in confusion to the town hall, and requested a piece of bread. The mayor came out to him, and began a "propaganda speech" stating that Jews were not allowed to be present in the city, and advised him "in a friendly manner", to leave as soon as possible, for if not he would be shot. However, the shoemaker was no longer afraid – and he did not leave. The mayor telephoned the gendarmes, who chased him to the valley next to the tannery near the jundenrat, where they shot him. Dozens of people were murdered in this manner.

The situation of the children of Sochaczew who hid in the surrounding forests, villages and properties is a whole other story. They had to be wary of the villagers who worked in the fields, or who tended to cattle in the villages. When the villagers recognized a Jewish child, they would fall on him, stone him with stones, and curse him with the curse "leprous Jew". There were cases where Jewish children who were being hidden by Christian acquaintances had to chase together with their friends after the unfortunate Jewish children, and join in the stoning and cursing, in order to disguise themselves. Nachman, the saved child of Hertzke Tilman, relates that during the time he served as a shepherd for a farmer who had known his father, he was forced to chase together with the local shepherds after Jewish children who were lost, in order to remove all suspicion from himself that he was a Jew. He was heartbroken at that time, however his life was hanging upon a hair.

There were numerous occasions where the Jewish children maintained contact with one another, and gave their lives together. Such an event took place in the fields of the village of Rybno, when the hunger stricken children stole potatoes from the fields, and the oppressors turned them over to the police. One of the children damaged the finger of one of the policeman by biting him.

The Christians knew that many Jewish children were hiding, seeking employment, and camouflaging themselves as Christians – and they were afraid to retain them without a birth certificate. It was very difficult to obtain such a certificate. Eleven year old Shlomo Jakobovitz, the son of Leizer the butcher, succeeded in obtaining a Christian birth certificate by fooling a priest. After some time, the Germans and their assistants who were stalking down the Jewish children, succeeded in revealing the secret as to how Jewish children were receiving forged certificates. From that time, the farmers refused to employ young shepherds who possessed certificates. The more respectable farmers were suspicious of their neighbors, and sent away the Jewish children. Thus did they wander from village to village, from farmer to farmer, downtrodden and hopeless.

The story of the saved youth Shmuel Jakobovitz is hair-raising. Even though his brother Hersch Leib disguised himself appropriately, and spoke Polish like the rest of the village youths, the neighbors recognized him as a Jew and informed the Germans. They came, and without uttering a word hauled the youth behind the barn and shot him. Shlomo heard the shot and fainted, and quickly told the homeowner that he was afraid that he would also be found out by an "official". He did not know where to go. He did not want to leave the ground that was wet with his brother's blood.

He gathered some of the blood with some clods of earth, and buried it. He left, but he did not want to wander far from the village of Kozlow Biskupi where his brother was buried. After he walked 45 kilometers by foot, he returned. However he was not able to remain, since they already knew that he was a Jewish boy.

Can we imagine the fear and suffering of the son of Hertzke Tilman, who was hidden in a village near Sochaczew, at the home of a Pole by the name of Dziwicki, and he overheard his wife saying that she wished that the Jewish boy should leave. She asked her husband to take him out to the forest and murder him with a razor.

This was not an isolated incident. Very few of the youths remained alive. They were killed in a variety of manners. In 1944, the son of Reuven Izraelovitz was murdered. He was hiding with a Christian who lived in the Christian cemetery and looked after him. It is probable that Christian children turned him in.

The situation of the remaining Jews of Sochaczew in the Warsaw Ghetto also worsened. They lived in desperation, stricken with hunger, supporting themselves by seizing bread, potatoes, and even pieces of clothing from the street – and then fleeing for their lives. This lot did not pass over the children. The hunger and epidemics shortened the lives of people without mercy. The victims included the wife of Yerachmiel Gersht, the daughter of Naftali the watchmaker, Yitzchak Bergzin, Berel Oklinski, Avraham Tilman, Yosef Muney, and Yoel Miller (the policeman).

Several Sochaczew natives fled in desperation to other ghettos, including Noach Levin, Simcha Kahn, Yitzchak Tilman, Fleischman, Shlomo Levin, and Shimon Krakov.

A few managed to sneak over to the Aryan side, and sustained themselves by selling the remnants of their belongings. Even there they lived in constant trepidation. Even there they suffered from a variety of tribulations, beatings and pillage. Many of the Jews of Warsaw lost their minds due to the great troubles, including Hertzke Berman and Yantza the porter of Sochaczew. Happenings took place which are beyond the comprehension of the average man, things that are aberrant to the normal order of human relations.

It is very difficult for the natives of Sochaczew to comprehend the actions of their co-villager Leibel Goldberg, who had always been a quiet and upright man, just as his father Chaim had been. He worked on the Aryan side, and made a deal with a Jew to sell him twelve kilograms of silver. In the evening, the seller brought him the silver. He went up with the seller to the attic where the silver was hidden, took it from him and murdered him. He hid the body under a pile of feathers. When this matter became known to the Judenrat, they turned him over to the Germans who killed him.

Those who followed in the footsteps of Cherniakov, who committed suicide, included the actor Aharon Kahn, the son of Meir; and the amateur actor Lipman Diament the son of Itze; as well as others. Hunger drove them to this.

The Jews of Sochaczew were murdered in the death camps, along with the rest of their brethren. A certain Moshe of Sochaczew was in Treblinka. He was suspected of being an informer, and the organizers of the revolt at Treblinka had to be cautious in his presence. (For more details, see: "Treblinka", by Wernick). However, it is difficult to establish his identity, as there were two people from Sochaczew by the name Moshe.

On the "bloody Sabbath", (March 1943), many victims fell from among the Jews of Sochaczew. The Germans took revenge for the killing of one of the German oppressors. Moshe Aharon, the grandson of Eliahu Yashinski; the young son of Aldslach; as well as others were killed in this event.

Approximately forty Sochaczew natives were still alive in the ghetto at the time of the uprising, including Moshe Graubard, the sister of Rachel Miller, Yechiel Zand, Yudel and Leizer Balas, the teacher Yitzchak Shapira of the "Tarbut" school and his family, Avraham Deichus, Hela Fein, as well as others.

The only way to salvation was to move over to the Aryan side, which was fraught with difficulties and mortal danger. One of the last was Hertzke Tilman. His son already worked at that time in the Aryan side, and he left the ghetto daily to go to work. At the outbreak of the revolt, Tilman wanted to remain in the ghetto for Passover. Tilman, his wife, Yitzchak Shapira and his family all hid in a bunker of 24 Franciszekonska St., near the border of the ghetto. When the Germans set the house on fire, Tilman moved to another hiding place that led to the sewer system. They were shot several times with gas bombs as they attempted to exit, and Tilman's wife was killed in the sewers. Tilman himself finally succeeded in joining up with a group of Jewish partisans, and today he lives in Paris with his son who survived.

Few of the Jews of Sochaczew survived. The rest perished in the midst of great torture. May G-d avenge their blood.

TRANSLATOR'S FOOTNOTES:

1. The "Tallit Gadol" or large prayer shawl, is worn primarily during prayers, while the "Tallit Kattan" or small prayer shawl, is a smaller garment worn at all times. Most Orthodox Jews wear it as an undergarment, however, some Hassidic Jews, primarily in Europe, wore it at all times on top of their shirt.

2. A Judenrat is a Jewish run leadership committee that was generally established by the Nazis to oversee the affairs of the towns and cities that they occupied. The Judenrat would primarily be responsible for providing Jews for work groups, and collecting money and goods from the Jews for the use of the Nazis. However, whenever possible, they would also concern themselves with the wellbeing of the Jews that they governed.

3. The Joint Distribution Committee – an American Jewish overseas aid organization.

Maidenak

{423 - Yiddish} {737 - Hebrew}

The Destruction of Sochaczew
by Reizel Rozenberg (Rosenkopf)
Translated by Jerrold Landau

There was no break in the suffering of the Jews of Sochaczew which began with the outbreak of the war. Already from the first day, when draft notices appeared in town, fear overtook the Jews of the town, in particular the parents of the draftees. On the third day of the war the Polish army retreated, and many packed their belongings in order to flee to Warsaw. On the next day the city was bombarded. Two Christians were killed. On that day, a bomb exploded in the synagogue, and several people were buried in the rubble, and were only saved with great difficulty. Almost all of the Jews fled in confusion to Warsaw.

In Warsaw, on 11 Orla Street, several people died: The Gothilf family, Moshe Jakobovicz and his child, and several people from the Shtzitner family, who were buried under the rubble of the bombarded houses. We returned to our town from Warsaw after four weeks, due to the difficult conditions, and we found many of the Jewish homes burned, and in the rest Christians were already residing. We were met with open hatred. The Jews crowded into rooms – several families in each room – however our repose did not last for very long.

The enlistment of Jews for the repair of the destroyed bridge began. Jews were beaten, denigrated, and cursed.

A few days later the town produced a list of 21 men, prominent citizens of the town, and a Judenrat [1] was established with Biderman as the head. The prime task of the Judenrat was to send the Jews to work, as well as providing various provisions to the governing authorities, using the money of the Jews. Itza Gelbstein and Monek Libert were responsible for turning over the provisions to the Germans.

Shortly thereafter, fifty young Jews were sent to the Majdanek death camp. When notice was received that they were starving for bread, the Judenrat decided to send them help, and gathered a significant sum of money for this purpose. The question arose as to who would deliver the money, since this task would entail life threatening danger. Lots were drawn, and Pinchas Rozenkopf and Mottel Bizniski were chosen. They set out for Lublin and found the men in very dire straits. They were engaged in the building of that frightful camp. The emissaries bought bread and butter to leave with the unfortunate people, and left money with the local community for their purpose. The "friendship" between Gelbstein and Libert and the Germans was sealed several days later, for they demanded that one be appointed as the head of the Judenrat and the other as his assistant . . .

This appointment caused a complete change within the Jewish community. Some established business connections with the Germans. The Shmeltz family, Aharon Kloska and Zelig Marienfeld, began to bring carloads of food to Warsaw. They participated in those days in the "good life", and ignored what was transpiring all around them . . .

One day Aharon Grossman arranged a birthday party for his daughter, and invited Shmeltz, Marienfeld, and other such people. Very quickly, the Germans appeared and "invited" the two of them to join them. They were separated from the rest, and the next day it became known that they were shot in the hospital. The rest of them began to regret their actions. Marienfeld's hand was broken. They were buried in the Jewish cemetery.

This murder was the beginning of the systematic annihilation of the community.

Immediately thereafter, it was decreed that the Jews were forbidden to walk on the sidewalks, and that they were required to tie special bands on their right arms. A wave of attacks and beatings on the streets began. Life became a free for all! One day, Yisrael Rotstein was summoned to the house in which the Germans dwelled in order to play and sing before them . . . they also brought several Jews to dance before them. They heard curses and calls for revenge. The situation continued to deteriorate. Nevertheless, nobody could imagine the bitter end that was coming.

In February 1941 a decree was proclaimed: all of the Jews were required to destroy the few houses that remained intact near the river, and the Ghetto would be set up there. The place was not large enough for everybody, so the rest would be expelled to Zyrardow. The crowding in the Ghetto was drastic, however the Jews believed that this was the end of their wanderings.

Two weeks after the establishment of the Ghetto, in February 1941, the decree was proclaimed that the town should become judenrein. In order to accomplish this, a Jewish police force was set up ("Ardenonges Dienst"), with Menashe Knot as the chief, however he was shot on that very day by a stray bullet. That night the gendarmes broke into the ghetto, beat the Jews fiercely, and expelled them all to Warsaw. I, along with other people from Sochaczew, had left for Warsaw previously.

The crowding in Warsaw was very severe. Those who had no other means were housed in warehouses, in filth and with great crowding. The Jews of Sochaczew arrived in Warsaw with the skin on their backs, starving. Berel Oklonski and Avraham Tilman ate at the table of my uncle Pinchas Rozenkopf, and Yaakov Aharon and his sick wife, as well as Eli Wishnia and his wife ate at my table.

The situation continued to deteriorate from day to day. Suddenly, the town of Sochaczew demanded the return of 150 from Warsaw for hard labor. Those who returned included: Balas,

Diament, Zolonka, Kloska, Chaim Bliachaj, Moshe Soliaj, and Yosef Mintz, who was the leader of the work group. Those people sent from time to time some food to their families in Warsaw, and this lightened the hunger to some degree. They were later returned to Warsaw. Twenty-one workers were left in the town, who were later taken out to be murdered in the Kaziosk forest. At the same time Itza Gelbstein and Libert were sent to a work camp in Warsaw, where they were appointed as foremen. Later, a typhus epidemic broke out in the camp, and all of the people were killed. Gelbstein alone managed to flee and survive. Some died a natural death, such as Meir Tilman, Rabbi Shlomo Goldstein, Aharon Leizer and others.

I remember frightening episodes. One day another person and myself were sitting in the house of Roza Fein (the wife of Pesach Eisenberg) when a poor person entered. We were startled. It was Itzel Bergzin. Mrs. Fein extended to him a gift and covered her head so that he would not recognize her. After he left we started to weep. Once as I was walking on the road with my son Zecharia, we met Meir Lewin, bloated from hunger. We hid so that he would not recognize us, and afterward my son gave him a gift. At first he did not want to accept it since he recognized my son, but he agreed after my son insisted. We also met the son of Gershon Izraelski withering away from hunger.

As the situation further worsened many of the Jews of Sochaczew fled to the nearby villages, including Macierzysz. My father and his family went as well. The first of our victims there were Noach Lewin and Heller, who were shot. Two weeks before Rosh Hashana an aktion took place there – ten thousand Jews were sent to Treblinka, including my father and his family. On that same day an aktion took place in Warsaw, and some of its victims included natives of our city, including Mania Bornstein, Pessi Hershkovitz and her daughter, the two daughters of Biderman, and Bracha Malenberg. Many "volunteered" to be sent away due to despair and lack of any means of existence, including Yisrael Rotstein and his family. My children and I hid for six weeks in the exhaust system of a factory. Aktion after aktion took place, and finally myself, my husband and our children ended up in the concentration area of those who were being sent away. We succeeded in bribing a German with a ten rouble gold coin – and we escaped for the time being, as we were included in a group of workers.

In the aktion of Yom Kippur, Paula Zaltzman and Liza Kahn were killed, among others. One the eve of the Warsaw Ghetto uprising the following natives of our town were sent for extermination, among others: Shlomo Mendel Bergzin and Hersh Nissan Moszenberg . Yossel Rotstein jumped off the railway car and broke his hand. Yitzchak Gringard, Nechama Plonska, David Izraelski, and my husband were also killed. They worked together, and were captured at their workplace. My husband jumped off the railway car at a distance of 40 kilometers from Otwock. He was severely injured and brought to Treblinka, where he lived until the liquidation of the camp.

During the Warsaw Ghetto uprising I did not have a bunker in which to hide. I was holed up in a room on Sczanszliowa St. for eight days, together with my children. I witnessed the frightening happenings in the ghetto from the window. The Germans eventually came to us. We were brought to the deportation grounds on Dzika St., walking over corpses. In that place where we were imprisoned, I recognized Matityahu Graubard (the son of Avraham). We broke out in weeping. His wife and children were also deported. We heard non-stop gunfire. We were finally placed on the transport trucks, with great crowding, without air and water. Thus we arrived at Majdanek. There I met Chana Plonska and David Izraelski. I was separated from my children. After searching for days I found them in a separate block, and they had changed almost beyond recognition.

In May 1943 they began to deport the children from Majdanek. I saw them for the last time on the 15th of the month. A kapo recognized me and beat me brutally. They spoke to me words of support: – "Mother, don't give up hope .. we will survive . . .". Two days later I saw a large bonfire in the field, and the kapo informed me that it was the children who had been deported on the 15th of the month who were being cremated in this fire. . . I broke forth toward the fire together with several other women, however the Germans pushed us back with the butts of their rifles. . .

We were transported to Auschwitz three months later. There was a group of us Sochaczew natives there – Melinberg, Sara Lewin, Golda Rotstein, Yoska Grossman, and Paula Shmeiser. Golda Rotstein became ill in her legs and was sent to the furnace. Paula Shmeiser became sick with typhus along with myself, but we continued to work nevertheless, and we were miraculously saved from the furnace.

With the approach of the Red Army in the winter of 1945, the Nazis began to liquidate the camp. We were brought to Ravensbruk by foot and transport truck. It was a frightful journey. From there were brought to the Radek camp near Berlin. I was there together with Yoska Grossman. There was great hunger there – we were given seven measures of bread and one liter of grass soup per day. There was also torture and backbreaking work.

We left the camp on May 1, 1945. After walking for two days on foot, I escaped to the forest together with Grossman. We starved for three days, and then we met the first soldier of the Red Army

We were liberated.

We arrived in Sochaczew after wandering for three weeks. It was a rainy, gloomy day.

The destruction spread out before us in its full force. We met Anshel Beker. None of our family members remained alive.

Israel Rothstein in forced to play for the Germans

A group of Jews brought back from Warsaw

{741}

Thus was I Saved
by Tova Moszenberg
Translated by Jerrold Landau

I did not return to Sochaczew after the conquest of Warsaw, and I remained at my job in the children's house on 124 Laszno St. I did come to my native town of Sochaczew around the time of the erection of the ghetto – and I again returned to my workplace, which was transferred to 24 Dzalona St., in the Jewish area. I witnessed the bitter end of our children with Korczak at their head [2] . Only four staff members, myself included, remained alive. I then went to work in the "shop" on 25 Nowolipki St.

I was among the last to be deported to Majdanek, after I had experienced all of the tribulations of the Warsaw ghetto. I was separated from my sister and her two children at the camp, who had been deported together with myself. At the camp, I worked in backbreaking labor.

From there I was brought, together with Roza Rozenkopf and others, to Auschwitz. Our block was next to the furnaces, and I went through five "selections", from which I was saved by a miracle of miracles. There were diseases, beatings, torture and horrors. On one occasion I escaped from the car which was taking me to the furnace, when I was only 20 meters away from it, and I hid under the wagons for an entire night in the freezing cold. One of the S.S. men recognized me. When I told him about my selection, he took off his tunic and coat, covered me with them, and brought me to the block of the sick. There I was beaten severely by one of the supervisors, a woman from Slovakia. She was the meanest of the gentile supervisors.

After I was moved to another block, I decided to escape. I escaped and hid among the dead bodies. I ended up in the hide factory, where I spent six months.

Afterward I was transferred to the Ravensbruk camp. We walked on foot in the snow, in hunger and thirst. The entire route was marked with stains of blood.

I was deported again to a camp near Leipzig. There, the situation improved slightly. However, the battlefront approached and we were sent away again. We were starving, and we slept in the open field. Later, most of our S.S. guards fled after disguising themselves with the clothing of the camp inmates.

I decided to escape along with my companion. We entered a German house, washed up, feasted to our hearts' content on bread and potatoes. This was the first night in weeks that we were able to fall asleep without beatings and being forced to arise at the break of dawn for roll call. We did not mention our Jewishness to our hosts. We explained that we were refugees who fled from a city that was conquered by the Russians . . .

Finally we were liberated by the Red Army. We returned to Poland.

{742}

In the Skarzysko Camp
By Zeev Sheynwald
Translated by Laura Yoffe
Donated by Anthony J. Stern and Elaine Goldman

After our dramatic escape from the Warsaw Ghetto, I, my brother Zvi (Hirsch) and Aharon Goldfarb, ran in the direction of Wyjarow Kalcki (a small town next to Opatow), where Shimon Krakow's family had escaped to before the explosion of Sochaczew. When we arrived in the shtetl it became clear to us that no one there would be able to help us. It would be impossible for us to remain in the shtetl, and so we had to hide in the surrounding area. We spread out into nearby towns. One day we learned that our mother had died in the Warsaw Ghetto and my brother decided to go there to bring out the rest of the family. He went. After some time he returned and a short time later my father Moshe, and three other brothers and sisters arrived. My father remained in town. After several days the Jewish police of the ghetto arrested my father.

After some time I was sent with 70 other Jews to Skarzysko Kamienna, where a work camp had been established for Jews to be put to work in munitions factories. There I worked for 27 months.

After a bout of typhus I was moved to the new camp which was located close to the munitions factory and not far from our neighbor camp "Markcza'. There were 4,000-5,000 people there. I was informed that there were 4 people from our shtetl who had arrived from Majdanek camp, namely: Yechiel Zand, Joshua Zevadski, Paula (Gittel Cohen's daughter) and Isaac Jelozko's daughter (Cohen's wife). The camp was well-known for its severe conditions: sixteen hours work a day producing explosives (day and night shifts), and everyone was yellowed with the yellow dust that covered their bodies and faces. Many died or lost the ability to work.

I made every effort to meet up with the people from my shtetl when they came to the shower. First I met with Zevadski. I also did something to help them insofar as I could, for I was already a veteran – 27 months in the camp. He told me of their bad situation, of the expulsion from the Warsaw Ghetto, of the suffering in the ghetto and afterwards, until he reached this camp. Later I met Jelozko's daughter, and she told me amid bitter tears that she was not going to survive, and so it was. Some time later she died of typhus. Zevadski told me this and he claimed that it would be his end as well. He weighed only forty kilos. Paula told me he died of starvation.

However, in spite of our dreadful condition there were times when all of us met together (five in number)

{p 743}

and we would speak together. We would reminisce and we had a 'homey feeling' at every such snatched meeting, remembering home and even the ghetto. Our sorrow was great when we learned that only three remained (in the end only two). And thus ends the chapter 'Skarzysko Kamienna' with people from Sochaczew. Before the final release I met Paula once more and then we parted ways, until I met her after the end of the war in Witlib.

{743}

In the Villages and Forests
By Hirsch Gothilf
Translated by Laura Yoffe
Donated by Anthony J. Stern and Elaine Goldman

Gradually the Jews adjusted to troubles – to hunger, to dispossession, to forced labor. One day in January 1940 the Germans put out a poster on behalf of the council, signed by the head of the council the Volkes Deutsch (ethnic German) Prouza, that all Jews between the ages of 14 and 60 must present themselves on Sunday at 8 am at the council. There was fearful talk in the community.

And then Prouza and his German escorts said that from this point on they would "take care" of us and "keep an eye" us ...For a Judenrat had been established whose leaders were: Biderman, Borstein, Lokstik, Levin, Velvel Pinczewski, P. Rosenkrantz, H. Libert and others.

Then the Judenrat began its official work – it had a secretary, attendants, and a door guard with a rubber whip in his hand. Immediately, messages and commands were sent to appear for work. Of course, only to those lacking in means to pay the ransom (five guilder a day).

I worked in a group dismantling the previously destroyed bridge over the Bzura. Gelbstein was the foreman, aided by the two sons of Shmeltz the tailor. Later he was appointed the head of the Judenrat.

A tragic new chapter of our lives began, which started with the sending of the best of our youth to the Belzec camp. And again, only those who could not afford the ransom. The first letter that arrived from the camp was from Herschel Yashinski, son of tall Bendet. A collection of money was initiated to save the tortured inmates.

Then a new notice appeared, signed by Gelbstein and Libert, that the city was in need of living space due to overcrowding. It was decided to transfer the people to Wiskiti near Zyradow. The Jews understood what was expected for them, and started bringing valuables to the Judenrat office: money, diamonds, jewelry, fur coats – life ransom.

At night the Germans would carry out searches for so-called weapons, at the same time robbing anything that came to hand.

{p 744}

In January 1941 it was decided to expel the entire Jewish population – all within the space of 24 hours. In the edict, it was said that anyone who refused would be handed over to the Gestapo.

The Judenrat (which was situated at the 'White House') got carts together – 10 carts for 2,000 people. Many walked by foot, their children and their babies with them, also the old and the sick.

Sochaczew was emptied of Jews. Only those of status remained.

It should be noted, by the way, that in the time of the ghetto that the Jews who lived outside the ghetto were also moved out of their dwellings, which were taken over by Christians. Then the Jewish police was also established.

And then came the time for the last of the Jews to be cleared. The expulsion was carried out with blows, with cruelty, with robbery.

The first to leave the city were members of the Judenrat, in a large vehicle, loaded with their luggage.

The head of the Gestapo, Priver, called the commander Menashe Knott and ordered him to provide him with a pair of boots in the few remaining hours before the expulsion. The latter came out to obey the order, turned to Graubard the shoemaker, but he [Graubard] answered that there was not enough time. The next day, the two of them went to the shoemaker's house – and he wasn't there. He had fled with his family. Priver shot Knott dead on the spot.

In the Warsaw Ghetto there was no contact between those who came from Sochaczew. I put a sewing machine in Taban's well-known shop, and I was accepted for work. Hunger and dread. In spite of this, many were envious of me.

Some of the people from Sochaczew were trying to establish trade links with the Aryan side - Moses Broker, Broitman, and Moshe Wiedislawski. The first to die and be buried, was Wolf Warshawski. Then the rabbi from Sochaczew died.

But life continued even under those horrible conditions. Sheynwald's son married Frieda Biezanski. The 'Jewish underground' operated from Taban's shop (14 Prosta St.). There were incidents of sabotage and arson.

I was taken to the hospital on Niska St. on account of illness. For three months typhus held me in its grasp. I came out in the middle of Passover, frail, and immediately bumped into David Wishnia on Zamenhoff St. and he asked me to help him home, for he was weaker than I was. On the way he snatched Matzoth from the hand of a woman who was passing ... hunger had made him go mad.

I also was hungry. I was compelled to sell even my Tallit. And my wife took out the gold teeth from her mouth, and together with her and my brother, we walked to the wire fence at the border of the ghetto, to bribe the guards to let us cross to the other side.

I arrived at the train station and amid the confusion I jumped up on to one of the trains that were just leaving. An unknown Christian woman saved me from the danger of the ticket inspection. At the station in Lewna I went with smugglers and later I continued my way to the village of Topolowa which is close to Sochaczew.

On the way I had to pass the village of Szymanow, in which there was a monastery, and I sat by it to rest and to consider the rest of my journey. There happened to be there a railway worker who noticed that I was Jewish.

{p 745}

He advised me to flee for my life for there were Gestapo officers in the monastery and he showed me the right way to Topolowa.

April 1942. I was staying in a village which lies seven kilometers from Sochaczew, where I there many people from our city. I found work as a tailor in a farmer's house, named Piatczak.

Once an official committee came to the village, asked me if I was Jewish, and a shower of blows came down upon me. They tied me up and put me on a cart. My landlord, the farmer, tried to have me freed. He invited all the members of the committee to a drink of brandy. At the same time, one of his sons untied me and told me to flee.

I fled to the forest, not far from Paszniki. After several days I returned to the same farmer who asked me to work for him. For several weeks I worked at his place and I withstood several trials. Once, at the call-up when I was sleeping on the threshing-floor, German hands, thinking me a Pole, grabbed me and ordered me to join those being sent for hard labor.

So there I was sitting in a vehicle with the rest of the Christian laborers, among them the three sons of the farmer in whose house I had found refuge. One of them told the foreman that I was Jewish, and immediately I felt his blows descending on me. It is difficult for me to describe the trial that I endured that time, as I stood, arms raised, awaiting my judgement.

Suddenly a German approached me and asked me if I knew him. I answered in the negative. I was very afraid. Then he said that we were old friends, his name was Engelbrecht, and that we had been at primary school together. I asked him to save me and he did. I hid in a cornfield. I lay there until dawn broke, then I made my way to the farmer's house.

The farmer crossed himself in shock. 'Thank God you were saved!' he exclaimed. I told him everything that had happened to me.

The next day I left the village. To where? I didn't know. I remembered that in the army someone from a nearby settlement had served with me, and his name was Kojawa. I went to him.

He was happy to see me but advised me to flee because it was not safe there, and gave me his father's address, in whose house I could stay for a while. So I stayed with his father for a certain time, and worked for trading food, which I set aside also for my wife who was in the ghetto. Finally my wife Bronia and her sister came to me.

In 1943 posters were published from the Germans that anyone who hid a Jew along with his family, could expect to die. On the other hand, anyone who handed over a Jew would receive a reward – a liter of brandy and three kilograms of sugar. This greatly aggravated our problems. We went from village to village, but no farmer was prepared by hide us. They would not even give us a drop of water to quench our thirst. We wanted to take our lives. Then we came to the village of Wyczolki, populated by rich farmers, and there, miraculously, I found work as a tailor.

I stayed a whole winter in that place. In spring we continued our way through other villages in the Sochaczew area. In the village of Biely I met some Jews from our town - Samuel Leib Gothilf, Hershel Roitman (my relative), Tindal and his wife and children, Tzalka Jakobowicz and her brother, Hershel Sheynwald, Rachtsha Skurnik and her child, the son of Pinchas Kahana, and others. All were murdered by the Germans in that village.

In one of the villages, a farmer by the name of Zaioncz asked me and Mendel Moiskit, the shoemaker to supply him every Sunday with a roasted goose and a liter of brandy. Otherwise he would hand us over to the Germans. We fled immediately from that place. We joined up with Tzilka Jakobowicz who was working then in one of the nearby estates.

I was hidden in the loft, and there also lay my injured wife.

During the second half of 1943 the situation in that area worsened unbearably. And then my wife's sister arrived (Esther Bzozowska) who had hidden in the nearby forest, and she brought us to her. Mendel the shoemaker from Wiskiti, whose sister had also hidden in the forest, also joined us.

We arrived in the forest on the 17 of July, on Shabbat. It was raining. In the forest were Jews who had fled from various towns, including Sochaczew. After the rain, farmers came to the forest to collect mushrooms, some of them came close to us. It turned out that they knew of the Jew's hiding place.

Shortly, thereafter, machine-gun fire was heard. My wife began to flee. I wanted to flee after her, but I encountered a German aiming his gun. I leapt into the bushes. Crawling, I arrived at the village of Nowa Wies.

A manhunt had been carried out against Jews in the forest. Alone I escaped to my last hiding-place, and luckily I found my wife, wounded in the arm. Persecuted like dogs as we were, I couldn't help her. A farmer had pity on me, and in lieu of payment, he let me lie her down in a pile of potatoes, and later in the loft.

Thus our wanderings and torments continued until January 17th, 1945, the day when the Red Army entered the village.

After several days we arrived in Sochaczew, there we found A. Pinczewski's family – the only Jewish family.

{747}

Pinchas of Blessed Memory (Pinia)
Translated by Jerrold Landau

Pinchas Weinberg

My dear brother, you were sixteen when I left my childhood home, when I went to the Land of Israel. You were energetic, enthusiastic with life, beloved of your fellowman, and known for your honesty.

You struggled within the walls of our small city due to your many talents, and you did not succeed in freeing yourself from it even in your final moments.

The evil winds that swept through took you away as the last victim of our town.

Perhaps as a reward for your great suffering, they brought you back to our town so that you can rest in the bosom of your mother [3] who loved you so.

In her arms you are not forlorn in the great and wide field, as if we abandoned you.

Raise up your dust that is dipped in blood, demand justice, and let your blood cry out from the land which swallowed you up in the midst of your life, and mercilessly forgot about you.

There is justice! There is a judge! Answer him!!!

Your sister,

Rachel

The grave of Pinchas Weinberg, murdered in Sochaczew in May 1945 after the conclusion of the war.

{752}

Who Would Make it that my Head Would be Water...
by Chana Frydman
Translated by Jerrold Landau

January 18, 1945. A notice in the newspaper appeared: Warsaw was liberated by the Soviet army. The paper adds: Warsaw that no longer has any Jews, and afterward, Sochaczew was liberated.

Yes, Warsaw was a city and a mother in Israel, and Sochaczew was one of its nearby daughters.

From the time of the war of destruction against the Jews of Europe, this was the first mention of Sochaczew, my hometown. How many memories are etched in my mind, and torment the soul without pause.

The bereft city! The hand of fate touched it already during the First World War, when it was almost completely destroyed. However, what a difference there is between then and now! Then Warsaw was saved from the battles which took place for a prolonged period near the town, and Warsaw, as if in a sign of gratefulness, later saved the residents of Sochaczew who found refuge there, as they fled while they were still alive. When they returned, they restored the destroyed town anew.

And now? My heart is not in pain over its destruction, but rather over the destruction of its Jewish residents, for our many relatives and friends who drunk from poisoned cup until it was emptied.

My heart, my heart goes out to you, my hometown! You, who were so full of life, how you have now turned into one large grave? Perhaps you don't even have a grave left anymore? You, who were so given over to the idea of the Land of Israel, and you expended great energies for it, how you have fallen without being able to rise up again! How hard is it to believe and to come to terms with this bitter and violent idea!

We here in the land, the few survivors – how great is our distress! Oh who would make it that my head would be a reservoir of water and my eyes a source of tears, for I would weep day and night for your victims along with all of the victims of the house of Israel... [4]

TRANSLATOR'S FOOTNOTES:

1. A Judenrat is a Jewish run leadership committee that was generally established by the Nazis to oversee the affairs of the towns and cities that they occupied. The Judenrat would primarily be responsible for providing Jews for work groups, and collecting money and goods from the Jews for the use of the Nazis. However, whenever possible, they would also concern themselves with the wellbeing of the Jews that they governed.

2. This is the same Korczak referred to in the Kampelmacher article. Janusz Korczak was an author and educator, who published several books on caring for children. He ran an orphanage for children in Warsaw, and as they were being deported in 1942, he was offered his freedom, but he refused, preferring to be taken to his death along with the children he cared for.

3. 'Mother' here seemingly refers to the hometown. On the other hand, it may refer to Pinia's actual mother if she had died in Sochaczew prior to the war, and Pinia was buried in close proximity to her grave.

4. A paraphrasing of a verse from the Book of Lamentations.

{414}

The German Murderers
by Lewkowicz
Translated by Jerrold Landau

On a January night in 1941, the German "Zunderdienste", or as we called them in Sochaczew "Szwarcze", conducted searches in all of the Jewish houses. They took whatever they wanted from the Jews and beat them soundly.

Two Jews, Aharon Zelig Marienfeld and Aryeh Szmelc, were taken from Grosman's house. They were murdered in a terrible manner that night. Their cries and shouts traveled through the entire town, and a terrifying pall fell upon the Jews. Unfortunately, nobody was able to help the unfortunate victims. At dawn, the Germans issued an order to the Judenrat to come to bury the two victims. At the burial, it became evident that the two victims were tortured terribly prior to their deaths. They had numerous holes in their heads and wounds on their necks. One of Marienfeld's hands had been dismembered.

The funeral of the two torture victims took place at night. The Germans did not permit a large gathering to take part.

The expulsion of half of the Jews took place on February 1. A ghetto was established for the other half. The living conditions in the ghetto were very bad. Ten to fifteen people lived in one room. My family and I remained in the Sochaczew Ghetto.

The ghetto did not exist for long – only for two weeks. The Germans posted signs indicating that the Jews must leave Sochaczew by February 15, 1941. The only direction was to Warsaw – to the Warsaw Ghetto.

A new hell began here. Things were tumultuous in the ghetto. One person runs to another to consult as to what to do. One makes various calculations – perhaps this is a lie. Perhaps they once again only refer to half of the Jews. However, very soon, Jews were traveling on their own to the Warsaw Ghetto. One looked at the other, and the few Jews bid farewell to their native town.

I also did the same as the others. I sent my wife and child, for I was not able to travel in the same car. Two other wives with two young children also traveled. There was no more room in the car.

I left Sochaczew about two weeks later, on February 12. Uniformed Germans found me along the way – the so-called "Szwarces". They beat me, and I arrived in the Warsaw Ghetto in such a condition.

The Judenrat had been the first to leave the Ghetto, and we were all left in a state of wantonness.

Izak Gelbsztejn was the chairman of the Judenrat. He left with his assistants a few days before the expulsion. He left Menashe Knot, the chairman of the Jewish Working Office, in charge.

The "Szwarczes" were terribly wild. They beat every Jew and asked: "Where are your representatives, why did they suddenly disappear?" They did not forgive the fact that the Judenrat did not fall into their hands, and they beat every Jew who crossed their path.

The Germans were not satisfied with those beatings. They captured Menashe Knot and took him to the home of Pinchas Graubard's son-in-law on Staszic Street and declared: "The chairman of the Judenrat hid a few pairs of boots for us in this house. When we came to take our boots, we found an empty dwelling." The Germans demanded that Knot present them with the boots. The chairman of the Jewish police was not able to fulfil this request, and he was murdered in that yard.

When I arrived in Warsaw, I ran into his father Leibish Knot by chance. I did not want to tell him the terrible news. A few days later, he found out about the death of his son.

I witnessed new Jewish tribulations in the Warsaw Ghetto. The people were starving, and they died on the streets. I saw the former respectable householders of Sochaczew extending their hands to beg for a piece of bread. There was nobody to help them. I saw that I was next in line. The little bit of money that I had saved was running out, and hunger would soon overtake my wife my child and me. I decided to leave the ghetto. On April 28, 1941, I left Warsaw along with my wife and child. We set out for Miêdzyrzec Podlaski.

We traveled on the train as Aryans. Polish anti-Semites recognized us as Jews and tormented us. However, our journey passed peacefully, and we arrived at our destination.

Life in Miêdzyrzec was significantly easier than in Warsaw. First of all, there was no ghetto there yet. Second of all, the cost of living was not that expensive, so one was spared from hunger.

Two weeks later, the following Sochaczew natives arrived in Miêdzyrzec with their families: Shlomo Lewin, Pinia Rozenkopf, Mottel Rojtman ("Kacew"), his brother Ben-Zion Retman, their nephew Yudka Berkowicz, Leib Helmer, his father-in-law Chaim Jochel, my sister-in-law Malka with her children, Pesach Rozenburg, Wolf-Itche Galek, and my parents with my entire family. The Sochaczewers suffered from hunger, and terrible tragedies ensued. Mottel Retman's daughter went crazy, for she could not bear the site of her father going around begging for a morsel of food. Their nephew Yudka Berkowicz died a bit later, in January 1942.

I had often met him in the village of ̄akowola Poprzeczna in the region of Radzyn, 13 kilometers from Miêdzyrzec. He worked there on the land for farmers. I was also employed there as a tailor, which was my trade.

In December 1941, the Germans issued a decree, under the threat of death, that Jews can no longer appear in the villages. I stopped going to the village. Yudka Berkowicz remained. He became ill with typhus. As the farmers told me, they wanted to bring him to Miêdzyrzec but they were afraid of the death penalty for holding a Jew.

One morning in January 1942, the mistress of the house in which Berkowicz lived went out to the stable in which Yudka lay ill, and found him dead.

The farmers immediately buried him, for they were afraid that the Germans would find out about the situation. Two days later, when the villagers came to me to take my wares, they informed me of Berkowicz' burial. They lay two bundles of straw in the grave, put more straw on top of him, and then filled the grave with earth.

Having been informed of the sad news, I set out to the Miêdzyrzec Judenrat with the Pole who informed me to inform them of Berkowicz' death. I requested that they bury him like a Jew, and they responded that they were unable to do so. The Sochaczew natives were also unable to bring their fellow native to a Jewish burial.

Leibel Helmer died in 1942. He was working at baking matzos during the week of Passover. He caught a chill at work, and died that week.

The first liquidation of the ghetto (known as an "aktion") took place on August 25, 1942 in Miêdzyrzec. Our natives were taken away in that liquidation. They were sent to the Treblinka extermination camp. I saw the Rozenkopf family at the gathering place (Umshlag platz), for they were seated beside my family and me. I did not see the other people of our town, for there was a crowd of more than 20,000 people gathered.

I worked in the Staug firm. The work consisted of building highways. When we were all gathered at the gathering place, the engineer Mosek of that firm arrived along with the work group, accompanied by the S.S., and removed all of their employees. Mosek said that the families would also be removed two hours later. The Germans played a trick. The families were sent to Treblinka.

We were immediately whisked away by car to work, where we waited for our families. To our great dismay, we did not see them.

Two days later, I returned to our dwelling, where I had the opportunity to have a good cry. I did not yet know that there was an extermination camp by the name of Treblinka. We only found out two weeks later, when my neighbor who had lived near me in Miêdzyrzec returned from Treblinka and told me how he had torn out of there, did I first realize that my relatives are no longer alive.

We continued to work. Each of us had a tear in his heart. We were not able to help ourselves and take comfort in the fact that this was G-d's will, and we must lovingly accept this.

Six weeks later, S.S. men along with Ukrainians surrounded us in the place where we worked for the Staug firm. They loaded us into vehicles and transported us to the Miêdzyrzec synagogue. They held us in the synagogue for three days without food or water. On the fourth day, they took us to the train to send us off to Treblinka. We were placed in covered transport wagons. They stuffed 80 of us into one wagon. People choked to death. In my wagon, five people choked to death in two hours. I decided that since they were transporting us to our deaths, I would jump from the wagon. Jumping was not so simple. The doors with small windows were tightly sealed. However, this occupied several men. We tore the bars off a small window, broke off the boards that sealed it off from the outside, and prepared to jump from the wagon.

We Jump from the Wagon

It was a difficult moment. The train was travelling very fast, like a speed train, and it was speeding before our eyes. I then decided that I would be the first to jump. I went out from the window, but did not jump immediately. I stood on the bumpers and waited until my two brothers also came out from the wagon and were standing on the same place as I was. Jumping was indeed terrifying. Death surrounded us from all sides. The Ukrainians who were driving the transport were shooting from both sides. However, without looking at what was going on around, my two brothers and I jumped from the speeding train. We were unharmed. We only remained there unconscious and a bit beaten. When we came to, we immediately went into the forest. We remained there for three days. We could not remain longer, as we had nothing to eat. The farmers from those villages did not want to sell us anything to eat. We had to suffice ourselves with various grasses, turnips, etc. Finally, we found it necessary to return to the city (Miêdzyrzec).

Three weeks later, the Germans made another aktion. My younger brother and I were again captured. We lay in a stable for two days, without food or drink. On the third day, the Ukrainians threw in a bit of bread for the large crowd through a window. As we struggled to get the bread, the Ukrainians shot us with machine guns. Five Jews fell dead. After the murder, they again led us to the train to send us to our deaths in Treblinka.

Now, I was once again with my brother in the sealed train. We had to jump once again. We tore open the window in accordance with our prior experience. However, we did not go out immediately. We waited for the children and youths who wanted to save themselves. They went out first. We held them by their hands, and let them down to the ground. Later my brother went out, and I followed.

The jumping did not go all that well for me. I was badly banged up, and I lay for quite a while until I regained consciousness. I started to look for my brother but could not find him. I again returned to Miêdzyrzec.

The journey was very difficult. The Germans had placed militia on all the routes. The militiamen were civilian Poles who had orders to capture Jews who jumped from the trains and take them to the Polish police, where they would be shot. They received 5 kilo of sugar for every Jew that they brought.

I did not fall into their hands, but my brother Binyamin did. He succeeded in escaping, because the militiamen were unarmed. Unfortunately, other militiamen captured him near the city. He tried to bribe them with money, to no avail. He tried once again to escape, but did not succeed. He was taken to the police.

Before his arrival, they had already shot 80 Jews. To his good fortune, an order was issued by the Uber-Sturm-Fuehrer that those who were newly captured by the militia should be sent to the Miêdzyrzec Ghetto. Thus was he saved, and we were in Miêdzyrzec until May 1, 1943.

On that day, a Saturday night going into Sunday, the Germans and Ukrainians surrounded the entire Miêdzyrzec Ghetto. They started the usual program: shots from all sides, and nobody knew where to flee. I wanted to go to my two brothers who lived not far from me, but it was not possible, since the Ukrainians were shooting from all sides. I found myself in a hail of bullets. I remained in my new hiding place "schran" and hid for two days.

I ended up in the hands of the Germans and Ukrainians for the third time. This time, I was separated from my two brothers forever. This was the last aktion in Miêdzyrzec.

During all of the aktions, the chairman of the Miêdzyrzec Judenrat, Klarberg, was in the good graces of the Germans. He even was permitted to live outside the ghetto. He was an optician, and lived on the Aryan side. During that aktion, the chairman and his wife were taken into the ghetto, where they were immediately shot. Thus, that aktion was to render Miêdzyrzec Judenrein.

In Majdanek and Auschwitz

I was now alone without my two brothers, once gain on a death train. I began to think, "What next? Should I jump again or not?" I was now loathing of my entire life. Jumping from the train and returning to Miêdzyrzec was pointless, as Miêdzyrzec no longer had any Jews. I thought that I should perish like my family. I and a few people broke a board from the wagon in order to breathe. We figured out that we were traveling in the direction of Lublin. It was impossible to remain in the train. People who had choked to death lay in the train, and we were dying of thirst. Things were so severe that I drank my own urine. Our only wish was to drink water and then die. Thus did we suffer until we arrived at Majdanek.

I arrived in Majdanek on May 4, 1943. A selection took place that day. I was fortunate, and was not selected for the gas chamber. The following Sochaczew natives were together with me in Majdanek: Shlomo Lewin and his son Moniek, and Avraham Kona, Jochel's son. I was with them in Majdanek until July 6, 1943, when they sent us from Majdanek to Auschwitz. There, we once again went through a selection. They drilled us four times, and lined us up at the fifth time.

I was standing in the same row as Shlomo Lewin and his son. At the final inspection, they took away Shlomo Lewin because he had swollen feet. His son remained together with me. That same day, they sent us to the Buna Camp near Auschwitz. There, I again met some Sochaczewers. Aside from the aforementioned Moniek Lewin and Avraham Kon, the following also were there: Yisrael Lichtensztejn and his brother Heniek, and Berish Lewkowicz and his son. At the end of 1944, Ch. Holcman came to us in the camp.

On May 15, 1944, a general selection took place. Hundreds of Jewish prisoners were sent to their deaths. Avraham Kon was among them. He even bade farewell to me. At our parting, he told me: "I know that I am going to my death, but unfortunately, you cannot help me." He did not want to take the package of food that I gave him. He wished me that the same fate would escape me.

We remained there until January 19, 1945. On that day, we were evacuated to Gliwice (Lower Silesia). We walked an entire day by foot. We remained an entire day in Gliwice. Later, we were loaded onto a transport train with open platforms and sent through Czechoslovakia to Buchenwald. The journey lasted for nine days, without food. We survived because the Czechs that we passed threw us bread. Along the way we took out our canteens, tied them with a string, and scooped up a bit of snow, so that we could sustain ourselves.

We were 124 prisoners in one wagon. Each one sat between the feet of his neighbor. It was to our good fortune that the wagons were not closed. Nevertheless, two people went crazy. When we arrived in Buchenwald, 30 corpses were removed from our platform. I did not see the Sochaczew natives again.

I remained in Buchenwald until February 9, 1945. Then, I was sent to another camp. There, we were treated well. They transported us in closed wagons, with 50 people in each wagon and 4 S.S. men, so that we had enough air. We also received food.

As we approached Erfurt, American flyers arrived and shot at the train, believing that the train carried German soldiers or ammunition. With the first volley of machine gun fire, I received five bullets in my right foot. I attempted to jump out, but the S.S. man aimed his gun at me. At that moment, he fell dead from an American bullet, which also hit me in my right hand. I remained lying down, and could no longer move. An order came from the transport leader, "Everyone off", so that the Americans could see that we were not militiamen, but rather innocent concentration camp survivors.

Everyone descended from the train. However, I was wounded and remained lying there with the dead. The American flyers stopped shooting. They looked around very well, and then looked away. The "half living" took that moment to flee. The S.S. had what to occupy themselves with, for there were many wounded and dead among them.

A sanitary unit was immediately formed. They took the ill and wounded to the hospital. The healthy ones continued on. I was brought to a provisional sick station, where they immediately removed the bullets.

The next day, I was taken to the Dora camp hospital. I remained in that hospital for a long time. I was liberated by the American army in the Dora camp near Nordhausen.

The liberation took place on April 11, 1945.

{437}

My Frightful Days
Tauba Moszenberg
Translated by Jerrold Landau

After the capture of Warsaw by the Germans, I did not leave my home in Sochaczew as all the Jews had done, but rather remained back in my old place and childhood home on Leszna 124. I went home to my parents shortly after the creation of the Ghetto in Sochaczew, and experienced the expulsion to Warsaw. There, I returned again to my childhood home, which located on the Aryan side on Dzelna 35. I worked there until the first "expulsion". As is known, children went to the first fire [1]. Our children, with Janusz Korczak[2] at the head, were taken away to Umszlag Platz. Having nothing more to do, since aside from me, only four staff member remained from the entire personnel, I went over to Szultz' shop on Nowolipki 25 and worked there until the complete liquidation of the large Ghetto.

During that time, I experienced numerous blockades. During one blockade, I was able to let myself down from the first floor. When the day of the liquidation arrived, I went to the designated bunker earlier, together with the remaining residents. However, we did not remain there for long, for after two days of sitting there, they mined the bunker and ordered everyone to leave. They told us that we would not suffer, that they would transport us to Trawniki[3], also a Szultz shop. Everyone came out, but resistance immediately broke out. Many people fell there. They took us to the "Umschlag-Platz", where we were left without a slice of bread or water. We remained there for two entire days. The beat us murderously as they loaded us into the wagons. They stuffed 100 or 110 people into each wagon, of whom only a half remained alive.

Our "trip" to Majdanek lasted for two days. There, they divided up the women separately, and mothers with children separately, and sent them immediately to other barracks, which were completely surrounded by wire. I, having no child, had to part from my sister, who had come here along with two children and went to a separate barrack. They immediately took me to the most difficult work – such as carrying rocks. Quickly, I was in a position to be able to buy a roll and an egg for the children. However, after three weeks, they put an end to the children. They were loaded onto heavy trucks together with the mothers and taken to the gas chambers.

In that time, there were no crematoria there yet. The poisoned corpses were brought to an empty field and thrown into dug out pits, where they were burned. At the same time, selections were conducted on the remaining women who did not have children. Those fit for work were taken to various other camps.

I and other friends who were also from my city, including Roza Rozenkop, were taken to Osweicim (Auschwitz). We had to remain in quarantine there for four weeks, as we were put to work immediately dragging wagons of garbage. After the quarantine, we were again taken to a work camp, where I had to port lime and bricks. Our block was directly opposite the crematoria. At that time, I took ill with malaria and was taken to the quarter[4]. Due to the good attitude of the Jewish doctors to me, I succeeded through various means of riding out seven selections that took place in the hospital. I was greatly weakened when I returned to the barracks, and I was afraid that they might take me, as they did to all of the ill people, to the 25th block, where they kept the candidates for gassing. I was registered in the 19th work crew, which also worked in lime and bricks outside the camp.

Hersh Nathan Moszenberg

Already on the first day when I came to the place of work, I was not capable of moving my hands. However, the German chief, who was by chance a good man, spared me from the work and ordered me only to sit with the spade and give notices, so that no other German would realize this. I did not remain there for long, for that same German was not able to watch as I tired. I was sent to a second work crew – the 18th – the worst in the entire camp. There, I ported wheelbarrows with lime, and was administered terrible beatings. With time, I became ill from the beatings. The work crew got smaller with each day. Some were killed on the spot, and others simply died.

I went to the authorities and registered in a different work crew, which also worked outside of the camp. The work was somewhat lighter. They did not administer beatings there. In the worst cold and frost, I went about barefoot and naked, with rags wrapped around my feet, for the two pairs of trepes[5] that my friend had given me, after having stolen them from someone else, were taken from under my head at night. There, I became ill again. I got a rash on my foot. I went to work for a few days with my ill foot, until the chief told me to go to the hospital.

I was unwilling to go there. I gave up my portion of bread to the block commander, who sent me to a block that she knew about where there was a Polish doctor who cured my foot.

As I was sitting thus on a bench with the Polish doctor, an S. S. man entered the hospital. When he saw me, he registered me into a different Jewish block, where people were taken for gassing.

There, they took naked people and loaded them into automobiles. One early morning, they took us to the transport autos and drove us to death. There were four S. S. men in each auto, who guarded us to ensure that we would not escape. I jumped off the auto about 20 meters before the crematoria, and the S. S. men did not notice. I hid in an iron wagonette that was standing by the side. I lay there naked for an entire night in the severe cold and frost.

I saw how the empty autos without people returned from the crematoria. Throughout the duration, the guards were changed. One of the S. S. men noticed me lying there. He quickly came to me and asked me what I was doing. I told him that I had escaped from the transport because I did not want to be placed alive in an oven. I fled because I preferred to be shot. He removed his military overcoat and took off his jacket. He gave them to me so that I could wrap myself up. He then took me to the "writing office". I was already black from cold, and could not move at all due to my sick foot. He took the jacket from me in the "writing office" and they took me to the sick block.

I received a bed on the third floor. The block commander, a woman from Slovakia, beat me terribly because I was not able to go up that high. When the German doctor came on the second day, she informed him that I had fled from the crematoria. The doctor "calmed" me by telling me that in the next three days, a second transport was being set up, and I would be selected as one of the first. I recognized the Polish block commander whom I knew from there. She came to the sick block and requested from the Jewish-Slovakian block commander that she should place my name on the second list as a blind or an old woman who would sooner or later be burnt. The Jewish block commander refused. Having no other means, my acquaintance went to the camp commandant Alej, and requested that he permit me to be discharged from the hospital, saying that they would yet see that I would be healthy.

After this intervention, I was indeed taken to a new work block, and I had to go to work every day. After being there for not more than two days, they conducted a "entlazung" (delousing), and took us into the bath. An acquaintance from Warsaw worked there, but as if out of spite, I did not make a point of encountering her at that time. I decided to flee from there because they were going to conduct a selection in the bath. With my sick foot, I would have surely been selected to go into the oven. They took our dresses from us, leaving us only our trepes[5] I took the trepes in my hand as well as an overcoat that I found, and went out through the corridor. The guards did not allow me to go further, but when I mentioned the name of my acquaintance and told them that she was my sister, they let me go. At the second end of the corridor, I climbed up the wall, made a hole in the pane of a small window, and escaped. My objective was to reach the hospital, where I had my acquaintance, the good block commander. At that time, there were "spares" in all the blocks, so they were making selections everywhere. I did not have anywhere to go. Dead bodies lay under the new block, with chlorine poured over them. I slipped in between the corpses and lay there hiding for over two hours.

As I was lying there, I heard the call "mitog holen" ("midday call"). I understood that the selection had ended. I went back into the bath, took my attire, and when asked if I had been registered, I answered that I had. Three days later, they came into the barracks and took out the people. One of the registered was hiding. When they could not find her, the block commander pointed to me. However, my number saved me, for the hidden person was registered in the books under a different number.

Through that time, my foot had healed, and I entered the best work crew of the entire camp, a leather factory. There I was a sorter of the garments of the gassed people, and also in the laundry of the S. S. that was used part time for "haeftlinge" (inmates). There, things were finally good for me. I was able to help other people. After six months of working there, the entire camp was liquidated and people were sent to other camps.

By my luck, I was taken to Ravensbruck. This was in the middle of winter, January or February. The journey lasted four weeks, for we went by foot as far as Leslau (Wlocklawek). We traveled over the snow, and whomever could not go further immediately received a bullet in the head. Several hundred people fell there, and the entire route was demarcated with human blood and scattered pieces of brains. When we arrived at Ravensbruck we were not given any water. When they finally brought a barrel of water, one person fell over the next. Many people died, and nobody got any water.

We received food once a day, mostly at night. It was a bit of dirty soup-water. From Ravensbruck we were sent to Malchau, but this time it was in a passenger train. We were given food for two days on the journey: a half a loaf of bread and a piece of sausage. When we reached our destination, we were led to the barracks. The beds were covered with straw, and we were told to lie down. Before going to sleep, the S. S. men conducted a search. We were left with only those items that were necessities. Everything else was taken away. The next day, we were led to the square and were given a lecture. Then we were given one loaf of bread for every ten people, and a bit of soup made of rape[6] and salt.

We suffered greatly from hunger there. Once, I suffered a misfortune. A friend and I went to the obikatzia[7]. I did not notice that a board was broken, and I fell into a deep pit of garbage, 8 meters deep. I would have drowned there, but people came in response to the shouts of my friend, and they pulled me out using ladders. I sat under a fountain for a couple of hours and washed myself. I washed my clothes at night with fresh water that I had prepared in my shoes. I left them hanging up at night so that they would air out. I sat on the doorstep of the barracks all night and aired myself out as I was naked, even though it was still winter.

After being there for a few weeks, they sent us to a camp near Leipzig. There, it was already a different world. We had a loaf of bread for eight people. We were able to wash up when we wished, and we received soup at a table. However, this good did not last for very long. After being there for a few weeks, the front approached and they drove us on further, rushing us on foot. Many people fell along the way. The American and Russian airplanes flew low over us, but when they saw that we were people from the camps, they did not shoot any of us. We were given nothing to eat, and the hunger was great. The "leaders" were afraid that we would be scattered, so they forced us to spend the nights in empty fields. The S. S. men, seeing that things were going badly, quickly changed their clothes into "pashkan"[8]. Many of them left us and fled. However, a portion of them remained and guarded us. The "haeftlinge" (inmates) remained mainly in groups.

My friends and I decided to flee. We broke loose from everyone and came to a German house. There, we changed into civilian clothing, and we wore the concentration camp clothing underneath. The army of liberation was already close by and around us, however the neighborhood was still in German hands. Therefore, we were still afraid to say that we were from the camps, so we posed as refugees. In a German house we washed up, got undressed, washed our clothes, and cooked some stolen potatoes. Then the German woman sent my friend with a bag to the bakery. There I requested a loaf of bread, and my friend also got a loaf of bread for herself. We were overjoyed when we saw the bread. We came home with our treasure, and went to the stable where the remaining women were waiting for us. The joy on account of the bread was very great. We ate it with cooked, peeled potatoes. That was the first night in some many years of torture that we went to sleep satisfied, slept through the night without beatings, and did not have to present ourselves to roll-call.

The sister of Yossel Chazen with her child.

The next day, we continued on to a second German peasant, and received a bit of potatoes and cream from him. This was not very far from the city of Ushatz[9] . There were rumors that the city had already been taken by the Americans. Early the next day, we left from where we were to go there. As we went a few kilometers, we saw along the way "Häftlinge" (inmates) with guns in their hands, who were stopping all German cars. They stopped us, but realized who were, they let us continue on further. The found a Polish camp not far from the city. The refugees procured horses and wagons, and drove to the city, where indeed nobody was present, for the Americans had not yet arrived, and the S. S. were stationed two kilometers from the city. They grabbed up the military magazines and loaded the best that the eyes could see onto the wagons. I also found such a "ridiculous convoy". They gave us something to eat and took us into the camp.

Above all, we did not identify ourselves as Jews. We desired to go into the city, and also to fetch something from there. In the street, we encountered four S. S. men dressed in full military uniform with guns and grenades in their hands. They called us over and asked us where we were going. We told them that we were refugees from a city that was taken over by the Russians, and we were going to search for something to eat for our children. After a brief conference among themselves, they permitted us to go further. They themselves went by bicycle into the forest.

On the same day, we saw Americans and Englishmen on the way to the city. This was shortly before May 1, and Berlin was soon to fall. This went on for two or three days, and we saw Russian soldiers who were returning from Berlin travelling though the town. They made a ruin out of everything. We decided to return home to Poland. No trains were running, so we went a few hundred kilometers by foot. In the meantime, the Russians captured us, took everything from us, and wanted to take us to a camp. At the same time, we encountered Polish soldiers. They realized that we were going to a camp, and they said that they would take us to Poland, not as the Russians had assured us. We escaped from the Russians, and followed after the Polish army.

Thus, we made our way to Poland. Lodz was the first city where we stopped to search for our relatives.

TRANSLATOR'S FOOTNOTES:

1. Probably referring to the tragedy that was to overtake them after the expulsion.
2. See biography of Janusz Korczak at http://www.us-israel.org/jsource/biography/Korczak.html. h
3. Trawniki is a labor camp near Lublin, Poland for Soviet prisoners of war and Polish Jews. In November 1943, 10,00 Jews were brought to the pits outside the camp and murdered.
4. 'Revir', usually means quarter or precincts, but perhaps here means the infirmary.
5. I am not sure of the meaning of this word. It is seemingly some type of undergarment.
6. Grape stalk
7. A Pashkan is some type of clothing – probably civilian clothing.
8. I am not sure of the meaning of this word. It is obviously some location or venue.
9. I could not identify this city. It does not seem to be spelled like Auschwitz, and in any case, they were already near Leipzig.

{446}

My Experiences Under the Nazi Regime
by M. Sh. Frejdenberg
Translated by Jerrold Landau

On May 5, 1941, my family and I decided to steal our way out of the Warsaw Ghetto. We succeeded. We went to a village near Bieliny. When we arrived in the village, we met up with our fellow natives: Dawidowicz, Hersz Rojtman, Korfiu, Goldman, Arkiewicz, and Bargoda. Ajzele's three children were also there, working as tailors. Tailors and shoemakers had much work with the farmers. However, we were very afraid and had to hide. Later, still more Jews from Sochaczew arrived. Among them were Izraelowicz's two children (tailors). His wife arrived from Sochaczew and died of hunger. In Sochaczew itself, the Jewish craftsmen (tailors, shoemakers, and carpenters) worked for the Germans, led by Balas. At a certain point, all the Jews were taken to the forest and shot. Things took a turn for the worse in the village. The Germans posted signs noting that the punishment for hiding Jews would be death. As time went on, the farmers themselves would capture Jews, bind them by their hands and feet, and give them over to the murderers. They would receive sugar, money and various other things as a reward. Among others, the farmers captured the son of Moshe Sztrykmacher[1], tied him up and gave him over to the Germans. They also gave over Ajzele's three children to the Germans. As the children fled, the farmers chased after them and captured them.

As a result of the informings, the police Germans conducted a search of the village. They came fully armed, in great numbers, and searched for Jews. Hershel Tendel, his wife and two children were shot. My family and I hid in a field among the tall corn stalks and were thereby saved from a certain death. During the search, they also shot Zalke Jakubowicz and his brother. At night, when it was already quite dark, we came out of the field and went to a farmer that we knew who advised us to flee, since the nearby farmers were conducting a large-scale search for Jews throughout the entire area. We left Bieliny and went near Rokotow, where once again hid in the tall corn stalks. We spent nine days there in great terror. We were not able to obtain any food. The large-scale search by the farmers of Bieliny began shortly after our escape. With clubs and other blunt objects in their hands, the murderers searched for Jews in all the fields and roads, and murdered without mercy. They found Hershel Pinczewski walking along a road. The farmers began to beat him soundly, but one of them said that he was a Pole, for he was nicely dressed. However, the beaters claimed that he was a Jew. To his fortune, a Polish acquaintance came by, who told the beaters that he knew him as a Pole who was a member of the A. K. (Armej Krajowa). The Poles left him alone. At the same time, a large number of armed Poles arrived, fought with the local farmers, and went away. Simultaneously, a letter came to Soltis informing him that he must demand that the farmers keep the peace and not inform on the Jews. If not, they would burn down the entire village. That threatening letter was effective, and the farmers calmed down. (The authors of that letter were partisans.)

We returned to Bieliny. Partisans came there every night and took various things from the farmers that they had left lying around. Our situation was a bit easier, for we were not afraid that the farmers would kill us. We wanted to remain there and continue to work, but the farmers did not let us enter their houses, to sell us food, or even to talk to us. Having no other choice, we had to set out on our wandering once again. As we left Bieliny, we found out that many Jews had been murdered there, including Mrs. Skornik, her child, and Knobel's sister and her child. We searched for a hiding place, and lived off of rotten potatoes that we stole from the fields. It took a long time until the farmer's hatred of us cooled off.

TRANSLATOR'S FOOTNOTES:

1. This is not necessarily a surname. It may mean "Moshe the ropemaker".

{448}

Memories

Moshe Gajer

Translated by Jerrold Landau

Five days after the outbreak of the war, the Jewish communal offices, Beis Midrash and synagogue were bombarded. This was the first bombardment. That day, all of the Jews fled to Warsaw with the thought that they would be able to save themselves there. The Hitlerist gangs entered on September 8, 1939. Since there were no Jews there, the Germans along with the local population robbed all of the Jewish possessions. As well, many Jewish houses and businesses were set on fire. The Jews of Sochaczew returned to their hometown after the fall of Warsaw. Along the way, the Germans gathered up all of the men and sent to them to camps in Pruszkow and Blonie. After three days of torture, they were released, leaving behind many dead. The first victims were the Liberman and Rozenperl families, who were shot in the village of Kampinos, 14 kilometers from Sochaczew. During the time of the bombardment of Warsaw, the Gothelf family and others, numbering more than 30 souls, were located in a house of Orla 11. The town was ruled by former secretary of the magistrate, the German Prause, who was nominated as mayor by the Germans. He manifested himself as an enemy of the Jews.

Formerly, he lived well with the Jews, to the point that the Jews helped him obtain a house. The mayor confiscated the remaining property for the magistrate. The returning Jews found their residences occupied. They were able to find rented premises with great difficulty. Immediately the next morning, a hunt started for the exhausted Jews, who were taken advantage of and conscripted into the most difficult and dirty of work. It is worthwhile to mention that the Jews bound their faces with kerchiefs in order to save their beards. Those people were persecuted more so than those who wore European clothing. The workshops and stores were not given back to the Jews. After a certain time, a Judenrat was created, headed by Liberman, the owner of the lumber warehouse. He fulfilled his role with great humanity. After him, Itche Gelbsztejn was appointed as the elder of the Jews, and his assistant was Moniek Libert. A certain group of Jews who were unable to tolerate the discrimination stole across the border to the Russian side. In February 1941, a ghetto was formed in the streets near the magistrate. The ghetto existed for three weeks in total. Then, the expulsion from Sochaczew took place. The Jews of Sochaczew were deported to Warsaw, and they suffered new anguish in that ghetto.

{450}

Dates to Remember
By Chaim Weisz
Translated by Dr. Heather Valencia
Donated by Anthony J. Stern and Elaine Goldman

8 November 1939: Germans march into Sochaczew

12 November 1939: The Germans seized a few hundred Jews in the streets and chased them to the Bzura River to mend the bridge there. While they were working they were beaten, and forced into the river where they had to remain for several minutes. Two Jews drowned on that day: Sheynwald and Chazan.

1 November 1940: The Ghetto was set up in Sochaczew on the following streets: Staszica, Reimant and Ond. The ghetto had no openings.

4 November 1940: Because not all the Jews were able to settle in the few little streets, 5,000 Jews remained homeless. The District Council, however, did not allow the Jews to wander around in the town and evacuated them to Zyradow. A Judenrat was created. Itche Gelbstein became President. The first job of the Judenrat was a terrible one: they made up a list of six thousand poor Jews and ordered that all those who wished to receive their required papers were to line up on the Rynek and take with them packs of up to twenty kilos.

The Judenrat sent out its police, who mercilessly dragged the Jews from their houses into the streets. The local Ukrainians received the Jews who were driven out, wickedly beating women and children and seizing from them all the belongings they had taken with them. When all five thousand were gathered on the Rynek they were loaded onto farmer carts and taken away to Zyradow. They were there for two weeks altogether and after that they were driven out of there and forced to go on foot to Warsaw, to the ghetto.

15 November 1940: The Judenrat gave out an order that all Jews regardless of age had to assemble that day on the Rynek. That morning there was a commotion in the ghetto: Ukrainians broke into the ghetto and, yelling wildly, they ran into people's houses robbing and murdering anyone who fell into their hands. Some Jews died that day.

When all the Jews of Sochaczew were assembled on the Rynek, Gestapo officers arrived, took over the Jews and forced them into the town baths, There they seized their remaining possessions, and chased them – half-naked – to the Warsaw Ghetto. Sochaczew was "Judenrein" (free of Jews in Nazi terminology.)

Some of the remaining tombstones in the Sochaczew cemetery

{452}

Expiring from Hunger and Cold
By A. Sochaczewer
Translated by Jerrold Landau

Jewish Sochaczew was wiped off the face of the globe.

On the eve of the outbreak of the war between Germany and Poland in 1939, I was mobilized into the Polish army. I was badly wounded on the front and remained in the hospital for a long time. This is the reason that I did leave with my brother Shlomo to Russia. I was released from the hospital one month later, in December 1939, and remained in my brother's residence in Warsaw. Here, I wish to write about the life and death of the natives of Sochaczew, with whom I was connected and together with whom I lived until my brother Immanuel's brother-in-law who lived together with my brother in Czestochowa took me out of Warsaw to join him.

My departure from the Warsaw Ghetto took place on September 15, 1942. Until then I lived with the Sochaczewers, of whom I believe that nobody other than myself survived, and is able to write about their life in the Warsaw Ghetto until their deaths. The main thing was regarding the poor of the Sochaczewers. It is about them that I intend to write the greatest part of what I recall. The first of them in Zeinwil Wyszogrodski (nickname was Zeinwil Chlaiak). His wife Freda, from the Gothelf family – Wolf Tregier's [1] daughter – died of hunger on Neia Dzika 20 along with her two children. In the same house, in the same timeframe, a few weeks later, the wife of Zlotnik the Shamash of the Sochaczew Chevra Kadisha (Burial Society) died. A bit later, Gedalia the Melamed (children's teacher) died in the same courtyard where a few hundred families of the Sochaczew poor lived. Somewhat later, Aryeh Leib Brojtman's wife (Yankel Gunner's daughter) died, and a few days later her stepmother Miriam Jablonska died. At the same time, Rachel Gothelf, Gedalia the Melamed's wife, died. Later, after my departure for Czestochowa, Aryeh Leib and his three children were removed from the Warsaw Ghetto and murdered in the village of Szwierczek, near Sochaczew. They are buried in the farmer Wagner's field.

Shimon Krakow's daughter and Leizer Grynberg's daughter were together with me in the camp in Czestochowa, until I was deported to Auschwitz. They survived. I met Moshe Yidel Gingold's son in Auschwitz. He was in the same block as I was. He was together with me until the march to Tyrol. He must have survived. I met Chaskel Holcman, Chaim Hirsch Holcman's son, in Dachau shortly before the liberation. He was liberated together with me and survived.

Regarding my martyrology and the suffering that I went through, I am not able to write about in any circumstance. Others are already familiar with everything, with all of the suffering that people went through. The main reason for my writing is to recall the people who were poor before the war, who knew nobody, and who perished from hunger and cold.

A few words regarding Chaskel Nasielski (Yaakov David Wasser-Tregier's [2] son). He was murdered and buried along with his son in Blonie, near the highway that goes into the Sereker

Court. This took place in May 1942. The farmers can show exactly where he lies buried with his son, because the Germans captured him when he was working with the farmers as a shoemaker.

Most of the poor people were murdered before they were deported. The rest were deported, already with the first "aktions"…

{454}

The Daughters of Yechiel and Lea Szmulewicz
Tortured by the Germans in France in the year 1942

Photo left: Beila Szmulewicz; right: Rachel Szmulewicz; center: Chaya Szmulewicz.

{455}

On the Aryan Side
By Roza (Wajnberg) Goldsztejn
Translated by Jerrold Landau

We returned to Sochaczew, after the capture of Warsaw by the Nazis. However, when I came through the door, I encountered a bitter disappointment: my calling card on the door was replaced with the calling card of the Polish merchant Przedpelski. His house had burnt down, and he took over our house. With a bitter feeling, I returned to the street where my family was waiting for me. (My husband and his brother were on their way to Warsaw a day earlier, and were captured by the Germans.) We set out for our second house on Parne Street, which had been partially destroyed. There the three of us, my uncle, my sister-in-law Bluma, and I, faced a bitter disappointment for the second time: This house as well had been taken over by a Christian who threw us off the steps. We decided to go to Mlodzieszyn with the thought that if that house were also to be destroyed, we would perhaps find a place with a farmer acquaintance. However, fortunately, this house remained in its entirety, and we settled there.

My husband and brother returned a few days later, beaten and robbed. We began to settle down. Here in Mlodzieszyn we had a field with some potatoes, and we received a permit from the military to dig it up. All of a sudden, many Volksdeutchen appeared with red ribbons on their sleeves, heavily armed, and began to persecute the Jews. We saved ourselves by hiding with a farmer acquaintance in a second village.

A few weeks later it became known that a border was created between the village and our town of Sochaczew, in accordance with decisions that were made by the German Third Reich. In order to avoid being cut off from the city, we decided to return to Sochaczew at night. However my parents did not want to go back, because they had their property there, so we returned to the town without our parents. Along the way, we were stopped by the Germans, but after searching us and not recognizing that we were Jews, they let us continue on, and we arrived in the town. Not having anywhere to go, we remained in the market. However we shortly found a dwelling, because many people had fled.

The Judenrat was created a few days later. The cruel decrees and persecutions increased day by day. At the end of 1940 we found out that Jasinski was murdered in some camp. Still later, they murdered Szmelc and Marienfeld. They we were ordered to wear white armbands, and life became increasingly difficult with each passing day. Suddenly, an order came from the Judenrat that a few hundred people must be presented for a deportation, but nobody wanted to present themselves for slaughter. People fled and paid large sums of money to have themselves struck off the list. Obviously, the first victims were the poor, who were not able to pay money to buy themselves off. Some were deported to Wiskitki, and some to Zyrardow. At the same time we realized that ghettos were being created in the cities, and we expected that we would find ourselves in a ghetto.

A ghetto was created in our town in January 1941, in the filthiest quarter of the town, and it was liquidated approximately three weeks later. All of the Jews were expelled to the Warsaw Ghetto. One day earlier, prior to the liquidation of the ghetto, our mother visited us briefly to bid us farewell. She already knew about the liquidation of the ghetto.

The Helpless Victims are Driven with Blows

The town was in a great panic. The Nazis had already driven the helpless victims with terrible blows towards the trucks, which stood ready to consume the people. My husband came in from the street and told us what was happening. He said that we must leave the house very quickly, for perhaps we can succeed in placing the child on the truck without beatings [3]. My mother grabbed the child from the cradle, wrapped him up in a kerchief and ran to the trucks. The trucks were parked in the market that bordered on the Aryan side, so it was necessary to take a leap in order to find oneself on the other side. Not knowing how we did it, my mother, my child, and I were on the other side in one instant. As quick as lightning, we ripped of the white armbands so that nobody would recognize us. Since we had an Aryan appearance, we did not draw the attention of the Christians. We immediately hired a horse cab, went to the train station, and set out for Warsaw. We went to the ghetto once we arrived in Warsaw in peace. The next day, my husband arrived in the Warsaw Ghetto with the rest of the family. A few days later the rest of the Jews of Sochaczew came to the ghetto. They told of the scenes of atrocities that took place in the town during the liquidation, and that our best friend Menashe Knott was murdered.

Seeing the Ghetto Burning from a Small Window

A "blockade" was set up in the Warsaw Ghetto in the autumn of 1942. They prodded all of the people to one place and conducted a "sorting": all of the workers who had work permits were left in the Ghetto, and all of those remaining were taken for deportation. To my luck, my husband received a work permit from an acquaintance. My father and my brother did not have such a paper, but they succeeded in intermingling with the workers and were sent to a workshop. I, along with my mother and my child, succeeded in hiding in the attic of the shop. We remained there for six days and barely succeeded in surviving.

At the same time, thousands of people were dragged from their hiding places and sent to their deaths. My husband bribed a S.S. man with a large sum of money, and he thereby took us out from the attic and took us into his house. It was quiet for three months after the aktion.

Another aktion came in January 1943. We hid for three days in an underground bunker. After the aktion, approximately 30,000 Jews remained in the ghetto. Having the deep conviction that a certain death awaits everyone (the Nazis "assured" everyone that all of those who remained who were workers would remain alive); we began to seek refuge on the Aryan side. We searched for contacts with Polish acquaintances. My husband sent my mother (thanks to her Aryan appearance) to a Polish acquaintance on the Aryan side with a large sum of money, in order to obtain a hiding place for us. The Pole agreed, and rented with that money a four room dwelling on Szliska Street number 50, where we would obtain a bunker. First, the Pole helped to bring over the last bit of belongings that we still possessed. Later, my mother and child were brought by the Pole through a tunnel on Moranowska Street to the dwelling. The remaining family and I were brought out of the Ghetto along with the "Einsatz Gruppen" (Worker-Groups) [4] and arrived at the dwelling where my mother and child were located. There, we were in the last room, and saw the fire of the burning ghetto through a small window.

Informers Chase Us

We did not go out at all into the light of day for several months, with the exception of my mother (due to her Aryan appearance) who would go for a walk on occasion with my child. Once, when my mother was outside alone on the street, she was recognized by a shiksa [5] from our village. However, mother did not notice the shiksa. She came home and did not tell anything. A few days later, while we were eating our evening bread, suddenly some policemen with agents came to us and wanted to take us away. We were able to bribe them with a large sum of money. We realized that the shiksa trailed mother and informed the police, who came to take only mother, but found us all. After that "visit" we decided to leave the dwelling out of fear, since tomorrow others could come, and we had no more money for bribery. That same night, we went over to a second Polish acquaintance on Moranowska Street. In the court there were garages with horses and stables, and the Christian hid us in an attic over a horse stable. My mother succeeded in changing her document to an "Aryan". She rented a room in a cellar on Twarda number 25 and took my child with her. There, in the attic, the four of us remained: my husband my father, my brother, and I.

Later in the evening, we would go out from the attic into the home of the Christian to eat something, and then we would go immediately back to the attic. Every few days, mother would pass by our home with my child, so that I could at least see the child through a crack in the attic. After some time, father caught a cold, and was not able to remain in the attic any more. He went out to our countryside, and hid with a farmer acquaintance.

Summer arrived, and it was terribly hot in the attic. It was literally stifling, however we had no other option and had to remain there. Around the same time the Christian told us that the Germans were suffering massive defeats on the front. This gave us this gave us the endurance to endure our pain. Later, severe air raids began to take place over Warsaw, and our hope to remain alive strengthened.

One day, after an air raid, my mother came to us in the attic due to her great longing. The child was already three years old, and we were afraid to let the child know about his parents. The child would play with Christian children, and we were afraid lest he say something to them. The same day, after mother left our hiding place with my child, the Polish uprising in Warsaw broke out, which lasted four weeks.

The daughter of Daniel Moszenberg, Roza.

{463}

From Aryan Documents
by Leib Lurie
Translated by Jerrold Landau

On the third day after the outbreak of the war, German bomber airplanes attacked Sochaczew and destroyed several houses in the Jewish area. During the bombardment, which lasted several days, Jews of Sochaczew fled to Warsaw and nearby towns and villages. My family and I fled to the village of Oryszew Gora[6]. In the meantime, Sochaczew was bombarded once again, The Jewish houses on Warszawer Street and the Market were destroyed. German military units appeared in the city on September 15. A stubborn battle began. The city passed from hand to hand several times. The bridge over the Bzura River was destroyed. The cannon shots destroyed houses as well as the Beis Midrash.

I came to the town a week later. Many refugees from Lowicz and Lodz arrived and told of the victories of the Germans and their approach to our region. We left for Ilow. Shortly thereafter, a bombardment began there as well. We set out once again on the route to Gabin. Along the way, we saw processions of police and Polish soldiers. The bombardment did not cease. We hid under a small bridge. The battle approached us. We saw the movement of German soldiers. We waited for the passage of the situation in terror and despair.

Suddenly, we noticed Germans with pointed guns who were shouting: "Hands up, come out". The approached us. We came out. Seven German surrounded us and asked if there were any soldiers under the bridge. My father answered that there were not. They ordered us to go to the other side. We were certain that they were going to shoot us. To our joy and surprise, they led us to an officer who did not ask us about our nationality. We were only brought into a house and told to wait. There were many people in the house, Jews and Poles. At about 6.00 p.m., the officer came in once again, and ordered that those present should go home and the refugees should go to Gabin. We set out for Gabin. We arrived in the city in the evening.

There was massive destruction in Gabin. Dead people, horses and cows lay in the alleys of the suburbs. Here and there, Germans stood at the watch posts. We went through the side streets and arrived at the house of an aunt.

The next morning, the Germans began to capture Jews for work – cleaning the city and clearing away the dead, among whom there were many Jews. On the third day after capturing the city, the Germans set the synagogue on fire. It burned down completely. A few Jewish houses were also destroyed with the fire.

Later, when the battle in Poland died down, we returned to Sochaczew. Jews of Sochaczew returned from Warsaw and other cities. A few set out toward the Soviet Union. My father went away to the U.S.S.R., with the intention that if things were good there, he would return to bring us there. It worked out otherwise: Father traveled to Bialystok, and from there, further on. There was no possibility of returning. My mother, sister and I remained in Sochaczew. We had no news of Father for a long time. Later, when a trade agreement was established between the Soviet Union and Germany, we received a letter and a package. Father was doing very well there, and he intended to bring us over in a legal manner.

Here, our situation under the Germans became significantly worse. The Germans conscripted the Jews to forced labor. We had to wear a special band on our sleeves. Jewish homes were torn down. An ordinance was issued on January 28, 1940 that the Jews of Sochaczew must leave the city and go to Zyrardow. The vast majority left, but approximately ten wealthy families remained, and a ghetto was created.

Shimshon (Szamek) Szlosberg, son of Yaakov and Bina. From Młodzieszyn, Sochaczew region.
Killed during a blockade in Warsaw, September 1942.

My family and I set out with the others to Zyrardow. We arrived in the city in the evening. The Zyrardow Jewish Committee was waiting for us. They treated us very well. We were billeted in the synagogue due to the crowded living situation. We received support from the Jewish committee throughout the entire time. A few days later, the vast majority were set up in private homes. However, we did not remain in the homes for long.

On February 10, 1940, the German authorities drove out all of the Jews who were found in Zyrardow. A great tumult broke out in the city. Jews sold everything quickly. The next day, everyone had to be at the train station. Uniformed Germans enumerated us at the station. We could take with us as much baggage as could be carried on our shoulders. Between the station and the wagons we had to undergo a "brand". Germans with rifles and automatic guns stood there, delivering death blows to everyone and prodding them onto the wagons. During the great tumult, the Jews left behind half their baggage that they had brought with them. The action ended after a few hours. The wagons were loaded. The wagons were so crowded that one could not move a foot. The train traveled under heavy guard. We arrived in Warsaw at night. At the station, the Germans once again prodded us by shouting, "Laus, schnell". Women and old men who were not able to hurry in such a way with baggage left their belongings along the way. We were taken to Jewish living spaces, and given over to the Jewish Judenrat.

We were billeted in former schools[7]. The cramping and crowding was exceedingly great. A few weeks later we found out that the Sochaczew Ghetto had been liquidated in a murderous way. Some Jews were shot, and the rest were transported to Warsaw.

In the Warsaw Ghetto, hundreds of people died each day from hunger and cold. Typhus and other illnesses spread. My brother and I registered for a work camp in order to get out of the ghetto. It was located near Wiskitki. There were many Sochaczew Jews in that camp. The work was very hard. We dug a river. The guards were civilian Ukrainians, who prodded us strongly. After a few days in the camp, we decided to flee to a village in the region of Sochaczew.

It was Sunday. I do not recall the date. We did not go out to work. It was raining all day. It was already dark before night fell. The Ukrainian guards were sitting in their booths. I was the first one to break through the barbed wire. I broke through and began to run. Thus did I run for about half an hour. Thoroughly soaked, I arrived at a village. I knocked on the door of the first house, and an elderly man opened the door. I told him the truth as it was. He invited me to the table and gave me kluskes[8] and milk. At that moment I felt fortunate – my dream of the last few weeks had been realized. I thanked him and set out again. I spent the night in the barn of a poor peasant in that same village.

I set out again in the morning and stopped at a farmer I knew behind Sochaczew. A few days later, my mother, brother and sister found me. I remained with the farmer, and tended to his cow. My mother, brother and sister went around to the villages seeking bread. A few other Jewish families were in that village, including Hollander and his family, and others whose names I do not recall.

After staying a few weeks with the farmer, he told me one day that I must leave his house, for a decree had been issued threatening the death penalty to those who hide Jews. I had to leave that village.

I knew that there was a ghetto with Jews in Gabin. The city belonged to the Third Reich. I tried to cross the border. The Germans captured me, and found nothing suspicious on me. They apparently did not realize that I was a Jew. I only received 25 lashes with a rubber stick, and they sent me back.

I tried to figure out a way to enter the Soviet Union. Hungry, tattered, and not knowing anything about the whereabouts of my family, I wandered on foot around the villages. From time to time I would beg the farmers for a bit of food. I met other homeless, hungry Jews along the way. I spent the night at the Jewish committee in Mińsk Mazowiecki. There was still a large number of Jews in that city. I set out on my way once again in the morning. I did not know how to enter the Soviet Union. One could not get through. I stayed with a farmer near Luckow, with whom I worked for a few months. Finally when he found out that I was a Jew, I had to move on. Thus did I wander on, with one shirt, torn clothes and boots, without a penny in my pocket. I set out again for Sochaczew. The journey took a few days. I passed through difficult times about which I don't have the energy to write.

I arrived in my native city, however I could not remain there. My acquaintances were afraid to let me into their houses. They told me that a pair of Sochaczew Jews who were wandering around the villages were shot, and the Poles who let them into their houses were sent to Auschwitz. I received a student identification card with the name of Tadeusz Matoszak from a Polish acquaintance. I obtained some trade tools and left Sochaczew. I knew nothing about the whereabouts of my family. I was told that my mother and sister returned to the ghetto, and that my brother was murdered in a nearby village.

I set out in the direction of Lowicz. There, I worked for several householders of the village. I manufactured household implements, including an apparatus for making liquor. I also worked at other household jobs. Thus did I live in filth, under terrible conditions, and with the constant fear of death. I hoped that the war would finally end.

Things again worsened. Several Jews were shot in the region of Lowicz. I spent the entire winter in the city. In April 1942, I set out for a neighboring city. With the recommendation of a farmer, I went to work for an elderly agriculturist who took me for a Pole. I worked for him until December 1942. Nobody knew that I was a Jew. The work was very hard, and the food was meager. I was happy, however, that nobody persecuted me.

On November 28, 1942, the German authorities in that area started sending Poles to work in Germany. One day, a neighboring farmer came to me and told me that he had received two notices for his son and daughter to immediately come to be sent to Germany. He suggested that I go instead of his daughter. I agreed to the proposal. I saw in this a means to save my life by obtaining Aryan papers in Germany. I made an agreement with the farmer for 2,000 zloty. I took the notice of his daughter, and that same day set out for Lowicz. I purchased a pair of boots and some clothes, and was left with 1,500 zloty.

The next day I went with another farmer's son to the work office in Lowicz. I was overtaken by fear when I saw the Germans there. I took hold of myself, and bravely entered the office. The officer treated me very nicely. I gave him the work notice and my student papers. He did not ask for any other documents. He registered the personal data, wrote me a card with "my name" Tadeusz Matoszak, and issued an order that the enlisted person should be taken to the camp. They took us to a work camp where there were smugglers and other criminals. There too, they treated us very well.

On December 7, 1942, when they had collected a transport of 1,000 people, they sent us under guard to Skariszewska Street in Warsaw, where the collection point was. We spent the first night in a cellar. The next morning they sent us back upstairs, where there were about 4,000 people. There were many thieves there, who stole even the hat from the head. We waited for a medical committee. Fear once again overtook me. When 30 of us were put into one bath, I made sure I was the last to get undressed. I waited until it filled with steam. After bathing, I got dressed immediately and went out to the corridor. I thought that I might be able to squeeze my way out of there. The next day, we went to the doctor's committee. There too, they saw 30 people at once. The doctors were mainly German. They examined us very superficially. It went very quickly. I put on such a "performance" that is hard to describe. The doctor thought that I was suffering from scabies, and sent me to the unit for infections diseases. I spent 3 days there. After the quarantine, they sent me again to the general unit, and a day later, I was sent off with a transport of 1,500 people.

We traveled for a full day. At about 7:00 a.m., we arrived in Stargard near Stettin. We were placed in a transit camp where we bathed and got haircuts. Two days later, we were sent to a medical committee to see if we were sick. There, I was afraid once again as I was in Warsaw. However, to my fortune, I came out unscathed. The food in that camp was worse than in Warsaw. For breakfast we received 200 grams of bread. For lunch – kohlrabi soup. For supper – black coffee. The work office then sent me to work on the telephone system. I was in a small camp near the post office. Until the end of 1943, nobody persecuted me. The camp grew. Ukrainians, Czechs, Frenchmen, Italians and Poles arrived. There were approximately 2,000 people there. My neighbor was a Ukrainian who caused trouble for me. I suffered from him for 4 months, and then he disappeared.

Thus did the days pass. New groups came to the camp directly from Poland. They told of the slaughter that had been perpetrated against the Jews.

With the approach of the front in 1945, bombardments began over that region, which often lasted for entire days. At the end, we were in the midst of the air assaults. The post office was taken over by the S.S. men, and we could not leave the camp under any circumstances. The entire city was destroyed. Houses went up in flames, and I had to fix the broken telephone lines.

A tumult broke out of February 15, 1945. The Russians began to attack Stargard. The Germans evacuated and led us to Stettin. We remained there until the Russians arrived. After all the years of tribulations, pain and fear of death, I was finally liberated.

I traveled to my native city of Sochaczew in January 1946. I found nobody from my family there. With deep sorrow in my heart, I left the city for Lodz, where I joined up with a Kibbutz. I left Poland a few weeks later.

TRANSLATOR'S FOOTNOTES:

1. Tregier is 'porter'.
2. Water carrier.
3. This is a very curious statement, and I am not sure exactly how to interpret. I suspect that the husband gave up, and just hoped to save his infant any suffering, whereas the resourceful grandmother had plans of how to escape.
4. This refers to a group of workers who go out for a specific task. It does not refer to the einsatzgruppen in the Nazi sense of the term (the groups of roving killing bands that rounded up Jews in the Soviet occupied areas and shot them – responsible for a full 25% of the Holocaust deaths). Although the more specific Nazi meaning is certainly derived from the more generic "worker groups".
5. A derogatory term for a gentile.
6. This village was not able to be identified on modern day maps.
7. Or synagogues. The Yiddish word is identical.
8. Kluskes are square noodles..

{470}

Thus Was the Sochaczew Community Tortured

B. Jarlicht

Translated by Jerrold Landau

There were no Jews there when the Germans entered Sochaczew. All of them had fled to Warsaw. Some of them were killed, including Chaim Leib Liberman and his son, and Aharon Rozenperl. In Sochaczew, the Germans found the only Jew, a sick person who was not able to flee, and they murdered him. I no longer remember his family name. They called him Zussel the butcher.

The Poles showed the Germans where there were Jewish houses, and the Germans set them on fire. The names of the Poles who helped the Germans were as follows: Wyktor Malinowski, Jan Zokowski, Sabczok who was a former policeman, and Gurski's son Francizek.

In 1940, refugees from Glowno, Zgierz, Lodz, and Janiki came to Sochaczew. Only a few families remained in Sochaczew. The rest were away in Warsaw, for they did not have anywhere to live.

The Judenrat was formed at the end of 1939. It was composed of the following 24 people: Biderman (chairman), Yossel Muney, Shmuel Libert, Velvel Pinczewski, Pinye Rozenkop, Leibish Keller, Brzozowski, Balles, Aharon Zelig Marienfeld, Berliner, Itche Gelbsztejn, Avraham Tilman, Yechiel Sztern, Shmuel Rotsztejn, and Maneh Bresler. I do not remember the rest of the names.

The Judenrat related well to the Jewish population. In 1940, a new Judenrat was formed with Itche Gelbsztejn as chairman, Shmuel Libert as treasurer, Maniele Libert (work office), Nachum Grundwag (secretary). The members of the Judenrat were: Aharon Zelig Marienfeld, Aharon Szmelc. High roles were played by Gelbsztejn, Shmuel Libert and his son. They imposed contributions upon people. When these people refused to pay, they compiled a list of the rebels and gave it to the Germans, who arrested them and tortured them so much until they gave over the money. On account of this money, the Judenrat members reveled with the Germans, and bought furs and jewels for themselves.

The Judenrat also activated "rescues" for Jews. There was an ordinance from the Germans that Jews were permitted to walk only in the middle of the street. The Judenrat worked things out so that Jews were able to go on the sidewalks. Jews worked in the dismantling of the iron bridge. They were greatly tortured during their work and received beatings. The Judenrat worked things out to ensure that the workers would not be beaten.

In the year 1914, at the request of the following Polish residents – Zelankewicz, Zokowski, Ratchimel, Balderski, the younger Balinski and others whose names I do not remember – a ghetto was created. The ghetto existed for a total of four weeks. The chairman Gelbsztejn lived in Sztechler's house, which was called the "White House". Libert lived in Urbinski's house. His "residence" was called "Belvedere".

On February 18, 1941, a deportation from the Sochaczew ghetto took place. Libert and Gelbsztejn fled and left the Jews to their own lot. The former "Waszny" of the financial office – Czelaniek – informed the Germans that the Jews were owing taxes, and one must collect the "debts" from them or else the Jews should be deported. The Land Council requested that the "black"[1] Volksdeutschen collate a list of the Jews who are owing taxes, and confiscate all of their belongings in lieu of the debts. At that time, the Jews were beaten and tortured, and their last bit of meager belongings were taken from them.

Balderski's daughter, her married name being Rozepczyk, had a consort who was a German officer called Blashau. She wanted the Jews to give her their jewels. After a long period of torture, the Jews were compelled to give her the demanded jewels.

Jews who had money had ways of surviving, whereas the poor expired from need. When the ghetto was created, half of the Jews were sent to Zyrardow. The expelled people consisted of the poor, who were not able to buy their way. Shmuel Libert wanted that the ghetto dwellers be divided into two groups, who would receive cards of different colors – white and yellow. Those with white cards would remain in the ghetto, and those with yellow would be deported.

The Jews celebrated all of the festivals in secret. These were festivals of tribulation.

The baker Jan Rzokowski gave a harmonica to a sheketz and ordered the Jews to go out with their kapotes and Jewish caps to the marketplace, and dance to the playing of the sheketz. The Jews danced in the marketplace for a half a day.

From right: Nachum Szmelc, Mendel Rozen, Baruch Flejszman, Yechiel Diamant, his wife (nee Segal) and daughter Feiga-Luba, Sheindel Lewkowicz.

The Jewish police commanded that the Jews not leave the ghetto. The penalty was death for going over to the Aryan side. When the Judenrat fled to Warsaw, there was no supervision in the ghetto. A "black" with the name Meps approached Menashe Knott with a demand that he give him boots. When Menashe did not give him any boots, the Volksdeutsche shot the Jew near Jarczewski's butcher shop.

When the Jews were deported from the ghetto, Poles stood by the highway and took the bags of from the Jews, saying to them that they would need them since they are most certainly going to their deaths. The elder Gorski rejoiced and said: "Finally, this is what we waited for. We have a Sochaczew that is empty of Jews." In the year 1943, Moshe Biznicki was captured by the "blacks" in the town of Dembsk. They burnt his eyes, chopped off his ears, and cut off his tongue. He gave up his soul amidst terrible torture.

Two months later, Hersch Graubard, the boot maker's[2] son, met a similar death in the village of Altanka. Shamai Flejszman was murdered in the village of Chodkow. The tailor Chudi was hiding in the same village with his wife and children. The "blacks" informed on them, and they were murdered. The three Jakubowicz butchers were murdered in 1943 in the village of Zukow by the A. K. (Krajowa Armie) – the Polish underground army under the command of the Polish government[3] in London. The miller Szpajzhendler was murdered in the village of Rybno in the second half of 1943. At the end of 1943 in the same village, the Germans capture Chaim Brzozowski, Yisrael Kimelman and other Jews whose names I do not remember, and led them to the cemetery. There the murderers cast lots as to which Jew would have to kill which. Chaimel Brzozowski seized the opportunity at that moment, and fled in the direction of the river. The Germans shot after him, but he succeeded in fleeing. Brzozowski hid in the villages. Approximately a half year later, the peasants captured him and turned him over to the gendarmes, for the Germans publicized an announcement that a person would receive a fortieth measure of liquor and a kilo of sugar for every Jew turned in.

Szewczyk: From among the number who helped hide the persecuted Jews.

I was hidden for a certain time with the peasant Szewczyk. That peasant told me about everything. People such as him were very few. I was sent deported to Warsaw on February 18, 1941. I was in the Warsaw Ghetto until the last days of Passover of 1941. I was captured for work on those days. I was sent to Garwolin. I worked at regulating the Wilga River. My brother-in-law Reuven Czemniarski, Asher Herneberg, Moshe Ber and others were also captured.

There were approximately 600 people in the camp. I found a few other Jews from Sochaczew there: Yidel Maszman and his brother, Mechel Marienfeld, Welman's son, Diamant's son, and others. The work was very hard. We worked from 4:00 a.m. until 11:00 p.m. We were standing in mud until the belt. As food, we received 10 deca[4] of bread, a liter of soup, and pieces of rotten beets. We were beaten mercilessly. Each of us was marked with yellow patches on the shoulders and a number in front. My number was 366.

The company that conducted the work by the Wilga River was called the "Rotszinski Firm". The chief engineer was Matola, and the technician was Doganski. The commandant of the camp was a Ukrainian named Bilas. All other officials were Polish. If we were 5 minutes late for work, a slaughter would begin. Diamant was murdered in such an attack. The chief murder in such "aktions" was Janek, a low ranking officer in the Polish army.

An epidemic of dysentery spread through the camp. People were swollen with hunger. 20-30 people died daily. New victims from Warsaw were brought to take the place of those that died.

On May 28, 1941, I discussed with Pinkus and Maszlanka the question of escaping from the camp, where an intolerable death was awaiting us. It was a dark night. We had no tools with which to cut the wire. We bit through the wire with our teeth, and the three of us fled. We went away in the direction of Lukow. We paused in the town of Stanin. There was no ghetto there yet. We found a few Jews from Sochaczew there: Noach Lewin and his son, Simcha Kotton, Necha and Baltsha Liberman, and the former resident Rachel Ajgelfeld. All of them were occupied with begging, for they had no means with which to live.

I went out to the village of Nowa Wroblina and worked there as a "Parawek" (servant) for the peasant Jaroslaw Donski. When the war between Germany and the Soviet Union broke out, an ordinance was issued that Jews can only travel on the streets until 5:00 p.m. Noach Lewin was murdered at that time. I remained with the peasant until December 1942. The peasant procured a document for me under the name of Stanislaw Michalski and did not wish to hide me any more.

I went away in the direction of Sochaczew, for I did not have anywhere to go. I arrived in Sochaczew in January 1943. At night, I went to Wyrt Draber, and he enabled me to go away to a village. He gave me 10,000 zloty, which my sister had left behind.

I spent the night in Felicks Koszinski's cellar. During the day, I went away in the direction of Gombin, and stopped in the village of Bibiampol at the home of Francizek Szewczyk. I hid for 18 months in Szewczyk's grove. Without the knowledge of his wife, he shared his last morsel of bread with me, for things were also bad for him. I lived in terrible conditions.

In July 1944, the Germans captured me as a Pole, for I had "Aryan" documents with the name Mikalski. They sent me to dig trenches at the Pilica and Warta rivers, for the front was approaching. Thousands of Poles from different parts of Poland worked there. They sent us to Pomerania when the work ended there. I remained there until February 2, 1945.

When the front drew near, the Germans wanted to send us to Germany. We went to a Pole by the name of Stanislaw Mazal. I begged him to save me, for I did not wish to go to Germany. He sent me off to the Tyrolian forests. There they supported up to 150 fugitives. I remained there until February

12, 1945. That day, in the morning, I was liberated by the Red Army. After the liberation, on July 28, I was wounded by assailants from the A. K.

Rotsztejn Shaul, Perl, Moshe and their daughter Sheindel – all from Bialymin.

Moshe Israelewicz and his wife.

TRANSLATOR'S FOOTNOTES:

1. This term "Schvartz" or "Schwartz" ("black" or "black one") was also used a few paragraphs earlier. Its connotation seems to be a means of referring to a Volksdeutsche – i.e. native German in Poland.
2. Komashen maker – a maker of gaiters or low laced boots.
3. In exile.
4. A deca is evidently a type of measure.

{478}

A Few Words
By Hersh Gotthelf
Translated by Dr. Heather Valencia

Gradually the Jews got used to their sufferings: to hunger, poverty and to being seized for work.

One morning in January 1940 the Germans posted a proclamation by the local magistrate, signed by the Bergermeister, a Volksdeutscher (ethnic German) from Sochaczew by the name of Prouza, ordering that all Jews between the ages of 14 and 60 years were to appear on Sunday at 8 a.m. before the magistrate. Various rumors circulated in the town. One person says the Jews are going to be expelled, a second says they are all to be taken to work, and so on, with various hypotheses and fears, so that we could hardly get through the days until we all assembled before the magistrate.

Prouza with his German companions appeared, and on their shouted command "Achtung" we all froze. They told us how well they were "looking after" us . Until today we had all been without "supervision"... but from today on we would have a Judenrat which would administer our affairs and look after us. He immediately produced a list and read out the names of the Judenrat. Leaders: Biderman, Borenstein, Lukshtik, Levin, Velvel Pinczewski, P. Rosenkopf, H. Libert and others.

The Judenrat began distributing work papers, but these papers were only sent to those who could not pay ransom money to the Judenrat. Anyone who could pay a zloty per day did not have to go to work.

One winter day a group of us went to work. Among us was Itche Gelbstein. The work was at the Bzura. We had to dismantle the bridge that the Germans had bombed. The Germans appointed Gelbstein as our supervisor, and from that day on the Germans did not come to fetch us, but instead Gelbstein took us to work. As his helpers he took the two sons of Shmeltz the tailor.

In the Judenrat there were beginning to be tensions with Libert's son Moniek who was the secretary. Biderman saw how the wind was blowing and resigned. With the agreement of all Judenrat members Gelbstein was elected President and the Gestapo then co-opted the elder son Nachem Shmeltz onto the Judenrat.

This was the beginning of the first tragedy in the work of the Judenrat. The flower of our youth is sent away to Belzec. Naturally only those who have no money were sent, and they were the majority.

The first sad letter from the camp arrives in Sochaczew: Hershel Yashinski (son of the tall Bendet) is dead. There is commotion and uproar, the others must be rescued. Money is collected, and the people who travel to Warsaw to get them come back with only eighteen out of the twenty, because Berish Katz's son had been shot on the very same day they were rescued from the camp. This was related by Avram Nashelewicz, my best friend, who was the leader of the group from Sochaczew.

The situation of the Jews was getting worse from day to day. A new "proclamation" signed by Y. Gelbstein and M. Libert announced that the town needs accommodation space, because it is overcrowded. Gelbstein, Libert and Shmeltz command all the Jews to assemble and announce that the Germans are going to help to evacuate the Jews to Wiskiti, near Zyradow. But we were given to understand that if we gave the Germans a large sum of money we could prevent the evacuation.

Every Jew began to bring to the Judenrat everything he possessed: money, diamonds, gold, jewelry, karakul sheepskin coats, and so on. Unfortunately there were among us some Jews who were living it up as never before. During the time of the evacuations and cruel decrees they organized entertainment at which the Germans were all present. One such entertainment was held to celebrate the birthday of the child of a certain Jew of Sochaczew who invited the "shishkes" (bigshots) of the Judenrat and Germans as well. In the middle of the celebrations two Germans rush in, the best "friends" of Shmeltz and Aharon Zelig Marienfeld. The Germans summoned both of them out and murdered them in a mysterious fashion.

Their murder shocked everyone. It was said that they ended up in this way because of the contributions they had taken for themselves. Shmeltz, Zelig and Gelbstein were the masters over the Jews of Sochaczew. They did whatever they wanted. There was no way of approaching them.

At night the Germans used to search for weapons among the Jews and threaten that they would do whatever they wanted to with us, the same as they did with "those Jews". And meanwhile they stole everything that came into their hands.

And so it went on until January 1941. Then the final decision came that the Jews of Sochaczew had to leave the town within 24 hours. In the announcements to the Jews it was said that if they did not leave within 24 hours they would be handed over to the Gestapo.

The Judenrat wanted to show that it was doing something and provided carts. For 2,000 people – 10 carts. Can you imagine how much one could take along when 8-10 families were packed in each cart?

There was a tumult. People who had received the evacuation notice had to leave the town. Since there were not enough vehicles, most of the people went on foot. They were walking along with tiny little children, old people, and ill people, all were hurrying to leave the town, because they were afraid of being late. The town was emptied of its Jews. Only the chosen few remained. It should also be mentioned that while the ghetto was being created, Jews who lived outside the ghetto had to leave their homes and the Christians took them over. But not all the Jews could get into the ghetto, because there were not enough dwellings. While the ghetto was being formed a Jewish police force was also created, in which the following served: Menashe Knott, and Lipman Diament. The most comfortable accommodations were taken by the members of the Judenrat. That house was called "The White House". The ghetto was opened on 24 January 1941 and it existed until the middle of February 1941. The people had not yet managed to get properly organized, when the order came that all the Jews from the town and the Sochaczew area had to leave the town within 48 hours. They were being evacuated to Warsaw. And so a new tragedy began.

The Judenrat was collecting contributions again, people were running round in confusion, horrified by the terrible decrees of the recent weeks. Jews were being mistreated, beaten to death, robbed and tortured. Farmers came in from the villages with carts and "bought" for a few groszy the Jews' furniture and their last remaining possessions.

The members of the Judenrat were the first to leave the town in this evacuation, in a big vehicle onto which they loaded their possessions. Only that worthy man Menashe Knott of blessed memory remained to supervise.

Gradually everyone escaped however he could. Some on foot and mostly at night. Priver the Gestapo leader called the Commandant Knott, and gave him an order that within the few remaining hours he was to provide him with a pair of boots. Knott went to Graubard the shoemaker and told him plainly that if he did not provide the boots for Priver by the next morning (by twelve midday no Jew was supposed to remain in the town), all the remaining Jews would be shot.

When the Gestapo leader Priver and Menashe Knott went to Graubard's house the next morning to get the boots they found that he and his family had fled. Leaving Graubard's house, Priver shot Knott and he fell dead on the spot.

In the Warsaw Ghetto

In the Warsaw Ghetto there was no contact among the people from Sochaczew. No one knew each other. There was no question of earning a living. Whoever had a little protection and a sewing machine could work in Teben's shop. I brought my machine in and began to work. There everyone got a serving of soup, which in the terrible conditions of the ghetto was a great thing. Money was paid every three months, there was terrible hunger. People with swollen-up bodies lay in the streets dying of hunger. Such were Hertske Moshke, Wideletz and others. But there were also Jews from Sochaczew who traded on a large scale on the Aryan side, yet it never occurred to them to help one of their townsfolk. At home they hadn't dreamt that something like this would happen to them. These were Moshe Bruker, Broitman and the brother Moshe Wiedislawski. The first who died was Hersh Wolf Warshawski. A few days later the Sochaczewer Rabbi also died.

But life went on. Some festivities took place. A son of Sheynwald's was married to Frieda Biezanski.

Working in Teben's factory was a very great advantage because each worker received an identity card. Everyone was jealous of me, because rumors were going around that those who had these identity cards would stay alive.

At the end of 1941 a transport of furs arrived in the factory which were to be made up and delivered to the Russian Front. The Germans promised that if the work was done by the deadline, they would reward us well for it.

At that time an underground movement was functioning in the factory, which didn't believe in German promises any more. When the transport was nearly finished the warehouse was set on fire and eighty percent of the furs were burned.

The next day when work was continuing again, the workshop, which was at 14 Prosta Street, was suddenly surrounded by the Gestapo, who immediately arrested some of the leaders, yelling that the Jews had carried out sabotage and threatening to burn us all as we had burned the furs.

The workshop became quiet. The work went on. Every day more people became ill from the soup that we were being given. I felt very ill and went to the shop doctor, who was on the spot. He gave me a note to go to the hospital, which was on Niska Street. There I lay sick for three weeks with typhus, under the supervision of Dr. Landner. The patients there were existing in terrible conditions. After lying there for three weeks I was "healthy". I left the hospital and not having any money for a rickshaw, I went on foot. This was in the middle of Passover 1942. On Zamenhof Street I met David Vishnia and asked him to help me home. He supported me under the arm and we went slowly. On the way he noticed in the distance a woman carrying matzos. He left me standing, ran quickly to the woman, snatched the matzos from her hand and ran away. With my last strength I dragged myself home to 58 Nowalipki Street.

At home there was terrible hunger. But there was no means of earning a livelihood. There was nothing to lie on. Everything had been sold. The only thing remaining was the tallis. Then my mother-in-law sold the tallis and for the money she cooked a meal.

After I had been at home for four days, I decided it would be better to die from a bullet than from hunger. There wasn't a zloty anywhere. My wife then took out the gold teeth from her mouth, gave me half of them, and I – still feeling pretty ill – went to the wire at the edge of the ghetto with my wife and brother. I bribed the police guard on duty and there we were on the other side, where human beings lived in freedom.

The common grave (literally "brother-grave") of the Sheynwald, Gotthelf, Berg, Kutnovski and Erlich families - who died during a bombardment in Warsaw on Orle Street in the first days of the war.

I went to the railway station. Hundreds of people were standing in queues. I stood among them. The trains were packed full, and I was too weak to push and shove. The train left and I remained in the station. I wandered around on the platform with my pack under my arm. Trains from abroad and from inland arrived and departed and I did not know which train is going to Sochaczew. It is already twelve o'clock. I notice that opposite on the other platform people are assembling. I drag myself over there and stand in the queue with the others. I notice that I am being observed and I begin to tremble. I stand impatiently with my heart fluttering. At last the train arrives. I am relieved, and in few minutes later I am in the train. Not knowing where it is going.

The train goes. Suddenly I hear "Get your tickets ready. Inspection". I give a start. I go hot and cold. I start shaking with fear and agitation. What shall I do? But at that moment a Christian woman turns to me (who probably saw my unease and understood what was going on) and asks me if I have a ticket. She takes my ticket and whispers to me that I should turn to the wall and look out of the window. When the ticket inspector comes, she gives him my ticket and hers. I am saved. We go on. I find out that the train is not going to Sochaczew, but to Bieliny. When the train stops, all the smugglers run on along the rails to avoid the inspection, and I do the same. But I haven't the strength to run like them and have to stop for a rest every few minutes. The smugglers laugh at me, saying that I won't get anything to buy. But I just pray that I shall have the strength to get to the village of Topolow near Sochaczew.

To get to the village of Topolow one had to go past the village of Szymanow in which there was a church. I sat down to rest not far from the church and wondered what I should do now. A koliazh (not sure of the meaning, but apparently some sort of Christian religious official) came up to me and asked me where I was coming from. He saw that I was a Jew. There was no point in denying it. I told him that I had come from the ghetto. Then he told me that the Gestapo was there in the church and advised me to leave and showed me the right way to the village of Topolow.

In the Village

In the month of April 1942 I arrived in the village of Topolow, which is situated seven kilometers from Sochaczew. There I met many people from Sochaczew. But I could not stay there for long. I found work as a tailor with a certain Pietczok with whom I worked at home.

Once a commission came to his house to look at his inventory. Seeing a tailor, one of them came over to me and asked if I was a Jew. And immediately blows started raining upon me. They bound me up with a rope and laid me on a cart. Seeing this, the farmer's sons quickly took their horses and went away to the field in order not to be there. The farmer, my boss, made every effort to rescue me. He invited the entire commission into his house for a schnapps. He said "let's have a drink" to them "before we take the tailor to the city". When they stopped to drink, one of his sons ran over, cut the string, and shouted "Flee quickly!".

I fled to the forest not far from Piaseczno. After a few days, I returned to the same farmer. He put me back to work. I worked for him for a few weeks when, as luck would have it, the same thing happened to me with the farmer. In the interim, they conscripted men for labor. Once when I was sleeping in the threshing-floor, I suddenly felt a brutal hand grab me. Several Germans stood near me and announced that I, along with the other Christians, must immediately go to work.

They crammed me into a Polish vehicle filled with Christians. I turned around and saw that the farmer's three sons were also in the vehicle. One of his sons announced in a loud voice that it would be best to inform the driver that there was a Jew in the vehicle. He spoke loud enough, and the driver immediately turned to me and placed his hand upon my head. I defended myself. He requested my documents. I handed him my documents. He read the name Gotthelf, and repeated it ten times. Then they turned me to face the car, with my hands raised, and in a moment they were going to take care of me. They informed me that there were Volksdeutschen and Reichsdeutchen (local ethnic Germans and Germans who are natives of Germany proper) in the area, who would certainly shoot me. It is difficult for me to put into writing what happened to me that night.

Suddenly, as I was standing with my hands raised, afraid to move at all, a Volksdeutscher approached me and asked me if I recognized him. I told him that I did not. Then he told me that we were friends. I was shocked. A German is my friend? However I soon recognized him, and remembered that we were together at the Volksschule in Ilowa Glaw, near Sochaczew, were we had previously lived. The German's name was Engelbrecht, and I did indeed remember him. I begged him to do something to save me, since they wished to kill me. He went away, and returned a few minutes later and told me that when I hear a shout I should immediately flee. That is indeed what happened. A few minutes later I heard a shout and I began to run with all my might. I immediately heard that they were shooting at me. I ran further. I was in a field, and hid in the grain. I remained there until sunrise. When it was light, I returned to the farmer with whom I had worked.

When the farmer saw me, he crossed himself three times. "Thank god that you are alive. We were certain that you were finished when we heard the shooting." The farmer's joy was very great, since I did not tell him from where they had taken me.

I left the village the next day. To where should I go? All the paths were locked with a hundred locks. I remembered that I had served in the Polish army with a friend who lived in Witoldowo. His name was Kojawa. I decided to go to that village.

He was happy to see me, and welcomed me warmly. However I could not stay there for long as nearby there was the town of Dembowko, which had only Volkesdeutschen. He advised me to leave shortly. He gave me the address of his father, where I would be able to stay for a certain time. That is what happened. I began to work for his father. I let myself be paid with food, and my wife found out where I was, and sent her sister from the ghetto in order that I should send them food.

The hunger in Warsaw was terrible. The atmosphere was tense. There were rumors of the uprising. I asked my wife Bronia and her sister to come to me. This was in June.

My sister-in-law Leah Bzozowska's children went to the ghetto every week with food. Thus passed the sorrowful days. There was no day and no night. Summer was easier, since we were able to hid in the grain fields.

My wife and I wandered around hopelessly. Then came the year 1943. A new year with new decrees. The Germans put up posters which stated that whomever harbored a Jew would be killed along with his entire family, and that whomever would hand over a Jew would be rewarded with one liter of vodka and three kilograms of sugar. This aggravated our suffering. No farmer would allow a Jew onto his threshold. They would not even let a Jew cross their fields, nor would they give a drink of water to a Jew, since they were afraid that this would upset the Germans. The situation worsened. We wanted to take our lives, however the will to live was stronger than the desire for death. Perhaps, perhaps it would be possible to be saved?. We must search for new ways. Then we came to the village of Wyczolki. This village was populated by rich farmers, and all tailors found work immediately.

So I stayed there the whole winter. Spring came and we went to a second village. All these villages are in the area around Sochaczew. In the village of Bieliny I met a lot of Jews from Sochaczew: Shmuel Leib Gotthelf, my cousin Hershel Roitman, Tendl with his wife and children, Tzalke Jakobowicz with her brothers, Hershel Sheynwald, Yitzchok, a son of Zalman Rakhtshe Skulnik with a small child, Pinchas Cohen – all of them perished later in the village at the hands of the Germans.

Once, when I was working for a farmer in the village, a farmer came in by the name of Zaioncz, calls me and the cobbler Mendel from Wiskiti, and tells us that since the Germans are demanding from them a contribution of food, he is demanding from me a roast goose to him and from the cobbler a liter of schnapps. We are to supply this every Sunday, otherwise he will hand us over to the Germans. We decide to flee. By chance I meet Tsalke Jacobovitch. He tells me that he is in a bunker in Skotniki and there is no lack of food, but it is embarrassing for him. He has heard, he says, that there are a lot of Jews in Bieliny. So he plans to rescue someone and take him with him. Hershel Roitman's son Yosef goes with him.

When I met Yosef again a little while later, he was talking to me but I could only hear his voice. I could not see him, because I was lying in an attic with my wife who was wounded. Yosef had come back to ask for his ring that he got as a present from his mother and he asked the farmer if he would give him back the ring, because it was very precious to him. It turned out later that Yosef left Jakobowicz because he had stolen various valuables from him. But the two Jakobowicz brothers did not manage to get back into their bunker. They were killed by the Germans when they were trying to get back to their bunker at night. That was in 1943, not far from Skotniki.

The second half of 1943. The situation is grave and hopeless. No farmer will now allow Jews to work for him. There is only one way out: to hide in the forest.

Not far from Bieliny there is an area called Wiskiti. There is a big forest, where Jews were hiding. Among them was my wife's sister, Esther Biezanski. As soon as she heard that things were getting very bad in the village she came to get us and took us into the forest. Mendel the cobbler from Wiskiti also came with us, because one of his sisters was also in the forest.

On Sabbath 17 July 1943 we arrived in the forest. During the night rain was falling. Together with us there was a man who had escaped from Bialystock , one from Treblinka, from Radomsk, people from Warsaw, Wiskiti and Sochaczew. After the rain Christians came into the woods to gather sponges. Some of them sat down beside us. They pity us because we are living more miserably than dogs. I ask my sister-in-law if she knows them and she answers that she does, and that we don't need to be afraid of them. The cobbler Mendel says to me: " Hershel, if to-day was not Sunday I would go back to Bieliny. I have a foreboding that there is danger here."

I negotiate with someone from Warsaw about a bunker, because they have a bunker and food. Suddenly we hear shouting and machine gun fire. My wife starts running. I try to run after her but I see a German aiming his gun. I throw myself down into the bushes. There is a deadly silence. I don't know my wife's fate. I hear footsteps. I decide to move. I start crawling on my stomach and on all fours until I come out into the village of Nowo Wies. That was on 18 July 1943. Then we knew that in the forest there were raids on Jews. The next morning I went back to Bieliny alone, sad and lonely. But the farmers gave me some hope – they said that my wife was alive. And so it was. My wife, Mendel's sister, and the boy from Warsaw had remained alive. My wife was only wounded in her left hand. On 23 July 1943 I met up with her again. It is difficult to describe our meeting. Apart from my wife all the others had died.

Despair seized me. My wife got a fever. The wound was open. There was nowhere I could even lay her down to rest. I pay a farmer money and he allows me to lay my wife in a heap of potatoes. There it was very damp and her fever got worse. Then I asked the farmer if he would allow me to take my wife up into the loft of the stable, where it was drier. The farmer's wife brought various leaves and the wound healed.

There were to be many hard days in our bitter time of waiting, until at last we lived to see the day, 17 January 1945 when the Red Army marched into the village.

A few days later we went to Sochaczew where me met only one family, the Pinczewskis. In the year 1951 we arrived in the Land of Israel.

{490}

Recall me – Remember
by Esther Shoham
Translated by Jerrold Landau

A Jew stands by an open book
In Israel's largest bustling city
It is his merit to praise the Creator –
The giver of life and the living law..

He begins, before the blessing, the words
Are stuck in his mouth;
He sees a personage approaching
He looks – and a shudder falls upon him!

It is a dead person in a white sheet
He waves to him with his hand,
He looks – his blood is congealed,
The man – he recognizes him!

"You know me – don't be afraid of me"
The words calmly emerge from him,
I am not a relative – but I beg this of you,
A good deed – the final one – do for me:

From my own, my dear ones, there is nobody
To recite Kaddish or to observe Yahrzeit;
The murderers did not leave behind anyone
To split open the heavens through tears.

As long as the shtetl still remembers
The people, the life, all together;
As long as the past is awake in the imagination –
Write, write, and omit nothing.

This Yizkor Book should be my monument
Its pages should be covered with tears;
They should call out the significant events
That the world, the deaf ones, did not hear.

This book shall remain for future generations
The murder and the terror are described therein
Not omitting the smallest taste
Not distorting the truth – this is a holy task!

My final request, I beg, do not forget!
He is now hovering over the bench
And the dead person vanishes from my eyes
One still hears: "Recall me, remember!"

Treblinka

{493}

Memories from My Time in Hiding
Tzvi Taubenfeld
Translated by Jerrold Landau

I was in Warsaw when the war broke out. I took part in the defense of Warsaw. Only 21 remained of a company that numbered 224 soldiers. Then I was taken captive and was taken to Lowicz. I remained there for six days, and then succeeded in fleeing to Sochaczew.

I found the entire family living together in a small room. A worker who had worked for us for fourteen years occupied the bakery. He did not even let us into work, claiming that as long as the Germans are in Poland, we have no more rights. Finding myself in the ghetto, I opened a bakery in partnership. It lasted for two weeks, until I was driven out to Warsaw along with all the Jews.

In Warsaw I lived without any means, and life was especially difficult. Having no choice, I along with my brother registered to work as bakers at Hrubieszow Lubelski, for the military. This work gave us the means to support ourselves and our parents. This lasted for eight months. Feeling that liquidation was awaiting us, I decided to go to Warsaw. My brother did not agree, and he remained in Hrubieszow. I miraculously arrived in Warsaw.

I thought and hoped they would not kill an entire city of Jews. Two days later, I contacted Hrubieszow by telephone. My acquaintance Brand told me that they had expelled all Jews. Then I registered with the Germans to work, which gave me the possibility to smuggle in a few products for my parents, for my sister, and for the Lewkowicz family. Thus did I work for seven months, until they began the so-called "lapankes" (conscriptions), which caused a panic. I worked with a different group in the Fli-Platz[1] in Okecie. We worked it out that they would permit us to remain in that place, in order to avoid entering the ghetto.

Berish Lewkowicz with his wife Gittel (nee Taubenfeld.

In 1939[2], we, four young lads – Gelbsztejn, Janowski (Bendet's son), Berish Kac (Aharon's son), and Meir Blumental's young son – were sent by the Jundenrat to work in Lublin. From there, we were sent to Parzniewice, near the Russian border. We lived in broken barracks along with thousands of Jews, in horrible conditions. The barracks had no doors or windows, and one person was on top of the other. Food consisted of a bit of watery soup. Many people became ill, and hundreds of Jews died every day. After four days, Janowski contracted a terrible case of dysentery, and through influence, he was allowed to stay in the barracks. However, he died the next day.

Berish Kac designed a plan to remain in the trenches and go over to the Russians at night. I do not know if his plan succeeded. I fled from the camp after being there for ten days. I went from town to town, from village to village, and thereby came to Sochaczew.

I came into contact with the German army in Okecie, and they surrounded us with a fence. They took us to work every day at 7:00 a.m.

There I came into contact with someone who was friendly with the head of our work, and worked out with him that he should open a canteen, of which we, along with two other people, would be the directors. We concerned ourselves with relieving the need. People were able to purchase various items through us. Thus was I able to make various connections, including with the Christian Jozef Kaleta, who promised to give me help.

In 1943, when things became worse and worse in the camp, I decided to hide. I organized a group of seventeen people, and turned to the aforementioned Christian. We set up two cellars with a disguised entrance and paid monthly rent. We also set up a kitchen in the bunker. After remaining in the bunker for a month, we heard that they had liquidated the entire camp and sent everyone to the Belzec death camp. We were discovered by the Polish police after being in the bunker for three months. They entered the bunker, beat us, ordered us to hold up our hands, and drove us from the bunker. They requested 1,000 Zloty a month from each of us, and if not, they would turn us in to the Gestapo. We collected 9,000 Zloty, gave them the money, and told them that we did not have any more. They, however, demanded the rest. After they left, Kaleta came to the bunker and declared that we must leave the place after the night. If not, he would take an axe and cut all of our heads off.

After his departure, we were left in despair. We wept and lamented, and did not know what to do. Finally we decided to leave the bunker at 4:00 a.m. Six of the eighteen people who had money decided that they were able to stay. Then, "acquaintances" entered the bunker, took them in a car, and transported them to Zoliborz. We later found out that they were soldiers, who took them out to the forest, stole everything from them, including their boots – and shot them.

We, the surviving twelve people, left the bunker in the morning and went into a village, not knowing the way. We obtained spades and dug trenches in a certain place, where we hid for a brief period. Among us there were women with a Christian appearance, who brought us food. However, we could not remain there for long. We suffered greatly from the cold. We then decided to go where our eyes would take us.

I, with a certain Menachem Pera, set out for a village. Along the way we encountered some concrete pipes. We hid in them, clasping each other and trembling with frightful cold. At night, a farmer with a wagon of cabbage passed by. The farmer noticed us as he descended from the wagon. He immediately came up to us and told us that he knew we were Jews. We began to weep, and begged him to help us, for we have not eaten for a long time. The farmer went away, and came back with a pot of cabbage and bread. We indeed did not know how to thank him, and we said to each other that it was for us like Simchat Torah… We remained there until the morning. However, we were not able to hide there anymore, for it was terribly cold in the pipes. In the meantime, children who were playing football noticed us. They were astonished, and shouted out "Jews are here!" They immediately ran home and reported this to the village. Soon, 10-12 farmers came and said to us: "Flee immediately from here, for the Germans will burn the village if they find Jews here. If not, we will immediately inform the Germans".

Having no choice, we returned to the bunker. My friend Pera knocked on the Christian Kaleta's door, while I hid in a toilet. He opened the door for him and immediately asked him: "Pera, do you have money?" He answered that he did. The farmer then immediately allowed him in. Pera paid him 500 Zloty and told him that Hershel Taubenfeld is here, in the toilet. The farmer than called out loud: "Heniek, come". He led us to a hayloft, and we thought that we were saved. Two more Jews came the next day. During the course of a few days, ten Jews whom he was hiding gathered together.

Our situation was terrible. We were left without money. We had sold all of our clothing. Miraculously, one of us found his wife on the Aryan side. She worked for a captain of the Polish underground movement. The wife knew that the captain was receiving money from England to support the partisans and those in hiding. Thanks to her, we had a contact with the outside world.

After a month, we were out of money to pay for the bunker. Then Kaleta warned us that he would throw us out if we did not pay him. We told this to Mrs. Goldman when she was visiting us. The next day, she came along with two women from the underground, gave us 5,000 Zloty and told us that each of us would from then on receive 50 Zloty a month. Our joy had no bounds.

However, our joy did not last for long. Six weeks after we established links with the underground, we again saw six Polish policemen in our bunker. "Jews, give money, for we do not want to turn you in", they shouted, and they beat us murderously. They were close to me. They tore at me and beat me, so that I was wounded on my entire body. Blood flowed from me. Without any option, I took out 1,500 Zloty and gave it to them. However, they demanded a monthly payment of 10,000 Zloty. Having no way out, we told them that we would give them the money.

Afterwards, Kaleta came to us, and ordered us to leave the bunker. We had to obey his orders. We hid ourselves in the attic in order to stay over for a day to avoid the hooligans, who were going to come to take the rest of the money that we had told them about. That is what indeed took place. They came and did not find us in the bunker. They went in to Kaleta and asked him where we are. Of course, he told them that he does not know anything. We heard the entire conversation between them as we were sitting in the attic.

That same evening, we, with the agreement of Kaleta, returned to the bunker. Thanks to the assistance of the underground committee, we were able to hide for six months. However, as fate would have it, due to our difficult conditions with hunger, terror, tribulations and anguish, the wife of our friend Menachem Pera became ill. We could not summon any doctor, and she died a few days later after terrible suffering. We buried her in the bunker.

That is the way our life continued until the end of the war.

We were liberated by the Russians in January, 1945. We were all broken and ill as we left the bunker. I could not walk. I could barely drag myself along while supporting myself on a cane. We had nowhere to go and nobody to turn to. I went by foot to Warsaw, and from there to Sochaczew.

I found Sochaczew completely destroyed. There was no sign of Jewish life. The area of the ghetto was flattened. Trees were planted, and a garden with benches, where there used to be Jewish houses. Then I went with my friend Menachem Pera to Lowicz. We found our bakery whole, and we quickly began to work. Later we went to Lodz, and spent a bit of time there before continuing on our way. I went to Israel, and my friend Pera went to Australia.

TRANSLATOR'S FOOTNOTES:

1. 'Fli-Platz' may mean Flight Place – i.e. aircraft factory – but I am not sure.
2. I am not sure how this story fits in with the above description. My guess is that the date here is incorrect. I would think it would be about 1941 by now.

{499}

A Letter to the Grundwag's Children
by Yozka Grossman
Translated by Jerrold Landau

Your letter arrived and I wish to respond to you. Why? Because this was the request of your father and my friend.

Warsaw looked like an inferno in 1942, during the large blockades. There was no place to hide. There were workshops, and one would give anything in order to be accepted to work for the Germans.

It was a terrible time. The blockades came day in and day out. Children were snatched from parents and parents from children. Everyone was sent to Treblinka. Among them were your beloved mother and sister Esther.

It is very difficult for me to write about this. However, unfortunately I must fulfil my obligation. They went with thousands of people. There was no salvation for them once they arrived at Umschlag Platz (the gathering point for deportation).

We, that is my husband and I, also worked in such a shop. My two children Tolle and Rene were in Wyszogrod. When that day came, we took a chance with their young lives and sent them to Wyszogrod. I cannot write about their departure. My heart was telling me that I was seeing them for the last time. A smuggler came, we bid farewell, and off they went. I did not weep, but I let out a scream.

They could not remain in Warsaw, because this time they were snatching children. There were risks even with their departure. What could I do? The situation was difficult. After much torment, they left for Wyszogrod.

In the meantime, the situation in Warsaw became more and more serious. Thousands of people were sent away every day, and thousands of victims fell every day. They buried people alive, and old people were buried half-shot. The city became a slaughterhouse.

Our turn came – that is, the shop workers. We had good bunkers. The bunkers were under the earth, where there was no light of day. There was no light, no air, no food and no drink. From the outside, all we heard was shooting, shouting, running, and the banking of locks. It was terrible. That is how we lived for days, weeks, months.

Your father also worked in the same shop as I did. When it was calm, he would eat with me at midday. His life was broken. I would say to him, "Nachum, do not be so much in despair. It is lost. But perhaps they live?" To this he had one answer, "I do not have Rivka and Esther. I do not have a life. I am already old and broken. Remember when they will take me to the blockade. You must remember the last thing that I ask of you. Write three letters for me: the first to Yossele in the Land of Israel, the second to Manie in Russia, and the third to Moshe Schwartz in America. You should write about our pain and our tragic life. They should take revenge for their parents, sister, brother and family." I said to him, "Why do you talk like this? And I will not go? Are we not all going the same way?" He said, "No, I am already old and broken, with swollen feet. You have more possibilities of remaining alive." He said, "If only I could see my children one more time, and then I would die in peace! It is so hard to remain alone! Where is my wife and my child?"

The heart was bursting from longing. The eyes were not dry. I had no words of comfort for him.

One day later, after a large blockade, my last friend, my last buddy was also snatched away! Nachum, where are you? Everybody was now gone! Lipman, Aharon Kohn, Machla, Mania Knott, and on and on.

My husband and I could not utter a word. Forlorn and alone, we could not control ourselves. I wept for an entire day. Where were those who were close to me? All of them were dragged to the crematoria of Treblinka, Majdanek and Auschwitz.

Suddenly, a letter arrived from my children. "We are travelling in a transport, to where, we do not know. Let us hope that we will see each other again." Then I knew very well where my children were. Together with my sister, brothers, and all the Jews, they were going to Auschwitz. The way was already very familiar to me. Everyone knew well what was going on the Auschwitz death camp.

I can not write any more, as my heart is bursting. My eyes are dripping blood. I have no more tears.

A few days have passed, and I am writing more. Now, our turn came. Lying in the bunkers, we have heard that Warsaw must become Judenrein, and everyone must leave. Like mice in a lair, we were taken out and taken to the designated Umschlag Platz on Nowolipki. We were surrounded with machine guns on both sides until we reached Umschlag Platz. The entire area was burnt, and we were dragging burnt people with us. They beat, they shot, and they murdered. The air was suffocating. We could not catch our breath. We saw that this was the beginning of our end!

We arrived at the place where thousands of people were waiting for us. I cannot describe the scene. All of Warsaw was ablaze. Every minute, we stumbled upon blackened, burnt corpses. They shot, they murdered, and they took everything that we had. We were living through atrocities. Then they stuffed us into wagons. People died, choked and suffocated. We traveled on and on. To where?

Majdanek, Auschwitz, it drilled through our heads. We regretted that we had not brought along poison like the others. We were jealous of those who had poison with them, and put an end to their lives.

Thus did we travel day and night. It seemed like an eternity. In the wagons, most of the people were already dead. Those alive were almost like dead. With his last strength, my husband said, "Lets persevere, maybe we will survive". He was speaking with his last strength. Thus did we travel on farther, and then we stopped. Where were we? In Majdanek?

"Move forward!" It was dark in the eyes! A noise rushed through the head as we stumbled on our feet. All around, we saw a black mass of men who were waiting for us with sticks and weapons. We were placed five in a row and told to walk. Beaten, sick, half wounded – we must all walk. Where were we going??? We all together said quietly: to the gas chambers...

Despite the fact that we were all half dead, nobody wanted to die such a terrible death. We moved on and trembled. People who still have their children hid them in their knapsacks during the selection, hoping that they could save their young lives. They lost them, and they were trampled underfoot.

Suddenly and order: stand still! We stood still. They divided us, men to the right and women to the left. My husband and I parted from each other. We already knew where we were going. We were going to where our children and friends had gone. My husband said that he would die calmly. He begged that I hold him, then he went right and I went left. It was a dark night. Even the moon did not shine. They could not see our pain. We went on and on without stopping. People screamed, people wept, until we arrived at the death place, where the men were already waiting for us. Our joy that we met up again with the men was indescribable. We lay down as if on hot coals. We knew that this was our last night. We had so much to say, but we were silent. Waiting for death was terrible! Even more terrible than death – – –

It started to get a bit light. We saw our murderers coming from afar. We were all asked to stand up. They lined us again in 5s, and the tragedy began. They divided us up, men together, women together, and children together. They tore children away from their mothers, they beat and they shot. Mothers sacrificed themselves. Old people were shot immediately on the spot. Younger people who were fit for work were left alive for the time being. The moment of separation was terrible. Thousands of people were searching for one another. We searched for people we knew. I did not take my eyes off my husband. I wanted to see to which category he would be assigned. To life or to death. However, I was not able to notice. Our eyes met. From afar, we expressed to each other the wish that we would see each other again, and then we went our separate ways.

I do not wish to write any more about my life in Auschwitz and Majdanek – about the hell and torture that I endured. Now I know only one thing, that I am in Sochaczew completely alone. No husband and no children. Everything is a bad dream. How terrible is my life. Of my entire family consisting of 36 people, I alone remained alive. Everything that I endured in the camps is nothing compared to today. Today it is worse. Where is my home? My children, my husband. I no longer hear "mother". The heart breaks. The head aches. My eyes have dried up. My Tolle would have now been 18 and Rene 16. How can one live? I live in the past. The nights are good, as I see my children. My life is completely empty. I am alone and forlorn. What can I hope for? Yes, one thing. I have a sister in America, but I do not have her address. Perhaps I will see her once again. I also have a brother-in-law in Israel, in Tel Aviv or Jerusalem. His name is Izak Saposznik from Wyszogrod. If I could get out of Sochaczew, far far away, perhaps my heart would not be so broken. I want to get away from here, so I can perhaps forget. Do for me what you can.

{504}

In the Ghetto

Mordechai Gebirtig

Translated by Jerrold Landau

Straight as steps on a sandy path
From the camps come tired slaves,
Dragging themselves into the ghetto for another day
Our sleepless nights...

The hours drag on, heavier than lead
Minutes full of terror and fear
For the time when the day will already be over,
The night will pass in peace.

One does not sleep at all, one listens and lies awake
Lest something terrible occurs

Upon whom will the lot fall this night
And become a victim...

Thus one lies, and the fear is great
Hearing the creaking of a door
The heart flutters when from hunger a mouse
Nibbles a piece of paper.

A limb withers away as is dragged around outside
Little pieces of paper in the courtyard by the wind
One sighs without any language, as a mute –
With mothers, wives and children.

And thus does one lie, with fear and terror
Driven and persecuted as slaves
And thus drags on our days
And our sleepless nights.

Numbers – Thousands, Millions

H. Lejwik

Translated by Jerrold Landau

Numbers – thousands, Millions,
All of the ways are filled,
One – and after them columns
Zeroes, zeroes, zeroes, zeroes.

All of the bodies are freezing,
All of the pupils of the eyes pass away,
When a one starts to march
With the long rows of zeroes.

Out with the essence and out with the form,
Out with the fullness of things,
When the zeroes in one row
Span over empty unpaved roads.

Forest – and trees, city – and houses,
Earth – and heavens without gods,
Dead lie in all the groups
On the level pages of numbers.

Also the numbers of the hours
Break out in a dance, in confusion,
Shouting and cracking like the crows
After the march of zeroes, zeroes

{506}

What I Saw and Heard in Sochaczew in 1939
Yitzchak Tilman
Translated by Jerrold Landau

I was freed on November 27, 1939 as a Polish captured soldier in the hospital of Rawa Mazowiecka. I traveled through Skierniewice. As soon as I set foot in the station at Sochaczew, I immediately felt the Nazi regime. Seeing myself as a captured soldier and finding myself in the hands of the Germans did not have the same strong impression upon me as seeing myself as a freed soldier. I found Sochaczew in the following situation:

Nothing could be recognized of the ruined houses up to the gymnasium. I saw the first one from afar (because going near was not permitted – Germans were found there). Almost no monuments could be seen in the cemetery. If one saw a stone, it was broken and crushed. Only the burnt, crumbling walls remained of the house of Sara Ajzman. No trace remained of Sara Ajzman's wooden workshop. The same was the situation with the wooden workshop of Deichus Ajzenberg. Germans, may their names be blotted out, lived in the house that was formerly the library. The house of the gentile Zwierzechowski was destroyed. The house where Rabbi Frenkel had lived was demolished. The Yavneh School, the synagogue and the Beis Midrash were all completely crushed. The building that housed the community offices and the areas near the Polish public schools and the castle – all were destroyed. The house in which I had lived was destroyed.

A Polish worker, named Kalski, worked in Taubenfeld's bakery. He drove everybody out and said: "Now is the time to take revenge upon the Jews. You must now pay me rent, and you can work for me as workers."

I asked about my friends Gutglas, Holcman, and Fursztenberg. I was told that they all went away to Bialystok.

The next morning, I set out to see what was going on in the city in general. None of my friends who remained in the city wished to go with me, because I wore a military uniform. I went out into the street alone. From where I was standing, I heard a shout and the sound of fleeing of the Jews. Suddenly, young Polish lads surrounded me and shouted: "Are you a Jew?". I answered them, "Yes, I am a Zyd". They immediately grabbed me and took me to the room of a German S. S. man with a black uniform. He asked me "Are you a Jew?". I answered "Yes". "Why have you remained and not fled?" I answered "I am a wounded Polish soldier, and have just been released from the hospital." The Germans immediately found me a place to sit down and continued to ask me: "Why are you still wearing a military uniform?". I answered them: "Because I have no other."

The young Polish anti-Semites immediately began to make noise. They shouted and ordered me to go with them. One motion of the hands and they would beat me. This was my first reception by my Polish brethren for whose fatherland I was willing to spill my blood and give my life.

After that, I went to the magistrate to give a report. As soon as I gave my report to the official Kranc, may his name be blotted out; he opened up his mouth to me with invective. I wished to respond to him but he did not allow me. He shouted out "Shut up Zyd!" Then some Gestapo agents came in and honored me with "Jew dog". They asked me why I was wearing a military uniform. I showed them my papers and demanded to speak to the mayor. They immediately took me to him. At the mayor's office I met his assistant Prauza who had worked for him before the war. The Jews had to dance "Mah Yafit" [1] before him. He treated me even "better" than the anti-Semite Kranc, with terrible curses. I was happy that he did not arrest me.

At that time, above all, I noticed the destruction of the city. The houses in the area from the building that housed the pharmacy to the house where Moshe Nelson lived, including all of the houses that my father left behind, were smashed to the ground. The houses remained intact only on Trajanower (Staszicer) Street. Christians lived in all the homes that Jews had lived in. All of the workshops that were not in the way were grabbed up by the Poles. There was a hodge-podge. Jewish children were going around in the street seeking their parents, weeping and lamenting. Parents were looking for their children. On primarily heard screams and weeping from the homes where Jews lived. People were afraid to leave the home. No Jew was seen on the street. Every day brought new attacks. Then I saw the ordinance that every Jew must wear a Star of David on the arm, or else he was no longer allowed to be seen on the streets. I did not wear a Star of David, for I went about in a military uniform.

Moshe Szwarc during his visit to the Sochaczew Cemetery in 1949 – standing next to the only standing monument. (From right: Yosef Grundwag, his wife, Maya.)

I could not remain sitting at home, and I had to go out to the street. I saw how they captured a Jew and gave him four cigarettes to smoke simultaneously. When he did this, they forced him to put the burning side in his mouth. When the pain from the fire became intolerable, and they threw the cigarettes out, they beat him with deathblows, as if the heavens might open up. They captured a second Jew, smeared his face with some type of grease, and made him run through the street shouting: "Thus did the Jews smear me!" He was then again dealt severe blows. My eyes were dark from shame, and I wanted to dispense with all joy. Thus I spent my time in great suffering during those fourteen days in Sochaczew. I thought about how to save my parents and myself, but I could not come up with anything. Around that time, an acquaintance, Tzvi Goldberg, told me that the entire Gothelf family, consisting of 31 souls, were killed in Warsaw by a bomb that hit the house on Orle Street.

And what happened with the entire family of Chaim Leib Liberman, who were neighbors of Nachum Grundwag? The family was away in Kampinos when the Germans entered the city. One son was in the army, and there they met up with their son. The Germans captured the entire family along with the sons. They took one son, Yehoshua, and ordered him to dig a grave. All of them were ordered to place themselves alive into the grave, and thus they were shot. Yehoshua had to cover them all, and when he finished, they shot him. However, he was only wounded, and he returned to Sochaczew at night.

After hearing such terrible things, I decided to flee to the Russians. I searched for a partner. I suggested it to Bergazen.. He did not wish to do so. Only Lewin, the son of the smith, agreed. We left Warsaw to Malkina. That was the border. From Malkina we went to Bialystok. There I met Nachum Grundwag's brother-in-law, Mendel Frydman and Manya, Mrs. Sender with Mendel Jakubowicz, and the families of Shmuel Holcman and Yosef Grundwag. I heard that many of them had already set off for work, such as: Puter, Tzvi and his wife, Nachum Tilman, Aharon and Leibel Fursztenberg with their wives, and others.

After I was in Bialystok for a few days, I wished to know what was going on in our town where I had left my family. After arriving in town I heard that they had captured the people of mixed background, and had murdered some of that group. I immediately returned to Bialystok, and from there I was sent to the far north. I came to Israel after remaining there for two years.

{510}

From the Last Days of the Warsaw Ghetto
Miriam Flajszman
Translated by Jerrold Landau

April 1943:

I alone remained of my entire family in Sochaczew. My sister Gittel, her husband Wolf Goldman and their children were already deported after the first aktions in 1942. My brother Melech, and my sisters Esther and Rachel with their husbands were deported at the same time.

I hid for a certain time with my sisters Chaya and Golda. When the situation became hopeless and it became murderously clear that the same end awaits all of us sooner or later, we decided to separate. My sisters, who were yellow-blond women with Aryan appearances, went out from the Ghetto to travel to Piotrkow, where they hid with gentiles in the surrounding villages. Unfortunately, no memory remains of them.

There in the Warsaw Ghetto, I met my cousin Shamai Flajszman, Avraham Shalom's son, by chance. He suggested that I should move over to Ostrowska 2, where he lives with his brother

Yitzchak in the cellars of a shot out house. Those cellars were connected with the cellars of the ruins, and this would be a safe "hiding place". I went over to there.

At the night of April 19th, a friend of ours who was a Jewish policeman informed us that the ghetto was besieged by heavy military troops. We went into the bunker with great fear. We were 70 people in total, men, women and a few children. We had electric light and also water there. We obtained air from a pipe that was connected to a tunnel.

For a few days, we had already been trembling in fear about the difficult uprising that was going on around us. We were lying pressed together, afraid of uttering the minutest rustle.

There were a few underworld personalities in our bunker, who had arms. They played the role of our "protectors". A sharp debate broke out among them over some shady matter, and the defeated one, Yisraelikl, was threatened with revenge.

Outside, we heard the shooting and bomb explosions from quite near. Houses were burning around us. The smelly smoke came in from around us. The air in the bunker was difficult to breathe. The eyes were tearing, the throats were strangling, and we were all choking. At night we opened the secret trap door to get some air. This also let us see what was going on outside. Suddenly, Yisraelikl was snatched out of the bunker. He disappeared. We had a suspicion that he would betray us. During the day we heard a strong explosion, and the lights went out. We were overcome by great terror. We heard Yisraelikl's voice near the trap door: "Here you have the group to be annihilated!" At that moment, the trap door opened and the order was issued: "Out!". A hand grenade fell into the bunker with a bang. There was a terrible stampede. We crawled out of the bunker with the fear of death. The wounded were dragged out by the Germans with terrible beatings from their guns and whips. Encircled by the armed Germans, we were taken to Umszlagplatz [2]. The entire way was flowing with blood. Dead bodies were wallowing in the streets. People were jumping from the balconies and windows, and smashed themselves on the cobblestones. Thus were we forced along our route of suffering to Umszlagplatz. There we found large masses of Jews surrounded by Ukrainians. It is hard to describe the cruelty of the Ukrainians. They drove us into buildings under the lashes of their whips. There they held us for 24 hours without water. The filth from the toilets overflowed to the floor. We stood in the filth and waited in rows to be loaded onto the cattle cars that were returning from their previous transport.

The next morning, the Gestapo and the Ukrainians began to lead us with murderous blows from the houses to the wagons. People fell and were trampled by the rows behind. Thus were we stuffed onto the wagons. The shouting and weeping of the women and children intermingled with the shooting.

Weakened and half dead, we stood, stuffed body to body. Finally, the train began to move. Among us there were a few doctors who had cyanide capsules. They swallowed them and extricated themselves from their cruel fate. The surrounding people in the wagons looked upon them with jealousy.

A few of us decided to tempt fate by jumping off. My cousin Shamai had a steel file hidden on him. At night, he began to file the bolt of the wagon door. A few other men helped him. The men filed endlessly all day. We waited until late at night, when the guards were napping in their guard cubicle. The finally succeeded in filing through the iron bar, and the door cautiously slid open. Shamai and a few others were the first to jump. After them, I did.

We heard shouts and shots. Obviously, when I jumped out I fell on the railway tracks and bumped myself badly. I do not remember for how long I lay unconscious. When I regained consciousness, I found myself in a thick forest. It was dark, but I felt as if I was completely covered in blood. I remained there for a certain amount of time. I heard the crowing of roosters. That meant that there was a village near me. I stood up with great difficulty and began to walk in the direction of the crowing roosters. I was terribly thirsty, and I wanted to go to the home of a farmer in order to quench my thirst and wash off the blood. I wanted to enter the yard and knock on the door. Then suddenly, a large dog fell upon me and bit me all over. Aroused by the barking of the dogs, a farmer woman came out and drove me away. I found a second cottage not far away. I knocked on the door. A farmer woman opened up the door and let me in. I washed up and rested a little bit. The farmer was away from home. He returned with a gang of shkotzim [3]. He demanded that I leave the house. I went out, and the entire gang went after me.

As we neared the forest, they demanded money from me. I had a few thousand Zloty on me, which I gave to them.

Melech Flajszman

TRANSLATOR'S FOOTNOTES:
1. A Sabbath song.
2. The depot in Warsaw from where the Jews were gathered for deportation to the death camps.
3. A derogatory term for gentiles.

{514}

The Partisans of Sochaczew
related by Yechiel Silber
Translated by Jerrold Landau

When the war broke out, everyone fled from Sochaczew to Warsaw. When the Germans entered Warsaw, people immediately began to flee back. This happened in my family as well. In the morning when we returned, we and many others no longer found our houses. The houses of the returning refugees had already been snatched by the Poles. The rest of the houses had been destroyed by the bombardment. We had to all live in one room, so long as we had a place to lie down.

The Germans immediately began to capture people for work. I was among them. They snatched men and women, young and old. I was sent to the train station with a group of women, including some Poles. The Germans ordered the women to wash the floors and to bring water. When the women asked the Germans for rags to do the washing, they were ordered to remove their undergarments, use them to wash the floors, and then put them back on. I was the only man among them, and when I saw their embarrassment and shame at the instruction of the Germans to remove and then put on again the wet, dirty undergarments, I decided on the spot: No, I will not remain here.

The next day, I and a group of friends – among them Vove Brzezinski, Gershon Hojker, Yisrael Gothelf, Lichtensztejn, Hollander, and Aharon Fursztenberg left the train, and fled from Sochaczew to Bialystok.

After spending about half a year in Bialystok, the group began to long to return home to Sochaczew. I told them that I was not going to return. The group was afraid to return without me, and they begged me to return with them and then go back alone to Bialystok. I could not withstand their begging, and decided to accede to their request. We went to the border village of Zareby Koscielne. There, we stole across the border.

I could not return to Bialystok, and therefore I decided to go to Stolpce. Skurnik lived there. When I arrived there, I found Mania Brzezinski, and Sara Skurnik with her brother, his wife and children. I worked in a Russian cartel until 1941. All of the residents left the city. It was only we whom the Russians did not allow to flee. When the Germans took the city, they immediately sent me back to my work as a tailor. When the Germans set up the ghetto, they did not order me to live in the ghetto. However, the Jews wanted me to live in the ghetto, because at that time they were organizing a group of rebels. They had found a stash of weapons in the place where I was working for the Germans. The Jews wanted me to help with the underground work. The German boss respected me, so I worked out with him that he would allow me to sleep in the ghetto.

At one time, the boss said to me, "Today you will not be sleeping in the ghetto, for tomorrow they will exterminate all the Jews there". After hearing the tragic news, I immediately ran to the Judenrat and told them what was to take place in the ghetto tomorrow. Then I went to the German boss and asked for his assistance in saving two families from the thousand who were concentrated there. He went to the ghetto with me and removed the two families.

The next day, the boss came to me and led me to the attic of the cartel, where he apparently hid me. Through the tiny window, I saw how the Germans and Latvians arrived with various weapons, and went straight into the ghetto. They immediately opened fire after entering the ghetto, until nobody was left alive. Finally, they found a few people still alive. They led them to a field and shot them there. After it was all over, the Germans and Latvians left. I then entered the ghetto to search for the bunker where a group of friends were hiding, and I rescued them from there.

A while later, they began to bring articles of clothing to the cartel where I worked. These were the garments of murdered Jews. They were sorted there. Many of them were distributed to the Polish people, who had to bring butter, fowl and other items in return.

At one point, the boss told me that he was going on vacation for a brief time, and that I was to keep things in order. A temporary substitute was appointed as boss. The substitute informed me that he requires 30 people for the work in the cartel. I entered the ghetto and brought 30 people. We decided amongst ourselves to smuggle weapons into the ghetto, and that is what we did. Everyone put weapons in their knapsack. We brought them into the ghetto. At approximately 10:00 p.m., we took out the hidden weapons and went out to set the cartel on fire. As we did this, we swore that we avenge the spilled blood. Then, as the cartel went up in flames, we all went out to the forest.

Only seven people survived from that group. After the liberation, two remained in Lodz and five went to Israel: Rivka Kantorowicz, Notek, Maniek Werthajm, and the writer of these lines. The other 23 did not witness the liberation.

Life in the Forest

The fleeing of the 30 who ignited the cartel succeeded, and all arrived in the forest in peace. At the first consultation it was decided that if the Germans were to find any of us, each of us would know how to take revenge. Whoever would remain alive would come to a designated point in the forest.

We were still new to the forest. We noticed a small house from afar, and we decided that three people would go there to take food. The others would remain at the border of the forest to guard the three. Along the way we shot a few times into the air in order to scare the peasant who lived in the little house. When he saw the three, he indeed gave them a loaf of bread, and he told them to come again the next morning to get a fresh loaf of bread. In the morning they set out again to the little house. As they approached, he opened fire upon them. They threw themselves upon the ground and began to retreat. At night, we all gathered at the designated point and decided to take revenge upon the peasant. Some of us went to set the house on fire.

In August, 1942, we joined up with a group of partisans. However, the gentiles warned us that in this region there is a group of partisans that go by the name Nekrasow, who rob everything from the rescued Jews and then shoot them.

A gentile advised us that we should go deeper into the forests, about 10-15 kilometers further on. There, the forests are larger, and we will be more secure. It became clear that there were some White Polish partisans there, who murdered any Jew that crossed their path. One night, they indeed opened fire upon our group and killed someone. We then took a stand against them, and another of our group fell. We had to move on from there and settle in the region of Humniska, where there were White Russians. We immediately began to dig pits and make dwellings, because winter was arriving. We dug three large pits: two for people and one for all other things. When we finished, we decided to collect food for a few months. We spread out far from our point, so as not to give any hints as to where we lived. Along the way, we took a horse and wagon from a farmer, and took as much food as we were able to. In the meantime, the farmer alerted the Germans about the situation. The Germans spread out along a certain way in order to capture us, but we avoided them by not following the straight path, but rather going by side fields. We hid the food very well, and sent the horse and wagon free far from the forest. That same night, we heard terrible shooting. The next morning, we came upon a nearby farmer and asked him about the shooting that night. We found out that a German patrol came upon the empty wagon that we had set free. They switched routes and went along the route where the second patrol was waiting for us at a certain place. They recognized the horse, and not knowing that Germans were sitting upon that wagon, they opened fire, being sure that they were shooting at us. The Germans sitting in the wagon themselves thought that partisans were shooting at them, so they shot back. 45 Germans from both sides fell.

At the end, they shot the farmer, for they suspected that he was involved in this situation.

When we heard from a farmer that they were preparing to liquidate the Stolpcer Ghetto, we decided to go to Stolpce to rescue Jews.

In Stolpce, we came across Sara Skurnik and her brother, already without the children, as well as Mania Brzezinski. We begged them to come with us to the forest, where they had prospects of remaining alive. Skurnik did not want to, for at the time he was conducting good business. Mania also did not want to, for she was working for a "good" German who assured her that he would save her.

We returned to the forest with great regrets. The Germans had a list of Jews who were in the forests, and from time to time they announced that a certain person had been captured and shot. Of course, we partisans did not trust anyone, but unfortunately, the Jews believed the Germans.

We became involved with a farmer named Karpowicz not far from the forest. We found out from him what was being said about the Jewish partisans. Through him, we also sent letters to Skurnik and Brzezinski in the ghetto, and begged them to save themselves, for the Germans decided to make the entire area of Stolpce Judenrein.

When the farmer returned, he told us that not one Jew remains in Stolpce.

Every evening, two different people of us went to the farmer, whom we called "Legalczyk" [1] in order to find out news. In January 1943, Natan and Maniek Werthajm, two brothers, went. This was on a Thursday. They found out that on Sunday, the wedding of a White Russian policeman would take place, for whom we had been searching for a long time because he had shot a Jew in Rubezhevichi. We immediately decided to take our revenge. One of our group went to Legalczyk, and he sent his wife to find out where the wedding was to take place. We received the news that the policeman we were looking for, along with two Germans and two other policemen, could be found there. When we arrived at the location of the wedding, we found those five people drunk. We immediately took them to us in the forest. We killed them when we reached our point.

The next morning, a group of police came to the village, arrested 200 people, and demanded that they inform them of the location of the Jewish partisans. However, none of them knew.

A short time after that event, the Legalczyk informed us that the Germans were preparing to take control of the forests, and would find all those who are located there. The farmer advised us to move from our point. After a meeting of all of us, we decided to move on and seek partisans. Only one, Leib Walecki and his wife said that we should remain there for the summer.

Every day, we received information from Legalczyk about the situation. We heard that the Germans were deciding to gather up many people for work. In the meantime, our departure from the place was delayed.

Once, in the month of March, when Rivka Kantorowicz was taking her turn on guard, she saw a woman near her, and close by to the woman a man. She became perplexed and did not know what to do. In the meantime, the two left, and Rivka came to tell us about it. We immediately went to search for the two. We could not find them, and decided to leave the place that night.

At 11:00 p.m., we heard a large explosion. We realized that they had broken into our place, being certain that they would find us there. A short time later, we left the area.

We set out for Naliboki Pushta[2]. The headquarters of the partisans was there. We thought that we might be able to join up with them, but we could not do so because it was impossible to come to within 100 meters of Naliboki Pushta. Therefore, we had to go a different way, to the forests of Rubezhevichi. There, we found approximately 150 Jews of Rubezhevichi.

They told us that partisans always come to them. They were very afraid of us, for we were all armed with weapons.

We found out from them that among the partisans that come to them, there are some who take the weapons and everything that they can find from the Jews. One was called Tolek from Kubinow's Otriad[3]. A second was Minin, a military commander of the high headquarters. They told us to be discrete, as they may soon come to take our weapons. At that rendezvous, the partisans told us that there is also a Legalczyk of Kuninow's Otriad.

I and Werthajm, a teacher from Mlawa went to Rajskie to talk to him. We told him how many people we were and how many weapons we had. We asked him to put us in touch with the partisans. He told us to come back on April 15, and one of the Otriad would be present.

We came at the designated time. There we found a group seated around a set table. We told them of our activities to that point, and they confirmed that they had heard about a group of Jews who were roaming around the area. We requested that they accept us into their partisan Otriad. Their answer was that the men could join, but not the women. We did not accept their terms, and decided to meet with them a second time. However, the second meeting also did not bring any results, for they held to their conditions, and we did not want to leave our women to their deaths. Thus, we departed with nothing.

In the interim, the winter ended. At the beginning of the summer, Jews with weapons began to come to us from the Baranovichy Ghetto. We became somewhat stronger with them. Then we decided to conduct some activities. We decided to go to the small town of Ivaniki not far from Rubezhevichi, we were found about 10 policemen, and finished them off.

On a specific night, we came to the place where the policemen were located. The policeman who was standing on guard perceived our arrival, and he immediately shot into the air. We immediately took up our posts and answered with fire upon the house. The shooting lasted for approximately a half an hour. We were not fired at from that house again. We became suspicious and felt that we were being surrounded. We decided to send a group of 7 people to the other side of the house and throw a grenade. When we saw that they also did not answer back to that, we decided that 10 people should enter the house to see what the silence was about. I and 9 others entered and found nobody. Apparently, they succeeded in fleeing. They left behind everything – products, animals, etc. We loaded everything onto a wagon, set the house on fire, and left.

The next day, a few partisan commanders arrived to seek out the Jews who conducted this piece of work. We introduced ourselves to them. They extended their hands to us, and sat down to eat and drink with us. They said that they would immediately send a notice to Moscow stating that a small group of Jewish partisans is being very helpful, and is conducting such fine work.

We once again presented our request to join their partisan group, so that we could do even more important work. However, they stuck to their condition: only without the women, and we did not want to abandon the women.

We heard that the Germans were preparing to conduct roundups in the entire region. All of the partisans began to retreat from the villages and enter the Pushta, the forests that were located up to Moscow.

We could not go into the Pushta because we were not official partisans. We had to remain in the region. We knew that the roundups would begin at the beginning of June, so we immediately divided into groups of three. Each group of three had to take responsibility for itself, and had to concern themselves with everyone.

The roundups began on July 10, 1943. First, they sent the gentiles[4], and the Germans followed after them. The roundups in the Pushta lasted for approximately three weeks, but in our area it was only for one day. The Germans asked the gentiles about the Jewish partisans, but the farmers were afraid of telling anything, for they wanted to protect their lives.

They left the Pushta after three weeks without any results, for they did not meet up with the partisans who were controlling the Pushta. After that, the partisans began to return to the villages. That night, I and Natan Werthajm went straight to a farmer. As we were eating, a commander of Kalinin's Otriad entered. Given that he had heard about us, he asked us about certain details, and then informed us that they had decided to accept us into the Kalinin Otriad. He told us that in two weeks, he would send to us a partisan with a letter, and he would bring us to the partisans of his Otriad.

Minin appeared during that time. He was somewhat drunk, and he shot three women and one man of the Rubezhevichi Jews. We were two kilometers from the place where the four Jews were shot. We immediately came to the place after we heard the shooting. We removed his weapons and wanted to shoot him on the spot. However, we decided to bring him to us alive, and not take revenge upon him at that point. In answer to our call, a partisan named Kolker, a Polimioczyk, came from the headquarters. He demanded that we turn over Minin, upon whom there was a writ of authorization. We refused to do so, and demanded that he bring a commander from his headquarters to judge him on the spot. We would only give him over if he was sentenced, for Minin warned us that if we were to kill him, his friends would kill us all.

The next day, the headquarters sent to us the Natshalik (official) Sztaba. We told him everything that had transpired. He requested that we turn over Minin and his machine gun, and they would judge him in their headquarters. We could not refuse his demand, and turned him over. We were interested in a trial, for we heard that they had not yet judged Minin. We had also heard that a group of partisans from their Otriad were preparing to take revenge upon us. We were prepared for anything, for we had once encountered their group of partisans. We loaded our guns with bullets so that we could defend ourselves. However, apparently they were afraid of engaging us, for they saw that we were prepared.

Thus did the relations between us become strained until the two partisans came to take our entire group into the Kalinin Otriad. Everyone in the Otriad knew that the "Charny"[5] group was joining them. (This is what they called our group, because of the writer of these lines, Yechiel Silber, who had dark hair.) They were very happy with us and did not believe that we were Jews, for Jews do not conduct themselves in that manner. They believed that Jews did not know how to take revenge, but only to sacrifice themselves in sanctification of the Divine name.

We then decided to inform the commander of the Otriad that Minin the military commander of the high headquarters, was found shooting four Jews. They told us that they would judge him, but we had not heard any news of a trial against him. On the contrary – he had threatened to take revenge upon us. The commander ordered us that the next day, two of us would travel to the brigade. That is indeed what happened. Two of our partisans traveled with him to the brigade, met with the Natshalik Asabavadiela, and told him about Minin. He assured us that in one week, they would arrange a trial about that matter.

On the designated day, we received an order that our entire group must come to the high headquarters.

Minin was already present, and upon our instructions the entire accusation was laid. He confessed, and defended himself by stating that he had been in a drunken state. After the declaration, the commander convened a general meeting of all the partisans of the high command. There, he read the protocol and demanded that those gathered carry out the sentence. The sentence was death. Everyone agreed that he was deserving of the death penalty.

Then, Minin himself turned to "Charny"[6] asking him if he wanted to shoot him. The answer was: "Yes! I am prepared to shoot such a dog." The order to shoot came immediately, and he shot Minin with 4 bullets – one bullet for each Jew that was shot.

Minin was wearing a fine leather coat. The commander ordered that a certain Zucker (today living in Tel Aviv) who was working as a printer in the high headquarters to remove the coat and keep it as a memento.

The partisans were weak until 1943, for there were many cases where the gentiles turned them in to the Germans. Later the partisans strengthened, and began to take over small settlements. They participated in regional activities and imposed taxes. Thus did they succeed in instilling a bit of fear in the peasant population.

The high command of all the partisans was located in the Pushta, where several thousand partisans were located, spread over an area of a few thousand square kilometers between Minsk, Vilna and Brisk.

Our region was Nowogródek and Nowojelnja. There were still many German soldiers in these towns, for these were two large railway hubs. The first activity of our group was to derail a train from the tracks. Four Jews and two Christians were sent out from the Otriad for this purpose. The Christians went to the Legalczyk when they arrived in the village. Every Otriad had its own Legalczyk. The group was served something to eat, and the Legalczyk went to the train station to find out when a train was coming. He returned and told us that no train was coming that week, because they were being redirected to another point to the right. We decided not to return with empty hands.

We went out into the area of Nowogródek. A peasant told us that he does not know when a train will be coming. However, he told us that the Germans usually arrive during the night. They bring clothing and kerosene, and receive in return butter, eggs, and other products. With this information, we decided to wait until the next morning in order to find out how many Germans come there. We divided ourselves into two groups. One group remained close and the other a bit farther out.

Suddenly, we saw three Germans arriving with sacks. We let them approached. As they came close to us, we opened fire upon them and saw as two fell immediately and the third was wounded. Then, we ordered them to raise their hands. They did so. We brought them to the village. The wounded one gave us important information. Then we brought them to the Pushta to stand trial.

It was clarified that everything that the Germans brought to the gentiles was from the Jews. After the trial, the commander gave the Germans over to my hands to shoot them. I awaited the order of the commander, and took the three Germans to Bielski in the Otriad.

The partisan chief was called Bielski. The commander gathered together all of the elders, women and children from Nowogródek and Nowojelnja, Lida, Baranovichy – Polish Jews and others. Approximately 1,500 hundred Jews whom he took care of and defended were gathered together. The three Germans were brought to them so that they could take revenge upon them. The commander himself gave over the three Germans to the Bielski headquarters as a present.

An older woman, Gittel Barkowski, immediately recognized one of the three Germans as the murderer who took her daughter out of the house and murdered her.

Bielski immediately called together the 1,500 Jews and said to the Germans:

"Here are the Jews with whom you made a great error, intending that you would do to the Jews whatever you want. Now they are here, and they want to take revenge upon you."

The woman Gittel Barkowski was the first to take revenge upon the German who had murdered her daughter. The other Jews carried out the sentence upon the other two.

A short time later, we received the news that a train was to arrive, and we should go about doing our work. When we went further out from our region, we were informed that a train would come that night along the Molodeczner Line.

In Molodeczno, we immediately got in touch with a Legalczyk, who was to give us all the information. He informed us that during that night, a train of soldiers would pass through on its way to Stalingrad. We began to plant mines close to the lines. Then, we distanced ourselves approximately 30 meters. At 3:00 a.m., we heard the train approaching. Then, we distanced ourselves further from the track and waited.

At that point the train began to slow down for the route was hilly. When it came to the mines, they all exploded. We heard the cries of the wounded when we were already quite far from the site. Early in the morning, we sent the Legalczyk to find out information about what happened, and how many Germans were there. He brought us an answer that the entire train was full of Germans – a few hundred Hitler youth.

When we returned to the Pushta, they already knew about our work. The chief immediately wrote on our chart: another train derailed from the line. For every partisan group had its chart in the headquarters.

The high command from Moscow issued an order not to permit the Germans to obtain help from any place that they had used.

One day they called me to the headquarters and told me: You are a Stolpcer and know the area well. There is a settlement called Œwier¿eñ a kilometer from Stolpce. There, there is a sawmill that works for the most part for the German airplanes. The sawmill obtains lumber from the forests. An order was issued by the chief of the sawmill that only Germans could obtain lumber from the sawmill. A few days later, some peasants came to obtain lumber, and he did not let them. We immediately got in touch with our Legalczyk asking him to find out what is going on with the Germans.

The Legalczyk informed us that there were many German aviators in the sawmill who could not travel home. On Sunday morning, the Germans would be sending three automobiles into the forest to put an end to the partisans.

On Saturday night, three Red partisans, belonging to three different groups, were sent out to surround the Germans with fire from all sides. We designated a point near the slaughterhouse approximately one kilometer from the sawmill, that is the point that we figured would be one kilometer from the place from which they would set out to drive, and they would still have to drive 10 kilometers from there.

At approximately 8:00 a.m., we already began hearing them singing: Germany, Germany... meaning that they still had to drive a long way. As they approached somewhat, the order was issued: Fire! None of them succeeded in putting their gun in their hand. All of them were shot. I finished off those who were only wounded. We removed the military fatigues from 90 Germans. All were placed in a pile, and an announcement was made: "Pardon them, Mr. Boss. The next time, when they will send more, they will come in better packaging"...

We returned to the Pushta was a great deal of arms.

In the Bielski Otriad

I met with Bielski and he proposed that I and a group of young partisans should go over to him, for he is having difficulty eating[7]. He has many older men, and the region in which they are located is quite poor. I approached the commander of my Otriad and told him that I wished to join Bielski's Otriad. At first he did not want to let me go, but then he took into account my great service and agreed.

There were several workshops in the Bielski Otriad, where almost everyone was employed. Through this, they greatly helped the partisan groups. There was a tailor workshop, a shoemaking shop, a hairdresser, a large bakery, various leather works, sausage factories, and a gun workshop. There were also hospitals for various illnesses.

I lived well in my new place. I had the feeling that I would end up in the Land of Israel. In general, Bielski's Otriad was called "Jerusalem". I co-opted seven people. The first thing that I did was to bring food. Wherever I went, they knew me as an old acquaintance, for at that time, they felt the fear that I instilled upon the population. Therefore, they treated me with all good things.

I was taken to within a kilometer from Nowogródek, where no partisan foot had yet walked. I obtained food from the population. I collected eight wagons of food in a brief period and then went away, for we began to hear shooting in the direction of Nowogródek. With great haste, I set out to the first point of the partisan regime, where the "Orzinikidzi" Otriad was located. We rested a bit, got something to eat, and fed the horses. The Otriad was 50% Russian and 50% Jewish. When we spoke to the Jews of the Otriad, the Russians, asked who is the commander of the group. I introduced myself to them, and then an order came from their commander: Since you took food from our region, you must give it all over to us.

I answered them: If you can bring in one peasant who can confirm that I took the food from him, it will go to you. Not only this, but also double and multiples. However, they were completely unwilling to give in, and they demanded the eight wagons of food.

I issued an order to lie down and load up the guns. I ordered the Jews of the Orzinikidzi Otriad to quickly distance themselves from there. They fulfilled my order because they were afraid of becoming involved or of mixing in to the matter. I ordered the commander of the Otriad to immediately run away from there.

When they saw that we were not "cold" Jews, but rather Jews who knew how to open fire, they began to distance themselves from the entire matter by saying that they were only joking when they demanded the food from us. However, I stuck hard to my decision that they must move away from there, for the Soviet Union did not have the authority to demand such a thing. When they heard these statements, they ran off. We immediately loaded the horses and returned to our Otriad.

I cannot describe the joy in our Otriad when we arrived with the wagons of food.

1944

In honor of the new year, we decided that the Bielski Otriad must not only sit and eat, but must also take revenge.

Karelic was a small town where there were many Germans, and even more police who subjugated the White Russians. We decided to shake them up a little.

We organized a few young forces and set out for a village not far from Karelic. A few of us acted as if we were drunk, and the others surrounded the village. We saw how a peasant went in to town, most certainly delivering the news that drunken Jewish robbers have arrived. Shortly, we saw an automobile with Germans. As they approached the border of the village, we greeted them with a hail of bullets and fire. Approximately 20 Germans were killed. We took their weapons, returned to the Otriad, and immediately organized new groups.

We organized a group whose task was to derail trains from the tracks. The first train was near Nowojelnja. It was full of weapons. The heads of all the regions arrived and began to divide up the weapons among themselves. Because of this, Bielski's Otriad became known as good fighters.

There was a brigade of Poles close to Bielski's Otriad. From time to time, they permitted themselves to exterminate Jews. Later, they even began to exterminate many Russian partisans.

Once, one of our groups entered a village in order to conduct a piece of work, and encountered the Polish partisans. They invited our group into a house, gave them something to drink, and immediately ordered them to put their hands up. They removed their weapons, and took them out into the forest at night to shoot them. Only one of them, Itche Berl, a youth from Rubezhevichi, succeeded in getting away in the following manner: At the time that the Polish partisans returned to the village in order to send peasants to bury those who were shot, he succeeded in escaping. He went to the Otriad and told them everything.

The chief command was immediately told about the matter. They transmitted the information to Moscow. A command was immediately issued from Moscow to remove the weapons from the Poles.

A few partisan Otriads organized themselves, and went out to the Poles to remove their weapons.

A plebiscite was conducted in the morning: who wishes to remain with the partisans and who wants to go home. All had to register. The camp had several thousand people, and only a few dozen chose to remain.

Those of the Poles who registered to remain as partisans were grouped into one Otriad told us that they had a directive to murder all Jewish and Russian partisans. Their headquarters was located in England, under the leadership of Nikolajczyk. The camp which was supposed to remain free was free to go to the other world...[8]

We then resumed our work of derailing trains and providing food for the old people, men and women.

June 1944

When the German army began to retreat, we received a command to remain on guard, for the Germans were retreating through the Pushta.

Thousands of Germans appeared. The Pushta was full with them, and since all the partisans were concentrated there, the Germans had to content with them.

Not one German left the Pushta alive.

Around July 20, a group of approximately 1,000 Germans suddenly appeared not far from our Otriad. Bielski issued a command to clean out all the Germans. We went out to them and negotiated with them to get them to surrender. Their answer was that they were willing to surrender to the Russians, but not to the partisans.

We immediately responded with fire. Another Otriad came to assist us when they heard our shooting. We and they finished it off. During the shooting, another large group of Germans approached our Otriad. Unfortunately, 10 people fell from our side, including young women.

A few hours later, another large group of Germans arrived. We immediately took up new points, and opened fire upon them. This lasted for 15 minutes. We sent a delegation to meet with a delegation from the Russian army. We were very happy, although our joy was mitigated due to the loss of 10 people, who fell in the last minute before the liberation. The Red Army arrived about 10 minutes later. It is impossible to describe what each of us felt at that time. The first question that each of us had was whether anyone from our families was still alive?

A command was issued that everyone to leave the reason and immediately return to his place. We returned to Nowogródek.

After the Liberation

On the first day, we guarded German captives whom we put to work. Each of us supervised 100 Germans.

A command was issued that all partisans must register. We were going to continue to conduct the war. All were informed that a command was issued to go to the front near Warsaw.

In the meantime, many Germans and White Russians concentrated around the points of the partisans. Then a command was issued that some of the partisans must remain to exterminate the remaining Germans in the forests.

The Istrobitelne battalion remained and joined up with the Otriads, and we began to conduct a battle. Every day, the "heroes" had to be given over to us, and we took captives.

Then they sent me to Vilna as a member of the militia. From there, I went to Kovno. There, I discussed with a group that, as the Red Army leaves, we should make our way to Romania, and from there, we would steal our way to the Land of Israel. This plan did not work out, for we were not able to reach the border of Romania. Therefore, we had to return to Kovno, where we lived until 1945, when Warsaw was taken.

We consulted with some of our group and decided to go to Warsaw. In Warsaw, I immediately met with Antek Cukierman, and we talked about the Land of Israel. "We were already waiting for a long time", said Antek. I assured him that I would return the week after next, for I wanted first to go to Sochaczew to see if any of my family or townsfolk were still alive.

I arrived in Sochaczew on April 30, 1945. I met Hershel Gothelf and his wife, Pinia Wajnberg and his wife, and a few other Jews. They told me that unfortunately, none of my family is alive. I went to see the yard in which we lived. When I saw that a Pole lived in our house, I immediately returned to the group of surviving Jews. I told them that I am immediately moving on, for the city of Sochaczew is no longer our city.

TRANSLATOR'S FOOTNOTES:

1. This term, used several times in this chapter, seems to refer to a local who served as an intermediary between the local population and the partisans.
2. Pushta is the Russian word for forest.
3. Otriad is a Russian word for a partisan detachment.
4. Probably a reference to local gentiles. Hebrew word is 'goyim'.
5. Charny (or variants thereof) means 'dark' or 'black' in Slavic languages.
6. He is speaking in the third person here, as it seems that Charny is the author himself.
7. Probably a euphemism for 'doing business'.
8. I suspect that this is a euphemism indicating that after this admission, they killed off the Polish partisans.

{533}

The Last Ones of a Family

Machla Lewin-Botler

Translated by Jerrold Landau

Maniek, the son of Shlomo Lewin.

In 1945, when the bloody war ended, I immediately wrote a few letters to my brother in Sochaczew, not knowing if he was living. I also wrote to P. Wajnberg, asking him if he had met anyone from my family on the way. I did not receive an answer. A few months later, I received an answer from Wajnberg's wife, in which she told me what had happened with her husband, and told me that she had seen nobody from my family.

The hope of finding anyone from my family died, and I felt doubly alone.

Some time later I received a notice from the Organization for the Search of Relatives under the auspices of the Jewish Agency, informing me that somebody was searching for me. It is easy to imagine my feelings. I literally shook from joy and expectation. I could barely wait until morning. I then went to the agency and found out that my brother's son Maniek was searching for me. He was the only one that remained alive of the entire family.

However, Maniek was sick, and the Joint [1] sent him to Italy. A different Jew was able to go to the Land of Israel on his certificate.

We corresponded in this manner until 1951. Then I traveled to Italy to bring Maniek to the Land. The joy upon our meeting was indescribable.

I traveled from Rome to Grotta Ferrata, where the institution in which my Maniek lived was located. We were both almost silent for the entire way. Finally, near the end, Maniek began to explain that immediately after the liberation, he went to Sochaczew to search for anyone from the family. However, he found nobody. He did encounter my letter with my address. His mother and two sisters were deported to Treblinka. He does not know what became of his father (my brother). He described how he had seen death before his eyes many times.

There were 360 young people in the institution in Italy in which he was housed. All of them loved him, and everyone was involved with him. He was a handsome and intelligent young man. I will never forget the few weeks that I was in Italy together with him. I loved Maniek with my full heart, just like my own child. He did not return with me, though, as he wished to complete his studies in Italy.

Some time passed. Finally, he decided to embark on his long awaited trip to Israel on July 26th 1952. However his fate was otherwise. I received a telegram on July 10th that I must come to Italy immediately, as Maniek was seriously ill. I arrived in Italy after a six-hour flight.

I was in Rome. I stayed by Maniek's sickbed and watched as he was dying. I watched as he was dying, and could not do anything to help him. I was powerless. I requested a permit from the management of the institution to take Maniek to Israel, even though I knew that I would not be able to take him. He would die on the way. The management refused.

On July 11, Maniek gave up his pure, tormented soul. He left behind a will that I should bring his body to Israel.

Six years have now passed, and this remains with me as a stone upon my heart. His last words that he whispered to me are etched upon my memory: "You see, when I will be able to travel to the land of Israel... to the Land of Israel".

His last words accompany my every step.

The last of the family.

{536}

From Among the First Victims
Rozka Szmulewicz (Rozenperl)
Translated by Jerrold Landau

Left: Avraham. Center: Hentche. Right: Aharon. The children of Reb Shlomo Rozenperl.

From among the first victims of Sochaczew, there is Chaim Leib Liberman, his wife Tirza, their daughter Esther, and their sons Yehoshua and Yaakov (Rozka and her older brother were in Warsaw.}

Since that family did not have time to flee from Sochaczew with all of the Jews, they fled to Kampinos. Shlomo Rozenperl's son Aharon and two Jews from Grodzisk whose names I do not remember were with them.

At the time that the Germans marched into Sochaczew and Kampinos, that group of Jews was taken from their hiding place by the Germans, due to an informant. They were all shot.

The oldest son Yaakov fell down from great terror. The Germans thought that he was dead. After the shooting, the Germans abused the dead -- and even the living Yaakov. He let them do what they were doing and did not demonstrate any sign of life. He lay with the corpses for a long period of time, until he heard that everything was quiet around him. He then stood up and buried his father, his brother Yehoshua, Aharon Rozenperl, and the Grodzisker Jews. He made a marker, and fled to Blonie. There, Avraham Rozenperl and his sister Hentche made every effort to bring the shot people back to Sochaczew for burial. However, all efforts ended with nothing. Later they succeeded – for a large sum of money – to bring them to Blonie for burial. That was in the winter of 1940.

The son who was the witness to this went with all of the Jews to the Warsaw ghetto. There he was captured during a roundup. Where he was taken is not known.

Bracha and Avraham Hirsch Libfreund, Rachl (nee Holcman), murdered by the Nazis.

A Memorial to our Fellow Native Yechezkel Adamczyk

M. L.

Translated by Jerrold Landau

Yechezkel Adamczyk of blessed memory.

The name of Yechezkel Adamczyk should be mentioned in our registry of martyrs with praise and love for his good character traits and good deeds, which he did with his heart and soul.

All of the Sochaczewers who served together with him in the Polish army in 1920 will never forget him.

TRANSLATOR'S FOOTNOTES:

1. The Joint Distribution Committee.

{539}

My Grandfather's Home
by Esther Shoham
Translated by Jerrold Landau

Today permit me to sing
About Sochaczew
The town in which my mother
Took her first steps.
Where my grandmother piously
Lit the Sabbath candles,
And my grandfather uprightly
Conducted his life.

In my grandfather's house
One could hear Torah,
Business discussions
Were also heard from his mouth.
It was noisy with grandchildren
Daughter-in-law and daughter
A joyous intermingling
Of holy and secular.

The twisted challas
Glance forth discretely
They tried hard
To bake them earlier.
The aromas
Of the tasty food entice,
The Sabbath Queen is arriving
She is already standing at the door.

Sabbath in the morning,
The grandchildren are still sleeping,
From the large room
Praying is heard.
The sweet melody of
The Torah reading awakens them,
They pay attention
Enchanted and thoughtful.

But now – where is the kingdom
Of my dear Grandfather?
Disrupted is the house
Which was always prepared
To make a wedding for a poor orphan

And no poor person
Had to leave empty handed.

Disappeared – gone
Like a lovely dream,
My grandmother is not here, my grandfather
Is no longer here.
And my mother had already for a long time
Been with them both,
Leaving me only with
Sadness and a tear.

For the loss
Of the holy purity,
For the heartfelt truth
Jewish grace.
The winds of fate
Blew it all away,
As if it
Never was.

But no – it has been so long
That my mind cannot comprehend
So long that blood
Flows through my veins.
For so long do they
Yet live in my imagination,
Indeed they did not
Live for naught.

Through thousands of miles
And decades of years,
Their voices yet ring to me
Day in and day out –
And sweeter than wine
Are my memories,
The blessing still beckons to me
From my grandfather's home!

{542}

The "Transfer"

Y. P.

Translated by Jerrold Landau

In the year 1948, the Tz. K. Jewish Historical Institute of Jews in Poland opened up a scientific investigation by T. Brustyn-Bernsztajn called "Transfer in the Warsaw Ghetto during the Time of the

German Occupation (1941-1942)". In that work, one can find official data regarding the number of Jews in Sochaczew prior to and during the German occupation.

According to table number 1, the number of Jews in the region of Sochaczew and Blonie was 19,000 in 1939, and 16,818 in 1940 – 16.818.

The data indicates a great change in the territorial division of the Jewish population that started after the completion of the war operations in December 1939, and mass transfer in the Generalgouvernement of Jews out of the province of "Warthenau" in East Prussia, which began in November 1939, and did not lose its momentum until January 1940.

"As a result of the transfer from these places that were incorporated into the Reich, the number of Jews in the Warsaw district grew…"

The author demonstrates the contradictions in the German sources from that time.

"The estimates exaggerated the number of Jews in Warthau Land… The Jewish source, constructed from the Joint material, describes a budgetary project for the assistance activity in the Warsaw district (excluding Warsaw), and the general number of Jews in the Warsaw district (excluding Warsaw) is approximately 250,000.

The author further states:

"One must regard these numbers exclusively in a general manner, and the number of Jews in 1939-1940 remains concealed, just as all previous numbers, for everything was an estimate."

These estimates will be left for the specialists. We are more interested in the migration, or as the author calls it: the transfer of the Jews from their places of residence to Warsaw, and their life there. It the chapter "The Transfer Politics" it states:

"The Jews from the western districts, that is from the Grodzisk, Sochaczew, Blonie, Lowicz, Skierniewice, and the western portion of the Warsaw district were transferred to Warsaw during the first quarter of the year 1941. For the most part they lived in areas for refugees. The greatest percent of those refugees died from hunger and communicable diseases caused by the meager conditions during their 1.5 years there. Human resources for the work camps were recruited first and foremost from among the refugees, and the first transports of Jews that were sent to Treblinka to be killed were from among the refugees."

The bitter fate of the refugees in Warsaw was the end of a long death process from hunger and epidemics that the author mentions: The transfer from the borders of the districts in the western area of the Warsaw district and the region of Warsaw-Land; the description of dark ghettos; the emptying of settlements in villages; brick factories; and at the end he also mentions – Sochaczew.

"In the regions of Blonie and Sochzaczew, the populations of five towns were gathered: Grodzisk, Sochaczew, Blonie, Mszczonow and Wiskitki… The Zyrardow Ghetto, which was cordoned off in December 1940, was settled with 900 Jews from Sochaczew (Ringelblum's archive, 353). The ordinance to create a ghetto in Sochaczew first appeared in the city after the time when a portion of the Jews of Sochaczew was shipped to Zyrardow. The remaining residents of Sochaczew were settled in the ghetto on January 24th and 25th, 1941"…

{544}

The Publication of the Book Du Prel
Magistrate Blumental
Translated by Jerrold Landau

The county office of Sochaczew-Blonie was composed of the former districts of Sochaczew and Blonie, and also of the city of Zyrardow. Four village regions that were close to the Wisla were included in East Prussia.

The county of Sochzczew-Blonie is approximately 1,690 square kilometers in size. Approximately 235,000 residents live there; including 4,000 Volksdeutchen. It is composed of 5 civic districts and 19 villages. The following are the cities:

    Zyrardow with 30,000 residents
    Groszisk with 18,000 residents
    Sochaczew with 13,000 residents
    Blonie with 8,000 residents
    Mszczonow with 5,000 residents

Prior to the world war (?)[1] the number of Jews in the town was ¾ of the population. See 355[2].

In the first edition of the official guide to the Generalgouvernement in Poland in 1940: "Dr. Mase Freiherr du Prel: "Das Deutsche General-Gouwernement Polen", the following statement is made regarding the city and district of Sochaczew.

The area of the district is 2,126 square kilometers, and consists of 5 free cities and 20 village organizations; 233,000 residents live there, including 8,000 Volksdeutschen and 20,000 Jews (See 210).

The county capital of Sochaczew, with 13,000 residents, is the seat of the county chief. At that time, it was Karl Adolf Patt. Branch offices of the county leadership were in Zyrardow (29,800 residents; land commissar was Wilhelm Denk), and in Grodzisk (18,600 residents; land commissar Richard Lisberg) (see 206, 207).

It is interesting that in the second edition of that book (from 1942) the number of Jews is no longer given; apparently the publisher knew that the Jews had already partially "disappeared" and the same fait awaits the few Jews that are still alive.

Regarding the ruins of the church, which was confused with a synagogue building, an official German publication gives the year as 1942, but it was really in 1911!

{546}

On the Ruins
by L. Fursztenberg
Translated by Jerrold Landau

Wherever I was on my wanderings since the time that I left Sochaczew on an autumn September day in 1939, I have always pined for my hometown. It is sufficient to close my eyes for me to see my town with its streets and lanes, even every alleyway, and the houses with their residents. Always before my eyes is the large market square and the new walking path by the Bzura where I used to bathe on summer days and spend time on the Sabbath. I lived there for 27 years and knew every stone. Then the bloody nightmare came. I realized that all those near to me were tortured by the Germans. Thus do I look upon my hometown.

In April 1946, after a seven year absence, I returned to Sochaczew, and I did not recognize the town. I could simply not believe that I was in the town in which I had lived for so many years.

Traveling to Sochaczew with a palpitating heart, visions from yesteryear floated before my eyes. I thought that, if nothing else, something would be remaining there and I would at least find a few Jews – perhaps someone from my family or perhaps a friend.

"Arriving in Sochaczew", shouted the conductor over my thoughts. I got out of the car. No! He must have made a mistake. I stood there numb, not moving from the place and not uttering a word – for there is nobody to whom to do so. This must be a hoax before my eyes. My head is pounding. Could this be my native town? I was standing in the place where Mendel Ajzensztadt's tavern used to be. All of the cars used to stop there. Now I see only an empty quadrangle there, lit up, sown with grass, even with benches put out – now it is a park. There, in the empty place beginning from the church until Kolejowa Street (Lewkowicz's house), the entire Jewish population was concentrated. Here, there were many fine houses. There was the narrow Shul-alleyway that led to the synagogue. All of the funerals passed by here on the way to the cemetery. Here stood the Beis Midrash with the eastern wall that abutted the mikva (ritual bath). A little farther on was the beautiful building of the Yavneh School, upon which was posted a large tablet with the inscription "Talmud Torah, Founded by the Sochaczew Relief Committee of Chicago". We then approach a tiny house which apparently had been part of a larger building – the location of the Jewish communal offices which were led for many years by Reb Yosef Wolkowicz. How many houses, how much Judaism had been in this corner of the city! If I was not mistaken, aside from one gentile, a shoemaker who lived in the house of "Yellow Beker", there are not even any gentiles living there.

Now the entire Jewish quarter is overgrown with roots. Even the foundations of the houses have been dismantled, without even leaving a remnant. That area that was once teaming with Jewish life, with many Jewish children, grandmothers, grandfathers, is now calm and peaceful – a square, sown with fresh, green grass...

On the other side of the market, the south side, Jewish mothers would walk with their strollers. There was a great deal of sun there. There was an entire row of Jewish houses, starting from Trajanower Street and extending until the new brick Magistrate building which contained many shops (Izik Waldenberg's house). Where are the houses of the Nelsons, Gerszt, Brot, Zajac, and Velvel Pinczewski Who now comes to the entire row of Jewish shops where Jews used to earn their living? And the last shop of Baruch Mordechai Cohen – a tiny general store – where has everything sunk?

Yes, the Magistrate building is whole, nothing has moved, exactly as it was from those days. It would have been a shame for those German murderers to destroy the Magistrate building. Germans built it during the occupation time of the First World War. In that Magistrate building, Jews were 50% of the council members, and there was a Jewish vice-mayor. And the mayor himself, despite being a gentile, was "one of us". They would refer to him as "the Zydowski Burmistrz" (Jewish mayor), for he was elected with Jewish votes and had to accede to Jewish demands.

Parne Street led out from the Magistrate building. Today it is empty and vacant. The Jewish houses and their residents were destroyed by the German murderers. They destroyed everything. There are not even any ruins of the houses left behind, they are covered with earth.

Here also are the houses of the Wajnbergs and the Czerwonieks, where the leader of the Zionist movement, the veteran Zionist activist Reb Simcha Grundwag used to live. Further on is Rozenperl's house and other small Jewish houses where Jewish laborers used to live. All of this no longer exists.

I arrived at the Farmer's Market. First I encountered the second building, the "Straszacke Shop". I recall various images from yesteryear: Jewish cultural events, readings, administrative meetings at which people battled, shouted and ranted, dance evenings, Keren Kaymet bazaars, and workers' meetings where the lofty struggle between the Bund and the Communists took place. The best Jewish actors performed on the boards of the small stage, such as: Ida Kaminska, Wyslice, Orleska, Maurice Lampa, Wladimir Gudak with all the demons, and the half resident of Sochaczew – Jack Lewi. How much Jewish spiritual life, how much esthetic pleasure took place in that very "shop" where the Sochaczew dramatic club was led by the talented Nachum Grundwag until the final days. How many blows did we, the white group of friends, receive from the old gentile Wrubel, the guard of the "Straszacke Shope" for coming into the hall for a performance, a concert or a lecture without a ticket.

Now it is deathly silent and gloomy. One meets very few people here in the market. Not the Jewish Shlomoles, Mosheles, Chanales, who used to cross the large marketplace with their ringing voices as they were playing.

As I was seeking the footprints of the pre-Holocaust Jewish life, I set out for the cream of the crop of Jewry – the rabbis house and the Beis Midrash.

Apparently, fate had it that a tiny remnant should remain as a memorial to the eminent Sochaczew courtyard. The Rebbe's Beis Midrash remained standing, and was not destroyed. However, woe to the state in which I found it. Who lives there and defiled it...

I recall that during those "good" times, we did not give the appropriate respect to those holy places. The Rebbe's Beis Midrash always served as Baumarder's small soap factory. More than once my group snuck into the Rebbe's orchard. There was fruit of all kinds, and there was no guard. We already knew what to do there. However at the same time I used to like to go into the destroyed rooms of the Rebbe. Images of various birds, palm trees and fruit of the Land of Israel such as grape vines and oranges were painted on the walls. Children would sit there and tell various stories. The Rebbe's room would inject a sort of fear mixed with reverence into our group.

Now everything is lonesome, strange and un-Jewish. I left that holy place in a broken mood. Sochaczew Jewry had been destroyed with all of its holiness.

The other half of the city was more alive. However, not like previously. Many people glanced at me. It seemed to me that soon I would encounter an acquaintance. I went quickly, nervously – was it indeed true that Sochaczew was indeed Judenrein, with no Jews left?

Suddenly I heard someone calling my name from a shop. I trembled, perhaps there was indeed someone? I entered the shop. No, this was Tzipora the apostate, the blot on our Sochaczew – she who embarrassed and mocked not only her pious father but also the entire Jewish city. She survived by remaining in hiding. For the Germans she remained a Jewess...

She peppered me with questions. She was interested in every surviving Jew – everything that was connected with Jewry. In our discussion she interspersed a few Yiddish words, as if she wanted to find out if she still knew a bit of her mother tongue.

I quickly left her. I was interested to see if there was any other surviving Jew. I went onto the Warszawska Highway. Nothing much had changed, except that the Jews were missing. I went into the street along which we used to go to the yard of the landowner (poretz) of Czerwonka. The street was as it was. The police building, the "dom Lodawi", and also the house of the "spole's", the large new building of the post office and the starosta – everything was as it was except... Now we are approaching Yosef Wolkowicz' house – the Jewish building is no longer there. Michalski's mill functions as before, with the entire apparatus, but they are no longer their own. The mill was nationalized. Now he is a worker there.

A new park was planted right by the mill in 1932. There used to be a horse market there every Tuesday and Friday, and we would play football there every Sunday evening. The oaks in that park have grown very tall, but there is no Jewish youth to admire them.

I did not want to go further on to the hospital on Trajanower Street. Everything was in order there. That was always a Christian area. I do recall, however how young couples in love would walk to the waterfall at Shabtai Libert's mill and watch with romantic glances for hours as the water noisily and powerfully turned the wheels of the mill. I do not want to go farther! Shabtai Libert and his family are not there, and the wonderful Sochaczew youth who used to stroll there are also no longer there. The waterfall continues to noisily spray its frothy waves, but no longer for Jews...

I turn back to Warszawska Street the second half of the street, starting from the Kolejowe. That half of the city was almost as it was. Most of the houses still stand, and are untouched. Just like the beginning – the new house of Czerniewski, opposite the houses of Bajernaczis and Hafenung. Further on is Mone Breslaw's small house, Borensztejn's and Chaikel Kara's house, Yisrael Rojtsztejn's houses, as well as that of the Holc's. That entire length of street was untouched. It seemed to me that I might enter the shops and chat with their Jewish inhabitants Gothelf, Kac, Plonski. Right here was the bungalow of Berl Ogledzki, who would sell anything from a need to a book or a newspaper with a joke, a chuckle and a good word. Opposite it was Zajac's fashion workshop and Biezanski's paint factory. Further on was Skotnicki's house, built in partnership with the gentile butcher Klott. The gentile's house still stands, and he continues to sell his non-kosher merchandise, but the feldscher's (medic's) house was reduced to its foundation. Not a great deal has changed in all the aforementioned houses – only the shopkeepers are newly arrived Polish homeowners, taking the place of the true ones, the Jews.

Chil-Meir Talman's three-story mansion, which was like a small village, is missing from the center of Warszawska Street. In this house one could find everything – various shops, a bank, organization, shtibels, all sorts of tradesmen, a shochet (ritual slaughterer), a scribe, a mohel (circumciser). The entire house was inhabited by dear, warm hearted Jews, and one gentile – a superintendent.

Wolf-Itche Galek with his wife Malka.

The post office. Images again float before me. How much Jewishness was in the post office! It was always full of Jews sending letters, telegrams and packages. They sent and received items from relatives in America, and arranged various monetary transactions with other cities. Boys and girls set the post office as a meeting place, where they would begin their "romantic" alliances. Of course, only gentiles worked in the post office. (I wish to make mention here of the postal official Przybysz, who was a friend of the Jews. He played the fiddle, made friends with Jews, and taught a young boy without means to play the fiddle without monetary compensation.)

It is worthwhile to enter the post office in order to see how it looks without Jews. I ascend the few steps. The post office was quiet. One customer stood there, and three officials looked at me through their windows, considering me as some sort of stranger. A melancholy and hollowness pervades there. I want to explain to them that despite the fact that Sochaczew Jewry was liquidated, a remnant remains, and there remains a great hope of continuity and existence. I order a postcard. I fill it with Yiddish letters and write the address with large clear letters, and I write only one word with Latin characters: ISRAEL.

For the last time in Sochaczew, I sent a postcard to my friend in the Land of Israel. I presented it to the window, and asked how many stamps I need. The employee, a woman whom I remembered from former times, was confused. She took the card and ran to ask the official. She did not know the price for it had been many years since such a strange postcard had passed through her hands. She returned, looked at me apparently without recognizing me, and told me the price without lifting up her eyes. I did not know why she did not look at me. Perhaps she understood something of the crime against our Sochaczew Jews, or perhaps she regretted that someone survived who writes Yiddish and was irritated with the fact that despite everything, Jews still remain and have their own place on the globe where they write with their own language. Secondly, I was wondering if my final letter from Sochaczew would reach its destination, or would the anti-Semitic officials destroy it. I left the post office without even saying "good day", and went on my final walk through the streets of Sochaczew. (The postcard arrived and can be found in Israel today.)

I had already almost walked through the entire town. To my great dismay, I found no Jews. Sochaczew was indeed Judenrein. The dream of the Sochaczew anti-Semites was indeed fulfilled. What they had not accomplished through various political and economic struggles against Jews, they achieved via the Hitlerist murderers. With fire, swords and gas ovens, the Germans actualized the ideals of the Polish nationalists.

Indeed, there was still one place in Sochaczew where one could find a memorial to the Jews – the Jewish cemetery. Binyamin Greber was certainly no longer there with his cemetery hut, but the monuments and the canopies of the Tzadikim of Sochaczew would certainly remain. What could they have against the dead? Thus was I thinking as I walked along the way to the place of eternal rest of our ancestors. However, there, an image unfolded before my eyes that remains etched in my memory forever, and that will always evoke hate and wrath against the desecrators of the graves of generations of Sochaczew Jews. I saw before me a field overgrown with wild grass, no grave markers, no monuments, and not one brick of the canopies over the graves of the great Sochaczew Rebbes. However, it was not empty. On the contrary, it was noisy and joyful, with horses running around and cows and goats grazing, defiling the holy ground in which the bones of our dear ones lie.

Animals graze in the destroyed Sochaczew cemetery.

I poured out my entire bitter heart, my great agony, and my great pain that has been building up all day on the shepherd girls. They did not say very much to me, but muttered something under their breath. However, on my command they had to round up the flocks and leave the holy place.

One marker remains indeed remains in the Jewish cemetery, like a bloody blot on the brow of the anti-Semitic Polish murderers. The monument over the grave of the youth, Pinchas Wajnberg, who was murdered by the Poles, remains. It is hard to describe the agonizing experiences and tough perseverance through which a Jew was able to remain alive during the bloody Hitler days. This happened with perhaps 30 Sochaczew Jews, among which was the young Wajnberg. His murderers were practicing more than homicide, more than Hitlerism. It is hard to comprehend what it means to lose one's life and suffer so many other tribulations in a terrible fashion on the day when the war ended.

The Survivors – Survivors from Sochaczew in Germany.

I bow my head over the fresh grave. I left the cemetery physically broken, agonized, and with great feelings of revenge.

Evening was falling. The sun was setting over the other side of the Bzura River. I must flee from Sochaczew very quickly. How terrible it sounds: to flee from my Sochaczew for which I had pined and waited for the moment that I could return. I decide to leave very quickly, not only from my hometown, but also from the land with its people, from the soil that soaked up the blood of our parents, brothers, sisters and young children...

Sochaczewers who returned from Russia.

{557}

Sochaczewers in the Land of Israel
Sochaczewers in America

{558}

Sochaczewers in Israel
by Yerucham Ejnes
Translated by Jerrold Landau

The thought of the return to Zion strengthened greatly after the First World War and after the Balfour Declaration. In our city as well there were many more adherents, not only from among the youth, but also from older, well-established householders. From the pulpits of the synagogues, emissaries from the Land of Israel appealed to the crowd to help build up the Land of Israel. The audience did not remain indifferent. The idea was spun in the hearts about a future in the Land of Israel, if not for themselves, then at least for their children.

Aharon Frydman Ish-Shalom of blessed memory traveled to Israel in 1920. His brother Yaakov of blessed memory also became involved in Zionist activities and traveled to Israel in 1921 together with his wife Rachel. My revered father Hertzke Ejnes left Sochaczew at the end of 1921 and made aliya to the Land of Israel. Machla Lewin-Butler and Miriam Lewin went in 1922.

The life of the new arrivals was not easy. The land was desolate. It was hard to find work. The prime work at the time was paving roads and draining swamps. People worked in terrible swamps and contracted fever. Cheap Arab labor worked in the orchards, and it was not easy to compete with them.

.Zalman Albert's wife Tauba Leah and her children, Fishel Wajnberg (Yisrael Karmi), Yosef Grundwag (the son of Simcha Grundwag of blessed memory), Moshe Frydman, Yitzchak Wajnstock, the Ejnes family, Bluma Wajnberg, Mendel Zaonc, Yisrael Balas, Eliezer Zalcman, Wolf Itche Geller, Yaakov Zadkoni (Rechtman) Moshe Brzezinski (Levanon), Rachel Wajnberg (Levanon), Moshe Ber Czerwank, Baruch Zalcman, Noach Walman and Itche Frydman all made aliya from Sochaczew to the Land of Israel in 1924, together with the so-called fourth aliya.

A larger aliya did not take place. The burden of earning of a livelihood was heavy for our Sochaczew Jews, and unfortunately, they did not have the energy and courage to leave...

Furthermore, not all of those who did come were able to adjust to the climate and the difficult living conditions. Those who had come earlier made efforts to help the newcomers. Yaakov Frydman organized the first work group, composed solely of Sochaczewers. The group existed for a long time, and when it disbanded its members went to Afula. Machla Lewin-Butler lived there with her husband, and she concerned herself with finding work for the Sochaczewers.

{559}

Gathering of Sochaczew Jews in Israel

Founding meeting, 1945.

A gathering of Sochaczewers in Israel with their fellow native Fleischman from America.

The first building group organized by Yaakov Frydman of blessed memory.

The following live in Afula: Moshe Levanon, Mendel Zaonc, Yisrael Balas, Frumowicz, Yosef Grundwag, Wajnstock, Czerwank and others. They lived together, they cooked together, and they took care of those who were unemployed. When the work in Afula finished, they turned to Aharon Frydman the head of the Y.R.Ch. group in Jerusalem to provide them with work. Aharon wrote that they should come to Jerusalem to take part in the work. They traveled to Jerusalem, and worked for Y.R.Ch. It was said that this should have been called the Sochaczew group.

Nevertheless, not all of the Sochaczewers were able to acclimatize themselves to the conditions, and some left the Land. There were approximately 80 Sochaczew families in the Land at the time of the outbreak of the Second World War. None of us was oblivious to what was going on with our families who remained in Sochaczew.

The Audit Committee of the Organization of Sochaczew Natives in Israel, 1957-1962.}

Sitting from right to left: Committee members Elchanan Katz, Shlomo Frydman, Yosef Grundwag. Standing from right to left: Leib Fursztenberg (Audit Committee), Golda Kirshbaum (Administrative Committee member), Shlomo Swiatlowski, Nathan Kipper (Audit Committee).

Missing from the photo is the Administrative Committee member Hertzke Graubard.

{561}

The Organization of Sochaczew Natives in Israel

It was September 1939. Tragic news came to us from Poland. Every day, the radio brought us news of Polish cities that fell to the Germans and of battles that were taking place near Sochaczew. On September 27, when Warsaw was taken, the Jews of Poland found themselves under the Nazi talon.

Dreadful news came from occupied Poland. New, terrifying concepts came from there: ghettos, aktions, roundups, Umschlag Platz, crematoria… The human mind cannot conceive of such horrors.

With the first call for help that came to us from the afflicted people, the Sochaczewers in Israel gathered together. The gathering took place in the home of Moshe Levanon on the intermediate days of Passover of 5705 (1945). From the news that was told to us, the extent of the terrible misfortune and the need to create an organization to help those in need and ease the pain of the survivors became clear. The "Organization of Sochaczew Natives in Israel" was founded. The first committee consisted of the members: Yaakov Frydman, Moshe Levanon, Yerucham Ejnes, and Moshe Eliezer Bornstein.

The organization made efforts to get in touch with the survivors who were scattered across Poland, Germany, Russia, etc.

The committee, and especially the chairman Yaakov Frydman, spend a great deal of time until they were able to make contact and establish a correspondence with them. Every letter told of the difficult experiences and tribulations that each person had experienced. It became clear that we should not only provide them with moral support, but that they also require material assistance to bring them to the Land, for they had lost everything. First and foremost they require a roof over their heads, and the means to set their lives in order.

The first sum of money came to use from the relief organization of our American townsfolk. The term "gemilut chesed" (doing of charitable deeds) was also well known to our Israeli townsfolk. The gemilut chesed cassa that was set up collected over 7,000 pounds, and obtained significant loans without interest and without the need for guarantors.

When the survivors started to arrive in Israel, it became clear that we must create a warm atmosphere for them. Various festivities were organized at which all of the natives of the town gathered together. A bond between all of us was forged. It is also worthwhile to note that we all participated in any joyous occasion of one of our townsfolk, or, Heaven forbid, a tragedy.

The presidium at a memorial gathering.

The organization also organized receptions for our Sochaczewers who came to visit Israel. Among others, the following people visited over the years: Itche Fleischman of blessed memory, Yisrael Brafman and his wife, Aryeh Muney and his wife, Moshe Schwartz, Pesia Fursztenberg and her husband, Shlomo Schmeiser, Chaim Nelson and his wife, David Wolrat and his wife, Speishendler and his wife and daughter. Recently our friends Chazan and his wife, Landau and his wife and Zabocki and his wife came to visit.

The ceremony to memorialize our martyrs takes place every year on the 29 th of Shvat. On that day, all of the Sochaczewers in the Land come together in order to publicly remember the destruction of our community. It is also timely and necessary for us to collect all the facts about the destruction of our community with its thousands of people. It was decided to found a historical committee which will collect everything that is connected to the life and destruction of our community in order to publish a book as a monument that will inform future generations of our life and our tragic destruction.

Sochaczewers from throughout the Land at a memorial for their martyrs.

Over time the Committee of Sochaczew Natives has requested several times that we not neglect our duty imposed upon us by fate to relieve the pain of those who endured the Hitlerist hell.

The life of the survivors in Israel was not easy. However the feeling that they are among our own has helped them to slowly lay down roots and organize themselves.

The spark of mutual assistance was not extinguished in the Jews of Sochaczew. It came to expression with the Organization of Sochaczew Natives and also through the activities of our committees that guard the memory of our martyrs and maintain the contact among our townsfolk.

As well, Rabbi Chanoch (Henech) Bornstein, the son of Rabbi Shmuel (the Shem Mishmuel) continued the traditions of Sochaczew Hassidism. His Hassidim travel to Jerusalem to their Rebbe, hear from him the Sochaczewer style of Torah, and continue on with the golden chain of Sochaczew Hassidism.

The Rebbe Rabbi Henech, the son of the Shem Mishmuel, who continues the tradition of Sochaczewer Hassidism in Jerusalem.

A Monument for a Dear Soul
by S. Swiatlowski
Translated by Jerrold Landau

Moshe Aharon Widelec of blessed memory.

Moshe Aharon, the son of Yechiel Widelec, had to start working already before his Bar Mitzvah.

In order to help with the livelihood in the house, he joined the ranks of the leftist circles.

During the time of the Spanish Civil War, he hid with a friend of his in the international Warsaw-Berlin-Paris train, with the intention of enlisting in the international brigade that fought on the side of the Spanish revolutionaries against the Dictator Franco. However, he was captured at the German border and shipped back to Poland.

He spent the last war under the Nazi talons and in Russian Siberia.

He came to the Land with his family broken and tired out from all of his wanderings. However, this did not deter him. With newfound strength, he set up a home for his family. He would express his contentment to all natives of his town. He was always prepared to help anybody in any way he could.

As he was driving his bicycle, he unfortunately slipped and lost his life at the age of 43.

A true lover of his fellowman and of the Jewish people passed away.

{568}

Yizkor

Translated by Jerrold Landau

Hertzke Ejnes, Chana Jalow (Ejnes), Sara Kaszman (Lewin), Reb Hershel Brzezinski

When one builds up a land such as the Land of Israel, every person who dies naturally or falls victim to the building of the Land is very precious.

Even though the group of Sochaczewites is small, they already have four graves in the Land of Israel.

It is our duty to perpetuate their names in our book, for they came to the Land of Israel and participated in its upbuilding in accordance with their powers. Not wishing to enter into an analysis of what brought them to the Land of Israel, the main point is: they indeed came to the Land of Israel and participated. "Even if only one brick in the wall was built", it is considered as if they participated. The bitter fate shortened their life and they died. It was certainly difficult and supernatural that they could not overcome physically.

When I arrived in the Land of Israel 25 years ago, to create, liberate and build the homeland, the Jewish home for its people, I did not think about death at all. When I arrived in the Land of Israel it was as if I was reborn. I was like a newborn, a child, who had just entered the world. The person who must now begin to reorder a new life under completely different circumstances, difficult and more strenuous life circumstances. First of all, he must become a worker, and endure difficult work conditions. As a chalutz (pioneer) and a Zionist, he accepts everything with love. Even if the new life breaks his body, the spirit of the Land of Israel encourages him and strengthens him. This is what the Land of Israel demands of its sons.

We know that we must bring sacrifices. We were educated with the concept that we must sacrifice for the Land of Israel; however, did we think that we would die a natural death? No. Such a thought did not even enter our minds, because we did not have time at all to think about extraneous matters. We lived constantly with one thought: that we are the pioneers of the Jewish people, and that we must go ourselves or send our children out on guard to protect Jewish life or participate in the creation of the Land of Israel.

However, the years run by, we get older, our strength slowly ebbs, the nerves weaken, our state of mind often becomes broken due to various circumstances, then we began to ask and press one another... whose heart is struck with despair, and whose eyes began to see things upside down... and we begin to cast doubts on that unnatural point in our lives, or when a person cannot comfort himself and begins to think only about what is broken – then he becomes completely broken physically and the end is – death before his time.

Reb Hertzke Ejnes of blessed memory, from among the first of the Sochaczew Jews who came to the Land of Israel.

{571}

Sochaczewers in America

{572}

Eliezer Meir Libert
by Yaakov Frydman
Translated by Jerrold Landau

Eliezer Meir was born in Sochaczew to fine, upstanding parents. His father Elchanan Libert wrote requests to the government authorities. It was difficult to earn a livelihood for the large family. When the children grew up, they learned various trades. Eliezer Meir left for London before the First World War. He returned to Sochaczew in 1919, then once again left for London, and then traveled to America. There, he became involved in the benefit organization for our townsfolk with his entire heart and soul. After the Second World War, he even hatched the idea of creating a colony for Sochaczew natives in the Land of Israel. He introduced me to the idea of creating a plan for such a settlement. However, the plan was too grandiose for him to actualize. When Eliezer Meir saw that the townsfolk in Chicago were distancing themselves from a large-scale assistance effort for their fellow townsfolk in Israel, he distanced himself from all of them. He once wrote to me: If people do not care to help their own townsfolk after the great destruction because Sochaczew is no longer for them, one can only regret it. Then people such as I have nothing more to do. Throughout 40 years, I never tired of giving of myself to help them. It is true that we no longer have the city, however the survivors who were saved from hell – for them it is still our duty to do something... We could have been in their place... He did everything. Immediately after the liberation, he sent 2,000 dollars to the Land of Israel in the name of the Chicago Welfare Organization. This concluded the activity of Chicago.

He displayed his warm feelings for the benevolent work of the organization in the Land of Israel from 30 years previously, when he arrived in America. He called together and encouraged things in Chicago, and the would have been prepared to receive the greatest help if only he would bring the small number of Sochaczew natives there. During the last part of his life, he stood with me and discussed the several hundred dollars that remained in the bank after the liquidation of the welfare organization in Chicago. He wished that this money would be used for the similar organization in Israel.

He was the president of the Sochaczewer Welfare Organization in Chicago for 30 years. At the same time, he was active in the Federation of Polish Jews. He was also active in and had an office in the General Clothing Union for the poor, and was involved in other organizations.

TRANSLATOR'S FOOTNOTES:
1. The question mark appears in the text.
2. This, and subsequent numbers of this nature in this section, are direct translations from the text and do not refer to the Yizkor book itself.

{574}

The Sochaczew Mutual Benefit Organization of Chicago
by Louis Libert
Translated by Jerrold Landau

I am grateful to have had the opportunity of being able to direct the constructive work of our small but active society for the fleeting period of 33 years.

Eliezer Meir Libert. Passed away in Chicago.

In 1914, due to a coincidental meeting of a few Sochaczew natives, the idea of founding a Sochaczewer Mutual Benefit Society was born. Before me now lies a copy of the original constitution, dated February 8, 1914.

The first task of the society at that time was to support the newly arrived immigrants from Sochaczew, and to help them to settle in their new home. We would provide for them respectfully until they were able to find their own means of livelihood. We would also support the families of the "greeners" from Sochaczew, as well as all other families who required support. The society also established a free loan organization here in Chicago to lend money to fellow natives without interest, when the need arose. The borrowers would be able to pay the loan back in small sums. That same year, the First World War broke out in Europe. Poland was occupied by the Germans, and no news came out of Sochaczew. The Sochaczew natives (landsleit) worried terribly. They worked extra hard to establish a fund, so that when the day of freedom would come they would be able to assist. The awaited day finally came. Without any request, help was sent along with a letter inquiring about the well being of the residents of Sochaczew, and indicating what our further support could accomplish. Their response came with a request asking if it would be possible for us to build a Talmud Torah (elementary school) for them, for the Jewish cheders were not fit for the children. Their request was accepted at our following meeting. A committee visited our native town, and plans were set.

When they returned, we commenced with the work.

In 1926, the president at the time, Mr. Hyman Rabinovitch, traveled to Sochaczew for the opening of the Talmud Torah. It was a very solemn opening. The school was the pride of all the Sochaczew Jews. Here, it was as good as there. We took care of the upkeep of the school. We regularly sent money, every year, to clothe the children, as well as help for poor children. We also sent help to all the organizations that existed up to the time of that accursed Hitler. Shortly after the murderers entered Poland, we heard that all the Jews of Sochaczew were expelled to the Warsaw ghetto. The Jews had ill fortune and were annihilated. The Talmud Torah was destroyed. The destruction of Sochaczew affected us greatly. We all decided to work toward and to eagerly await the great day when our greatest hater would be destroyed. Nobody would have been able to believe that so many of our people were destroyed. More than three-quarters of the people from our hometown were murdered.

Aside from the support that we sent via the federation, we at that time did much assistance work. We received letters from the small remnant of our natives who were scattered in all parts of the world. We sent them packages of food and money. We also received letters from natives of other areas who were searching for their relatives. We did what we could to connect them with their relatives.

Sochaczew is no more. As faras we hear, the entire city has turned Polish. All signs of Judaism were erased. We are still bonded to our hometown of Sochaczew with thousands of threads, and we wish that Jewish Sochaczew would still live. We carry with us the hope of establishing a Sochaczewer settlement in the Land of Israel. We will attempt to realize our dream. It should be said about our fruitful work on behalf of our organization is thanks to the constant hard work of people such as Mr. Yitzchak Landau, who held office for more than 25 years already; Mr. Benny Beister, the ex-president[1]; H. Rabinovitch, Mr. J. Rabinovitch the treasurer; G. Beister and others, such as myself[2], who held the office of president and recording secretary for 20 years.

Chicago District
November 1947

Deceased Members of the Relief Committee [3]

Pinchas Graubard	Vova Rosenberg
Max Graubard	Max Landau
Henry Miller	Tzalel Nelson
Eliezer Rosen	Fanny Borenstein
Meir Plamiak	Phillip Nelson
William Muney	Hyman Goldberg

Yisrael Keller   Sam Leifer

Jack Leifer

Sitting from right to left:
Chava Benzer, Shirley Lesinger, Esther Shpeizhendler, Becky Winter, Chana Hodes Rosen.

Standing from right to left:
Sam Winter, Shimon Neiten, Moshe Geier, Isadore, Silverstein, Moshe Shpeiznendler, Hermen Nelson, David Wohlrat, Al Weitzman, Bella Weitzman, Avraham Shorkin, Joel Roth, Mendel Gombinski, Yosef Chazan.

Missing from the picture:
Moshe Kipper, Y. Jacobi, Molly Solomon, Yetta Spikler, Sydney Landau, Klara Leifer, Chava Zuckerweiss.

{577}

Sochaczewers in New York
by Ch. L. Ludzki
Translated by Jerrold Landau

Regarding the first Sochaczew Jews in New York, when did they come, how did they earn their livelihood in their new home, their social and spiritual state, how did they acclimatize in their first years, how many returned to Poland, etc. – about all this, unfortunately, we have no written documents, and also no accurate details.

There are no record books, letters or books that tell about this. They do not exist. After a great deal of searching, we can find grave markers with letters that are peeling off in the old Jewish cemeteries that are no longer used today. On these, we can make out the word "From Sochaczew" beside the personal data of the deceased. There is no other reminder of the great immigration of the Sochaczew Jews who took up their wandering sticks and came to the Golden Land along with the great stream of Jewish immigrants from Poland and Russia at the end of the 19th century.

I had no choice other than to collect in a primitive manner the meager data from the remaining aging Sochaczew natives who remember themselves or who had heard stories told by their parents about their first years in New York. I will attempt to relate here that which I have collected.

The information goes back to the end of the 1870s, and I can state with certainty that at the beginning of 1880, there were already groups of Sochaczew Jews who not only came to worship in the Hassidic Shtibels that were located both on the East Side and in Harlem, but also served as gabbaim (synagogue trustees), prayer leaders, Torah readers, and other official positions in a number of groups of Polish Jews. They also took part in all of the institutions that began to arise during that time that were needed for the newly arrived immigrants who were fleeing the Russian pogroms. We find our Sochaczewers in the Beis Midrashes, in the beer halls, and also in the parks and gardens where they came to search for work or where they came on their day of rest with one objective: perhaps they might find a newly arrived immigrant with a warm greeting from the old country.

Thus do we find the names of Sochaczewers in the membership lists of the first Warsaw, Lodz, Vilna and Berdichev organizations. They were active in the work of these organizations.

For the first time in 1881, a small number of Sochaczewers in New York began to organize their own societal life, as well as assistance activities for their own fellow natives, who would be ashamed to ask for help from others even during their time of need – but they would be willing to accept assistance from their own people from the same city, and they would not be ashamed of pouring out their difficult situation...

In that year, a group of Sochaczewer worshippers at the "Great Beis Midrash of the East Side" founded the first Sochaczewer institution.

Despite the fact that its original name was not indicative of any unique Sochaczew origins, as it was called "Chevra Bnei Rachmanim" (The Organization of the Merciful Ones), and also offered assistance to other Jews in need. All of the unique Sochaczewer institutions and societies that exist until this day stem from it.

Among the first group of activists one finds names such as Chaim Slomak, Zindel Segal, Yeshaya Spiegel, Yona Sheinbaum, Yaakov Lewin, Aharon Zelig Leitheld, Yaakov Switzman, Yehoshua

Goldberg, Shalom Leib Hershkowitz, Pinchas Keller (later the shamash at the Ludlow Street Synagogue), Tovia Speiss, Avraham Greenberg and others who later assisted in the founding of the "Young Men's Organization".

I wish to mention here the scholar Ashenheim who assisted with the first institution with his entire energy and soul. In those days he was not yet an official rabbi, and he worked at various jobs such as a mashgiach (kashruth supervisor) and learning holy studies with youths so that he could sustain himself.

It also seems that the Sochaczewers in New York did not form an independent Sochaczewer organization, for with meager means it would not be possible to obtain their own building. They were centered around the beautiful synagogue on 117 Ludlow Street, which was founded in 1898 by almost the same group of people and activists.

Its first worshippers were members of the Bnei Rachmanim. Later, a group of Sochaczewer Jews gathered around the Chevra Mishnayos synagogue on Suffolk Street.

The fervent activity first began in 1894, when a new cemetery was needed for the members who died during that year. The members desired that the synagogue should have its own cemetery, as did other organizations. This led to the founding of the "Chevra Kadisha Anshei Sochaczew" that exists to this day, and has maintained an important set of records. (President Issie Silverstein, Chairman H. Landau, Treasurer Sidney W., Landau). For example, they transferred the remains of the long deceased members from the old cemetery, for the place was needed by the city for other purposes...

To that end, two areas in the Washington Cemetery were purchased as a cemetery for the members of the synagogue. Later, they also purchased a place in the Beth David Cemetery in Long Island.

A mikva (ritual bath) was also constructed at the synagogue. It was called "The Kosher Mikva for all Jewish daughters", and was still in existence at the end of 1928, when the bathhouse attendants provoked a scandal and the president of the time, Meir Slomak had to call a special meeting where the announcement that was sent to all of the Sochaczewers was read. It was tragic enough even for those times.

In the Yiddish and English invitation from the middle of October, 1928, we read: "Worthy Members! You are called to attend a regular and special meeting on Tuesday, October 30, 1928 at 8:00 p.m. in the synagogue, 121 Ludlow Street, New York.

The purpose of this meeting is very important: the current circumstances of our synagogue and what will be the conclusion.

As you already know, the synagogue is undergoing a difficult situation with the bathhouse attendants who accused us. The trial will take place shortly. Also, since the contract with the bathhouse attendants expires in the month of April, we must begin to discuss and debate what we will do so that the name of our synagogue should not Heaven forbid be debased, the synagogue will not be driven to the ground, and the name of our city of Sochaczew will not be shamed – so that we can continue to maintain a synagogue. At the last meeting, it was decided to send around circulars to every member to remind them to be present and take part in the meeting for this holy purpose. We have already existed for 45 years, and we must not, Heaven forbid, be driven into the ground through this terrible crisis.

It is impossible now to describe the situation in writing about all the years that we have toiled for the synagogue. We request that all the members come to the meeting with pure hearts and proper thoughts, to do what is needed, since the time is short.

The day is short and the task is great. If you do not attend the meeting, we will leave the synagogue in an abandoned state, as well as our portion of the cemetery with its plots. Nobody will be able to protest.

You should know that in our synagogue we have a member who has been sick for six months, and the synagogue has done what it could do. Now his family has set up a theater benefit. So that we can further help this member, every member must purchase a ticket. Every member who does not show up at the meeting will be charged a three dollar fee, which will go toward this sick member.

We are hoping that none of our members will be absent from this important meeting – by the order of the president:

Meir Slomak, President, Tzemach Pomerantz, Secretary"

I have especially included the meeting announcement from 1928, and even brought it down with its original orthography and language, in order to illustrate a small snippet of the large scale and multi-faceted work that has taken place throughout the years when, aside from serving as a holy place for worshipping, the synagogue served as a devoted home for our Sochaczewer immigrants who for the most part arrived alone and without their families. In the synagogue, they found familiar people and friends, and first and foremost, a warm, brotherly atmosphere and environment that was somewhat of a substitute for the old home.

At the time that I write a little about the long history of the Sochaczewer community in New York it is indeed our great duty to express to a small degree our great fondness for the builders, and to mention with respect the honorary list of the first group of activists, who did not hold back any money and time as they worked for the benefit of their society.

Among the original activists for the benefit of the Sochaczewers, we find the important names of Michael Landau, Yaakov Switman, Aharon Leidhold, Zindel Segal, Yeshaya Hershkowitz, Aharon Speiss, Hyman Hirsch, Sam Bauman, Shlomo Goldshneider, Max Landau and Rabbi Ashenheim, the first rabbi of the Sochaczewer Synagogue. He assisted the endeavor during the early period for a very small salary. He also learned with the Chevra Mishnayos group and played a very important role in forging the spiritual form of our society, which had to accustom itself to the new American style and customs.

The synagogue had two eras: the first one until 1920, and the second one until 1956. During the first period, its spiritual leaders included the rabbis Ashenheim, Efraim Einman, Landau, and others.

In 1920, a very large renovation of the synagogue took place. It took on the appearance of a modern, stately building, comparable with the large synagogues of New York. The work was done voluntarily and with great proficiency under the supervision of Moshe Cooper, who gave of his entire free time and experience. At that time, the prime activists included: Zindel Segal, Hyman Nelson, Hyman Hirsch, Max Bauman, Yaakov Switman, Max Landau, Shlomo Goldshneider, as well as the younger people Sidney Landau, David Segal, Reverend Louis Rosen who was the sexton of Reb Yitzchak Graubard, and others.

The synagogue existed until the year 1956. Its last president was A. G. Silverstein. However, since the entire areas now had fewer Jews, and most of the Sochaczew builders and worshippers moved to other areas just like most of the Jews, a decision was made to sell the synagogue at a general meeting of its members.

The sum of 35,000 dollars was used for a very important project which was certainly very important to our fellow natives.

Rabbi Yitzchak Graubard of blessed memory, one of the synagogue activists in New York.

It was decided to donate the sum of 25,000 dollars to the eminent Bar Ilan University. A special, modern tablet with the names of all of the deceased members and worshippers of our Sochaczewer synagogue in New York was to be put up in the synagogue that was to be built at the University. This would serve as an eternal light, and on every yahrzeit date, a light would be turned on next to the name of the deceased, and someone would recite Kaddish. For this purpose we gave 15,000 dollars in cash and 10,000 dollars in Israel bonds. The rest of the money would be kept for cases of need in New York as would be determined through a regular meeting of the committee.

That first group of activists who came in 1900 included the founders of the broad based organization that is called to this day the "Independent Sochaczewer Young Men's Sick Benefit

Organization". It was officially founded on November 27, 1900, and conducts its activities to this day with a large membership.

It is interesting to bring down here a small snippet of its constitution, which was published in Yiddish and English in a 55 page booklet at the time that it was amended on December 28, 1939. (The booklet was published at the beginning of 1940.)

I will only bring down the first article of the constitution:

The name of this society will be – the Independent Young Men's Sick Benefit Organization.

The name of the society will never be changed.

The society must not be disbanded as long as thirteen members wish that the society should continue its existence.

All of the business of the society must be written in minutes in Yiddish or English.

The funds of the society must be used only for the following purposes:

Sick benefit.

Death benefit.

Shiva benefit.

Assisting and supporting members in need and assisting those who are in need because of the death of a member.

Publications that are needed in the interests of the society.

A further article: Members, that is a member or his widow, who become apostates, meaning that they abandon the Jewish faith, will be suspended from the society. Furthermore a member who marries a wife from outside the Jewish faith, or a Jewish wife who does not follow Orthodox Jewish practice, will be suspended.

From this small excerpt, we can get a bit of idea about the work in both the national and the social areas, as well as the concerns of the society during its early years, when the need of newly arrived townsfolk were a daily phenomenon, and they had to be helped during their time of need.

It would take up too much space to tell about the entire 60 years of its activity, and also to mention all of the activists, most of whom have already passed away. I will suffice myself with mentioning a number of the first elected officials, organizations and builders who lovingly gave of their time, health and monetary savings for the benefits of the community of Sochaczewers in New York.

The society was founded with 18 members.

Its father and actual founder was Max Eisenstop of blessed memory, who also served as president for the first six months. A few years later, he again served in that important office once again due to his important work.

The first committee consisted of Barney Greenberg of blessed memory, who served as vice president; Alex Gottlieb of blessed memory, treasurer; Harry Berman of blessed memory, financial secretary; Yaakov Friedman of blessed memory, recording secretary; and the members Benny Lewin of blessed memory, Hyman Slomak of blessed memory, Abe Rotstein of blessed memory, and Louis Schwartz of blessed memory.

They raised the number of members to 45.

The second president was Aharon Zelig Leitheld. Under his leadership, in May 1901, the area of 12 plots in the Mount Sinai Cemetery was purchased in May 1901. A. Z. Leitheld did a great deal more during his term of office as president.

The third president was Solomon Goldshneider of blessed memory. He excelled in intelligence, knowledge and tact, which gave a great deal to the society in those times.

The fourth was Louis Brokman of blessed memory.

The fifth was Mendel Frankenstein of blessed memory. He also simultaneously served as the treasurer.

The sixth was M. D. Helfand of blessed memory.

Max Sheinberg, who at that time was one of the first and the eldest members, was elected as president several times. He also arranged for the construction of the beautiful fence with an inscription around the Sochaczewer area in Mount Sinai Cemetery.

Aside from serving as president, Moshe Metchnik served several times as financial secretary. Aside from being among the first organizers, Barnet Kolsky served as president in 1910.

Aside from serving as the first financial secretary, Harry Berman was the president from 1910 to 1912, and he later took on many other positions of responsibility.

Yosef Miller, also one of the founders, was the president in 1913. In 1915, at the 15th anniversary of the society, a special souvenir collection of 50 pages with an accounting of the first 15 years of work, as well as photos of the first activists, both those who had already passed away and those who were still alive and active in the activities was published. We can take the names from this booklet.

These are: Aharon Z Leitheld, Harry Berman, Max Muney, Barney Greenberg, Moshe Metchnik, Henry Cohen, Chaim Slomak, Max Eisenstop, Barnet Kolsky, M. Frankenstein, Yosef Miller, Louis Schwartz, David Ohlberg, Max Lewin, Avraham German, Herman Jacobs, Arthur Sofron, Avraham Berman, David Miller, Yaakov Laosher, Avraham Rotstein, Max Sheinberg. The members included: V. Enis, B. Enis, D. Auerbach, Y. Berman, Yosef Berman, M. Berman, Y. Berger, A. Benzer, Y. Besserman, Meir Bauman, Y. Binder, L. Brzasky, M. Bernstein, L. Boznicky, Sh. H. Becker, A. Boznicky, A. Cohen, Y. Cohen, L. Cohen, R. Cohen, M. Cohen., Sh. Sholk, B. Cohen, Sh. Cohen, S. H. Diamond, M. Temple, H. Epstein, Y. Friedrich, Y. Felt, L. Pritz, L. Friedman, S. Finkel, Y. Goldflus, H. Greenberg, Y. Greenberg, S. Grobshmit, Y. Gursky, M. Greenwald, H. Heiman, D. Helman, S. Holtz, A. Innfeld, L. Jakobovitch, S. Jacobs, Y. Kozshinsky, A. Kotshinsky, V. Kornfeld, Pinchas Keller, V. Kopeld, Y. Lusky, H. Lewin, D. Lions, A. Levy, Sh. Levy, S. Levy, D. Lustig, L. Lisser, Y. Levkovich, Yosef Lewin, Sh. Miller, S. Miller, H. Miller, A. Miller, Y. Miller, Y. Mashman, A. Mashman, T. Morenfeld, H. Notan, P. Nelson, Y. Foster, Y. Putter, A. Peters, Sh. Rosen, Sol Rosen, H. Rotstein, L. Rappaport, Meir Slomak, B. Slomak, Y. Slomak, L. Slomak, Y. Speiss, M. Speiss, Y. Sofer, Y. Stromfeld, L. Stromfeld, A. Stromfeld, Sh. Schwartz, A. Schwartz, Sh. Schwartz, H. Silverman, M. Silver, B. Solomon, Sh. Sochaczewsky, M. Sherel, M. Zuckerwise, M. Temple, Sh. Weingard, H. Weingard, M. Wishinsky, S. Vidaver, Y. Wagner, Y. Weisman, L. Weltmsman, S. Zemel, L. Zand, M. Weisman. As well as the following people whose photos were not present:

S. Bauman, Y. Birnbaum, D. Balterman, H. Blinderman, S. Boznicky, L. Cohen number 1, M. Cohen, Dr. D. Diamond, Dr. H. B. Elster, Dr. H. Y. Friedman, P. Gorlik, S. Gilder, H. Goldman, Zimmerman, A. Gutman, Y. Gordon, Mrs. A. Greenwald. A. Greenwald, A. Greisman, H. Graubard, L. Grusky, A. Hershkowitz, Dr. M. D. Keller, H. Kramer, T Marenfeld, S. Moshkovich, L. Rappaport, S.

Reiter, Y. Sofer, S. Solomon, A. Schlesinger, Y. Silber, B. Sochaczewsky, Mrs. H. M. Starkman, S. Starkman, Sh. Sneiberg, Y. Sh. Ohlberg, S. Weinberg, A. Wilhelm. N. Winter, Z. Zanger.

It would be interesting to give over a little bit of the financial and activity report of the first 15 years, which began with a small sum of dollars and at the anniversary year almost reached the sum of 6,000 dollars. In the treasury there was the sum of 2,300 dollars.

It is also very important to give a small list of the first people who were buried in our own cemetery. We can see from this that our town natives underwent a difficult struggle for their existence during the first years. We see from the death information that the oldest was 45 years old and that the youngest deceased was 25 years old (in the picture of the first graves in the aforementioned anthology).

In the later years we find among the active members the names of: secretary, Y. Donowitz (1915-1922), Yosef Sharfstein of blessed memory, M. Libert, Herman Nelson, Sol Levy, Nathan Slomak, S. Becker of blessed memory, Herman Hirsch, S. Solberg, Morris Cooper, Max Landau, Sam Miller, Aharon Nelson, Yosef Mittleman, Hyman Zabosky, Milton Robinson, Nat Dolow, Harry Temple, Hyman and Irving Nelson, Isadore Greenberg, and others.

In the booklet that was published for the 60th anniversary of the society, we find the following activists from 1960: ex president Sol Levy, President Nathan Slomak, vice president Shmuel V. Becker, Recording secretary Nat Dolow, Financial secretary M. Robinson, treasurers Aharon Boznicky and Isadore Greenberg. We also find a list of over 50 members who were active in the activities. We also find the names of the former presidents Shorl Cohen, Nat Dolow, Morris Feld, Morton Friedman, Herman V. Hirsch, Sol Levy, Herman Nelson, Yaakov Nelson, Robert Putter, Sam Solberg, Nat Slomak, and Sam A. Temple. We also find the names of the members in good standing, which reached a number of 270. This demonstrates the usefulness and the brotherliness of the society at its 60th anniversary, just as it was 60 years previously.

Our Young Men's society was called upon for every case of Jewish need, both for local as well as for general Jewish causes.

We also find in the annals of the first Jewish Relief Committee that was founded immediately after the First World War in order to assist Jews in Europe who were victims of the war and the Russian Revolution – our large sums of assistance money that was raised with heart and soul by the general committee.

Aside from this, in those years we conducted a special activity for our Sochaczew natives, by giving power of attorney to our dear brother Hymie Nelson so that he could do what was necessary for our brothers in the old country.

Hymie Nelson is one of the sons of the elder Sochaczew native Reb Shmuel Nelson of blessed memory, who was one of the first of Chovevei Zion in the town. He came to his children in 1924, and died on April 1, 1931 in New York.

The "United Sochaczewer Relief" was founded at the end of 1939, a the time when the sword of destruction of Polish Jewry was launched – among them being our townsfolk who found themselves under Hitler's bloody rule.

The relief committee was comprised of all of the Sochaczewer organizations in New York. There were representatives from the Young Men's Society, the synagogue, the Lady's Assistance Organization, and from Branch 337 of the National Workers' Union.

The following people were on the first committee: Hymie Nelson, Harry Miller, David Wolrat, Sam Winter, Chava Zuckerwise, Bella Weitzman, Max Graubard, Moshe Speisshendler, Vove Rosenberg,

Pinchas Graubard, Betzalel Nelson, Yisrael Moshe Zuckerwise, Shimon Neiten and Meir Menzer. The first president was David Wolrat, and the secretary was Pinchas Graubard. His term lasted until the end of the war in 1945.

Immediately after the war a new committee was created which had the great task of aid and rescue. Under the leadership of Hymie Nelson as president, Bella Weitzman as recording secretary and Moshe Speisshendler as financial secretary, we began to forge contact with the survivors of Hitler's death camps and those who returned from the forests and Russian exile.

We got in touch with friends and acquaintances in the German camps, in Poland, in Austria and Italy. Aside from packages with food and clothing, we also sent them our warm feelings. We sent over 500 packages to townsfolk in all corners of the world. We helped them with various sums of money to enable them to emigrate from the camps to the State of Israel, South America, Australia and the United States. We also offered our brotherly assistance to help them acquire dwellings and furniture when they propitiously arrived in their new homelands. We gave them general assistance so that they would be able to begin a new life after the dark Hitler and Stalin years. We assisted the Sochaczewer Charitable Fund in the State of Israel with a large sum of money so that those in need could find a source of livelihood, so that they could support themselves on their own two feet.

Yisrael Moshe and Chava Zuckerwise.

We did everything for those Sochaczewers who wished to come to America – we helped with papers, affidavits, and other material and moral assistance. Here, they were able to experience our best family relationships, so that they were able to quickly acclimatize to our environment in our Sochaczewer Society.

In April 1952, on the 10th anniversary of the Warsaw Ghetto uprising, we arranged a large memorial gathering. Close to 400 Sochaczewers came to pay their respects to our martyrs.

The gathering took place under the chairmanship of our member Vove Rosenberg of blessed memory. The program included speeches about our hometown, about the martyr and writer M. Demblyn, and about our townsfolk the folklorist and scholar Pinchas Graubard of blessed memory. The memorial prayer was recited by our esteemed fellow townsman Cantor and Rabbi Leifer.

The current activists in the relief committee include Hyman Nelson – chairman, Isadore Silverstein – treasurer, Moshe Speisshendler – financial secretary, and Moshe Geier – recording secretary. They never refuse, and are always prepared to assist Sochaczewers in need, either personally or through others. We regularly send assistance to those in need in the State of Israel.

Aside from all of the Sochaczewer institutions of various forms, on March 18, 1934, a special institution with a different purpose was founded. This was the Sochaczewer Branch 337 of the National Workers' Union of America.

In the group of the first ten activists we find Sam Winter, Shimon Neiten, Max Zuckerwise, Yosef Winter the recently deceased Moshe Birnbaum, Meir Benzer, Chaim Fleischman, Meir Slomak, Mendel Graubard and Jack Leifer. They did not suffice themselves with all of the activity of all of the previous organizations that took on solely a material character and rarely concerned themselves with the national and spiritual life.

Their first task was to establish connection with Sochaczewers who had recently left Poland and had settled in the Land of Israel. To this end, they paid great attention to those organizations that worked for the chalutzim (pioneers), for the Histadrut Campaign, for the Keren Kayemet LeYisrael (Jewish National Fund) and its branches. Aside from this, we took part in all of the activities for the JOINT and for the United Jewish Appeal. Our program attracted a number of nationally conscious townsfolk. Today, the "Branch" consists of 35 families who are one Sochaczewer family. The branch participated in and continues to participate in all activities to strengthen Jewish life in all countries. We conduct special undertakings to help our townsfolk who survived and came back from the great Jewish destruction.

Aside from what was sent through the relief, we sent our own 500 packages of food and clothing to needy people in the German camps and in Poland. We helped a number of our townsfolk in Israel with their needs. To this end we arranged a special event every year, with the entire proceeds going to the State of Israel. Each of us in the branch separately purchased Israel bonds, the sum of which has already reached 20,000 dollars. We expended the effort and succeeded in bringing two of our townsfolk to America on our affidavits. We helped them and their families settle in to the United States.

The following friends were active in the branch throughout the 25 year period: Sam Winter, Eliahu Weitzman, Abe Shorken, Issie Brafman, Moshe Speisshendler, Shimon Neiten, Yoel Rotstein, Yosef Winter, Menashe Baron, Saul Weiss, Max Lieder, Avraham Hirsch, Mendel Gombinsky, Mrs. Becky Birnbaum, Henry Weiss, Herbert Berkovitch, Anshel Pinczewski, Henry Olewing, Irving Brafman, Max Zuckerwise, David Speisshendler, Walter Speisshendler, Yisrael Brafman, David Speisshendler, and others.

We hold a monthly meeting which deals with all matters of the branch, and our own cemetery which we have had since 1950.

We wish to dedicate a few lines of memory to one of our builders who fell in the line of duty in the war against the Nazis during the Second World War. This is our former dear comrade Chaim David Neiten (Shlomo Neiten's son), who was killed by the Germans at the age of 24 during the air raids over London on April 28, 1944. May he rest in peace!

Our current officers are:

Sam Winter – chairman, Yosef Winter – vice chairman, Abe Sharken – financial secretary, and Irving Brafman – recording secretary.

Chaim David Neiten, fell on the 5th of Iyar.

{592}

The Activities of our Women's Help Organization in New York

In the winter of 1934, after letters and sorrowful greetings from our relatives in our old hometown began to arrive, describing the difficult Jewish situation and the increasing level of need due to Polish anti-Semitism, a group of women townsfolk met in the house of our townsfolk Becky and Sam Winter in Brooklyn and decided to found a special women's organization, which would occupy itself with assisting the needy in our old home.

The organization grew from the first group of twelve founders. Today it plays an important role in the work of the Sochaczewers in New York.

Some of the original group are unfortunately no longer alive, but their names must be mentioned honor.

These include the longstanding chairwoman and recording secretary Feiga Bornstein and the activists Chava Winter, Floris Speiss, Malka and Chava Tenner, Becky Graubard and Mrs. Fleischman.

פנחס גרובארד	וואווע ראזענבערג
מאקס גראובארד	מאקס לאנדו
הערי מילער	צלאל נעלסאן
אליעזר ראזען	פעני בארענשטיין
מאיר פלאמיאק	פיליפ נעלסאן
ווילאם מוני	היימאן גאלדבערג
ישראל קעלער	סעם לייפער
	דזשעק לייפער

We must also mention those of the first group who were actively constantly until today. These include Becky Winter, Chava Benzer (the wife of the late activist in the Sochaczewer Landsleit Organization Meir Benzer of blessed memory. Their son Seymour, who affiliates as a child of Sochaczew natives, is one of the ten most famous scientists in all of America[4]), our first chairwoman Rae Baron, Becky Birnbaum, Fleischman, Clara and Polly Leifer, and a number who today do not live in New York.

Dozens of women followed voluntarily, who gave of their precious time and money, going around to all of the Sochaczewers in New York to collect money for assistance that was later sent back home to Sochaczew.

Thus did the work progress until the war in 1939.

We held our meetings in our old synagogue on Ludlow Street in order to save a few dollars that we utilized to send help.

We undertook various activities. We arranged various theatrical performances in English and Yiddish. The ticket sales and benefits went toward the assistance effort.

Through our common efforts we collected various items and raffled them off, with the entire proceeds going toward those in need...

This took place between the years 1939-1944. During that time, the former president and secretary Bella Weitzman excelled. She brought the work to a higher level.

The highest level of our activity began at the end of the Second World War, when Chava Zuckerwise was elected as chairwoman and Mali Solomon as secretary. They assisted in the founding of the much needed Sochaczewer Relief Committee, to which all of the Sochaczewer organization of New York belong today. These include the Sochaczewer Young Men's Society, the synagogue, Branch 337 of the National Workers' Union, and our Women's Help Organization. All of them together raised the capital for help and rescue of the surviving Sochaczewers after the huge Jewish destruction.

Aside from the general assistance through the relief committee, we ourselves with our own means – through the help of our women – sent hundreds of packages of food and clothing, as well as medicine and other necessities to those who miraculously survived Hitler's death camps, to those who returned from their wanderings in Russian, and to those who remained alive in the bunkers and hiding places in the Polish forests.

Already from the first day of their liberation, we sent the needed assistance along with our good wishes to those who were in Poland as well as Germany, Austria and Italy. We saw to it that they would remain in contact in us and not feel lost after their difficult experiences.

We assisted them and continued to assist them as they settled in the State of Israel or here in America. We offered both individual and collective help.

We adopted two war orphans and gave 600 dollars for their maintenance, at first in a home in Paris and today in Israel. Throughout the time, we sent them whatever they needed.

This took place over a period of 15 years of daily work, which we conducted with love, in order that those who required our assistance should feel as part of one Sochaczewer family.

Finally, I wish to mention our active activists who give of their assistance and hearts for our organization. Let us mention with honor the late activists such as: Reverend Louis Rosen who never refused any undertaking of ours, and helped with words and deeds; the shochet (ritual slaughterer) Reb Naftali Geshen and his wife Sarah of the Neiten family; the prominent Vove Rosenberg; Reb

Yitzchak Graubard (called Reb Yitzchak Shamash) and his son Mendel Graubard; Yisrael Moshe Zuckerwise; Max Shpilker and the writer Pinchas Graubard.

I also wish to thank the active workers Chava Benzer, Bella Weitzman and Sarah Lessinger.

I especially wish to stress the great material and moral assistance from our friends Max and Ida Zuckerwise, Issie Fen and Moshe and Becky Cooper, without whose help we would have had to restrict our activity.

Our current committee consists of: Chava Zuckerwise – chairwoman, Chana Esther Green – vice chairwoman, Yetti Shpikler – social secretary, Becky Winter and Pearl Rosen – managing committee, and Mali Solomon – general secretary.

The marketplace in the center of the city.

TRANSLATOR'S FOOTNOTES:

1. It is not clear if the title 'ex-president' belongs to the preceding name or the following name. I guessed at the preceding name. The same applies for the title 'treasurer'.
2. Literally 'mein veinikeit', which means 'my smallness', which is a humble way of referring to oneself.
3. It is not clear if the people on this list, and those listed in the caption of the photo on the following page, are from the Chicago group, or some other group. There is no indication one way or another on these pages.
4. Seymour Benzer, a physicist, molecular biologist and geneticist, died just last year on November 30, 2007. See the Wikipedia article:
   http://en.wikipedia.org/wiki/Seymour_Benzer.

Shopping center.

Shabtai Weinberg and his wife

z bratem żony/ i Posztergowie
z Młodzeszyna/

Z mojej rodziny/ Albert Kac
i tp/ nikt przy życiu nie pozostał.

Materialnie jest nerazie nie źle
ale mamy dosyć tego wszystkiego
i chcielibyśmy szybko uciec tam
gdzie są nasi. Wyobrażacie chyba
sobie jakie tu u nas smutki kiedy
tyle tysięcy cienie zmartych otaczają
nas

Cieszymy się że żyjemy ale
tęsknimy za dawnymi czasami
Pozdrawiam Was serdecznie
Bracia od rodziny Wasz
P. Weinberg

mój adres:
P. Weinberg
Sochaczew
Reymonta-9

[Stamp: KOMITET ŻYDOWSKI W Sochaczewie]

חנה פרידמן

מי יתן ראשי מים....

18.1.45. ידיעה בעתון: וארשה שוחררה על־ידי צבאות ברית המועצות. והעתון מוסיף: וארשה שאין בה יהודים. אחריה שוחררה סוכצ'וב.

כן, וארשה, עיר ואם בישראל, וסוכצ'וב אחת מבנותיה הקרובות. מאז מלחמת ההשמד על יהדות אירופה נזכרה סוכצ'וב, עיירת הולדתי, זו הפעם הראשונה. ומה רבים הזכרונות המנקרים במוח ומענים את הנפש ללא הרף.

עיירה אומללה! יד הגורל פגעה בה עוד במלחמת העולם הראשונה ונהרסה כמעט כליל. אך מה ההבדל מאז ועד עתה! אז ניצלה וארשה מפאת הקרבות שנמשכו זמן רב ליד העיירה, וזו, כאילו לאות תודה, הצילה אחר־כך את תושבי סוכצ'וב שמצאו בה מקלט, בברחם כל עוד נפשם בם. ומשוחזרו הקימו מחדש את הריסות העיירה.

ועתה? לא על הריסותיה לבי דוי, אלא על תושביה היהודים, על קרובינו וידידינו הרבים ששתו את כוס התרעלה עד תומה.

לבי, לבי לך, עיירת הולדתי! את שכה שקקת חיים, איך נדמת ונהפכת לקבר גדול אחד? ואולי גם קבר לא נשאר לך? את, שהיית כה מסורה לעניו ארץ־ישראל, ולא מעט גם פעלת למענה, איך נפלת ללא קום? מה קשה להאמין ולהשלים עם רעיון מר ונמהר זה!

ואנו פה בארץ, השרידים המעטים — גדול כים שברנו! מי יתן ראשי מים ועיני מקור דמעה, ואבכה יומם ולילה על חלליך יחד עם כל חללי בית ישראל...

{753}

Those That Passed Away

{754}

In Memory of Mother of blessed memory
by Chana Frydman 19 Kislev 5709 (1950)
Translated by Jerrold Landau

Today marks the conclusion of one month from the day that mother of blessed memory passed away. It is strange, I am not a young girl, but the impact is so great that it is difficult for me to be comforted. Perhaps this is because I lived together with her until the last moment, and I suffered with her. She suffered greatly from the murder of her eldest son, the pride of the family, in Poland. The siege of Jerusalem broke her completely, and she was not able to find comfort. And now the house is empty! Apparently it is only one soul, however in every corner something is missing. The completeness of the family has been damaged, and it so difficult to get used to the thought that mother is not here anymore. How great is the lack. Woe unto our loss, and we will not forget. May her fine soul be bound in the bonds of eternal life.

19 Cheshvan, 5710 (1951)

The first yahrzeit has arrived. A year has passed, a year of sorrow and mourning. I have just returned from the grave, where a small bush grows near the head. The bush is small and modest, just like the life of mother of blessed memory. In moments that I unite myself with her memory, I see her as in the last day of her life, alive as she was before that bitter day. She fought with her last strength against the bitter death, and she was not able to overcome it... her heart weakened; however the glow on her face was sublime. As the sun prior to sunset, we see and feel the approaching sunset and then the thread is cut and detached forever, this was mother! Dear mother! She is no more! Blessed be the true judge! G-d gives and G-d takes, may his name be blessed.

6 Cheshvan 5712 (1953), thirty days after the passing of father of blessed memory

A month has now passed from that terrible day when I became completely orphaned. With the passing of mother of blessed memory three years ago, he comforted me. A father remained in the house, and the completeness of the family was damaged, but not destroyed. Now the house is completely empty, for the glory of the house has been removed, and mourning encompasses it.

How quickly did this all happen, for he was only ill for a few days. We were together with him until his last moments, and we suffered with him. From the time that he found out about the death of his eldest, illustrious son, of whom there are not many like him, during the Holocaust which afflicted Polish Jewry, and furthermore, there was no remnant of his own family, he was not able to be consoled. He often wept bitterly over this, when nobody was looking. When he knew that somebody was around, he regained his composure quickly and swallowed his tears, so that nobody should see him in his weakness. He found some small comfort by studying his books, for he inherited the literary tendencies of his son, however his sensitive and pained heart continued to weaken until it broke completely.

Father of blessed memory was one of the rare personalities of our time, of those Jews who are complete in their faith, with all their resources and soul. He did not know any aberration or compromise. He was pure and upright, his entire life being dedicated to the service of the creator. He made his nights like days and set aside time to study the Torah. He never missed going to the Beis Midrash, whether in wind, rain, or snow, and even during the times of mortal danger during the siege of Jerusalem. Everyone admired him there since he always awakened people for prayer, and he inspired them with a love of Torah. He was willing to do anything on behalf of those who studied Torah, even to serve them, due to his boundless modesty and humility. Even in the house, every moment was dedicated to study, fulfilling the adage: "and you shall study it day and night". He was diligent in fulfilling the commandment of visiting the sick, as well as arranging for the funerals of those who passed away in our neighborhood, even when it was already difficult for him to walk due to his weakness. In addition, father of blessed memory was very charitable. In order that he should not be lacking any coins for this purpose (he would not take any money from his daughters for this purpose, but would only take from the fruits of his own labor), he supervised the physical order of the Beis Midrash for a small salary.

I will never forget how father of blessed memory welcomed the Sabbaths and festivals. He prepared the first Chanukah candle, cleaned and organized the Chanukah menorah, prepared the wicks, and poured only the finest oil that it was possible to buy. He did this all with devotion, with holy awe and great concentration. I enjoyed so much standing before father of blessed memory at such moments, enjoying his splendor and warming myself from the holy fire that was within him. I enjoyed hearing his enthusiastic singing, and his stories about the miracles and wonders that took place at that time, in this season. He would then sigh and add: "without the miracles that the blessed G-d performs for us at every moment, we would not be able to live. How could we stand up before all of the dangers and tragedies, if it were not for his great kindness.". Those feelings returned at every holiday and appointed season. He prepared for Yom Kippur with great awe and fear – even though he himself was pure and upright, and would not even hurt a fly on the wall, he was so afraid of the judgement. I could not understand this.

All of the sublime traits were found in father of blessed memory, and perhaps these stood in his merit as he left life, for his holy and pure soul left him as he was standing in prayer, enwrapped in his prayer shawl, on the Sabbath day of the 6th of Tishrei, 5712.

His holy memory will be deeply engraved in our hearts, with love and longing.

Woe unto our loss! We will not forget! May his soul find bliss, and may the clods of his earth be sweetened.

{756}

Aharon Ish-Shalom (Frydman)
by Y. P.
Translated by Jerrold Landau

He was the son of Menachem and Sara (nee Ashenheim). He was born in 1896 in Sochaczew to an activist, popular, Hassidic family. He was the grandson of Shalom Tzvi Frydman. He joined the active Zionist movement when he became an adult. He was one of the activists of the People's Library, and he dedicated himself with all his might to the communal activity that was placed upon him. He filled his public duty in the city until he made aliya to the Land.

In 1919, an aliya group was founded consisting of four young men: Aharon, Avraham Yitzchak Weinberg, Tzvi Lewin of blessed memory, and Maroz Mlodaz, may he live long. I helped them steal across the border. They dressed up as Polish youths and succeeded in absconding to Germany. When they got there, they went to work in a coal mine in order to earn money for the journey. They were caught at the Italian border. Tzvi Lewin remained in Germany, and the rest of them were returned to Poland. Weinberg and Maroz were conscripted to the army, and Aharon was freed, since he was below the age of enlistment. In the summer of 1920, Aharon went on his journey again, and succeeded in reaching the Land for the festival of Shavuot. He immediately went into the agricultural preparatory work in Dileb, which is today Kiryat Anavim, and from there he went to Petach Tikva, Tiberias, and he returned to Jerusalem, where he remained until his last day.

{Bottom of page 756 – a newspaper from the Keren Kayemet of Israel in Sochaczew, dated the second day of Sukkot, announcing that an academic guest is coming to visit from the Land of Israel, Aharon Ish Shalom (Frydman).}

He was a man of Jerusalem, and served it in all facets. He worked at many jobs, in particular in building, and he founded the "Yerach" building group in the new city of Jerusalem. This group built the first houses in the neighborhoods of Beit Hakerem and Bayit Vagan. Afterward, they went to Mount Scopus and fixed up the old buildings for the future university.

Aharon at the grave of his father on his visit to Sochaczew in 1937. The grave is of Mendel Frydman the son of Shalom Tzvi, who died on the 5th day of Tammuz 5693 (1933) when he was 64 years old.

They built Kiryat Moshe. He was one of the founders of the Haganah and was active during all of its years of existence. He was one of the founders of Hapoel, and one of the protectors and leaders of the Histadrut house. He transferred to the advisory board of the builders of Jerusalem, and to the union of building workers. From there he went to a contractors office, and finally to Solel Boneh, where he worked until his death. Whoever came in contact with him through work or communal matters, whether they were workers, contractors, or building owners, valued his fine demeanor, his faithfulness, and his dedication to the institution and to the Histadrut house. On occasion, the contractors offered him a position for a high salary, and he refused. He also was a weapons supervisor for the Haganah outside of Jerusalem (in the Borochov neighborhood), and was one of the defenders of Jerusalem. He filled many roles also during the War of Independence.

His spirit was almost broken during the defense of Gush Etzion, for his son Amnon was also one of its defenders. His joy was great when his son returned from prison in Transjordan, however this matter left its mark upon his health. He continued on with dedication in looking after his family, his business ventures, and his communal work, and he merited to witness Jerusalem as the capital of the State of Israel.

He was an example of uprightness and faithfulness in all his endeavors, including in the political area (Mapai), and for the workers of Jerusalem, whom he served with love and leadership for 33 years. His name is perpetuated on the field of Hapoel in Jerusalem.

He died at age 57 of a heart attack on the 5th of Tishrei 5714 (1953).

Tzipora Baum (Albert)
by Y. P.
Translated by Jerrold Landau

Tzipora Baum

Tzipora Baum, or as she was known in our town – Feiga Reshil, was born in 1894 in Sochaczew to her parents Reb Zalman Albert and Tova Leah (nee Fleischman).

Her father was an orthodox Jew, and the owner of a store for iron utensils. He was known to everybody as Reb Zalman the visitor. He dedicated his time to healing the sick of the impoverished people, and he was diligent in this for many years. Even during the time of the First World War, when there were refugees from Warsaw, he expended great efforts in healing the sick of the refugees. The local pharmacies would accept his prescriptions, which were signed with his initials.

The days of Tzipora's youth were in the first decade of the century, during the time when the youth of the cities of Poland, as well as the Maskilim and workers were tossing about with new ideas. Tzipora was one of those who were taken by the new ideas, and she began to dream about going to the wide-open world.

When she was fifteen, a tall and slender girl, she suddenly told her parents that she wished to obtain general knowledge. Her father saw this as a deviation from tradition, however her strong stand caused him to give in. She spent day and night in her studies, which included the best of Polish, Russian, and German literature. She was especially fond of Yiddish literature and Jewish folklore, even after she made aliya. In a short time, she became proficient in the Hebrew language. Hebrew became the language of her daily use.

In those days, she established connections with the workers and poor people who lived in her parents' neighborhood, and she would visit them, learn about their lives, and play with their children. She remembered their personalities, characters, sayings, and mottoes for her entire life.

Tzipora became involved with the Poale Zion movement, and she joined the group that had recently been established in the city, and became active in it. She spread her ideas among the youth, in particular among the well-connected youth. As can be understood, she came in conflict with the influence of the Bund. However, her work paid off, and her influence infiltrated into the homes of the Hassidim and general populace. The parents took objection to this, and alerted the Rebbe's courtyard, and strongly castigated her father Reb Zalman, claiming that he does not stand up to this. He was forced to promise the Rebbe that he would take steps against this. He attempted to influence his daughter in a gentle manner, but it was to no avail. The domestic peace was broken, and her parents began to oppose her and oppress her. At that time, she decided to leave her parents and the city. She packed a small bag of her clothes and slipped away from home.

Her sudden disappearance shocked her family and caused a commotion in the city. They attempted to trace her footsteps in order to appease her and return her to her home, however all investigations were for naught. After a certain time, her parents received a letter from her with a postmark from Lodz, in which she requested that they forgive her for the pain that she inflicted upon them, and explained to them that she could not continue on in that situation. However, she did not reveal her address.

She lived in the home of friends, and she worked as a seamstress and pattern maker's assistant in a large women's clothing factory. Very quickly, she began to enjoy her new surroundings, and she made connections with the Poale Zion group, as well as other groups. The period of Lodz forged her character.

Finally, her parents found out her location in Lodz, and one day, her mother appeared. This was an emotional meeting. However all of the pleas and tears of the mother did not influence Tzipora to return home. Only after her father visited and promised her that she would be given complete freedom in the home to act as she pleased, did she agree to return home.

After her return, she already had different mannerisms, and she was full of self-confidence. Her group of friends and associates listened to her words with respect and seriousness.

In the spring of 1911, she organized a small group of youth to make aliya to the Land of Israel, including David Baum from the town of Leczna, Rafael Shotland from the town of Bielany, Pinchas Graubard from Sochaczew, and others. Tzipora maintained a correspondence with her two friends Baum and Graubard. The latter, after living in Israel for a few months, returned to Sochaczew disappointed. At that time, the connections between Tzipora and David Baum became stronger, and they agreed that she would make aliya. David returned to his town in 1913 for that purpose. He visited Tzipora in Sochaczew. Tzipora's parents did not object to their journey, on the condition that they would get married prior to leaving. Therefore, after she married David Baum, they made aliya to the Land in the spring of 1914.

Their first place of sojourn in the Land was Chavat Kinneret. David Baum was invited there by his friends that he had made while he was working in Degania and Kinneret. He hoped that Tzipora would be accepted as a student in the agricultural school of Chana Meisel, however the teachers refused, saying: "It is too bad David, I don't have any faith that the fine and delightful girl which you brought with you will be able to be a farmer in the land"... She became ill in Kinneret, so she moved with her husband to Hadera. The community of workers and guards in Hadera accepted Tzipora enthusiastically, and she felt herself to be in a good position. This was until the First World War broke out, and the Jewish settlement was subject to the whims of the Turkish government. Many of the community of workers in Hadera decided to leave by ship to Egypt and from there to America. This included many close friends of Tzipora and David. David had money in the Ango-Palestine Bank, which his father transferred to him to purchase land. However his greatest concern was for her lot. She declared: "No David, don't worry about me. I will not leave here, and I will not flee from the land. The lot of the Yishuv (Jewish settlement) will be my lot." Tzipora and David remained in the land. They were forced to become Ottoman subjects. David was conscripted into the Turkish army. When she was alone, she suffered from hunger, loneliness and illnesses. She was forced to change her place of living on occasion, however she accepted all of her tribulations with love, and she supported those who were in similar straits.

After her husband deserted the army, they lived in Metulla, and attempted to set up a small farm. She began growing vegetables. At that time, men and women were snatched for army service, however Tzipora did not pay attention to that danger.

After the land became free, she and her husband became part of the Tel Chai settlement, and there her first daughter Ariela was born. During the time of troubles, she took her daughter, covered her in a coat, and with the help of A. Hertzfeld, she left the place and succeeded in arriving safely to Rosh Hanikra. David served at that time in the mounted police with veteran members of Hashomer, and was far from home. However, her spirit did not abandon her.

Tzipora and her husband were among the first conquerors of Emek Harod in 1922, and among the first families that settled in Kfar Yechezkel.

In 1933, she answered a call from the council of workers and the central agricultural organization to come to assist the farm of the workers in the Borochov settlement for one year, for agricultural affairs were lax. It was not easy for her to leave her family and her own farm that she had built. After deliberation, she responded to the request. She gathered all of her energy to set up this important institution for new immigrants. She succeeded. Instead of one year, the work continued until 1941, for they did not want to release her from her position.

When she came home, despite her weariness and many pains, she again became involved in farm work. However her health took a turn for the worse, and she was forced to abandon the farm. They moved to Haifa, and she continued her life there for only a few years, however they she was also very dynamic and active until her last day. She suddenly passed away while she was visiting with friends in her home. The earth of Kfar Yechezkel received again, after her death, the faithful and dedicated member from the day that the farm was founded, who worked its land with her blood and sweat.

Our first Halutz (pioneer) died, the member of the Second Aliya from Sochaczew.

{763}

Tzipora Baum
by Yisrael Rozen
Translated by Jerrold Landau
About her personality, and in her memory.

Sochaczew – 1912.

It was a small town in Eastern Europe. Apparently, it was a town like any other Jewish town, and like any other small town in the world in any era, in which it was never thought that anything worthy of attention would occur. It is clear that the peace and quiet, the gray monotony, the poverty and limited horizons, the state of being closed off from the outside world were all only external, only seen by someone who looks in from the outside. From within, there was effervescent life, which was punctuated on occasion by dramatic moments. Under the Jewish veneer there beat a warm human hart, the heart of youth who were engaged in youthful activities, who hoped for freedom and redemption. They pined for love, purity, truth, and in their imaginations they traveled to a better world.

Who can count the thousands of Jews who came from such towns who made history, who forged new paths and changed the face of the era? They acted discreetly and quietly, everyone in his own area. As a result of their blessed efforts, life began to build toward the future.

There was one of these types of people in our own town, Tzipora Baum of blessed memory who died in the midst of her activities, struggles, trials and tribulations.

All of us are proud of the State of Israel and its accomplishments, of the generation of pioneers and workers of the land, workers and defenders, of the Jezreel Valley which is dotted with towns that are developing, such as Nehalel and Kfar Yechiel. Such towns were founded through the efforts and struggles of hundreds of pioneers, including our Tzipora!

Twenty-three young people conquered the land of Kfar Yechiel with their blood and sweat. Tzipora was not only one of them, one of the founders of the village, but she also lived in the village for decades. She was not only a pioneer and a farmer, the owner of a farm, but she was also an activist who found time and energy to work in social and educational work. She dedicated herself to the agricultural education of the young generation. She was a pioneer who influenced a generation of pioneers!

She never looked for the easy way out; she did not swim with the current but rather against it. She searched out new ways, and was always one of the first. She was active, and influenced others to be active. She was energetic and imbued others with energy. In her hometown, she started a fundamental revolution due to the new influences. She was convinced of her path, which she set out upon while she was still a young girl.

Already in Sochaczew, in her youth, she displayed an independent and revolutionary spirit, rebelling against the norm.

Her contemporaries related that while she was still a young girl, more than fifty years ago, she set up a meeting hall in the city, a room which served as a meeting place for the progressive youth, those who were freethinkers, those who were though of as 'revolutionaries' in those days. This was for those young boys and girls who felt constricted in the traditional homes of their parents, who were exacting and parochial. They eventually felt that there was no way out. Tzipora suffered from all these things. She was a refined and feeling person, with an open and understanding heart. She showed the youth of our town, fifty years ago, that not all paths were closed off, and it was not necessary to accept one's fate; that another world existed. She introduced the "other world" to the youth at first through books that she gave them to read. She gobbled up these books and obtained them with dedication and diligence. She had many books, a veritable library, private books that she obtained at great monetary cost and with the opposition of her parents. These books granted some sort of salvation to her tormented soul, and they established her world of the spirit.

When young boys or girls, whose eyes were already opened, could no longer continue their lives between the two worlds, the narrow, gray and sad world of the town, and the world of their imagination portrayed in the books – books by Tolstoy, Dostoyevski and Gorki; or when a young boy or girl fell in love and the parents did not agree at all to the mate, or the parents of the mate, lest the family pedigree be tainted (if for example, the mate was a tailor or a simple artisan...); – in such cases Tzipora would offer advice to the young people. She would say to the young girl: "you can forgo your dowry and do what you want, however you must become independent by entering a trade, by working in order to establish your own power, and then you will be able to leave your home and do as you wish... When your parents realize that you are no longer dependent on their support, they will make peace with your desires and chosen path at the end."

Thus, many young people went, through the influence of Tzipora, to large cities such as Warsaw or Lodz, without the approval of their parents, in order to learn a trade, to work, and to marry those whom they desired. Tzipora herself also left, even though she did not require work in order to exist, and even though she enjoyed a large degree of independence in her home, for she had learned over the years to "educate" her parents to respect her will and ways. She achieved this through her diligence and stubbornness.

Tzipora decided to make aliya to the Land of Israel. Why? Because this was the most difficult, most revolutionary thing she could do!

She lived in the Land of Israel for approximately fifty years, and throughout all these years she continued in her manner, for her life was a continuation of the strong path and living out of the dreams of her youth.

Thus was Tzipora Baum, and thus will her memories remain. We miss her. May her memory be blessed.

{765}

Yaakov Frydman of blessed memory
by Yisrael Rozen
Translated by Jerrold Landau
(About his personality)

Yaakov Frydman of blessed memory

Only very few of us knew Yaakov Frydman when he was still in Sochaczew, prior to his aliya. A few of us met him here in the Land, however, most of the natives of our city who are now in Israel first met Yaakov not in Sochaczew, and not here in Israel, but on the journey, that is to say when they were wandering around as refugees from the holocaust in Russia or Siberia, in far away camps and places of exile, or as survivors who were lived in hiding in such places, among the gentiles.

Yaakov Frydman searched all of this out, and these people received their first greeting from a different world from him – from a world of freedom, a world that was not destroyed.

The name Yaakov Frydman was more than a name – among us holocaust survivors from our city of Sochaczew which once was and is no longer; this was an address or more accurately "the address" or focal point to where the scattered ones of our city were gathered, and from where they hoped for a warm and encouraging word. They received such words from him.

Yaakov left our town approximately forty years ago, when he was still a youth. He only spent a small period of his life in our town. He left and made aliya – to the desolate land which "eats its inhabitants"[1], in order to realize the dream of his life. He showed the way for his charges in the first pioneering Zionist youth movement of our town, Hashomer Hatzair.

He left the city for exalted reasons, but he did not leave it permanently. He left, and there, far away, he set up a sort of settlement for our city. He left, and took the name of our town with him. He was among the first to make aliya, however he knew that even though he was among the first, he would not be alone there. He did not make aliya merely to improve his lot, not to have an easy life – for he could have found an easy life in any other place other than the Land of Israel, for the whole world was open, even enchanting America – but rather he and his wife Rachel, may she live long, chose our small and poor land, perhaps because this was the most difficult route, which required the most sacrifice, and which promised the least reward – hard work (when there was work), sweat, partial famine, disease, and a life of danger due to the enemies, as well as almost unbearable natural conditions. He lived in a small hut in the Borochov neighborhood, which was a neighborhood of workers, of which Yaakov was a founder and builder. He gathered and organized the first immigrants from our town, who came after him. He set up a builders union for them, and concerned himself with getting them settled in the land. When the axe was set upon the Jews of Poland, and the fate of our hometown Sochaczew was sealed, Yaakov established for himself the objective of rescuing whomever he could: he did not rest, he made contact in various manners with those that remained alive – until he succeeded in finding all of the exiles from our city. He maintained correspondence with them in order to encourage them; he concerned himself in sending them necessities. For many of these people, the letters of Yaakov and his loving care restored their faith in mankind, the faith that "Israel will not be abandoned", the faith that "the nation of Israel lives". They realized that they were not alone – they have a relative, an address – and that is Yaakov.

Yaakov's letters were very long, and full of emotion. He did not only write as the chairman of our organization. His letters were not official, but rather intimate and personal. The survivors of our city longed for those type of letters, and not terse, dry, official letters.

The organization of Sochaczew émigrés was not the only of its kind in Israel. There were many like it. However, Yaakov gave our organization its uniqueness, and made it stand out from the other organization. The other similar organizations saw it as their duty to help their brothers who survived the holocaust, for it was for that reason that they were founded – however there is help, and there is help. It is possible to give a person a bank draft along with a wish of good luck, and with that finish one's "care"! On the other hand, it is possible to give to a new immigrant a small bank draft, however to establish a warm relation with that person, who is taking his first steps in a new land, to help him form friendships, to allow him to open up his heart, to listen to him, to comfort and support him, to invite him to your home immediately, to host him, to go with him and ease his dealings with the offices and institutions, to accompany him as he searches for accommodation and later work – and afterward – to remain close with the new immigrant as he becomes accustomed to the land, to his work, to his living quarters and his new community.

Yaakov did all this, along with his faithful wife Rachel, may she live and be well. Is it possible to assign a value to such personal care? Is it possible to equate this with the granting of an official check, as was customary among the other organizations?!

I remember, during one of my visits with Yaakov and Rachel, they told me that a few days ago they visited "the children". They did not mean their own children, but rather the children who Yaakov had discovered while they were still in Poland among the gentiles. He concerned himself with bringing them to the Land of Israel. Is it any wonder that they saw the home of Yaakov and Rachel Frydman as their own home, and visited them constantly, just as one would visit actual parents?

I saw these "children" among the group that accompanied Yaakov to his final resting-place. I also saw all of the residents of the Borochov neighborhood, with whom Yaakov had walked for forty years, from the time he lived in a poor hut until the neighborhood became the center of an important city in Israel – Givatayim!

It was symbolic that the funeral procession went from his house that was near this hut to the city hall – in order to emphasize that this city did not arise on its own. Only thorns, thistles, and other wild plants grow on their own. However, with regards to a tree, one must plant it, and tend to it with love and dedication. Yaakov was one of those who "planted" the neighborhood, and "tended to it". Next to his home, he grew trees and tended to them (and in his last years he looked after the "Magen David Yarok"[2]. He also raised his own children to love the country, work, defense of the land, and pioneering.

There are those that felt that Yaakov's communal work was old fashioned, not modern, and even somewhat "inefficient" – but nothing could be further from the truth. In truth, which other communal activist would inconvenience himself to travel to a far off Kibbutz, an elderly and not well man, along with his wife, in order to represent our town at the circumcision ceremony of one of the new immigrants who had no other relatives? Which other modern communal activist would inconvenience himself to travel to Kibbutz Negba every year in order to visit the grave of a young person from our city who fell in the War of Independence?! Which other modern communal activist would trouble himself to make regular visits to every new immigrant – at least once a year – in order to see how they are getting along and acclimatizing? Indeed, only an "inefficient" person would do this! However, these types of "inefficient" people built the land, these types of "inefficient" people gave us our country, for the "inefficient" people are always the salt of the earth who give meaning to life.

I remember my first meeting with Yaakov. It was in 1942 or 1943, when the world was still suffering from the tribulations of the Nazis against our people, and it was clear that the holocaust was rapidly approaching. Even at that time, Yaakov spoke of the danger that our town was in, that it may be wiped out without a memory, Heaven forbid. He said that we must act immediately and gather information. He wished to obtain details about the extent of the holocaust, about everything that preceded it, about our town prior to the war, and our town in previous generations. We must gather facts about our town, and its Jewish community in particular, in order to gather them and perpetuate the town in a book which will serve as a monument to our town, which was about to be wiped out, so that it will not be forgotten that it was an important Jewish city, part of the glorious Jewish community of Poland; data about the town that was popular, well rooted, struggling, and effervescent.

Yaakov nurtured the idea of the book of Sochaczew and worked for it. He wrote a great deal, he prodded others into joining the effort, so that they should write and perpetuate their memories – so that we will not forget.

The book became the prime goal of our organization, and it became the prime work of his life, and the crowning achievement of all his years of work for our organization.

Yaakov would say that the Book of Sochaczew is the monument for Sochaczew. He said this, but did not realize that he was also building a monument for himself. His personality and activity for the book and for our organization remain engraved on this book, just as his memory will never be erased from our hearts forever.

Those who are proud of his accomplishments in the Land throughout the past forty years mourn the passing of this unique person. Many are indebted to him so much for their work, their efforts, and accomplishments.

The life of Yaakov Frydman was a life full of activity and content.

May his memory remain forever!

{769}

Moshe Eliezer Bornsztejn of blessed memory
by M. B. Stein
Translated by Jerrold Landau
A monument in his memory

Moshe Eliezer Bornsztejn of blessed memory

Moshe Eliezer was the son of the Admor Rabbi Shmuel of holy blessed memory, and the grandson of the Admor Rabbi Avrahamele. He was born in Sochaczew in the year 5655 (1895). He was educated and grew up until the time of his Bar Mitzvah in the atmosphere and environment of the Hassidic court of his illustrious grandfather, in whom Torah and Jewish wisdom were found in one bundle.

When he reached the age of Bar Mitzvah, at the command of his grandfather, he went to study with the Gaon Rabbi Yaakov Aharon of blessed memory, the Rabbi of the city of Konstantynow, which was close to Lodz. Rabbi Yaakov Aharon conducted a Yeshiva there for older boys.

When he returned to Sochaczew, in his sack he had a notebook of his own Torah innovative ideas, and he continued to study in the courtyard of the Rebbe, while at the same time becoming active in the city. He was particularly interested in the various special personalities who came to the Hassidic court, as well as the average people of the city.

After his wedding, he underwent a change of outlook, and during the First World War he moved to Lodz, and later to Warsaw. There, he became associated with the literary group of Y. M. Weissenberg, who influenced him greatly with his literary style. He collaborated in writing with other people, and he wrote essays and stories. His play "Himmel un Erd" ("Heaven and Earth"), which portrayed the Rabbi of Kotzk, described the deep personality and character of the Rabbi of Kotzk. He also published the play "Di Churba" ("The Ruin"), which was also on the topic of Hassidism in Galicia.

Moshe Eliezer had a constant internal struggle, and he expressed this in his saying: "Anyone who is drawn to the writers pen, carries with him his package. The package of Hassidism is drawn after me, and it is doubtful if I can ever discard this burden.".

During the world war, he stayed in Warsaw, and suffered from the Nazi rule. He succeeded in reaching Vilna, and from there, after many difficult tribulations, he reached the Land in 1941.

There, he established himself. He was for a short time the secretary of a Yiddish literary group, and he also participated in various publications. In the latter years, he was the editor of "Das Vort". He played an active role in the editing of the Yizkor Book in memory of our town.

He was involved with the people of our city, and he was the chief writer of the events of the city, which was destroyed.

He died in Jerusalem, and was buried on the 13th of Shevat, 5721 (1961).

The people from our town will always remember him with reverence and honor, as a good person, and a friend.

May his memory be blessed in our midst.

{771}

Chana Kaplan (nee Greenberg)
by Yerucham Ines
Translated by Jerrold Landau
A tear over her fresh grave

Chana Kaplan

Chana was the lone survivor of a large family. Alone, she saved herself from the frightening claws of the Nazis. Her father, Reb Eliezer Greenberg, her mother Mindel Toiba, her sisters and all members of the Greenberg family numbering dozens of souls, as well as her husband and her young son – all were killed. She remained alone as the lone survivor of her family, and a witness to the terrible tribulations.

She attempted to reconstruct her life after the war. She remarried, and her entire desire was to make aliya to Israel and to raise her only daughter in the Land, among Jews.

She succeeded in arriving in Israel with her young daughter in 1956, and after some time her stepdaughter also arrived and joined them. Her wish that her husband would liquidate his business in Poland and come to Israel, so that they could all live together and build their family anew was never realized.

Chana was a proud woman, and despite her weak health, she went to work in a factory in order to support herself honorably. However the difficulty in adapting caused her illness, which she had already contracted during the holocaust, to worsen. She valiantly fought for her life, for the sake of her young daughter the hope of her life, but in vain. On the second day of Rosh Hashanah 5721 (September 12, 1961), she succumbed to her cruel illness. She was only 51 at the time of her passing.

May her soul be bound in the bonds of eternal life.

{772}

Those Who Fell in the Battle for the Homeland
Translated by Jerrold Landau

{774}

Shmuel Avraham Bornsztejn

He was the son of Aharon Yisrael and Rivka (nee Morgenstern), and a grandson of the Admor of Sochaczew and Sokolow. He was born on the 4th of Adar 5688 (1928) in Sokolow, and made aliya to the Land in 5694 (1934). He completed the Bilu School and Haskala high school in Tel Aviv. He worked in a textile factory, excelled, and reached the rank of technician. He intended to continue his studies in the United States. He was a member of the cadet corps from age fourteen, and later on, of the Haganah. He interrupted his work and activities in the Haganah twice due to drawn out illnesses, however, due to his dedication and capabilities, he quickly made up what he missed, excelled in his studies, and gained thorough knowledge of both Hebrew and general literature. He had extensive knowledge of music and its literature.

He intended to travel to study in the University of Philadelphia in 1947, however with the worsening of the national situation, he did not want to leave the land. He said: "the concern for the public is more important than my private concern". At the time of the announcement of the U. N. partition decision, he was in the hospital with a serious illness, and when he was released, he enlisted in January 1948. He concealed the remnants of his illness and his weakness from the physicians, and he entered into full duty. He completed the sergeant's course, and he was in charge of new conscripts. He cut off his connection with his childhood friends due to their evading of military duty. He participated in the battles of Mishmar Haemek, and was appointed as company commander. He refused an opportunity to serve behind the lines, and chose to be with his men on the front line. He fell in battle along with his group while protecting the harvesters in the fields of Tel Adashim on Lag Baomer, the 18th of Iyar 5708 (May 25, 1948). His body was brought from Nazareth to Tel Aviv, and he was brought to rest in the Nachalat Yitzchak cemetery on July 30, 1948.

Shmuel Avraham Bornsztejn

May his soul be bound in the bonds of eternal life.

{775}
Shmuel (Shmulik) Jasinski

He was the son of Menashe and Dina. He was born on May 30, 1929 in Sochaczew. He ended up in the Warsaw ghetto at age 10, and he hid in the municipal sewer system and was saved from extermination. He suffered from the tribulations of hunger and wandering. After the war, he went to Germany and Italy. He went illegally to the Land of Israel[3] and was exiled to Cyprus. He was permitted entry as part of the Youth Aliya in 1947. He joined the Yosef Kaplan group, and began working in agriculture in the Negba. The tribulations of his youth left their mark. Even after he got used to the life of a free person, he remained quiet and closed within himself, however he finally became accustomed to the work. He particularly enjoyed working as a wagon driver.

He participated in the defense of the Negev, and he performed bravely and valiantly in battle, until he was shot in the head by a sniper of the Iraqi army[4]. He was buried in Negba on June 2, 1948.

Shmuel Jasinski

We had encouraged him to overcome his thoughts about the time that he went through the ghetto. We walked with him, and he eventually revealed his emotions. In once sentence, he said everything: "I have not yet recovered from the nightmare of the ghetto. I cannot forget the life in the sewer system. The odor of the sewage in the sewers remains in my nostrils even today… and furthermore, the horrible, tragic images." This was the secret of his reticence.

He worked faithfully in the Negba Kibbutz, and he was affectionately called "Shmulik". I received a short letter from him, with a photo, two days before his death, as if he had a premonition of what was to come.

A few years after his death, I found out that his sister had survived and lived in a remote village in Poland. He had been certain that she had been murdered along with everyone else after they had parted.

May his memory be blessed and holy!

By Y. P.

TRANSLATOR'S FOOTNOTES:

1. A reference to the difficult physical existence in Palestine at the time. This is a quote from the book of Numbers, when the ten spies referred to the land as being a good land, but one that eats up its inhabitants.

2. Literally, the "Green Magen David", seemingly some sort of society for the care of nature.

3. This refers to the Haapala, or illegal immigration, which took place during the final years of the British Mandate of Palestine, when the British imposed quotas on the number of immigrants allowed in to Palestine.

4. Iraq was one of the Arab countries that sent its army into the newly founded State of Israel in 1948, even though it does not share a border with Israel.

2.

{776}

Tzvi (Hershele) Lewin

He was the son of David and Chana. He was born in 1930 in Sochaczew. He was imprisoned in the ghetto by the Nazis at age nine, however he managed to escape, and lived in the home of Christian farmers as their child. After the conclusion of the war, he went to the Halinbok children's home, and left Poland with his friends to go to the Land of Israel. On the way, he was imprisoned in Cyprus for three-quarters of a year, and arrived in the Land on September 26, 1947. His desire was to settle on a Kibbutz. He went through his Kibbutz training in the house of pioneers (Beit Hachalutzot) in Afula, and at the conclusion, he joined the Palmach in May 1948. He fell during the course of duty in the war for the liberation of Jerusalem on July 17, 1948. On the 11th of Adar 5710 (February 28, 1950), his body was transferred to the Har Herzl cemetery in Jerusalem.

Tzvi (Hershele) Lewin

Prior to his enlistment in the Palmach, he came to ask for his posting. I refused, and I requested that he finished his preparations, to regain his strength after what had transpired to him, and to learn the language. He promised to fulfil my request. After a short time, we received a letter from the Palmach training camp, in which he wrote: "You are my parents, my father and mother. You should think of me, and forgive me that I have promised and not fulfilled. Given that I have survived – I wish to help free Israel along with all the Jewish youth. I have told you everything, since you are my parents. I will keep in touch with you with any information."

A short time thereafter, I received the official announcement from the Zahal representative: "Tzvi Lewin has fallen". Prior to going out to the final battle, he informed us that you are his parents, and I am fulfilling his will and our duty – you should be comforted". He left me the official announcement and left – we both burst out crying...

Several weeks later, a Palmach representative arrived and announced in sorrow: "Tzvi Hershele commanded before his death that we should give you his bag with his belongings. You should certainly remember him through it, and each year remember his memory."

May his memory be blessed and holy!

Each year we go up to visit the graves of the two: Shmuel Jasinski and Tzvi Lewin.

By Y. P.

{778}

Meir Orbach

He was the son of Yitzchak, and the grandson of Mordechai Schlesinger.

He was born in 1909 to a committed and respected Hassidic family, the descendents of rabbis. His family moved to Warsaw during the First World War. Afterwards, his beloved mother died, and it was very difficult for him in the house with his stepmother. He moved to the home of his paternal grandfather, however, he could not find a common language with him, so he became closed and inwardly turned. His grandfather was a Maskil and a lover of Zion, and he educated his grandson in that manner. There, he found out for the first time about the books of Mapu, and studied bible. His studies in school were not orderly; therefore he left and started working to support himself. He had technical capabilities. He became active in the youth movements.

His father's house and its business did not attract him. When he had the opportunity to visit a glass factory (his father was a middleman for glass products), he chose to remain there as a worker. He aided in publicity with the workers, and aided them in their organization. "I cannot not be a socialist" – he said – "just as I cannot not be a Jew".

From the glass factory, he transferred to agricultural work and trained with weapons. These were his preparations for military duty. At age seventeen, he volunteered for the Polish army in order to train in the use of weapons.

When he made aliya to the Land in 1929, he served as a guard and watchman for the Talpiot district of Jerusalem. From that time on, he became very dedicated to the Haganah, and studied matters of security.

Meir Orbach

In his first period in the Land, he suffered from many difficulties. He worked in the groves of Petach Tikva, and suffered from shortage of work and hungry, however he never turned to his father for assistance. He trusted in the resourcefulness of the Hebrew worked in the Land in general, and on the Moshava in particular. He said about his friends that left the Moshava: "They left because they left themselves". He always demanded a great deal of himself, and saw himself as an example, however he never demanded from anyone else more than he could do himself.

He transferred to work in the groves in the area of Ramat Gan. He served as a foreman and trainer. He always had his flute and broken harmonica with him, as well as his revolver. He trained in signaling, and became an expert signaler.

In 1933, he moved to Gan Yavneh, and was one of its builders and protectors. He struggled for the rights of the workers in the institutions of the Moshava.

In 1936, from the time that the troubles broke out, he did not leave Gan Yavneh even for a day, and especially not for a night. He dedicated himself completely to the defense of the place. The work during the days and guard duty at night had an ill effect on his health, and he weakened. When they urged him to travel to a sanatorium, he refused. His response to his father who requested that he come home for a visit was as follows: "It is not proper to leave the Land even for a short period, and to give up on its stand.". He believed in the future, in peace, but he did not merit to witness it.

He and his friend Avraham Cohen traveled to Tel Aviv for urgent Haganah business and returned to Gan Yavneh in the afternoon. They sat on the first seat near the driver, and kept their eyes open on the roadway, ready to answer any fire. When the bus reached a grove between Pardes Warberg and Mishtarat Beit Dagon, the bus was suddenly shot a few times. Two bullets penetrated the walls of the bus and hit them both simultaneously – his friend Avraham in the head and Meir in the chest. Cohen succeeded in shooting one shot with his revolver, and then he fell, wallowing in his blood. Meir died immediately. Thus did the two fall, the two who stood on guard for the security of Gan Yavneh. They both gave their lives simultaneously while fulfilling their security duties. Meir was the right hand of his friend Avraham Cohen in matters of guarding and defense. He was 29 years old when he died. He left a wife who at that time was a teacher in Gan Yavneh.

{780}

Epilogue
by Yaakov Tzidkoni
Translated by Jerrold Landau

If a person dies, people pay their final respects, eulogize him, mourn for him, and place a monument upon the grave.

If the person is an average person, his community, and in particular his family, are saddened by his death. They arrange a funeral according to his status, recite the 'tziduk hadin' [1], and bring him to a Jewish grave.

If a Torah luminary or other illustrious person passes away, many come to pay their final respects, including honorable scholars, who speak about his praiseworthiness and lament his passing.

If a disaster occurs in a community, such as an epidemic, fire, or other such calamity, the event is recorded in the town's record books as an eternal record of the mourning.

... And there is no greater calamity in the annals of Israel than the terrible disaster that took place to us in our generation. Millions of Jews were slaughters, including people of Sochaczew.

If an entire community is destroyed, the records, council hall as well and the town annals are also burned. How can we now remember and relate to those who come after us, until the final generation, about the terrible holocaust that came onto us?

The reality gave rise to two customs that were accepted by the holocaust survivors.

An annual memorial day for the loss of the dear ones is observed by the town's natives on the anniversary (true or approximate) of the slaughter – and 'Yizkor books' are published.

At the time of the memorial gathering, which is like a collective Yahrzeit, we unite ourselves with the memory of our holy martyrs. We light Yahrzeit candles. Heartfelt eulogies are delivered, which penetrate the heart of the listeners.

The Yizkor book, which is a living monument for perpetuity, is different. The book is written by simple people who are moved by deep feelings from the soul. The survivors, who feel the pain of their community that was cut off, weep over the destruction and establish a memorial. On the one hand, it is good that the books are not published too soon, so that they can create a more removed perspective, which enables an appropriate evaluation of the terrible events. On the other hand, it is good that the publication is not pushed off too long, so that the opportunity does not pass, lest friends be forgotten.

Here we have before us a memorial monument, full of content and deliberations, which was set up with love and self-sacrifice by the natives of the city. Whenever we read it, we are carried by the locks of our ears [2] back to our town, and our eyes are once again filled with visions of the streets, alleyways and stores, and of those who lived there – whom we loved so much – and are no longer alive.

In conclusion, we extend a "yasher koach" [3] to those who helped in the publication of the book, to those who participated in the writing and editing, to the members of the committee of the Organization of Sochaczew Émigrés in Israel, and to those who extended financial help.

TRANSLATOR'S FOOTNOTES:

1. A funeral prayer in which the righteousness of G-d's judgement is acknowledged, even if we do not understand it. https://www.jewishgen.org/Yizkor/Sochaczew/so753.html - 1rt

2. A reference from the book of Ezekiel, when Ezekiel was carried in a dream by the locks of his ears from his exile in Babylon to the Holy Temple in Jerusalem.

3. "May your strength go forward", a traditional good wish extended to people who participate in a holy task.

דעם הייליקן אָנדענק פֿון די סאָכאַטשעװער קדושים, װעלכע װערן דאָ אויסגערעכנט, און אויך די װעמענס נעמען ס'איז אונדז, ליידער, נישט געלונגען אויפֿצונעמען — אַלע די װאָס זענען אומגעקומען על קדוש־השם װעל קדוש־העם, איז געװידמעט אונדזער בוך.

לזכרם של קדושי סוכצ׳וב המפורטים כאן, וכן לאלה אשר לא הצלחנו, לגלות שמותיהם, — לכל אלה אשר נספו על קדוש־השם וקדוש־העם, מוקדש הספר הזה.

Names of the Martyrs
Translated by Jerrold Landau

(Note: Page numbers and translator comments are enclosed in brackets.) Page numbers of the page numbers of the original Yizkor Book, not this translation.

Aleph

{783}

Ovitzki	Avraham		Eisenstein	Mendel
	Mania			Malia
	Chava Lea		Eisenstein	Yisrael and family
Avraham Yitzchak	(the wigmaker's son) and his family {last name not provided}		Eisman	Moshe
				Freidel
				Rozshka
Adamchik	Miriam		Eisman	Yisrael
	Yechezkel (Chaskel)			Sara
	Feivish		Albert	Yosef
Auerbach	Yitzchak (Itche) and his family			Bluma
Indik	Zalman		Albert	Yechiel Nathan
	Tauba			Rachel
	Baruch			Baruch
	Yitzchak			Gella
	Zanwil		Alberg	Beila
Inklus	Wolf		Alberg	Lea
	Yehoshua		Alshevitz	Esther
	Sara			Binyamin
Inklus	Moshe			Yitzchak
	Mania			And daughter
Eisenberg	Yaakov		Alshevski	Moshe
	Chana			Gella
	Polia		Opozdover	Yisrael
	And family			Chana
Eisenberg	Pesach			Genia
	Rozsha			Karola
	And family			Moshe

Opozdover	Meir	Oklinski	Berl
	Reizel		Hugra
	And family	Oklinski	Chana
Opozdover	Avraham and family		Chaim
Opozdover	Eliezer (Luzer) and family	Oklinski	Leibel
			Freda
Opozdover	Yitzchak (Itche) and family	{784}	
Akavitz	Meir Wolf	Oklinski	Tzvi (Hershel)
	Rachel		Feiga
	Shmuel	Oklinski	Moshe
	Chana		Sara

Bet ב

Bauman	Fishel	Baruchovitch	Shprintza
	Sara		Abba
	Rachel		Chava
	Mendel	Bornstein	Aharon
Baumarder	Avraham Moshe		Mania
	Ezriel		Feiga
	Mottel		Yetka
	Nechama (Chuma)		Lea
	Yechezkel (Chaskel)		Sima
Balas	Yudel	Bornstein	Yechezkel (Chaskel)
	Yisrael		Chava
	Eliezer (Leizer)		Yehoshua (Shia)
Balsam	Polia	Bornstein	Eliahu
	Chaya		Chaim Wolf
	Bronia		Wolf
	Yitzchak		Sara

	Sima		Gittel
	And children		Libe
Bornstein	Moshe	Bzozovski	Yisrael
	Malka		Hendel
	Sheina Yenta		Wolf
	And children		Tzvi (Hersch)
Bornstein	Michel and family		Rachel
Bornstein	Esther	{785}	
Bornstein	Avraham and family	Bzozovski	Gershon
Boznitzki	Eliahu	Bzozovski	Berl
	Lea		Tzirel
	Tovia		Baruch
	Hinda Esther		Shmuel
	And children		Lea
Boznitzki	Moshe	Bzozovski	Meir
	Reizel		Lea
	And children		Esther
Bzozovski	Tzvi (Hershel)		Bracha
	Hadassah	Bzozovski	Beila Feiga
	Chaim		Hinda Esther
	Tova		Bracha
	Henia	Bzozovski	Meir
	Moshe		Feiga
Bzozovski	Shlomo	Bzozovski	Moshe
	Tzirel		Yenta
	Chaim Yaakov		And children
	Yeshayahu (Shia)	Bzozovski	Feivel

	Asher		Miriam
	Avraham	Beigelbeker	Mendel
	Machla Sara		Esther
Brzezinski	Hugra		And children
	Nachman	Beitshman	Shimon Wolf
	Mania		Pessa
Biderman	Yaakov		Ita Rivka
	Shrpintza		Malka
	Hela		Zisman
	Dora		Yisrael
Bienenthal	Meir Yechiel	Beitshman	Yaakov Shimon
	Sheindel		Malka
	And family	Beitshman	Avraham
Bister	Blima		Chana
Biezanski	Mordechai	Beitshman	Yisrael Avraham
	Yocheved		Feiga
	Meir	Beitshman	David
	Yitzchak		Breindel
Biezanski	Feiga	Beitshman	Kaufman
	Sima	Blum	Shaulka
Biezanski	Yudel		Roiza Gittel
	Tirza		Rikel
	Batia		Yechezkel
	Hugra		Shrpintza
Biezanski	Avraham	Blum	Hersch Yosef
	Feiga		Esther Liba
Biezanski	Chana		Chaim

Blumenthal	Meir		Ita
	Miriam	Bergazin	Mendel
{786}			Frimet
Blumenthal	Naftali		Sara
	Eliahu		Yaakov
	Chana Roiza	Bentshkovski	Simcha
	David		Yaakov
Blumenthal	Naftali		Levi
	Golda	Beker	Chaim Pinchas
	And children		Yitzchak Mordechai
Blumenthal	Avraham	Beker	Chana
	Nechama	Beker	Yudel and family
	Chaya	Berliner	Moshe
Blumenthal	Yitzchak and family		Golda
Blumenthal	Naftali		Kova
	Pinchas		Balbina
	And family	Berman	Sara Yenta
Berg	Nachman Leib		Sheva
	Rivka Lea		Rivka Eidel
	Yaakov Yona		Berish
	Chaya Esther	Berman	Hertzka
	Tzvi		Hinda
Bergazin	Yaakov		Shalom
	Chaya		Zilpa
	Feivel	Berkovitch	Meir
	Rivka		Chana
	Shimon		Roiza

	Yudel	Brandshpigel	Necha
	Sheindel	Brochovski	Shmuel
	Zlata		Rachel
Berkovitch	Eliahu		Sara
	Chava		Keila
	And children		And children
Berkovitch	Yissachar	Brochovski	Naftali
	Michal		Yentel
	Feiga		And children
Berkovitch	Malia	Broitman	Wolf
	Chaya		Esther
Berkovitch	Itshe Zalman		And children
	Keila	Broitman	Leib
Berkovitch	Chana Breindel	Broitman	Roiza
Broder	Shlomo		Malia
	Feiga		Betzalel
	Yechezkel (Chaskel)	Broitman	Hertzka
Brott	Rachel		Sara Lea
	Motta		Chava
	Sender	Broitman	Chaya
{787}		Brof	Tsharna
Brand	Leizer Yosef		Tzvi (Hershel)
	Esther Gella	Bressler	Tzvi (Hershel)
	Dvora		Pinchas
	Pessa		Yona
	Rachel		Sheindel
	Michal		Fela

	Tema		Leibel
Bressler	Mania		
	Chaya Reizel		
Gimel ג			
Gotthelf	Tzvi (Hershel)		Rachel
	Malka Beila		Moshe
	Matel	Gotthelf	Shmuel Leib
	Berka		Ethel
	Shmuel David		And children
	Dreizel	Gottlieb	Hershel
	Freda		His wife
	Eliezer (Leizer)		Avraham Yitzchak
Gotthelf	Gedaliahu	{788}	
	Miriam Beila	Gottlieb	Golda
	Hendel		Mania
	Shaul		Chaya
	Mordechai		And other children
	Dreizel	Goldberg	Yitzchak
Gotthelf	Chava		His wife
	Yisrael		Berl
Gotthelf	Roiza		Sara
	Dova		Shlomo
Gotthelf	Binyamin		Mania
	Frimet	Goldberg	Sara
	Chaya		Eliahu
	Dreizel		Shmuel
Gotthelf	Gedaliahu		Hinda

	Rachel	Goldberg	Feivel
	Yenta		Lea
Goldberg	Chaim		Blima
	Alte Lea		Avraham
	Leibel		Kalman
	Chaika	Goldberg	Zalman
	Sara		Sheindel
Goldberg	Getzel		Chaim
	Chana		Freda
	Freda	Goldberg	Getzel
	Eliezer (Leizer)		Chana
	Yehoshua (Shia)		And children
Goldberg	Yehoshua (Shia)	Goldberg	Dvora
	Tauba Rachel		Yudel
	Tzvi (Hershel)	Goldberg	Chaim
	Beila		Dvora
	Esther	Goldberg	Chanina
Goldberg	Pessa		Breindel
	Friedel	Goldberg	Feiga
	Yehoshua (Shia)	Goldman	David
	Gitman		Chana
	Chaya		Gittel
Goldberg	Dvora		Rivka
	Eliahu		Zissel
Goldberg	Shmuel		Yisrael
	Friedel	Goldman	Wolf
	Rachel		Gittel

	Malka		David
	Shmuel		Chana
	Tzirel		Hinda
	Yitzchak		Shmuel
Goldman	Yitzchak	Goldstein	Moshe
	Blima		Feiga
	Avraham		Chaya
Goldman {789}	Yudel		Hadassah
			Avraham
Goldman	Eida		Shmuel
	Mendel	Goldstein	Baruch
Goldman	Moshe		Pessa
	Chaitsha		Hinda
Goldfarb	Shmuel Hertzka		Hadassah
	Aharon		Avraham
	Shifra	Goldstein	Yehoshua
	Sara		Gittel
	Eliahu		Chana Sara
Goldfarb	Yisrael		Yaakov
	Feiga		David
	Pessa	Goldstein	Mordechai Menachem
Goldfarb	Hersch Gedaliahu		Pessa
	Pessa	Goldshlak	Moshe Aharon
	Yaakov		His wife
Goldstein	Yehoshua (Shia)		Yitzchak
	His wife		Michal
	Yaakov	Galek	Shlomo

	Bracha	Gottglas	Shmuel
	Wolf		Heniek
	Golda Lea	Guttman	Pinchas
	Avraham		Chaya
	Yocheved	{790}	
	Rivka	Guttman	Chaim
Galek	Feivel		Keila
	Sara	Gutthart	Yechiel Meir
	And children		Yenta
Gombinski	Yehoshua (Shia)		Yaakov
	Malka		Etka
	Alter	Gidalevitch	Yudel
	Bronia		Chana Reizel
	Rivka		Yaakov Shimon
Gombinski	Yosef		Yitzchak
	Sara Malka		Hugra
	Chaya	Gidalevitch	Moshe
	Ber		Malka
Gombinski	Melech		Hinda Rivka
	And family		Chaim
Gottglas	Moshe	Gidalevitch	Yaakov
	His wife		Reizel
	Shmuel		And children
	Meniek	Gidalevitch	Chava
Gottglas	Yisrael		Her husband
	Chaitshka	Gidalevitch	Chaim
	Saliek	Gingold	Moshe Yudel

	Sara	Gelman	Freda
	Zeev (Hershel)	Gersht	Yerachmiel
	Yocheved		Sara
Gingold	Yitzchak Eizik		Tila
	Esther		Chana
	Tzvi		Shlomo
	Baruch		Baruch
	Betzalel		Shmuel
Gingold	Wolf	Graubard	Mordechai
	Freda Lea		Hinda
	And children		Blima
Gines	Chaim		Yaakov
Gips	Pessa	Graubard	Motta
	Pinchas		Feiga
Glikzeliker	Yitzchak (Itshka)		Avraham
	His wife		And children
	Mordechai	Graubard	Noach
	And children		His wife
Getlichman	Moshe		Berl
	Tsharna		Feivel
	Yisrael		And children
	Rachel Lea	Graubard	Yudel Leib
Gelbstein	Yoel		Hendel
	Rachel	Graubard	Chana
Gelbstein	Yitzchak (Itche) and child		Chava
		Graubard	Moshe
Gelbstein	Machla	Grodzitzki	Mordechai

	Chana Chaya		Levi
	Yitzchak		Yosef
Grossman	Aharon	Greenberg	Yerucham
	Tauba		Avraham
{791}			Yenta
Grossman	Rivka		Machla
Grossman	Tauba		Elka
Grondwag	Simcha	Greenberg	Eliezer (Leizer)
	Sara Rivka		Mindel
Grondwag	Nachum		Yenta
	Rivka	Greenberg	Chava
	Esther		Yaakov
Grondwag	Chana		Rachel
Groinem	Zanwil		Yitzchak (Itshe)
	Tauba Gittel	Greenberg	Chana
	Yudel		Yisrael
	Tzvi (Hershel)		Moshe
Gringard	Yitzchak and children	Greenberg	Tzvi (Hershel)
Grinspan	family		Gutsha
Greenberg	Shmuel Hersch		Yoel
	Golda	Greenberg	Aharon
	Sara		Tzirel
	Hertzka		Menachem
	Chana	Greenberg	Avraham
	Shlomo		Chana
Greenberg	David		And children
	Chana	Greenberg	Moshe

	Miriam		And children
	And children	Greenberg	Blima
Greenberg	Avraham		Velvel
	Chaya	Greenberg	Yaakov
Greenberg	Perl Zlata	Gritzhendler	Eliezer (Leizer)
	Feiga		Gittel
Greenberg	Shlomo		And children
	Miriam		

Dalet ד

Davidovitch	Feiga		And child
	Yaakov	Davidovitch	Leibel
	Blima		Michal
	Mordechai		And child
Davidovitch	David	Weiss	Eliezer (Lozer) {this entry is out of place alphabetically}
Davidovitch	Shlomo		
	Rivka		Rivka
{792}		Davidovitch	Tzvi (Hershel)
Davidovitch	Chana		His wife
	Rachel	Davidovitch	Meir
Davidovitch	Moshe	Davidovitch	Ozer
	His wife		His wife
	Sala	Danziger	Yisrael
	Esther		Taubcha
Davidovitch	Motta		Simcha Binem
	Freda		Necha
	Yitzchak		Gittel

Danziger	Leizer Yitzchak	Deichus	Noach
	Frimet	Deichus	Avraham
	David	Degenshein	Wolf
Dzigan	Yosef Aharon		Hodess
Dzigan	Ita		Frimet
	Chana	Dreifus	Alter
	Avraham		Rachel
Dzigan	Yehoshua (Shia)		And daughter
	Chana		

(Note: Page numbers and translator comments are enclosed in brackets.)

Hey ה

Haberman	Moshe
	Freda
	Ziskind
	Berl
	Sara
Haberman	Yosef
Hochbaum	Yerachmiel
	Roiza
Hollander	Yitzchak (Itshe)

{793}

Hollander	Esther and her child
Hollander	Chaim
	Miriam
Holtzman	Mordechai
	Machla

Diament	Meir
	Sheindel Lea
	Yudel
	Beila
	Aharon David
Diament	Yudel
	His wife
	Aharon
	David
	Berl
	And child
Diament	Yechiel
	Batia
	Chaya Liba
Diament	Lipman
Diener	Yitzchak (Itshe)
	Miriam
	And children

	Chana	Helmer	Meir
	Rozka		Hinda
	Esther		Eidel
Holtzman	Chaim Hersch		Yechezkel (Chaskel)
	Frania		Tzvi (Hershel)
	Meir	Helmer	Tzvi (Hershel)
	Gittel		His wife
Holtzman	Moshe		Chaim
	Sheva		Yitzchak
	Shmuel	Helmer	Leibel
Holtzman	Chaya Tauba		Rachel
	Yosef	Herbstein	Pessa
	Nathan		Zlata
Holtzman	Feivish		Chaya
	Miriam		David
	Shmuel		Rachel
Holtzman	Motta		Menashe
	Blima		Sara
	And children		Lea
Holtzman	Malka		Miriam
	Yenta	Herbstein	Shlomo Zalman
Hofenung	Meir		Pessa
	Shifra		Esther
Hirschbein	Keila		Zlata
	Aharon		Sara
Hillel	Treger {This entry is alphabetized by first name}		David
			Lea

		Michal		Chaya Rivka
		Shlomo Zalman		Hinda
Herbstein		Menashe		Batsha
		Michal	Hershberg	Moshe
Hershkovitz		Nachum		Rachel
		Pessa		Esther
		Reizel	{794}	
		Hertzka	Hershberg	Asher
		Avraham	Hershberg	Rachel
		Gittel		
Hershberg		Kalman		

Vav ו

Waldman	Chaim Yaakov		Shmuel
	Yenta Malka		And family
	And children	Warshavski	Nachum and family
Waldenberg	Shlomo	Wiedislavski	Moshe
	Rozsha		Sara
Varman	the lawyer and family	Volkovitch	Yosef
Wasserman	Sender		Leibel
	Pessa		Motta
	Chana		Sheina
	Kudesh	Walman	Leibel the judge
Warshavski	Hershel	Walman	Moshe David and family
	Regina		
	Esther	Walfish	Nathan
Warshavski	Hersch Wolf		Blima Gittel

	And children		Nachshon
Videletz	Yechiel	Vimberg	Hugra
	Chana	Vishnia	Eliahu
	Bronia		Machla
	Shalom		Moshe
Wittenberg	Shifra and family		Berl
Winter	Yechiel	Vishogrodski	Chaya
	Moshe		Leibish
	Sara	Weiss	Eliezer (Leizer)
Winter	Fishel		Blima
	Michal		Rachel
Wiener	Chaim David		And children
	Shlomo	Weiss	Shmuel
	Mottel	{794}	
	Tsharna	Weiss	Roiza
	Rivka		Eliezer (Lozer)
	Binem Meir		Blima
Wiener	Zigi		Avraham
	Avraham		Yisrael Yaakov
	And family	Weiss	David
Wiener	Shimon and family		Tauba
Wiener	Yitzchak		Meir
	Esther		Moshe
Winkler	Berish		Menashe
	Chana Reizel		And three other children
	Feiga	Weinstock	Rachel
	Avraham		

	Sheindel		Chaya
	Chaya		Yisrael Nathan
	Rivka		Rivka
	Moshe		Mordechai Binem
Weitzman	Sender		
	Lea		

Zayin ז

Zavadzki	Yehoshua (Shia)	Zaltzman	Betzalel
	Roiza		Frimet
	Zissel		Berish
Zavadzski	Chaim David		Chava
	Reizel		Feiga
	And children		Golda
Zaonz	Chanoch (Henech)	Zaltzman	Yechezkel
	Sara		Paula
	Lea	Zaltzman	Yaakov David
	Moshe		Lea Elka
	Alter		Betzalel
	Shlomo		Chava
Zaonz	Yitzchak		Eliezer
	Chaya Reizl		Tzvi (Hershel)
	Lea	Zaltzman	Moshe
Zaonz	Alter		Machla
	Blima		Yitzchak (Itshe)
Zaonz	Motta		Dvora
	Tsharna		Sara

	Aharon David	Zaltzman	Beila
Zaltzman	Pinchas	Zand	Avraham
	Yenta Lea		Chaya Sara
	Yaakov		Hertzka
	Rachel		Grunem
	Chava		Yosef
	Shalom	Zand	Yaakov
Zaltzman	Moshe Yudel		Esther
	Chava		Avraham
	Meir	Zand	Aharon
	Gittel		Tauba
	Ita	Zand	Leibel
{796}			Sheindel
Zaltzman	Eliezer	Zander	Moshe
	Rachel		Beila
	Sheina Yenta		Betzalel
	Paula		Bronia
Zaltzman	Yechiel Meir	Silber	Gavriel
	Keila		Dvora
	Eliahu		Avraham
	Yenta		Sonia
Zaltzman	Shmuel		Tzipora
	Gittel	Silberman	Yisrael Meir
	Meir		Chana
Zaltzman	Berl		Reiva
	Lea	Silberman	Yehoshua (Shia)
	Efraim	Silberstein	Yosef

	Miriam		Sara
	And children	Jelechovski	Eizik (Mikvenik)
Silberman	Yisrael Meir		Perl
	Rivka		Sara Nechama
Silberman	Yehoshua		Breindel
Zisman	Eliezer (Leizer)	Zelonka	Moshe
	Lea		Beila
	Rachel		Rota
	Avraham		David
	Moshe		Sender
	Yitzchak Meir	{797}	
	Eliahu	Zelmanovitch	Avraham
Zeifman		Zemel	Moshe
Zlotnick	Avraham		Rivka
	Chana		And children
	Tzirel	Zranov	Shimon
	Esther		Chana
Zlotnick	Baruch Shimon		
	Freda Lea	Chet ח	
	And children	Chazan	Lea
Jelozko	Yitzchak (Itshe)	Chaitshek	Leibel
	Rachel		Sara
	Shaul		Meir
	Yisrael		Chava
Jelechovski	Eizik	Chaitshek	Chana
	Perl		Sara
	Breindel		Malka

		Meir		Gittel
Chaimovitch	Mordechai			David
		Eidel	Taubenfeld	Avraham
Chaimovitch	Malka			Lea
		Hinda	Taubenfeld	Chaim Leizer and family
		Chava		
		Chaya	Taubenfeld	Nachman
		Avraham		Rozka
		Yoel	Tilman	Yitzchak
		Rachel		Rachel
Chaimovitch	Rachel			Nachman
		Leibel		Malka
Chaimovitch	Avraham			Yisrael
				Rivka
Tet ט				Dvora
				Eidel
Taub	Moshe		Tilman	Moshe
		Friedel		Chaya
		Avraham		Ita
		Tauba		Yenta
Taub	Yosef			Malka
		Rachel		Tzvi (Hershel)
Taubenfeld	Leibel		Tilman	Yerucham
		Chaim Leizer	{798}	
		Sara	Tilman	Breina and child
		Sheindel	Tilman	Ita and daughter
		Yitzchak	Tilman	Shmuel
Taubenfeld	Yitzchak			

	Sara		Bina
	Necha		Yeshayahu (Shia)
	Meir		Esther
Tilman	Michal	Tsharka	Yaakov
Tilman	Sara		Lea
	Meir	Tsharka	Libka
	Necha		Krusa
Tilman	Mechel and family	Tsharka	Tzvi (Hershel)
Tilman	Avraham		Shrprintza
	Rozsha	Tshinkus	Shlomo
	Tzvi		Lea
Tilman	Chaitsha		Velvel
	Binyamin	Tshernievski	Moshe
Tilman	Yechiel Meir		Hentshe
	Esther Lea		Avraham
Tikotshiner	Moshe		Renia
	Ita	Tshernievski	Zechariahu
	Abba		Lea
Tshervoniek	Zelik		Rachel
	His wife	Tshernievski	Reuven
	Chaim		Rozka
	Yechezkel (Chaskel)		Moshe
	Hinda	Tempel	Avraham
Tshervoniek	Yechiel (Chil)		His wife
	Rachel	Tempel	Manes
Tshervoniek	Moshe Ber		Sheindel
Tshervinski	Yosef Meir	Terner	Avraham

	Sheindel		Sara
			Yehoshua (Shia)
Yod			Perl
Jablonski	Moshe		Gedaliahu
	Rivka		Sima
	Yaakov		Shamai
	Leib		Lea
Jablonski	Avraham		Sheindel
Jablonski	Chava	Jakobovitz	Moshe
	Yaakov		Esther Feiga
Jablonski	Meir		Sara
	Chaya		Chaya
	Yaakov		Gnedel
{799}			Sonia
Jablonski	Miriam		Binyamin
	Chava	Jakobovitz	Shalom
	Lea		Rivka
Jablonski	Moshe		Rachel
	Rivka		Sara
Javitz	Helena		Beila
Jazinek	Dora		Betzalel
	Shmuel	Jakobovitz	Berl
	Sheindel		Chaya
Jazinek	Shaul		Yosef
	Dina		Chava
	Chaim		Glika
Jakobovitz	Bracha	Jakobovitz	Alter

Jakobovitz	Rachel			Nathan
	Betzalel		Jakobovitz	Moshe
	David			Chaya
	Tzvi (Hershel)			Eliahu
Jakobovitz	Chaim			Tauba
	Mindel		Jakobovitz	Yoel Mechel
	Bendet			Feiga
	Sara			Betzalel
Jakobovitz	Tzvi (Hershel)			And children
	Eidel		Jakobovitz	Yosef
	Shaul			Reizel
	Aharon Zelik			Akiva
Jakobovitz	Yaakov		Jakobovitz	David
	Malka		{800}	
	Shmuel Yossel		Jakobovitz	Mindel
	Dvora		Jakobovitz	Feiga
Jakobovitz	Tzirel			Rachel
	Sara		Jakobovitz	Eliezer (Leizer)
	Berish Leib		Jakobovitz	Shlomo
	Sina (Saneh)		Yashinski	Bendet
Jakobovitz	Yudel			Rivka
	Tsharna			Mendel
	Moshe			Yaakov
	Sara			Feiga
Jakobovitz	Chaim Yisrael			Tzvi (Hershel)
	Chaya			Yudel
	Berish Leib		Yashinski	Bendet

	Tauba	Izralevitch	Shmuel
	Blima		Malka
	Gittel		Lea
Yashinski	Bendet		Sara
	Feiga		Chana
	Dreizel		Yitzchak
	Tzvi (Hershel)	Izralevitch	Avraham
	Esther		Chaya
	And three children		Lea
Yashinski	Elazar		Yitzchak
	Rachel		Blima
	And children	Izralevitch	Hershel
Yashinski	Chana		Pessa
Izralevitch	Moshe		Yisrael
	Chana Sara		Bendet
	Tzvi (Hershel)		Moshe
	Leibish	Izralevitch	Reuven
	Avraham		Feiga
	Yitzchak		Bronia
	Henna Liba		Yitzchak
Izralevitch	Tovia		Binyamin
	Chaya	Izralevitch	Gitman
	Henia		Sheindel
Izralevitch	Yitzchak		Freda
	Chana	Izralevitch	Yitzchak
	Zechariahu		Machla
	Avraham	Izralevitch	Avraham

Izralevitch	Feivel		Chana
Izralski	David		And children
	Gershon		Moshe Aharon
	Chaya		Hodess
	Gnedel		And children
Yarlicht	Mordechai	Cohen	Michael and child
	Malka	Cohen	Gutsha
	Renia		Lipka
		Cohen	Avraham
{801}			Chaya
		Cohen	Grunem

Chaf כ

Chmiel			Aharon
Cohen	Velvel	Cohen	Avraham
	Sara		Feiga
	Zilpa		Yitzchak (Eizik)
	Chana Roiza	Kahana	Pinchas
	Mendel		Mattel
	Rivka		Feivish
Cohen	Chaim		Tzvi (Hershel)
	Rivka		Binem
	Chaya	Kahana	Shmuel
	Yocheved		Sheindel
Cohen	Simcha	Kahana	Feiga
	Machla		Shlomo
	Gitel	Kahana	Yehoshua (Shia)
	Tzipora		Mania
Cohen	Eliezer	Katz	Berish

	Eidel Miriam		Tirza Beila
	Yechezkel	Katz	Moshe
	Avraham Leizer		Dvora
	Feiga		And children
	Shmuel Yosef	{802}	
	Yaakov	Katz	Chana
Katz	Shmuel		Wolf
	Esther Sheindel		Lea
	Yisrael	Katz	Bendet
	Yudel		Malka
	Chaya		Avraham
Katz	Rachel		And children
	Yenta	Katz	Lozer David
	Shmuel		Ethel
	Eliahu		And children
	Matel	Katz	Yisrael
Katz	Berish		Chana
	Sheva	Katz	Shlomo
	Chava		Feiga
	Yitzchak	Katz	Shlomo
Katz	Tzipora		Sara
	Yosef	Katz	Tzvi (Hershel)
	Baruch (Butshe) Tovia		Sara
	Mordechai	Katz	Aharon and family
Katz	Avraham	Katz (Kuznitshiner)	
	Liba		

Lamed ל

Lasman	Moshe
	Leibish
Lasman	Yechiel and children
Laskovski	Avraham
	Miriam Beila
	And children
Lustman	Henele
	Lola
	Mietek
	Frania
	Lili
Lustman	Meir
	Chana Lea
Lukshtik	Yudel
	Yenta
	Shlomo
	Baruch
	Tzirel
	Lea
Lukshtik	Yosef
	Rachel
	David
	Yitzchak
	Yudel
Libfreund	Avraham Hersch
	Bracha
	Machla Sara
	Eliezer
Libfreund	Mendel
	Chava
Liberman	Chaim Leib
	Tirtza Michel
	Rozka
	Esther
	Pinchas
	Yaakov
	Yehoshua
Liberman	Shmuel Chil
	Avraham
	Chava
Liberman	Berl and family
Liberman	Binem and family
Liberman	Yaakov and family
Litvak	Chaim
	Liba
	And family

{803}

Litvak	Miriam
	Chaim
Lichtenstein	Chaim
	Perl
	Naftali

	Moshe		Meir
	Yeshayahu		Yaakov
	Chaya		Motta
Lisser	Leibish		Tzvi (Hershel)
	Naska (Ziska)	Levin	Shlomo
	Reuven		Zissel
	Kazczik		Mendel
Lisser	Yaakov		Esther Sara
	Gella	Levin	Gittel
	Aryeh	Levin	Noach
Lisse	Shmuel		Sara
Listenberg	Shmuel		Yoel
Leifer	Berl		Gittel
	Tauba	Levin	Yosef
	Sara Zissel		Shifra Lea
	Shia	Levin	Pinchas
	Feivel		Rachel
	Yosef Eli	Levkovitch	Betzalel
Lederman	Shlomo		Golda
	Sara		Yisrael Leib
	Beila		Freda
	Yudel		Tzvi Zeev
Lederman	Mendel		Moshe
	Chaya		Efraim
Levin	Berl	Levkovitch	Mania
	His wife		Eidel
	Mendel		Meir Yitzchak

	Yisrael	Levkovitch	Shmuel Mordechai and family
	Nathan	Levkovitch	Leib
	Tzvi (Hershel)	Libert	Shmuel
	And two other children		Lea
Levkovitch	Berish		Asher
	Gittel	Libert	Moniek
	Sheva		Ita
	Machla	Libert	Chanan (Chana)
	David		
	Avraham	Mem	
Levkovitch	Mendel	Moser	Moshe Aharon
	Henia		Chaya
	Meir		Sara
	Malka		Genia
	Yudel	Moser	Yitzchak
Levkovitch	Wolf		Zissel
	Chana Sara	Malazh	Keila
	Miriam Roiza		Yechezkel (Chaskel)
	Shmuel		Velvel
	Moshe	Montshik	Avraham
Levkovitch	Eliezer (Leizer)		Liba
{804}			Yechezkel (Chaskel)
Levkovitch	Malka Beila	Mann	Melech
	Chana		Mendel
	Kodesh		Shlomo
Levkovitch	David	Mann	Eliezer (Lozer) and family
	Mirl		

Monkovitzki	Tzadok (Tzudik)		Chaya
	Chaya		Bracha
	Yaakov		Malka
	Esther		Lea
	Rivka	Moshenberg	Chaya
Motzna	Shlomo		Sara
	Zelda		Pessa Malka
	Tauba	Moshenberg	Tovia
	Chana		Tauba
Motzna	Eliezer (Leizer)		Avraham
	Chaya	Moshenberg	Hersh Nathan
Moshman	Yudel		Perl
Moshman	Tovia		And family
	Freda	Moshenberg	Shaul
Moshman	Tzipa	{805}	
	Pessa	Moshkovitch	Moshe
Moshenberg	Daniel		Pessa
	Sara Lea	Moshkovitch	Pinchas
	Frimet		Tauba
	Roiza	Moshkovitch	Eizik
	Bracha		Necha Lea
Moshenberg	Yosef Yona		And children
	Rachel	Marienfeld	Aharon Zelik
	Tzipa		Gittel
	Yaakov		Dina
	Hirsch Nathan		Ita
Moshenberg	Moshe Aharon	Marienfeld	Eliahu

	Machla		Beila
	Sheindel	Muneh	Yosef
Marienfeld	Yokel		Helena
Marienfeld	Tauba Roiza		Shmuel
Marienfeld	Michael	Miller	Yoel
	Feiga Rivka		Rachel
Muneh	Yechiel	Moshe Chaim	Berek and his family {alphabetized by first name}
	Rachel		
	Shmuel		
	Bendet		

Nun ב

Nadelhaft	Naftali		Meir
	Chana (Chantsha)		Rivka
	Yosef	Nashelevitch	Hinda
	Yisrael		Eliahu
	Yenta		Avraham
Novinski	Chava Rachel and children	Nashelevitch	Chana
Nashelski	Yechezkel (Chaskel)	Nashelevitch	Yaakov
Nashelevitch	Avraham		Chaya
	Chana		Eliezer
	Asher		Dvora
	Sheina Esther	Nashelevitch	Berish
	Chaya		Breindel
	And their mother		Yenta
Nashelevitch	Avraham	Nashelevitch	Yona
	Chana		Chana
			Yitzchak (Itshe)

Nashelevitch	Yosef		Moshe
	Reizel		Shamai
	And children		Efraim
Nashelevitch	Chaim Lozer and family	Sotenberg	Yeshayahu (Shia)
			Machla
Nashelevitch	Yechiel Yona		Menucha (Nicha)
	Simcha		Yosef
Nashelevitch	Michal	Sotenberg	Avraham
	Yenta		Masha
Neirat	Aharon		Tirtza
{806}			Yosele
Neirat	Chava and children	Sotenberg	Avraham
Neiman	Yitzchak (Itshe) and family		Chana
			Malka
Neiman	Nachman	Sochaczevski	Ozer
Neiman	Tshipa		Lea
	Miriam		Moshe Aharon
Neis	Yisrael		Shmuel Nathan
	Sara Lea		Avraham
Nelson	Moshe		Yaakov
	Rachel	Sochaczevski	Leibish
	Chana		Sara
	Lipa	Sochaczevski	Miriam
Nelson	Yitzchak	Safer	Shmuel David
			Chava
Samech ס			Beila
Sotenberg	Yona		Bendet
	Rachel		

	Avraham		Sima
Segal	Berish	Ines	Berl
	Sheindel		Zelda
Segal	Mordechai		David
	Yocheved	Ines	Yechezkel
Senderovitch	David		Rachel
	Sara (Sala)		Avraham
	And child		And family
Senderovitch	Gittel	Ines	Moshe and family
Senderovitch	and family {perhaps the family name was repeated in error here}	Ines	Yitzchak
			Frania
Sendatsh	Gittel	Ines	Chaim
Skotnitzki	Herman		Miriam
	Marta	Edlitz	Itshe Netta
Skotnitzki	Sala		Esther
Skurnik	Mina		Tzvi (Hershel)
	Yitzchak (Itshe)		Zalman
	Chana Sara		Moshe David
	Blima		Rivka
		Elbaum	Moshe
Ayin ע		Engel	Sara
Ines	David		Moshe
	Gittel	Engelman	Shlomo Aharon
Ines	Eliahu		Esther
	Avraham	Efraimovitch	Tzvi (Hershel)
{807}			Yirmiahu
Ines	Moshe		Meir

	Yehoshua		Ita Lea
	Ita		Malka
Efraimovitch	Rivka		Freda
	Meir	Erdbaum	Chaim
	Frimet		Chasha
	And two children	Erlich	Yehoshua (Shia)
Efraimovitch	Eizik		Rachel
	His wife		Shmuel
	Asher		Freda
	Ita		Rivka
Efraimovitch	Shia		Chana
	Mania		Beila
Efraimovitch	Rachel	Erlich	Zalman
	Asher		Esther
	And one child		Moshe
Erbst	Eliahu	Erlich	Yisrael
	Pessa		Sara
	And family		And children
Erbst	Feiga	Erman	Yudel
Erbst	Yosef		Chaim
	Tzila		Rivka Lea
	Aharon	{808}	
	Kalman		
	Feiga	Pe/Fe פ	
Erbst	Fishel and family	Pozanski	Eliahu
Erbst	Ozer		Mania
	Frimet		And children

Pomerantz	Itshe Meir		Batia
	His wife		Nachman
	Chana		Yosef
Putter	Chaim Yisrael	Pertchak	Fishel
	Elka		Keila
	Esther		And children
	Moshe	Perelgritz	Eliezer
	Ronit		Gittel
	Mordechai		Feigele
Putter	Feivel		Tirza
	Esther		Yisrael
	Simcha		Esther
	Shaul	Ferkal	Tzvi (Hershel) Rabbi
	Rivka		Odel
Putter	Tzvi (Hershel)		Aharon Pinchas
	Rozshka		Yitzchak Wolf
Pzhepiorka	Perl	Prashker	Moshe
Pinchevski	Chaim		Bracha
	Yenta		And children
	Manes	Pshititzka	Chuma
	And other children	Forman	Lea
Pinchevski	Velvel and children		Yeshayahu
Piernik	Yechiel Meir		Shamai
	Gittel		Shmuel
	And children	Fein	Mordechai
Pletshevitzer	Eliahu		Malka
Plonski	Mendel		Rachel

	Rivka		Moshe
	Yocheved	Fleischman	Shamai
	Yehoshua (Shia)		Marila
Fleischman	Avraham Shalom	Fleischman	Esther
	Miriam		Her husband
	Chava Roiza	Fleischman	Shmuel Aryeh
	Yitzchak	Feferkovitch	Chaya Yehudit
	Freidel		Shalom Yitzchak
	Gittel		Roda
	Sara	Feferkovitch	Lea
	Tzirel		Esther
	Efraim		Hershel
	Rachel	Feferkovitch	Gershon
	Rivka		Zissel
{809}		Feferkovitch	Avraham and family
Fleischman	Lea	Fuerstenberg	Eliezer
Fleischman	Yaakov		Miriam
	Golda	Fuerstenberg	Moshe
	Rachel		Aharon
	Melech		Eliahu
Fleischman	Golda		Shmuel
	Lea		Chana
Fleischman	Golda		Noach
	Melech	Fuerstenberg	Tovia
Fleischman	Shaul		Zalman
	Rivka		Meir
Fleischman	Rachel		Rachel

Fuerstenberg	Rivka	Findek	Daniel
	Pessa		Beila Roiza
Fuerstenberg	Avraham		Berish Leib
	Ronia		Lea
Friedman	Yechiel	Findek	Motta
	Nicha		Perl
	Yehudit		Berish Leib
Friedman	Shimon		Itzik
	Chana	Findek	Azriel
	Moshe		Perl
	Yechiel		Berish Leib
	Shmuel		Yechezkel
Friedman	Shlomo	{810}	
	Esther		
	Mates	Tsadek צ	
	Lea	Zwerman	Dvora
Friedman	Chaya		Pinchas
Friedman	Tzina	Zwerman	Meir
	Feiga		Rivka
	And two children	Zwerman	Shlomo and family
Frielich	Beinish Kalman	Zuckerweitz	Yitzchak
	Chana		Elka
Findek	Aharon		Beila Gittel
	Tauba		Kalman
	Michael	Zibola	Yisrael Meir
	Hershel	Zibola	Miriam
	Hinda		David Moshe

	Eliahu		Feiga
	Perl		Sara
Zibola	Yitzchak (Itche)	Kampelmacher	Bernard
	Chana	Kampelmacher	Berta
Zibola	Veichna		Edek
	Gittel	Kaplan	Fishel
Zimereinski	Aharon Leizer and family		Yocheved
		Kaplan	Dr.
Zimereinski	Fishel and family	Kapla	Yudel
			Chana
Kuf ק		Kapla	Paula
Kaufman	Zissel	Kofetz	Shmuel
	Chana		Rachel
	Fishel		Bracha
	Yehudit (Yides)	Karo	Moshe
	Sara		Chaikel
Kaufman	Chanoch (Henech) and family		Nissan
			Rachel
Kaufman	Berl and family	Kartozenski	Moshe
Kaufman	Chaim David and family		Chana
			And children
Kolski	Moshe	Katzovitch	Dina
	Chaya		Aliza
	Chaim	Kutnovski	Mordechai
Kalinski	Nachum	{811}	
	Dvora	Kutnovski	Roiza
	Mottel		Pessa
	Shmuel		

Kulson	Yisrael	Kloska	Tzvi (Hershel)
	Hersch		Pessa
	Tsharna	Klein	Chana
	Henna		Dvora
	Sara		Michal (Mechel)
Kufert	Avraham Chaim	Kleiner	Yitzchak
	Chava Dvora		Chana
	Rachel		Gittel
	Frimet		Ita
	Sheindel		Moshe
Kufert	Shlomo	Knobel	Mordechai
Korbitsh	Shlomo	Knobel	Hinda Freda
Kloska	Adam		Nissan Leib
Kloska	Chaya Freda	Knobel	Yisrael Meir
	Zelik		Aharon
	Wolf	Knott	Yechiel
Kloska	Nissan		Mania
	Rachel Lea		Hershel
	Moshe		Saba
	Beila Gittel	Knott	Leibish
Kloska	Shalom		Pessa
	Rachel	Knott	Menashe
	Bella		Perl
Kloska	Shalom	Keizman	Wolf
	Bella		Zlata
Kloska	Eliezer	Keizman	Sara
	Paula	Keller	Meir

	Malka		Rozsha
	Shamai	Kronenberg	Eliezer (Leizer) and family
	Shaul		
	Bracha	Krakow	Shimon
Keller	Chaim Tzvi		Chana
	Sara	Krock	Chaim Hersch
	Mordechai		Hendel Miriam
	Tzipora		Sara
	Chava	Kriger	Sender
Keller	Simcha		Dvora
	Tirza		Mendel
	Rachel		
	Tzeshe	Resh	ר
Keller	Leibish	Rabinovitch	Menachem
	Feiga		Chana
	Mordechai		Malka
Kenigstein	Yaakov	Rabinovitch	Dintsha
	Yadzsha		Aharon
Kefer	Avraham		Feiga
Kraianka	Avraham		And children
	Chava	Rabinovitch	Naftali
	Eliezer (Leizer)		Mala
	Yudel		Yitzchak
	Freidel		Blima
{812}			Binyamin
Kraianka	Motta		Avraham
Krotshik	Yosef	Rabinovitch	Shamai

Rosen	Yaakov	Rosen	Mordechai Zalman
	Malka	Rosenbaum	Reuven
	Avraham		Freda
	Moshe		Rozsha
	Michael		Malka
Rosen	Mordechai	Rosenbaum	Freda and four children
	Lea Gittel	Rosenberg	Mordechai
	Chava		Roiza
	Breindel		Shaul
	Pessa Bina		Moshe
	David		Menucha (Nicha)
	Reuven		Perl
Rosen	Yentel	Rosenberg	Binyamin
	Etka		Chana
	Mendel		Shmuel Yona
Rosen	Velvel	{813}	
Rosen	Michael	Rosenberg	Mordechai Zalman
	Shifra		Sheindel
	Tzirel	Rosenberg	Yosef
Rosen	Eliezer and family		Chana
Rosen	Chaim		Sara
	Roiza		Shaul
	Yaakov	Rosenberg	Chaya Reizel
	Sheva		Sara
Rosen	Moshe		Yisrael
	Feiga	Rosenperel	Avraham
	And children		Chava

	Shlomo	Rachman	Yaakov
	Aharon		Keila
	Hentsha	Rachman	Yenta
	Dovtsha		Beila
Rosenperel	Yechiel		Yechiel Meir
Rosenperel	Botsha	Rakovski	Shalom
	Freidel		Zissel
Rosenkopf	Pinchas		Moshe
	Reizel		Chana
	Yissachar		Yosef
	Shlomo		Yona
Rosenkopf	Shmuel	Roitstein	Esther
	His wife		Tzvi (Hershel)
Rosenstein	Yosef		Bracha
	Feiga		Melech
	Malka		Leibel
	Avraham	Roitstein	Shlomo
	Gittel		Rachel
Rosenrat	Avraham		Baruch
Rothbaum	Moshe		Efraim
	Ita	Roitstein	Tzvi (Hershel)
	Yitzchak (Itche)		Bracha
	Velvel		David
Rothbaum	Tzvi (Hershel)	Roitstein	Yisrael
	Chana		Miriam Beila
	Moshe Itsche		Itzik
Rothbard	Yaakov	Roitstein	Mates

	Dina (Mates' mother)		Feiga
	Michael		Wolf
Roitstein	Avraham		Esther Rivka
	Sara	Reitman	Chana
Roitstein	Yitzchak (Itche) and family		Lipa
Reitman	Berish Leib
Ribner	Shmuel and family		Chana Ita
Ringel	the lawyer and family		Freda
Ringelblum	Yechiel Meir		Malka
	Perel		Zissel
	Keila		Binyamin
	Yocheved	Reitman	Ben Zion
Reitman	Ben Zion		Hodess
{814}			Roiza
Reitman	Esther		Zlata
	Yudel		Rivka
	Binyamin	Reitman	Yona
	Tzvi (Hershel)		Rachel
	Baruch		Roiza
	Chaim Leizer		Zlata
Roitman	Motta	Reitman	Esther
	Nechama	Reitman	Yokel
	Yocheved		Sara
	Chava		Paula
	Sheindel		Lidsha
	Zlata		Tzvi (Hershel)
Reitman	Moshe Avraham	Reitman	Yechiel

	Yaakov	Schwartzhar	Tzvi (Hershel)
Reitman	Tzvi (Hershel)	Schwartzhar	his wife
	Yocheved		Esther
	Ruth		Binyamin
	Yudel	{815}	
Reitman	Abba and family	Schwartzhar	Binyamin
Reitman	Mordechai		Baltsha
	Ethel	Shviatlovski	Hinda
	And children	Steiglitz	Shlomo Zalman
Reitman	Tzvi (Hershel)	Steiglitz	Chaya
	Gutsha		Moshe
Reitman	Chana		Necha
	Hendel	Stoltzman	Paula
Rechtman	Meir	Stern	Zisha
	Sheina Esther		Sara
	Eliezer (Leizer)		Moshe Yudel
	Leibish		Hinda
	Sara	Stern	Hertzka
	Ita Lea		Sara Yenta
Rechtman	Shmuel	Stern	Yaakov
	Reizel	Stern	Moshe Yudel
	Ita		Pessa
Rechtman	Rivka and family		And children
		Stern	Yechiel
			Chana
Shin ש			And children
Schwartzhar	Machla		
	Binyamin	Strum	Yehoshua (Shia)

	Yitzchak (Itche)		Yitzchak
	Sara		Chaya
Sheinbaum	Yosef	Sheynwald	Zalman
	Shoshana		Yitzchak
	Sara		Chaim
	Hersch Leib		Sheindel
	David	Sheynwald	Hersch Yankel
	Chaya Gittel		Freda
	Leib	Sheynwald	Nathan
	Paula		Sara
Sheynwald	Moshe	Sheynwald	Yosef
	Lea	Shladov	Berl
	Tzvi (Hersch)		Roda
	Rachel		Tauba
	Feiga		Chana
	Chaim		Yaakov
	Yaakov		Masha
	Beila	Shladov	Yechezkel
Sheynwald	Moshe	Schlossberg	Shamai
	Freda	Shmuel Ribnes' children	{alphabetized by first name}
	Eliahu		
	Pessa Rivka	Shmulevitz	Malka
	Pessa Rivka {probably duplicated in error}		Yitzchak
			Chaya
	Tema		Yaakov
Sheynwald	Yaakov		Rachel
	Tauba	Shmeiser	Meir

	Sara Raizel	Shmeltz	Naftali
	Nechama (Chuma)		Reizel
	Rachel		Mendel
	Chaim Aharon		Hendel
	Nachman	Shemiantek	Pessa
	Yaakov		Shmuel Yudel
{816}			Leib Yosef
Shmeiser	Tauba		Malka
Shmeiser	Ozer	Shemiantek	Sara
	Sara		Mordechai
	Feiga		Frimet
	Henna	Shemiantek	Sheindel
Shmeiser	Abba	Shemientek	Moshe
	Eli		Perl
	Shmuel Hertzka	Shemientek	Leib Yosef
	Rikel		His wife
Shmeiser	Ethel	Shemientek	Golda and children
	Miriam	Shpeizhendler	Wolf
Shmeiser	Yisrael Abba		Hinda
	Yenta		Chaim
Shmeiser	Sara		Sheina
Shmeltz	Chaim		Shmuel Aharon
	His wife	Shpeizhendler	Moshe
	Yehoshua (Shia)		Pessa
	Aryeh		And children
	Lea	Shpeizhendler	Moshe
	Yitzchak (Itche)		

{817}

Index
Translated by Jerrold Landau

Translator's notes:

The spellings in this index may not match the spellings in the text. During the various stages of text translation, different spelling conventions were used. Later on, it was decided to use a Polish spelling of surnames, except for cases where the person was known to be living in America or Israel, where an Anglicized version was often used. This index follows the later convention, and the text was not revised for consistency.

First names use a transliterated spelling rather than a Polish spelling. Some entries in this table of contents include first names only.

I spot-checked some of the page references. There are cases where the page numbers do not correspond to the actual name occurrences in the text. Some of these errors were likely introduced when the index was first produced, well before the age of computers. Others are not really errors, but rather inconsistencies due to cases where the Hebrew and Yiddish text overlapped, and the translation (and therefore the online version) was based on the Hebrew translation. During translation, no effort was made to ensure correspondence of the names to the text. In fact, it seems that in several cases, particularly in the historical sections, it appears that the Yiddish section, which was not directly translated, has more detail than the apparently equivalent Hebrew section.

CAUTION: Page numbers are the page numbers of the original Yizkoe Book, not this translation.

Alef	Bet	Gimel	Dalet	Hey	Vav	Zayin	Chet	Tet	Yod	Kaf
Lamed	Mem	Nun	Samech	Ayin	Peh	Tsadek	Kof	Resh	Shin	Tav

Reb Avrahamele Sochaczewer, Rebbe	57, 58, 59, 60, 64, 69, 79, 80, 82, 84, 85, 86, 88, 89, 90, 91, 92, 93, 229, 242, 243, 249, 282, 288, 323, 324, 342, 348, 349, 393
Reb Avraham Czechnower, Rabbi	65, 70, 80, 235

Avrahamele Morszalek	235
Avraham Meir Leizer's	305, 306
Ogrodnik	133
Adamaszek Yechezkel	358
Reb Aharon	342
Reb Aharon Shmuel Kadynower	227
August Stanislaw	37
Auerbach D.	585
Ochanski, Chelmer Bishop	20
Olewing Henry	590
Elberg David	585
Urbinski	471
Achad Haam	190
Igielfeld Rachel	475
Izraelski Zelig	174
Izraelski Gershon	429
Izralski David	393, 431, 433
Izraelowicz	204
Izraelowicz	404
Reb Itche Meir the Gerrer Rebbe	58, 231, 241
Itka	342
Itche Berl	529
Ajgens Yehoshuale	83
Eidel Pese	328
Ajzman Yisrael	201, 219

Ajzman Sara	216, 506
Eizele	446
Ajzenstat Reb Meir the "Panim Meorot"	17, 227
Ajzenberg Avraham-Natan	229
Ajzenberg Deichus	506
Ajzenberg Pesach	428
Ajzensztejn Mendel	393, 546
Eisenstop Max	584, 585
Einman Efraim	581
Ajsman Yisrael	126, 127, 131
Reb Ichel, Rabbi	77
Einfeld A.	585
Ohlberg Sh.	585
Albert Zalman	181, 232, 295, 296, 297
Albert Tauba	558
Reb Elimelech the Rebbe of Lizhensk	65, 72
Reb Eliezer HaKohen of Pultusk	57, 229, 324, 325, 393
Reb Eliezer Tzvi Charlop	323, 324
Oldszlok	410
Oliwa Jozef	18
Aleksander Rebbe	83
Aleksandra	32
Alef-Beit	190
Omboros Berl	114, 157

"Omnibus"	330, 332, 333
Anna Dutchess	34
Antek	532
Anthony the Holy	258
Antonius Mark	182
Enis B.	585
Enis V.	585
Anski Sh.	107, 214, 276, 277, 320
Anshel Becker	436
Ostrowczer Rebbe	81
Esther	98, 500
Opatoshu	262
Opatowski	201
Efreiml	243
Oklanski Berl	136, 405, 427, 550
Oklanski Hershel	186
Reb Aryeh Leib Charif	88, 155, 228, 230
Aronowicz	201
Aronson Shamira Dr.	201
Arleska	548
Arnold Professor	30
Ish Shalom	106, 144, 181, 262, 265
Aszkinazy Meir	57
Ashenheim Rabbi	581, 578
Orkowicz	446

Bet ב

Balas Yisrael	470, 558, 560
Balas	220, 398, 427, 446
Balas Eidel	399 (translator's note, says 939 which seems to be a typo), 398, 410
Balas Leizer	395, 399, 410
Balaban Professor	20
Bobe Chaya	277
Boshinski A.	585
Bozuchowski Tovia	412
Balderski	471
Balterman D.	585
Balinski	471
Boleslaw III (Cziwosty)	31
Balczerska	392
Balfour	99, 558
Bona King	93
Benderowicz Stanislaw	45
Bombas Yankel	176
Bombas Nachum	176
Baumarder	549
Baumarder Mottel	118
Beserman Y.	585
Baron Menashe	590
Baron Rae	592
Baronow	384

Borbis Enri	128, 130
Borochowicz Lewek	26
Bortnowski General	389
Bornsztejn Reb Chanoch Rebbe	564
Bornsztejn Moshe Eliezer	561
Bornsztejn Yechezkel	173, 393
Bornsztejn	201, 550
Bornsztejn Reb Shmuel Rebbe	325
Bornsztejn Reb Meir	98, 349
Bornsztejn Monia	530
Bornsztejn Feiga	592
Borkowski Gittel	525
Borkowski	126, 127, 135
Boznicky L.	585
Boznicky S.	585
Boznicky Aharon	586
Reb Bunim of Przysucha Rebbe	57, 77, 228, 241
Bozasky L.	585
Brzezinski Hershel	196, 245, 245, 568
Brzezinski Yehoshua	192
Brzezinski Sender	195
Brzezinski Avraham	402
Brzezinski Vove	514
Brzezinski Moshe	558

Brzezinski Mania	515, 518
Brzezinski	470
Bzozowski Leah	486
Bzozowski Esther	488
Bzozowski Bronia	394
Bzozowski Meir	195, 405
Bzozowski Berl	173, 294, 299
Bzozowski Avraham Yaakov	211
Bzozowski Chaim	473
Bialer Rabbi	82
Bialik Ch.	141
Bialiskenski	201
Biderman	201, 470, 478
Biznicki Moshe	473
Biderman Yaakov	118, 392, 449, 470
Biderman Yankel	138
Bejles	475
Birnbaum Y.	585
Birnbaum Moshe	585
Birnbaum Becky	590, 592
Biezanski	550
Biezanski Mordechai	392
Biezanski Hershel	245
Biezanski Freda	482
Biezanski Mottel	294, 207, 425
Biezanski Eliahu Moshe	294

Bichowski Z. Dr.	160
Biernacki	550
Beinish Shamash	17, 18
Beister G.	576
Beister Benny	576
Bauman Sam	581, 585
Bauman Meir	585
Blaszow	471
Bluma	455
Blumenthal Nachman	40, 544
Blumenthal Eliahu	118, 138
Blumenthal Meir	196, 494
Blumenthal Pinchas	196
Blumenfeld Diana	132
Bliastshik	391, 392
Blimele	350
Blinderman H.	585
Binyamele "Crower".	327
Binyamin Blochasz	115
Binyamin Graber	552
Ben Y.	189
Beznicki Moshe	401
Baal Shem Tov	64, 65, 79, 81
Benzer Nathan	587
Benzer Shimon	587
Benzer Meir	589, 592

Benzer Chava	592, 594
Benzer Seymour	592
Benzer A.	585
Bendekowski Moshe	42
Bester Aharon	50
Benczkowski Yaakov	138, 57, 207, 209
Benczkowski Chana	139, 237
Becker	400
Becker Sh. H.	585
Becker Yankel	196
Becker Pinchas	196
Becker S.	586
Becker Shmuel	586
Ber Moshe	474
Berish	342
Berl Chazir	273
Bergelson David	123, 133, 182, 264
Bergajzen	509
Bergajzen Yitzchak	405
Bergajzen Itche	429
Bergajzen Shlomo Mendel	431
Berman Harry	584, 585
Berman Avraham	585
Berman Y.	585
Berman Moshe	195
Berman Aharon	195

Berman Alter	195
Berman Hertzke	195, 330, 407
Berman David	196
Bernstein M.	585
Bernsztejn Ignace	277
Berson M.	28
Berkowicz Yudka	416
Berkowicz Yakov	24
Berkowitz Herbert	590
Berszadski	28
Broder Feiga	174
Bronia	486
Bronka	281
Brot	547
Brot Reizl	221
Brot Sender	174
Brand	493
Brafman Yisrael	562, 590
Brafman Yitzchak-Meir	196
Brafman Henech	196
Brafman Irving	590
Brafman Issie	590
Broker Moshe	425
Brokman Louis	584
Baruch Ber	332
Baruch Shamash	327

Brusztejn	542
Bruker Moshe	482
Brojtman Hertzke	294, 299
Brojtman Aryeh-Leib	452
Brojtman	482
Breindel the daughter of the Liser Rebbe	240, 243
Bargoda	446
Bressler Mania	470
Bressler Yona	131
Bressler Pinchas	118
Breslauer Mone	550

Gimel ג

Gudak Wladimir	548
Godel Melamed	159
Gothelf Hirsch	207, 289, 389, 394, 400, 478, 532
Gothelf Bronia	400
Gothelf Esther	400
Gothelf	206, 424, 448, 550
Gothelf Rachel	453
Gothelf Shmuel-Leib	487
Gothelf Yisrael	514
Gottlieb Alex	584
Gotteskind M. K.	160
Galek	194

Galek Wolf-Itche	186, 416, 551
Galek Malka	551
Galek Feivel	111, 157, 299
Galer Wolf-Itche	558
Golda	510
Goldberg Yehoshua	578
Goldberg Binyamin	115
Goldberg Leibel	408
Goldberg Chaim	399, 408
Goldberg Tzvi	508
Goldberg Simcha	115, 116, 138
Goldberg	400
Goldman H.	585
Goldman Wolf	510
Goldman	128, 446, 497
Goldman Gittel	510
Goldfarb Meir	201
Goldfarb Yisrael	390
Goldfarb Hertzke	202
Goldshneider Shlomo	581
Goldshneider Solomon	584
Goldsztejn Reb Shlomo Rabbi	428
Goldsztejn Baruch	294, 299
Goldflus Y.	585
Goldfaden	107, 123, 181, 291
Gombinski Mendel	589, 594

Gordon Yaakov	107, 123, 144, 181, 291
Gordon Y.	595
Gorki Maxim	128, 260
Gorelik P.	585
Gedalia Melamed	453
Goszik David	253
Gutglas	506
Gutold Yosef	505
Gutman	395
Gutman A.	585
Gutgieztaldt Hirsh	207
Gutejn Kuba	214
Gurski Frantiszek	470
Gurski Y.	585
Gurski	205, 473
Gitajn	111
Gitajn Shmuel	173
Giterman Yitzchak	253, 272
Gilder S.	585
Gincburg Naftali Hertz, Baron	320
Gincburg Nachum	323
Gincburg	277
Gingold Moshe-Yidel	453
Gingold	201
Gejer Moshe	116, 204, 448, 589
Gebertig Mordechai	504

Gelbsztejn Itche	393, 424, 448, 449, 450, 470, 479
Gelbsztejn Yoel	39, 399
Gelbsztejn Itzik	415, 479
Gelbsztejn	494
Gelbsztejn Zelig	196
Gelman Sh.	158, 160
Gabel Max	178
Gesundheit Reb Yankel Rabbi	241
Gepner Avraham	253
German Avraham	585
Geshen Naftali	594
Geshen Sarah	594
Gerszt	405, 547
Gerszt Yerachmiel	201, 405
Gerszon	514
Grachower Rabbi	308, 312
Grabski	152
Grodzinski Mottel	186
Grodzinski Moshe	311
Grossman Yozke	499
Grossman Aharon	174, 396, 425
Grossman Yoska	434, 435
Grossman	414
Graubard Pinchas	105, 174, 176, 272, 274, 275, 276, 277, 330, 365, 587, 589, 594, 778
Graubard Leibish	193, 274

Graubard Hertzke	165
Graubard Motte	167
Graubard Moshe	410
Graubard H.	585
Graubard Max	587
Graubard Mendel	589, 594
Graubard Yitzchak	581, 582, 594
Graubard Becky	592
Graubard Mates	432
Graubard Avraham	432
Graubard Hershel	39, 155, 165, 186, 473
Grubszmidt S.	585
Grundwag Simcha	106, 107, 118, 123, 126, 131, 138, 145, 158, 164, 178, 191, 232, 236, 285, 287, 289, 374, 379, 548
Grundwag Nachum	107, 108, 122, 123, 131, 132, 133, 143, 145, 165, 176, 180, 181, 185, 291, 375, 470, 508
Grundwag Yosef	174, 180
Grundwag Yossel	186, 500, 508, 509, 558, 560
Grundwag Machla	145, 174, 180
Grundwag Rivka	180, 181
Grundwag Dina	180
Grundwag Mania	374, 540
Grundwag Y. M.	158, 379
Grundwag Esther	499
Grosky L.	585
Groszka Yitzchak	196
Grynberg Leibish	159

Grynberg Aharon	138, 203
Grynberg Uri Tzvi	261
Grynberg Leizer	453
Greenberg Avraham	578
Greenberg Barney	584, 585
Greenberg H.	585
Greenberg Y.	585
Greenberg Isadore	586
Grynberg Machla	374
Grynbard Yitzchak	431
Gryngard	427
Greenwald M.	585
Greenwald A.	585
Green Chana-Esther	594
Grynszpan Aharon	237
Greisman A.	585
Graetz Professor	160

Dalet   ד

Dovrish (the mother of the Sochaczewer)	79
Doganski	474
Dawidowicz	167, 176, 446
Dolow Nat	586
Don Qixote	271
Dancis Mordechai	279

Reb David Rabbi	60
King David	193
Dombrowski Henryk	35
Donski Zadislaw	475
Donowicz Y.	586
Jawicki	404
Dziezanowski Mikolaj Archbishop	18
Deichus Noach	193, 206
Deichus Meir	244
Deichus	313
Deichus Avraham	313, 410
Diamant	475
Diamond D. Dr.	585
Diament Lipman	123, 174, 409, 480
Diamand	123
Diament Aharon	174
Diament Zalman	174
Diament	395, 427
Diament Shaul	174
Diament Yechiel	472
Diament Feiga-Luba	472
Diament S. H.	585
Diament Perl-Leah	42
Daniel Szuster	145
Degiensztajn Frimet	203
Denk Wilhelm	544

Demblin M.	589
Der Liser	240, 241
"Der Kleiner Moshe Dudl"	237
Draber	115, 116, 135, 137
Driszan Tzvi	201

Hey   ה

"Hagiladi"	190
Hodel (the daughter of the Baal Shem)	79
Holtz S.	585
Holcer Rachel	132
Holcman Yechezkel	453
Holcman Meir	123, 133, 182
Holcman Feivish	196
Holdman	211, 506
Holcman Ch.	421
Holcman Shmuel	509
Holtzman Rachel	537
Holander	514, 466
Holander	400
Halbersztadt Reb David the Sosnowiecer Rebbe	252
Halpern Yisrael	27
Hafenung	550
Hamer David-Yitzchak	193

Horonczyk Shimon	269
Horowicz Pinchas	228
Hindes T. Dr.	160
Hirsch Porczewer	238
Hirsch Herman	586
Hirsch Hyman	581
Hirsch from Blonie	114
Hirsch Avraham	590
Hirszbein Peretz	123, 144, 181
Heilpern Reb Leibush Charif	57
Hejman Mordechai	176
Heiman H.	585
Helmer Leib	416, 417
Helmer Hirsch	217
Heler	429
Helek	172
Helczel	27
Helman D.	585
Helfand M. D.	584
Hendel Avraham	251
Hershel Shochet	280
Herman V. Hirsch	586
Hermalin	184
Hertzl Dr.	159, 162, 279, 289
Hernberg Asher	474
Hershowitz Shalom-Leib	578

Hershkowitz Yeshaya	581
Hershkowitz A. Dr.	585
Herszkowicz Pese	430

Vav ו

Wagner	453
Wagner Y.	585
Wolf Strykower	235
Wolf Lipsker	240, 241
Wolrat Yisrael	196
Wolrat Pesach	94, 176, 175
Wolrat David	92
Wolicki Leib	519
Wolman Noach	558
Wolman Reb Leib, rabbi and teacher	237
Wolman K.	158, 160
Wolkowicz Bracha	374
Wolkowicz Perl	375
Wolkowicz	200
Wolkowicz Yosef	119, 138, 203, 232, 382, 547, 550
Wolkowicz Chaim-Mordechai	232, 282
Waldenberg Izik	118, 547
Wolfstat Avraham	132
Wanwild M. (Sh. L. Kowa)	279

Wasiotinski Bogdan	27
Warszawski Ozer	105, 117, 165, 167, 257, 258, 259, 261, 262, 263, 264, 266, 268, 330, 351
Warszawski Gedalia	105, 158, 163, 165, 232, 267, 330
Warszawski Hirsch-Wolf	398, 427, 482
Warszawski Hershel	116, 126, 138, 203
Warszawski Tzvi	205
Warszawski Yitzchak	165
Warszawski Sh. N.	160, 174
Warszawski Nachum	174
Warszawski Shlomo	163
Vidaver S.	585
Widelec Yechiel	39, 566
Widelec Moshe-Aharon	566
Widelec	481
Wilhelm A.	585
"Wilner"	123
Wiener	313, 424
Wiener Mordechai	119
Wiener Yitzchak	119, 138, 203
Winter Becky	592, 594
Winter Chava	592
Winter Sam	587, 589, 590, 592
Winter N.	585
Winter Yosef	589, 590
"Wiernik"	235
Wiernik Y.	409

Wiewiorka Avraham	333
Wymaslowski Simcha	379
Wisznia Eli	427
Wisznia David	482
Wiszlicki	342
Wyszogrodski	111
Wyszogrodski Freda	452
Wyszogrodski Zeinwil	452
Wishinsky M.	585
Widislowski Moshe	482
Wojciech Milner	18
Weiter A.	144
Weinberg	548
Wajnberg Fishel	558
Wajnberg Pinia	131, 211, 221, 532, 533
Wajnberg Roza	455
Wajnberg Pinchas	118, 126, 131, 138, 211, 221, 553
Wajnberg Bluma	108, 145, 180, 558
Wajnberg Rachel (Levanon)	108, 146, 180, 558
Weinberg S.	585
Wajnberg Avraham Yitzchak	211
Wajnsztejn	204
Weingort Sh.	585
Weingort H.	585
Wajnsztok Yitzchak	39, 186, 558, 560

Weiss Saul	590
Weiss Henry	590
Weiss Chaim	450
Weisman Gavriel	5
Weisman Y.	585
Weisman M.	585
Weisman Itche-Meir	395
Weisberg S.	585
Weislic	548
Weisenberg Y. M.	105, 230, 260, 261, 262, 263, 268, 269, 273
Weitzman Bella	587, 593, 594
Weitzman Eliahu	590
Weitzman Zelig	168, 172
Wladislaw the Fourth	37, 38
Welstman L.	585
Weksztejn	109
Wertheim Nathan	518, 520, 522
Wertheim Moniek	516, 518
Wrubel	548

Zayin

Zeev-Nachum Rav	79
Zawocki	562
Zawoski Hyman	586
Zawadzki	186
Zajac Henoch	244

Zajac	487, 547, 550, 560
Zajac Mendel	558, 560
Zalcman Felia	431
Zalcman Eliezer	196, 558
Zalcman Baruch	558
Zalcman Yechiel-Meir	115, 156, 174
Zalcman	174, 313
Zalcman Leibel	196
Zalcman Yaakov David	196
Zalcman Pinchas	196
Zalcman Betzalel	196
Zalcman Shmuel HaKohn	195
Zanger Z.	585
Zand L.	201, 221, 585
Zand Yechiel	410
Reb Zusia Rabbi	72
Zusia, butcher	470
Zusman eliezer	138
Zwitkower Shmuel	26
Zwirchowski	506
Zygmunt	461
Zygmunt the Third	37
Zygmunt August, King	16, 19, 36
Silber Yechiel	514, 523
Silber Y.	585
Silberman Yisrael-Meir	197

Silbersztejn Avraham	176
Silverman H.	585
Zymler Yechezkel	44
Zymler Chana-Rachel	44
Zymler Dvora-Reizl	44
Singer Y. Y.	262
Zeidman Hillel	250, 252, 253
Seidendorf Gutcha	176
Zeinwil Grunem	201
Zielonka	427
Zielonka Moshe	399
Zelmanowicz Shalom	154
Zylber Yisrael	43
Zemba Menachem Rabbi	254
Zemel S.	585
Zlotnik	452
Zlotniszek Lewek	24
Dzulkowski	426
Zokowski	471
Zokowski Jan	392, 470, 471, 472
Zmiaowski	137
Dzeloska Yitzchak	395
Dzelonkewicz	471
Ziemowit the Second	32
Ziemowit the Third	32
Ziemowit the Fourth	32, 34

Ziemowit the Fifth	34

Chet ח

"Chidushei Harim"	83, 229
Reb Chanoch Shlita	60
Reb Chanoch Henoch the Aleksander Rebbe	66, 68
Reb Henoch	83
Chazan	562
Chaya	227, 510
Reb Chaim Sanzer, Rebbe	65, 67
Reb Chaim Miszerwiczer	160
Chaim Leizer	177
Chaim-Yokel	416
Chaim Bliachosz	427
Chaim Nissan	307, 312
Chaikl the wagon driver	307, 308, 309, 310, 311, 312, 313, 314, 315, 316, 317
Chanale	370
Chana-Rachel	44
Chetzroni A.	57, 97

Tet ט

Tabenfeld Leibel	195
Tabenfeld Tzvi	493, 496
Taub Avraham	131

Tolek	520
Tol	499, 502
Tolstoy	107, 123
Thomashefsky	178
Taras Bulba	266
Tarnowski Jan	37
Tovim Julian	130
ThonYehoshua	190
Turkow Jonas	132
Tauba Leah	296
Tilman Hertzke	131, 134, 201, 389, 402, 410
Tilman Yechiel-Meir	140, 157, 208, 383, 428, 551
Tilman Moshe	392
Tilman Nachman	395, 402
Tilman	404
Tilman Ch.	405
Tilman Avraham	405, 427, 470
Tilman Yitzchak	405, 506
Tindel Hershel	446, 487
Tykociner Moshek	39
Tener Chava	592
Tener Malka	592
Tempel	294
Tempel Chaim	162
Tempel M.	585
Temple Harry	586

Temple Sam A.	586
Trunk Y.	11, 27, 28, 36
Trunk Y. Y.	342
Trunk Yeshaya	271
Triwaks Y. Y.	278, 279
Reb Treitel, Rabbinical teacher	229
"Czarni"	523
Czudnik Shmuel	89
Czelianek	471
Czemniarski Reuven	474
Czerwonek Moshe-Ber	558
Czerwonek	548
Czernikow Adam	251, 273
Czerniewski	550
Czernikow	410

Yod   י

Jablonka Beniek	174
Jablonska Miriam	453
Jagiello Wladyslaw, King	32, 34
Jagiellonczyk Kasimiersz, King	34
Joaszon B.	94, 95
Janek	475, 513
Yantsha	407
Yantsha	207

Jasinowski lawyer	100
Jakobs Herman	585
Jakobs S.	585
Jakubowicz Mendel	509
Jakubowicz L.	585
Jakubowicz Lewek	25
Jakubowicz Tzalka	446, 487
Jakubowicz Shlomo	389, 403
Jakubowicz Mendel	509
Jakubowicz Hirsch-Leib	45, 403
Jakubowicz Berl	195
Jakubowicz Shamai	328
Jakubowicz Pesach	424
Jakubowicz (Moshe Lodzer)	106, 138
Jakubowicz Shmuel	138
Jakubowicz Betzalel	173
Jakubowicz	400
Jarzynek Chaim	196
Jarczewski	473
Jasinski	494
Jasinski Brona	130
Jasinski	456, 494
Jasinski	400, 479
Jasinski Hershel	479
Jasinowski	231
Reb Yoav Yehoshua,	58, 99

Kinczker Rabbi	
Yoel Wyski	333
The Holy Jew	57, 64, 88, 228
Judika A.	320
Reb Yochanan HaSandlar Rabbi	252
Yochanan, surgeon	27
Reb Yehoshuale Kutner	83
Reb Yehuda Leib Rabbi	227, 229
Reb Yehoshua	159
Reb Yehoshuale	342
Reb Yona Nachum HaKohn	227, 229, 234
Yosef-Leib	145
Yosef-Yona	154
Yosef the teacher	155
Izraelewicz	475
Reb Yechiel-Meir Gastiniger	79
Reb Yaakov of Lissa	57, 229, 240
Reb Yaakov Tomaszower	227, 229
Reb Yaakov, Rabbi	229
Yaakov Camber	334
Yaakov-David	401, 453
Yaakov-Aharon	427
Yaakov Ben-Zion	24
Yaakov	17
Yaakov Ben-Yitzchak	24

Yaakov Z. N.	190
Yaakov Yosef	65
Yaakov Doctor (or Rabbi)	16
Yaakov the Schvartzer (the black)	22
Yaakov (Yankel) Beker	196
Reb Yaakov Melamed	245
Yentel (Reb Michel Zlotczewer's grandmother)	79
Reb Yitzchak-Meir the Gerrer Rebbe	58
Rabbi Yitzchak-Elchanan of Kovno	58
Reb Yitzchak Werker	342
Yitzchak	342, 344, 400
Yakor Shuster	193, 194, 196, 244, 245, 303, 336, 337
Jarlicht B.	470
Yerachmiel	343
Yisrael Sofer	322
Reb Yeshayale of Przebosz	57, 228
Reb Yeshayahu Yona	245
Yisraelikl	511
Yisrael "Shechter"	407

Kaf   כ

Kohn Michael   118, 126, 138, 190

Kohn Avraham	124, 125, 126, 130
Kohn Simcha	108, 126
Kohn Tzvi	370
Kohn Baruch-Mordechai	547
Cohen Henry	585
Cohen A.	585
Cohen Y.	585
Cohen L.	585
Cohen R.	585
Cohen M.	585
Cohen B.	585
Cohen Sh.	585
Cohen M. Dr.	585
Kohn Yankel	124
Kohn Shoshana	132
Kohn Finka	167
Cohen Sharl	586
Kohn Aharon	123
Kohn Avraham	124
Kahana Pinkus	487
Kac Hershel	108, 146, 180
Kac Yechezkel	195
Kac Elchanan	292, 479
Kac Berish	494, 196
Kac	550
Kac Moshe	195

Kac Shmuel	195, 207, 402
Kac Avraham	126
Kac Eliezer-David	211
Kac Meir	229
Kac Tzipa	293
Kasher Menachem Rabbi	250
Carmi Yisrael	585
Katriel the bag maker	379
Chabarnik Moshe	395
Chaberes Mendel	478
Chaberman Yossel	427
Chudi	473
Chazen	443, 450
Chmiel Freda	183
Chmielnicki Miriam	276

Lamed

Labencka Dorota	17, 18, 19, 36
Lazencka	17, 18, 19, 36
Lozer Malosz	324
Lateiner Yosef	178
Lampa Maurice	132, 548
Landau Rabbi	335, 388
Landau Reb Shmuel-Yitzchak Rabbi	40, 235, 244
Landau Ari Leib	254

Landau	562
Landau Yitzchak	576
Landau Sidney V.	579
Landau H.	579
Landau Michael	581
Landau Max	581
Landau Sidney	581
Landau Max	586
Landauer Dr.	882 (this page number is seemingly an error)
Lasher Yaakov	585
Levanon Moshe	227, 338, 558, 560, 561
Levanon Rachel	558
Lub Rachel	432
Lubieniecki	20
Lubienska Jadwiga	24
Lubetkin Tzvia	412
Libert	428
Libert Chanan	196
Libert Moniek	224, 449
Ludwig, King of Poland and Hungary	32, 33
Ludzki Ch. L.	577
Reb Levi Yitzchak Berdichever	65, 68
Lustig D.	585
Lusky Y.	585
Luksztyk Yosef	138, 145, 392

Luksztyk Yudel	135, 173, 478
Luksztyk	201, 478
Luria Leib	463
Reb Leibish from Korowa	57
Reb Leibish	324
Reb Leibish Charif	57, 230
Leibish Feldscher	244
Libert M.	586
Libert Moniek	449, 479
Libert Shmuel	220, 392, 470, 471
Libert Maniele	470
Livert H.	478
Libert Shabtai	550
Libert Eliezer-Meir	146, 375, 572, 574
Libert Elchanan	282, 572
Libert Louis	574
Liberman Baltsha	475
Liberman Necha	475
Liberman Yaakov	536
Liberman Shmuel Yechiel	217
Liberman Chaim-Leib	470, 508, 536
Liberman Tirtza	536
Liberman Esther	536
Liberman Yehoshua	207, 536
Liberman	448
Libfrajnd Avraham-Hirsch	537

Libfrajnd Bracha	537
Lider Max	590
Litowski Wolf	42
Litwak A.	145
Lions D.	585
Lewek H.	506
Leizer the butcher	400
Leitheld Aharon-Zelig	578, 581, 584, 585
Lajpctkier Wolf	240, 241
Leifer Rabbi	589
Leifer Jack	589
Leifer Klara	592
Lajfer Berl	106, 378
Leifer Polly	592
Lichtenstajn G.	158
Lichtenstajn David	244
Lichtenstajn	514
Lichtenstajn Yisrael.	421
Lichtenstajn Heniek	421
Lilit Ella	548
Lisberg Richard	544
Liser L.	585
Lipomano Francis	17, 36
Lipomano Alajzi	17, 36
Lipman	123, 174
Lipman	500

Lipman Eliezer	97
Legalczyk	518, 520, 524
Lejman Shmuel	271, 272, 273, 276
Levy Jack	182, 548
Levy A.	585
Levy Sh.	585
Levi S.	585
Levy Sol	586
Lewi (Levy)	27
Levy Rachel	584
Lewin	28
Lewin Pinchas	196
Lewin Sh.	393
Lewin Noach	405, 429, 475
Lewin Shlomo	405, 416, 421
Lewin	411
Lewin Maniek	421, 533
Lewin Meir	429
Lewin Benny	584
Lewin H.	585
Lewin Yosef	585
Lewin-Butler Machla	374, 533, 558, 560
Lewin Miriam	558
Lewin Yaakov	578
Lewin Louis	28
Lewin Sara	434

Lewita	100
Lewin Max	585
Lewek Dr.	22
Levkovich Y.	585
Lewkowicz Yosef	414, 493, 547
Lewkowicz Berish	421, 494
Lewkowicz Gittel	494
Lewkowicz	547
Lewkowicz Avrhaam	335
Lewkowicz Esther	335
Lewkowicz Sheindel	472
Lewkowicz	184
Lewkowicz Binyamin	419
Lewkowicz Moshe	195
Lessinger Sarah	594
Lesman Moshe	424
Lefkowicz Chwacza	145

Mem   מ

Mahler R. Dr.	28
Meir Binyamin	304, 305
Mazal Stanislaw	476
MatusekTadeusz	467
Matola	474
Malinowski Victor	470
Malenberg	434

Malenberg Bracha	430
Manczasz	130
Manczyk	138, 201
Mania Nachum's	374
Moska Hertzke	481
Macna Shlomo	196
Marienfeld Eliahu	196
Marienfeld	396, 456
Marienfeld Yankel	399
Marienfeld Aharon-Zelig	414, 470, 480
Marienfeld Zelig	425
Marienfeld Ch.	585
Marienfeld Mechel	474
Morgensztern Yaakov	43
Markesh Peretz	261
Marek	277
Moszenberg Hersh-Nathan	431, 438
Moszenberg Tauba	437, 473
Moszenberg Roiza	203, 459
Moszenberg Daniel	154, 459
Moszenberg Moshe-Aharon	154
Moszenberg Bracha	203
Moszenberg Yosef	154
Moszenberg Yona	154
Mosman Yudel	203, 274
Maszlanka	475

Mosman Y.	587
Mosman A.	587
Moshko	311
Moszkowicz S.	585
Moszkowicz Lewka (Leib)	38
Moszkowicz Lewek	24
Muney Yosef	108, 126, 145, 241, 375, 393, 399, 405, 470
Muney Aryeh	562
Muney Max	585
Munia Jozek	39
Muney	201
Mocha Marek	16
Mocha Feliks	16
Mosek	417
Muszikowski	106
Mitelman Yosef	586
Reb Michel Zloczower	79
Michael	16, 37
Michael ben Shlomo	16
Reb Michele Magid	228
Michalski	214, 550
Michalski Stanislaw	475
Miler Yoel	126, 138, 405
Miler Julek	201
Miler Rachel	410
Miller David	585

Miller Sh.	585
Miller S.	585
Miller H.	585, 587
Miller A.	585
Miller Y.	585
Miller Sam	586
Miler	220
Miller Yosef	584, 585
Minin	520, 522, 523
Minc Yosef	427
Melech	510
Malka	416
Reb Menachel Mendel the Kocker Rebbe	57, 58, 66, 69, 70, 76, 78, 79, 81, 82, 83, 97, 238, 241, 324
Mezhericher Maggid	65
Mendelson Shlomo	281
Mendelson Klara	132
Mendele Mocher Seforim	133, 263, 264
Mendel	487
Mendel the Shochet's	398
Mendel Hitelmacher	195
Meps	473
Mecznik Moshe	584, 585
Mordechai (Marek) ben Shlomo	16
Reb Moshele Charif	88, 224, 227, 228, 258, 323
The Gaon Reb Moshe	57

Reb Moshe Sochaczewer	17
Reb Moshele Grodzisker	167
Moshe Sztrikmacher's son	446
Moshe Temes	111
Moshe-Itcha the teacher	155
Moshe of Sochaczew	228, 409
Moshe-Davidl, teacher	237
Moshe Betzalel	252
Moshe-Aharon Shulklaper	193, 196, 283, 286, 292, 301, 302
Moshe-Itche	154, 245
Moshe the son of Shmuel HaKohn	311
Moshe Stoliar	37
Moshe Shneider	176

Nun　　　　　　　　　　　נ

Nadelhaft Yosef	203, 205
Notan H.	585
Notek	516
Nomberg H. D.	144, 237, 261, 264, 277, 281
Noelson Yochanan	27
Noelson Levi	27
Napoleon	327
Naszelewicz Meir	160, 196, 217, 379
Naszelewicz Avraham	180, 186, 479
Naszelewicz Zilpa	328
Nasielski Yechezkel	453
Nut Yona	43
Rabbi Nachman of Breslov	70

Reb Nachman	258
Noach	177
Nina	281
Niemcowicz Julian	29
Nikolajczyk	530
Neiten Shimon	589, 590
Neiten Chaim-David	590
Neiten Shlomo	590
Najman Baruch	245
Najman Itzik-Izak	42
Namran	334
Nelson Moshe	507
Nelson Moshe	110, 111, 196
Nelson Chaim	562
Nelson P.	585
Nelson Herman	381, 586
Nelson Aharon	586
Nelson Hyman	586, 589
Nelson Irving	586
Nelson Jakob	586
Nelson Shmuel	587
Nelson Shmuel	284, 288, 379, 380
Nelson Betzalel	587
Nelson Tzvi	195
Nelson Lipa	195
Nelson	547
Naftali Hirsch	197
Naftali	405
Reb Natan Ari	228
Natan-David, teacher	155

Samech ס

Sabczok	470
Satenberg Yosef	196
Socha Yosef	17, 18, 22
Socha Yaakov	17, 18, 22
Socha Treitel	17, 18
Socha Beinish	17, 22
Sochaczewski Miriam	229, 328
Sochaczewski B.	585
Sochaczewski Sh.	585
Sochaczewer A.	452
Solomon Dr.	118
Solomon Mali	593, 594
Solomon B.	585
Solomon S.	585
Solberg Sam	586
Solberg B.	586
Solzasz Moshe	427
Sofer Y.	585
Soperman Shalom	195
Safran Arthur	585
Sochasznik Izak	503
Sokolow Nachum	160, 188, 190
Surowiec	37
Switman Yaakov	578, 581
Stanislaw	45
Strindberg	107, 181
Strogacz Yosef	132
Stefan	18
Stopnicki Sh.	281
"Stoag"	417
Segal Zindel	578, 581
Segal David	581
Silver M.	585

Silverstein A. G.	581
Silverstein Isadore	589
Silverstein Issie	579
Slomak Chaim	578, 585
Slomak Meir	579, 580, 585, 589
Slomak Nathan	586
Slomak Hyman	584
Slomak B.	585
Slomak Y.	585
Slomak L.	585
Sliwa Jan	392
Segal Mordechai	196
Segal (Diament)	472
Semianowska	38
Speiss Floris	592
Speiss Tovia	578
Speiss Aharon	581
Speiss Y.	585
Speiss M.	585
"Sczutner"	111
Skotnicki Lutek	106, 108, 126, 127, 131, 145, 176, 180
Skotnicki Herman	176
Skotnicki Moshe	264, 296
Skotnicki	374, 550
Skurnik Rachtshe	487
Skurnik Sara	515, 518
Skurnik	447, 515
Skurnik Itche	186
Skurnik David	173
Skurnik Ezriel	113
Skurnik Yehoshua	173
Skurnik Shmuel	196

Skrent	127, 130
Sklodkowski	135

Ayin   ע

Edelman Mark	412
Ejnes Hertzka	558, 568, 569
Ejnes Yerucham	558, 561, 568
Ejnes Chana-Jalob	568
Ejnes David	392
Eltster H. B. Dr.	585
Engel Reb Yosef	58
Engielman	155
Engielman Yitzchak	233
Engielman Moshe	244
Engelbrecht	485
Epstein H.	585
Erlich Henryk	127
Erlich Yitzchak	195
Erlich	483

Peh   פ

Podliszewski	160
Poznanski Eliahu	303
Poznanski Berl	196
Poznanski Shaya	196
Poznanski Chaim	196
Poznanski Eli	399
Pozner Meir	228
Fett Karel Adolf	544
Patalowski	165, 166
Fatom	154
Poniatowski Jozef	35

Pomeranc Tzemach	580
Foster Y.	585
Putter Robert	586
Putter Y.	585
Przybysz	551
Przerembski Jan	20
Przedpelski	455
Piast	30
Pinia	177
Pinczewski Mordechai	53
Pinczewski Velvel	214, 393, 470, 478, 547
Pinczewski Anshel	590
Pinczewski Hershel	447
Pinczewski Chaim	116, 138, 204
Pinczewski	489
Pindyk Motte	176
Pinski David	144
Pinskier L.	159
Pinkus	475
Pietczok	484
Piernik Yechiel-Meir	111, 157
Reb Pinchas Koreczer Rabbi	65
Pinchas Becker	196
Plonski Mendel	112, 113, 156, 207
Plonski	550
Plonska Nechama	431, 433
Plucer	166
Fen Issie	594
Perkal Hershel Rabbi	150, 203, 236, 237, 506
Perla Yehoshua	276, 277
Festman M.	158, 160, 162, 376, 379

Festman Bina	108, 145, 180
Festman Naftali	377
Peters A.	585
Frost Marcel	260
Priwer	481
Prilucki Tzvi	278
Prilucki Noach	127, 272, 274, 276, 277, 278, 280, 281
Peretz Y. L.	132, 133, 134, 145, 261, 277, 280
Polonto	31
Fan Fess	27
Fuchs A. M.	262
Furman Yaakov	24
Finkel S.	585
Fejn Hele	410
Fejn Rosza	428
Feiga the granddaughter of the Baal zshem	79
Fajgenbaum Yitzchak	58, 99
Feivish	231
Feivel the Torah reader	311
Flichta Jan	402
Flejszman Chana-Tzirl	295
Flejszman Chaya-Reshel	108
Flejszman Shaul	195
Flejszman Leibel	195
Flejszman Baruch	196, 472
Flejszman Itcha	562
Flejszman Shamai	473, 510
Fleishman Chaim	589
Flejszman	405, 592
Flejszman Miriam	510
Fleiszma Yitzchak	510

Flejszman Chaya	145, 180
Feliks Dr.	16
Feld Morris	586
Feld Y.	585
Feferkowicz Yechiel	195
Feferkowicz Gershon	173
Pera Menachem	496, 498
Fursztenberg Leibel	133, 213, 221, 309, 506, 509, 546
Fursztenberg Pese	174, 562
Fursztenberg Aharon	174, 509, 514
Fursztenberg Zalman	174
Fursztenberg	309
Prouza	391, 398, 448, 478, 507
Franco General	567
Frankenstein Mendel	584
Fromer Aryeh-Tzvi	60, 99, 256
Fromer Mendel	230
Fromer Aryeh Tzvi	60, 99
Fromer Yitzchak	60
Fromer Aryeh-Leib	237
Frumer Binem	53, 193
Frumer	39
Frumet	348
Fromowicz	560
Frydman Alexander-Zisha	105, 117, 237, 248
Frydman Mendel	116, 127, 194, 131, 133, 138, 286, 509
Frydman Menachem	103
Frydman Mania	509
Frydman Yaakov	146, 164, 168, 180, 189, 285, 300, 320, 376, 558, 560, 561, 572, 584
Frydman Aharon	146, 211, 375, 558,

560

Frydman Hersch	159, 275, 296, 381
Frydman Gershon	196
Frydman Shaya	196
Frydman Yechiel	398
Frydman Yehoshua	105
Frydman Chava	221
Friedman Rachel	558
Friedman Moshe	558
Friedman Itcha	558
Friedman L.	585
Friedman Martin	586
Friedman H. Y.	585
Friedrich Y.	585
Fryman Hirsch Frydman	249, 283, 284, 286
Paritz. L.	585
Freida	338, 340
Frajdenberg M. Sh.	446
Freund Menashe	325
Frenkel Rabbi	203, 398

Tsadek   צ

Comber Yaakov	344, 349
Reb Tzadok HaKohn from Lublin	70, 81
Zadkoni Yaakov	558
Zweckweiss	558
Cunzer	333
Zucker	523
Zuckerwise Yisrael Moshe	587, 588, 594
Zuckerwise Chava	587, 588, 593, 594
Zuckerwise Max	589, 590, 594
Zuckerwise Ida	594

Zuckerwise Leizer	196
Zuckerwise Yisrael Moshe	196
Zuckerman Antek	531
Tzina Rebbetzin, the daughter of the Kocker	347, 349, 350
Zimmerman	558
Zimerinski Menashe	193, 195, 196, 232, 292
Cejtlin Aharon	79
Ceszer	182
Tzipora	549

Kof ק

Kohn Baruch Mordechai	196
Kohn Chaim	196
Kohn Yosel	174
Kohn Meir	160
Kohn Michael	190
Kohn Liza	491
Kohn Aharon	500
Koze Sh. L.	279
Koznitz Maggid	65
Kasimierz the Great	32
Kasimierz, Duke of Mazowia	32
Kasimierz Jan, King	37
Katyn Simcha	475
Kotshinsky Y.	585
Kotshinsky A.	585
Kolobielski Chaim-Meir	173
Kalinin	522
Kolkier	522
Kolsky Barnet	584, 585
Kolsky	506

Kaleta Jozef	405, 496, 497
Kaliszer	190
Columbus	269
Kampelmacher	120, 121, 213, 214, 215, 216, 217, 218, 220, 221
Kampelmacher Berta	220
Kampelmacher Erek	220
Kampelmacher Lundek	220, 222, 223
Kaminska Ida	132, 548
Kamen Yosef	132
Kon Simcha	145, 405
Kon Avraham-Yaakov	395
Kon Mordechai	392
Kon Moshe	42
Kon Aharon	174, 409
Kon Avraham	421
Kon Zilpa	206
Kon Liza	431
Kantarowicz Rivka	5616, 519
Konrad I Duke of Mazowia	31
Konrad III	15
Kosowski Ignacy, Starosta	24
Kaplan Dr.	126, 138
The Kocker	65, 66, 79, 81, 238, 323
Kac Adam	203
"Kacap"	155
Kac	42
Kac Berish	495
Korczak Janusz	120, 437
Korotkin	162
Karel Gustav	23
Kara Nissan	344

Kara Chaikel	550
Kornbajser Sara	276
Karpowicz	518
Karpa	446
Kornfeld V.	585
Kotshinsky Y.	585
Kotshinsky A.	585
Kotszuska	26, 35, 38
Kubinow	520
Kutner Gaon	83
Kutnowski	483
Kumec	186
Cooper Morris	586
Cooper Becky	594
Cooper Avraham-Chaim	244
Cooper	585
Kopeld V.	585
Koszinski Feliks	475
Kwiawa	486
Kojfman Zissel	195
Kielman Yisrael	473
Klott	550
Klorberg	420
Kluska Adam	115, 156, 174
Kluska Aharon	425
Kluska Hirsch	154, 196, 294, 298, 299
Kluska Zelig	154
Kluska Abba	195, 294
Kluska	399
Kalman-Yankel	338, 339, 340, 341
Knott Menashe	126, 127, 130, 131, 133, 191, 375, 396, 415, 427, 457, 473, 480, 481

Knott Mania	500
Knott Leibish	196, 415
Knott Menachem	395
Knott Moshe	126
Knobel Mordechai	173
Kaszman	568
Kaszman Yechezkel	196
Kaszman Yosef	186
Keller Yisrael	116
Keller Pinchas	585
Keller Leibush	244, 470
Keller Pinchas	578, 585
Keller M. D.	585
Kefer Nachshon	195
King Leo	257
Grundwag Nachum	392
Kranc	507
Kroma H.	585
Krakow Shimon	204, 453
Kraszinski	20
Krongold Chaim	172
Krojn Ben-Zion	160
Krizowski A. Y.	278
Krel Yosef	252

Resh ר

Rabinowitz Hyman	575, 576
Rabinowitz J.	576
Rabinowicz Chaim	116
Rabinowicz Menashe	159
Rabinowicz Binyamin	195
Rabinowicz Naftali	195, 207

Rivka	500
Rawicz King	268
Rosen Louis, Reverend	581, 594
Rosen Sh.	585
Rosen Sol	585
Rosen Chana-Hadas	594
Rosen Perl	594
Rozen Mendel	472
Rozen Yontl	116, 138
Rozen Lozer	176, 178
Rozen	39
Rozen Michael	43
Rozenberg Reizl	423
Rozenberg Nina	281
Rozenberg Bronka	281
Rozenberg Vove	106, 108, 146, 176, 180, 280, 281, 282, 587, 589, 594
Rozenberg Pesach	416
Rozenberg Simcha	176
Rozenfeld Lozer	176, 177, 178, 324, 379
Rozenfeld Yosef	278
Rozenfeld Pinchas	176, 178
Rozenfeld	39
Rozenfeld	158, 162
Rozenfeld Shaya	167
Rozenperl	448
Rozenperl Aharon	470, 536, 537
Rozenperl Hentche	536
Rozenperl Avraham	207, 536, 537
Rozenkop Kalman	204
Rozenkop Pinchas	393, 416, 425, 427, 429, 470

Rozenkop Pinia	470
Rozenkop Roza	439
Rozenkop Zecharia	129
Rotsztejn Shmuel	470
Rotsztejn Yossel	431
Rotsztejn Golda	434
Rotstein Abe	584
Rotstein Avraham	585
Rotstein Yoel	590
Rotstein H.	585
Rotsztejn Yisrael	177, 394, 426, 430
Rotsztejn Yisrael-Shaya	196
Rotsztejn Moshe	177
Rotsztejn	170
Rotstein H.	585
Rotsztejn Chaim	177
Ratner Chaim	208
Ratchimel	471
Ratszinski	474
Rajak M.	389
Rolan Roman	128, 167
Roslow Priest	16
Rappaport L.	585
Rapoport Nachum	323, 324
Rapoport Mendele	154
Rapoport Simcha	154
Rapoport Yaakov	154
Rapoport Aharon	154
Ratze	345
Robinson Milton	586
Robinson M.	586
Rozepczyk	471
Roczimek Yitzchak	37

Rumianek Aharon	167, 232
Rojtman Hirsch	446, 487
Rojtsztejn Yisrael	550
Rites S.	585
Rizel	201
Richter Moshe	175
Ringelblum Emanuel	26, 28, 272, 543
Rajzen Avraham	264, 331
Rejtman Hirsch	399, 446
Rejtman Abba	207
Rejtman Mottel	416
Rejtman Ben-Zion	416
Rachele	312, 370
Rachel	510
Rechtman Shmuel	220
Rechtman Moshe	193
Rechtman	155, 167
Rene	499, 502

Shin ש

Sholk Sh.	585
Chopin Friedrich	217
Sharfstein Yosef	586
Szacki Y.	28
Sharken Abe	590
Shoham Esther	490, 539
Swiatlowski Shlomo	115, 154, 174, 207, 295, 409, 566
Swierzynska Janina Magister	30, 39
Schwartz Louis	584, 585
Schwartz Sh.	585
Schwartz A.	585
Szwarc Binyamin	395, 479

Szwarc Moshe	106, 108, 115, 141, 146, 154, 157, 174, 180, 207, 280, 295, 409, 566
Szwarc Rivka	108
Szwarc Machla	108, 174
Szwarc Shaul	174
Szwarcer Rivka	175, 176
Szwarcer	145
Szwrcer	374
Szwarcer Moshe	374
Swarcsztejn Meir-Yoel	249
Szulc	251
Szubec Mendel	427
Szulc	437
Szulsztejn Moshe	133
Szuster Yaakov	167
Starkman H. M.	585
Starkman S.	585
Stiglic Mendel	195
Stiglic Jame	115, 116
Stiwniak	173
Sztift Herman	178
Sztejn M. B.	85, 105, 238, 249, 335
Stajnman Eliezer	64
Sztejnberg	20
Sztern	405
Sztern's son	405
Sztern Yechiel	395, 470
Sztechler	471
Stromfeld	585
Stromfeld L.	585
Stromfeld A.	585
Streicher	201

Szapa A.	173
Sziper Y.	28
Szajnwald	450
Szajnwald Moshe	200
Szajnwald Hershel	487
Szajnwald Yitzchak	119
Szajnwald Pinchas	196
Szajnwald Chaim	203, 204
Sheinberg Max	584, 585
Sheinbaum Yona	578
Shach (Siftei Cohen)	227
Szlodow Berl	206
Shalom Aleichem	107, 123, 144, 181, 264, 266
Shlomo Grodzisker	244
Reb Shlomo Yisachar Dov Ber	228
Shlesinger A.	585
Rabbi Shimon Bar Yochai	255
Shimon Ben-Natan	26
Reb Shmuel Rabbi	324
Reb Shmuel Trajanower Rabbi	235
Reb Shmuel	384
Reb Shmuel (Shem Mishmuel)	60
Shmuel Yechiel, Shochet	235
Shmuel Yitzchak	235
Simcha Pelcenmacher	296
Reb Shmuel Kadynower	227
Rabbi Shmuel the Sochaczewer	60, 91, 95, 96
Rabbi Shmelke of Nikolsberg	65
Shmuel Zwitkower	26
Simcha-Yehuda Sznejder	155
Shmuel Czudnik	39
Szmulewicz Yechiel	454

Szmulewicz Leah	454
Szmulewicz Rachel	454
Szmulewicz Chaya	454
Szmulewicz Beila	454
Szmulewicz Ruzka	536
Szmajser Bina Gittel	328
Szmelc Aharon	470
Szmelc Aryeh	414
Szmelc	396, 425, 456, 480
Szmelc Nachum	472, 479
Szmelc Aharon	470
Szmeiser Paula	434
Szmeiser Shlomo	562
Szmejser Bina Gittel	328
Sznejder Aryeh-Leib	155
Sneiberg Sh.	585
Rabbi Shneur Zalman	65
Szewczyk	474, 475
Semiantek A. L.	138, 160
Szepiatowska	404
Szepietowski	31
Szepielowski	426
Szeparski Anzi, Rewer Wojewoda	16, 19
Shakespeare	182
Szereszewski Rafael	250
Sherl M.	585
Szpiegel Yeshaya	578
Szpiegel Hinda-Esther	42
Spinoza	134
Shpikler Max	594
Shpikler Yeti	594
Speisshendler	473, 562
Speisshendler Moshe	399, 587, 589, 590

Speisshendler David	590
Speisshendler Walter	590
Speisshendler David	590
Szapira Dr.	201
Szapira Kalonimus, Piaseczner Rebbe	552
Szapira Reb Moshe-Natan Rabbi	97
Szapira Yitzchak	201, 410
Skolek	115, 156, 174
Szpetrik	131, 133
Szitner	424
Sczapa	404
Sara-Yentl	390
Sara Tzina (daughter of the Admor of Kock)	97

Index of the Hebrew Section
Translated by Jerrold Landau

Page numbers are the page numbers of the original Yizkor Book and not the page numbers of this translation.

Alef	Bet	Gimel	Dalet	Hey	Vav	Zayin	Chet	Tet	Yod	Kaf
Lamed	Mem	Nun	Samech	Ayin	Peh	Tsadek	Kof	Resh	Shin	Tav

Alef

Rabbi Avraham, Admor of Sochaczew	612-621, 623, 625-628, 631, 632, 700, 709, 769, 774
Rabbi Avraham, Admor of Ciechanów	620
Avigdor Leibish	636
Aurswald (Ghetto Commissar)	638
Admor of Grochow	713
Unger Yoel	684
Oklanski Berl	734, 738
Auerbach Yitzchak	778
Auerbach Meir	778, 779
Orlean Yehuda Leib	681, 682
Egier the Gaon Rabbi Shlomo	677
Asz Reb Chaim Yisrael of Zurich	685
Ajsman Meir	702
Ajzenberg Pesach	739

Ajzenman Gavriel	677
Ajzensztadt Rabbi Meir (author of Panim Meorot)	609
Ajzenszteajn Mendel	730
Izraelowicz	734
Izraelski Gershon	735
Izraelski Gershon	739
Ejnes David	730
Ajsman Yisrael	654, 656
Albert Zalman	759, 760
Aldslach	735
Alter Rabbi Avraham the head of the rabbinical court of Pabianice	685
Alter Reb Moshe Betzalel (brother of the Gerrer Rebbe)	685
Alter Reb Mendel, head of the rabbinical court of Kalisz	638
Alter head of the rabbinical court of Pabianice	638
Rebbe Elimelech of Lizhensk	613, 622, 624
Rabbi Elimelech, Admor of Grodzisk	700
Rabbi Eliezer Lipman, the son-in-law of the Admor of Radomsk	628
Rabbi Eliezer Shalom the rabbi of Zadnoska Wola	634
Rabbi Eliezer HaKohn head of the rabbinical court of Sochaczew	720, 730
Ambaras Berl	650
Engelbrecht	745

Erlich teacher	684
Erlich Heinrich	654
Ish Shalom	659

Bet ב

Baum Arele	761
Baum David	761
Baum Tzipora	759-764
Balas Yudel	730, 732, 735
Balas Leizer	731, 732, 735, 738
Balcarska	730
Barbis	654
Bochner-Szteier	684
Rabbi Bunim of Przysucha	626
Bornsztejn Rabbi Avraham, Admor – see Rabbi Avraham	
Bornsztejn Aharon Yisrael	633, 674
Bornsztejn Ita Leah, wife of the Admor Rabbi Shmuel	628
Bornsztejn Esther, wife of Reb Meir	629
Bornsztejn Esther wife of the Admor Rabbi David	632
Bornsztejn Rabbi David Admor	632, 633, 635, 639, 640
Bornsztejn Volvish of Czestochowa	634
Bornsztejn Yechezkel	730
Bornsztejn Rabbi Meir, brother and son-in-law of the Admor Rabbi Avraham	629, 634

Bornsztejn Mirl wife of the Admor Rabbi Shmuel	628
Bornsztejn Mendel (of Siedlice)	633
Bornsztejn Mania	739
Bornsztejn Moshe Eliezer	604, 648, 769, 770
Bornsztejn Rivka	774
Bornsztejn Rabbi Shmuel Admor	628, 630, 632, 634, 769
Bornsztejn Shmuel-Avraham	774
Bornsztejn Sara Tzina wife of the Admor Rabbi Avraham	628
Burkowski ("Brodka")	654
Bursztejn	743
Brzozowski Esther	746
Brzozowski Bronia	730
Boznicki Moshe	733
Biezanski Mordechai	730, 737
Biezanska Freda	744
Bienkowski	657
Biderman	737, 739, 743
Biderman Yaakov	653, 657, 730
Biderman Rabbi Yaakov Meir the brother-in-law of the Gerrer Rebbe	
Beinish the Shamash	609
Bajkowski Dr. Z.	620
Blumental	657
Blumental Eliahu	653

Baumhertzer Mottel	653
Bliaschik (German captain)	730
Ben-Natan Shimon	610
Ben-Shlomo Mechel Mordechai (Marek)	608
Binyamin the smith	652
Becker	733
Rabbi Ber the Magid of Mezherich	613
Besht (Baal Shem tov) Rabbi Yisrael	612, 688
Brand (head of the Gestapo)	638
Bergzin Yitzchak	734, 739
Bergzin Shlomo Mendel	739
Bergelson	661
Brojtman	744
Bronia	745
"Broko" the enemy	657
Brokier Moshe	744
Berliner Neta Yerucham	682
Berman Hertzka	729, 734
Berman Sara Yentl	729
Bresler Yona	654
Bressler. Pinchas	652

Gimel ג

The Gaon of Vilna (the Gra)	688
Galek Feivel	649
Reb Gidel the teacher	670

Guzik David (the director of the JOINT)	684
Gothelf Hirsch	730, 732, 737
Gothelf Shmuel Leib	745
Goteskind (children's teacher)	670
Goldberg Chaim	732, 734
Goldberg Leibel	734
Goldberg Simcha	652, 657
Goldberg (the cobbler)	732
Goldman	654
Goldfaden	659
Goldfarb Aharon	742
Goldfarb Yisrael	729
Goldsztejn Yehoshua	705
Rabbi Shlomo Goldsztejn	739
Rabbi Y. Goldszlag head of the rabbinical court of Pieszyce	
Gordon	659
Gurski M.	645, 764
Guthajm	649
Gajer Moshe	652
Glebsztejn Itza	730, 737, 738
Gelbsztejn Yoel	732, 743
Gelman Sh.	670
Gerszt Yerachmiel	734
Graubard Leibish	708, 723
Graubard Moshe	735

Graubard Matityahu	739
Graubard Pinchas	601, 604, 648, 723, 761
Graubard (shoemaker)	744
Grosjman Aharon	731
Grosjman Yoska	740
Grundwag Simcha	648, 652-654, 657, 692, 693
Grundwag Rivka	659
Grundwag Nachum	648, 654, 659, 693, 730
Grundwag Machla	659, 669
Grundwag Dina	659
Grundwag Yossel	656
Grynberg Aharon	657, 658
Grynberg Eliezer	771
Grynberg Leib	670
Grynberg Mindel-Tauba	771
Gryngard Yitzchak	739

Dalet ד

Rabbi David Admor of Sochaczew	632, 633, 635, 639, 640
Dostoyevski	764
Jiwicky	735
Diament Itza	735
Diament Lipman	731, 735

Deitcher Moshe (Censor from Krakow)	682
Derber (head of the P.P.s.)	652, 657

Hey ה

Haber Yosef Moshe (head of the community of Kalusz)	684
Hollander	732
The Holy Jew (Rabbi Yaakov Yitzchak, Admor of Przysucha)	612, 613, 635
Hajnter Meir	682
Hindes Dr. T.	670
Hirsch (communist from Blonie)	650
Hirzbejn Peretz	659
Halbersztam Rabbi David (Rabbi of Sosnowiec)	685
Heler	739
Hendel Avraham	684, 690, 691
Rabbi Henech Admor of Aleksander	614, 617
Hermelin (actor)	661
Hertzfeld A.	761
Herskowicz Pessi	739

Vav ו

Wajsenberg Izak	657
Warszawiak Reb Pinchas (the brother-in-law of the Gerrer Rebbe)	689
Warszawski G.	669, 671

Warszawski Hershel	653, 654, 657, 658
Warszawski Wolf	744
Warszawski Yosef	732
Warszawski Ozer	601, 647
Warszawski Reb Sh. N.	670
Wazninski	733
Wolman K.	669, 670
Wiedislawski Moshe	744
Wajnberg Avraham Yitzchak	756
Wisznia Eli	738
Wisznia Eli	744
Wajnberg the Gaon Rabbi Avraham (Reb Avraham Stucziner)	634, 637
Wajnberg Bluma	659
Wajnberg Pinchas	653, 654, 656, 657, 668
Wajnberg Rachel	659
Wajntraub Y.	670
Winer Yitzchak	653, 657
Winer Mordechai (Mottel)	653
Wajnsenberg Y. M.	648, 770
Wyszogrodzki (secretary from Wyszogrod)	649
Waldenberg Izak	653, 657
Wolkowicz Yosef	653, 702
Wachler Reb Mendel (Rosh Yeshiva)	633

Zayin ז

Zawadski Yehoshua	742
Zajac	746
Zand Yechiel	735, 742
Zwitkower Shmuel	610, 677
Zhokowski Jan	730
Zygmunt August (King of Poland)	609
Rabbi Zusia of Anipoli	622
Zysman Eliezer	657
Zolonka	738
Zolonka Moshe	732
Jelozko Yitzchak	731, 742
Zalcman Yechiel-Meir	652
Zalcman Meir	661
Zalcman Paula	739
Zmiaowski	657
Zemba the Gaon Rabbi Menachem	678, 683

Chet ח

Rabbi Chaim Halberstam Admor of Sanz	613, 616, 632
Rabbi Chaim head of the rabbinical court of Konstantyn	634
Chaim Bliacharz	738
Chaim Nissan the son of Chaikel	713
Rabbi Chanoch Henech, Admor of Aleksander	614, 617

Chaikel the wagon driver	602, 712, 714
Chofetz Chaim (The Gaon Rabbi Yisrael of Radun)	688
Chetzroni A.	57, 97

Tet ט

Tabans (Shiff)	744
Taub Avraham	656
Tovim	654
Tolstoy	654, 764
Tilman Avraham	734, 738
Tilman Hertzka	656, 733, 735
Tilman Yechiel-Meir	658, 704, 739
Tilman Yitzchak	734
Tilman Moshe	730
Tilman Nachman	731, 733
Tindel Hirsch	666, 746
Temes Moshe	649
Tritel (father of Yosef and Yaakov) Sucha	609
Trukenhajm Yaakov	685

Yod י

Yancha (the porter)	734
Jasinowski lawyer	670
Jasinski Eli	735
Jasinski Dina	775

Jasinski Hershel	654, 743
Jasinski Menashe	775
Jasinski Moshe Aharon	735
Jasinski Shmuel (Shmulek)	775, 777
Rabbi Yehoshua (the son of Rabbi Eliezer HaKohn)	669
The Gaon Rabbi Yoav Yehoshua head of the rabbinical court of Kinczak (author of the Chelkat Yoav book)	631
Yosef Sucha	609
Yaakov Sucha	609
Yochanan (surgeon and obstetrician of the city)	610
Yaakov the son of the Shamach Beinish	609
Yaakov the doctor (or rabbi)	609
Rabbi Yaakov Aharon head of the rabbinical court of Konstantyn	769
Yaakov Aharon	738
Rabbi Yaakov Aryeh Admor of Radzimin	637
Yaakov David (water drawer)	733
Rabbi Yaakov Yitzchak of Przysucha (the Holy Jew)	612, 613, 635
Jakubowicz Leizer	732, 733
Jakubowicz Hirsch Leib	734
Jakubowicz Moshe	648, 737
Jakubowicz Tzalka	746
Jakubowicz Shlomo	733, 734
Jakubowicz Shmuel	657

Rabbi Yitzchak Zelig Morgiensztern Admor of Sokolow	774
Rabbi Yitzchak Meir, Admor of Ger (Chidushei Harim)	614, 621, 627
Rabbi Yitzchak Mendel Danziger Admor of Aleksander	638
Rabbi Yitzchak Shlomo Liberman	632
Yakir the shoemaker	602, 716, 717
Rabbi Yisrael Besht (Baal Shem Tov)	612, 688
Rabbi Yisrael the Magid of Kozienice	613
Rabbi Yisrael Morgensztern Admor of Pylow	634
Rabbi Yisrael Zelower rabbi and teacher in Radomsk	634
Rabbi Yissachar Kohn of Gustinin	637

Kaf כ

Kohn Avraham	654, 656
Cohen Avraham – Gan Yavneh	779
Kohn Gittel	742
Kohn Michael	653, 654, 658
Kohn Paula (the daughter of Gittel)	742
Kohn Simcha	648, 654
Kohn Pinchas	746
Chmiel Freda	661
Kac Hershel	659

Lamed ל

Lodzer Moshe (Jakubowicz)	657
Lewkowicz Shlomo	702
Lawancka (or Lazancka) Dorota	609
Levi Zak	661
Rabbi Levi Yitzchak of Berdichev	613, 616
Lewita (father of L. Lewita)	670
Lewin	743
Lewin Rabbi Aharon head of the rabbinical court of Rzeszow	681
Lewin David	776
Lewin Chana	776
Lewin Rabbi Yitzchak Meir	678, 679, 682, 684
Lewin Meir	739
Lewin Menachem Zeev	700
Lewin Noach	734, 739
Lewin Tzvi (Hershele)	776, 777
Lewin Tzvi	756
Lewin Shlomo	730, 734
Lewin Sara Leah	700, 740
Lewintal Rabbi Lipman Tzvi, head of the rabbinical court of Cialadz	634
Laufer Berl	648
Luksztyk	743
Luksztyk Yosef	658, 730
Laznowski, Rabbi Baruch, head of the rabbinical court of Ujazd	634
Lazar Aharon	739

Libert H.	743
Libert Munik	730, 737, 738
Libert Shmuel	730
Leibishel the small	708
Leizer Droszkosz	666
Leizer the butcher	733
Leist, German ruler	638
Lichtensztejn Y.	669
Lipszyc Rabbi Shlomo Zalman (Chemdat Shlomo) head of the rabbinical court of Warsaw	638
Landenberg Falik	681
Laskowski Rabbi Eliahu head of the rabbinical court of Dobrut	634
Lejman Shmuel	601

Mem   מ

Meir Hauser	732
Meir Binyamin	698, 699
Rabbi Meir Yechiel, Admor of Ostrowiec	700
Muney Yosef	648, 654, 730, 732, 734
Montcik	656
Montcik	657
Mokotowski Reb Avraham	675, 682
Moszkoski Mayor of the city	648
Moszko, smith	712

Mazor Eliahu	679
Rabbi Michel, head of the rabbinical court of Biala	627
Meisel Chana	761
Miller Yoel	654, 657, 734
Miller Rachel	735
Minc Yosef	738
Miszrowicer Rabbi Chaim	670
Mechel and Mordechai (Marek) son of Shlomo	608
Malinberg Bracha	739, 740
Mendele Mocher Sefarim	656
Mendel (shoemaker from Wiskiti)	746
Rabbi Menachem Mendel the Admor of Kock	613-616, 625-628, 632, 770
Mendelsohn Klara	656
Maroz	756
Marienfeld Aharon Zelig	731, 738
Marienfeld Yaakov Y.	732
Rabbi Moshe Sochaczewer the son in law of the "Panim Meirot"	609
Moshe of Sochaczew	735
Moshe Soliaj	738
Moshe Aharon "Shulklaper"	697, 698
Moszenberg Hirsch Nisan	739

Nun ׳

Nadbornik Moshe	731
Noelson Levi	610
Rabbi Nachman of Breslov	620
Neihaus Rabbi Meir Bunem	633
Nelson Moshe	649
Nelson Shmuel	697
Naftali (watchmaker)	734
Nasielewicz Avraham	659
Nasielewicz Rabbi Meir	670

Samech ס

Sokolow Nachum	670
Strawinski (Financial director of the Z.T. A.S.)	698
Strindberg	659
Salomon Dr.	652
Sliwa Jan	730
Rabbi Y. Sender of Posen	685
Skotnicki Lutek	648, 654, 656, 689
Skrunik Azriel	650
Skrunik Rachtsha	746
Skrant	654

Ayin ע

Elbingier Reb Yosef	638
Elbingier Reb Yitzchak Meir	638

Elbingier Leibel   634

Peh   פ

Podliszowski A.	670
Piatczak	745
Poznanski Eli	732
Pola	743
The Rabbi of Piatek	634
Fajgenbaum the Gaon Rabbi Yitzchak the head of the rabbinical court of Warsaw	631
Fajn Hella	735
Fajn Mordechai	666
Fajn Roza	739
Fajngold Y. L.	638
Pinczowski A.	746
Pinczowsk Velvel	730, 743
Pinczowski Chaim	652, 657, 658
Pinczowski Mottel	702
Fisher (German ruler)	638
Plonski Chana	739
Plonski Mendel	650
Plonski Nechama	739
Feliks, Jewish doctor	608
Flajszman	734
Flajszman Chaya-Rashel	659
Flajszman Tova-Leah	759

Rabbi Pinchas of Korec	613
Rabbi Pinchas, the author of "Haflaah"	613
Pestalozzi	710
Festman A.	669
Festman Bina	659
Festman M.	670
Prouza Julian	729, 732, 743
Farbsztejn Reb Heshel (Sejm representative)	679
Frum Leibel	681
Frumer the Gaon Rabbi Aryeh Tzvi (Rosh Yeshiva of Chachmei Lublin)	631, 633, 634, 636, 637
Pruszynowski Reb David	633
Freda, wife of Kalman Yankel	718, 720
Frydman Aharon Yehoshua	675
Frydman Aleksander Zisha	601, 647, 674-691, 705
Frydman Amnon	758
Frydman Gisha	701
Frydman Taba	700
Frydman Yehudit	703
Frydman Yechiel	700
Frydman Yaakov	604, 659, 765-768
Frydman Mendel	652, 654, 656, 657, 700
Frydman Menachem	756
Frydman Nicha	703

Frydman Friman Hirsch (Shalom Tzvi)	670, 696, 697, 700, 705, 756
Frydman Shlomo (Grodzisker)	700, 703
Frydman Shimon (Chilkele)	732
Frydman Sara	756
Frejdenson Reb Eliezer Gershon	682, 684
Priwes Reb Eliezer	677
Priwes Reb Yeshaya	677
Prever (head of the Gestapo)	744
Prilucki Noach	654
Perkal Rabbi Tzvi	666, 703-705, 731, 732
Fersztynberg Leibel	656

Tsadek   צ

Rabbi Tzadok HaKohen, the Admor of Lublin	620
Zimerinski Reb Eliezer	705
Zimerinski Reb Menashe	700
Czerniakow Adam	638, 683, 684, 689, 734

Kof   ק

Kon Aharon	735
Kon Liza	739
Kon Reb Meir	670
Kon Meir	735

Kon Mordechai	730
Kon Simcha	734
Kon Chaim Nissan	730
Kojawa	745
Korczak Janusz	710, 741
Kirszbraun Reb Eliahu	679, 688
Kluska Adam	652
Kluska Aharon	738
Klioski (shoemaker brothers)	732
Kalman Yankel	664, 718, 720
Keller Yisrael	652
Kampelmacher	653, 704, 710
Knott Avraham Yaakov	731
Knott Menashe	644, 656, 731, 738, 744
Kaplan Dr.	654, 657
Kaplan Chana	771
Kaplan Yosef	775
Korotkin	670
Krakow Shimon	734, 742
Krojn Reb Ben-Zion	670
Krongrad Avraham Meir	684
Carlebach Dr. Emanuel	676

Resh ר

Rabicz, teacher	684

Rozenberg Vove	601, 604, 648, 659
Rabinowicz Reb Menashe	670
Rabinowicz Tema	652
Radzinski Yaakov (Mizrachi activist)	685
Rogowy Avraham Mordechai	681, 684
Rozen Yuntel	652, 657
Rozenfeld A.	669, 670
Rotsztejn Golda	740
Rotsztejn Yossel	739
Rotsztejn Yisrael	731, 738, 739
Rotsztejn Shabtai	702
Rolen	654
Rozenkop Pinchas	730, 737, 738, 743
Rozenkop Roza	741
Rotenberg Aharon the son-in-law of the Admor Rabbi Shmuel	633
Rajtman Hirsch	732, 746
Ringelblum Dr.	687, 689
Rechtman Avraham	706
Rechtman Reb David	706
Rechtman Malka	706
Rechtman Moshe	708, 723
Rechtman Pinchas Eliahu	709
Rappaport Aharon (from Bielec)	685
Rappaport Yaakov (from Bielec)	685
Rappaport Simcha (from Bielec)	685

Shin ש

Szafran David	684
Szwarc Binyamin	731
Szwarc Moshe	648, 659
Swarcsztejn Meir Yoel	676
Szotland Rafael	761
Swiatlowski Shlomo	652
Szulc	685, 690, 691
"Shulklaper" Moshe Aharon	697
Steiglic Ziama	652
Sztejn A. Sh.	604
Sztern Yechiel	731
Szajnwald (son of Yankele the teacher)	653
Szajnwald	744
Szanwald Moshe	742
Szanwald Tzvi (Hirsch)	742, 746
Shalom Aleichem	659
Sleznger Mordechai	778
Rabbi Shlomo the Admor of Radomsk ("Tiferet Shlomo")	628
Rabbi Shlomo Zalman Lipschitz ("Chemdat Shlomo")	638
Rabbi Shmuel the Admor, see Bornsztejn Rabbi Shmuel	
Szmiontek	657
Szmiontek A. L.	670

Szmajser Paula	740
Szmelc (tailor)	743
Szmelc Menachem	731, 738
Rabbi Shmelke of Nikolsburg	613
Shimon ben Natan	610
Rabbi Shneur Zalman of Liadi (the "Tanya")	613, 620
Szpotrik (dental technician)	656
Szapira Asher	682
Szapira Yitzchak	735
Szapira Rabbi Moshe Natan, the head of the rabbinical court of Kosienice	628
Szapira Rabbi Kalonymus Admor of Piaszczyna	685
Sczitner	737
Szereszewski (banker)	677

Appendices

The following following appendices are not in the original Yizkor book

Sochaczew map

Produced from memory by Mr. Yosef Grundwag of Jerusalem (label 16)

Note from translator: I labeled the Hebrew/Yiddish inscriptions from 1-63. I did my best to verify the spelling of cities and towns. For street names, I tried to match Polish spelling, but it is probable that the spelling that I provided is not exact in most cases. I put my own comments in parentheses. In the two cases where street names had parentheses in the original (presumably these are alternative street names), I put them in square brackets so as not to confuse with my own comments.

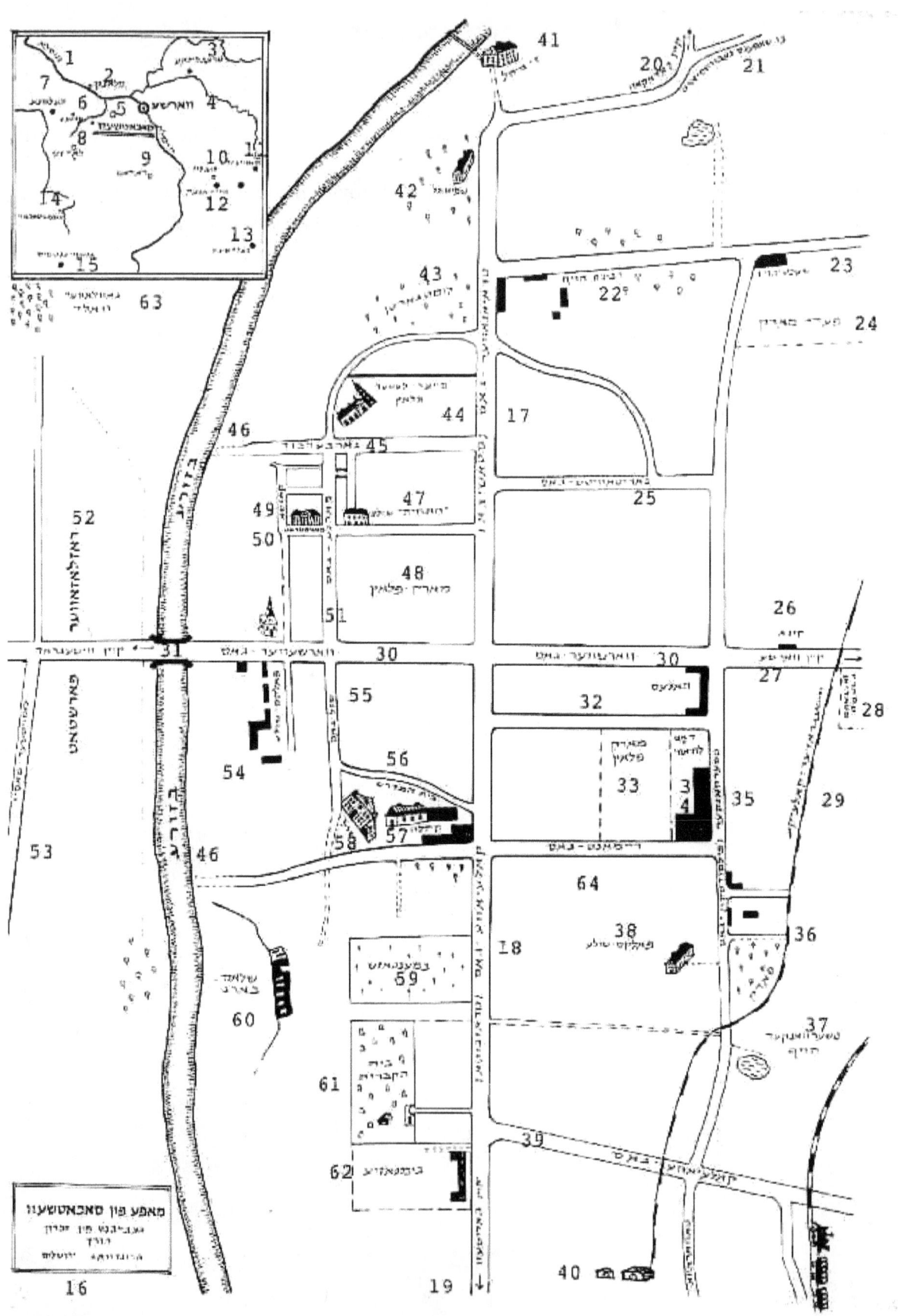

Small Map in Upper Left Inset

The small map inserted at upper left is a map of Sochaczew in relation to major cities and concentration camps of Poland. Cities are denoted on map by circles, and Concentration Camps by black dots.

1. Wysla (River)
2. Plock
3. Treblinka (Concentration Camp)
4. Warsaw
5. Sochaczew (underlined)
6. Kutna (a city, but noted on map with a black dot, so presumably a Concentration Camp as well, although not a well-known one.)
7. Chelmno (Concentration Camp)
8. Lodz
9. Radom
10. Lublin
11. Sobibor (Concentration Camp)
12. Majdanek (Concentration Camp)
13. Belzec (Concentration Camp)
14. Czestochowa
15. Auschwitz (Osweicim – Concentration Camp)

Main Map

Directions are not labeled, however, since the note (27) at rightmost edge of main street crossing City (Warsawer Street) notes that direction is to Warsaw, and Warsaw is almost directly east of Sochaczew, it can be deduced that the rightmost edge is east, and consequently, the top edge is north. These directions may not be exact, as it is doubtful that the main streets which cross from top-bottom and right-left are exactly north-south and east-west respectively, however from the labels, it is obviously that they are close to that.

16. Main label – Map of Sochaczew, produced from memory by Mr. Yosef Grundwag of Jerusalem.
17. Trajanower Street [Staszica] – upper segment of main north-south Street
18. Kolejova Street [Traugutta] – lower segment of main north-south street
19. To Boryszew (village south of Sochaczew)
20. To Chodakow (town northeast of Sochaczew)
21. To Chopin's birthplace
22. Rabbi's Hauf (not sure what Hauf means, perhaps a high place)
23. Slaughterhouse
24. Horse Market

25. Narutowicza Street
26. Movie theater
27. To Warsaw
28. Sport stadium
29. Wyszogroder train line
30. Warsawer Street
31. To Wyszogrod (town north of Sochaczew)
32. Hales (perhaps from Polish Hala – a hall)
33. Market place
34. The Ludawi (people's hall)
35. Czerwanker [Pilsudski] Street
36. Park
37. Czerwanker Hauf
38. Folk School
39. Kolejova Street
40. Towarowa
41. The Mill
42. Hospital
43. Lustgarten
44. Pierrer Laszer place
45. Garberbuch
46. Bzura River
47. "Hatechia" school
48. Marketplace
49. Kazsza
50. Magistrate
51. Farna Street
52. Roszloszower suburb
53. Lowiczer highway
54. Folk School
55. School Street
56. The House of Study (Bais Medrash)
57. The Community Offices
58. The Synagogue
59. Cemetery (Christian)
60. Schloss Mountain
61. Cemetery (Jewish)
62. Gymnasia (high school)
63. Gowlower Forest
64. Remont Street

The Committee of Sochaczewites in Israel
by Joseph Grundwag

The Sochaczew Committee in Israel (the Committee) is the group that wrote the Sochaczew Yizkor book, relating their and other Sochaczewite survivors' memories. The Yizkor Book, Pincas Sochaczew, lists 2,467 of the Sochaczewites who were killed in the Shoah. However, this is not the full number of the victims as Sochaczew's Jewish Community totaled over 5,000. Some victims are, therefore, not included.

The Committee has existed since the 1950's, with an executive committee that moved between Jerusalem and Tel Aviv over the years. Joseph Grundwag has been the Secretary for the past 12 years. Mr. Grundwag left Sochaczew in 1934 to become a student at the Hebrew University in Jerusalem, having taken part in all the wars Israel has fought. He spent 37 years as the director of the Jerusalem branch of the Jewish National Fund.

Among the most important activities of the organization are:

1. The establishment of a memorial monument at the Holon Cemetery in Israel, including the burial of ashes from the extermination camps in Poland.

2. Conducting an annual memorial service in memory of the Sochazewite Holocaust victims.

3. Saving the grounds of the Jewish cemetery in Sochaczew from total deterioration and preventing the Polish authorities from demolishing it in order to build new low-cost housing, as they did elsewhere. This was accomplished after a meeting held in 1988 between the Mayor of Sochaczew, Committee members Arieh Firstenberg and Joseph Grundwag.

4. The construction of a metal fence around the Jewish cemetery in Sochaczew, with the financial assistance of Mr. Yehuda Widavski, a Sochaczew hassid.

5. In 1991, the Committee built a huge memorial wall within the cemetery grounds in Sochaczew, with metal plaques in four languages: Hebrew, Yiddish, English and Polish. Adjacent to the monument is a symbolic grave built of the fragments of the shattered gravestones found in the area.

6. Members of the "younger generation" have started to participate in the Committee's activities. The Committee also established a scholarship fund for higher education, which is granted annually to children or grandchildren of original Sochaczewites living in Israel. Three scholarships were awarded in 1999 (August 31, 1999) for the eighth consecutive time.

7. Following the construction of the said memorial wall, the Sochaczew Hassidim built by an Ohel Yizkor, containing two graves of the Admors (Hassidic Rabbis) Rabbi Shmuel and Rabbi Avreimel, of blessed memory. This followed excavations to uncover the remains of the two rabbis. Many visitors now flock to the site and in November 1999, 40 rabbis from Israel visited.

The Sochaczew memorial

(Photographs donated by Mr. Yosef Grundwag of Jerusalem)

The unveiling ceremony of the memorial plaque on the "remembrance wall" which stands in the Sochaczew cemetery.

23rd July, 1991.

The right side of the remembrance wall. Standing: Aryeh Firstenberg Ze'ev Szianwald and Yosef Grundwag (speaker).

The deputy mayor addressing the audience.

From left to right: Yosef Grundwag (Sochaczew Organization Secretary), Ze'ev Szianwald (former Organization Chairman), the "chazan" David Vishniya (formerly from Sochaczew, a Holocaust survivor currently living in the U.S.) and Shlomo Friedman (of blessed memory - was former chairman of the Sochaczew Organization).

Poland Trip 2001 (July)
Photographed by Jan Meisels Allen

These photographs were taken in July 2001 by Sochaczew Yizkor Book translation coordinator, Jan Meisels Allen on a trip to Poland to visit her ancestral shtetls. They are representative of how the Sochaczew is today.

Sign upon entering the town

Gate to Jewish Cemetery

Ohel sign

Inside ohel with graves of Bornsztejn rabbis

Memorial stone

Cemetery memorial stone

Back of memorial stone with defacing "Jude" and a swastika

*Area of former Jewish community
(synagogue, community offices)*

Area of former Jewish community looking toward rynek [market]

Castle hill (Schloss Mountain) with castle remains

Looking across town square to museum and new church

Museum

Museum exhibit poster on Jews of Sochaczew

Photographs from Treblinka

Photographed by Jan Meisels Allen

These photographs were taken in July 2001 by Sochaczew Yizkor Book translation coordinator, Jan Meisels Allen on a trip to Poland to visit her ancestral shtetls. They are representative of how the Treblinka camp is today.

(* Click on the photographs to enlarge)

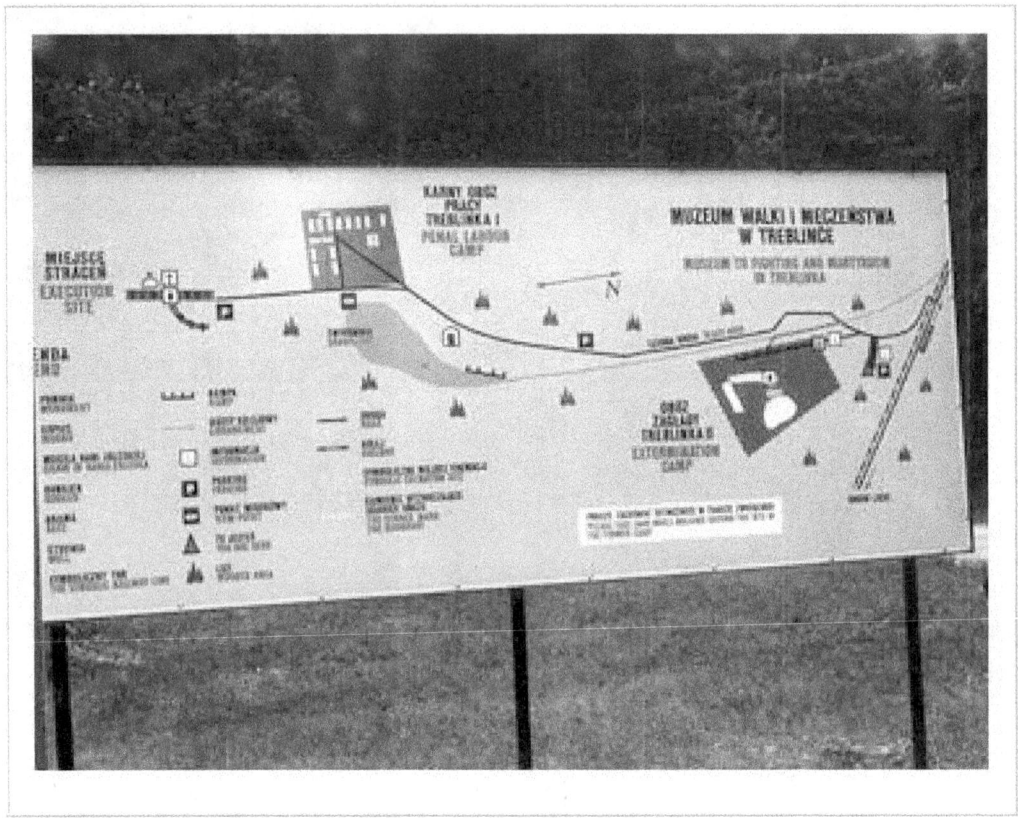

Treblinka Sign

Treblinka Sign

Stone Sign

English Memorial Stone

Line of stones in different languages

Stones representing railroad tracks

Field of stones representing destroyed towns

Sochaczew Stone

Memorial

Aerial photographs of Sochaczew

These photographs are from the Records of the Defense Intelligence Agency Record 373, Captured German World War II photographs available from the National Archives and Records Administration II Cartographic Section.

Sochaczew, Poland 1944

Captured German Aerial Photograph, 1:41,200
National Archives and Records Administration
Cartographic Section, RG 373~TUGX353~SK 122

Aerial photograph

National Archives and Records Administration

Cartographic Section RG 373~TUGX353~SK 122

Aerial photograph (without arrows)
National Archives and Records Administration
Cartographic Section RG 373~TUGX353~SK 122

Numbers in parenthesis refer to numbers in Yizkor Book
1. (46) Bzura River
2. (30) Warszawer Street
3. (57/58) Jewish Community Center
4. (60) Schloss Mountain (Castle Hill where castle ruins are)
   See also Sochaczew map

World War II German Captured photographs

These photographs are from the Records of the Defense Intelligence Agency Record 373, Captured German World War II photographs available from the National Archives and Records Administration II Cartographic Section.

Sochaczew Synagogue
Sochaczew Yizkor Book, Page 19

Sochaczew Synagogue
Sochaczew Yizkor Book, Page 19

Street with burning houses in the city that was just captured by German troops
September 19, 1939
National Archives and Records Administration
Cartographic Section 242-GAP-203-S-12

Totally destroyed building
September 9, 1939
National Archives and Records Administration
Cartographic Section 242-GAP-203-S-8

Bombed Sochaczew Synagogue
September 20, 1939
National Archives and Records Administration
Cartographic Section 242-GAP-203-S-24

Burning building

September 19, 1939

National Archives and Records Administration

Cartographic Section 242-GAP-203-S-15

Sochotzover Society of Greater New York, Membership 1977

Dedicated to the Memory of:

Bernice Phyllis (Mann) Knee (nee Mittleman)
Beloved Sister of Sandra Mittleman Robinson,
Granddaughter of Sochotzover Society Member Charles Miller
Donated by: Sandra and Ken Robinson

Note: While the membership list is from Greater New York, there were members from other states, namely, California, Florida and New Jersey. The information was input exactly as it appeared in the membership roster. Telephone numbers were eliminated as they would no longer be valid. Not all persons had their zip codes included.

Sochotzover Society of Greater New York Membership List 1977-1978

Surname	First name & MI	Office held	Committee name	Street address	City	State	Zip
DARLOW	Nat	Ex-President	Officers	220 West Jersey Street	Elizabeth	NJ	
BECKER	Samuel	President	Officers	555 Kappock St. Apt 1J	Bronx	NY	10463
ROBINSON	Milton	Vice President	Officers	250 Prospect St.	East Orange	NJ	7017
KITMAN	Myer	Secretary	Officers	4520 12th Avenue	Brooklyn	NY	11219
DARLOW	Nat	Treasurer	Officers	220 West Jersey Street	Elizabeth	NJ	
DARLOW	Nat		Past-president				
LEVY	Sol		Past-president				
SALBERG	Sam		Past-president				
NELSON	Irwin G.		Trustee				
ROBINSON	Milton		Trustee				
COOPER	Nathan		Trustee				
DARLOW	Nat	Chairman	Ways & Means Cmte				

ROBINSON	Milton		Ways & Means Cmte				
COOPER	Louis		Ways & Means Cmte				
	and elected officers		Ways & Means Cmte				
DARLOW	Nat	Chairman	Social Committee				
COOPER	Louis		Social Committee				
COOPER	Nat		Social Committee				
ROBINSON	Milton		Social Committee				
	and elected officers		Social Committee				
COOPER	Morris	Chairman	Charity & Reserve Fund				
ROBINSON	Milton		Charity & Reserve Fund				
NELSON	Irwin G.		Charity, & Reserve Fund				
	and elected officers		Charity & Reserve Fund				
ROBINSON	Milton	Chairman	Finance Committee				
NELSON	Irwin G.		Finance Committee				
COOPER	Nat		Finance Committee				
	and the elected officers						

Membership

Surname	First name & MI	Street address	City	State	Zip
BECKER	Sam S.	555 Kappock St. Apt. 1-J	Bronx	NY	10463
BENSON	Bernard	402 Barnard Avenue	Cedarhurst	NY	11516
BENZER	Rose	36K Amberly Drive	Englishtown	NJ	7726
BERMAN	David	64-20 Saunder St.	Rego Park	NY	11374
BERMAN	Rose	134-54 Maple St. Apt. 5-P	Flushing	NY	11355
BERMAN	Augusta	321 West 24th St.	New York	NY	10011
BERMAN	Mrs. Pearl	10989 Rochester Ave. Apt 109	Los Angeles	CA	90024
BERMAN	Mrs. Ruth	c/o Prince Michael 2618 Collins Avenue	Miami Beach	FL	33139
BESOFSKY	Sophie	2245 Barker Avenue	Bronx	NY	10467
BINDER	Tessie	70-10 Parsons Blvd. Apt. 3B	Flushing	NY	
BLUCHER	Philip	200 Hudson St.	New York	NY	10013
BORENSTEIN	Louis	800 West Ave. Apt. 718	Miami Beach	FL	33139
BORENSTEIN	Rubin	1445 44th Street	Brooklyn	NY	11219
BROTHMAN	Helen	1953 70th Street	Brooklyn	NY	11204
COHEN	Florence	1200 N.E. Miami Gardens Drive	No. Miami Beach	FL	33179

COHEN	Mrs. Hilda	31-19 33rd Street	Astoria	NY	
COHEN	Mrs. Ida	412 East 4th Street	Brooklyn	NY	11218
COHEN	Mrs. Rose	19 Maplewood Avenue	Elmwood Park	NJ	7407
COOPER	Jacob	609 Palmer Rd.	Yonkers	NY	10701
COOPER	Louis	3201 Grand Concourse	Bronx	NY	10468
COOPER	Morris	2132 Wallace Ave. Apt. 345	Bronx	NY	
COOPER	Nathan	1147 East 214th St.	Bronx	NY	10469
DARLOW	Nat	220 West Jersey St.	Elizabeth	NJ	7202
DIAMOND	Dr. Abraham I.	3500 Washington St. Apt. 515A	Hollywood	FL	33021
DIAMOND	Louis	1654 East 13th Street	Brooklyn	NY	11229
DIAMOND	Jenny	RR #3 Box 510	Monticello	NY	12701
DOLDERER	Anna	6309 23rd Avenue	Brooklyn	NY	11204
DUBROW	Harry A.	3 Strathmore Gardens	Matawan	NJ	7747
FELD	Eva	241 Charles Street	Clifton	NJ	7013
FINKELSTEIN	Irving	Fortie Towers 1000 West Ave. Apt. 401	Miami Beach	FL	33139
FLEISCHMAN	Maurice G.	3535 Kings College Place	Bronx	NY	10467
FLEISCHMAN	Mrs. Sadie	728 East New York Avenue	Brooklyn	NY	11203
FREDERICK	Nathan	c/o Albert Frederick	Brooklyn	NY	11235

		4750 Bedford Avenue			
GERMAN	Mrs. Edna	205 East 17th Street Apt. 607	Brooklyn	NY	11226
GOLDBERG	Mrs. Molly	c/o Mrs. F. Golub 5980 North West 64th Avenue	Ft. Lauderdale	FL	33313
GOLDSTEIN	Morris	1849 Sedgwick Avenue	Bronx	NY	10453
GOODMAN	Ms. Sophie	2525 Batchelder St.	Brooklyn	NY	11235
GOSS	Max	c/o L. Goss 3010 Grand Concourse Apt.2-N	Bronx	NY	10458
GREENE	Albert	Box 59 E. White Plains Station	White Plains	NY	10604
GREISMAN	Bernard	2100 Linwood Ave. Apt. 5-J	Fort Lee	NJ	7024
HABERMAN	Lena	218 Soundview Avenue	White Plains	NY	10606
HEILMAN	Rose	3021 Avenue W	Brooklyn	NY	11229
HELLMAN	Irving	2894 Shore Road	South Bellmore	NY	11710
HEUMAN	Robert S.	5950 Bathurst St. Apt. 203	Willowdale, Ontario CN		
HOLTZ	Minnie	920 Theriot Avenue	Bronx	NY	10472
KELLER	Charles	2928 West 5th Street Sect.A	Brooklyn	NY	11224
KELLER	Louis	9020 Avenue K	Brooklyn	NY	11236

KELLER	Sam	6611 17th Avenue	Brooklyn	NY	11204
KOTCHER	Samuel	80-35 Springfield Blvd.	Queens Village	NY	11427
LAPOW	Harry S.	40 East 9th St.	New York	NY	10003
LEFF	Joseph	106-15 Queens Blvd.	Forest Hills	NY	11375
LEFKOWITZ	Max	1599 West 10th Street	Brooklyn	NY	11204
LEINWAND	Ben	1388 West 6th Street	Brooklyn	NY	11204
LESSER	Dr. Hal	224 Jericho Turnpike	Floral Park	NY	
LEVENTHAL	Rebecca	140-2 Alcott Place	Bronx	NY	10475
LEVENTHAL	Bessie	125 B 19th Street	Far Rockaway	NY	11691
LEVINE	Jack	3500 DeKalb Avenue	Bronx	NY	10467
LEVINE	Beatrice	1801 Bedford Terrace Apt 234J	Sun City Center	FL	33570
LEVINSON	David	Wellington B-203 Century Village	West Palm Beach	FL	33409
LEVY	Leo	8302 229th St.	Queens Village	NY	11427
LEVY	Milton	8102 229th Street	Jamaica	NY	11427
LEVY	Sol	1411 Meridian Avenue	Miami Beach	FL	33139
LISTENBERG	Jack	c/o Zatkowsky 933 Douglass Terrace	Union	NJ	7083
LUBARSKY	Sam	2975 West 33rd Street	Brooklyn	NY	11235
MAMBER	Rose	6901 21st Avenue	Brooklyn	NY	11204

MARENFELD	Rose	458 East 51st Street Apt. D9	Brooklyn	NY	11203
MILLER	Irving	1 Mallard Road	Manhasset	NY	11030
MILLER	Max J.	44 West 77th Street	New York	NY	10024
MiILLER	Mrs. Tessie A.	31 East 12th Street	New York	NY	10003
MITTLEMAN	Joseph	1401 Euclid Avenue	Miami Beach	FL	33139
MORENFELD	Abraham	9330 Lime Bay Road Bldg. # 17 Apt. 306	Tamarac	FL	33319
MUNEY	Rebecca	P.O. Box 4301	Fort Lauderdale	FL	33338
MUNEY	Mrs. Helen	30-10 Marcos Drive, Apt. R 109	Point East No. Miami Beach	FL	33160
NAIDORF	Isaac	3280 Lake Osborne Drive	Lake Worth	FL	33460
NELSON	Frieda	2192 Morris Avenue	Bronx	NY	10453
NELSON	Irving	69-11 261st Street	Floral Park	NY	11004
NELSON	Irwin G.	35 Rochelle Terrace	Mt. Vernon	NY	10551
NELSON	Josh	305 Linden Blvd.	Brooklyn	NY	11226
NEWDORF	Nat	1700 Albermarle Road	Brooklyn	NY	11226
OCEAN	Rachel	31 East 21st Street Apt. 5D	Brooklyn	NY	11226
PASTOR	Mrs. Daisy	2200 West Cornwallis Drive	Greensboro	NC	27408
PASTOR	Isadore	62-60 99th Street	Rego Park	NY	11374

PELTZ	Abraham	12 Tudor Road	Hicksville	NY	11801
PORTER	Dorothy	Presidential Apartments Jefferson House City Line Ave	Phila.	PA	
RABINOWITZ	Meyer	140-9 Debs Place	Bronx	NY	
RABINOWITZ	Mrs. Minnie	65-20 Booth Street	Forest Hills	NY	11374
ROBBINS	Samuel	62-05 Douglaston Pkwy	Douglaston	NY	11362
ROBINSON	Milton	250 Prospect Street	East Orange	NJ	7017
ROSEN	Benjamin	635 8th Street	Miami Beach	FL	33139
ROSEN	Fred	900 S.W. 10th Terrace Bldg S19	Hallandale	FL	33009
ROSENBERG	Charles	6917 Collins Avenue Apt. 1009	Miami Beach	FL	33141
SALBERG	Sam	1010 Pennsylvania Ave. Apt 4	Miami Beach	FL	33139
SAMERS	Edith	68-40 78th St.	Middle Village	NY	11379
SCHARF	Mrs. Marion	103-97 No. Kendall Drive # W3	Miami Beach	FL	33176
SCHNEIDER	Cynthia	3800 South Ocean Drive #305	Hollywood	FL	33020
SCHOENBERG	Murray V.	295 Elm Drive South	Levittown	NY	11756
SCHWARTZ	Ida	807 Arnow Avenue	Bronx	NY	10467
SCHWARTZ	Michael	c/o Schwartz Bros. Memorial Chapel	Forest Hills	NY	11375

		Queens Blvd & 76th Road			
SHERMAN	Mrs. Nellie	129 Norman Drive	East Meadow	NY	11554
SLOMACK	Mrs. Bella	1355 NE 167th Street	No. Miami Beach	FL	33162
SLOMACK	Irving L.	932 Annette Drive	Wantagh	NY	11793
SLOMACK	Sidney	76-26 113th Street	Forest Hills	NY	11375
SPEISS	Mrs. Anna	2386 Walton Avenue	Bronx	NY	10473
SPEISS	Samuel	1966 Newbold Avenue	Bronx	NY	10473
STROMFELD	Louis	300 California Avenue	Santa Monica	CA	90403
SUSSMAN	Mrs. Stella	2870 Grand Concourse	Bronx	NY	10458
TEMPLE	Harry	56-33 231st Street	Bayside	NY	11364
TEMPLE	Mrs. Judith	30 Lenox Rd.	Rockville Centre	NY	11576
TULL	Seymour	693 Wildwood Road	West Hempstead	NY	
UHLBERG	Leon	12 Dunwoodie Road	Lake Carmel	NY	10512
UHLBERG	Sarah	1751 Second Ave. Apt. 29-S	New York	NY	10028
VIDAVER	Elaine	176 West 87th Street Apt. 5-C	New York	NY	10024
WAGNER	Joseph	1902 Avenue L	Brooklyn	NY	11230
WAX	Louis	3405 NW 48th Ave Apt. J-404	Lauderdale Lakes	FL	33313

WAYNE	Henry	1323 209th Street	Bayside	NY	11360
WERNER	Jack M.	1320 15th Street	Miami Beach	FL	33139
WOLMAN	Frances	2006 Seagirt Avenue	Far Rockaway	NY	11691
ZEMEL	Mrs. Esther	1355 East 18th St. Apt. 2B	Brooklyn	NY	11230
ZIIMMERMAN	Louis	759 46th Street	Brooklyn	NY	11220
ZUCKERWISE	Mrs. Anna	1016 50th Street	Brooklyn	NY	11219
ZUCKERWISE	Louis	369B Woodbridge Drive	Ridge	NY	11961
ZUCKERWISE	Sam	67-20 Parsons Boulevard	Flushing	NY	11365

The scanned photo of the plaque and list of members at the Mt. Lebanon Cemetery

NAME INDEX

This is the name index for this English Translation

A

Adamchik, 448
Adamczyk, 380
Agala, 245
Aharonson, 50
Ajgelfeld, 343
Ajzenberg, 157, 361, 497, 556
Ajzenhendler, 219
Ajzenman, 151, 153, 557
Ajzensztadt, 156, 385, 557
Ajzman, 361, 496, 497
Akavitz, 449
Alberg, 448
Albert, 95, 159, 219, 392, 426, 448, 497, 557
Aleichem, 95, 108, 178, 179, 553, 578
Aleksandrower, 251
Alemi, 186
Allen, 1, 590
Alshevitz, 448
Alshevski, 448
Alter, 136, 172, 203, 457, 461, 465, 470, 504, 557
Ambaras, 81, 115, 116, 557
Amshenover, 203, 251
Anski, 3, 247, 498
Anszkin, 187, 188
Arkiewicz, 326
Arnold, 14, 498
Aronovich, 140
Aronson, 140, 498
Asch, 95, 108
Ash, 177, 178, 179, 181, 182
Ashenheim, 406, 407, 423, 498

Auerbach, 410, 448, 496, 556
Ayzman, 141

B

Baal Shem Tov, 45, 63, 64, 207, 210, 502, 568
Bajernaczis, 387
Balas, 153, 294, 296, 297, 300, 302, 326, 392, 394, 449, 499, 558
Balcarska, 294, 558
Balderski, 340, 341, 499
Balinski, 340, 499
Balles, 340
Balsam, 449
Balterman, 410, 499
Bar Yochai, 174, 175, 553
Bargoda, 326, 505
Barkowski, 372
Baron, 247, 413, 416, 499, 507
Barter, 206
Baruchovitch, 449
Baum, 426, 427, 429, 430, 558
Bauman, 407, 410, 449, 502
Baumarder, 386, 449, 499
Baumhertzer, 83, 560
Becker, 410, 411, 498, 503, 541, 560
Begun, 206
Beigelbeker, 451
Beister, 403, 502
Beitshman, 451
Beker, 136, 298, 304, 385, 452, 525
Bencjanowski, 162
Benczkowski, 116, 145, 146, 503
Bendkower, 21

Bentshkovski, 452

Benzer, 404, 410, 413, 416, 417, 502, 503

Ber, 157, 255, 343, 392, 457, 469, 503, 504, 522, 553, 560

Berg, 144, 348, 452

Bergazin, 452

Berglas, 179

Bergzin, 299, 303, 560

Berkovitch, 413, 452, 453

Berkowicz, 317, 504

Berliner, 200, 340, 452, 560

Berman, 136, 293, 299, 409, 410, 452, 503, 504, 560

Bernstein, 410, 504

Bernsztajn, 382

Bernsztejn, 187, 504

Besserman, 410

Bester, 27, 503

Betzalel, 125, 136, 172, 203, 412, 453, 458, 465, 466, 470, 471, 476, 518, 523, 536, 537, 557

Bialik, 106, 501

Bialiskenski, 140, 501

Bichowski, 118, 502

Biderman, 83, 92, 140, 201, 294, 301, 303, 308, 340, 345, 451, 501, 559

Bielski, 372, 373, 374, 375

Bienczkowski, 92

Bienenthal, 451

Biezanski, 136, 221, 294, 298, 309, 347, 351, 387, 451, 501, 559

Bilas, 343

Binder, 410

Binyamin, 81, 136, 223, 224, 225, 243, 244, 245, 296, 318, 389, 448, 454, 469, 470, 472, 488, 489, 491, 492, 502, 506, 532, 548, 551, 560, 570, 578

Birnbaum, 410, 413, 416, 501

Bister, 451

Biznicki, 342, 501

Bizniski, 302

Blashau, 341

Bliachaj, 303

Blinderman, 410, 502

Blum, 451

Blumental, 20, 354, 384, 559

Blumenthal, 83, 92, 136, 452, 502

Bochner, 202, 558

Bombasz, 128

Bondanowicz, 23

Borenstein, 47, 50, 52, 57, 140, 234, 345, 403

Borensztejn, 31, 32, 72, 74, 162, 387

Borkowski, 85, 500

Bornstein, 7, 294, 296, 303, 395, 397, 415, 449, 450

Bornsztejn, 3, 125, 249, 250, 267, 434, 437, 438, 500, 558, 559, 578, 593

Borstein, 308

Boteler, 276

Botler, 376

Boznicky, 410, 411, 500

Boznitzki, 450

Brafman, 396, 413, 414, 504

Brand, 56, 353, 453, 504, 560

Brandshpigel, 453

Breslaw, 387

Bresler, 340, 560

Bressler, 83, 90, 453, 454, 505, 560

Brochovski, 453

Broder, 126, 453, 504

Brof, 453

Brofman, 136

Broitman, 309, 347, 453

Brojtman, 221, 330, 505, 560

Broker, 309, 504

Brokman, 410, 504

Brot, 130, 153, 385, 504

Brott, 453

Bruker, 347, 505

Brustyn, 382

Brzasky, 410

Brzezinski, 2, 133, 167, 168, 292, 366, 368, 392, 399, 451, 500, 501

Brzezonski, 145

Brzezowski, 148

Brzozowski, 125, 221, 340, 342, 559

Butler, 392, 531

Bzozovski, 450

Bzozowska, 310, 350

Bzozowski, 136, 295, 501

C

Carlebach, 195, 576

Cejtlin, 62, 545

Chaimovitch, 468

Chaitshek, 467

Charif, 68, 498, 513, 529, 535

Charlup, 249

Charyf, 32, 156, 157, 249

Chazan, 135, 293, 328, 396, 404, 467, 520

Chazen, 325, 527

Chernikov, 56

Chetzroni, 32, 73, 520, 566

Chilkile, 297

Chlaiak, 330

Chmiel, 95, 473, 527, 568

Chmielnicki, 187, 258, 527

Chopin, 151, 152, 551, 583

Cohen, 32, 37, 56, 75, 79, 83, 85, 90, 93, 156, 238, 258, 273, 307, 350, 385, 410, 411, 443, 473, 526, 553, 568

Comber, 265, 266, 267, 544

Cooper, 407, 411, 417, 547

Cukierman, 375

Czemerynski, 216

Czemiernicki, 159

Czemniarski, 343, 522

Czerniakow, 207, 575

Czerniewski, 387, 522

Czernikow, 171, 185, 202, 522

Czerwank, 392, 394

Czerwonieks, 386

Czestochower, 63

Czundik, 69

D

Dajchus, 167

Dancys, 189

Danziger, 460, 461, 568

Darber, 81, 82, 91

Davidovitch, 460

Dawidowicz, 122, 128, 326, 510

Degenshein, 142, 461

Deichus, 135, 144, 300, 361, 461, 497, 511

Demblyn, 413

Denk, 384, 511

Deutscher, 200

Diamant, 21, 125, 126, 341, 343, 511

Diament, 296, 299, 303, 346, 461, 511, 539, 562

Diamond, 410, 511

Diener, 461

Doganski, 343, 510

Dolow, 411, 510

Dombrowski, 17, 511

Donowitz, 411

Donski, 343, 511

Draber, 343, 512

Dreifus, 461

Drizhan, 140

Droshkosh, 101

du Prel, 384

Dzigan, 461

Dziwicki, 299

E

Edlitz, 481

Efraimovitch, 481, 482

Eiger, 196

Eines, 294

Einman, 407, 497

Eisenberg, 303, 448

Eisenstat, 11

Eisenstein, 294, 448

Eisenstop, 409, 410, 497

Eisman, 85, 90, 448

Eiz, 203

Eizenman, 196

Eizman, 228

Ejnes, 392, 395, 399, 400, 540, 557

Elbaum, 481

Elbinger, 52, 56

Elchanan, 33, 134, 138, 192, 216, 395, 401, 525, 526, 529

Elster, 410

Engel, 32, 481, 540

Engelbrecht, 310, 350, 540, 557

Engelman, 481

Engelmans, 115

Engielman, 159, 167, 540

Enis, 410, 498

Epstein, 410, 540

Erbst, 482

Erdbaum, 482

Erlich, 85, 136, 202, 348, 482, 540, 558

Erman, 482

F

Fajgienbaum, 75

Farbsztejn, 197, 574

Feferkovitch, 484

Feferkovitsh, 136

Feigenbaum, 32, 49

Fein, 102, 300, 303, 483

Feingold, 56

Feld, 411, 543

Feldfevel, 206

Feldscher, 167, 529

Felt, 410

Fen, 417, 541

Ferkal, 483

Festman, 94, 108, 117, 118, 278, 279, 281, 541, 542, 574

Findek, 485

Finkel, 410, 542

Fischer, 56

Flajszman, 219, 363, 365, 573

Fleischman, 94, 99, 136, 299, 393, 396, 413, 415, 416, 426, 484

Fleishman, 136, 271, 542

Flejszman, 108, 341, 342, 542, 543

Forman, 483

Foster, 410, 541

Franco, 197, 203, 399, 543

Frankenstein, 410, 543

Frejdenberg, 326

Frejdman, 212, 214, 219, 285

Frekal, 142

Frenkel, 361, 544

Frenkiel, 157, 162

Freund, 250, 544

Friedenson, 200, 202

Friedman, 4, 7, 109, 162, 188, 409, 410, 411, 485, 544, 589

Friedrich, 410, 544, 551

Frielich, 485

Fromer, 35, 158, 162, 173, 543

Frum, 200, 574

Frumer, 20, 28, 29, 49, 52, 55, 75, 135, 543, 574

Frumowicz, 394

Frydman, 2, 77, 81, 85, 90, 92, 94, 117, 120, 122, 131, 135, 136, 139, 148, 162, 168, 170, 171, 172, 173, 174, 186, 193, 194, 195, 196, 197, 198, 199, 200, 201, 202, 203, 205, 206, 207, 208, 209, 210, 221, 225, 226, 227, 230, 241, 243, 247, 277, 278, 281, 284, 285, 297, 312, 363, 392, 394, 395, 396, 401, 421, 423, 424, 431, 433, 434, 543, 544, 574, 575

Fuchs, 177, 181, 542

Fuerstenberg, 484, 485

Furman, 268, 542

Fursztenberg, 126, 148, 154, 238, 361, 363, 366, 384, 395, 396, 543

G

Gabel, 129, 508

Gajer, 327, 561

Galek, 80, 115, 130, 221, 317, 388, 456, 457, 505, 506, 560

Gastininer, 62

Gebirtig, 359

Gefner, 173

Geier, 81, 143, 404, 413

Gelbart, 195

Gelbstein, 136, 294, 297, 302, 303, 308, 328, 345, 346, 458

Gelbsztejn, 19, 316, 328, 340, 354, 508, 561

Geller, 392

Gelman, 117, 118, 458, 508, 561

German, 410

Gerrer, 32, 165, 172, 190, 203, 207, 208, 251, 284, 496, 525, 557, 559, 563

Gersht, 140, 299, 458

Gerszt, 385, 508, 561

Geshen, 416, 508

Gesundheit, 165, 508

Getlichman, 458

Gidalevitch, 457

Gilder, 410, 507

Gincburg, 247, 249, 507

Gines, 458

Gingold, 140, 330, 457, 458, 507

Ginzberg, 157, 187

Gips, 458

Gitejn, 125

Giterman, 173, 207, 507

Glikzeliker, 458

Godel, 117, 505

Goldberg, 81, 92, 297, 299, 363, 403, 406, 454, 455, 506, 561

Goldfaden, 95, 506, 561

Goldfarb, 140, 141, 293, 307, 456, 506, 561

Goldflus, 410, 506

Goldhaft, 142

Goldman, 86, 134, 139, 140, 307, 308, 326, 328, 356, 363, 410, 455, 456, 506, 561

Goldschlag, 52

Goldshlak, 456

Goldshneider, 407, 410, 506

Goldstein, 230, 303, 456

Goldsztejn, 221, 331, 506, 561

Gombinski, 404, 457, 506

Gombinsky, 413

Gordin, 95

Gordon, 108, 410, 507, 561

Gorky, 177

Gorlik, 410

Gorski, 144, 342

Goszik, 173, 507

Gothelf, 145, 327, 330, 363, 366, 376, 387, 505, 561

Gothilf, 295, 297, 301, 308, 310

Gottglas, 457

Gotthelf, 144, 345, 348, 349, 350, 454

Gottlieb, 409, 454, 505

Gozik, 202

Graubard, 4, 7, 78, 120, 122, 128, 130, 135, 184, 186, 187, 188, 189, 233, 253, 271, 288, 289, 300, 303, 309, 316, 342, 347, 395, 403, 407, 408, 410, 411, 413, 415, 417, 427, 458, 508, 509, 561, 562

Graubards, 115

Graubert, 19

Greber, 389

Green, 95, 417, 440, 510

Greenberg, 92, 93, 117, 141, 177, 181, 182, 406, 409, 410, 411, 436, 459, 460, 510

Greenwald, 410, 510

Greisman, 410, 510

Gringard, 303, 459

Grobshmit, 410

Grodzisker, 122, 167, 225, 251, 379, 536, 553, 575

Groinem, 140, 459

Groman, 130

Grondwag, 459

Grosman, 126, 315

Grossman, 296, 302, 304, 357, 459, 508

Grundwag, 1, 79, 83, 85, 90, 92, 94, 95, 107, 108, 111, 117, 120, 126, 127, 128, 129, 130, 132, 133, 159, 162, 210, 211, 276, 277, 281, 294, 340, 357, 362, 363, 386, 392, 394, 395, 509, 548, 562, 581, 583, 585, 586, 587, 589

Grushko, 136

Grusky, 410

Grynberg, 181, 276, 330, 509, 510, 562

Grynszpan, 162, 510

Gudak, 386, 505

Gunner, 330

Gurski, 340, 507, 561

Gursky, 410

Guterman, 185

Gutgiesztaldt, 145

Gutglas, 361, 507

Gutman, 410, 507

Guttgold, 143

Gutthart, 457

Guttman, 457

H

Haber, 202, 563

Haberman, 461

Hafenung, 387, 512

Hakohen, 52, 156, 157, 158, 160, 163

HaKohen, 64, 168, 250, 497, 575

Halberstam, 51, 203, 565

Halbersztadt, 172, 512

Hamer, 135, 512

Hasandlar, 172, 174

Heiman, 410, 513

Heinter, 200

Hejman, 127, 513

Helfand, 410, 513

Heller, 102, 303

Helman, 410, 513

Helmer, 151, 317, 462, 513

Helpern, 32

Hendel, 172, 203, 208, 209, 450, 454, 458, 488, 492, 494, 513, 563

Henech, 40, 43, 65, 167, 212, 397, 398, 465, 486, 504, 563, 565

Herbstein, 462, 463

Herneberg, 343

Hershberg, 463

Hershkovitz, 303, 463

Hershkowitz, 406, 407, 410, 514

Hertzfeld, 428, 563

Herzl, 117, 118, 120, 123, 210, 281, 440

Hindes, 118, 513, 563

Hirsch, 23, 81, 137, 145, 162, 163, 168, 170, 188, 193, 212, 213, 214, 219, 221, 222, 223, 226, 230, 297, 307, 308, 330, 379, 407, 411, 413, 478, 505, 513, 515, 523, 529, 537, 544, 547, 551, 561, 563, 566, 567, 571, 575, 577, 578

Hirschbein, 95, 108, 462

Hitlmacher, 136

Hochbaum, 461

Hodes, 404

Hofenung, 462

Hojker, 366

Holc, 387

Holcman, 148, 319, 330, 361, 363, 379, 512

Hollander, 297, 337, 366, 461, 563

Holtz, 410, 512

Holtzman, 136, 461, 462, 512

Horowitz, 156

I

Indik, 448

Ines, 2, 100, 104, 436, 481

Inklus, 448

Innfeld, 410

Ish-Shalom, 124, 392, 423

Israelewicz, 344

Isserles, 75

Izraelovitz, 299

Izraelowicz, 326, 496, 557

Izraelski, 126, 294, 303, 496, 557

Izralevitch, 472, 473

Izralski, 473, 496

J

Jablonka, 126, 522

Jablonska, 330, 522

Jablonski, 470

Jacobi, 404

Jacobovitch, 350

Jacobs, 410

Jagiello, 15, 16, 522

Jagiellonczyk, 16, 522

Jakir, 167

Jakobovicz, 301

Jakobovitch, 410

Jakobovitz, 79, 92, 297, 298, 470, 471

Jakobowicz, 136, 310, 350, 351

Jakubowicz, 23, 105, 125, 252, 326, 342, 363, 523, 567, 569

Janek, 343, 522

Janowski, 86, 354

Jarlicht, 340, 525

Jasinowski, 118, 523, 566

Jasinski, 332, 438, 439, 441, 523, 566, 567

Javitz, 470

Jazinek, 470

Jelechovski, 467

Jelozko, 307, 467, 565

Joaszon, 72, 522

K

Kac, 22, 109, 134, 136, 142, 145, 148, 156, 216, 217, 354, 387, 526, 527, 546, 568

Kadynower, 156, 496, 553

Kahan, 136

Kahana, 310, 473, 526

Kahn, 126, 132, 144, 294, 299, 303

Kaiser, 128, 257

Kalabielski, 125

Kaleta, 355, 356, 546

Kalinski, 486

Kalisher, 133

Kalski, 361

Kaminska, 386, 546

Kampelmacher, 84, 85, 87, 149, 150, 151, 152, 153, 154, 155, 229, 235, 236, 313, 486, 546, 576

Kan, 108, 118

Kantorowicz, 367, 369

Kapla, 486

Kaplan, 85, 92, 436, 438, 486, 546, 576

Kara, 387, 546, 547

Karmi, 392

Karo, 240, 295, 486

Karpowicz, 368, 547

Kartozenski, 486

Kasher, 171, 527

Kaszman, 399, 548

Katriel, 281, 527

Katriels, 122

Katz, 292, 346, 395, 473, 474

Katzovitch, 486

Kaufman, 136, 451, 486

Kavel, 237

Kawe, 189

Kazimierz, 15, 16, 18, 29

Kefer, 136, 488, 548

Keizman, 487

Keller, 81, 167, 340, 404, 406, 410, 487, 488, 548, 576

Kenig, 175

Kenigstein, 488

Kezman, 136

Khazer, 185

Kiejzman, 130

Kimelman, 342

King August III, 18

King Boleslaw III Krzywausti, 14

King Ludwig, 15, 16

King Stanislaw August, 18

King Wladyslaw IV, 18

King Zygmunt August, 11

Kipper, 27, 395, 404

Kirshbaum, 395

Kirshborn, 206

Kirszbraun, 197, 576

Kiszka, 114

Klarberg, 319

Klein, 487

Kleiner, 487, 512

Klioski, 297, 576

Kloska, 81, 302, 303, 487

Klott, 387, 547

Kluska, 114, 115, 126, 136, 220, 221, 547, 576

Knee, 184, 190, 264, 281, 284

Knobel, 125, 327, 487, 548

Knot, 276, 302, 316

Knott, 85, 90, 134, 136, 246, 295, 296, 309, 332, 342, 346, 347, 358, 487, 547, 548, 576

Kocker, 165

Kofetz, 486

Kohan, 21

Kohen, 122, 156

Kohenof, 249

Kohn, 358, 525, 526, 545, 568

Kojawa, 310, 350, 576

Kolski, 486

Kolsky, 410, 545

Kon, 319, 546, 575, 576

Kona, 319

Konrad I, 14, 546

Kopeld, 410, 547

Korbitsh, 487

Korczac, 236

Korczak, 305, 313, 320, 326, 546, 576

Kornbajser, 187, 547

Kornfeld, 410, 547

Kosciuszko, 13, 17, 19, 45

Koszinski, 343, 547

Kotshinsky, 410, 545, 547

Kotton, 343

Kozshinsky, 410

Kraianka, 488

Krakov, 299

Krakow, 15, 16, 17, 32, 142, 199, 200, 206, 250, 307, 330, 488, 548, 563, 576

Kramer, 410

Kranc, 362, 548

Krawski, 188

Krel, 172, 548

Kriger, 488

Krock, 488

Kroin, 89, 118

Kronenberg, 488

Krongard, 202

Krongold, 124, 548

Krotshik, 488

Kufert, 487

Kulson, 487

Kumok, 130

Kuper, 167

Kutner, 65, 75, 266, 524, 547

Kutnovski, 348, 486

L

Lajpcykier, 163, 164, 165

Lampa, 386, 527

Landau, 4, 6, 9, 13, 14, 20, 31, 32, 38, 46, 50, 57, 62, 66, 70, 73, 77, 94, 100, 105, 106, 114, 117, 120, 122, 125, 127, 130, 132, 145, 148, 161, 162, 163, 166, 170, 173, 175, 182, 184, 186, 190, 193, 204, 210, 212, 214, 216, 218, 220, 221, 231, 233, 235, 241, 243, 244, 245, 247, 253, 259, 260, 264, 268, 271, 273, 276, 278, 281, 284, 285, 286, 288, 293, 301, 305, 311, 312, 315, 320, 326, 327, 330, 331, 335, 340, 352, 353, 357, 359, 360, 361, 363, 366, 376, 378, 380, 381, 382, 384, 392, 396, 398, 399, 401, 402, 403, 404, 405, 406, 407, 411, 421, 423, 426, 429, 431, 434, 436, 437, 444, 448, 495, 527, 528, 556

Landner, 347

Laosher, 410

Laskovski, 475

Laskowski, 52, 570

Lasman, 475

Lateiner, 129, 527

Laufer, 79, 569

Lawancka, 12, 18, 569

Lazancka, 12, 569

Laznowski, 52, 569

Leder, 128

Lederman, 476

Lefkowicz, 108, 532

Lehman, 4, 184, 185

Leidhold, 407

Leifer, 280, 404, 413, 416, 476, 530

Leist, 56, 570

Leitheld, 405, 410, 530

Leizer, 101, 136, 296, 297, 298, 300, 303, 330, 449, 453, 454, 455, 459, 460, 461, 464, 467, 468, 471, 474, 477, 478, 486, 488, 491, 492, 496, 499, 510, 520, 530, 545, 558, 567, 570

Leizers, 136

Lejwik, 360

Lejzers, 244

Leman, 187

Lendenberg, 200

Lesinger, 404

Lessinger, 417, 532

Levanon, 2, 109, 156, 260, 392, 394, 395, 516, 528

Leventhal, 52

Levi, 13, 39, 42, 97, 452, 459, 528, 531, 536, 569, 572

Levin, 136, 226, 294, 299, 308, 345, 476

Levkovich, 410, 532

Levkovitch, 476, 477

Levkovitz, 136

Levy, 410, 411, 531

Lewi, 386, 531

Lewin, 197, 199, 200, 202, 276, 303, 304, 317, 319, 343, 363, 376, 392, 399, 405, 409, 410, 423, 440, 441, 531, 532, 569

Lewita, 118, 532, 569

Lewkowicz, 227, 257, 315, 319, 341, 353, 354, 385, 532, 569

Liberman, 145, 151, 327, 328, 340, 343, 363, 378, 475, 529, 568

Libert, 109, 136, 154, 192, 277, 294, 302, 303, 308, 328, 340, 341, 345, 346, 387, 401, 402, 411, 477, 528, 529, 570

Libfreund, 379, 475

Lichtenstein, 117, 475

Lichtensztajn, 167

Lichtensztejn, 319, 366, 570

Lieberman, 50

Lieder, 413

Lions, 410, 530

Lipman, 46, 52, 73, 126, 296, 299, 346, 358, 461, 511, 530, 531, 557, 562, 569

Lipoan, 18

Lipschitz, 57, 578

Lisberg, 384, 530

Lisse, 476

Lisser, 157, 163, 164, 165, 410, 476

Listenberg, 476

Litowski, 22, 530

Litvak, 475

Lodzer, 79, 92, 523, 569

Lokstik, 308

Loksztyk, 125

Lukshtik, 140, 345, 475

Luksztik, 294

Luksztyk, 108, 528, 529, 569

Lurie, 335

Lusky, 410, 528

Lustig, 410, 528

Lustman, 475

Lutwak, 108

lzralevitch, 143

M

Machla, 94, 108, 126, 276, 358, 376, 392, 451, 458, 459, 461, 464, 465, 472, 473, 475, 477, 479, 480, 492, 509, 510, 531, 552, 562

Malazh, 477

Malenberg, 303, 532, 533

Malewicz, 97

Malinowski, 340, 532

Manczyk, 145, 533

Mann, 184, 190, 264, 281, 284, 477

Mantshik, 140

Marek, 11, 187, 533, 534, 535, 560, 571

Marenfeld, 410

Marienfeld, 136, 296, 297, 302, 315, 332, 340, 343, 346, 478, 479, 533, 571

Markish, 177, 181, 182

Markisz, 181

Mashman, 410

Maszlanka, 343, 533

Maszman, 343

Matola, 343, 532

Matoszak, 338

Matsno, 136

Mazal, 343, 532

Mazur, 197

Meisel, 427, 571

Melinberg, 304

Mendel, 2, 31, 32, 39, 40, 41, 46, 52, 73, 80, 81, 85, 90, 92, 115, 136, 145, 158, 163, 165, 166, 178, 214, 222, 226, 249, 285, 294, 303, 310, 341, 350, 351, 363, 385, 392, 394, 404, 410, 413, 417, 424, 448, 449, 451, 452, 456, 471, 473, 475, 476, 477, 483, 488, 489, 494, 497, 503, 506, 509, 518, 523, 527, 535, 541, 543, 549, 552, 557, 559, 560, 564, 568, 571, 573, 574

Mendelson, 90, 191, 535

Menzer, 412

Metchnik, 410

Michalski, 343, 387, 534

Mikalski, 343

Mikhalski, 150

Miler, 153, 534, 535

Miller, 85, 92, 141, 184, 190, 264, 281, 284, 299, 300, 403, 410, 411, 479, 534, 535, 571

Minin, 369, 370, 371, 535

Mintz, 303

Mishmuel, 35, 46, 47, 48, 50, 51, 52, 53, 60, 62, 73, 74, 162, 163, 397, 398, 553

Mishrowitzer, 118

Mittleman, 184, 190, 264, 281, 284, 411

Mlodaz, 423

Moiskit, 310

Mokotowski, 194, 200, 570

Monia, 19, 500

Monkovitzki, 478

Montshik, 92, 477

Morenfeld, 410

Morgensztern, 22, 533, 568

Moser, 477

Moshenberg, 142, 478

Moshke, 347

Moshkovich, 410

Moshkovitch, 478

Moshman, 142, 478

Moszenberg, 114, 303, 305, 320, 322, 334, 533, 571

Moszikowski, 79

Moszkowicz, 18, 534

Motzna, 478

Munaj, 276

Muney, 79, 85, 108, 140, 294, 297, 299, 340, 396, 403, 410, 534, 570

Myszonower, 251

N

Nabarnik, 296

Nadelhaft, 143, 479, 536

Najman, 22, 167, 265, 537

Nambergen, 108

Napoleon, 129, 251, 536

Nashelevitch, 479, 480

Nashelevitz, 118

Nashelewicz, 136, 346

Nashelski, 479

Nashelwicz, 94

Nasielewicz, 130, 151, 252, 281, 572

Nasielski, 330, 536

Naszelewicz, 292, 536

Neihaus, 52, 572

Neiman, 480

Neirat, 480

Neis, 480

Neiten, 404, 412, 413, 414, 416, 537

Nelson, 80, 136, 214, 222, 281, 282, 283, 292, 362, 396, 403, 404, 407, 410, 411, 412, 413, 480, 537, 572

Nelsons, 385

Nemerin, 257

Nezer, 31, 33, 48, 49, 50, 51, 53, 54, 57, 58, 59, 61, 62, 63, 158, 160, 161, 162, 250

Niemcewicz, 13, 29

Noelson, 13, 536, 572

Nomberg, 162, 177, 179, 181, 187, 191, 536

Notan, 410, 536

Notek, 367, 536

Notta, 138

Novinski, 479

Nut, 22, 536

O

Ogledzki, 387

Ohlberg, 410, 411, 497

Oklanski, 130, 498, 556

Oklinski, 299, 449

Oklonski, 302

Olewing, 413, 496

Opatoshu, 177, 182, 498

Opatowski, 182, 498

Opotovska, 140

Opozdover, 448, 449

Orbach, 442

Orleska, 386

Orlian, 200

Ovitzki, 448

P

Palet, 138

Parcower, 163

Patalowski, 121, 540

Patt, 384

Peperkowicz, 125

Pera, 355, 356, 543

Perec, 181

Perelgritz, 483

Peretz, 90, 91, 95, 108, 177, 181, 182, 187, 190, 513, 533, 542, 563

Perkal, 102, 541, 575

Perla, 187, 188, 541

Pertchak, 483

Pesse, 252

Pestalozzi, 235, 574

Peters, 410, 542

Piatczak, 309, 573

Piernik, 116, 483, 541

Pinchevski, 483

Pinczewski, 28, 29, 81, 92, 93, 143, 228, 294, 308, 311, 327, 340, 345, 385, 413, 541

Pindek, 127, 128

Pinsker, 117

Pinski, 108, 541

Plamiak, 403

Pletshevitzer, 483

Plonska, 303, 541

Plonski, 80, 115, 145, 387, 483, 541, 573

Plucer, 121, 541

Podlishewski, 118

Pomerantz, 407, 483

Poniatowski, 17, 540

Posnanski, 237

Pozanski, 482

Poznanski, 136, 297, 540, 573

Pozner, 156, 540

Prashker, 483

Praust, 177

Prekal, 112, 228, 229, 230, 297

Prilocki, 85

Prilucki, 185, 186, 187, 188, 190, 191, 542, 575

Pritz, 410

Priver, 309, 347

Priwes, 196, 575

Proshinowsky, 51

Prouza, 294, 297, 308, 345, 543, 574

Przedpelski, 331, 541

Przedwozer, 156

Pshititzka, 483

Putter, 410, 411, 483, 541

Pzhepiorka, 483

Q

Quixote, 184

R

Rabicz, 202, 576

Rabinovitch, 136, 403, 488

Rabinovitz, 117

Rabinowicz, 145, 548, 577

Rabinowitz, 81, 548

Rachman, 490

Radzinski, 203, 577

Rajc, 293

Rakovski, 490

Rapaport, 172

Rapoport, 249, 550

Rappaport, 203, 410, 550, 577

Ratchimel, 340, 550

Ratner, 146, 550

Rawicz, 182, 549

Rechtman, 122, 135, 153, 231, 232, 233, 235, 289, 392, 492, 551, 577

Rechtmans, 115

Reisen, 179

Reiter, 411

Reitman, 297, 491, 492

Rejtman, 145, 551

Retman, 317

Ribner, 491

Ribnes, 493

Ringel, 491

Ringelblum, 185, 205, 208, 292, 383, 491, 551, 577

Robinson, 184, 190, 264, 281, 284, 411, 550

Roczimek, 18, 550

Rogowi, 200, 202

Roitman, 310, 350, 491

Roitstein, 490, 491

Rojtman, 317, 326, 551

Rojtsztejn, 387, 551

Rosen, 81, 92, 403, 404, 407, 410, 416, 417, 489, 549

Rosenbaum, 489

Rosenberg, 4, 7, 79, 94, 99, 403, 411, 413, 416, 489

Rosenfeld, 117, 118, 275

Rosenkopf, 143, 294, 301, 345, 490

Rosenkrantz, 308

Rosenperel, 489, 490

Rosenrat, 490

Rosenstein, 490

Roth, 404

Rothbard, 490

Rothbaum, 490

Rotstein, 227, 295, 302, 303, 304, 409, 410, 413, 550

Rotsztejn, 127, 128, 340, 344, 550, 577

Rozen, 20, 22, 127, 128, 129, 235, 341, 429, 431, 549, 577

Rozenberg, 109, 128, 190, 301, 549, 577

Rozenburg, 317

Rozenfeld, 19, 122, 127, 128, 129, 188, 249, 281, 549, 577

Rozenkop, 321, 340, 549, 550, 577

Rozenkopf, 302, 306, 317

Rozenperl, 145, 327, 340, 378, 379, 386, 549

Rozepczyk, 341, 550

Rumianek, 122, 159, 551

Rutshteyn, 136

Rzokowski, 341

S

Sabczok, 340, 538

Safer, 480

Salomon, 83, 572

Sapirman, 136

Saposznik, 359

Satenberg, 136, 538

Schenirer, 206, 210

Schlesinger, 411, 442

Schlossberg, 100, 493

Schmeiser, 396

Schultz, 172, 173, 203, 208, 209

Schwartz, 79, 94, 99, 296, 345, 357, 396, 409, 410, 551

Schwartzhar, 492

Sefarim, 90, 571

Segal, 136, 341, 405, 407, 481, 538, 539

Sendatsh, 481

Sender, 130, 136, 203, 363, 453, 463, 465, 467, 488, 500, 504, 572

Senderovitch, 481

Shafran, 202

Shamash, 159, 167, 194, 216, 330, 417, 502, 504, 559

Shapira, 47, 140, 200, 229, 300

Sharfstein, 411, 551

Sharken, 414, 551

Sheinbaum, 405, 493, 553

Sheinberg, 410, 553

Shemiantek, 118, 494

Shemientek, 494

Sherel, 410

Sheynwald, 84, 136, 140, 142, 143, 307, 309, 310, 328, 347, 348, 350, 493

Shimiontek, 92

Shladov, 493

Shladow, 144

Shmaltz, 296

Shmeiser, 304, 493, 494

Shmeltz, 302, 308, 345, 346, 494

Shmulevitz, 493

Shochet, 190

Shoham, 352, 381, 551

Sholk, 410, 551

Shorashewski, 204

Shorken, 413

Shorkin, 404

Shotland, 427

Shpeizhendler, 404, 494

Shpikler, 417, 554

Shpilker, 417

Shpotrik, 90

Shtipt, 129

Shtzitner, 301

Shulklaper, 134, 241, 242, 536, 571, 578

Shulklapper, 136, 213, 216, 218, 222, 223

Shuster, 134, 135, 136, 259, 525

Shviatlovski, 492

Siemanowska, 18

Silber, 366, 370, 411, 466, 518

Silberman, 137, 138, 466, 467, 518

Silberstein, 466

Silver, 174, 199, 410, 538

Silverman, 410, 519

Silverstein, 404, 406, 407, 413, 539

Skornik, 80, 125, 130, 327

Skotnicki, 108, 128, 167, 219, 276, 387, 539, 572

Skotnitzki, 79, 85, 90, 94, 99, 481

Skrent, 86, 540

Skulnik, 350

Skurnik, 136, 310, 366, 368, 481, 539

Sliwa, 294, 539, 572

Slomak, 405, 406, 407, 409, 410, 411, 413, 539

Sneiberg, 411, 554

Socha, 12, 538

Sochaczevski, 480

Sochaczewer, 11, 63, 64, 66, 158, 264, 330

Sochaczewski, 252, 538

Sochaczewsky, 410, 411

Sofer, 23, 248, 410, 411, 525, 538

Sofron, 410

Sokolov, 133

Sokolow, 93, 118, 131, 157, 437, 538, 568, 572

Solberg, 411, 538

Soliaj, 303, 571

Solomon, 404, 410, 411, 416, 417, 506, 538

Sotenberg, 480

Speishendler, 396

Speiss, 406, 407, 410, 415, 539

Speisshendler, 411, 412, 413, 554, 555

Spiegel, 405

Spikler, 404

Starkman, 411, 552

Starwinski, 208

Staug, 317, 318

Steiglitz, 81, 492

Stein, 7, 78, 434

Stern, 134, 139, 140, 295, 307, 308, 328, 492

Stieglitz, 136

Stopnicki, 191, 538

Streicher, 82, 140, 552

Strindberg, 95, 538, 572

Stromfeld, 410, 552

Strum, 492

Strykower, 161, 514

Stuciner, 55

Swarcsztejn, 195, 552, 578

Swiatlowski, 81, 114, 126, 145, 218, 220, 395, 398, 551, 578

Swierzynska, 14, 19, 20, 551

Switman, 407, 538

Switzman, 405

Szapira, 172, 203, 555, 579

Szereszawski, 196

Szereszewski, 171, 554, 579

Szewczyk, 342, 343, 554

Szikorski, 23

Szkalek, 126

Szlosberg, 336

Szmejser, 252, 554

Szmelc, 315, 332, 340, 341, 554, 579

Szmulewicz, 331, 378, 553, 554

Sznajder, 114, 128

Szpajzhendler, 342

Szpigiel, 21

Sztechler, 340, 552

Szteiner, 202

Sztejn, 1, 2, 66, 163, 170, 259, 552, 578

Sztejnman, 38

Szteper, 115

Sztern, 126, 340, 552, 578

Sztszafa, 125

Szultz, 320

Szwarc, 106, 109, 116, 126, 190, 362, 551, 552, 578

Szwarcer, 127, 128, 276, 552

Szwarcsztajn, 170

Szwercer, 108

T

Talman, 387

Tarnowski, 18, 521

Taub, 90, 468, 520, 566

Taubenfeld, 136, 353, 354, 355, 361, 468

Teben, 347

Telman, 284

Temes, 80, 140, 536, 566

Tempel, 94, 217, 469, 521

Temple, 63, 102, 145, 235, 410, 411, 445, 521, 522

Tendel, 326

Tenner, 415

Terner, 469

Thomashefsky, 129

Thon, 132

Tikotshiner, 469

Tilman, 89, 90, 91, 93, 140, 229, 294, 296, 298, 299, 300, 302, 303, 340, 361, 363, 468, 469, 521, 566

Tindel, 101, 521, 566

Tolek, 369, 521

Tomaszower, 156, 524

Trawka, 188, 189

Treger, 462

Tregier, 330, 339

Trepiasz, 116

Trukenheim, 197, 203

Trunk, 9, 29, 184, 264, 522

Tsharka, 469

Tshernievski, 469

Tshervinski, 469

Tshervoniek, 469

Tshinkus, 469

Turower, 161

Tykoczlner, 19

Tylman, 116, 146

Tzemach, 57, 407, 541

Tzidkoni, 231, 233, 235, 444

Tzina, 31, 46, 73, 266, 267, 268, 485, 545, 555, 559

U

Ungar, 202

Urbinski, 340, 496

V

Valencia, 134, 139, 140, 328, 345

Varman, 463

Vidaver, 410, 515

Videletz, 464

Vimberg, 464

Vishnia, 348, 464

Vishogrodski, 464

Volkovitch, 463

W

Wachsler, 52

Wagner, 330, 410, 514

Wajnberg, 108, 148, 153, 154, 331, 376, 377, 389, 392, 516, 564

Wajnbergs, 386

Wajnstock, 392, 394

Wajnsztok, 130, 516

Wajsenberg, 181, 183, 563

Wajsman, 123, 124

Waldenberg, 83, 385, 463, 514, 564

Waldman, 463

Walecki, 368

Walfish, 463

Walman, 392, 463

Wanwild, 189, 514

Warshavski, 463

Warshawiak, 207

Warshawski, 4, 77, 81, 85, 92, 93, 117, 118, 141, 142, 143, 297, 309, 347

Warszawski, 120, 122, 126, 159, 175, 176, 177, 178, 179, 180, 181, 182, 183, 253, 268, 515, 563, 564

Warszawskis, 115

Wasser, 330

Wasserman, 463

Wazenberg, 92

Weinberg, 52, 56, 83, 85, 90, 92, 94, 104, 109, 311, 312, 411, 418, 423, 516

Weingard, 410

Weingut, 51

Weinstein, 143

Weinstock, 19, 464

Weintraub, 117

Weisenberg, 177, 178, 179, 181, 183, 517

Weisman, 410, 517

Weiss, 413, 460, 464, 517

Weissberg, 77

Weissenberg, 185, 435

Weissman, 5

Weisz, 328

Weiter, 108, 516

Weitzman, 404, 411, 412, 413, 416, 417, 465, 517

Wejszman, 1, 2

Welkowicz, 227

Welman, 117, 118, 343

Weltmsman, 410

Wernick, 299

Werthajm, 367, 368, 369, 370

Widelec, 19, 398, 399, 515

Wideletz, 347

Wiedislavski, 463

Wiedislawski, 309, 347, 564

Wiener, 464, 515

Wilhelm, 384, 411, 511, 515

Winer, 84, 92, 93, 141, 142, 564

Winkler, 464

Winter, 404, 411, 413, 414, 415, 416, 417, 464, 515

Wishinsky, 410, 516

Wishnia, 302, 309
Wittenberg, 464
Wohlrat, 404
Wolert, 224
Wolkowicz, 84, 92, 128, 141, 159, 276, 284, 385, 387, 514, 564
Wolman, 162, 514, 564
Wolrat, 70, 122, 127, 136, 396, 411, 514
Wolwowicz, 153
Wosk, 256
Wosky, 256
Wrubel, 386, 517
Wymaslowski, 281, 516
Wyslice, 386
Wyszogrodsky, 80

Y

Y. F., 221
Yakovitz, 192
Yarlicht, 473
Yashinski, 299, 308, 346, 471, 472
Yoffe, 307, 308
Yorzinek, 136
Yudiki, 247

Z

Zabocki, 396
Zabosky, 411
Zadkoni, 392, 544
Zaioncz, 310, 350
Zajac, 385, 387, 517, 518, 565
Zajdendorf, 128
Zajdman, 170, 171, 172, 174
Zajonc, 167
Zalcman, 115, 116, 126, 392, 518, 565
Zalman, 39, 126, 143, 159, 218, 219, 350, 392, 426, 427, 448, 453, 455, 462, 463, 481, 482, 484, 489, 492, 493, 497, 511, 543, 554, 557, 570, 578, 579
Zaltzman, 81, 95, 136, 303, 465, 466
Zand, 141, 153, 300, 307, 410, 466, 518, 565

Zander, 466
Zanger, 411, 518
Zaonc, 392, 394
Zaonz, 212, 465
Zavadzki, 465
Zavadzski, 465
Zawadski, 260, 565
Zawadzki, 130, 517
Zawitkower, 196
Zeidman, 193, 519
Zeifman, 467
Zelankewicz, 340
Zelmanovitch, 467
Zelmanowicz, 114, 519
Zelonka, 297, 467
Zelwer, 22
Zelzoko, 295
Zemba, 173, 197, 201, 519, 565
Zemel, 410, 467, 519
Zevadski, 307
Zhokowski, 294, 565
Zibola, 101, 103, 485, 486
Ziemowit II, 15
Ziemowit III, 15
Ziemowit IV, 15, 16
Zilberman, 138
Zimereinski, 486
Zimerinski, 135, 136, 226, 230, 545, 575
Zimler, 22
Zimmerman, 410, 545
Zinger, 177
Zisman, 295, 451, 467
Zlotnick, 467
Zmiaowski, 92, 519, 565
Zokowski, 340, 519
Zolonka, 303, 565
Zranov, 467
Zucker, 371, 544
Zuckerweiss, 404
Zuckerweitz, 485

Zuckerwise, 410, 411, 412, 413, 416, 417, 544, 545

Zuckerwitz, 136

Zusman, 92, 518

Zwerman, 485

Zwierzechowski, 361

Zwitkower, 13, 518, 553, 565

Zygmunt III, 18

Zylbersztejn, 128